COUNSELING PARENTS OF
THE ILL AND
THE HANDICAPPED

COUNSELING PARENTS OF THE ILL AND THE HANDICAPPED

Compiled and Edited by

ROBERT L. NOLAND

Professor of Psychology
University of Dayton
Dayton, Ohio

CHARLES C THOMAS • PUBLISHER

Springfield • Illinois • U.S.A.

Published and Distributed Throughout the World by

CHARLES C THOMAS • PUBLISHER

Bannerstone House

301-327 East Lawrence Avenue, Springfield, Illinois, U.S.A.

Natchez Plantation House

735 North Atlantic Boulevard, Fort Lauderdale, Florida, U.S.A.

©*1971, by* CHARLES C THOMAS • PUBLISHER

Library of Congress Catalog Card Number: 79-130934

*With THOMAS BOOKS careful attention is given to all details of
manufacturing and design. It is the Publisher's desire to present books that are
satisfactory as to their physical qualities and artistic possibilities and
appropriate for their particular use. THOMAS BOOKS will be true to those
laws of quality that assure a good name and good will.*

Printed in The United States of America

RN-1

Contributors

LAWRENCE E. ABT, Ph.D.
D. W. BARUCH, Ph.D.
GASTON J. BAUS, M.D.
KENNETH L. BECKER, M.D.
KEITH N. BRYANT, M.D.
R. G. B. CAMERON, M.B., M.R.A.C.P.
JOSEPHINE CATENA, M.S.W.
FRANK CERULLI, M.D.
PAUL CHODOFF, M.D.
RUTH M. CLARK, Ph.D.
ALBERT V. CUTTER, M.D.
LYDIA SANTIAGO DE COLON, M.S.S.
ERIC DENHOFF, M.D.
HARRIET W. DUBNER, M.A.
ARTHUR A. EISENSTADT, Ph.D.
NOAH D. FABRICANT, M.D.
ANDREW FLYNN, M.A.
ANNE C. FRENCH, Ph.D.
STANFORD B. FRIEDMAN, M.D.
WALTER J. GAMBLE, M.D.
RICHARD A. GARDNER, M.D.
RICHARD GLADSTON, M.D.
FLORENCE B. GOLDY, M.S.W.
LAWRENCE GOODMAN, M.S.W.
CHARLES E. GOSHEN, M.D.
MORRIS GREEN, M.D.
DAVID A. HAMBURG, M.D.
LEROY D. HEDGECOCK, Ph.D.
ANGELA HEFFERMAN, M.D.
J. COTTER HIRSCHBERG, M.D.
RAYMOND H. HOLDEN, M.A.
VIVIEN INGRAM, M.A.
ELIZABETH J. IVES, M.B., D.P.H., F.R.C.P.

CECIL B. JACOBSON, M.D.
WENDELL JOHNSON, Ph.D.
ELIZABETH JOLLEY, M.D., M.P.H.
PAUL H. JORDON, M.D.
THOMAS E. JORDON, Ph.D.
ALFRED H. KATZ, D.S.W.
GLADYS C. KINNIS, M.S.W.
RUTH LEDERER, Ph.D.
L. LAVERGNE LETSON, M.A.
M. LEVBARG, M.D.
ROBERT P. LISENSKY, M.S.
LUIS SANCHEZ LONGO, M.D.
HENRY T. LYNCH, M.D.
STANLEY C. MAHONEY, M.S.S.W., M.S.
JOHN W. MASON, M.D.
DOROTHEA MCCARTHY, Ph.D.
EUGENE T. MCDONALD, Ed.D.
MERLIN J. MECHAN, Ph.D.
H. MICHAL-SMITH, Ph.D.
ELSA A. MILLER, M.A.
HYMEN MILLER, M.D.
DORIS H. MILMAN, M.D.
MARIAN H. MOWATT, Ph.D.
GODFREY P. OAKLEY, Jr., M.D.
J. WILLIAM OBERMAN, M.D.
RICHARD B. PATTERSON, M.D.
RALF A. PECKHAM, M.A.
CLEO E. POPP, M.A.
ELEANOR S. REID, Ph.D.
JULIUS B. RICHMOND, M.D.
EDITH RUSSELL, R.S.W.
BETSY SAFRAN, M.S.W.
ERIC K. SANDER, M.A.

To parents of children with major illnesses or handicaps, a word of perspective as written over three centuries ago:

> *"Deformities and imperfections of our bodies, as lameness, crookedness, deafness, blindness, be they innate or accidental, torture many men; yet this may comfort them, that those imperfections of the body do not a whit blemish the soul, or hinder operations of it, but rather help and much increase it."*

— ROBERT BURTON
The Anatomy of Melancholy

Introduction

No society has been as responsive as ours to the plea "heal the hurt child." While much more can and should be done, we are witnessing the fruits of an unparalleled marshalling of the forces of related specialties in medicine, psychology, social work, rehabilitation, and education for the care of the seriously ill or handicapped child. Advances in molecular genetics research offer, in genetics counseling, the prospect of prevention of certain genetic errors; new and innovative diagnostic and remedial techniques are now being used in the prenatal period; other increasingly sophisticated diagnostic and treatment procedures are daily adding to our capability of helping the child with a major illness or handicap. But there is, of course, another side of the coin. There are many chronic illnesses and physical handicaps for which the word *cure* is inapplicable and for which the goal of relative *adaptation* must be substituted. Thus for the child, the parents, and the parent-counselor, reason and realism must rule over emotion and fantasy, sensitive objectivity must replace the anarchy of subjective feeling, and developmental planning and implementation must replace either apathetic fixation or blind impulsivity.

Three major hypotheses underlie the rationale for the collection of articles as represented in this book. The first hypothesis is that the phenomenological reaction of the parents to the child's illness or disability may well be as crucial — and in some cases more so — as the actual disability in terms of impact on child. The second hypothesis is that the child's illness or disability may serve as a source of severe disruption, especially psychologically, to parental and family adjustment. Our third hypothesis is that in most serious illnesses, especially terminal, and disabilities, a therapeutic-type relationship with a competent professional in the field is needed if the parents are to make an objective, integrative, and wholesome adaptation to the child's disability. Such an adaptation would imply that all relationships would be considered (i.e., parent-child, parent-parent, parent-family) as in need of psychological maintenance, not just the issue of the child's care.

While the seminal insights of Sigmund Freud, Alfred Adler, Rene Spitz, and others, have been widely publicized for many decades, it was not until recently that the major helping professions recognized just how much parents influence the psychological perception and adjustment of their children, and how important it is for parents of children with major handicaps to receive comprehensive instructional and therapeutic counseling.

Parents of children with handicaps are like other parents; they have their own unique assets and liabilities, their own self-concepts, their own hopes and fantasies regarding their children. They did not expect that their child would be handicapped, but on the other hand they are not rendered different as a result of their child's handicap. Each parent will bring to the situation his own differential perceptions of the child and the handicap, his own assets and limitations for handling his role in the situation. Some will accept the challenge with fervor and skill of remarkable proportions; others will be overwhelmed, guilt-ridden, impotent. To most parents, though, it is a painfully difficult, threatening, and highly ego-involving experience to face the reality of major illness or handicap in a child.

Recent studies on the diagnosis, treatment, and education of handicapped children continue to emphasize the importance of the parents' adjustment to and role in the child's overall maturation and psychological adjustment. Both research and clinical and social case studies have furthered our knowledge of the gross and subtle interaction patterns existing between the handicapped child and his family, thus focusing more and more on the need for improved methods of parent education and counseling. It has long been known that children can — and often do — reflect the emotional and social adjustment patterns of their parents. This being so with the normal child, imagine the degree to which this relationship could be magnified in the case of the severely ill or handicapped child who is typically more home bound and more parent bound, both physically and emotionally.

From the frame of reference of the parent, the child's condition is very likely to affect the parent's personality and adaptation. The parents' past successes and failures in important challenges, their present mental health, their age, physical health, and socioeconomic status are examples of major factors which will affect their capacity to adapt to the child's disability. One crucial additional factor is selective perception: one parent may perceive a relatively minor handicap in his child as an almost overwhelming catastrophe, while another is able to accept a much more severely disabled child without undue strain on his psychological security and adaptational abilities.

A distinction should always be made, despite their interactional nature, between the socioeconomic and rehabilitative efforts of the parents in caring for their child and those both tangible and intangible psychological and emotional cues which reveal genuine love and acceptance or masked rejection of the child as a real and fully accepted member of the family unit. All parents probably make many mistakes in the child-rearing process. If the overall relationship, however, is one of genuine and openly communicated love and respect for the child, then many mistakes can apparently be made without disrupting the positive growth tendencies of the child. It is likely that similar mistakes made in dealing with the handicapped child will be more deleterious to the psychological health and self-concept of the child. Certainly the parents face more difficult child-rearing conditions in such a case in any event. If the parents become overly concerned about the impact of their behavior, they may transmit, rather than their deep feeling of love and concern, the characteristics of fear, guilt, anxiety, indecision, inhibition, and so on, thus increasing the probability that the child is going to be psychologically handicapped as well as physically ill or handicapped.

Not only must the parents face the challenge of some degree of role reorientation in order to maximize their effectiveness with the child, but so too might other children in the family be forced into some adaptational requirements. This, of course, depends upon such factors as the nature and severity of the handicap, its social stimulus value, and so forth. The parents will face other adaptational requirements with, for example, their close relatives, neighbors, the school and the local community.

Parents of children with serious illnesses and handicaps usually come in contact with representatives of several of the following fields: medicine and medical specialties, clinical and counseling psychology, rehabilitation specialists, social casework; education and special education. Some representatives of these disciplines are, in addition to their expertise in child diagnosis and treatment, well trained and experienced in the parent-counseling area. Still others do not possess the skill or the confidence in the parent-counseling relationship which they possess in their specific area of specialization. Then again there are professional workers in many of the aforementioned fields who have never really thought that much about anyone in the family other than the child with the illness or handicap. Thus while some counseling of the highest quality and value is being carried on with parents of handicapped children, there is much room for continued upgrading of this activity. A perusal of the literature reporting on parental reactions to interviews of this sort indicates that in far too many cases the parents leave the counseling session with mixed feelings of frustration, confusion, bewilderment, denial, and guilt. Accompanying the feelings may be incomplete information, misunderstood information, and selectively perceived information. That some parents may be using defensive reactions such as denial, insulation, projection, displacement, and selective perception is somewhat understandable. It seems, however, that some of the unfortunate parental reactions are the result of counseling interviews which failed. That is, some of the primary goals of the counseling session were not reached because of an incorrect or changed diagnosis, evasion or distortion of the child's condition and prognosis, seemingly brutal callousness and frankness in the initial informing session, and perhaps no provision for the very important follow-up interviews with the parents. Well-prepared and well-conducted parent interviews are an important part of the treatment and rehabilitative procedures of people functioning in any sort of counseling relationship with parents of handicapped children, be they family physicians, pediatricians or other medical specialists, or psychologists, social workers, rehabilitation experts, or educators.

In hopes of furthering this professional interest in parent counseling, the writer has collected this series of articles from the world's literature dealing specifically with the counseling of parents of seriously ill and handicapped children. The articles selected were originally published in journals representing the United States, Canada, Puerto Rico, England, Australia, and Switzerland. Thirty-four different professional journals of high professional distinction are represented, as are seventy-nine contributors.

As there is already available voluminous information regarding problems relating to diagnosis, classification, and treatment of the illnesses and handicaps represented in this book, such topics will be given only peripheral treatment in this book. The major criterion used in selecting articles for this collection was the relevance of the article to the topic of counseling parents of ill or handicapped children. Some exceptions to this will be found in the rather general and introductory articles of the first part of the book and in a few of the articles on genetics counseling which stress more an explanation of the genetic bases of certain handicaps. In the final analysis, however, the articles were chosen with the hope and the belief that the interested reader would find the insights and techniques shared by the authors to be of value to them in contacts with parents who look to them for so much.

The range and diversity of childhood illnesses and handicaps are such that not all forms would be represented in a single volume. However, since many conditions would be dealt with in basically the same fashion in a counseling relationship with the parents, there is no essential need that all disturbances be represented.

The collection of readings is divided into seven major sections. Part I includes articles intended as an orientation to the broad area of parent-child-therapist interaction and the implications of disability. Part II focuses on the parents of the mentally retarded child. The articles focus on topics such as the role of the family physician, the initial informing interview, continuing treatment of the family with a retarded child, and group counseling of parents. Part III contains articles dealing primarily with counseling of parents of children with epilepsy and cerebral palsy. Part IV includes articles on counseling parents of children with speech, hearing, and visual handicaps. Articles on individual, group, and genetic counseling are found in this section. Part V contains only four articles as brief representations of the problems involved in counseling parents of children with cardiac, hemophilic, diabetic, and asthmatic conditions. Somewhat like the preceding section, Part VI includes articles dealing not so much with the traditional concept of handicapped children as with that of the child suffering from terminal-type illnesses. The articles included in this section are representative, we think, of the growing body of evidence now becoming available on the need to deal therapeutically with the parents of children suffering from critical and terminal illnesses. Part VII deals with genetics counseling and its use with parents of children with genetically based disorders. Several of these articles were chosen to explain recent findings in the area of medical genetics. The articles were primarily chosen, however, for their usefulness in providing to counselors from all disciplines clear and meaningful explanations of the genetic bases for that large number of disorders where heredity plays a major role.

It is hoped that this collection will serve as a useful and convenient source of information, insights, case studies, and specific techniques for use in counseling parents of ill and handicapped children. The book may also be used with profit in college courses in certain of the medical specialties, clinical and counseling psychology, social work, rehabilitation, and special education courses dealing with the exceptional child and his parents.

Acknowledgments

THE editor wishes to express his appreciation to the authors of the articles contained in this book. Thanks are offered both for their contributions to the area of parental counseling and for approval to reprint their articles in the present collection. To the extent that compilations such as this book of readings are of value to the professional medical and counseling community, they are so because of the merit of each contributor's paper.

The articles represented in this collection represent important contributions initially published in journals in the United States, Canada, Puerto Rico, England, Australia, and Switzerland. Thanks are therefore expressed to editors of the following journals for permission to reprint articles from their journals:

American Journal of Diseases of Children
American Journal of Mental Deficiency
American Journal of Psychiatry
Annals of Allergy
Annals of the New York Academy of Sciences
Archives of General Psychiatry
Association Medica de Puerto Rico Boletin
Canadian Journal of Public Health
Cerebral Palsy Journal
Children
Clinical Pediatrics
Crippled Child
Eye, Ear, Nose and Throat Monthly
Group Psychotherapy
International Journal for the Education of the Blind
J.A.M.A. (Journal of the American Medical Association)
Journal of Jewish Communal Services
Journal of Pediatrics
Journal of Rehabilitation
Journal of Speech and Hearing Disorders
Medical Journal of Australia
Medical Social Work

Mental Hygiene
New Outlook for the Blind
North Carolina Medical Journal
Orthopedic and Prosthetic Appliance Journal
Pediatrics
Postgraduate Medicine
Psychotherapy and Psychosomatics
Rehabilitation Literature
Sight-Saving Review
Social Work
Transactions, American Academy of Opthalmology and Otolaryngology
Volta Review

R.L.N.

Contents

Page

Contributors . . . . *vii*

Introduction . . . . *ix*

Acknowledgments . . . . *xv*

PART I

Parents of the Child with a Disability

Chapter

1. The Psychology of Physical Handicap: A Statement of
   Some Principles — *Lawrence Edwin Abt* 5
2. Physical Disability in Children and Family Adjustment
   — *Thomas E. Jordon* 10
3. The Guilt Reaction of Parents of Children with Severe
   Physical Disease — *Richard A. Gardner* 27
4. Understand Those Feelings — *Eugene T. McDonald* 44
5. Helping Parents of Handicapped Children — *Eleanor S. Reid* 52
6. The Interpretive and Summing-up Process with Parents
   During and After Diagnostic Studies of Children
   — *Albert V. Cutter and Elsa A. Miller* 62
7. Misdirective Counseling — *Ralf A. Peckham* 78

PART II

Counseling Parents of the Mentally Retarded Child

 8. Mental Retardation and Neurotic Maternal Attitudes
    — *Charles E. Goshen* 87
 9. Problems in Helping Parents of Mentally Defective and
    Handicapped Children — *S. L. Sheimo* 101
10. Helping Parents Understand Their Mentally Handicapped Child
    — *Cleo E. Popp, Vivien Ingram, and Paul H. Jordan* 110

Chapter   *Page*

11. Helping the Parents of a Retarded Child, the Role of the
    Physician — *Keith N. Bryant and J. Cotter Hirschberg* 117
12. The Family Physician and the Mentally Retarded Child
    — *E. H. Watson* 144
13. The Physician and Parents of the Retarded Child
    — *J. William Oberman* 160
14. Observations Concerning Counseling with Parents of
    Mentally Retarded Children — *Stanley C. Mahoney* 170
15. Continuing Treatment of Parents with Congenitally
    Defective Infants — *Lawrence Goodman* 179
16. Parent Counseling as a Means of Improving the Performance
    of a Mentally Retarded Boy, a Case Study Presentation
    — *Anne C. French, M. Levbarg, and H. Michal-Smith* 189
17. Small, Short-term Group Meetings with Parents of Children
    with Mongolism — *Mary L. Yates and Ruth Lederer* 200

PART III

Counseling Parents of Children with Epilepsy and Cerebral Palsy

18. Group Sessions for Parents of Children with Epilepsy
    — *Gaston J. Baus, L. LaVergne Letson, and Edith Russell* 213
19. A Group Work Experience for Mothers of Adolescents
    with Epilepsy — *Lydia Santiago De Colon,*
    Richard D. Trent, and Luis Sanchez Longo 219
20. Group Therapy with Parents: An Approach to the Rehabilita-
    tion of Physically Disabled Children — *Doris H. Milman* 227
21. Emotional Conflicts of Handicapped Young Adults and
    Their Mothers — *Marian H. Mowatt* 233
22. A Letter to the Parents of a Brain-injured Child
    — *Merlin J. Mecham* 242
23. Therapeutic Aspects of Parent Associations for the Handicapped
    — *Alfred H. Katz* 248
24. Understanding Parents: One Need in Cerebral Palsy
    — *Eric Denhoff and Raymond H. Holden* 255

Chapter *Page*

25. How Parental Attitudes Interfere with Counseling
— *Andrew Flynn* 264

PART IV

Counseling Parents of Children with Speech, Hearing, and Visual Handicaps

26. Language Disorders and Parent-Child Relationships
— *Dorothea McCarthy* 269
27. Parent Counseling by Speech Pathologists and Audiologists
— *Elizabeth J. Webster* 285
28. An Open Letter to the Mother of a "Stuttering" Child
— *Wendell Johnson* 299
29. Counseling Parents of Stuttering Children — *Eric K. Sander* 311
30. Group Therapy for Parents of Preadolescent Stutterers
—*Ruth M. Clark and Murray Snyder* 327
31. Procedures for Group Parent Counseling in Speech Pathology
and Audiology — *Elizabeth J. Webster* 335
32. A Speech Pathologist Talks to the Parents of a Nonverbal
Child — *Harriet W. Dubner* 342
33. Emotional Adjustment of the Mother to the Child with
a Cleft Palate — *Gladys C. Kinnis* 348
34. What Parents Should Be Told About Cleft Palate
— *Noah D. Fabricant* 353
35. The Family and the Deaf Child — *Robert P. Lisensky* 356
36. Counseling the Parents of Acoustically Handicapped Children
— *LeRoy D. Hedgecock* 366
37. Psychological Problems of the Parents of a Blind Child
— *Arthur A. Eisenstadt* 377
38. Infancy: Counseling the Family — *Frank Cerulli and
Estelle E. Shugerman* 385
39. Preadolescence: The Caseworker and the Family
— *Josephine Catena* 391

Chapter   *Page*

40. Genetic Counseling with Specific Reference to
    Visual Problems — *Elizabeth Jolly* 395

PART V

Counseling Parents of Children with Cardiac, Diabetic, Hemophilic, and Asthmatic Handicaps

41. On Borrowed Time: Observations on Children with
    Implanted Cardiac Pacemakers and Their Families
    — *Richard Galdston and Walter J. Gamble* 405
42. Psychotherapy of Parents of Allergic Children
    — *Hyman Miller and Dorothy W. Baruch* 413
43. An Experiment in Group Therapy with the Mothers of
    Diabetic Children — *Angela Hefferman* 423
44. Social Adaptation in Hemophilia — *Florence B. Goldy*
    and Alfred H. Katz 432

PART VI

Counseling Parents of Children with Severe and Terminal Illnesses

45. Helping a Mother Face Medical Crisis in a Child
    — *Betsy Safran and Frances Spiegel* 445
46. Behavioral Observations on Parents Anticipating the
    Death of a Child — *Stanford B. Friedman, Paul Chodoff,*
    John W. Mason, and David A. Hamburg 453
47. Psychologic Aspects of Management of Children with Malig-
    nant Diseases — *Julius B. Richmond and Harry A. Waisman* ... 481
48. The Psychologic Management of Leukemic Children
    and Their Families — *Godfrey P. Oakley and*
    Richard B. Patterson 492
49. Psychologic Considerations in the Management of
    Deaths on Pediatric Hospital Services
    — *Albert J. Solnit and Morris Green* 507

PART VII

Genetic Counseling and Parents of Children with Handicaps

Chapter *Page*

50. The Impact of Genetic Counseling upon the Family Milieu
    – *Robert L. Tips and Henry T. Lynch* 523
51. Genetic Counseling – *R. G. B. Cameron* 534
52. Genetics and Genetic Counseling – *Elizabeth J. Ives* 545
53. Genetic Counseling in Clinical Pediatrics
    – *Margaret W. Thompson* 557
54. Genetic Counseling in Obstetrics and Gynecology
    – *James G. Sites and Cecil B. Jacobson* 580
55. Translocation Mongolism – *Kenneth L. Becker* 588

Index 601

COUNSELING PARENTS OF
THE ILL AND
THE HANDICAPPED

PART I
PARENTS AND THE CHILD WITH A DISABILITY

Chapter 1

The Psychology
of Physical Handicap*
A STATEMENT OF SOME PRINCIPLES
LAWRENCE EDWIN ABT

W E are in the beginning stages only of our understanding of the factors that are important in the psychology of physical handicap. My experience in working with the physically handicapped has been limited both by inclination and opportunity, and I suggest the following psychological principles in only a tentative way. I believe that they are among the more important principles that may ultimately be developed into a full-scale psychology of physical handicap.

1. The emotions, desires, and drives of the handicapped individual are not different from those of the normal individual.

This principle insists that with respect to his intellectual and emotional equipment, the handicapped individual is not different from the normal. The particular means by which desires are satisfied and drives satiated depends to a very large extent upon the personality of the handicapped person, the nature and extent of his disability, and the social opportunities available to him for gratification of personal strivings. There may be more similarity between two individuals, one of whom is handicapped and the

---

Note: Reprinted by permission of the author and the *Orthopedic and Prosthetic Appliance Journal, 8*:19-22, 1954.
*For a more complete statement of this material, the reader is referred to my chapter, "Psychological Factors in the Adjustment of Amputees," in *Human Limbs and Their Substitutes,* edited by P. E. Klopsteg and P. D. Wilson, New York, McGraw-Hill Publishing Co., 1954.

other of whom is nonhandicapped, than there may be between two nonhandicapped individuals.

2. Under conditions in which the handicap has necessitated prolonged hospitalization and convalescence, repression of the activity drive may occur.

Most individuals by inclination have a strong activity drive which may, however, become greatly modified through certain personality trends. In the same manner, prolonged convalescence may force upon the physically handicapped an attitude that physical activity is neither possible nor desirable. As a result, there may occur a considerable restriction of the physical world of the disabled person which does not find its sanction in incapacity to be active.

3. Trivial disabilities are often sources of intense conflict.

As a result of injury, there may occur an increased sensitivity toward and interest in the body. Such an interest may find expression in discovering and magnifying bodily defects which all individuals may be presumed to have. Owing to the increased sensitivity, certain trivial disabilities acquire a degree of importance which may be totally unrealistic but which often serve as means for the handicapped individual to work out personal and social problems to which the trivial disabilities are actually unrelated.

4. The handicapped resent segregation.

Actually, many physically disabled individuals have ambivalent attitudes. They both want to be treated as normal individuals and, at the same time, need to be treated as handicapped persons. Such attitudes fluctuate and may be presumed to be a function of the possibilities of realizing certain goals in different social situations. That attitude which is likely to be dominant is calculated to permit the physically disabled most readily to gratify his needs in different social contexts. On the deepest levels of personality, however, it must be presumed that most handicapped individuals have a strong need to identify with all other people. It is this situation which accounts for their resentment toward any efforts at their segregation.

5. The handicapped resent sympathy but seek understanding.

Like the nonhandicapped person, the handicapped individual

feels that expressions of sympathy place him in a position of social and personal inferiority, force him to entertain ideas of inequality and inadequacy, and disturb his level of self-confidence. Hence, most physically disabled persons develop deep resentment when others extend sympathy to them, since they cannot always be sure of the motives of the other person which have aroused sympathetic expressions. At the same time, in common with all others, they sense a deep need to be understood and fully accepted in the social world.

6. *The handicapped individual is inclined to be lonely, morose, self-conscious, sensitive, and suspicious of the opinions of others.*

For all his efforts at maintaining himself in the social community and identifying fully with the nonhandicapped, the physically disabled person finds it exceptionally difficult, just as the nondisabled person does, to see the world through the eyes of someone else whose physical status is different from that of his own. The inability fully to participate empathically in the larger social environment may increase his sensitivity, sense of non-belonging, and suspicion of others' motives and opinions.

7. *Many handicapped do not have an adequate understanding of the physical and mental aspects of their conditions and are fearful of the possible consequences of their disabilities.*

Because of a lack of sufficient understanding of the meaning of their disabled conditions, many physically disadvantaged individuals impose unnecessary restrictions upon themselves and their activities with considerable loss to themselves and their adjustment to the social environment.

8. *An underlying anxiety, which may be exacerbated by repeated failures growing out of or related to the disability, may become focused on minor ailments.*

This is similar to principle 3 and differs only in the sense that repeated failures tend to build up in the handicapped individual a "psychology of failure" which pervades his whole life and which may cause him to rationalize his shortcomings not only by means of his disability but also because of other minor ailments which he may have. His attention is thus more readily directed to such ailments, which tend to increase in their importance to him.

9. *Defects of personal appearance give more worry to the*

disabled than defects which are not readily visible.

Visible defects catalyze more anxiety for the disabled individual because they tend to have social psychological implications, invite the attention of other persons, and may force the handicapped individual to explain or even defend his physical status.

10. The sudden trauma of disability may reactivate whatever fears and anxieties are latent within the individual.

Every person, normal or handicapped, carries with him at all times a number of fears and anxieties which, through learning, he usually manages to handle in such a way that they affect to a minimum degree his interpersonal relationships. Individuals differ widely in the amount of anxiety which they have learned to tolerate and in the extent to which fears and anxieties may remain latent. Under the stress imposed by severe trauma of sudden onset, anxiety and fears, formerly latent and potential, may become overt and actual.

In addition to the above principles, there is a social psychological aspect of physical handicap that it is helpful to keep in mind. At present it is possible to suggest this only in broad outline.

To understand the social psychological problems of the physically handicapped, it is helpful to think of them as members of a group among whom certain loyalties have become established, certain attitudes developed, and for whom certain behavior has come to be appropriate and to have acquired sanction. The physically handicapped may be considered to represent one of the marginal groups in the culture. As a minority group, the physically disabled, as other minority group members, tend to feel underprivileged.

The physically disabled often find it difficult to identify themselves with the nonhandicapped, whom they may regard as a group whose lot in life is more fortunate than their own. On the other hand, there disabled persons who have learned that, although they may discover advantages in identifying themselves with others who are also physically handicapped, such identifications may seriously restrict their activities and social contacts to an extent that leads to personal conflict and frustration.

The status needs of the physically handicapped can perhaps best be understood precisely in terms of their group membership in a minority segment of the population toward which nonafflicted individuals frequently express ambivalent and strongly conflicting attitudes. Like other marginal group members, the physically disabled tend to develop special zones of sensitivity that are easily invaded, often quite unconsciously, by the nonafflicted. Because of membership in the marginal group, many physically afflicted individuals think of their social and personal status as precarious and have learned that because of the very physical limitations that have made them members of the underprivileged group, their social status cannot be materially improved. Among the physically disabled, therefore, it is not difficult to see why there are those who experience deep and painful feelings of social rejection that often they cannot correct.

Living in a subordinate position in our society, the physically afflicted may come to find that many of the normal cultural goals that they are disposed to strive for are inaccessible. A forced change in the level of aspiration of a handicapped person may lead to deep frustration, and the imposition of a ceiling on their position in society may deepen the feelings of membership in the minority group.

There is another important social psychological consideration to which I should like briefly to invite your attention. I refer here to the importance of the attitudes of the physically handicapped persons's family toward the handicap or injury and the extension of this feeling to the disabled person as a whole. Sometimes, for example, the rejection of a cosmetically unacceptable injury spreads into a rejection of the person who has suffered the injury, to the great detriment of the disabled individual.

There are many other social psychological factors that deserve our attention and interest, but I have had to omit them in the service of brevity. In conclusion, I would like to mention one, however, that seems to be of transcendent importance, that is, *our attitude toward our client and his disability*. I cannot stress to you too much the importance of our own attitudes in dealing with clients, for the reservations we may entertain, whether verbalized or not to the client, tend to become known to him and to influence significantly his outlook on the future and his attitude toward his own disability.

Chapter 2

Physical Disability in Children and Family Adjustment

THOMAS E. JORDON

THE twentieth century has been described as the century in which a large proportion of mankind has been freed from material want. People today believe that happiness in the conventional sense is an attainable goal rather than a fortuitous accident in a lifetime of hard work and deprivation. The deliberate protection of our rights to "life, liberty, and the pursuit of happiness" extends from childhood through adulthood. It is of course clear that expectations of happiness are generally sound. Most young people make the transition from adolescent happiness to marital happiness without too much difficulty. This is a matter of probabilities and can be predicted on the basis of personal maturity and adjustment. Young persons establishing their families will be successful for determinate reasons arising partially from their backgrounds of experience and the nature of their concept of family living.

Several things may seriously affect the extent to which a couple successfully establish a home. Their personal qualities and their personal expectations are important factors. A third matter beyond their control, but of particular interest in this context, is the set of realities presented by the birth of children.

In most cases the reality and the expectations coincide; occasionally they do not, and a family attempts to cope with a child whose deficiencies are unexpected. The impact of such an

Note: Reprinted by permission of the author and *Rehabilitation Literature, 24*:330-336, 1963.

Dr. Jordan is Professor of Education, University of Missouri, St. Louis, Missouri.

event is partially determined, as is the success of the marriage, by the personal resources of the couple who married and established the family.

This paper will consider the effect that disability in a child can have on the life adjustment of families with handicapped children. It will attempt to describe the events and to understand their implications. The organization of these remarks will have a structure I would like to make clear. The concept of development is valuable in understanding the impact of disabled persons on their families. Development means the following things:

1. An event, like a person, has a present, but it also has a past from which it emerges and a future whose form is partially determinate.
2. A family, like a person, has a cycle of growth, and it too emerges from a past state and changes as its members age or mature.

Into this life cycle there may be introduced concepts whose value is to illuminate a facet, or conceivably several aspects, of problems. Some concepts help us understand processes — happenings — and others help us understand people. Further, some processes are helpful at one stage but not at another. In a few cases concepts at one stage in the existence of a family may help predict subsequent events. Obviously, this last idea is important, since it would help us anticipate problems and make plans.

We may begin by considering, say, a child with cerebral palsy. The selection of one with this condition is deliberate. Cerebral palsy is in many ways a model disease. It incorporates just about every possible type and degree of disability. It offers limited but not illusory possibilities of progress. It produces every conceivable reaction because of the endless combinations of symptoms and corresponding reactions. It calls on just about every discipline in the development of a therapeutic regimen.

THE CRISIS AT BIRTH

The birth of a child is an occasion of stress for the entire family. The expectant mother has experienced increasing discomfort, and the father and children have realized that further adjustments in family living are probable. Attention shifts from the several members of the family to the mother and from her to the child. A certain degree of stress is normal, and the delivery becomes a source of stress reduction; possibly family attention will eventually be refocused — diffused — in an approximation of the previous pattern. Put another way, the birth of the baby is the object of attention, but it seems probable others will get their previous share of family attention. This means father as well as the children!

The end of pregnancy sometimes can bring the delivery of a child with visible signs of neurological damage, accidental or developmental. In this case, rather than the delivery signaling the end of a tolerable degree of anxiety, it marks the transition to a period of sustained indecision and heightened anxiety.

This atmosphere of crisis is not unique to cerebral palsy, of course; it applies to other conditions such as mongolism, spina bifida, and other obvious errors of prenatal growth. (The matter of "visibility" is a separate issue to be considered later.) So, in that sense specific disease entities lose their singularity, although the topic we are considering is properly formulated as family reactions to the class of events we call congenital anomalies.

The anxiety that families radiate during the crisis surrounding the birth of a child with obvious defects arises from several sources. First there is the general lowering of the threshold for tolerating problems because of fatigue and upset of family routine. This is normal and subsides within several days in usual circumstances. However, the birth of the sick infant generates more anxiety. Parents expect that a typical baby will be a perfect baby, a child without blemish — an expectation to which exceptions are common and inevitable. There is shock as a consequence of birth of a defective infant, and there is a natural tendency to look for a reason. A feeling of personal responsibility for the child's condition is a common reaction, as is one of attaching blame to the other parent. The mother may feel responsible in a vague way and have feelings of inadequacy that feed on imaginary failings while pregnant. Zuk (26) and Boles (2) have called attention to the mediating role that a mother's values play. If she has certain religious convictions, she may feel more anxious as a consequence.

On the other hand, religious values may depersonalize guilt and responsibility, leading to an ill-defined anxiety. The gap between expectations of perfection and the reality may lead literally to flight. One such mother is known to have gathered her clothes and, within a matter of hours after delivery, vanished into the night, abandoning her ill-formed baby to whatever care fate might provide.

The reactions of fathers are also diverse. Fathers seem to have a more ready mechanism at their disposal: simply putting the entire matter in the wife's lap is all too common. In such cases the basis is laid for an entire pattern of subsequent behavior — largely built around avoiding responsibility.

THE EARLY YEARS

The early years of life for families with cerebral palsied children are not smooth. Feeding commonly is a problem, and fragility raises many health problems. A delicate child is a source of worry, and health problems that are thrown off routinely by other children are only slowly emerged from by young children with cerebral palsy. (A recent study indicates that the cerebral palsied have a death rate considerably higher than is found in the general population (20).) Colds become more than nuisances, they become sieges of debility that last for weeks. They become occasions for serious nursing, and energy normally allotted to other members of the family is diverted into the care of the sick child. The secondary consequences of the period of sickness are feelings of neglect in other children and a disturbance of the normal household routines. Brothers and sisters may become hard to handle, and the father may feel neglected, creating discord. As with all such family crises, the reactive process is circular or spiral in nature, and the situation becomes more aggravated until relieved by the return to good health of the child.

Emerging Symptoms

It is entirely too simplified to view the delivery of an unfinished child as an immediate matter of heightened anxiety and subsequent reactions. In many cases, as we know, congenital disabilities are invisible. Cerebral palsy may not be apparent unless the infant is moving. Medical personnel can detect neuromotor difficulties of a gross sort in infants. But to parents, particularly young parents having their first child, all babies wiggle in a useless random sort of way, and disturbances of tonus are not perceptible. In such cases an invisible disease that they have been told their baby has becomes a mysterious source of worry. What is the "it" that is apparent to nurses and physicians? Will it be outgrown? How about a vaccine as in the case of poliomyelitis? Is it *really* true there is something wrong? This is anxiety, but of a different sort. It is anxiety in the face of the unknown. It is anxiety that comes and goes as motor symptoms dissolve into peaceful sleep, only to appear when the child wakens.

Since cerebral palsy is not always recognized at birth, it does not follow that all mothers of the cerebral palsied are overwhelmed from the time they leave the hospital. The anxiety that we find in many − but not all − parents of the cerebral palsied arises a year or so after the child is born. Recognizing a nonvisible disease may not be easy, particularly if a child meets all the expectations parents hold for babies. Inexperienced parents may believe most infants have feeding difficulties and that theirs is no exception. They may only later come to realize their child is not demonstrating the kind of motor activity expected during the first year.

Normally the Moro reflex is gone by the end of the first three months of life, as is the tonic neck reflex. The persistence of these primitive responses is abnormal and is highly indicative of delayed neuromotor development. Not every parent is aware of this, and we consider it normal for them to be oblivious to clinically important signs. A less obscure matter is head control, which babies usually attain by the time they are three months old. This is an overt type of behavior that may be recognized by an alert parent. Such a parent is probably well informed and consults Dr. Spock's book conscientiously and frequently. Here then is an element of importance in understanding why parents react differently to the rates at which infants develop. Well-educated, alert mothers are more likely to perceive that there are norms of attainment to which children usually conform. Also, an experienced parent, one with older children, is more likely to perceive and then assess the rate at which a youngster is growing that will a new parent. (This is not restricted to parents of handicapped children; there is the example of the mother with a boy with an IQ close to 200. She thought that all boys talked in sentences at 12 months!) In such matters ignorance is bliss for a limited period of time; it begins to give way to doubt and anxiety as youngsters fail to reach developmental levels at the usual time.

Dependence

There is another factor in parental reaction to physical disability not apparent immediately that is a concomitant to delays in motor development. Infants are not bundles of reflexes, they are complex little people with personalities that are distinct at an early age. From infancy children are social creatures and they exhibit patterns of social behavior. Bathing a baby is a happy time, giving pleasure to mothers – and to fathers. As we say so often, they are so helpless and so lovable. In fact, they are helpless; they depend on us for their food, for the love that makes them grow, and for the care that protects them. Their very dependence on us is satisfying and helps us toward maturity as we help them.

The total physical and psychological dependence of infancy is normal, and it is to be expected. In the case of physically handicapped children, however, the normal stage of serious dependence may mask an abnormal degree of dependence. The pattern of interaction of mother and child in matters of feeding and care is typically one of early serious dependence, which normally gives way to a lessened degree of dependence as a child attempts self-care and self-feeding. Parents of children who are cerebral palsied may for a time not realize that dependence that is normal and delightful at one age is inappropriate later. This is a kind of problem that ticks away and evolves into anxiety only with the passage of time. The neuromotor problem exists, but without concern or worry in parents. Parental anxiety slowly emerges as a child at fifteen months shows little willingness to walk, to feed himself, or to grasp toys. A child at two years may fail to progress socially, to make spontaneous moves towards independence. In this case parental reactions may be due to social rather than neuromotor problems. Obviously, parental reactions on social grounds alone occur in children whose physical limitations are not extreme.

At this point friends and relatives are inclined to advise that children will "grow out of it." Of course this does not happen, since it would require a doubling of the developmental quotient in many cases to allow a child to catch up. Such alterations in the rate of maturation are not common, and parents may now realize that "something" — vague and unspecified — is wrong.

THE SCHOOL YEARS

Let us pursue the development cycle a little farther. Starting school is an experience for more than just children. Parents tend to prize this step because of the achievement potential their children represent. A child's succeeding in kindergarten, our values tell us, will open the door to success in elementary school. This in turn may lead to high school success and college. Fantasy about our children's success is normal, and we all realize the crucial role that education plays. Today's technological revolution seems to make school success a corollary of economic and social success. Failure at the bottom rung of the educational ladder consequently produces parental concerns. These are likely to be more naked reactions when children have physical disabilities. It seems that visible defects in children make parental perception less distorted, as Zuk has pointed out (25). We may expect, therefore, that a child's reaching school age is important and can precipitate family reactions.

In line with this general desire of parents that their child make the progress expected of most children, you may recall the change for the good in family attitudes that occurred in parents of trainable children about ten years ago when schools and classes for them were opened. These parents felt better because their children were doing what other children were doing — going to school. For the purposes of this discussion it really does not matter that the schools sometimes were not very good or that the children made little academic progress; the point is that the children engaged in an activity expected of children during the middle childhood years. A reduction of anxiety in the parents was understandable, since their own needs relating to their children were now being met.

Adolescence

Adolescence is a period of stress in families with nonhandicapped children. It follows that to parents of physically handicapped children adolescence is a period of stress producing a variety of responses. The form the responses of families take depends largely on what is perceived in the handicapped adolescent.

In some adolescents with physical handicaps problems may arise where before none existed to a serious extent. For example, handicapped adolescents may produce anxiety in their parents by engaging in fantasies with worrisome content. A boy or a girl may entertain unrealistic vocational goals, dreaming of becoming a member of a profession. In some cases adolescents may entertain ambitions whose lack of a realistic base is obvious to parents, but not to the children. To some extent we — society that is — may be responsible. There is an unfortunate tendency to offer as models the superman who has triumphed over all obstacles, enticing the handicapped adolescent into unprofitable fantasy. As we know, all too often a person's predictable failure to become outstanding, indeed even adequate, produces its own reaction, further complicating the self-concept of the adolescent with whom the family must cope.

The need for self-acceptance of one's physical appearance can make problems for the family of an adolescent. Physically disabled adolescents find the discrepancy between their appearance and that of other boys and girls distressing. Added to the normal discomfort of adolescence, which is partially neurotic, is a reality-centered discomfort. This arises as the young person recognizes the failure to be normal in appearance.

A little later this sense of personal devaluation may give way to problems arising from the conventional expectation of earning a living and raising a family. Many handicapped persons, of course, do earn a living, but many do not. Probably only a minority marry, which is particularly true of the cerebral palsied.

THE ECOLOGY OF DISABILITY

Now, it might seem that this catalog of human ills and limitations inevitably produces intense family maladjustment. In many cases this is so. Certainly much of the research bears this out. Farber's studies (6-10) and those of Klebanoff (15), Boles (2), Holt (11, 12) and Schonell (21, 22) demonstrate this. On the other hand, family reactions to disability are sometimes excellent. Excellence in this context has several connotations. An excellent reaction may be no reaction; when disability is mild, a family may find its routines altered only slightly and its expectations barely modified. Excellence may be attributed to realistic and therapeutically oriented attitudes toward a child with serious limitations. In some families such attitudes exist, and the result is that team efforts at rehabilitation are successful, within the neurological limits of the child. In such situations positive attitudes do not usually arise spontaneously, but are the result of deliberate attempts to create them. Excellent attitudes are as much a therapeutic goal for parents as speech or mobility for children. This means that treatment for physically disabled children includes the attempt to assist their families. Failure to consider this is the consequence of a limited and inadequate concept of disease. Current concepts of disease recognize that it is ecological — that it affects the diseased person directly and also produces a secondary effect on other people. This effect is as real when a person is cerebral palsied as it is when a person has an infectious disease. Attitudes and anxieties are social components of physical disability and are as contagious as microbes. Unfortunately, bad attitudes are usually more difficult to eradicate and feelings of guilt and worry may be suppressed, only to appear as irritation and petulance among members of the family.

NEED FOR RESEARCH

Let us now consider disability and its impact on family life as a challenge to our ingenuity. The object is not to consider tricks of "researchmanship" but to try to identify aspects of the problem that may be profitably explored.

Review of Research

A brief review of pertinent research seems in order. First, there have been the sociological studies on retardation by Bernard Farber of the University of Illinois (6-10). These have been classic studies in which theory and concepts were applied to the families of retarded children and the situations that arise. Saenger (18, 19) has given a picture of mental disability and the scope of adjustments brought about, using slightly less technical concepts. Equally helpful have been the pictures of family adjustment to a variety of conditions in children by Davis (4), Little (16), Denhoff and Holden (5), Stein and Longenecker (23), Westlund and Palumbo (24), and Farber (9). Zuk has given a personal, or subjective, dimension to the problem by looking as a clinician at family reactions (25, 26). Jordan (13) applied the Parent Attitude Research Instrument to mothers of retarded children and found an interesting relationship to aspects of child growth. In a further study (13) a similar pattern of values was identified in mothers of cerebral palsied children. Collins (3) has found Catholic mothers of cerebral palsied children more introverted and depressed than non-Catholic mothers. Both groups were more introverted than a control group of mothers. Much of this literature has been reviewed elsewhere by Jordan (14).

After we have noted these contributions, there are few left to consider. This is because the concept of disability as a family issue is not particularly old. There are many unraised questions, of course, and the answers to some are undoubtedly being sought by conscientious investigators at this moment. Saucier at McGill University is conducting research on the familial consequences of chronic illness in children, using a socioanthropological model of family structure.

Problems of Application of Research

All of this research is fine, but physical disability produces problems at the level of application. What does the conscientious worker say and do to help a family? How much is possible? Who should do what, and how, to help a family cope with a moderately involved cerebral palsied child? The answers are too often locked in the private thinking of experienced workers. Clearly more exchange of information is needed to capitalize on what we know informally. I should like to suggest some modes of inquiry into this problem area.

Suggested Problems for Research

An ideal approach would be to take a chronically ill child, study his family, cure him, and study the family during the process. I wonder if we do not have a paradigm for studying pieces of this problem: We might analyze the self-concept and psychodynamics of obese children. They experience much of the doubt and self-rejection that really sick children experience. Obesity is often a condition that yields to diet. Without a doubt this condition is a useful paradigm, and it can help us understand child and family relationships over a period of time.

The pattern of adjustment or maladjustment — depending on the condition — is slow to emerge in some families. In others it is rapid. There are some conditions in children that produce family reactions quickly, instantaneously in some cases. This kind of problem can yield to serious study. Accidents involving fire or lye burns can produce swift crises in families. In such situations families respond differently.

Research may be profitably directed to family patterns of reaction that have a slow rather than swift onset. Attention should be paid to the patterns of reaction that emerge in children who are moderately ill for a long time but that shift eventually as the child enters the terminal phase of illness. Leukemia is an example, and its slow but merciless development produces a pattern of reaction in the family that might offer an opportunity for profitable study.

All patterns of reactions to disability present fundamental questions. Are patterns of reaction disease-specific? By this we mean, is there a pattern of family adjustment or style of reaction specific to a given disease. Looking at the matter in another way, we may ask if patterns of adjustment and reaction are consistent for visible disabilities. Do parents or brothers and sisters of mongoloid children react in a determinate response to the visibility of mongolism? Are such parents more reality oriented at the same level of functioning than, for example, parents of children with metabolic forms of mental retardation?

There are the standard questions concerning ecological variables. Do rich and poor, white and colored, well and poorly educated families develop consistent patterns of adjustment to a given disease?

How a child's physical disability affects different persons can be measured by noting discrete events in their lives. Using this approach we can identify a series of incidents: minor arguments between members of a family, nerves frayed by the task of coping with a physically dependent child who is heavy and hard to manage, an incautious comment creating a storm. The set of events may conclude in the tragedy of family disintegration. This approach is fragmentary, however, and it usually consists of anecdotal materials that rarely do more than arouse one's sympathy even when they occur in a long and comprehensive list.

A more productive approach is needed if families are to be helped. We need to establish dimensions of reaction so that our analysis will be more than a catalog of human predicaments and dilemmas.

A useful dimension is integrity of family patterns; that is, we identify expected patterns of neighborhood and community activity and patterns of interaction within the extended family circle. Deviation from the expected patterns, a simple hypothesis of discrepancy, becomes an indicant of family response to physical disability in one of its members.

A theoretical issue of considerable interest may be noted at this point. Families react to the reality we as outsiders perceive, but they also react to what they think they see; that is, there is a *phenomenal* reality to which a family reacts. Frequently there is a discrepancy between the reality, in the disease sense, and the formulation of that reality, its phenomenal nature. This discrepancy between what a disease is and what it seems to be is a major dimension of disease of all types. Over twenty-five years ago we had our first and practically only piece of work on what disease means to afflicted children (1). It is important for us to understand how the pivotal person in the family — the sick child — perceives his own condition. It may be that this is a key to the reactions of other members of the family and as a testable problem can be applied to virtually every form of handicap in children and adults.

Complementary to the issue of families and their goals is that of parents and siblings and their individual goals. The goals may be formulated as successive social roles usually entered into. Girls normally progress from marginal family responsibilities to full responsibilities when they establish their own homes. In some families this normal evolution of responsibility may be speeded up as siblings share the heavy burden imposed by another child. The girls also may not establish their own homes at all, a consequence of choice or of necessity as would-be suitors perceive the presence of a chronically ill brother or sister. Parents also experience change in role. They were not parents when they married, nor will they normally remain so, in the nurturing sense, once the youngest child has left home. When there is a member of the household who is physically dependent, the "youngest" child (meaning the handicapped person) never does leave home. Parents do not continue role change; they do not evolve into grandparents but, rather, remain parents of a young child for the rest of their days. Evolution of personal roles within the family circle is an index of progress toward family goals; it becomes, therefore, a measure of adaptation to the presence of a physically handicapped person.

A vital subproblem here, of theoretical and practical importance, is the repertoire of role constructs that relatives of handicapped persons use to order their personal lives. Both role constructs and semantic differential techniques could be used to advantage to shed light on the personal dimensions of response of relatives to the problem.

Another class of questions may also be raised. Many of us who have worked with handicapped children and their families have noted the circularity of adjustments to children's traits and the determinate effect a family has on many of those traits. For example, a family reacts not to the number of damaged cells in the system of a brain-injured child, but to the behavior projected from the neurological substratum. Fortunately or unfortunately, the skills a child projects are partially determined by the values and attitudes the family exhibits. The circularity emerges as those very attitudes emerge as a reaction to perceived child traits. Obviously, the disability state in many cases, for example, organically caused retardation, cannot change, but family patterns of reaction can change. By designating the family unit as an object of our assistance through counseling, we insure the probability of our own efforts reaching their potential level of effectiveness. A family assisted to react and adjust will at least be less likely to hinder rehabilitation and, if experience is not too cautionary, to assist actively at times. Family participation in the rehabilitation process becomes a research topic of importance, since it is a vital element.

An obvious subject for research is the process of socialization in handicapped children. Since we know little of the socialization process in nonhandicapped children we have little knowledge on which to presume. It may seem strange, but it is true. The amount of useful information on how normal children grow is very small. The amount of information on how handicapped children grow is even smaller. We need to know if growth potentials in infancy are always met. We should ask at what point mothers of handicapped children treat their youngsters differently and whether it is always necessary. Mothers probably train many children to be handicapped — in the personality sense. How can we minimize a process until we know what it is? Let us hope to see more work on the basic processes of socialization of children, handicapped children in particular (17).

Roles of the Disciplines

We must consider which professional disciplines can give new insights on family reactions. To a surprising extent much of our knowledge of family reactions to disability has come from psychologists and sociologists, but comparatively little of a fundamental sort has come from social workers. Because of their heavy work load they have failed to report what they know, which is unfortunate in view of the strategic nature of their contacts with families. The social caseworker, if an alert observer, can reach useful conclusions after sustained contact with families in difficulty. Social workers generally adopt a frame of reference in their work that decreases the probability of mere repetition in their family contacts. Using concepts of change and growth they try to move families in positive directions and are sensitive to changes in family integration. Perhaps more than some other professional personnel social workers can give breadth and vitality to current concepts of families and their problems. In a complementary fashion psychologists can contribute to the study of the problems. Assisting both social workers and rehabilitation counselors, psychologists can design studies that will produce realistic conclusions. These, in turn, can lead to more productive and strategic intervention in the process of family reaction to the presence of a physically disabled child.

In conclusion it may be observed that we are slowly turning our attention to nonmedical aspects of physical disability. As we apply our energies to the family aspects of physical disability in children we contribute in a fuller way to the understanding of human behavior. We begin to see that the behavior of handicapped persons is explained partially by disease processes and partially by social factors. When all aspects of disability are considered we may well conclude that the challenges to our professional ingenuity posed by psychological and social factors are at least as important as those produced by medical considerations.

REFERENCES

1. Beverly, B. I.: The effect of illness upon emotional development. *J Pediat, 8*(5):533-543, May, 1936.
2. Boles, G.: Personality factors in mothers of cerebral palsied children. *Genet Psych Monographs, 59*:159-218, 1959.
3. Collins, H. A.: Religious Values and Adjustment in Mothers of Cerebral Palsied Children. Unpublished paper, 1963.
4. Davis, F.: Polio in the Family; A Study in Crises and Family Process. Unpublished dissertation, University of Chicago, 1958.
5. Denhoff, E., and Holden, R. H.: Family influence on successful school adjustment of cerebral palsied children. *Exceptional Child, 21*(1):5-7, Oct., 1954.

6. Farber, B.: Effects of a Severely Mentally Retarded Child on the Family. In Trapp, E. P., and Himelstein, P. (Eds.): *Readings on the Exceptional Child.* New York, Appleton-Century-Crofts, 1962.

7. Farber, B.: *Effects of a Severely Retarded Child on Family Integration.* Lafayette, Child Development Publications, 1959. *(Monographs of the Society for Research in Child Development, 24:2,* Ser. no. 71, 1959.)

8. Farber, B.: *Family Organization and Crises: Maintenance of Integration in Families with a Severely Mentally Retarded Child.* Lafayette, Child Development Publications, 1960. *(Monographs of the Society for Research in Child Development, 25:1,* Ser. no. 75, 1960.)

9. Farber, B.: Interaction with retarded siblings and life goals of children. *Marriage and Family Living, 25*(1):96-98, Feb., 1963.

10. Farber, B.: Perceptions of crisis and related variables in the impact of a retarded child on the mother. *J Health and Human Behavior, 1*(2):108-118, 1962.

11. Holt, K. S.: The home care of severely retarded children. *Pediat, 22*:4 (Pt. I):744-755, Oct., 1958.

12. Holt, K. S.: The Impact of Mentally Retarded Children upon Their Families. Unpublished dissertation, Sheffield Univ., 1957.

13. Jordan, T. E.: *The Mentally Retarded.* Columbus, Merrill Books, 1961.

14. Jordan, T. E.: Research on the handicapped child and the family. *Merrill-Palmer Quart, 8*(4):243-260, 1962.

15. Klebanoff, L. B.: Parental attitudes of mothers of schizophrenic, brain-injured and retarded, and normal children. *Am J Orthopsychiat, 29*(3):445-454, July, 1959. (Part of a doctoral dissertation in clinical psychology, Boston University Graduate School, 1957.)

16. Little, S.: A note on an investigation of the emotional complications of cerebral palsy. *Nervous Child, 8*(2):181-182, Apr., 1949.

17. McKenney, J. P., and Keele, T.: Effects of increased mothering on the behavior of severely retarded boys. *Am J Ment Defic, 67*(4):556-562, Jan., 1963.

18. Saenger, G.: *The Adjustment of Severely Retarded Adults in the Community.* Albany, New York State Interdepartmental Health Resources Board, 1957.

19. Saenger, G.: *Factors Influencing the Institutionalization of Mentally Retarded Individuals in New York City.* Albany, New York State Interdepartmental Health Resources Board, 1960.

20. Schlesinger, E. R., Allaway, N. C., and Peltin, S.: Survivorship in cerebral palsy. *Am J Public Health, 49*(3):343-349, Mar., 1959.

21. Schonell, F. J., and Rorke, M.: A Second Survey of the Effects of a Subnormal Child on the Family Unit. *Am J Ment Defic, 64*(5):862-868, Mar., 1960.

22. Schonell, F. J., and Watts, B. H.: A first survey of the effects of a subnormal child on the family unit. *Am J Ment Defic, 61*(1):210-219, July, 1956.

23. Stein, J. F., and Longenecker, E. D.: Patterns of mothering affecting handicapped children in residential treatment. *Am J Ment Defic, 66*(5):749-758, Mar., 1962.
24. Westlund, N., and Palumbo, A. Z.: Parental rejection of crippled children. *Am J Orthopsychiat, 16*:271-281, Apr., 1946.
25. Zuk, G. H.: Autistic distortions in parents of retarded children. *J Consulting Psych, 23*(2):171-176, Apr., 1959.
26. Zuk, G. H.: The religious factor and the role of guilt in parental acceptance of the retarded child. *Am J Ment Defic, 64*(1):139-147, July, 1959.

Chapter 3

The Guilt Reaction of Parents of Children with Severe Physical Disease

RICHARD A. GARDNER

THE author studied 23 parents to test the hypothesis that psychological processes other than the classical process might explain the inappropriate guilt reaction of parents of severely ill children. Some of the parents did suffer guilt for reasons described by the classical process, i.e. it was related to unconscious hostility toward the child, but the guilt of some of the others is more readily explained by the alternative hypothesis that it represents an attempt at control of the uncontrollable. In some parents neither mechanism seemed to be operative.

The author has observed that most parents of children with severe diseases such as leukemia, cystic fibrosis, cerebral palsy, and brain injury exhibit at one time or another an inappropriate guilt reaction concerning their child's illness. Typical comments include "It's my fault he got measles encephalitis. I shouldn't have sent him to camp." "We had sexual relations during the last month of my pregnancy. Maybe that did it." "God punished me for not going to church."

Note: Reprinted by permission of the author and the *American Journal of Psychiatry,* *26*:636-644, 1969, Copyright 1969, the American Psychiatric Association.

Dr. Gardner is associate in child psychiatry, College of Physicians & Surgeons, Columbia University, and is on the faculty, William A. White Psychoanalytic Institute, New York, N. Y.

This paper was the recipient in 1967 of the Gralnick Foundation Award, given to a recent psychoanalytic graduate for an original contribution to the field.

The author wishes to thank Dr. Norton Garber for his valuable assistance to the study while he was a senior medical student at New York University College of Medicine.

Freudian psychoanalytic theory (2) holds that this inappropriate guilt reaction is related to unconscious hostility against the stricken child and that the illness represents the magic fulfillment of these unconscious hostile wishes, therefore the guilt. Freud's theory of a constant association between repressed hostility and guilt has become so deeply ingrained that many psychiatrists do not consider exaggerated or inappropriate guilt to stem from any other cause. The fact that one can almost always ferret out some hostility toward the person over whose misfortune the patient feels guilty has further served to strengthen this connection.

So ubiquitous is this guilt reaction that the author wondered whether in some of these parents other processes might be operative. If the classical hypothesis were the only one, then one would have to assume that most parents are secretly so hostile that they wish their child to have suffered the catastrophic illness. One plausible alternative is that the guilt might be an attempt to gain some control over this calamity, for personal control is strongly implied in the idea, "It's my fault." When guilt is used in this way, not only is the individual convinced that he had the power to prevent the illness, but also implied is his ability to avert its recurrence in the sick child as well as its appearance in siblings and possibly even in the parent himself. Such inappropriate guilt may stem, then, not from hostility but from love and affection, from the desire to see the illness undone and/or prevent it in the future.

A study of these parents was carried out in an attempt to determine the psychodynamics of this guilt reaction. Although the study was structured specifically to compare the likelihood of the classical explanation with the author's alternative, it did allow for the possibility that neither was an appropriate explanation and that other mechanisms might be present.

Freudian psychoanalytic theory holds that these guilt-ridden parents suffer from at least one of three psychopathological processes.

The first hypothesis holds that the parents harbor an excessive amount of unconscious hostility toward the stricken child and that the illness represents the magic fulfillment of these unconscious hostile wishes. The guilt, then, is appropriate to this hostility, and it is postulated that were these parents not so hostile to their children, they would not feel so guilty. In summary, the essential elements in process one are as follows:

1. Excessive hostility.
2. Normal inhibition of hostility.
3. Magic thinking.

The second classical hypothesis maintains that the parents' hostility against the child is not excessive but that the superego is unduly intolerant of even the normal degree of hostility that any parent at times feels toward a child. Here, too, the illness is regarded as the magic fulfillment of the parent's hostile feelings. Accordingly, the guilt is related to a conscience that is overly critical of even normal hostile feelings that occasionally arise in the healthiest parent-child relationship.

The essential elements in process two are as follows:

1. Normal degree of occasional hostility.
2. Excessive guilt over normal hostility.
3. Magic thinking.

The third Freudian hypothesis is a combination of the first two processes. The individual is inordinately hostile and feels excessively guilty. The guilt is greater than what might be appropriate even to the exaggerated hostility because the parent feels responsible for the illness, which he regards as the magic fulfillment of his hostile impulses. The essential elements in process three are as follows:

1. Excessive hostility.
2. Excessive guilt over hostility.
3. Magic thinking.

If the author's hypothesis were valid, process four, comprising the following elements, would be operant:

1. Normal degree of occasional hostility.
2. Normal inhibition of hostility.
3. Magic thinking.

With this theoretical construct in mind, the study was conducted as follows: Parents of severely ill children at the inpatient and outpatient departments of the Babies Hospital, Columbia-Presbyterian Medical Center, New York City, were told that a study was being conducted to learn more about the reactions of parents in their situation so that doctors would be in a better position to counsel them. They were advised that participation would entail five to six hours of interviewing and testing; in addition, they were told that the examiner would be available to assist them in handling their reactions to the child's illness.

Thirty parents were approached, and twenty-three participated in the study to its completion. The inquiry was divided into four sections.

THE STUDY

Section 1

The primary purpose of this section was to determine if the inappropriate guilt reaction was present. It was originally decided to place parents exhibiting the guilt reaction in the experimental group and those without it in the control group. However, some parents, although not blaming themselves, did blame others (e.g., the doctor). Therefore, two experimental groups were formed: group A for those who blamed themselves and group B for those who blamed someone else. The control group, group C, exhibited no need to blame anyone.

Although it was recognized that there might be different parental reaction patterns to each illness, the guilt reaction focused upon did not appear to be related to the nature of the disease, and therefore the parents were not grouped according to the child's disorder.*

The interview was structured and the questions were asked so as to provide the greatest likelihood that the parents would describe the guilt reaction *de novo*. Other background information was obtained so that the parents would not realize that the primary focus of the interview was the guilt reaction. Questions posed early in the interview were designed to elicity general reactions to

---

*For the reader's interest, the children of the 23 parents studied suffered from the following illnesses: cerebral palsy, 7; leukemia, 3; hemophilia, 2; chronic glomerulonephritis, 2; congenital esophageal atresia, 1; multiple systemic congenital anomalies, 1; chronic asthma, 1; nephrotic syndrome, 1; craniosynostosis, 1; cystic fibrosis, 1; pontine glioma, 1; intra-atrial septal defect, 1; and chronic peritonitis, 1.

the child's illness; during this period the guilt reaction was sometimes described. Later questions made more specific reference to the guilt and blame reactions, and if they were present, further details were elicited to ensure that the parent was being placed in the proper group — either experimental (A or B) or control (C).

Section 2

A scale consisting of three sections was devised which attempted to specifically evaluate in an objective way the relative degree of both loving and hostile feelings that the parents felt toward the child. A parent whose feelings of affection markedly predominated over those of hostility (some of which is expected even in the most loving parent) would obtain a high score. The parent whose hostile feelings predominated over the loving feelings (some of which also exists even in the most hostile parent) would obtain a low score. Each parent's score was expected to fall at some point on a continuum between marked affection and marked hostility on the Affection-Hostility scale.

Section 2A

This section was devised to evaluate the parent's scores on the Affection-Hostility scale for material *in conscious awareness.* Mothers were given thirty-three questions and fathers twenty-one.* The questions were in part derived from Levy's criteria for the determination of maternal feeling through observations and questions (9-12), but additions and elaborations were made by the author. Typical questions for the mothers included, "When you were a child, what were your feelings about playing with dolls?" "When you were a teen-ager, what were your feelings about helping care for younger children and/or babysitting?" "Before you were married, how many children did you hope to have?" "Why that number?" "Do you have any pictures of your

---

*Space does not permit the complete inclusion of these as well as subsequent scales to be described in this article. However, all questionnaires with guidelines for scoring are available from the author.

children?" "May I see them?" "What kind of feelings do you have when you see a new baby?" "Are you the kind of woman who likes to cuddle new babies?"

Of the thirty-three questions posed to the mothers, twenty-one were appropriate to the fathers as well, providing a separate conscious Affection-Hostility scale for each sex. Face validity only is claimed for these criteria. Since the author's criteria have incorporated many of Levy's, his scale cannot be compared with mine to establish content validity. Since no other scales measuring maternal affection are known to the author, content validity of his criteria will have to await future work.

Instead of using Levy's somewhat vague 1 to 5 scoring system, a more rigorous system of +1, 0, and −1 was utilized in an attempt to make the data more meaningful. A question was scored by +1 if the answer definitely indicated warm, loving feelings toward children, −1 if the reply revealed hostility, and 0 if the question was not appropriate or the answer gave no clear-cut information in either direction. The mothers' scores could range from −33 to +33 and those of the fathers from −21 to +21. An attempt to establish reliability was made by having the other examiner independently score a response, and then disagreements were discussed for possible resolution. If differences could not be resolved, a 0 score was given. No claim is made that this represents true statistical reliability, but is was an attempt in this direction.

Sections 2B and 2C evaluated *unconscious factors* operant in determining the parents' position on the Affection-Hostility scale.

Section 2B

The parents were presented with a series of twelve pictures, each selected because it tended to elicit data about intrafamilial relationships. Seven were chosen from popular magazines and five from the Thematic Apperception Test (TAT) (14) (cards 1, 2, 7GF, 13B, and 19). The parents were told, "This is a test of imagination, one form of intelligence. While looking at the picture, try to make up as dramatic a story as you can. It is part of a test of creative ability. So let your imagination have its own way as in a myth or fantasy. Give it free rein." Scoring was done according to the same criteria employed in section 2A. Scores could range from −12 to +12.

Section 2C

The parents were presented with a series of thirty-five short phrases for sentence completion designed to elicit a response involving children. Some of the questions were taken from the Miale-Holsopple Sentence Completion Method (7). Miale-Holsopple items 1, 6, 8, 16, 30, 40, 58, 70, and 73 were utilized. Other items were designed by the author, e.g. "The sick kitten. . . . ," "Boys and girls. . . . ," "Mothers often. . . . ," "Kids are. . . . ," and "The lame animal. . . ."

The parents were instructed:

> This is a test to see how rapidly you can make up an end to these uncompleted sentences. Although it is hard, try to tell me the very first thought that comes into your mind, as rapidly as you can. Most people give some responses that are embarrassing, difficult to say or seem silly, but try to be as honest as you can. Most people take less than a second to respond. I will measure your speed with a stopwatch. See how fast you can do this. It is one measure of intelligence.

Then, one or two trials were made with nontest items such as "Bread and. . . . ," and "The tree. . . ."

Scoring was done on the +1, 0, and −1 basis as in sections 2A and 2B. The score of 0 was given for all responses begun after three seconds. Scores could range from − 35 to +35.

Scoring in sections 2B and 2C was based on each examiner's interpretation, and an attempt at reliability and the minimization of bias was made by independent scoring by each examiner; an attempt at resolution of differences was made, and a score of 0 was assigned if such agreement could not be obtained.

The total score on the Affection-Hostility Scale was determined by adding the totals of sections 2A, 2B, and 2C. It could vary from −80 to +80.

Section 3

The only scale the author learned of that purported to test hostility inhibition was that of Siegel (16). His scale is derived from questions of the Minnesota Multiphasic Personality Inventory (MMPI), and he claims validity via its correlation with a scale of authoritarianism. I not only questioned this assumption but the face validity of some of Siegel's items as well.

According, a Hostility-Inhibition scale of twenty-eight true-false questions was designed by the author. Its purpose was to specifically evaluate the degree of inhibition in the conscious awareness of and the expression of hostility. As with the items in Siegel's scale, some were taken from the MMPI (6), but others were designed by the author. Twenty-five MMPI questions were utilized: numbers 26, 30, 75, 82, 91, 96, 105, 150, 162, 195, 201, 225, 232, 277, 282, 316, 368, 382, 426, 438, 443, 502, 503, 509, and 536. The author devised three questions: "A pacifistic approach has enabled me to avoid many arguments and conflicts." "Once a week or oftener something happens that gets me angry." "I make it a rule to avoid discussing religion or politics because it most often leads to differences of opinion and even arguments." Face validity only is claimed for these questions.

The questions were presented on a mimeographed form that included directions requesting the parent to mark each statement as true or false as it most closely applied to himself. After the parent had written his answers, the test was reviewed to ensure that all questions had been understood and answered appropriately.*

Scores could range from −28 to +28, with − 28 representing ideally healthy, free, and appropriate handling of hostility and +28 a pathologic degree of inhibition of hostility.

Section 4

The author could find no scale for evaluating magic thinking. Accordingly, a scale was designed to ascertain the degree to which the parent utilized magic-thinking processes to control events generally not considered controllable. Questions concerned beliefs

---

*It was surprising that many parents did not understand a question, yet marked it true or false just to place an answer in a box, or if they did understand it, placed their answer in a box inappropriate to their intended response. The verbal review was necessary to be sure that the most accurate data were being used.

in such subjects as faith healing, the power of prayer, fortune-tellers, horoscopes, superstitions, Christian Science, and predicting the future. Face validity only is claimed for these items. An attempt to achieve reliability was obtained by independent scoring and matching as described above. Fourteen questions were asked in an open-ended manner, similar to section 1. Responses were scored $+1$, 0, or -1 depending upon the degree of magic thinking implied in the response. The score could range from -14 to $+14$, with -14 representing relative freedom from magic thinking and $+14$ a marked degree of utilization of magic thinking.

Table 3-I summarizes the scores to be expected of parents in group A, i.e., parents exhibiting the inappropriate guilt reaction if the psychodynamics of their guilt were to be explained by each of the four postulated psychodynamic formulations.

TABLE 3-I

ANTICIPATED RESULTS FOR EACH OF THE FOUR
PSYCHODYNAMIC FORMULATIONS

	Section		
Process	2 *(Affection-Hostility Scale)*	3 *(Hostility-Inhibition Scale)*	4 *(Magic Thinking Scale)*
1 (Classical)	Low	Normal or low	High
2 (Classical)	Normal	High	High
3 (Classical)	Low	High	High
4 (Author's)	Normal or high	Normal or low	High

RESULTS

Of the 23 parents who completed the study, ten were placed in group A (inappropriate guilt reaction), three in group B (blame reaction), and ten in the control group, group C. The results are tabulated in Table 3-II.

In discussing the data, I will confine myself to groups A and C since group B consisted of only three parents.

The ten parents in group A had a significantly lower average score on the Affection-Hostility scale ($+4.1$) than the ten control

TABLE 3-II

RESULTS OF THE STUDY

				Section		
Parent	*2a*	*2b*	*2c*	*2(total)*	*3*	*4*
Group A						
RA	(+ 3	− 2	+ 5)	+ 6	− 10	+ 2
AM	(+ 13	− 7	− 7)	− 1	+ 5	0
MM	(0	− 4	− 2)	− 6	+ 1	0
MC	(+ 9	− 5	+ 3)	+ 7	− 28	− 12
MMc	(+ 4	− 9	0)	− 5	− 10	− 4
CK	(− 4	− 4	+ 5)	− 3	+ 4	+ 1
AF	(+ 18	0	+ 3)	+ 21	− 4	+ 4
JB	(− 21	− 4	+ 3)	− 22	− 11	− 1
ES	(+ 25	+ 1	+ 6)	+ 32	− 4	+ 3
EM	(+ 9	− 2	+ 5)	+ 12	+ 1	+ 1
Range				− 22 to + 32	− 28 to + 5	− 12 to + 4
Average				+ 4.1*	− 5.6	− 0.6
Group B						
WH	(+ 11	− 8	+ 1)	+ 4	− 4	+ 6
SK	(− 2	+ 2	+ 8)	+ 8	− 22	+ 10
TF	(+ 8	− 9	+ 6)	+ 5	+ 1	+ 1
Range				+ 4 to + 8	− 22 to + 1	+ 1 to + 10
Average				+ 5.7	− 8.3	+ 5.7
Group C						
EM	(+ 9	− 1	− 5)	+ 3	+ 9	0
AG	(+ 13	+ 6	+ 10)	+ 29	− 3	+ 3
CM	(+ 1	− 2	+ 2)	+ 1	+ 9	− 4
SB	(+ 16	+ 3	+ 5)	+ 24	− 10	− 2
RL	(+ 19	− 2	+ 2)	+ 19	− 3	− 11
MS	(+ 3	− 4	+ 3)	+ 2	+ 5	+ 6
BB	(+ 12	+ 1	+ 3)	+ 16	− 12	+ 2
MH	(+ 22	− 1	− 1)	+ 20	− 9	+ 2
PH	(+ 14	− 4	+ 5)	+ 15	− 10	− 2
GG	(+ 13	+ 3	+ 1)	+ 17	− 10	− 7
Range				+ 1 to + 29	− 12 to + 9	− 11 to + 6
Average				+ 14.6*	− 3.4	− 1.3

*Differences between groups A and C significant at the 0.05 level (Sum of the Ranks Test).

parents (+14.6), suggesting that the guilt group on the whole harbored more hostility toward children than the parents without the guilt reaction. The difference between these two groups was significant at the 0.05 level on the Sum of the Ranks Test. Groups

A and C showed similar averages on the Hostility-Inhibition scale (section 3) and Magic Thinking scale (section 4).

More important than average figures are individual scores that, on analysis, are more meaningful in establishing the presence or absence of any of the four postulated psychodynamic formulations. The scores of each of the ten parents in group A were studied to determine if they fell into any of the patterns outlined in Table 3-I. Before this could be done, normal ranges had to be delineated for each of the sections in the group C data. This was done by listing the results of each section in group C in numerical order and ascertaining a natural cutoff point for the few highest and few lowest figures. Such cutoff points usually delineated the middle two-thirds as the normal range. The results of these determinations are shown in Table 3-III.

TABLE 3-III

HIGH, LOW, AND NORMAL RANGES FROM THE ANALYSIS OF GROUP C DATA

	Section		
Range	*2* *(Affection-* *Hostility* *Scale)*	*3* *(Hostility-* *Inhibition* *Scale)*	*4* *(Magic* *Thinking* *Scale)*
High	+ 21 or above	+ 6 or above	+ 1 or above
Normal	+ 10 through + 20	− 9 through + 5	− 2 through 0
Low	+ 9 or below	− 10 or below	− 3 or below

These criteria were then used to decide whether a section score in a group A parent was in the high, low, or average range and thereby to determine whether a score pattern fit into any of the four processes of psychodynamic formulations. To facilitate this, the specific high, low, and normal ranges were substituted for the categories outlined in Table 3-I. The results are shown in Table 3-IV.

Of the ten parents in group A, five did not obtain scores that would place them in any of the four categories. Of the other five (see Table 3-V), two had scores suggesting that their guilt could be explained on the basis of classical psychodynamics, and three by the alternative hypothesis suggested by the author.

These three parents had the highest section 2 scores of the ten

TABLE 3-IV

ANTICIPATED SCORES FOR EACH OF THE FOUR PSYCHODYNAMIC
FORMULATIONS (TABLES 3-I AND 3-III COMBINED)

	Section		
Process	2 *(Affection-Hostility Scale)*	3 *(Hostility-Inhibition Scale)*	4 *(Magic Thinking Scale)*
1	Low (+ 9 or below)	Normal (− 9 through + 5) or low (− 10 or below)	High (+ 1 or above)
2	Normal (+ 10 through +20) or high (+ 21 or above)	High (+ 6 or above)	High (+ 1 or above)
3	Low (+ 9 or below)	High (+ 6 or above)	High (+ 1 or above)
4	Normal (+ 10 through + 20) or high (+ 21 or above)	Normal (− 9 through + 5) or low (− 10 or below)	High (+ 1 or above)

TABLE 3-V

GROUP A PATIENTS WHOSE SCORES FELL INTO
ONE OF THE FOUR PSYCHODYNAMIC PATTERNS

	Section			
Parent	*2*	*3*	*4*	*Process*
AR	+ 6	− 10	+ 2	1*
CK	− 3	+ 4	+ 1	1*
AF	+ 21	− 4	+ 4	4†
ES	+ 32	− 4	+ 3	4†
EM	+ 12	+ 1	+ 1	4†

*Classical hypothesis.
†Author's hypothesis.

parents in group A, i.e. they rated highest in parental affection.
One of the three obtained a score of +32, which was eight points
higher than the highest control group score in section 2. This
would lend further evidence to the author's view that the guilty
reaction can arise out of affection and devotion and not
necessarily hostility. No attempt is made to explain the psychodynamics of the remaining five parents.

To translate this into perhaps more meaningful clinical terms,
the protocol of two parents who demonstrated psychodynamic
processes 1 and 4 will be summarized.

Case 1. C. K., a 53-year-old Jewish housewife, was the most striking example of process 1: She exhibited a high level of hostility, normal inhibition of hostility, and a high degree of magic thinking. Her 14-year-old daughter had cystic fibrosis. The symptoms had been present since infancy, but a definite diagnosis was not made until she was 11. In the more than three years since learning the diagnosis, Mrs. K. suffered with feelings of guilt. The guilt centered around ideas that she had not done enough for the child when she was younger and that she might have made mistakes during the girl's upbringing but did not know exactly what these were. Other guilty preoccupations were with biblical quotations in which God punished people for their sins through their children. These obsessions were associated with anorexia and insomnia. On numerous occasions she had mentioned these feelings to physicians and had been told "not to think that way."

Mrs. K.'s score on section 2 (Affection-Hostility) was −3, placing her lower than any member of the control group (range +1 to +20) and eighth among the ten parents in her own group A (guilt) group.

As a child, Mrs. K. had not enjoyed playing with dolls or helping her mother with housework. She never enjoyed baby-sitting or caring for younger siblings. She did not breast-feed her child. Typical responses in section 2B included "The children looked intently at the apples, but the mother doesn't like the way the apples look, they're rotten or something, so she doesn't buy them." To TAT card number 1 she responded: "He'll never be a musician. He's just not cut out for it. He thinks you'll get somewhere by just sitting there and staring."

This parent's magic thinking exhibited itself in a deep involvement with the rituals of orthodox Judaism, continuous use of prayers, belief in miracles, faith healing, and mental telepathy, and marked adherence to common superstitions.

Clinically, Mrs. K. was observed to be an angry woman whose hostility to her daughter could not be overtly expressed. Guilt over her daughter's illness was probably related to her unconscious hostility toward the child. This anger, she probably felt, was magically realized in her daughter's illness.

Case 2. E. S., the parent whose scores most confirmed the author's hypothesis, showed the highest maternal feelings of the twenty-three parents in the study. She also manifested normal inhibition of hostility and an abnormally high degree of magic thinking. She was a 41-year-old Catholic housewife whose 8-year-old son had an intra-atrial septal defect that had been known to the family for six years. During this period the mother was intermittently obsessed with the idea that the cardiac defect was caused by the baby's having fallen off the bed when she was lax in watching him one day when he was about one-year old. Numerous reassurances by physicians that this could not have been the cause did not assuage her guilt. In addition, she felt that because she was a divorced Catholic, God was punishing her by making this child of her second, "sinful" marriage a defective one.

During her childhood she had enjoyed caring for her younger brothers and liked playing with dolls. As a teen-ager she frequently baby-sat for her nieces and nephews and asked to do so without pay. Prior to marriage she planned on having four to six children. At the time of the study she did indeed have six children, whose pictures she proudly displayed to the examiner. During interviews she would caress and soothe her child, and she smiled with pride when the examiner made a complimentary comment about the boy. Of the thirty-three questions in section 2A she scored twenty-six pluses, six zeros, and one minus. Her only negative response was that she had wanted a boy during her pregnancy and had only chosen a boy's name.

In section 2B some typical responses were, "They'll buy apples from the lady and go home and make pies and enjoy themselves." "The teen-age children are entertaining their friends, dancing is going on. Upstairs there's either a son or daughter in college studying." For one picture, she was the only one of the twenty-three parents who described the main female figure as being pregnant. Of the ten parents in group A, Mrs. S. achieved the highest score in this section.

She also scored higher than any other parent in section 2C and was third highest of the twenty-three parents in the total study.

Her score in section 3 revealed a normal degree of inhibition of hostility.

The score of +3 in section 4 indicates a greater than average amount of magic thinking. She was sure that God directly helps each doctor do his work; she prays frequently, believes in miracles, clairvoyance, and fortune-tellers, and has many superstitions.

This mother well demonstrates that parents with high scores on the Affection-Hostility scale can nevertheless exhibit the prolonged inappropriate guilt reaction, and she supports this author's thesis that predominantly loving, not hateful, feelings toward the child can be a significant factor in the psychodynamics of this guilt reaction.

The clinician should be aware of this possibility when working with parents who exhibit an inappropriate guilt reaction to their child's illness. To assume that only the Freudian formulation is correct may lead to a false interpretation of the situation and can serve to unnecessarily increase the parent's burden. Dredging up every shred of even normal hostility to explain the guilt reaction along classical lines may only increase the guilt and cause humiliation. Moreover, telling such guilty parents that the situation is not their fault is usually of little clinical value. Whether the guilt is due to unconscious hostility, the need to control the uncontrollable, and/or related to other mechanisms suggested by this study, it is an essential mechanism that can best be resolved through its understanding and analysis.

It has been the author's experience that those parents whose guilt arises from the need to gain control over the uncontrollable can be helped by encouraging participation in the child's treatment program. Feelings of impotency and helplessness are thereby reduced, and the resultant need for magic power, diminished. The author has had considerable experience with such recommendations for the parents of minimally brain-injured children (3) and has found that encouragement of parental participation in the child's education, drug management, and psychotherapy have been useful in alleviating this guilt.

It has been my intent in this study to demonstrate that it is *possible* to explain the inappropriate parental guilt reaction along lines that do not require a problem concerning hostility to be present. Although statistically proven validity and reliability are not claimed, and the number of patients in this study is small, the data strongly suggest that the psychodynamics of only two patients out of ten appear to fall into the classical pattern; the other eight follow other mechanisms, one of which relates to the excessive need to control the uncontrollable. If I have been successful in demonstrating that other mechanisms do exist and that one of these can be related to an exaggerated need to control, I will have accomplished my aim.

DISCUSSION

This study presents an attempt at clinical confirmation of the author's thesis that guilt can be utilized as a defense mechanism in the handling of existential anxiety. The term "existential," as used here, refers *only* to its dictionary meaning, viz., that which pertains to existence. Existential anxieties arise in man by virtue of his existence in the world. They include anxieties over death and harm from one's fellowman as well as from the overpowering forces of nature. Man experiences these anxieties because of his relative impotence in controlling such forces. The term does *not* refer to its more specific use by the so-called existentialists, although there is certainly some overlap between their and my use of the term.

Although most defense mechanisms and neurotic symptoms are considered devices to ward off, protect against, and handle anxiety, guilt is not usually included (1, 15). The use of guilt as an alleviator of existential anxiety has occasionally been described. Kierkegaard (8) described a type of guilt that he equated with responsibility. He felt that the concept of fate leaves man impotent to change his environment, but with guilt and its implication of personal responsibility, the individual commands a certain degree of control over his milieu.

May (13) refers to Kierkegaard, and in discussing this type of guilt he mentions chronically ill tuberculosis patients who become panicky when reassured by well-meaning friends that the disease was due to accidental infection by the tubercle bacillus.

> If the disease were an accident, how could they be certain it would not occur again and again? If, on the other hand, the patient feels that his own pattern of life was at fault . . . he feels more guilt, to be sure, but at the same time he sees more hopefully what conditions need to be corrected in order to overcome the disease.

Such references are rare, and in general psychoanalysts have not given this mechanism the attention it deserves.

The author holds that a fuller appreciation of this guilt mechanism lends greater understanding to a variety of psychological processes. In another work (5) I have elaborated upon its utilization in the formation of certain symptoms of involutional depression and schizophrenia and have demonstrated how this concept contributes to a better understanding of such phenomena as the origin of religious belief, original sin, scapegoatism, and prejudice. Elsewhere (4) I have shown how this concept of guilt lends greater understanding to the biblical Book of Job.

REFERENCES

1. Freud, A.: *The Ego and the Mechanisms of Defense.* Trans. by C. M.

Baines. London, Hogarth Press, 1937.

2. Freud, S.: *Civilization and Its Discontents* (1930). London, Hogarth Press, 1951.

3. Gardner, R. A.: Psychogenic problems of brain injured children and their parents. *J Amer Acad Child Psychiat.*, 7:471-491, 1968.

4. Gardner, R. A.: Guilt, job and J. B. *Medical Opinion and Review* 5(2):146-155, 1969.

5. Gardner, R. A.: The utilization of guilt as a defense mechanism against anxiety. *Psychoanal Rev*, in press.

6. Hathaway, S. R., and McKenley, T. C.: *The Minnesota Multiphasic Personality Inventory, Revised.* Minneapolis, University of Minnesota, 1968.

7. Holsopple, J. Q., and Miale, F.: *Sentence Completion – A Projective Method for the Study of Personality.* Springfield, Charles C Thomas, 1954.

8. Kierkegaard, S.: *The Concept of Dread (1844).* Trans. by Wetter Louvie. Princeton, Princeton University Press, 1944.

9. Levy, D. M.: Problems in determining maternal attitudes toward newborn infants. *Psychiatry, 15*:273-286, 1952.

10. Levy, D. M.: Maternal Feelings Toward the Newborn, presented at the World Federation for Mental Health, Berlin, Germany, August 13, 1956 (unpublished).

11. Levy, D. M.: *Behavioral Analysis.* Springfield, Charles C Thomas, 1958.

12. Levy, D. M.: A Method of Analyzing Clinical Observations of Relational Behavior. In Hoch, P. H., and Zubin, J. (Eds.): *Current Approaches to Psychoanalysis.* New York, Grune & Stratton, 1960.

13. May, R.: *The Meaning of Anxiety.* New York, Ronald Press Co., 1950.

14. Murray, H. A.: *Thematic Apperception Test.* Cambridge, Harvard University Press, 1943.

15. Noyes, A. P., and Kolb, L. C.: *Modern Clinical Psychiatry.* Philadelphia, W. B. Saunders Co., 1963.

16. Siegel, S. M.: The relationship of hostility to authoritarianism. *J Abnorm Soc Psychol, 52*:368-372, 1956.

Chapter 4

Understand Those Feelings

EUGENE T. McDONALD

The observation that handicapped children generally make handicapped families is almost a cliché today. More and more parents are seeking help for their own problems and professional workers concerned with the habilitation of handicapped children are recognizing that attention must not be given to the child alone but to the child as a part of a family unit. There are many evidences that parental reactions to the handicapped child's condition often result in the development of psychological problems, which must be given attention if the family unit is to be fully rehabilitated. The genesis of these problems of psychological adjustment is not hard to trace, for they have their beginnings in very common attitudes and feelings. When these natural reactions are not properly understood and channeled they sometimes develop in unwholesome ways. While, of course, the specific problems differ from family to family, there seems to be considerable similarity in the general pattern of parental reactions.

Since the birth of a child is anticipated for several months, the parents during this time usually look forward eagerly to its arrival and have bright dreams of its future. It never occurs to many

Note: Reprinted by permission of *Crippled Child,* *32*:4-6, 29, 1954, and National Society for Crippled Children and Adults.

Eugene T. McDonald, D.Ed., is director of the Speech and Hearing Clinic at The Pennsylvania State College where he obtained his doctor's degree. He is a member of the Executive Committee and Board of Directors of the Pennsylvania Society for Crippled Children and Adults as well as consultant in speech therapy to several county chapters of the society. In 1952 he was awarded one of the Alpha Chi Omega scholarships for special study in cerebral palsy. Dr. McDonald is president elect of the American Association for Cleft Palate Rehabilitation and editor of the association's publications. He is also chairman of the Committee on Clinical Certification of the American Speech and Hearing Association and holds professional membership in the American Psychological Association.

parents that their child will be anything but perfect and, while others are aware of the possibilities of having a handicapped child, they hope and pray that this will not happen to them. Few parents are prepared for having a handicapped child, so it is easy to understand why many parents report being shocked and confused upon learning of their child's condition. One young father has described how, while in this disturbed state, he had walked the streets from 4 a.m., when his cleft palate baby was born, until late the next night worrying about what would have to be done, where he would get the necessary money, how he would tell his wife, whose fault it was, and a "million other things." Many parents of cerebral palsied children have also reported their feelings of bewilderment upon being informed of their child's problem. Professional workers have observed that the most traumatic period in the lives of parents of handicapped children is the period between the moment it is learned that their child has a handicap and the time when they learn what they can do about it. Confusion comes naturally from a lack of information about the child's problem and the absence of a directed treatment program. If not redirected, these feelings of confusion sometimes lead to the parents feeling balked, defeated, and frustrated.

It is characteristic of man to be disappointed when he does not get what he wants or when something turns out to be different from what he was expecting. We should not consider it abnormal, therefore, for parents who have been expecting or hoping for a "perfect" child to feel deeply disappointed upon learning that their child is handicapped. A mother of a cerebral palsied daughter expressed this feeling when she said, "Ann will never be able to wear the pretty clothes I wanted to make for her" and a father when he said, "I just can't do any boasting about my boy." Sometimes these feelings of disappointment are so deep that they prevent the development of warm, loving feelings toward the child. Without understanding why, or perhaps without being aware of their feelings, disappointed parents may find it increasingly difficult to play with their handicapped child, take him visiting, or in other ways show the affection which children need in order to feel wanted and accepted.

Deep concern about the handicapped child's welfare is also an early parental reaction. Not only do parents worry about their child's physical pains, but they worry about his future social and economic adjustments. Our culture places a premium on such skills as walking, talking, and writing. Even the most elementary social relations require the participants to move about and talk. The parents of a child whose handicap might interfere with the development of these skills have reason to be concerned about their child's "social" future. In our culture, parents always hope that their children will "do better than Dad and Mom." Parents today expect their children to attend school, to get a job, to get married, to have a family, in short, to adjust well to a complex social structure. They are aware that this adjustment is often difficult for nonhandicapped persons. It is very natural for them to ask such questions as, "Will my child be able to take care of himself; if not, who will take care of him after we're gone?" Anxieties develop when parents are not helped to find answers to these questions. If not properly directed, these concerns sometimes result in oversolicitousness and overprotection, which rob a child of his opportunities for developing independence.

Embarrassment is one of the most common emotional disturbances. Everyone has been momentarily disconcerted and has felt his cheeks turn red when attention has been turned toward him. Most people have felt the discomfiture and mental distress that occur when an idea that was strongly supported proves to be wrong or impractical. It is usual to feel upset and disturbed when something we have done has not turned out well. Such feelings are quite natural for it is very difficult to divorce our personalities from our ideas, to be objective when evaluating things we have done, to think clearly about persons or things to which we are emotionally attached. A young mother exhibited these feelings when she said, "I just go to pieces inside when I think of having our relatives see our child." Many parents have reported being embarrassed, and often angered, by their friends' expressions of sympathy or pity, or the way people look at their handicapped child. Unless the causes and developmental pattern of such feelings are recognized, they may lead to hostility toward other people including those who are trying to help habilitate the child. Often during early conferences the clinician will find parents displaying hostile feelings which have grown from such small beginnings.

Parents often report that they feel they are to blame for what has happened to their child. One of the major causes of such "guilt" feelings is the lack of accurate information about the nature of the child's handicapping condition and the causes of it. In the absence of reliable information, parents often feel that the handicapped child is their punishment for having committed some sin. The nature of these sins varies greatly. Sometimes a husband or wife reports feeling that the child was born handicapped because they had not wanted to have a baby. Again, it is natural for us to look for an all-powerful hand in things which we do not understand, and since most of us subconsciously expect to pay for our sins, it is very easy to understand why parents might assume that having a handicapped child is their way of paying. Guilt feelings sometimes arise, too, from the parents' feeling that they have not done enough for the child or have not done the right thing. This attitude was illustrated by a mother when she said, "I'm a poor mother. John would probably be able to walk today if only I'd taken him to a doctor sooner." A father kept blaming himself repeating, "I just can't understand now why we kept thinking everything was going to be all right. We should have started his treatment three years ago." These attitudes often lead the parents to be overaffectionate to their children. They are unable to be firm with the handicapped child, and they try to protect him from experiences which might be painful or difficult. As a result, their children often fail to make the physical and social development of which they are capable. There is another natural outgrowth of guilt feelings which it would be helpful for parents to recognize. Just as our bodies try to develop defenses against diseases, our personalities attempt to develop protective mechanisms to keep us from being hurt emotionally. It is not unusual, then, for parents who feel that they are in some way to blame for their child's condition to become very defensive. They are already hurt by their thinking that they are responsible for their child's condition so they develop defenses to protect their feeling from being hurt more. Therapists and counselors often find it difficult to break through these defenses in order to provide the family with the kind of help which is most needed.

Another reaction which sometimes result from a lack of information about the child's difficulty is that one parent becomes suspicious of the other. Being unable to recognize anything in his life for which punishment has been meted out, the parent assumes that the mate is at fault. One mother confided, "I guess I just didn't know my husband well enough before we were married. His past sounds all right but how can I be sure?" Sometimes a parent assumes that the child's condition is hereditary and, finding no history of abnormality in his family, feels sure that there is a skeleton in the closet of the mate's family. It is easy in our natural desire to protect ourselves to permit such wonderings and suspicions to grow until they affect all family relations.

Family problems often develop because the handicapped child creates unusual demands on finances, time, and energy. Mothers, for example, often become hostile toward fathers because they do not do their share in caring for the child. Fathers become hostile because the mothers devote most of their time and energies to caring for the child and then have little time or energy left for the normal activities of family life. As one father complained, "She just doesn't seem to think of me any more. Doesn't she realize that I still need some affection and attention?" His wife had earlier remarked, "I'm completely worn out after I get the children to bed. If John would only help more it would be so much easier." Family finances may become strained by the expenses of providing medical care, therapies, and the other many special attentions which handicapped children need. Financial worries make a fertile ground for the development of tensions which further aggravate family problems. While these feelings start from very simple beginnings, they can come to pervade all interpersonal relations between a husband and wife.

These are not, of course, all the problems which might develop in a family where there is a handicapped child. Like those described, though, other problems will have simple beginnings in the natural feelings and reactions of parents and, unless understood, they may develop into complex personal adjustment problems which may affect the future behavior and adjustment of every member of the family. Many families are finding the following program helpful in working out their problems.

BECOME INFORMED ABOUT THE CHILD
AND HIS PROBLEMS

As has been pointed out, confusion, anxiety, guilt feelings and other emotional disturbances often develop because of lack of information about the nature of the child's problems. Several types of information will be helpful to parents:

First, parents should recognize that shopping around from one specialist to another produces only an uncoordinated and generally ineffective approach to their problems. Instead of looking for someone to perform a miracle or to tell them the optimistic things they naturally want to hear, they should have a detailed study made of their child under the guidance of one specialist who can coordinate the work of other specialists and then integrate all their findings for a better understanding of the child's problems. Included in this study should be a thorough medical and psychological evaluation. The results of this study should be discussed with the parents by a qualified professional worker so that they will have an understanding of the present nature of the child's condition, what might have caused it, and the child's potentialities and limitations. While it is not necessary for parents to understand all the details of the medical findings, it is important for them to have misconceptions cleared up and to learn enough to enable them to carry out their role effectively.

Second, the parents should become familiar with the patterns of growth and development of children. Unfortunately, parents are always amateurs. They expect to have to learn to drive a car, or to sew, for example, but they usually don't realize that they must also learn how to direct the growth and development of their children. Consequently, parents who recognize that their young child is physically not mature enough to carry a sack of potatoes and would not expect such a feat from him become disturbed because he can't play without fighting or doesn't know the difference between "right and wrong". Learning that emotional and intellectual development, as well as physical development, follow certain patterns will not only make child rearing a more pleasant experience but will also help prevent the development of many psychological problems in both the child and the parents.

Because parents have not had an opportunity to observe the development of a large number of children from infancy to maturity, they have no frame of reference within which to evaluate the behavior of children. They very naturally tend, therefore, to react to each emotional outburst, each infraction of the rules, or each violation of the social amenities as an isolated bit of behavior. Parents have spoken disparagingly about books dealing with child psychology because these books have not given specific answers to the question of how to handle these disturbing episodes. If a father and mother will take the time to read and discuss a good book on child growth and development, they will gain the perspective that is necessary to interpret these episodes as part of an unfolding pattern. With this orientation, much of the previously disturbing behavior will no longer seem so alarming and more effective techniques can be worked out to manage those episodes which really require attention.

Third, parents should become familiar with the broader aspects of their child's problem. Knowing something about the number of other children in the country who are similarly handicapped, the facilities available for the care and treatment of these children, etc., will help parents see their problems in better perspective. Many parents have reported feeling better able to carry on when they realized that they were not alone but that many other parents were facing these same difficulties. The awareness that specialists have been studying these problems and have accumulated knowledge and skills which can be applied to the treatment of handicapped children is in itself encouraging.

DEVELOP A POSITIVE ACTION PROGRAM

Probably nothing is more effective in helping parents adjust than the feeling that they are doing things which will help their child develop and which will improve his welfare. The first action step should be to see that the child receives all the medical attention which has been advised by the specialist who is coordinating their program. Second, parents should make those arrangements which are necessary to obtain the special therapies which have been recommended. Third, determine, through conferences with the therapists, exactly what part home training should play in the child's program and carry this out conscientiously. Fourth, identify with the cause. This does not mean that parents should become missionaries or gadflies to prod their communities into action. Rather, they should affiliate with organizations which have competent professional advisors and should make contributions both in time and money to worthwhile programs for handicapped children.

TALK OUT ALL PROBLEMS

When problems are kept bottled-up, they often increase in seriousness. Talking about them will not only make them seem less important but will also lead to solutions. Several types of discussions are important. First, husbands and wives should realize that only by their mutual understanding and cooperation can the handicapped child be optimally habilitated. Together they should become informed and together they should plan and carry out the positive action program. Against this background of information and action, they should discuss all problems as they develop. Second, opportunities should be sought to discuss problems with other parents. Parent counseling groups in which parents meet to work out their problems with the help of understanding professional workers have proved very effective. Many parents are helped just by talking with another parent of a handicapped child. Third, parents should not hesitate to consult a professional worker who specializes in dealing with emotional problems if some disturbing feelings or attitudes persist after these discussions. Psychological terms such as "anxiety", "hostility", "guilt feelings", "rejection", and so on, sometimes make parents feel afraid or ashamed, and they are reluctant to discuss their feelings with anyone because they are afraid of being stigmatized. As has been described, however, these feelings have very natural beginnings. It is only when they are not understood and properly directed that these natural reactions develop into more serious adjustment problems. Talking with other parents or with professional workers is one of the first steps in learning to understand these feelings and to direct their development into wholesome channels.

Chapter 5

Helping Parents of
Handicapped Children

ELEANOR S. REID

FEW, if any, parents know instinctively how best
to help a handicapped child, and how best to handle the intense
feelings of disappointment, guilt, and resentment which pour over
them when they realize that their child may never walk or talk, or
learn, or love as other children do. Learning to live with their
handicapped child, and with their feelings about him, imposes
upon parents the necessity for tremendous spiritual growth and
intellectual understanding. This does not come overnight. Finding
out what the child needs and how to give it to him is a slow
learning process. Parents need wise and patient guidance if the
lesson is to become an integrated part of their thinking and being.

Handicapped children belong to emotionally healthy and
mature parents and to neurotic and insecure parents. Most often
they belong to average parents, who are able to withstand a
moderate amount of stress and strain, but who may develop
serious problems of adjustment if the stress becomes very great. In
other words, the typical parent of a handicapped child is, like
most of us, a person who can take just so much and no more. This
parent is subject to great emotional strain, which may affect his
ability to plan appropriately for his child and himself unless relief
in the form of counseling and other professional services is
available.

Note: Reprinted by permission of the author and *Children,* 5:15-19, 1958, published by
the United States Department of Health, Education, and Welfare, Children's Bureau.

Dr. Reid is Field Associate Professor in the Graduate School of Social Work,
University of Pittsburgh, Pittsburgh, Pennsylvania.

Severely handicapped children do not, like normal children, "just grow." The growth of a normal child is governed by an inner law of development. The child will "just grow" − as a physical being and as a personality − if granted a reasonably favorable physical and emotional environment.

But the inner law of development which governs the growth of a child who was born with cerebral palsy, for example, has lost its reliability. Who, then, knows how it will operate? Certainly not the child's poor parents − at least, not at first. They are apt to be average − not exceptionally bright, not exceptionally slow. They are familiar with the way their average children grow, and they are doing fairly well by them. But what now? Their little girl is eighteen months old and she does not even crawl, or say "mama," or feed herself cookies. The doctors say she will probably always be handicapped but hasten to add that there is much that can be done to help her.

It is that word "much" that does it. Remember, the little girl's parents are the kind of people whose tolerance for stress is just average. They can take so much but no more. And here comes much more − hours of exercises, speech stimulation, assistance in feeding and dressing, plus days and weeks of discouragement and frustration when there seems to be no tangible reward for such a great investment of effort. The goal? Well perhaps the little girl may, at some far distant day, reach that goal her brothers and sisters achieved without even trying − functional independence.

On whom will the final responsibility for achieving this goal rest? Not on the child alone; only partially on doctors, nurses, social workers, and therapists. It will rest chiefly, in the long run, on the child's parents. They are the ones who must face the major responsibility for stimulating artificially the physical and emotional development of a child whose natural potentialities for development have been disastrously tampered with. No wonder that a handicapped child's parents often say, in one way or another, "This is too much to ask of me."

PARENTS AS PEOPLE

There are many ways in which parents of handicapped children say, "This is too much." Social workers and nurses have heard them all again and again.

When a parent of a handicapped child says, in effect, "But I have my own life to lead," he means that the burden of his handicapped child is becoming too heavy and that he is asking, however indirectly, for help. This reaction to stress is sometimes labeled "parental rejection." On the surface that is what it seems, but the professional person who looks farther may find that it is a fairly wholesome response to an almost intolerable pressure.

Twentieth-century American parents who read a great deal about child care in the periodicals are likely to come to the conclusion that our society regards them as less important than their children. Our child-centered culture expects parents to make great sacrifices in order to provide their children with "security" — that "elusive" goal of modern living. So saturated are most of us with the concept of the almightiness of the child, that we recoil when we hear a parent protest, "But I have my own life to live!" When we hear the parent of a handicapped child say this, we recoil farther. "How selfish and self-centered can a parent be?" we ask.

A professional person should not be dismayed when a parent of a handicapped child protests, "But I have my own life to live!" After all, he speaks the truth. He is right, and he needs to be told he is right. He cannot be a good parent if he does not have some of the satisfactions and rewards, which he needs as an individual in his own right. He cannot give up his whole life for his handicapped child and expect to be a well-adjusted, self-respecting, contributing member of society.

Professional persons must accept the task of lightening the load for such parents and giving them a chance to be free — free of guilt, remorse, and resentment and free of a twenty-four-hour a day schedule of child care and therapy. We can say, in effect, "You do have your own life to lead, and you should be free to lead it. We will help you by sharing the physical burden, by giving you knowledge of why and how this happened so you won't feel so badly about it, and by finding adequate financial assistance for you so that the cost of medical care will not leave you bankrupt."

This approach involves the professional person in a threefold responsibility:

1. Sharing the physical burden may mean helping the parents secure admission for the child to a treatment facility, a hospital school, a special camp or a day center. In some instances, it may even mean helping the parents to make a decision in favor of permanent institutionalization and acquainting them with appropriate facilities for long-term care. In either event, the professional person must share with the parents a sound knowledge of the resources available for handicapped children and must pave the way toward referral.
2. Supplying the "know-why" and "know-how" involves the professional person in individual or group counseling with the parents, usually over an extended period of time. In some cases, this may require the combined efforts of a professional team including doctors, psychologists, social workers, and parent-education specialists. It also requires the professional person to participate in public-information campaigns.
3. Securing adequate financial assistance for the care and treatment of a handicapped child means that the professional person will probably have to refer the parents to the services equipped or responsible for meeting their needs. This may be a clinic for crippled children, run under public, semipublic or voluntary auspices, where medical care can be secured free or at low cost; or a local welfare department, service club, or voluntary social agency, which can help out with the expense of braces, wheel chairs, prostheses, or other appliances.

Such services can go far toward restoring to a parent his own life to lead as he sees fit. They do not take from a parent any of the rights or responsibilities which are inherent in his parenthood. They merely give him a little more time, a little more assurance, a little more security, which he can share with his family and his community. Everyone benefits, particularly the handicapped child.

UNSURE PARENTS

Some parents have another way of saying that they need help.

They say, "I do not have patience to work with a handicapped child. I cannot give my little boy what he needs. I am too nervous."

A professional person who looks behind this statement may find that the child's parents are young and unsure of themselves, and that grandma, experienced and very sure of herself, has taken over: she compulsively follows every order the doctor gives; having hours to devote to the child, she decides he might as well live with her and benefit from her determination and devotion; she exercises limbs, she fortifies diets, she stimulates speech; she does everything.

In such a situation, the young parents feel more helpless than ever and decide that they can never be as adequate as they must be to meet the child's needs. They have had so little chance to get to know their own child that he is a stranger to them. They find it increasingly difficult to find a place in their lives for him. Eventually, he is deprived of normal family experiences, his parents feel guilty about their rejection and withdrawal, and grandma continues to overprotect him because of her own need to control and dominate. For this little boy personal relationships are badly snarled. He gets his therapy daily and his vitamins every morning. But he does not know who he is or where he belongs, and his disposition is deplorable.

This illustration does not mean that grandparents are not useful and necessary to the family of a handicapped child. It means, however, that there are grave dangers for the handicapped child inherent in any situation which takes ongoing responsibility away from the natural parents.

A similar situation sometimes develops when a handicapped child is placed in foster care by official authorities because his own parents are neglecting his physical care. Like grandma, the foster parents may be determined to do everything just right. But foster homes often fade fast, since the care of handicapped children is more demanding than many foster parents ever dream. So these children all too often lose their foster parents. Who then takes their place? Who has been growing up to the ongoing responsibility of meeting their emotional needs? Not the parents — they have no permanent responsibility and know it.

The truth is, no one has grown up with the problem. The child's own home is lost; the foster home is lost; the child, unfortunately, is probably lost, too. Too late we may recognize the hard, cold fact that half a home of his own is better for the child than no home at all and that ineffective parents are better than none. The professional person's task is not to find new parents for handicapped children — except in rare instances, substitute parents just do not work out on a long-term basis — but whenever possible to help natural parents with their load so that they will be better able to carry it.

Moral support is what insecure parents need and the offer of concrete services together with recognition that they have a hard row to hoe. Once granted respect by the community and relief from the burden of ignorance and debts under which some of them stagger, these parents often show a remarkable ability to handle responsibility which might once have been taken away from them.

DENIAL OF REALITY

There is a third way in which parents of handicapped children tell us that they are beginning to crack under the strain of their responsibility. With what appears to be unrealistic optimism they say, "Billy is doing just fine. We are pleased with his progress."

Denial of reality as a reaction to stress is found among the parents of severely handicapped children, and especially among those whose physically handicapped children are also mentally retarded. During such a child's infancy, his parents may have gradually learned to accept the fact that he is crippled. But this seems to be as far as they can go. As the child advances in chronological age but fails to advance mentally, the parents cannot accept the additional stress of a second disability, and although they have been told repeatedly that their child is mentally retarded, they say, "We are convinced that our little boy is a bright child. It is only his physical handicap that holds him back."

It is true that the parents of the handicapped must have help. But it must never be given in a patronizing "I know better — now you listen to me" way. In the final analysis, the parents know their child better than the professional person does and they will probably tell the truth about him if given a chance, for a defense usually crumbles in time before a truly sympathetic listener. They'll need to be absolutely sure they are not in disrepute for past shortcomings, or that an honest confession will not be used to cut off their access to services. The professional person who understands that "he is doing just fine" is merely a defensive verbal barricade against deeply feared reality, and not the expression of an unshakable conviction, will be better able to help.

Of course, there are parents whose denial of reality becomes so extreme that only intensive psychotherapy can help them. The professional person has to find out how severe this reaction is before he can judge whether or not it can be handled successfully without psychiatric help. Nurses and social workers know that they are not competent to treat severely aberrant reactions in the parents they seek to help. But recognition of their limitations should not block them from doing what they can to ease anxiety in deeply disturbed parents. They need never be afraid to listen sympathetically to persons in distress. This may not help, but it will never hurt. Afterwards they will want to consult with a competent psychaitrist about the next step to take.

THE HOPELESS

Not so different from the unrealistic optimists are the unduly pessimistic parents who say, "It's a lost cause." They are afraid to be hopeful lest their hopes be dashed. Fearing that they cannot sustain the emotional stress of another disappointment, they say, "We expect nothing. If progress occurs in our child, we'll regard it as a miracle."

These parents react to stress with a defeated attitude; they are afraid to keep trying. A professional person should remember that when the parents of a handicapped child sound a note of defeat, they are probably trying to defend themselves against an overpowering fear. He should let them know that *he* knows how hard it is to be cheerful in the face of cruel disappointment. But he must turn the focus to the hopeful facts — the child's strengths, his potential for improvement. He should offer services and let the parents know that a treatment center, a hospital school, a speech correctionist, or whatever is needed will share the burden of their fears and help them make appropriate plans for their child's habilitation. In such cases, nothing succeeds like success. When such parents learn about their child's potentialities and about the services available and see the child improving under appropriate treatment, the truth frees them of their fear of failure. But always the professional person must remember never to deviate from the truth, never to hold out unjustified hope.

PROJECTION AND WITHDRAWAL

There is a fifth way in which parents tell professional persons that they need help. They say, "It was all the doctor's fault. He was careless when the baby was born," or "He should have known I was Rh negative. The baby should have been transfused at birth," or "It runs in my husband's family."

Some of these parents are factually right. Some are very wrong. But whatever the facts, they are reacting to stress by projecting blame for the cause of their predicament upon someone else. This relieves them of a sense of full responsibility for their own actions and attitudes, and so stands in the way of their planning a sound program for their child. Such parents need the kind of counseling which can help them express their feelings and free themselves of any sense of guilt they might have in regard to the child's retardation.

There is yet another way in which parents of handicapped children tell professional persons that they need help. They simply do not say a word. They withdraw into their shells and do not talk about their child. They seem ashamed and sometimes even try to hide their imperfect child from the world to avoid embarrassment. Such parents are saying, in their silent way, that they cannot carry the weight of their shame about their inability to produce a normal child. They see their offspring as a product of their own imperfections. The child is a constant reminder of their inadequacy. Lest this inadequacy be paraded before the world, the parents keep themselves and their child from society and the child grows up without normal social experiences.

In its extreme forms, this type of withdrawal indicates deep-seated mental illness. In milder forms, the warm support of a professional person can do much to encourage such parents to make normal social contacts for themselves and their child. "Ego-supportive treatment" is the term social caseworkers use to describe the process which seems to be most helpful in relieving the anxieties of those who tend to withdraw. The parents are warmly approved for any positive steps they make toward regaining contact with society. They gain confidence in their own worth from the knowledge that their doctors, nurses, and social workers like them, esteem them, and care about them as individuals. With more self-assurance, they begin to appreciate the worth of their child, however handicapped he may be. Having learned to relate in a new way to a person whose friendship offers them longed-for security, they find confidence to face the world.

GUILT REACTIONS

Some parents indicate when the strain of their burden is becoming too great by showing feelings of guilt in regard to the child's handicap. "I blame only myself," they say. "It is not the child's fault."

Some of these parents know why they feel guilty. They tell about not having secured proper medical care for a sick baby, having allowed the child to go swimming during the polio season, not having followed diet instructions during pregnancy, or having taken the child to a chiropractor instead of to a physician. Others are pervaded through their whole being with a sense of guilt, the source of which they cannot name. The guilty feeling, then, may stem from deeply buried fears of religious or sexual error, the child's handicap being regarded as a punishment from God for the parents' sins.

To care for a crippled child under a heavy burden of guilt is a heavy task. The guilt-laden parent needs immediate help. He needs counseling, education, services — everything that will help him regard the handicapping condition not as a punishment but as an accident. When his energies are no longer totally invested in inner conflict but free to make plans and find care for the child, then the whole family, including the handicapped child, stand to gain immeasurably.

PARENTAL ATTITUDES

These are a few of the ways in which families of handicapped children give warning that they are faltering under their burden and ask for help. Let us hope that the ears of doctors, nurses, and social workers will be tuned to hear the true meaning of what is being said, and that their professional services will be broad enough and flexible enough to meet the needs. For if the families of handicapped children can be salvaged, the children can probably be salvaged, too. But if the parents are lost, the cause is lost.

Chapter 6

The Interpretive and Summing-up Process with Parents During and After Diagnostic Studies of Children

ALBERT V. CUTTER and ELSA A. MILLER

T HE staff of the Guidance Center of Buffalo, in its diagnostic studies of emotionally, physically, or mentally deviant children, early became aware of the large number of parents who had been running from one diagnostic facility to another, sometimes over a period of years, unable to accept the professional advice they had sought. Since many of the previous studies had been made by reputable diagnosticians, parental inability to accept the findings could not be explained solely on the basis of inadequate diagnosis or parental distortion. There were times when there had been incomplete or inadequate diagnosis or when explanations to parents had been too brief or too technical, but these were at a minimum. A careful study of cases that did not fall into that category revealed that the greater part of parental inability to accept diagnostic findings was based on certain underlying dynamic considerations within the family constellations.

A generalization that can be made is that parents intuitively sense that their child is mentally or physically different or severely

Note: Reprinted by permission of the authors and *Mental Hygiene, 42*:321-333, 1958.

Dr. Cutter is medical director and Mrs. Miller chief psychologist at the Guidance Center of Buffalo, Buffalo, New York.

emotionally disturbed. They develop intense feelings of failure and personal inadequacy. The presence of the child in the home furthers these feelings. The parents react in accordance with their individual and collective security and maturity. Mature parents, though hurt, are able adequately to accept the child and meet his physical and emotional needs. Less mature parents, or parents who have conflict in their relationship, react quite differently. They have normal parental feelings for the child but feel guilty because of incomplete or ambivalent acceptance of the child's condition. The child may appear to be normal in specific respects and deviant in others. The parents have difficulty in equating the differences of functioning. They are confused by this and by hollow reassurances of relatives and well-meaning friends. They witness failure of their many efforts to meet the needs of the child. The repeated frustrations lead to mounting negative feelings and to a parent's giving up in some situations. The guilt, anxiety, and confusion call forth self-protective defenses which partially block him from giving freely of himself to the child or to the other parent. One parent may play down observed signs of deviation in attempting to make things easier for the spouse and for himself. However, the similarly upset spouse may interpret this as indifference, callousness, or lack of concern, and react strongly. One parent may claim complete blame for the condition and bear the burden in masochistic fashion. He may so dote on the child that the other parent reacts to feeling shut out of his own family. The child in turn reacts as if he interprets as rejection the well-intentioned but inadequate supply of love, acceptance, and understanding. Thus the stage is set for conflict in the relationships in the family.

In attempting to handle mounting feelings people characteristically present a wide variety of defensive patterns. We could roughly classify in three groups the parents of the children studied:

Those who protest that the child is normal. Fathers seem to protest louder than mothers. The parents may subject the child to undue educational and social pressures, and involve him in cultural pursuits far beyond his capacity. For example, a severely mentally retarded, brain-damaged and somewhat physically handicapped girl was put into a dramatics and dancing class. The teacher finally forced the protesting parents to remove the child. The parents continued to pressure other teachers to take the child into a class of normal children.

This group of parents seems to use denial or reaction-formation-like ego defenses against recognition of the handicapping condition. These are primarily for their individual self-protection and for the protection of family status in society. They are afraid to face the marital partner or society with their true awareness for fear of hurting the spouse, and they possibly receive a deeper narcissistic wound in return. The show of overprotectiveness is actually nonprotective in that the limited child is forced to function as a normal child. These parents are as a rule very inconsistent in their handling of the child. Many of the children are as anxious and confused as are the parents, and evidence reactive or deeper emotional disturbance.

Those parents who accept that there is something wrong with the child, but who hold to a diagnosis that is hopeful or emotionally acceptable. The parents of Paul, a seven-year-old, held that he was physically and intellectually normal but that he was an emotionally disturbed child. Study revealed the boy to be brain damaged and severely mentally retarded.

The parents of this group hold to a condition which is more ego acceptable to them and which may be treatable. Through their protestations they evidence insecurities and intolerance of the true findings. However, they reveal their true awareness of the condition as they describe the child. The parents of Paul, while still protesting, presented an accurate picture of the brain damage and the mental retardation. They were very upset at having given birth to a severely impaired child. For self-protection they partially blinded themselves by saying symbolically, "Paul is not severely impaired. He has a condition which is reversible. We got him into this and we can help him."

With parents of this group there is a basic psychological dynamic for denial of realities. They do not protest that the child is normal, and they do protest that there is something wrong with the child. However, they do not find the true diagnosis tolerable. They substitute for it one which is more acceptable and not so final.

A few parents are overly accepting of the diagnosis. They force the symptoms on society and on the diagnostician. There is so much pressure to "tell all" that one gets the feeling that the parents are talking about something inanimate — a symptom. The empathy for the child has been blocked by the narcissistic blow of discovering that the child is "different." For self-protection the parents seem to say, "We know that our child has this condition. We know all about it and accept it. We are doing everything possible to help him. Our actions and understanding show that we love, understand, and fully accept him. You can't and shall not tell us anything." This is a surface reaction aimed at disarming and fending off others. It helps the parents to retain their disturbed *status quo*. The natural parental feelings are present, but are submerged and bottled up.

For example, the parents of Sally, an eight-year-old girl, asserted that she was normal except for her blindness. They brought out supporting evidence and in a very intellectual way talked on blindness and all that they had done for Sally. As they talked about Sally herself, and as they were seen with the girl, a coldness and distance was felt in the relationship which had essentially become a relationship between the parents and "blindness" rather than between the parents and Sally.

There is both overlapping and variety of dynamic patterns in the three groups listed, but a common factor that emerges is the anxiety and fearfulness these parents have in facing the diagnostic findings. They want and appreciate an honest and sincere statement of findings in their child but have been psychologically unable to absorb or apply the findings. Thus they become "shoppers" — that is, they are "shopping" ostensibly for a diagnosis of their child but in reality for help for themselves.

Recognition of the dynamics of the parental disturbance in these cases suggested a diagnostic approach which has proved to be a satisfactory method of preventing "shopping" in most cases. This paper represents the fruits of five years of self-critical study and practice in over a hundred such cases.

THE DIAGNOSTIC PROCESS

The diagnostic process consists of the child's being seen by the psychologist, psychiatrist, and varied consultants as needed to gain a full understanding of the condition in the child. The psychologist sees the child in three or four or more sessions in administering a battery of psychological tests. The child's intellectual capacity, with the range, present level and possible potential of functioning, is ascertained if possible. Specific learning problems and special abilities and disabilities are studied. Ego strengths and weaknesses and total personality functioning are evaluated. The psychiatrist sees the child in from one to three sessions in gaining a clinical impression of the degree of emotional upset, and in doing a cursory physical and neurological examination. The child is referred to consultants or clinics for special studies indicated by our evaluation of the child.

In most cases, the parents are involved in the diagnostic process through meeting with a psychiatric social worker or with the psychiatrist during each visit of the child with a diagnostician. Some criteria of selection of the staff member to work with the parents are these: the level of skill required, the degree of disturbance in the individual parent, the degree of disturbance in the parental and parent-child relationship, the complexity of the medical aspects of the problem, and the feelings the parents have toward the medical profession.

The approach to the parents is not one of history getting; it is, rather, one in which they become deeply involved. The parents are helped to reveal, examine and gain an understanding of their anxieties, fears and confusions in relationship to their own disturbed feelings and the feelings provoked by the chiild and his condition. This is accomplished through the worker's dynamically pointing up the expressed or implied feelings which become evident during the interview. Also, the parents are helped to bring out their true awareness of the child as the worker utilizes information transmitted by the diagnostician in brief conferences following each contact with parents and child. Similarly, the diagnostician may utilize with the child dynamic material gained from the parents and from the diagnostic evaluation. The brief conferences serve to keep the process constantly integrated. By the end of the diagnostic process, parents have faced and gained understanding of their problem and that of the child. Thus they are prepared for full acceptance of the diagnosis and recommendations.

The summing-up interview with the parents follows an evaluation conference in which the findings of the various staff members are integrated. The psychiatric social worker, psychiatrist, or psychologist may individually or in combination meet with the parents. In this interview the social, emotional, intellectual, and physical findings are shared and fully discussed with the parents. At the close of the interview the parents are helped to outline recommendations. Conferences may be held with schools, social agencies, physicians, or others. Contact is kept with the family through follow-up at stated intervals, and in some cases a reevaluation is recommended after a specific lapse of time.

To illustrate this process, two cases are presented with the focus on the work with the parents. Implicit in the illustrations are the dynamic considerations presented earlier. These must be understood by the worker if the process is to be helpful. The first case is about a child with a host of physical symptoms which, we found, sprang from an underlying emotional disturbance. The second is about a child found to be severely retarded mentally whose parents had previously protested her normalcy despite a variety of diagnoses to the contrary.

Case 1. Billy C, a 9-year-old boy, was referred by a neurologist for study. The neurologist had seen the boy for possible psychomotor epilepsy but clinical findings were negative. The boy had been seen by 56 doctors, had been in 4 hospitals and in 2 institutions, and had been followed in clinics. There were repeated complaints of sore gums, sore throat, sore ears, headaches, sleep difficulties, temper tantrums, bed wetting, soiling, tearing of the eyes, pain and bloating of the stomach, refusal to go to school and, more recently, "spells" which had been diagnosed as psychomotor epilepsy.

The parents were confused, fearful, and discouraged about their son. They were sure that he had epilespy, a brain tumor, and leukemia. For years they had feared Billy would die. They excused their lax and ineffective discipline on the basis of their fears saying, "We are afraid to upset him. We know he's sick. It's better to do nothing than to possibly kill him." Angry with doctors and hospitals, they said, "They give us the run around and don't tell us the truth. They take our money, though." The medical expenses had mounted rapidly and indebtedness was now at about $8,000. The father was forced to work at extra jobs, and his income was such that he was not eligible for public asistance. Neither parent evidenced insight into the why of the boy's behavior. Review of voluminous medical reports showed no medical basis for the many complaints.

The present pattern was one of Billy's being sick each morning at school time. He had coughing spells or complained of sore throats, headaches or stomachaches. The parents could not understand the morning sicknesses because "Billy is a brilliant boy and loves his teacher and school work." During the day he had "spells" in which he ran wildly about the house. The mother was unable to stop him. On a couple of occasions Billy stopped long enough to talk his younger brother into joining him. The spells did not occur when the father was at home.

The decision in an intake conference was for the psychiatrist to meet regularly with the parents while Billy was being studied. The decision was on the basis of the parental confusion, the medical aspects and the feelings the parents had toward the medical profession.

The diagnostic process for Billy consisted of his being seen by the clinical psychologist in four sessions and by the psychiatrist in one formal interview and briefly on several other occasions. Psychological tests administered were the Stanford Binet (Form L, 1937), WISC performance tests, Draw-a-man and other drawings, Symonds picture test, Bender *gestalt* and Rorschach.

In the first contact with the parents, the psychiatrist stayed within the content revealed in referral and in the intake interveiw. Billy complained of bloating of his stomach and was seen briefly by the psychiatrist, who could find nothing of physical significance. After this first clinic visit by child and parents, the psychiatrist and psychologist discussed their preliminary findings and feelings in a brief conference. The tentative feeling gained was that Billy was a dull normal intelligence, that he used his physical symptoms as a possible defense against facing failure in school, and that the parents were completely confused by the controlling behavior and hollow threats.

During the second contact with the parents, the findings and impressions were used in helping the parents to a realistic appraisal of Billy. For example, the parents had claimed that Billy was brilliant. They were asked, "In what ways is Billy brilliant?" and "Does Billy seem to be quick in book learning or is he better with his hands?" The parents talked back and forth in response to the questions and the father finally said, "He's like me. I was always a good talker but I had a hard time learning from books. Like me, Billy is good with his hands. He can take things apart and put them together again. He is a big help around the house if he wants to be." Both parents went further in expressing their false hope that Billy would fulfill their own unfulfilled educational desires.

Similarly, the question of "sickness" was gone into. "How sick a boy is Billy?" "Do you think that his spells are epilepsy or that he has some hidden disease?" After considerable discussion shared by father, mother, and psychiatrist, the father said, "Billy doesn't like to go to school. He has a hard time keeping up. He's gotten himself way behind. He knows how scared his mother is. All he has to do is cough or hold onto his belly and she puts him to bed and calls the doctor. I have told her and told her that there is nothing wrong with Billy, but she won't listen." The mother came back strongly, "I know there's nothing wrong with him, but if I try to force him to go to school or do some work he has one of his spells or fights me. I'm afraid he will hurt me, himself, or his brother. He gets so wild, and he's getting big." She paused. "You're a big help — never at home when I need you. And when you are there, all you do is sit around and read the paper. Can't you see that I need your help?"

Their recognition that Billy was "using" symptoms, that they had negative feelings in their relationship, and that the father had given up at home was gone into extensively.

After this second clinic visit a brief integrating conference was held. The psychologist revealed confirmation of dull normal intelligence. She had utilized the findings and the tentative feeling arrived at the week before. To her questions and comments, Billy was able to bring out the why of his dislike for school, to express his feeling of a lack of unity in the home, and to admit to the use of physical symptoms as an escape. The psychiatrist shared what had gone on with the parents. He brought out his feeling that the parents were making good use of the interview situation, that they were realistically facing the problem, and that despite a show of negative feelings there was a basically strong relationship between father and mother.

The third contact with the parents went further into discussion of the findings and into the ambivalent feelings in the relationship between father and mother. They vented their terrifically negative feelings toward doctors. The fears of death dated to the boy's infancy. He had had "bloody flux" and pneumonia. He was expected to die and the parents were told that if he should live he would always be weak and "not quite right." Billy later had glandular enlargements and an abnormal blood picture. The boy was said to have leukemia. The parents had a friend who died of this. Now, with the spells, they were told that the boy had epilepsy with this possibly being caused by "something going on in his brain." The parents projected full blame for their confusion onto doctors and hospitals.

The psychiatrist pointed out that doctors were partially to blame, but that the parents themselves had a part in adding confusion to their confusion: "Not only have you confused yourselves through your lack of confidence in doctors and your running around, but you have certainly confused and very possibly angered doctors." The parents discussed this and the father summed up the discussion by saying, "We have made lots of doctors mad at us and they were right. We didn't give them a chance. I guess we just lost our heads."

Third contact with the psychologist more openly revealed the pattern of escape from failure. When faced with difficult material, Billy began to cry and complained that his head ached, his stomach felt funny, and that the watering of his eyes made it impossible for him to see the work. The psychologist faced Billy with what was going on and the boy was soon applying himself to the tests. In discussing his spells he brought out, "I don't have the spells when I don't need them." To inquiry he enlarged on this by saying that at times the physical symptoms were not enough to gain his end; he therefore resorted to spells which "scare mother." He said that he didn't have the spells when his father was at home — "he would lick me."

Again a brief conference was held to integrate the findings.

The fourth session with the parents went more deeply into the breakdown in the parental relationship and their ambivalent relationships with Billy, and the findings of the psychologist were utilized in helping the parents to a realistic picture of their son.

In the fourth session with the psychologist Billy revealed full awareness of his use of physical symptoms and said that already he did not have so strong a need for these. His mother did not scare so easily, and she was now disciplining him for his misbehavior. Also, he was now going to school. The revelations tied in with the personality tests, which showed a pattern of immaturity and of reaction to upset in his milieu.

The clinical impression of the psychiatrist very closely approximated the findings of the psychologist.

A staff evaluation conference was held to integrate the total findings and to set forth recommendations. It was felt that the parents should be seen in another interview or two and that this case should be carefully followed up. The family physician and the school should be helped to understand the problem. It was felt that the further work with the parents would solve the problem and that Billy was not disturbed to such a degree as to require treatment.

The next meeting with the parents was a summation interview in which they were helped to bring out their full understandings of Billy and the part their parental anxieties played in his symptomatic picture. A full interpretation of our findings was then given. The parents expressed great relief and the feeling that for the first time the boy had really been studied and that they had been given true findings. They also felt they had profited by sharing and gaining an understanding of their anxieties, fears, confusions and resentful feelings. The parents were helped to arrive at recommendations.

The findings were shared with the school, the neurologist and the family doctor. The school welcomed the findings as fitting in with a realistic picture of the boy as they saw him.

The parents were met with on several occasions for a continuation of the process. Three months after closing the case the father reported that the mother and a new baby were doing well. Billy had had no symptoms for two months, was attending school regularly, was a far happier boy and was responding well to parental leadership and discipline. The father, "now able to think," had worked out plans for financing his debts. With this he was able to ease up on work and spend more time at home with the family. Subsequent follow-ups indicate that Billy is progressing as expected in school. At home "he is no angel, but he is like most boys of his age."

Case 2. Barbara S, an 8-year-old white girl, was referred by a pediatrician, who stated that the father and mother had a serious problem with the girl and with their own relationship. The father, a physician newly arrived in Buffalo, wanted the girl placed in a public school. He had run into some "red tape" because of some medical reports he presented. The school wanted further data on the girl. The pediatrician learned that the girl had been studied for possible deafness, brain damage, mental retardation, aphasia, speech diffi- culties and endocrine disturbance, and for possible emotional disturbance. The parents argued and were very contradictory in what they brought out.

The medical reports were reviewed before the parents were seen. At no point had an integration of the reports been made. The parents had gone to many outstanding clinics in the eastern part of the United States. The psychiatrist was assigned to meet with the parents because of the complexity of the medical reports and findings and because the father, himself a physician, would bring in a great deal of medical material.

The intake interview started with a lengthy review of the medical data. The parents were very critical of diagnosticians, who had given them a wide variety of diagnoses — that is, that Barbara was deaf, mentally retarded, brain damaged, possibly autistic and possibly just emotionally disturbed. They called up evidence to explode each diagnosis and expressed the feeling that the girl was normal. The father in particular used medical textbook pictures of syndromes and went further in similar vein in postulating what might be wrong with the girl. He spoke of how her coordination was poor at times, of how she tended to pull away from people, and of her being a slow learner and possibly mentally retarded. As his own contradictions and confused thinking were pointed out, the father waxed eloquent in his damning of diagnosticians. He felt that the truth had been withheld from him because he was a physician. The suggestion was made that the intellectualizing, the contradictions, and the verbal striking out were defenses against his own insecurities and that his attitude shaped how others reacted to him. The father protested and again projected the blame onto others.

Allowance was made for placing some of the blame on others, but he was told, "You have a definite part in reinforcing your own insecurities. It is not that you are to blame — you have tried your darnedest to do what you felt was right for Barbara. You have made many personal sacrifices in your 'shopping around' with Barbara. However, your well-meant efforts have backfired and helped to make you and Mrs. S more insecure, and Barbara has reacted to your confusion. If you (Dr. and Mrs. S) and Barbara are to be helped, you will have to face the part you have played in the mix-up." The parents agreed that this was correct and furthermore felt they had no idea what they were really seeking in their running around.

Both parents became less defensive and began realistically to consider what was needed. The mother brought out that no diagnostician had been able to get a valid picture of the girl because of her hyperactivity and distractibility, her clinging to her mother and her uncooperativeness. After one interview each diagnostician had given up. The parents wanted to see if we would be able to study the child and get some concrete findings which could be shared with them. They elected to wait until completion of the studies before again coming together.

The diagnostic study consisted of three sessions with the clinical psychologist and two with the psychiatrist. Our findings indicated that the diagnosis would be incomplete without further study. Barbara was therefore referred elsewhere for a general physical examination and a complete neurological study.

Barbara was noted to have stigmata suggestive of mental retardation and neurological impairment. Facies were "blank," there was occipital flattening without compensatory bossing, and there was poor coordination in the use of arms and legs. Study revealed the girl to be severely retarded developmentally. Head measurement indicated microcephaly. No localizing neurological lesion was found. The hearing problem was one of lack of comprehension. The poor speech and coordination resulted from the severe mental and developmental retardation. She was also seen as an anxious little child.

Barbara clung to her mother tenaciously. Mrs. S was in the psychologist's office during the first session. It was virtually impossible to test the child. Barbara did not seem frightened but was felt to be a very controling child. The mother was insecure and reluctant to leave her. Barbara had learned to take advantage of the mother's inability to function effectively under such circumstances.

The brief conference following the session focused on the need to effect a separation.

The second session started as did the first. However, the clinical psychologist told the mother what we felt was going on. After the discussion the mother reluctantly left, but stayed close to the office. Barbara put up a storm, but quickly quieted and began to cooperate in testing when she realized that she was not in control of the situation. A similar pattern followed in the third contact with the psychologist and in the sessions with the psychiatrist, the neurologist and encephalographer. Our knowledge of how to effectuate the separation was transmitted to the others, and they were able to study the child with relative ease. Thus an adequate study of Barbara was made.

After each of the sessions the psychiatrist met briefly with the mother to set up the next appointment and to tell her of the findings. Also, the psychiatrist and psychologist met in brief conferences to integrate the process and share thinking.

An evaluation conference was held to integrate findings and arrive at recommendations. The neurologist and encephalographer participated. It was felt that the girl would quickly quiet down if the parents could be helped to accept the findings and go along with the recommendation that she go to a school for severely mentally retarded children.

The clinical psychologist and the pyschiatrist met with the parents in the summation interview. The parents were very anxious and the father in a tentative way reached out for discussion of the weather. His wife jumped at this. Recognition was given to the why of the anxiety. The father opened by stating that he was frequently misunderstood by other doctors. He felt he tended to give the impression that he knew more than they did. This he felt angered them. The suggestion was made that the father was afraid he would scare us off and in doing so would not get the true findings and would be forced to "shop" further. He and his wife were told that we were aware of their knowledge of Barbara and that it would not be far different from our findings. We assured them that we would be open and honest and requested that they raise questions if they did not understand points being made.

The parents were then asked for their opinion of Barbara. The father said he felt her to be like a 3 1/2 to 4 1/2-year-old. However, she was able to do a few things at her chronological age. After further discussion between father and mother, they arrived at a mental age of 3 1/2. Our finding that Barbara had a mental age of 3 years 9 months was brought out. With this there was a lengthy and intense discussion of intelligence measurements. The clinical psychologist was able to spell out what intelligence tests measure in comparison to what the parents were relating from direct observation of the girl. Also, the psychologist was able to get across the concept of a range of functioning. Barbara evidenced a potential of functioning, but in actuality was functioning at a somewhat lower level. The "turning of a deaf ear," which led others to believe that Barbara was deaf, was due to the girl's lack of comprehension of many things. She could converse adequately at a very simple level. The "turning of a deaf ear" was also seen as a way that Barbara escaped situations which frustrated and overwhelmed her.

The question was now raised as to why Barbara was the way she was. The parents felt that something happened that they could have prevented. Their guilt feelings were discussed. It was then pointed out that we felt this problem to be entirely on a developmental basis — that Barbara had been different since the union of the egg and the sperm. For confirmation of this, the uncomplicated mental retardation and the microcephaly were cited. The normal pregnancy, birth, and postnatal periods were tied in. The parents readily accepted this as the logical possibility. The poor coordination and the speech difficulty were seen as a result of the severe developmental retardation.

Mrs. S now said, "There is a lot Barbara can do if she wants to. She starts to do something and then all of a sudden goes away from it. Also, I can't get her to do things on her own. She won't let me out of her sight." This led to further discussion of limitations, of natural findings with this degree of impairment, and of emotional problems. We pointed up the separation problem and the basis for it, and discussed the emotional problems in the parental relationship and in the relationships with Barbara. The parents brought out frankly that they had had need for the girl to function as an 8-year-old, saying "We have tried to kid ourselves and other that she is normal."

Dr. and Mrs. S asked for practical suggestions about discipline for Barbara and her siblings. Once they realized that we could not tell them specifically what to do, they felt they could work together on this now that they understood Barbara and the problem. Dr. S recognized that all of the children had resented the constant attention demanded and received by Barbara. Now, with their feet on the ground, things would be different.

Recommendations were discussed in closing the interview. The parents brought out the need for specialized schooling for Barbara and decided to enroll her in a local center. They spoke of the severe handicap and of the limited help she could receive. They would now start saving their money for education for the other children and for some pleasures for the family and themselves. They did not feel a need to return for further discussion, but wanted to know that they could come to talk with us from time to time. The door was left open to them. Their changed attitudes, the ability to face the problem squarely, and their realistic picture of Barbara gave us the feeling that the "shopping around" was at an end.

A conference and written report of findings brought about placement in a special program. Barbara has been happy there for close to three years. There have been a number of contacts with the school, and Barbara has been reevaluated with the earlier findings confirmed. The parents have been seen in several follow-up interviews, and there have also been a number of telephone contacts. Things have gone well for Barbara and the family. It is of interest that the parents have to a degree sublimated disturbed feelings in P.T.A. activities and in becoming involved in community mental health efforts.

DISCUSSION AND CONCLUSIONS

The two cases presented give a picture of overall design of diagnostic study. It can be seen that there is no stereotypy. There are as many variations as there are cases. Flexibility is needed if the family problem is to be met. The first case illustrates our use of graduated interpretation of findings, the second our way of handling the presentation of findings in a summation interview. The cases indicate the breadth of application of the process for diagnostic situations. This encompasses physical or emotional problems or a combination of the two. The cases also illustrate the effective work that a clinic can do in families of varied educational, social and intellectual backgrounds. The basic parental problem in the cases is seen to be the same – anxious, confused parents who were on the defensive and on the run. The first family had limitations in the intellectual, social and financial spheres. The second family had none of these. Because of limitations the first family "shopped" locally, while the other "shopped" on a national scale. Both were able to profit with equal effectiveness and solved their problems. The first situation was solved in realistic and practical terms. The second, having a continuing problem of a severely impaired child, went beyond handling mixed feelings to becoming closely identified with community efforts.

All of the foregoing adds up to our conviction that there is more to satisfactory diagnosis than the findings of a specific condition in the child. The most important aspects of the process described are these:

1. The parents are directly and actively involved in the process. The worker shares findings with the parents and helps them consider every aspect of the child's functioning. The goal is to help in the total problem presented rather than to focus on the narrower aspect of the diagnosis itself.

2. A dynamic approach helps the parents to understand their individual feeling of inadequacy, their confusions, anxieties, and guilt feelings. Parents gain insights into their relationships with each other and with the child. They gain a full understanding of the diagnostic findings and are helped to an emotional acceptance of the impaired child. The summing-up interview particularly helps the parents to an integration and crystallization of the complete findings. Parents rediscover and rebuild faith in themselves. Thus they are helped to assume normal parental roles and to function more effectively within the family and with people generally.

3. The total process meets the needs of parents as expressed through their complaints about prior studies. Findings are presented completely and honestly with no hollow reassurances given. Instead of giving direct advice, we help the parents to make their own decisions and recommendations. The parents are talked with in language they can comprehend.

4. To achieve these results, the worker and diagnosticians must have a good understanding of the process and the dynamics in the case. This is effected through supervision and through staff conferences in which the consultants, if active, participate if at all possible. The team members thereby gain in security and in their positive and accepting attitudes towards the confused and upset parents. Thus, for example, negative and antagonistic feelings expressed by the parents can be accepted, securely handled and placed in proper perspective.

5. It is therefore evident that the team approach, which implies constant integration of the case, is necessary for a successful outcome. For this to work, there must be good

understanding and mutual acceptance of the skills of the various disciplines.

The process is time-consuming and costly, but our conviction of its worth has led us to adopt it as a valid approach and to gear our clinic practices to its use. Through our periodic reevaluations — repeat diagnostic studies — and through our follow-up contacts, we find that the very high percentage of successes completely justifies our effort. Not only are the parents stopped in their running and "shopping," but both they and the child are therapeutically helped through diagnosis.

Chapter 7

Misdirective Counseling

RALF A. PECKHAM

THE counseling kettle has long since boiled over between the directivists and nondirectivists, and the tea of compromise has been poured; but there still remains another pot upon the fire, and it may be high time to stir the beans. The divergence that here provides food for thought is between the counseling visionaries and the counseling realists, regardless of their choice of methodology.

Actually, this may be of concern to all counselors; but the prime concern here is with counselors in the field of rehabilitation — those who participate in assisting physically or mentally disabled individuals to overcome their handicaps by planning and implementing programs of medical restoration services, special vocational training, and ultimately, job placement and personal adjustment. Typically, these counselors have at their disposal certain public monies which they employ "in the public good" to defray the necessary costs of implementing the plans, decisions, and goals that are worked out by the counselor and his client. In addition to public tax money, there are involved contributions from other sources and from the client himself. Over and above these considerations is the cost to the client and all his family during this sometimes long and painful process — their investment of time, their experience of mingled hope and anxiety and aspiration.

But there is something else that is crucial here, too.

To what kind of risk has the counselor committed this tangible and intangible capital? Are the counseling dreams and schemes staked on a one-chance-to-a-hundred gamble, or are the odds much nearer to the even chance or better? Anyone who has been in

Note: Reprinted by permission of the *Journal of Rehabilitation, 19*:3-6, 1953.

Mr. Peckham is associated with the Michigan Division of Vocational Rehabilitation.

counseling for long has noted the parallel. Counselors have the same kind of "psychology" as their fellow beings at the race track. Some are partial to the long shots, some take an occasional fling, and some just stick to the favorites. It may be all very well for the racing fan, since it is his money that he is risking, and it is only just horses that are winning or losing the contests; but for the counselor it is not his money, *and it is not just horses.*

Let us get down to cases. What could be more familiar than the problem of the very bright but terribly involved victim of cerebral palsy? Let us consider one whose speech is almost unintelligible, whose hands and arms jerk so that he can scarcely feed himself. He is precarious of balance, and very slow of gait. His IQ is 130, and he wants to go to college! Recognize him? You ought to, because he has been sent to college by every state in the nation, everywhere, with the endorsement of rehabilitation counselors and the underwriting of public money for his support.

And so he got his degree — maybe he was even on the honor roll — but then what? His counselor participated in building into him the image of the "college-trained" man; then, with this added handicap, he went out to seek that one chance in a hundred wherein someone would employ his college-trained brain, and in addition, hire an extra person to discover what went on in that brain, answer the telephone for it, type out its messages, and see that it was moved around to the various points where management desired to have it function.

Perhaps this kind of visionary counseling scheme *sounds* ridiculous to the overly practical counselor. Well, it often sounds ridiculous to the overly practical business man, too. And so our embittered young spastic is not hired for the job in which he received college training. But perhaps, if he is lucky, he marries someone less handicapped than himself, and the two of them (mainly the wife) earn a very modest living operating a chicken farm.

WHEN IMAGINATION RUNS RIOT

Many of these 100-1-shot counseling plans depend upon some sort of Siamese factor for their ultimate success — "Siamese" in the sense that the client must be tied in as a package deal with some other individual. This other person may be cast in a subservient role — a sort of robot — to serve as eyes, ears, hands, or legs for a severely limited client; or the situation may be inverted and the client trained to contribute some one of these auxiliary services in behalf of a "superior" — with his own vocational destiny inextricably imprisoned within the area defined by the generosity of the individual upon whom he has been grafted.

Thus in the first instance our more celestially minded counselor envisions a role in industry in which our college-trained spastic will be supported by a kind of manservant, the latter's wages to be derived from the bountiful consultation fees earned by his master. In the alternative instance, the counselor uses a little wand-waving to solve the problem of the disabled adult who is perhaps also mentally retarded. Instead of training him in the job sophistication and the simple requirements of the dishwashing trade, or guiding him to a similar level of endeavor, he places the client in a training program for some such highly skilled trade as upholstering. The idea is not that he could ever be a completely qualified upholsterer in his own right, but that *when paired with a skilled upholsterer* who would always tell him where to tack, where to cut, and where to pound, he might get along as an upholsterer of sorts, and at rather high wages to boot.

Sometimes this Siamese pairing involves linking the client with not just one individual but many: some of the homebound, for instance — arthritics who can move neither legs nor arms, quadraplegics who are totally paralyzed, and others with involvement similarly severe. Most down-to-earth counselors are inclined to believe that little more than a greeting card or magazine subscription service business can be worked out for these situations, and even that is done with the tacit acknowledgment that most of the simple business transactions connected with such a modest endeavor will very likely have to handled by some other member of the family. But not all counseling is so unimaginative. What counseling veteran has not heard of a program somewhere in which one of these individuals — say, a total paralytic — is given some training in theory of bookkeeping with the idea that the managers of small businesses in the community will deliver each week, or each month, their receipts, due bills, and accounts to his rural home, where he — unable to physically operate an adding machine or even to write with any degree of efficiency — is somehow, with the aid of his family in whatever spare time they have, to work out the balances, do it on time, and do it well enough to equal or surpass his competitors for this kind of business? These latter crass practicalities tend to obscure the free play of the imagination, and are accordingly minimized if not altogether overlooked. At any rate, a counseling plan so intricate and so overextended seldom, if ever, works out according to its original conception.

THE WAY IS POINTED BY THE WILL

But there are levels of counseling, and there are levels of error or misdirection. One can correctly appraise a client's limitations as well as his abilities, interests, and aptitudes, can correctly interpret the job market, and yet participate with the client in making a crucial counseling mistake: the mistake of failing to take a penetrating view of the client's level of *motivation*. When a counselor looks back over his "great rehabilitations," he cannot but be impressed with the determination and will-to-succeed that distinguished each of them. Nor were these unusual or highly imaginative counseling cases of the 100-to-1-shot variety. Most probably they were ordinary programs involving the provision of some special training or special equipment, and leading toward an immediate and obtainable goal. What made these cases so startling was that after the first goal was reached, the client went on and on under his own power, climbing ever farther to the uppermost rungs of the ladder to success. But conversely, when the counselor looks back on so many of the other kinds of cases — the clients on whom was lavished so much of money, time, and attention, only to have them drop out or return to public assistance — then he is struck with the invariable absence of a constructive motivation.

Motivation is not to be confused with wish for status or yearning. Motivation implies an overpowering *will to do;* it is action, not fantasy. Yet all too often the daydreams of the unable are treated by the more visionary of counselors as though these were mature interests, clamoring for release; hence too many mentally retarded clients (cases of the milder sort) are now being trained as watch and clock repairmen, or as bookkeepers, or radio mechanics — getting ready for jobs in which they cannot possibly operate at maximal efficiency or make a satisfying social contribution. Properly directed counseling does not accept a client's statement about a goal and proceed to plan toward the highest placement for which that individual has some capacity, without giving every consideration to the degree of service that he will be able to render on the job. Perhaps we can even succeed in placing a retarded person in watchmaking or in bookkeeping; *but how would we feel about letting him keep our books or fix our watches?* Is it fair to him, to his employer, or to his prospective customers?

CURB ON GREAT EXPECTATIONS

To look at motivation in one of its other aspects, one may well consider the *operational level* of an individual's performance. This brings us squarely onto the target of what a person will do, not what he would like to do. There are some 65,000,000 employed "nonhandicapped" persons in the United States, most of them of average intelligence, employed at noncomplex jobs. This represents the general operational level for this middle group. They would like to be supervisors or business owners; but they are not, and they will not be. There are exceptions, of course. Some among them go to night school or business school, or take correspondence courses; others seek in other ways to improve themselves; but as for the rest, they represent the average person doing the average things — a person not at all disposed to give up his television, his sports, his "neighboring," his relaxations, for the grind of study or the indefatigable pursuit of promotion.

CONSIDER, AND AGAIN CONSIDER

The operational level of performance may be very different from the potential level. Not all individuals with IQ of 140 want to go to college; some of them are content to pump gas in a filling station and will expend no energy to go beyond that. It would be poor counseling to match the potential talent to the maximal job if the individual habitually operates on a lesser level. There is nothing terribly abnormal about squandering or wasting one's talent. To adopt a harsh attitude toward others in this regard is to invite a close inspection of how fully we ourselves have been wont to utilize that which we possess. Self-indulgence is rather a frequent temptation for us all; so is pleasure-seeking; so is avoidance of responsibility. The wise counselor is not one who moralizes on what a client should do with his talents (and proceeds to build a plan around it); rather he seeks to determine what the client *will do,* and then assists him in a maximal adjustment thereto. This poses a somewhat different viewpoint in counseling the rehabilitation client. Rather than aim toward training and placing the client on the highest level of job for which he has capacity, one might better point him toward the highest level of job at which he can and will operate; and one need be not too dismayed if in some instances "operational level" is markedly below "capacity level." Thus, for the counselor with pragmatic outlook, a sound appraisal of the whole motivational concept may prove to be the key to many of his counseling problems.

This discussion contains little of flattery for the cloud-centered counselor; but it is not intended to indulge the earthbound too much, either. Misdirective counseling is a problem to all, and it has been the intent of this presentation to sharpen the focus on the sports where we may be weakest. In addition, there is frankly implied the existence of a definite cleavage in rehabilitation counseling. At the one extreme will be found those who would risk personal and public capital on some kind of a long-shot plan which — if perfectly executed — would totally dissolve all major impediments to maximum adjustment. At the other extreme are those whose counseling goals are less spectacular in objective, and are based on high probabilities for attainment, with a minimum risk to any capital outlay involved. Is there a middle ground for compromise between these two viewpoints?

What do you think?

PART II

COUNSELING PARENTS OF
THE MENTALLY RETARDED CHILD

Chapter 8

Mental Retardation and Neurotic Maternal Attitudes

CHARLES E. GOSHEN

THE RESEARCH OBJECTIVES

T HE project was launched in 1950 and was carried on continuously through 1962, except for a two-year interruption (1957-1959). Initially, the objectives were (1) to determine the critical periods of an infant's life when language learning begins and (2) to determine the significance of maternal attitudes and activities on the rate of language development. Rather soon after the project got under way, the objectives were broadened to the study of the more general question of the influence of maternal attitudes on childhood development, with specific reference to the influence of *neurotic* maternal attitudes on childhood development. Still later, and finally, the objectives were narrowed down to the study of the influence of neurotic maternal attitudes on the development of mental retardation in children, with particular reference to language development. The following report summarizes the findings of this aspect of the study. The reason for restricting the project to the study of neurotic maternal attitudes was that the subjects available for study became limited to neurotic mothers. Although the broader study of the influence of

Note: Reprinted by permission of the author and *Archives of General Psychiatry*, 9:168-174, 1964. Copyright 1964, American Medical Association.

Associate Professor, Department of Psychiatry, School of Medicine, Vanderbilt University.

The reader interested in additional information on this topic is referred to Noland, Robert L.; *Counseling Parents of the Mentally Retarded: A Sourcebook* published by C C Thomas, 1970.

neurotic maternal attitudes on childhood development in general has been continuously carried on, a more specific emphasis on mental retardation came about as a result of recognizing a certain urgency in exploring this area; the sense of urgency, in turn, being determined by the realization that this has been a relatively unexplored area, while having immediate and practical clinical implications.

THE RESEARCH METHOD

From among a large number of patients coming for evaluation or treatment to three different psychiatric treatment centers over the ten-year period, those mothers who had mentally retarded children were selected for study. About 5 percent of the patient population fell into this category. In some instances, the presenting problem was that of diagnosis or disposition of a retarded child. In about an equal number of instances, the retarded child was incidental to some other presenting psychiatric problem. Since no statistical analysis is being offered in this report, the actual number of subjects will not be specified. Because of the widespread variation in the degree of resistance and of cooperation in any population of (voluntary) psychiatric patients, there was a considerable spread in the depth to which the subjects were studied. This factor imposed a self-screening quality to the amount learned about the various subjects, since the most cooperative were also those who were the least serious, psychiatrically speaking, and became the ones who contributed most to what was learned.

The subjects were further selected according to certain characteristics of their retarded children. They were limited to those whose retarded children were under twelve years of age (in the earlier part of the study, the limit was placed at 6 years). The children were invariably those who demonstrated no organic pathology, no history of birth injury, no history of encephalitis, and no other developmental abnormality except for mental retardation. In each instance, the child (and in one instance, 2 children of 1 mother) had been readily recognized as retarded by physicians or schools, and their IQ's as measured by standard psychological tests ranged from 50-80. All children lived with their mothers, that is, were not institutionalized, at the beginning of each study.

The technique employed was a psychotherapeutic one, in which the subjects reported at regular intervals (usually 1-hour session per week) to the office of the project director and engaged in an individual, face-to-face psychotherapeutic interview. Through this medium, both intensive and extensive investigations were conducted, seeking to answer the following questions:

1. What was the customary way by which the subject went about the business of making decisions?
2. What were the usual contents of the subject's phantasies?
3. What were the characteristic types of relationships the subject established in her life with other people?
4. What were the usual ways by which the subject faced her responsibilities, and what were her characteristic ways of discharging these?
5. What were the specific ways in which all of the above influenced the manner in which the subject related to the retarded child?
6. What was the detailed history of the course of these factors during the lifetime of the retarded child, especially as the ups and downs in the subject's psychological history were related temporally with critical periods in the child's life?
7. What was the nature and extent of the influence of other people on the child's life?

Since the amount of useful information elicited from each subject was unrelated to the number of visits, there was a wide variation in the number of contacts, ranging from a minimum of 2 to a maximum of 150 (including some contacts with the fathers) for each subject. In general, the group having the larger number of visits consisted of those presenting a current psychiatric problem in which the problem of the retarded child was an incidental factor, whereas the group with the smaller number consisted chiefly of those whose presenting problem was that of the retarded child. When the latter was the case, the issue raised was either that of making a differential diagnosis or of making a suitable disposition of the child.

RESEARCH FINDINGS

Soon after the study was inaugurated, it became evident that the data to be collected would need to be classified according to the personality, or life, characteristics of the three principals in each unit of study, these principals being: the subject (mother), the retarded child, and the subject's husband (child's father), while the other individuals potentially involved (such as the siblings of the retarded child) could serve as controls in the study. The findings can be conveniently summarized under the following headings: (1) generalizations, or the common denominators; (2) the typical history, which would represent, more or less, the equivalent of the statistical average; and (3) specific examples, cited for the purpose of illustrating the findings.

Generalizations

Presence of Psychiatric Problem in Subject

In each instance, there was a clearly recognizable state of psychiatric disability present in the subject for a substantial period of time during the retarded child's early life. In most cases, there were also one or more other children whose *early* life did not coincide with a corresponding period of psychiatric disability, and in those children there was no evidence of mental retardation. In two thirds of the subjects, the psychiatric difficulties in question were still present to a serious degree at the time they were being studied, and in only one third was the nature of these difficulties evident by history alone.

Nature of Psychiatric Problem in Subject

In each instance, the nature of the psychiatric disturbance was characterized by a severe diminution in activity, by a lack of interest in people, by an extensive avoidance of responsibility, by a great resistance to making any decisions, by a poverty of spontaneous verbal communication, and by a deep, brooding introspectiveness. Such states are usually diagnosed, psychiatrically, as "depressions," and in these subjects they were usually recognized as such by other people, but in only a few cases brought to the attention of a psychiatrist early. Otherwise, from a diagnostic point of view, there was a range of variation between conditions which could be classified as "psychoneurosis" to those classifiable as "schizophrenia." However, there was no behavior sufficiently bizarre, destructive, or overtly psychotic to lead to psychiatric hospitalization. In some cases, however, brief periods of hospitalization took place for pseudomedical reasons. In brief, if all possible degrees of psychiatric incapacitation were rank-ordered according to severity and these cases fitted into the list, they would fall in the middle group.

General Personality Characteristics of Subjects

In all subjects, there was present a substantial degree of immaturity existing prior to, and subsequent to, the early life of the retarded children in question and present to a marked degree at the time they were introduced to the study. The psycho-therapeutic attack was directed at this, even though, in some instances, there was not then present any serious psychiatric state. The characteristics of this immaturity were most evident in the reluctance and/or unreadiness of these subjects to make decisions for themselves and secondarily in their general tendency to present a mechanical kind of social conformity to the world. The more rebellious or reckless kind of immaturity which is sometimes seen was not evident.

Characteristics of the Husbands (and Fathers)

In each case, the husband of the subject (and father of the retarded child) presented certain unique characteristics, also. They were, invariably, ineffective, remote men whose relationships with the retarded children were exceedingly distant. In a few instances they were alcoholics who had very little contact with the family, and what contact there was tended to be limited to the wife (subject), and then in a sporadic manner. In one instance the husband died soon after the birth of the child in question. In the majority of instances, the husband was an insecure, apprehensive person who tended to be dominated by the wife (subject) and inclined to relate to her in an appeasing manner. In no instance was the husband a person who assumed the initiative in caring for the child in question or in assisting the wife with the depressive state she was in, although there was clearly a problem in these areas. Instead, these husbands tended to respond mechanically to the demands made by the wife and were usually ready to seek medical (but to resist psychiatric) assistance.

Critical Period in Children's Lives

The critical period of the child's life during which the depressive features of the subjects were most significant and prominent appeared to be the period between the ages of six and eighteen months.

Significant Historical Events in Children's Lives

In no instance was anything noticed in the child's early development which seemed unusual up to the age of nine to twelve months. (One child was jaundiced at birth, but this did not appear to be associated with any other difficulty. His two older siblings [not retarded] had also been jaundiced at birth.) The first evidence of abnormality in the development was only slowly apparent and was manifested by lateness in the development of talking and walking. In retrospect, it was usually evident that the children showed considerable fear of trying anything new, such as walking, but this fear did not seem to be recognized by the parents at the time. By the age of three to four years, there was also evident a fear on the children's part of separating from the mother. Usually the parents had recognized the existence of a developmental problem by this time and in most cases recognized this fear of separation, but they had found no solution to this problem.

Characteristics of Interaction of Subjects and Children

The subjects uniformly manifested their depressed state in a characteristic way of relating to those children who later came to be known as mentally retarded. In the first place, the deepest period of depression developed after the child was several months old, but always within the first year, and was usually not conspicuously evident immediately after delivery (in other words, not a typical postpartum depression). The type of relationship then established between the mother and child assumed a peculiar, contradictory quality. On the one hand, the subjects were inattentive to the children, unresponsive to them, and consistently disinclined to assume any initiative in meeting the children's needs. On the other hand, they tended to remain consistently in the presence of the children and to be nearly the sole person to care for them; but the nature of their participation was silent, mechanical, resentful, gloomy, and lacking in any spontaneity. Most significantly, there was a minimum of interest expressed in eliciting any emotional response from the children and a maximum of interest expressed in keeping the child quiet and inactive. These attitudes or activities were colored by a powerful effort to control in a restrictive, negative way.

Characteristics of the Type of Retardation in the Children

The children with which this study was concerned ranged in age from 4 to 12 years. The most striking aspect of their retardation was in the area of language, and in many instances it appeared that this was primary. In contrast, there was relatively little evidence for motor retardation except for a general slowness in development of motor skills. There tended to be a wide scatter in the quality of performance in different areas, being at the lowest level in those fields where they were required to meet the demands of others (such as school). In other areas there was usually found a surprising level of accomplishment in some task which was outside the province of what society demanded (such as skill in doing jigsaw puzzles.) Uniformly, the language retardation was evident in the form of scanty and immature use of English, although there was often a fair degree of mastery of sign language. The nonuse of intelligible verbalizations often appeared to be the result of a positive, active resistance to speaking, with some of the children showing an obvious determination to make no sounds whatever.

The language difficulty tended to serve the purpose of making these children excessively dependent on their mothers. In no case was the school performance of the over-six-year group adequate for remaining in graded classes. As a result, nearly all members of this older group were either placed in ungraded special classes or had been dropped from school altogether.

Characteristics of the Sibling Controls

Three fourths of the subjects had children other than the retarded child in question, and, in the remaining instances, the retarded child was the only child. In one instance, both of two children were retarded, but in all other instances the siblings showed no striking degree of retardation. The retarded child was usually either the oldest or the youngest; rarely was he in the middle of the sibling group. Invariably, the sibling controls showed evidence of disturbed adjustment to some degree and were about equally divided between personality types characterized by excessive submissiveness or excessive rebelliousness. It was generally quite apparent that these were modes of adjustment to a dominating mother.

Outside Influences

There was a striking absence of outside influences on these retarded children. The subjects' (mothers') controlling tendencies frequently took the form of excluding contacts with older people. The net result was to the effect that the mothers represented the overwhelmingly most significant person in the lives of these retarded children, meaning that the quality of her influence was not ameliorated or neuralized by other kinds of influence, except insofar as it was transmitted through her. The absence of a contrary kind of influence from the fathers was especially conspicuous.

The Typical Case

A reconstruction of a "typical" case which would be

representative of the group could be summarized as follows:

The subject (Mrs. AB) was a 30-year-old woman with three children, ages 6, 3, and 1. The retarded child in question was the oldest, a boy. The subject was an only child from a lower-middle-class household in which the mother was a person who was excessively concerned about her health, constantly preoccupied with special diets and visits to doctors and frequent complaints about nonexistent illnesses. The father was a distant person, a "good provider" but rarely engaged in any interesting or spontaneous activity with the family. He was generally sympathetic with the subject, but "hard to talk to" and never offered any leadership. The family had very limited social relations with others, and what social life there was, tended to be stilted, formal, and frequently concerned with meetings concerning the deaths and illnesses of relatives. The mother, particularly, was excessively concerned with public opinion and required of the subject a strict conformity with old-fashioned restrictive social customs, with much more emphasis on the letter than the spirit of conformity. The mother tended, consistently, to undermine the subject's self-confidence with expressions of fear concerning the outcome of any new venture. The subject became dependent on the mother in a rather passive way and tended to try to avoid trouble by avoiding situations which were novel or unfamiliar. She performed adequately but unspectacularly in school, completed high school, and took a job as secretary in a small office. She took very little interest in other people, had no hobbies, avoided travel, but, nevertheless, went to great pains with her appearance. With boys she had a reputation of being attractive, but otherwise uninteresting and inclined to complain freely over minor discomforts. She married a man her own age who worked as a bookkeeper in the same office. She immediately quit work and spent all her time compulsively grooming a small apartment. From the beginning, the relationship with her husband was of a formal, ritualistic nature wherein the only interest they shared was mutually complaining about the failures of other people, presenting an image of ultrarespectability in a do-nothing kind of way. She was slow to agree to having children, although the husband, characteristically, did not press this. When it was agreed, four years after marriage, it was done on the basis of its being "the thing to do." Although pregnancy was accompanied by a great deal of complaining, an excessive weight gain, and almost complete inactivity, neither the husband nor the subject regarded it as an especially trying period. Delivery occurred uneventfully after two false starts, and the baby seemed normal in every way. For the first time in her life, the subject seemed to take a deep interest in something by caring for the baby, although in retrospect her activities were found to be directed away from instead of toward the baby itself. She became unusually preoccupied with preparation of formulas, decorating a nursery, buying baby clothing, etc, while treating the baby as another lifeless object comparable to the accouterments associated with it. She regimented her care of the baby to a precisely timed schedule, and the slightest sign of alertness on the baby's part was a signal to her to restore him to a state of sleep. As a result, the baby was essentially never hungry, never cold, never wet, hardly ever touched or fondled — in other words, never stimulated. Progress on the baby's part was measured almost solely by his weight gain, and since this was satisfactory, the first several months of his life were regarded by the mother as outstandingly successful. The sterile environment in which he lived was also characterized by the mother's setting up impenetrable barriers to other people coming in contact with him, and since she, too, was isolated from others, the baby contracted no infectious diseases during his first year and was thus robbed of the experience of having to suffer discomfort in that area.

When the baby was about nine months old, a creeping sense of disappointment and failure set in on the mother's part. Her discouragement did not seem to be directed at any realization of unsatisfactory progress on the child's part, but at a growing awareness that some great and magical change that she expected to happen to her had not taken place. Mostly, this change she expected was a recognition by others of her great worth as a righteous, self-sacrificing mother. No such recognition occurred. Her husband seemed to regard her preoccupation with the mechanics of baby care and her efforts to exclude him from contacts with the baby as a blessing rather than an evil and was unaware of any problem. The disillusionment which set in produced a rather deep, brooding depression which lasted for about two years, during which time she was even less communicative and even more isolated from others than usual. She continued, however, to maintain complete control, herself, over the care of the baby. It is illustrative of the two parents to note that, during this period, the husband often went for a couple of weeks at a time without ever seeing the baby awake, so diligent was the mother in keeping it quiet and in keeping him away from it.

A most striking quality which, retrospectively, was seen to characterize the mother's attitude was the absence on her part of any effort or interest in stimulating the baby to respond to her. It was not until the baby was about 15 months old that she became aware of the fact that there was no sign of language development. She compared this with books on child development and decided this must be a medical problem, so she took the baby to a pediatrician. The latter saw nothing remarkable and reassured her. She did not become concerned again until the baby was about 18 months old, when his attempts at ambulation did not progress beyond the crawling phase. By the time he was 2 years old, he was walking unassisted, but still made no effort to communicate (and she did not, either). For the first time, he began to show evidence of curiosity and sought to explore cupboards, closets, etc. She responded to this activity with a smothering kind of restrictiveness which only rarely became punitive. Detectable emotions were recognized then by the mother as fear of punishment and prompted her to avoid such provocation. By the time the child was 3 years old she finally decided a serious problem existed and made more diligent attempts to seek medical assistance. After a round of visits to pediatricians and psychologists, she was told the child was retarded, that he would never develop like a normal child, and that he would eventually have to be institutionalized. For a period of a few months, she was able to rationalize this news in such a way as to absolve herself of any sense of failure, and her spirits brightened to the ordinary pessimistic level which characterized her mood before she became depressed. She then began to get impatient with the child, regarding it more and more as an intrusion, and was surprised to find him responding to her show of feeling for the first time. He began to make sounds indicating obvious anger, which though unintelligible, conveyed a meaning which was understandable. At this time the child was 4 years old, and she entered the research project as one of the subjects. Remarkably, she came with a cogent question that the child's lack of intellectual development might have been a result of her own lack of understanding in how to stimulate and guide it. More characteristically, she also expressed the hope of proving wrong the pessimistic predictions made by pediatricians and psychologists. After a year of psychotherapy, the mother and child were communicating with each other and with other people, and by the time the child was six he entered public school and seemed much like the other children his own age, although he still showed a fear of separating from his mother. In many ways, this mother succeeded in creating in the child her own distorted goal of happiness – a state having no need, no stimulation, no emotion, no noise, no trouble. Her cooperative attitude in the research project was largely due to her own disillusionment over this image.

Specific Examples

Following are some very brief sketches of some of the other subjects in the study:

Case 1. Mrs. BC was a 35-year-old woman who married a first cousin and had two unplanned, unwanted pregnancies. She faced her pregnancies and deliveries with a strong conviction that the consanguinity of her marriage would be productive of abnormal children. When the first child (boy) was born, she was somewhat reassured, however, when nothing unusual was noted in the baby, and this reassurance continued for about six months or so. By this time she became impatient about eliciting proof that the baby was normal and made feeble, sporadic efforts to teach it language (prematurely). Her failure to achieve this precipitated a profound depression which lasted almost two years. This boy never learned any language, was severely retarded, and when he was 6 years old was institutionalized, after which he developed a series of infections and died. The second pregnancy occurred during the third year of the first child's life, and almost an identical history developed. This child, too, turned out to be severely retarded, and the mother entered the project when he was 3 years of age (at the time the first was institutionalized). She was still deeply depressed, had made several suicidal attempts, and remained in this state until the second child was also institutionalized.

Case 2. Mrs. CD was only 19 when her only child was born and was seen in the project when she was 25 and the child 6. She was an extraordinarily immature person who seemed to be exclusively preoccupied with entertainment and clothes. She seemed to face the prospect of raising a child with utter surprise, as if she did not know that any effort would be required of her. During the first few months of the child's life she made such half-hearted attempts to care for the child that her in-laws began to exert pressure on her to remove the care of the child from her hands. She reacted to this pressure by becoming very possessive and by diligently preventing anyone from coming in contact with the child. For a period of about a year and a half she seemed angry and bitter toward everyone else, avoided social contacts, and determined to demonstrate "what a good mother she was" by keeping the child completely quiet and unobtrusive. She frequently resorted to the use of sedatives to accomplish this. Although she came out of this state of feud with her in-laws, her subsequent contacts with people were lacking in any warmth or spontaneity. Meanwhile, the child had failed to develop intellectually and demonstrated only the most primitive kind of language. She came into the project at the time the child would enter school, and on the advice of the school.

Case 3. Mrs. DE was a 29-year-old woman with two children, the retarded one being the younger of the two. The development of the first child (girl) was uneventful except that she was a rather fearful child, mirroring the many phobic fears of the mother. The second child passed through its first eight months without incident; then the subject's husband suddenly and unexpectedly died (coronary disease at age 35). The subject then had to face the prospect of caring for her home and children, and at the same time resolving many complications in her husband's business affairs. She first ignored the children almost completely and concentrated on the business, but became increasingly more frustrated in her efforts to understand it, then gave up altogether. For over a year she lived as a recluse with her two children in a deep depression and resisted the efforts of anyone else to intrude. The period of depression extended from the ninth month of the second child's life to the twenty-fourth month. Her entrance into the study was occasioned by the retarded child's reaching school age, demanding some sort of appraisal. She had previously consulted a pediatrician about his retarded development and seemed to accept unquestioningly his judgment of there being a permanent state of retardation present.

Case 4. Mrs. EF was a 31-year-old woman with three children, ages 12, 7, and 6, the retarded one being the oldest. She faced the task of raising her first child with many rigid, preconceived ideas based on a determination to make his life better than the one she had as a child. What she did for the baby bore no relation to the child itself, but followed a ritualistic pattern of feeding, etc. She apparently assumed that at a certain point in the child's life, it would automatically begin speaking intelligible English. When, instead, rather unintelligible noises were produced she sought to suppress them. As a result, the early ingredients of communication between the two were absent, and the mother merely waited expectantly for the child to blossom forth with a complete vocabulary. When this did not happen toward the end of the first year, she decided the child had some organic defect of hearing or speech and began to make extensive shopping tours of doctors to find out "what was wrong." The relentless search continued sporadically until she came into the study. Meanwhile, her relationship with the child was comparable to that of an observer of some mysterious drama in which she was not, herself, a participant. Strangely, when the other two children came along, she had forgotten about her rituals of baby care and treated them much more humanly, although her relationship with them seemed more like that of another child than of a mother. The retarded child, by age 12, was in an ungraded class in school.

CLINICAL IMPLICATIONS

This research project suggests mechanisms by which certain types of mental retardation result as a by-product of certain types of maternal attitudes. Specifically, it suggests that neurotic maternal attitudes which are characterized by a failure to stimulate and evoke meaningful signals during critical periods of life can result in failure on the child's part in grasping the significance of language, thus proceeding to a state recognizable as mental retardation. Extrapolating from these findings to the broader problem of mental retardation in general, it seems reasonable to assume that many cases of mental retardation (perhaps 50% of the retarded population) which demonstrate no brain or sensory abnormalities have been produced in this way. To test this hypothesis for any particular case of mental retardation, the following clues are suggested: (1) look for evidence of gross inattention to the child by the responsible adult (usually mother) during the six months or so preceding and following the child's first birthday; (2) look for evidence of deep psychological depression on the part of the mother during the child's infancy; (3) look for evidence on the mother's part of a combination of personality traits characterized by a tendency to exclusive control of the child on the one hand and a tendency to be mechanical, unresponsive, and uncommunicative on the other hand; and (4) look for evidence that shows a primary language failure as basic to the retarded condition.

An important question not fully answered in this project requires further investigation. This question refers to the probable reversibility or irreversibility of mental retardation produced in the way described above. One example is described where the retardation was reversed, and a normal child resulted. Perhaps the successful outcome was determined by the fact that the child was only four years old at the beginning of the change. Perhaps it was due to an unusual degree of cooperation on the part of the mother. It is conceivable that there exists a critical period during which a reversal is feasible.

One important clinical implication is suggested from this project which might prove effective in reducing the number of such cases in the future. When a mother develops a deep psychological depression during the first year of a child's life, it would seem to be an urgent necessity to place the child in the care of a healthy adult until the mother comes out of the depression.

Chapter 9

Problems in Helping Parents of Mentally Defective and Handicapped Children

S. L. SHEIMO

THE emotional conflict in which parents of mentally defective or handicapped children frequently become entangled is one with which general practitioners, pediatricians, and psychiatrists are often confronted. The intense anxiety frequently aroused is manifested in many different ways, and the problems encountered in helping such parents overcome their conflicting attitudes toward their child are often difficult and time consuming. Although there has been an abundance of material reported in the literature discussing the mentally defective child as an individual, it seems significant that relatively little has been written concerning the parental attitudes toward such a child. Even less has been written concerning the difficulties the clinician experiences in attempting to be of help to the parents.

In a review of the literature of the past ten years, there have been some who have reported and emphasized the importance of dealing with the parental attitude and anxiety. H. C. Schumacher (8) stresses the treatment and helping of the parents, the removal of the significantly disturbed persons from the child's environ-

*Note:*Reprinted by permission of the author and the *American Journal of Mental Deficiency,* *56*:42-47, 1951. Copyright 1951, American Association on Mental Deficiency.

Dr. Sheimo is Clinical Instructor in Psychiatry, University of California School of Medicine, and the State of California Department of Mental Hygiene, The Langley Porter Clinic, San Francisco, California.

ment, and/or transfer of the child to a more stable environment. W. Wardell (2) reports on her experiences in dealing with the anxieties within the parents of institutionalized mentally defective children. She feels that the exra therapeutic casework effort is rewarding in its help to the parent, and its contribution to a greater ease of institutional adjustment for the child. Westlund and Palumbo (10) report on the parental attitudes in parents with crippled children, and specifically those with infantile paralysis. They recognize and discuss the tendency toward increased parental rejection of the child, with the consequent guilt and anxiety in the parents as the severity or chronicity of the debility increases. They also report a case in which a mother and handicapped daughter were seen regularly by a psychiatric social worker and a psychiatrist in therapeutic interviews. E. W. Coughlin (5) reports on parental attitudes in parents with handicapped children. He feels that these parental attitudes are perhaps no different from the attitudes of parents toward so-called normal children. He felt, rather, the disability brought deep-seated feelings to the surface, which might otherwise have been suppressed. Marguerite M. Stone (11) dealt with this aspect of the problem in an article more recently. She too was impressed by the paucity of the published literature on this subject. She classified the parental types according to degrees of awareness of the retardation or disability, and studied the feelings of parents as recorded in the interviews in a series of forty-four cases. She did this both before and following several diagnostic interviews with the parents. She discussed the parental guilt around the tendency to reject the child, and how the defective child, often quite unconsciously, becomes the pawn in the battle between marital partners. At the same time, she recognized the importance of the skill, training, and experience of the worker, and the many difficulties involved in actually helping the parents. She thought there was an evidence of growth, during the diagnostic process, in the ability of the parent to face the problem.

Others (4, 6, 7, 9) speak of how parents should educate and train the defective or handicapped child, with special projects for woodworking, needle craft, weaving, and so on. They stress the importance of better facilities including expanded foster home placement programs, parent and public education, home training under the supervision of a staff of social workers to relieve the parents of the wearing task of constant supervision of the particular child, and education to give the parents a better understanding of the child's mental capacity and thus postpone placement. Others (1) write of "unworthy parental attitudes," as evaluated by the parents' failure to visit, send letters, and give gifts to their institutionalized child. Another (3) evaluates the hereditary genetic factor and IQ levels of parents of retarded children.

This author's experience consists of working with several families, each of whom came to this clinic with an obviously defective or handicapped child. The ages of the children ranged from a mongolian idiot, twenty-one months old, to a fourteen-year-old mentally defective child. In one of these cases, the experience consisted of working with the mother in biweekly therapeutic interviews for a period of two years. The others were seen for a briefer period, ranging from four to twenty interviews. Further investigation was made in a review of 150 cases of mentally defective children in a state institution.

This discussion is limited to situations in which the mental deficiency and/or physical handicap of the child has been established. The difficulties in differentiating between mental deficiency due to impersonal, organic factors, and subnormal functioning due to emotional conflicts, with a consequent inhibition of intelligent behavior, will not be dealt with in this paper. This presents an aspect of another problem and so will not be considered here.

The uncertainty as to whether or not a child is congenitally defective obviously makes it more difficult for the doctor to deal with the parental conflict. The most relevant factor at such a point is for the doctor to clinically establish the status of the child. To whatever extent he is still uncertain, a frank expression to the parents might then liberate him from a feeling that he *has to know,* thereby making him better able to deal with the anxiety of the parents.

An outstanding factor in these cases is the extended attempt of the parents to seek help from other sources prior to their referral to this clinic. More frequently than not, most professional services had concurred in their opinion that the child was congenitally defective or handicapped. The parents' inability to accept this fact seemed to be expressed by the frequent change of doctors and clinics, and the continued search for some new medication or treatment for the child. In some cases the time, energy, and great financial sacrifice that the parents had made in search of some help has very impressive. As a result of these observations, we are faced with the question of what conflict or conflicts are possibly serving as the motivating force behind such manifestations. In attempting to evaluate this further, some of the problems encountered by the professional person become more evident.

Even though there is no question as to the clinical evaluation and diagnosis of the child's condition, the parents' initial concern is, nevertheless, centered around the condition of the child, discussion of previous experiences with doctors, and doubt as to the opinion and diagnosis of these doctors. The insistence that they believed something more could be done for the child was frequently expressed in terms of requesting glutamic acid injections, endocrine therapy, and so on, (referring to some current periodical they had read), and even wanting to "offer" their child for some surgical or medicinal "experimentation."

As interviews progressed and the parents began to feel free to discuss their feelings, the meaning of the above-mentioned behavior became clearer. Initially they expressed self-blame, feeling they were in some way at fault and had "caused" the condition of their child. Invariably, the parents had some idea as to the intellectual level of the child, and would say, "He acts like a one- or two-year old child," and would almost give the exact mental age level which psychological tests would subsequently reveal. The parents would say that a part of them knew all along that this was so, but that they felt an "inner urge or force" to do everything to disprove it.

Perhaps the most striking common factor was the intense guilt and conflict in regard to the impulse to reject the child. In one of the cases, this impulse was actually of a murderous degree. In each case, with only quantitative variations, the frequent changes of doctors, the often fantastic expenditure of energy, time, and money seemed to be a manifestation of the aforementioned conflict.

It is also became progressively more evident that the doctor's mere presentation of clinical diagnosis and recommendation was neither sufficient nor perhaps *really* what the parents were seeking. Advice and suggestions seemed to be of no avail and unconsciously impossible for the parents to accept and find useful. In an attempt to help these parents, it is necessary for the doctor to become more sympathetically aware of the conflicting attitudes of the parents toward such a child. The parents' denial of the child's deficiency seemed to be an important element in their defense mechanism and very necessary in the maintenance of their self-esteem. The issue of the "child's defectiveness" frequently seemed to become, quite unconsciously, as Marguerite M. Stone states it, "the pawn in the battle between marital partners."

It is felt that the attitude of the particular doctor, whether he be pediatrician or psychiatrist, becomes an integral factor in aiding these parents. To be aware that the parents usually *know* their child is handicapped and defective and that their anxiety is predominantly an expression of their own internalized conflict, increases the possibility of being of real help to the particular parents. To tell parents that they *should* institutionalize the child, should, in a sense, "get rid of him," often tends to increase the guilt and strengthen the defense against this already forbidden impulse. The doctor fulfills his medical responsibility when he quite frankly states his clinical diagnosis — both in regard to mental and physical status of the child — estimates the probable future difficulties, and recognizes the added burden which such children are to parents. He becomes a physician in the true sense of the word, however, when he *recognizes* and *respects* the parents' right to decide what *they* want to do in terms of their total situation, including their own ambivalence and conflict. This implies that the doctor be ready to accept whatever decision the parents make, whether it be to keep the defective child in the home or to place him outside the home. The doctor's offer to discuss some of the parents' difficulties in arriving at a decision becomes a beginning move in the direction of a possible resolution of the conflict.

If the doctor's efforts at being of help are directed, not toward a decision, but rather toward a resolution of the conflict and consequent relief of anxiety, it begins to liberate the parents from feeling they must come to an immediate decision. Also implicit in this is that an approach on the part of the parents toward a resolution of the conflict need not necessarily mean a decision to place the child outside the home. In the doctor's sympathetic understanding of the realistic aspect of the added burden and emotional drain such children are to parents, as well as the impulse within parents to reject such a child, he actually becomes to help in reducing the intrafamilial tension. The parents may then feel easier and consequently more ready to keep this child in the home indefinitely. In the meantime, the fruitless searching for a "cure" as a manifestation of the unresolved conflict no longer becomes as necessary. As has already been suggested, the ambivalence and uncertainty within the clinician when he faced with the task of dealing with these parents becomes a point at which parents, perhaps quite unconsciously test and react. Opposing attitudes are not infrequently expressed by clinicians: on the one hand, "feeling sorry," oversolicitude, and an attempt to "soft-pedal" the truth; while on the other hand, impatience, and even annoyance, that his position as an authoritative person has been questioned. It is understandable that doctors do appreciate and are sensitive to the unpleasantness of such a situation for the parents. To some it may seem unkind or even brutal to be frank with the parents as to the truth of the situation. Yet perhaps at just such times nothing short of an honest statement is really helpful to any of the members concerned, including the child. If the doctor is able to stand firm and strong in his convictions while at the same time he allows the parents to react with what sometimes may be even intense rage and denial by stating that they do not and will not believe the doctor, he often proves, in the long run, to be of real, integrative value to these parents. At such moments, the doctor may not even get the satisfaction of having been of help, but in the ensuing months and years the parents may either attain a greater decisiveness or return to that particular clinician for help.

For the doctor to have the attitude that it seems illogical, if not "superhuman," for parents to expect the same degree of satisfaction from a defective child that can be received from a more "normal" child may be of help in reducing the parents' guilt and anxiety about being "unworthy" or "bad" parents. Likewise, it is important for the doctor to be aware of the fact that the attitudes and pressures from other children and neighbors, both toward the defective child as well as toward the parents, do add to and aggravate the existing inner turmoil and sense of dissatisfaction. This is not to imply that the clinician "warns" the parents of these factors, but rather that these concepts be a part of his attitude. In this way parents can experience simple honesty with another person, who neither has to be unsympathetic, impatient, and authoritarian, nor oversolicitous and hesitant. It behooves the clinician to recognize that these parents invariably *know* the degree of the deficiency and that their intense anxiety around the child's defectiveness is the way in which their conflict is manifested. He must therefore not wittingly participate in this manifestation.

In the case of a 4-year-old male mongolian idiot, the parents had spent three years searching for some "cure" for the boy. Following several sessions, the mother became more able to discuss some of her own feelings in relationship to this child as well as toward her husband. She discussed her fears that this child might fall into their swimming pool, and then later, with much anxiety and guilt, related the impulse she once had to push this child into the pool. The significance of these feelings as related to this mother's earlier childhood conflicts in relationships with her parents and siblings was not gone into. Nevertheless, this mother subsequently was able to come to a clearer decision to place this child outside the home.

Another case was that of a 7-year-old congenitally blind, mentally defective girl. In this case the work with the mother was more intensive and prolonged, consisting of biweekly therapeutic interviews for two years. This family had been to ten different sources for help. Treatment had consisted of five surgical operations on the child's eyes, numerous efforts in special schools, and temporary placements outside the home. This child's father died when she was five, two years prior to beginning treatment at this clinic. During the course of treatment the mother related with much uneasiness and guilt how she had felt "initially glad" that her daughter was born blind, because then she would not have to take care of her. Because of the guilt associated with this feeling, it became necessarily suppressed and in the ensuing seven years the mother spent her time searching for treatment. After a year of regular interviews, the mother was able to come to a decision to place her daughter in a state institution. During the subsequent year of treatment, the mother related how unhappy her marriage had been, her regret in her choice of a marital partner, and the intense guilt she felt around the sense of relief she experienced at her husband's death. The fear which she felt over the years that it would "hurt" her daughter too much if she were placed permanently away from her became clearer as a manifestation of this mother's earlier experience of feeling rejected and excluded at the birth of her sister when she was 4.

Perhaps these cases were those in which the parental conflict was more severe. Nevertheless, it is felt that the difference between these cases and those where some decision in regard to the child is either made earlier or more readily is quantitative rather than qualitative. The many efforts that such families make — frequent change of doctors, great financial sacrifice, and so on — is something that has been observed by many who are called upon to be of help in such situations.

In a survey of 150 defective cases in a state institution, the direction and extent in which the parental conflict was manifested seemed significant. The pressure from parents on the particular institution in regard to the type of treatment their child was getting, the food, and so on, consumed a phenomenal amount of time on the part of all professional persons concerned. This pressure often extended to local city and county resources, State Department of Mental Hygiene, and, not infrequently, to the executive departments of the state government. At times the manifestation of the conflict seemed to be of a paranoid degree. The average age of admission (13 to 14) seemed to be in part an indication of the years of struggle the parents had been going through before finally *having to* institutionalize their defective child.

It seems important to the author not to underestimate the intense repressed forces which become mobilized in parents who have mentally defective and/or handicapped children. At such times, to center one's attention on the defective child rather than toward the parental conflict might be attempting to deal with the least relevant factor in the total situation.

REFERENCES

1. Thorne, Frederick and Andrews, Jean S.: Parental attitudes toward mental deficiency. *Am J Ment Defic, 50*:411, 1946.
2. Wardell, Winifred: Case work with parents of mentally deficient children. *Am J Ment Defic, 52*:91-97, 1947.
3. Berry, R. J. A.: Investigation into mental state of parents and siblings of 1,050 mentally defective persons. *Bristol Med Chir J, 56*:189-200, 1939.
4. Nugent, M. A.: Home training and teaching of mentally deficient children by parents in home. *Am J Ment Defic, 45*:104-109, 1940.
5. Coughlin, E. W.: Parental attitudes toward handicapped children. *Child,* Vol. *II,* No. 11, May, 1947.
6. Horsefield, E.: Suggestions for training mentally retarded by parents in the home. *Am J Ment Defic, 46*:533-537, 1942.
7. Rautman, A. L.: Mental deficiency as a problem in general practice. *Wisconsin M J, 41*:771-776, 1942.
8. Schumacher, H. C.: Contribution of child guidance clinic to problem of mental deficiency. *Am J Ment Defic, 50*:277-283, 1945.
9. Johnstone, E. L.: What should we do with the mentally deficient? *Ment Hyg, 30*:296-302, 1946.
10. Westlund, N., and Palumbo, A. Z.: Parental rejection of crippled children. *Am J Orthopsychiat, 16*:271-281, 1946.
11. Stone, Marguerite M.: Parental attitudes to retardation. *Am J Ment Defic, 53*:363-372, 1948.
12. Sampson, Alan H.: Relations with parents of mentally deficient children. *Am J Ment Defic, 52*:187-194, 1947.
13. Waterman, John M.: Psychogenic factors in parental acceptance of feebleminded children. *Dis Nerv Syst, 9*:184-187, 1948.
14. Kanner, Leo: Exoneration of the feebleminded. *Am J Psychiat, 99*:17-22, July, 1942.
15. Barry, H., Jr.: Study of bereavement in parents — approach to problems in mental disease. *Am J Orthopsychiat, 9*:355-359, 1939.
16. Millman, C. G.: Mental deficiency: responsibility of practitioner. *M Press, 201*:525-528, 1939.
17. Haskell, R. H.: Mental deficiency over 100 years. (Brief Historical Sketch of Trends in this Field.) *Am J Psychiat, 100*:108-118, 1944.
18. Dawley, Almena: Interrelated movement of parent and child in therapy with children. *Am J Orthopsychiat, 9*:748-754, 1939.
19. Ingham, C. W. J.: Private practice and public services: mental deficiency services. *M Press, 216*:38-44, 1946.
20. Schumacher, H. C.: Program for dealing with mental deficiency in children up to six years of age. *Am J Ment Defic, 51*:52-56, 1946.

Chapter 10

Helping Parents Understand
Their Mentally Handicapped Child

CLEO E. POPP, VIVIEN INGRAM, and PAUL H. JORDAN

Most parents desire to have their children lead happy, well-adjusted lives, and to become adequate social beings. This desire brings into sharp relief the inadequacies of the mentally handicapped child, inadequacies which increase as he develops and is measured over and over against his own brothers and sisters, his neighborhood playmates, and later his school companions. As the mentally handicapped child approaches school age, his parents feel increasingly frustrated and helpless.

The primary needs of the mentally handicapped child are no different from those of any child. The parents alone cannot provide all these needs, nor can the school alone. Since the child is a part of society, many agencies of the community must cooperate with the parents to satisfy these needs. The problem, therefore, lies *first* in helping the parent to understand the needs of the child, his growth and development, his limitations, his frustrations, and his relationships with family and peers. And *second,* it lies in helping the parent to know his community so that every and any

Note: Reprinted by permission of the authors and the *American Journal of Mental Deficiency, 58*:530-534, 1954. Copyright 1954, American Association on Mental Deficiency.

Cleo E. Popp is Chairman of Special Education and Vivien Ingram is Supervisor of Tests, Measurements, and Guidance, Flint Public Schools; Dr. Paul H. Jordan is Director of the Flint Child Guidance Clinic, Flint, Michigan.

In addition to the authors the following were intimately involved in the planning for and conduct of the course: Manilla Campbell, Mental Hygiene Nurse, Flint Child Guidance Clinic; Frances Potter, Principal, Institution School, and Ruth M. Selleck, Director of Education, Lapeer State Home and Training School.

agency that can help his child may be used. Within the last few years when parents have come to the school with problems about their mentally handicapped children, the school and the Child Guidance Clinic have tried to work with these parents on an individual basis, but such a method is time consuming. Since all parents can profit by a knowledge of basic principles which are common to such groups, it was soon apparent that much work could be done more successfully on a group rather than on an individual basis. Further, it was realized that the sharing of these common problems might provide a release for some of the inevitable frustrations which these parents are bound to feel. Therefore, early in 1952, members of the staff of the Lapeer State Home and Training School, the Child Guidance Clinic, and a public school representative compiled a list of parents of retarded children under ten who had been excluded from school. These children may or may not have had a trial in kindergarten or first grade before they were thought to be uneducable. This list also included parents of children who were waiting to be admitted to state institutions for the mentally handicapped.

THE PROJECT

These parents were invited to meet at the Clinic with the psychiatrist and the mental hygiene nurse. The purpose of the meeting was to learn whether these parents were interested in coming together to discuss their common problems and, if so, to suggest what should be the program for future meetings. The response in numbers was good, with twenty-two parents, representing seventeen severely retarded children, reporting. In the course of the subsequent discussion, the parents expressed concern about many things. A few are suggested here: need for special training facilities in Flint; habit training; social experience; problems of insecurity, hostility, undesirable habits, sexual feelings in the child; recreational outlets; understanding convulsive disorders and brain injury; and the child's relationship to family and community.

Following this first meeting with the parents, a planning committee was formed to outline subject matter for the course, using as a guide the expressed interests of the parents. Subsequently, the psychiatrist and the mental hygiene nurse met again with the parents and presented for their consideration the tentative course outline which the parents adopted unanimously without a suggested change. The planning committee met again and worked the course outline into a complete prospectus encompassing subject material, instructors, teaching methods and teaching aids. The course which evolved was subsequently accepted for inclusion in the Adult Education Program of the Flint Public Schools and the Mott Foundation.

The following is a summary of the subject material presented or discussed and the teaching aids and methods used. Each of these broad areas encompassed one to three class sessions. The psychiatrist and mental hygiene nurse were always present, but other personnel carried the responsibility for instruction under the supervision of the psychiatrist.

Causes and effects of mental retardation was the subject of the first several sessions. With the use of books, charts, and projector, this subject was discussed by the psychiatrist. This covered the causes of mental retardation, including a discussion of the neuroanatomical changes, the effect of brain damage or retarded development on the function of the human organism, the effect on neurological and intellectual function and emotional control, the effect on qualitative and quantitative learning, and the limitations, emotional, social and educational, that are imposed by the fact of retardation. These sessions with the parents gave the background and setting for the rest of the course.

The second general subject discussed was how the child feels and what his emotional needs are. The presentation of the materials in this area of information was made by an educator, and a psychologist. The basic primary needs of all children and the special needs of the retarded child were included in the content of this session, and a film, *Preface to a Life,* provided background for discussion.

Relationship of the retarded child in the family and neighborhood provided the area of discussion for several class sessions. In presenting this subject, role playing, with parents participating, was used as the principal technique in making real the feelings of parents, sisters and brothers, the child himself and the feelings and reactions of playmates in the neighborhood. Instructors for these sessions included a psychologist and a psychiatric social worker.

A Saturday inspection trip to Lapeer State Home and Training School under the guidance of the Director of Education and the Principal of the Institution School was the next part of the course. There the parents observed all phases of the school program, much of the training program, and the very stimulating work which is being done with the so-called custodial children. At the next meeting of the class the instructors aided the parents in evaluating what they had observed on the field trip.

Following this, three full class periods were spent discussing what parents can do to meet the child's needs. The films, *Children Learning By Experience* and *When Should Grown-ups Help* were used for motivation. Areas of discussion included handling of dependence-independence, habit training, provision of appropriate stimulation, learning experience, and constructive recognition. Time was also spent on how to provide appropriate social experience, with help in learning to meet social demands and to operate within limits imposed by society, and on how to train toward development of occupational skills.

The first semester closed with discussions on what the community can do for the retarded child and what its limitations are. Representatives from public schools, the Lapeer State Home and Training School, social work agencies, and recreation agencies provided a panel to cover this subject material. Areas discussed included the special education facilities provided by tax funds, the program in the public school and state training school, as well as a review of facilities through private training schools. The exploration with parents of existing community recreation programs and how to use them, and a description of the clinical agencies and their functions provided material for several class periods.

RESULTS

One naturally asks the question, what are the results of such a project? We do not know yet what the full effects may be, but certain observations appear significant and certain trends seem to be developing. An average of twenty-two parents have attended the sessions. They did not begin to participate actively in the discussion until the third session, and the use of role playing in the fourth session definitely led to more participation with more spontaneity and more interaction on the part of the parents, and for the first time, a highly intelligent but depressed mother of a severely brain-injured child really began to talk. A week later her husband reported that she had become more relaxed and was beginning to take part in group discussion for the first time in years. Since the field trip to Lapeer another bright mother of a brain-injured child has been more relaxed, friendly, and less defensive than any of us have known her to be. Also, since the field trip the parents of three severely retarded children have become interested in giving their children the advantages of the facilities at the State Home and Training School where as formerly they were resistant. Two of the above mentioned families are now filing for commitment. A number of parents have expressed a growing awareness that they had expected too much of their children, and have evidenced a better acceptance of the limitations of their children. In the sixth session a mother of a three-year-old mongoloid child asked, "What can we parents do now to provide our children with the social experience and training they need?" Since then this same question has been raised by the parents of two other children.

We see the following trends developing: (1) relief from feelings of guilt, anxiety and shame on the part of many parents, (2) marked reduction in expression of hostility toward the public schools, (3) practically a disappearance of any fear of the state training school, (4) better acceptance of their retarded children, (5) a growing interest in developing a cooperative nursery school to provide habit training and social experience for their children, (6) formation of a Flint Chapter of the Michigan Association of Parents and Friends of Mentally Retarded Children.*

---

*Developments between December 1952 and May 1953. In the early spring, a chapter of the parents for Mentally Handicapped was formed and they have been very active on several projects. (1) They have set up a car pool so that five of the children in the group are participating in a day-school program at the Lapeer State Home and Training School twenty miles from Flint. (2) They are working with the City Recreation Department on a summer recreation program for their children.

The several agencies that have actively participated in this course have also received some benefits and have gained new perspectives. The Flint Public School is contemplating reevaluating their special education program, especially in respect to meeting more effectively the needs of the uneducable but trainable child.*

The responsiveness of the parents has been stimulating to those instructors from the Lapeer State Home and Training School and provided added and well-deserved recognition for their work with retarded children. There has been a decrease in pressure on the Child Guidance Clinic from parents of severely retarded children.

The second semester of the course is yet to come. Enrollment will be limited to those parents who attended the first semester. It will consist largely of the clinical discussion of the children whose parents are enrolled in the course. It is expected that two cases will be covered each night. The clinical "team" will consist of a psychiatrist, psychologist, mental hygiene nurse, the director of the education program at Lapeer, and a member of the Special Education Committee of the Flint Public Schools. The discussions will be based on full clinical case studies on the children concerned, and it is hoped that further gains may be made in dealing with this frustrating problem.†

EXTENSION OF PROJECT TO SLOW LEARNERS

Although the parents served in the course described in this paper were parents of severely mentally handicapped children, who had been excluded from school, there probably is just as great

*Developments between December 1952 and May 1953. The Board of Education of the Flint Public Schools has authorized the setting up of two rooms for the severely mentally handicapped child and has worked out a very flexible working relationship with the State Home and Training School through the Probate Judge. This makes it possible to try the child in a training situation and then move him if it is found that his needs and best interest may be served by a different agency.

†Developments between December 1952 and May 1953. These clinics proved to be very successful. The attendance of parents held up to the last. The therapeutic value could not be measured, but it was evident, that parents relaxed and were willing to bring their problems out before the group. The planning by the panel for each child and the discussion of problems by the whole parent group opened the way for a complete understanding of the child's problems and resulted in a satisfactory plan for the parent and child. Furthermore, parents were able to see their own problems in their proper perspective and were ready as a result, to work as a unit for all the children rather than just for their own child.

a need for such help for parents of children who are in school but who are beginning to show unusual behavior patterns because they are "slow learners." Since much of the course outlined covers the primary needs of *all* children, there would need to be very little modification of the content to make the course profitable to parents of children who are less severely handicapped and who will probably become socially competent citizens if given the proper chance to develop. With less emphasis on causes and classifications of handicaps and more emphasis on the development and needs of the child, the background information in the course could be the same for the parents of the "slow learner group."* The desired outcomes would be very much the same as those that seem to be emerging from the experimental course; namely, relieving parents of feelings of guilt, anxiety and aloneness and helping them to accept more readily their child's limitations and to be more relaxed in dealing with his problems.

---

*The program was outlined in this paper is to be repeated for the coming year.

Chapter 11

Helping the Parents of a
Retarded Child
THE ROLE OF THE PHYSICIAN

KEITH N. BRYANT and J. COTTER HIRSCHBERG

THE physician who will take the time to listen, to understand, to support, and to counsel parents of the retarded child will do them a great service, but many parents of retarded children who have taken their child to their family doctor are not satisfied with the help they receive (1). For this reason we decided to examine the parents' dissatisfactions for clues about how the physician might increase his usefulness to such families.

Part of the parents' dissatisfaction about the help they had received represented their own difficulties and distortions, springing from their intense feelings about their child's problems (2). Nonetheless, the complaints in part often seemed to be justified (3). In a surprising number of instances, the physician had treated the parents in ways which seemed to reflect his own uncertainty about his role. These parents described with hurt and anger the doctor's seeming misunderstanding of them and their retarded child, and his inability to help them with the difficult problems that such a child posed (4).

The anxiety of the parents, their tenacious questioning, their sometimes aggressive approach, may lead the physician to avoid

Note: Reprinted by permission of the authors and the *American Journal of Diseases of Children, 102*:52-66, 1961.

J. Cotter Hirschberg, M.D., Children's Service, The Menninger Clinic, Topeka, Kan.

Children's Service of the Menninger Clinic. Senior Child Psychiatrist (Dr. Bryant); Senior Child Psychiatrist and Training Director in Child Psychiatry (Dr. Hirschberg).

"getting involved." However, if he can think of their behavior as not related to him personally, but stemming from their un-happiness and anxiety, and if he can free the time to examine and listen and understand, then he will be richly rewarded for his efforts to help them (5-6). To work with these parents and their retarded child with tact, with sympathy, and respect, the physician must remember that the retarded child is still a child with feelings, needs, wishes, and desires to which the parents respond. The physician needs to ally himself with the parents in their struggle with the dilemmas which having a retarded child create (7). If he cannot deal objectively with the problems, or is not interested in this demanding work which involves more listening than "doing," or if he is already overburdened and cannot free the time, then when possible, he should tactfully refer them elsewhere (8). It is not an example of poor practice to refer such cases — it is rather practicing good medicine to appraise accurately what one can do, and parents will respect such integrity and be grateful for it.

It is our hope that this paper will give some guidance to the physician in deciding whether he can help cases of retarded children and, if he elects to do so, to make his task a little more understandable and rewarding.

THE DIAGNOSIS

Parents of the retarded child want from the doctor a *total* understanding of the problem, both with reference to the child and to themselves (9). While we cannot entirely do this nor grant the wish of the parents that the child be cured, we can, nevertheless, try to help them to achieve the best solution for their problem.

In recent years, it has become clear that mental retardation in itself is *not* a diagnosis. It is no longer sufficient to arrive at a diagnosis through only an estimate of the child's intellectual level of performance (10), and it is important to appreciate the immense *variability* in the clinical picture that such children (and their parents) present. Report No. 43, *Basic Considerations in Mental Retardation,* by the Group for the Advancement of

Psychiatry (11) stated the diagnostic problem as follows

> It would be preferable to classify mental retardation on the basis of etiology, but present knowledge makes this difficult. . . . Evaluation of mental retardation must include organic, psychological and social factors which are closely interwoven. . . .
>
> The diagnostic process is by no means complete with a mere determination of "mental retardation." An adequate diagnosis is concerned with the implications of the specific prognosis and a comprehensive program of care, treatment and training. Diagnostic study and the subsequent treatment of the mentally retarded not only requires collaboration between the psychiatrist and pediatrician, but often calls for the help of many other medical specialists because of the frequent coexistence of multiple handicaps.
>
> The role of other professions such as education, nursing, psychology and social work cannot be overemphasized.

The goal then is represented by the ideal combination of the aforementioned services. Yet even where these are available, it is still usually the physician to whom the parents first turn with their problem, and he must make the initial diagnosis of mental retardation. Then frequently he must direct the family to and help them to use other community resources. Many parents, at the time of diagnosis, are not ready for a referral of their child for a psychiatric evaluation, and they may only come to this gradually; nor may it be the wisest time to refer the child. When the referral is made, the physician may have to coordinate the referral services — he may have to gather and interpret for the parents the various findings and recommendations from a number of different specialists and resources. Ideally each community should have a center with a totally coordinated program from diagnosis through continued training and treatment as needed over the years, but in most communities this is not yet available (12). Even after the referral is made, the physician frequently must continue to guide the family, since some parents cannot immediately act upon the recommendations, or the child is referred, at various points in his growth, back to the physician for further medical evaluation. It is important to realize that the initial diagnostic study is only the beginning of the helping process.

Parents who are angry because "the doctor looked at our child and said he was retarded and needed to be put away" have been approached in a way that is not helpful to them. New knowledge about mental retardation, and the parents' reactions to it, made it imperative for the physician to deal carefully with even the most severely retarded child and his parents. The kind of help they need may require from the doctor a series of visits, often repeated over years, as the parents *continue* to help their retarded child. The physician must show the parents he is not going to be hurried or blunt with them, but that he is willing to *share* in their task over a span of time. Even in those cases where it is clear from the very beginning that the child must be referred for psychiatric study, the physician will still need to spend a great deal of time on the case, and it may help to clarify this with the parents at the outset, so that they will expect to be charged for the necessary time spent with them as well as for the time spent with the child.

As the physician obtains a history and diagnoses the condition of the child, he will also seek answers to such questions as the following:

1. What brought the family to seek help at this particular time?
2. What is the effect of the child on his family and community?
3. What is the effect of the family and community upon the child?
4. What adjustment have the parents made to the problems that having such a child is posing for them?
5. What resources has the community to offer them?
6. How will the parents react to the findings?

The physician must gauge the parents' readiness to understand and their willingness to act on that understanding — and these do not necessarily occur at the same time. Omissions or distortions in the parents' accounts are significant, but a rigid outline for the history taking is not recommended because much significant material is best brought out spontaneously by the parents. A formal outline should be used only as a framework for thoughts and then in a flexible fashion, allowing the parents to shift topics at will.

A comprehensive diagnosis can scarcely be done in only one brief examination or interview. Each case is unique and requires individual appraisal and planning. Variations in cases may range from a *relatively* simple one, such as the uniformly and severely retarded child within a relatively normal family, living in a community with food facilities, to a more complex one, where there are different levels of retardation in various areas, to those where there is also a marked psychological disturbance in the parents, who are further plagued by intolerant neighborhood attitudes or poor community facilities.

Even when the parents and child must be referred for specialized studies and help, if the physician accepts the case at all, he should go as far as he can in his own understanding of it so as to make the best referral. He is still the medical doctor to whom the parents have come; they will ask many questions, and the more thorough his study has been, the better he can help them.

THE RECOMMENDATIONS

One recommendation the physician may elect to make at some point in helping the family is to refer them to a psychiatric clinic for a more comprehensive diagnosis, or for further treatment and training for the child, and further guidance for the parents. The physician may elect to make a referral when he feels he does not understand adquately the problems and needs at a particular point in the child's development. For example, a baby may be recognized as retarded at birth or shortly after, but it may not be helpful or necessary then to recommend a psychiatric evaluation, whereas by the time the child would normally be starting school, it may be important to get a comprehensive picture of the child's resources. Referral might also be indicated because the physician is unable to deal with the parents' disturbances, or because he does not have the necessary time to be of genuine help to the family. Availability of local resources and the readiness of the parents and child to use these resources may govern the physician's decision about referral.

Even in this present age of relative enlightenment, parents may still feel some hesitation about a psychiatric consultation. They may also be disappointed and feel that the physician is not interested in their difficulties or that he believes they themselves are emotionally disturbed and require special treatment. When these feelings arise, they need to be dealt with carefully. The physician should describe to the parents and the child what will happen to them at the referral center. The evaluation and the referral for it always need to be made a therapeutic experience for the parents and the child, and if it seems like some kind of vague, mysterious process, this will increase their anxiety about it. The procedure involved will vary, of course, from clinic to clinic.

At our center, for example, usually the parents and the child spend a week, during which time the examination of the child includes approximately five hours of play interviews with the psychiatrist, six to eight hours of psychological testing by the psychologist, an examination by the neurologist, and certain laboratory procedures, such as skull x-rays, electroencephalogram, and urine examination for phenylketonuria. Occasionally endocrinological and other special studies are done. During this time, the parents are also involved in interviews with the social worker and with the psychiatrists who is seeing the child, a process taking a number of hours, and one in which an attempt is made to assist the parents in understanding the total problem of their child as fully as possible and to help them formulate a plan of action to deal with the problem in a constructive fashion.

The need for specialized studies, of course, becomes more apparent where one is attempting to evaluate the relative roles of what have come to be known as "organic" impairments and those which represent "functional" inhibition (13-16). Especially in cases of mild mental retardation, psychological and environmental factors may determine the kind of help the child will need and what he will be able to achieve (11). The effects of psychological deprivation on children are now better understood, and it has been shown in some cases of apparent retardation that these factors have impinged upon the developing child so that he suffers from a pseudoretardation (17-18). It has even been suggested that every case of apparent retardation in a child should be given a trial of psychotherapeutic treatment (19). While this would not be indicated where severe brain damage is clearly the cause of the retardation, there have been cases of apparently severe retardation which proved to be based on a disturbed environmental and parent-child interaction and which responded dramatically to treatment.

Perhaps a word of warning is necessary at this point, however. Although many retarded children are also emotionally disturbed (since retarded and brain-damaged children have feelings just as any other child, and often need psychotherapeutic help with these feelings just as any other child) (20), a recent tendency has developed to label any seriously disturbed child who does not have very obvious stigmata of congenital maldevelopment, as "schizophrenic" (21). As a result, probably a number of retarded children — so labeled — are receiving expensive psychotherapy in a futile attempt to correct what a competent diagnostic evaluation might clarify as basic retardation. This tendency to view every disturbed child as being so only because of environmental factors is no doubt a reaction to the fact that until recently many seriously disturbed children were considered to be severely retarded and were mistakenly placed in institutions for mentally deficient children (22-23). Careful diagnostic study can now in many instances eliminate such doubts. When doubt persists, a thorough trial of competent psychiatric treatment should be tried, and this *may* help clarify the child's condition (24-25).

Constitutional and environmental factors never, of course, operate in isolation from one another. Montague states:

> ... there is little that is final about constitution, for constitution is a process rather than an unchanging entity ... constitution is not a biologically *given* structure predestined by its genotype to function in a predetermined manner. The manner in which all genotypes function is determined by the interaction of the genotype with the enivronment in which it undergoes development (26).

A misconception occasionally conveyed to parents is that if the child is emotionally disturbed, it is their fault, whereas if the child is brain-damaged, then the parents are not to blame. This is a false concept and of no practical use. There are many children with schizophrenic reactions where it is extremely difficult to see a degree of disturbance in the parents which would cause such a devastating reaction in the child. Likewise, there are mildly mentally retarded children who are emotionally disturbed because, it would appear, of improper understanding and management. Of course, neither diagnosis — brain damage nor emotional disturbance — is ever of any comfort or reassurance to parents. Each condition is so disconcerting that saying a child has one or the other does not provide any relief. Also, many parents "feel to blame" for producing a congenitally defective child anyway, even though logically they know they had nothing directly to do with it. (27-28).

Another false concept is that if the child is brain damaged, nothing can be done to help him (which is certainly not necessarily true), and that if the child is schizophrenic, then something can be done to help him (which is also not necessarily true). What is true is that the kind of treatment program needed may be considerably different in each case, although many children with brain damage also need and respond well to psychotherapy, in addition to the special educational and training techniques they may require (29).

A recommendation the physician will frequently have to consider is whether to place or not to place the child away from home. Here the mistake may be made of seeing placement as the complete solution. If the child is obviously severely retarded, placement in an institution may best fit the need. However, the physician must examine his own attitudes toward retarded children and toward the parents of retarded children before making recommendations. Society has always valued persons who contribute something positive to it and has placed a premium on creativity and intelligence (28). Such an attitude may interfere with the physician's adopting a sympathetic yet objective role because he fails to see adequately the needs and values of the child. Such children are commonly regarded as a burden, and the fact that some of them contribute much to the family and are dearly loved, not only by the parents but also by the other siblings, is overlooked. A recent study (29) found that siblings, in general, accepted the attitude of the parents toward their retarded brother or sister being in the home.

What do the parents want for their child? Papish, in the *Proceedings of the 35th Conference of the Child Research Clinic of The Woods Schools* stated it this way:

> They want a place of dignity in human society for their child. They want their child to be treated as all children are treated, with due recognition, of course, for the children's differences. And they want as nearly a normal life as possible for the family, recognizing that it can never be *really* normal because of the handicapped child. They

want a chance for their children to develop within their limited capabilities, to lead as useful a life as possible (30).

Studies (31-33) show that many retarded children are better off at home, especially during the early years of life. The psychological trauma and resulting physiological disturbances associated with removing an infant from his mother have been well documented (34-35). The too frequent practice of telling parents when the child is abnormal at birth to "put him away immediately before you get attached to him, so you can forget him more easily," is psychologically unsound advice. As Jolly has pointed out (32), the mother *has* been attached to the child long before birth; and has already made a great investment in him before he is born. If the parents send the child away and try to forget about him, it may only increase their guilt. Obviously, it is impossible for parents to "forget" about any child they have, and it would be pathological if they could do so. By keeping the infant at home during the early years, the parents will learn whether they can adequately care for the child and will be more accepting of placement if they decide they cannot manage with the child at home.

The immediate placement after birth of the retarded child "to forget about him" will affect the siblings. They will sense some kind of guilt and a hiding of something by the parents. All kinds of distorted fantasies may arise in the children's attempts to understand and explain this secret. This tension may disturb the family unit more than the presence of the retarded child. The siblings' "shame" — if any — about having a retarded brother or sister probably will be less destructive than knowing that one of them for unclear reasons has been put away somewhere and is never to be mentioned or seen again. This arouses anxieties around the idea of abandonment and may be seen as a potential rejection or punishment if the placement is not explained and adequately discussed with them.

Which factors make it possible for the child to be kept at home and which determine that the child cannot stay? Intellectual functioning is only one aspect of the total number of factors which go into this determination (36-38). Some retarded children need to be placed in an institution at a *relatively* early age; others are better off at home. This is not clear-cut or definite in most instances. Each case must be evaluated and reevaluated over a period of time, with much flexibility in planning in each of these evaluations. For example, beginning school or entering adolescence is often a time of stress, and changes may have to be made in the child's program. The child in a rural home may not have as much stress placed upon him as may a child in an urban home. On the other hand, urban families may have greater help available in caring for such a child. So one cannot say that the rural family can better deal with the retarded child and the city family will necessarily have to place the child; actually the reverse may be true. However, Krishef (39) found that retarded children discharged from a state school made a more satisfactory adjustment in a rural environment in spite of the better facilities available in urban communities.

In regard to the questions of placement, the Group for the Advancement of Psychiatry *Report* (11) states

> Accepted psychiatric principles do not support the separation of any child from his family if the only purpose is to make an educational program available to him. In recent years more communities have developed special public school programs for the educable mentally retarded and some now also include provisions for the trainable children. When such facilities are available, the admission of a retarded child to a residential setting is determined by the severity of other related factors — psychological, social or somatic.... A mildly retarded individual is seldom admitted to a residential center on the basis of his impaired intelligence. However, the disintegration of the family constellation, distorted sociocultural attitudes and the lack of available community facilities and programs often result in further psychological impairment in the retarded child. He may then become a psychiatric casualty and, since adquate help is rarely available to him in his own community, placement in a residential facility becomes necessary even though it could have been avoided had other resources been available.

One must further consider also the changes that will take place in the family over the years (such as new reactions to the child as he becomes older and as his siblings become older, the birth of other children, alterations in the financial situation) and in the community, which may disturb a shaky adjustment and thus alter the parents' being able to keep the child at home. In our culture —

a culture that is essentially one of optimism, in which everything is expected to turn out well, *especially* for our children – a retarded child is always a grave problem (40-42). It may impair marital relationships, interfamily relationships, and the family's relationships in the community. Additional financial strain, additional stress and worry in contending with the everyday problems, along with the anxiety about the future, may lead to serious trouble in the total family unit. Having a retarded child may, however, have an opposite effect and serve to mobilize the strength of the family members and bind them together to meet the problem imposed upon them.

SHARING THE FINDINGS

The physician's most difficult task with the parents is to explain the findings from the examinations in words they can understand and to gain their acceptance of the findings. The implications of the findings may indicate to the physician the best way to tell the parents (43-44). Ideally, the parents wish to achieve a full understanding of the total problem, but in some instances this is not even the parents' conscious intent. Their aim toward the ideal goal is always accompanied by enormous worry and fear and mixed feelings of doubt about wanting to find out. These conscious, mixed motives and deeper unconscious ones, complicate the task.

What measures can the physician adopt to gain the cooperation and trust of the parents? His attitude is of paramount importance in imparting the findings; if he is sympathetic and understanding, the parents will be less defensive and can absorb more accurately the findings. He might use the following as a guide:
1. Allow yourself sufficient time to do as thorough an examination as possible.
2. Be objective but kindly toward the parents and child.
3. Be sympathetic without being patronizing.
4. Accord to the child and his parents the proper dignity and respect.
5. Show them your support but do not take over in an authoritarian fashion.

6. Allow the parents sufficient time to raise questions, absorb the findings, and work at reaching their decisions.
7. Allow them to mobilize their own strengths to come to mature decisions which are best for them and their particular family and child.
8. Be prepared for them to have to postpone action on the recommdentations for awhile.

When parents ask "Where do we stand?" tell them the truth, but at the pace at which they have individually indicated they can absorb it. This varies greatly from parent to parent, so that no set rule can be given for it. Usually the parents will give some clue about the most helpful way to tell them. Many parents already have guessed the condition of their child (45) and prefer an immediate and direct confirmation of their fears. Some can face only a gentle question or an observation in the first steps of their preparation. Then plan interviews for exploring further facts as they can tolerate them. Some know, but will not say so until the doctor does, hoping he will say there is no problem and that magically then there will be none.

When the physician is in doubt about the diagnosis, he should say so; then as new evidence comes along, it can be given to the parents. Never conceal the retardation by telling the parents the child may "grow out of it." When the child does not "grow out of it," the parents naturally distrust and are hostile toward the physician. When in doubt, an honest "I don't know" should be given. A delay in giving all the findings may be necessary with some parents, who themselves usually give the clue for such a delay. Occasionally parents can move ahead constructively only when they are given clear-cut directions, which they will then solicit. Severe personality disturbance in the parents sometimes requires direct and authoritative action by the physician — for example, when they are too depressed or too emotionally exhausted to act, or when the parents are psychotic or extremely emotionally immature. Here the physician must maintain an objective attitude to be of maximum benefit to all concerned — a feeling of having to rescue the parents from the child or the child from the parents will not be conducive to maximum help to both.

Many parents are overwhelmed and numb after hearing the

doctor's report. They say, "I heard his words but they went over my head." Details may have to be repeated a number of times, and the parents may have not absorbed what has previously been discussed with them. They did not hear because they could not face the painful facts. It is important to realize the chagrin, the discouragement, the depression, the shame, and the anxiety such findings arouse. Technical jargon naturally should be avoided, and the terms "moron," "idiot," and "imbecile" should never be used to describe the child because of the emotional meanings these words have in our society. One does much better by speaking of degrees of retardation or levels of intellectual functioning. Even this is not very helpful to the parents who really want information about what the child can and cannot do. Giving them an intelligence quotient is of little practical use.

In the interviews, questions do not arise in an orderly fashion but come up as the parents go from one concern to another and back again. The following is a representative, but by no means complete, sample of the information they will be seeking:

1. Will the child need to be institutionalized?
2. Can he progress further?
3. What areas might he advance in?
4. What special treatment and training will he need?
5. How should he be managed?
6. Will he be difficult to look after?
7. What degree of independency will he be able to achieve?
8. What will be his effect on the other children?
9. What should they tell the other children and neighbors?
10. What about his sexual development, and will he be able to marry?
11. What is the cause of his illness?
12. Does heredity play a part, and will it show up in future generations?
13. Can they safely have other children?
14. Isn't there a drug or an operation that will help?

Frequently (perhaps in an attempt to convince doubting parents of the retardation), only the negative and pathological aspects are stressed, and assets and capabilities are ignored. This mistake makes the parents feel the child has not been fully understood, or it may burden them unnecessarily. It will be much easier for the parents to accept the facts if, along with the negative and pessimistic findings, hopeful and positive ones can be given; for example, predicting that the child is intelligent enough to be able to learn simple arithmetic so that he can become at least to some degree self-sufficient. Even in a more severely retarded child, if one can assure the parents that he will be capable of being toilet trained or of dressing himself, this will make a significant difference. The parents must always be told what to expect in having the retarded child at home. For example, the occurrence of physical illness is greater in a mongoloid child, has more serious consequences, and must be managed more carefully than is true for a normal child (46). The more concrete information of this kind which can be supplied to the parents, the better they will be able to deal with the problems. The physician will also need to inform the parents about additional sources of help for them (such as parent groups and educational services) and for the child (such as remedial education, vocational training, and placement facilities).

Merely telling the parents not to feel guilty about their child is of no use — active support is needed. Much has come recently from organized groups where parents discuss with each other their own problems and difficulties (47). The experience is invaluable and the parents no longer feel isolated. Occasionally in some groups an extreme attitude develops, e.g. that no child should be placed in an institution and every child is better off in the home. If neighbor and community attitudes are increasing the parents' guilt and remorse about necessary placement, or if relatives interfere, then the parents will very much need the physician's support in taking the needed step. He should also emphasize that placement is not always by any means "a last resort" or a negative step. The child may need the special remedial and educational opportunities and be much happier with peers of his own level of functioning in an institution especially designed to meet his particular needs (48). Unfortunately, not many institutions adequately meet these needs, and it is understandable why parents are reluctant to place their children in institutions which are overcrowded, have inadequate facilities, and a shortage of properly trained staff. The physician should be familiar with the conditions which prevail at the institution in which he is suggesting placement so that he can supply the parents with factual information and help them weigh the pro's and con's.

The final decision about placement must be left to the parents. They must determine the plan of care they believe best for their child and their family. Circumstances sometimes force parents to keep their child at home even though he would be better off in an institution, or vice versa.

The frequent pattern of "shopping for a cure" by some parents is not always entirely negative. It may mean that they are dissatisfied with inadequate examinations and unclear recommendations and are persisting in their efforts to understand. True, their search often reflects their denial of the retardation or belief in a magical cure. But it is natural, as one family reported, to "go to the moon if they were a possibility of getting help for our child." It would appear that "making the parents accept" the diagnosis has been overemphasized and that we tend to become annoyed or discouraged when they refuse rather than trying to discover why they cannot "accept" the facts. In some instances, it is necessary for us to "accept" the unreadiness of certain parents to face the difficulties of their child. Mandelbaum and Wheeler comment (49) upon this problem of why professional people feel a desperate need to help parents *accept* the diagnosis of mental deficiency:

> Perhaps this is in part due to our own frustration and guilt that parents come to us for help and we must tell them that the child's condition is irreversible, which is akin to saying there is no help. Then, too, there is our own resistance against accepting the child's condition. We are angry that we have to be the bearers of such sad tidings. In ourselves there are magical wishes and profound protests against this "senselessness of nature" which has happened to another human being. . . . We are often appalled by the suffering, by the burden, by the way of life they have assumed and how they misuse themselves. . . . Our sense of values may dominate so that we may not properly understand the feelings of the parents and the values which they have needed to take on for themselves. We fail to see their sufferings through their eyes but rather through our own feelings. . . . If the pain or conflictual feelings can be made more tolerable, less punitive, or less guilt arousing, the parents will then

find whatever solution is possible for them. As for the parents, the concept of "acceptance" is difficult for them because there are some things which can never be accepted. The first is the knowledge that a major portion of the child's limitation can never be reversed. The child will always remain with some important limitations. The help for the child can never go as far as the parents wish it to go.

The physician sees the parents not only for the taking of the history of the child's development but also to see how they feel about the problem. It is important to see both parents *together* at least initially. If there is conflict between the parents, or difficulty in their speaking freely in the presence of one another, then separate interviews may also need to be arranged. Another reason for seeing both parents is that one may blame the other for the child's retardation and lack of progress, or one parent does not believe the child is retarded, or they disagree about placement. A father may be against placement because he is not aware of the burden that the child creates, since he is not with the child all day. One parent may exaggerate the findings or distort them without knowing it, the parents may disagree on management, or they may have concerns which they have not told each other. Also one parent may forget relevant information that the other can supply. A parent may not wish to come because he fears the information that might be revealed or wishes to escape a painful situation. (Ocassionally it is helpful to see other members of the family — the grandparents, for example — who, not understanding the problem, interfere and cause trouble for the parents and child.) If one parent declines to participate, the problem around the retardation will likely not be fully dealt with, since the absent parent shows resistance to a full understanding of the case. Reasons given for absence, such as lack of time, or having to work, are almost always found to be a defense against involvement in the process. One of the major purposes of the examination is to unite the family, whenever possible, to meet the challenge of having a retarded child, and this unity will not be established when one parent is absent.

In the helping process, where only the *content* of the diagnostic findings are given, the parents often come away saying they have not been helped — because the *content* of the diagnostic findings is not enough. Not infrequently in our experience, we have told the parents nothing essentially new or different from what they have already been told at other centers, as far as facts are concerned. Yet follow-up reports have shown that some of these parents have gone away with a sense of real gain, because their fears and concerns were dealt with. A reduction of their defenses and anxieties, effected by the physician by establishing a tolerant and comfortable relationship with the parents, enabled them to view the findings more realistically. The need to overcome the emotional obstacles that make it impossible for the parents to face the findings is often overlooked (50-51).

ATTITUDES WHICH CREATE PROBLEMS IN THE HELPING PROCESS

What are the attitudes and feelings of the parents of the retarded child? These must be understood before the physician can help effectively (52-55). Because acceptance of the diagnosis and the planning recommendations rests on such feelings and attitudes, it seems worthwhile to consider some of them in detail. These are not described here for the purpose of having the physician discuss them with the parents (rarely is it helpful to go into such deeper meanings with them, and at times it would be extremely unwise to do so), but forearmed with general knowledge about the possible parental attitudes, the physician can gauge the direction the process should take and what conflicts the parents must be helped in resolving in order to move in that direction. The focus of this paper thus now shifts from the more practical aspects of management to some of the dynamic considerations which lie behind the practical considerations. The attitudes to be described are generalizations; one must remember that each individual case is different; for example, one colleague insisted that the parents must feel great concern about separation and have much guilt about it — because most the the parents of retarded children he had been seeing did have these feelings. However, he failed to recognize that in this particular case, the parents had worked past these feelings before coming to him, and they were angry that he did not understand this.

Parents express great anxiety about their inability to meet their child's needs — they are not confident about their handling of the child. If the mother is not secure in her feminine role, a retarded child will create special dilemmas for her. Some mothers handle this conflict by having another child, thus hoping to prove their adequacy. However, the mother may react in an opposite way and not have another child even though there is no reason why she should not. Having another child often stirs up guilt because it takes time away from the retarded child; not having another child may result in unconscious anger and resentment toward the retarded child, and in blaming him for the decision not to have another child. Another solution may be to adopt a child; but unless the negative feelings have been resolved, this solution also contains possibilities for further conflict and difficulty (28).

The parents may feel frustrated because the child's handicap itself is felt as a blow to their own success as parents. If they are parents who can love the child only by seeing themselves in the child, then they will always be discontented about what the child can never be or do. They will feel anger and frustration because of their own unrealistic demands on the retarded child, which because of his handicap he can never meet. They may feel angry and frustrated because of the dependent demands the retarded child necessarily makes on them; such parents cannot give the extra care required, and they may need to deny the retardation in order to deny the need for the extra care. Or the parents may wish to place the child in an institution when such a placement would not ordinarily be indicated, except for their own feelings toward the child. Opposite emotional feelings, such as love and hate, toward the child commonly coexist and act unconsciously and independently of each other.

An emotionally disturbed mother may be so afraid of her own anger toward the child that she has to isolate herself from him. Her depression over the child's handicaps may prevent her from providing the emotional support and additional care that is required. She may make a "negative identification" with the child — that is, the child is seen as a "throwback" to a despised or unsuccessful member of the family, and this may prevent a positive relationship. The effect of the retarded child upon other members of the family and upon other children in the community is a concern of all parents, and if they view the child as the result of "bad blood," they will not be able to assess these concerns realistically. Parents who had problems with their own sexual development may worry unduly about their child's sexual development; parents who had difficulties in school or in social adjustment, may exaggerate the retarded child's problems in these areas. Of course, every parents has aspirations and desires for his children and feels grieved and concerned when these aspirations can never be fulfilled.

Parents may also feel they have caused the retardation by negligence during the pregnancy, and if the child was not wanted, or if there were wishes or actual attempts to abort the child after conception, then the guilt will be greatly compounded. Their guilt feelings about producing a handicapped child will be accentuated if religious concepts of sin and suffering get intermingled in the parental attitudes toward the child. Parents with these attitudes sometimes act as though they are being punished by fate or by God; the retarded child is a penance they must do. This may cause them to devote an unrealistic amount of time and money to the care of this child to the neglect of the other children. However, one rarely achieves much change by pointing this out to the parents, since stressing the effects of this child on the others or on themselves only increases their anger because they feel this is a burden they *have* to bear. Such guilts may make them determine never to have another child, feeling they do not deserve anything better in life and that they do not have the right to a normal child.

To conceal their anger from themselves and others, parents may be unable to discipline the child or to demand that the child do what he can adequately do. They overprotect the child and keep him close to them, not being able to have him away in special classes of facilities. It may be this need to "prove" they are "good parents" which prevents them from placing the child away from the home when it is obviously needed. But even the most normal parents will feel they are abandoning the child when he is sent away from home and will be haunted with doubts about whether he is being properly cared for and whether they should be doing something further. Here good relationships with the admitting institution and confidence in its staff and facilities will greatly help in handling the more conscious aspects of this problem. Unfortunately, not many institutions as yet work actively with parents on a regular and continuing basis.

Parents may feel so ashamed and guilty about their child that they are unable to keep him at home even though this would be the best solution. Here the physician should try to encourage them to keep the child in the home at least for the younger years. However, the parents' needs must also be met, and some may not be able to bear the burden such a child places on even the most normal and stable home. The social stigma of having a retarded child may continue to be a factor in the parents' reactions, even though they intellectually know it is something about which they should not be guilty or ashamed.

These unconscious conflicts may also make the parents deny the reality of the child's handicap and maintain false expectations regarding the child's education or treatment. Instead of blaming themselves, which is the one extreme, they blame the community and ascribe the child's failure to the incompetence of the teacher or of the doctor, rather than to the disability. Such parents question the professional advice given them, and appear sometimes quite irrational in their views, often to the bafflement of those who deal with them. They will turn to charlatans, or repeatedly seek new sources of professional help. Then they will use the minutiae of differences in findings of one physician against the other, or they will use one of the more developed areas in the child's functioning to deny the existence of greater problems in other areas. Only a careful, understanding approach will help them to obtain a more realistic view of the problem and to interrupt their costly and painful shopping pattern.

In spite of the physician's best efforts, and his spending of extra time with them, such parents may still complain of his lack of concern and accuse him of being biased and prejudiced. Thus it becomes obvious that as well as having special attitudes toward the retarded child, the parents also come to the doctor with certain unrealistic attitudes and expectations. They may have magical expectations in which they are doomed to disappointment, no matter what the physician is able to do for them. They may carry over attitudes they held toward their own parents to the physician and expect him to be critical, depriving, hostile, or authoritarian, or conversely, to be all-giving and understanding, taking over and solving all the problems for them, as they believe a good parent would.

What are some of the other possible implications of the parents' coming to the doctor beyond obtaining a diagnostic study of the child? Sometimes it may be a bid for treatment of themselves, or they may come to solve a marital problem, but displace this difficulty onto the child. One parent may be using the child's problems to criticize the other; one parent may be coming for self-justification and for reassurance that he is doing the right thing for the child. An important question always is how is the child used in the individual parent's own needs and in the marriage. Occasionally a child may be used to maintain a neurotic balance in the marriage and may be what holds the marriage together, with this situation preventing the parents from taking constructive steps to help the child. In other marriages the child may be the final blow that leads to the disruption of the family, with the child representing an area of extreme disagreement between the parents and being used as a conductor of hostility between them. In some marriages, each parent competes for the retarded child's love and thus they are unable to initiate any discipline or achieve any separation from the child, because each sees this as a lack of love rather than as something beneficial for the child. Or the reverse may be true, hostility between the parents may lead one parent to refuse to send the child to a special school in order to oppose the views and wishes of the other.

Unconscious and conscious attitudes of the parents toward themselves, toward the child, toward the community, and toward the doctor greatly influence what can be done in providing them with help. Anyone who plays a role in his situation, even at the parents' request, is bound to be exposed to irrational feelings. Strong denial of defects, or great anger and resentment toward the physician, or toward others in the community need to be understood in part in terms of their underlying origin — arising from fear, anger, guilt, disappointment, and despair. With such understanding, one can tolerate these attitudes, even though they are unjustified, and will be able to help the parents in their painful struggle with reality.

CASE ILLUSTRATIONS

To clarify some of the foregoing comments, these brief case illustrations are given: (1) the physician could have been of help if his orientation and understanding had been different; (2) the physician was of great benefit to the family; (3) referral for specialized study was needed; and (4) neither the referring physician nor the psychiatric center could make much progress in working with the parents.

Case 1. Mr. and Mrs. X. brought their second child, Tommy, age 3 years, for diagnostic study because their physician had told them their child was retarded and "should be put away." They were concerned about the child at a relatively early age, but had been told the child would "grow out of it." The hurt and bewildered parents now insisted the doctor was wrong, desperately related examples of how well the child could perform, and almost pleaded with us to find the child adequate.

Had the physician's approach been different, and had he given the parents an opportunity for frank and understanding discussions, he would have learned about their anxieties, their fears for the future, and their current difficulties with the child. It became clear that the parents knew the child was not developing normally, and with support and guidance, they were able to think about his limitations and make constructive plans for his future. Fortunately, the child's difficulties did not preclude his being kept at home, at least for a few more years. With the beginning of school, the situation might become different, as again it might in adolescence or later life.

Case 2. This case illustrates a child and family with about the same kinds of problems as Case 1, but they were handled differently by their physician. From an early age, the physician and parents had concern about the child's development. The doctor told the parents he was not able to say with certainty that the child was retarded; then as the evidence of slow development increased, he discussed this with the parents, helped them with planning, and at an appropriate time referred them to the psychiatric clinic for an examination to check on his own suggestions and recommendations. The physician has continued to serve them in a guiding role and when necessary has the child and parents return to check on what has been accomplished, what still can be done, and what cannot be done. The physician recognized the family's strength, that they had much love for the child and were able to provide in the home much which could not at her age be provided in an institution. The physician has helped the parents recognize that at some point, as the child gets older, special training away from home may be the most helpful course and that only time will tell what degree of independence the child will be able to achieve and maintain.

In this case, in contrast to Case 1, the parents had an entirely different attitude toward their physician — and to the clinic he referred them to. They looked upon him as a wise, supporting person whom they trusted, whereas the family in the first case lost confidence in their doctor and had difficulty at first in making constructive use of the clinic's resources. In this second case, the parents could make a smooth transition back and forth from their family doctor to the guidance center because they trusted their doctor.

Case 3. This case illustrates another reason for referral. The family physician had made a diagnosis of retardation when the child was age 2 years, and then began to doubt his diagnosis, suspecting an emotional basis for the disorder. He referred the family to the psychiatric clinic for further diagnostic study when the child was 5. Although it was found that the parents too were emotionally disturbed, the child's disturbance was basically a reaction to his primary organic deficit, and he was not a schizophrenic child as the physician had suspected. When such a question arises, it is wise for the doctor to refer the child to the best psychiatric center available to obtain as accurate a picture as possible on which to base future treatment and plans.

Case 4. This case illustrates a situation where the family physician made a referral because of the complications of the case. Our psychiatric center also was unsuccessful in really helping the parents much because of these same complications.

Harold was the only son of a prominent and wealthy family in a large city. Throughout the boy's 13 years, the family physician had repeatedly and skilfully attempted to help the parents seek special training and guidance for their child, who was obviously moderately retarded, but who had some abilities a little more advanced in certain areas than in others. However, neither parent would accept the fact of their son's retardation. The father could not because of the loss of self-esteem this would mean to him — he was a self-made and self-centered man, this was his only child, and he was determined that his son should take over his position in his numerous business enterprises. The father himself was a disturbed person and in fighting off a depression would go on severe alcoholic and gambling binges; it had proved impossible over the years to get him to seek psychiatric aid for himself. The passive mother turned to her son for the dependency and the support which her husband did not provide — the son was her only source of security and solace, and thus it was impossible also for her to see the child's real limitations or to consider his leaving the home for the special training he needed. Harold found himself exposed to increasingly difficult problems both at home and in the community. His retardation became more obvious as he advanced in school, and he had more and more difficulty in making and keeping friends. The father blamed the mother for all the difficulties, and the mother felt helpless.

In desperation, the parents finally heeded the advice of their family physician and came to the psychiatric clinic for help. Unfortunately, because of the complex and deep-seated nature of their problems, it was not possible to resolve their difficulties. Although they did agree to enroll the boy in a special school — one of the best available for their child's problems — they continued to be dissatisfied and constantly complained, blaming the school for their son's lack of progress. In such situations one has to settle for limited goals with the family, sometimes very limited ones. The most useful thing one can do for the parents in this case is to remain a friendly ally to whom they can hopefully return as their needs increase. Eventually they may recognize their own need to become involved more actively and consistently in treatment for themselves.

CONCLUSION

If the physician can free himself of biased judgmental attitudes and can take sufficient time to listen, to understand, to support, and to counsel the parents, he will do them a great service. If he believes in the inherent strength of the parents to reach with his help or with additional outside help the best possible solutions for themselves and the child, then he will have the patience and the objectivity it takes to assist them with dignity in reaching these solutions, and he will be able to serve as coordinator and guide to the family which works toward the maximal growth both of the retarded child and of the family itself.

REFERENCES

1. Waskowitz, C. H.: The parents of retarded children speak for themselves. *J Pediat, 54*:319-329, 1959.
2. Smith, E.: Emotional factors as revealed in the intake process with parents of defective children. *Am J Ment Defic, 56*:806-811, 1952.
3. Koch, R.; Graliker, B. V.; Sands, R., and Parmelee, A. H.: Evaluation of parental satisfaction with the medical care of a retarded child. *Pediatrics,*

23:582-584, 1959.

4. Wolf, L.: The impact of the mentally defective child on the family unit. *J Pediat, 42*:521-524, 1953.

5. Sheimo, S. L.: Problems in helping parents of mentally defective and handicapped children. *Am J Ment Defic, 56*:42-47, 1951.

6. Bird, B.: *Talking with Patients.* Philadelphia, J. B. Lippincott Company, 1955.

7. Bustek, F. P.: The non-judgmental attitude. *Social Casework, 34*:235-239, 1953.

8. Winn, H.: Brief psychiatric approach for the clinician. *JAMA, 172*:226-228, 1960.

9. Murray, M. A.: Needs of parents of mentally retarded children. *Am J Ment Defic, 63*:1078-1088, 1959.

10. Gibson, R.: Changing concepts of mental deficiency. *Ment Hyg, 43*:80-86, 1959.

11. Group for the Advancement of Psychiatry: *Report No. 43, Basic Considerations in Mental Retardation: A Preliminary Report.* New York, the Group, 1959.

12. Kelman, H. R.: The function of a clinic for mentally retarded children. *Social Casework, 37*:237-241, 1956.

13. Cassel, R. H.: Differentiation between the mental defective with psychoses and the childhood schizophrenic functioning as a mental defective. *Am J Ment Defic, 62*:103-107, 1957.

14. Benton, A. I.: The concept of pseudo-feeblemindedness. *Arch Neurol Psychiat, 75*:379-388, 1956.

15. LeVann, L. J.: A concept of schizophrenia in the lower grade mentally defective. *Am J Ment Defic, 54*:469-472, 1950.

16. Kanner, L.: Feeblemindedness: absolute, relative and apparent. *Nerv Child, 7*:365-397, 1948.

17. Gelinier-Ortigues, M. C., and Aubry, J.: Maternal Deprivation, Psychogenic Deafness and Pseudo-Retardation. In Caplan, G. (Ed.): *Emotional Problems of Early Childhood.* New York, Basic Books, 1955, pp. 231-242.

18. Cutts, R. A.: Differentiation between pseudo-mental defectives with emotional disorders and mental defectives with emotional disturbances. *Am J Ment Defic, 61*:761-772, 1957.

19. Caplan, G. (Ed.): *Emotional Problems of Early Childhood.* New York, Basic Books, 1955, pp. 482-488.

20. Stacey, C. L. and DeMartino, M. F. (Ed.): *Counseling and Psychotherapy with the Mentally Retarded.* Glencoe Free Press, 1957.

21. Kanner, L.: The "emotional block." *Am J Psychiat, 113*:181-182, 1956.

22. Craft, M.: Mental disorder in the defective: a psychiatric survey among in-patients. *Am J Ment Defic, 63*:829-834, 1959.

23. Garfield, S. L., and Affleck, D. C.: A study of individuals committed to a state home for the retarded who were later released as not mentally

defective. *Am J Ment Defic, 64*:907-915, 1960.

24. Hirschberg, J. C., and Bryant, K. N.: Problems in the differential diagnosis of childhood schizophrenia, in neurology and psychiatry in childhood. *Proc Ass Res Nerv Ment Dis, 34*:454-461, 1954.

25. Fuller, D. S.: A schizophrenic pattern of behavior in a child with brain injury. *Bull Menninger Clin, 18*:52-58, 1954.

26. Montague, M. F. A.: Constitutional and Prenatal Factors in Infant and Child Health. In Senn, M. J. E. (Ed.): *Symposium on the Healthy Personality.* New York, Josiah Macy, Jr. Foundation, 1955, pp. 148-210.

27. Stone, M. M.: Parental attitudes to retardation. *Am J Ment Defic, 53*:363-372, 1948.

28. Mandelbaum, A., and Wheeler, M.: The meaning of a defective child to parents. *Social Casework, 41*:360-367, 1960.

29. Caldwell, B. M., and Guze, S. B.: A study of the admustment of parents and siblings of institutionalized and non-institutionalized retarded children. *Am J Ment Defic, 64*:845-861, 1960.

30. Papish, M. F.: The Pre-Adolescent Exceptional Child, in Understanding the Needs and Desires of the Parents of the Retarded Child. *Proceedings of the 35th Conference of the Child Research Clinic of The Woods Schools.* Langhorne, Pa., May, 1953, pp. 53-55.

31. Farrell, M. J.: The adverse effects of early institutionalization of mentally subnormal children. *Am J Dis Child, 91*:278-281, 1956.

32. Jolly, D. H.: When should the seriously retarded infant be institutionalized? *Am J Ment Defic, 57*:632-636, 1953.

33. Slobody, L. B., and Scanlan, J. B.: Consequences of early institutionalization in mental retardation. *Am J Ment Defic, 63*:971-974, 1959.

34. Spitz, R.: On Hospitalism. In *The Psychoanalytic Study of the Child,* New York, International Universities Press, Inc., 1945, Vol. 1, pp. 53-74.

35. Bowlby, J.: Maternal care and mental health. *Bull WHO, 3*:355-353, 1951.

36. Kirman, B. H.: Prognostic difficulties in mental retardation. *Rec Med, 172*:197-203, 1959.

37. Hormuth, R. P.: Symposium on mongolism. Home problems and family care of mongoloid child. *Quart Rev Pediat, 8*:274-280, 1953.

38. Heilman, A. E.: Parental adjustment to the dull handicapped child. *Am J Ment Defic, 54*:556-562, 1950.

39. Krishef, C. H.: The influence of rural-urban environment upon the adjustment of discharges from the owatonna state school. *Am J Ment Defic, 63*:860-865, 1959.

40. Schonell, F. J., and Rorke, M.: A second survey of the effects of a subnormal child on the family unit. *Am J Ment Defic, 64*:862-868, 1960.

41. Farber, B.: Effects of a severely mentally retarded child on family integration. *Monogr Soc Res Child Develop,* Serial No. 71, Vol. 24, No. 2, 1959.

42. Braun, S. J.: The psycho-social adaptation of a family to a mentally retarded child. *Psychiat Quart (Supp.), 32*:259-264, 1958.
43. Tudor, R. B.: What to tell parents of a retarded child. *Lancet, 79*:196-198, 1959.
44. Rheingold, H. L.: Interpreting mental retardation to parents. *J Consult Psychol, 9*:142-148, 1945.
45. Schulman, J. L., and Stern, S.: Parents' estimate of the intelligence of retarded children. *Am J Ment Defic, 63*:696-698, 1959.
46. Schipper, M. T.: The child with mongolism in the home. *Pediatrics, 24*:132-144, 1959.
47. Weingold, J. T.: Parents' groups and the problem of mental retardation. *Am J Ment Defic, 56*:484-492, 1952.
48. Stevens, G. D.: An analysis of the objectives for the education of children with retarded mental development. *Am J Ment Defic, 63*:225-235, 1958.
49. Mandelbaum, A., and Wheeler, M.: Personal communication to the authors.
50. Doll, E. A.: Counseling parents of severely mentally retarded children. *J Clin Psychol, 9*:114-117, 1953.
51. Mahoney, S. C.: Observations concerning counseling with parents of mentally retarded children. *Am J Ment Defic, 63*:81-86, 1958.
52. Kanner, L.: Parents' feelings about retarded children. *Am J Ment Defic, 57*:375-383, 1953.
53. Waterman, J. H.: Psychogenic factors in parental acceptance of feeble-minded children. *Am J Ment Defic, 56*:475-483, 1952.
54. Stone, M.: Parental attitudes to retardation. *Am J Ment Defic, 53*:363-372, 1948.
55. Grebler, A. M.: Parental attitudes toward mentally retarded children. *Am J Ment Dis Nerv Syst, 9*:184-187, 1948.

Chapter 12

The Family Physician and the Mentally Retarded Child

E. H. WATSON

IN general medicine as in pediatrics, the nature of practice has changed fairly rapidly in a generation. Less and less time is spent in treating acute infections and their sequelae and more on diagnosis and management of anomalies and handicaps. In this connection, the physician must become a counselor to the family. In some instances, the family and afflicted child can be referred to a surgical specialist, as in the case of congenital heart disease. If, however, there is no present treatment, as in cases of mental deficiency, the physician cannot simply present the family with the diagnosis and send them away. Parents expect the physician to have knowledge and advice of kinds not fully covered in medical school curriculums. Physicians should not leave the parents to the care of semiprofessional counselors but rather should, I believe, accept the role of chief counselor, enlisting help from specialties as needed.

All of the family physician's art and skill as a counselor will be called on when he delivers a deformed or obviously mentally defective child. The latter would be a child with marked microcephaly or macrocephaly, or a child who had unmistakable stigmata of mongolism. Other types to congenital mental deficiency may not be obvious until weeks or months after birth. Other anomalous conditions (not commonly associated with

Note: Reprinted by permission of the author and *Postgraduate Medicine, 25*:301-309, 1959.

Dr. Watson is with the Department of Pediatrics and Communicable Diseases at the University of Michigan Medical School in Ann Arbor, Michigan.

mental retardation), such as clubfoot, congenital heart disease, harelip, or even myelomeningocele, at least carry with them the possibility of probability that something can be done to correct the situation.

In the case of mongolism or extreme microcephaly, it is rather evident from the beginning that the child's future, so far as mental development is concerned, can never be normal. The physician can do much to help the family in this tragic situation. That he can fail to be as helpful as he might, or even, sometimes, may add to the family's confusion and prolong the time when an accurate diagnosis and acceptable plans for the future can be made is, of course, entirely possible. Accurate diagnosis of congenital defects during the early neonatal period has been made more difficult by the fact that the time the newly born infant spends in the hospital has been progressively decreased until it is only a few days in most instances. This means that in a week or less the physician and his professional assistants, including house officers and nurses, have a shorter time than formerly to decide whether the infant is, or is not, normal.

There are certain signs or symptoms which arouse the physician's suspicions. These include disproportion between the size of the head, usually the occiptolfrontal circumference, and the length and weight of the child. These three measurements should be taken promptly on all newly born infants. Obvious deviations from normal, such as the signs of mongolism, microcephaly, or macrocephaly, are usually rather obvious. However, it goes without saying that the physician must be as certain as he can that the child is, indeed, abnormal before he makes definite statements to this effect to the family. So long as he only suspects the presence of one of these abnormalities, the best course is to put a carefully worded note on the infant's chart with an outline of a definite plan to continue observations and to get consultation as needed to make a definite diagnosis before acquainting the parents with the strong probability of such a serious thing as mental defectiveness.

The intelligent mother notoriously expresses concern and asks for reassurance that her baby is entirely normal, often when there is not the slightest doubt in anyone's mind that this is the situation. If there is some doubt in the physician's mind, but he does not wish to commit himself, he must be rather careful how he answers the mother's questions. I have had parents ask if I thought that their physician really knew that their child was not "right" but that he was afraid to tell them, or sometimes they are not quite so generous to their physician and ask bluntly, "Why didn't my doctor recognize this?" It often requires all of the art of the practice of medicine to avoid the appearance of inconclusiveness or evasiveness on the one hand and the unwarranted arousing of parental fears for the future development of their child on the other hand.

The unstigmatized child who later proves to be grossly mentally deficient may look as normal as another for the first days and weeks of life. Some of the signs which do occur shortly after birth may serve as a warning to the physician. These, of course, are failure of the infant to do those things which normal infants do, such as to cry, to suck, and to feed normally. Conversely, the appearance of abnormal signs such as cyanosis, twitchings or frank convulsive seizures is ominous. However, these do not necessarily indicate that the central nervous system is abnormal or that it has been damaged beyond complete recovery. As all physicians know, a child may appear to be severely damaged following a long or traumatic birth only to recover completely without any subsequent demonstrable brain damage. As a matter of fact, this is the rule rather than the exception.

Growth and development during the first few weeks and months proceed rapidly, and the experienced physician should be able to recognize signs of delay of development by the time the child is three or four months of age. The intelligent and experienced mother will also have her suspicions aroused at about this time or shortly thereafter. For this reason, the monthly checkup should certainly include observations and a notation on the chart of the child's approximate developmental stage. One expects the child of one month to have gained approximately 2 pounds over his birth weight, to have gained 2 or 3 inches in length, to still retain the Moro and tonic-neck reflexes, and one is satisfied if the child makes any attempt at all to look at objects in front of him. At two months of age, he should be paying attention to his surroundings, to the extent that he will look at persons or objects directly in front of him and will follow to a limited extent as objects are moved laterally in his field of vision. He may not yet be able to turn his head to enable him to follow objects moving out of his field of vision. Both the Moro reflex and tonic-neck reflex will be present, and he usually will have added another 1 1/2 pounds at least to his weight.

By three months of age, he can look at objects near him and can follow an object moved through a circle of 360 degrees in front of him. As Gesell has said, he seizes objects with his eyes before he can seize them with his hands. As yet he knows no fear of strangers, and can be picked up by the physician without signs of alarm. It is probably too early for most mothers to detect signs of delayed development, but I believe that the physician may be able to do so if he has had much experience with infants, and I regard the eyes as the best indicator of the child's normal mental development. If I cannot get an infant to look at me as I examine him at three months of age, I am worried about his mental development or his eyes. The short attention span and lack of interest in his surroundings, so typical of the mentally retarded child, can be detected sometimes as early as three months of age.

By the time the child has reached four or five months of age, the mother will probably be aware of the fact if her child is not developing at somewhat near the normal rate. This is, of course, more likely to be true if she has other children. If she has not had experience in this connection, the child may well be six, seven or even eight months of age before the mother, through comparison with infants of her friends, realizes that her child is not coming along as rapidly as they are. She will hesitate at first to ask the physician, sometimes because she does not want to appear to be overly anxious and sometimes because she is afraid of the answer that she will receive. If she does raise questions about the child's development, I think that the physician must again be very careful of his answer unless he is absolutely sure of the situation. I do not think that he should put the mother off with some offhand statement to the effect that children vary so much in their development that comparisons are unwise and unfair.

A common bit of advice which may subsequently plague the

physician is to the effect that "Your baby is doing just fine; give him time and he will be perfectly all right." This soothing statement may be exactly what is needed when the physician is convinced that the baby is, indeed, normal, and that the mother is overly apprehensive. However, if the mother's fears do prove to be well grounded and subsequent events prove that the child is retarded, the parents are very likely to remember the physician's words and to be critical of him. They may even conclude, rightly or wrongly, that the baby's development would have been better had the physician recognized the condition earlier and instituted treatment. It is well to remember that we have educated our patients to the general principle that a great many human ills can be bettered or cured if diagnosed early and given proper treatment. The mentally retarded child learns much during the preschool years, and early recognition of his condition may result in his getting special training and may also prevent the development on the part of anxious parents of attitudes of rejection unfavorable to the child.

When the physician is consulted about the mental or physical growth of a child that he has not followed from birth, the diagnosis of mental retardation may be relatively easy, but the cause or causes and the best program to be instituted for the child and his family often take a considerable amount of thought and working out. The physician often has to call on certain medical specialists or other auxiliary services in order to get the best possible arrangement in such instances. Again, I would remind you that the physician is considered by his patients to have the ability to counsel on some matters that are not included in the curriculum of medical schools. For example, when a child is not doing well in school, the physician is consulted. It seems to me that physicians not only should be able to check the child's vision and hearing and to determine in general if the child is physically able to enter into the school situation in a normal fashion, but they should also be able to advise the family what to do if it seems certain that the child's school troubles are due simply to a mental development incompatible with an education as it is offered in our public schools.

There is considerable confusion about one common complaint,

TABLE 12-I

CAUSES OF MENTAL DEFICIENCY

I. Hereditary causes
  A. Several genes involved (common)
  B. Single genes involved (rare)
      1. Phenylpyruvic oligophrenia
      2. Galactosemia
      3. Tuberous sclerosis
      4. Cerebral angiomatosis
      5. Neurofibromatosis
      6. Sturge-Weber syndrome
      7. Friedreich's ataxia
      8. Laurence-Moon-Biedl syndrome
      9. Gargoylism
     10. Tay-Sachs disease (cerebral lipoidosis)

II. Prenatal causes
  A. Infection
      1. Syphilis
      2. Toxoplasmosis
      3. Rubella
  B. Iso-immunization (kernicterus)

III. Metabolic disorders
  A. Galactosemia
  B. Phenylpyruvic oligophrenia
  C. Hypothyroidism (poor prognosis)
  D. Hypoglycemia

IV. Other causes
  A. Mongolism (multiple causes; anoxia)
  B. Primary amentia

V. Cranial maldevelopment
  A. Microcephaly
  B. Craniostenosis
  C. Hypertelorism

VI. Cerebral injury
  A. Natal
      1. Hemorrhage
      2. Anoxia
      3. Subdural hematoma
  B. Postnatal
      1. Poisoning
      2. Infection
      3. Sequelae of infection

VII. Degenerative disorders
  A. Tay-Sachs disease
  B. Heredodegenerative disease
  C. Hurler's syndrome

TABLE 12-II

CAUSES OF PSEUDOMENTAL DEFICIENCY

Sensory defects
  Hearing defects
  Sight defects
  Language difficulties
  Aphasia
  Reading defects
Cerebral palsy
Chronic illness
Emotional disturbance
Psychosis (schizophrenia)
Unstimulated child (environmental retardation)

namely, that the child has not yet learned to talk, or that his speech is defective. The easiest way for the physician to dispose of such a patient is to refer him to the speech correctionist, but I believe that we have failed our patients if the child's defective speech is a part of defective mental development, and it has been my experience that this is usually the case. The majority of children who are not talking by the time they are three or who have grossly defective speech as they are about ready to enter school will also be found to exhibit other evidences of mental retardation. One exception of this statement is the emotionally upset child who, because of lack of proper care and stimulation or because of a long-continued unfavorable emotional environment, has not developed speech in a normal fashion. Again, it should not require much questioning of the family concerning relationships among its members for the alert physician at least to suspect that the child's abnormal speech development is based on emotional disturbance or deprivation.

As I have indicated already, there is more than one reason for failure of mental growth and development to proceed in a normal fashion. In order that a correct and complete diagnosis may be made, the physician should keep in mind the various causes of mental deficiency and pseudomental deficiency. In its broader sense, the term *pseudomental deficiency* is used to designate the condition of a child who is not behaving in a normal manner at a given time, but who subsequently is not found to be mentally retarded. The various causes of mental deficiency and pseudomental deficiency are listed in Tables 12-I and 12-II. It is necessary for physicians to be as accurate as possible in making a diagnosis of mental deficiency if they are to be effective as counselors for their patients.

As I mentioned previously, when a physician is dealing with a child who appears to show evidence of mental retardation he, will find it necessary to enlist the aid of other professional services. I have found the experienced psychologist of the greatest aid in helping distinguish the mentally retarded child from the pseudomentally retarded one, and also to distinguish a child with a brain injury from the simple, genetically mentally inferior child. He can make this distinction with a high degree of accuracy by applying three or four standard psychometric tests as commonly used.

Often the services of an otologist or ophthalmologist may be needed in order that the child's hearing or sight may be accurately evaluated. However, as part of his routine examination of the child even before one year of age, the general practitioner can be fairly certain whether or not a severe deficit in hearing or sight exists.

There are state and national agencies* on which the physician can call for help and advice to the parents of the blind or deaf preschool child. A great deal is lost if these defects are not recognized until the child is ready to go to school. Just like other children, they are capable of learning a great deal in the preschool period of properly handled. A somewhat similar situation exists with respect to the child who shows evidence of brain injury acquired natally or at some time during the postnatal period. Any physician can make a fair neurologic examination, but it is sometimes helpful to have a specialist as a consultant when the neurologic signs are not clearcut or when their implications are confusing.

Today, most school systems have the services of a speech pathologist or speech correctionist. Many counties have such a consultant who spends a few hours a week in several different schools. This is very helpful for the school child with speech difficulties but, again, some help for the preschool child is often needed. Previous mention was made of the speech difficulties of mentally retarded children. However, there are others who have speech difficulties on an emotional basis. It is obvious that the child's speech should be as good as possible by the time he enters school, for the mere fact of defective speech will inevitably pose certain problems for the child and may result in emotional disturbances and a dislike for school.

There is one very important area where the family physician must assume to a certain extent the role of a psychiatrist. A physician's gestures and his words, even including their intonation,

---

*Parents should write to their State Department of Health, Division of Maternal and Child Welfare, for information on state schools for children who are mentally retarded or otherwise handicapped. Parents of deaf children should write to the John Spencer Tracy Clinic, 924 West 37th Street, Los Angeles, California, for correspondence courses for deaf children of preschool age. The Volta Speech Association for the Deaf, 1537 35th Street, Northwest, Washington 7, D.C., also supplies pamphlets for parents of deaf children. The Lighthouse, 111 East 59th Street, New York, New York, supplies a manual for parents of blind children of preschool age.

are of great import when a situation is one of counseling parents of a child who has a serious defect. It has been my experience that it is desirable to have more than one session with parents when the problem is one of counseling what to do in these tragic situations. Unless the family is especially well prepared, only a part of what is said at the first interview will actually get across, particularly when that part is to the effect that they have a seriously handicapped or defective child whose prognosis for normal growth and development is hopeless. It seems rather useless to attempt to go ahead and outline in detail just what will happen in the next several years. I say this because many of my patients come from considerable distances for consultation, and it is not easy for them to return several times. However, since these conferences in which the physician tries to impart to the distraught parents the exact nature of the child's defect and its implications for the future are very important, I think both the physician and the parents may well devote as much time as is needed to get those matters thoroughly understood.

It sometimes is advisable to have young parents bring along their parents to some of the counseling sessions; however, I try to emphasize to the father and the mother of the defective child that the problem is primarily theirs and one which they alone can decide, and that above all they must come to a decision which is acceptable to both of them; then they must stand firmly together against all others who would attempt to deter them from the course which seems best. All of us know how much help in-laws can be in such circumstances and also how much hindrance they can offer by such cruel remarks as, "Nothing like this ever happened on our side of the family."

There has recently developed in many areas throughout the country a movement known as the NARC or National Association for Retarded Children. Branches of this organization are found in many towns and counties. The officers of the local chapter of the NARC often can perform a service for the parents of a defective child which the physician cannot offer. In my own area, I know that parents have had moral support from the local NARC members and that a program of parent education and mutual support goes forward. Often, such groups support day schools for the preschool child or for the school child who has been excluded from regular schools because of his severe mental deficiency. While these cooperative efforts seldom lead to very effective training or education of severely defective children, these day schools do serve the purpose of giving the mother some relief from the constant demands of her defective child and, in addition, the parents feel that the child is at least getting a chance to do whatever he can in a school situation. There is the added value of some degree of social maturity which might otherwise be denied the child who is excluded from school and largely from the play of normal children. Physicians can perform a service to such groups by giving talks when asked to do so, and, in general, serving in an advisory capacity. It is understood that the cooperative day school here mentioned is mostly for severely retarded children who cannot be educated but can assimilate training. The educable retarded child is admitted to special classes in most school systems.

GENETICS AND MENTAL DEFICIENCY

A trained geneticist can be of great assistance to the physician and his patient, but this service usually is available only in connection with large medical centers. Most physicians must serve as their own geneticists and, fortunately, can do so because of excellent books which are available on the subject. Sometimes, it is possible to answer the anxious parents' question, "If we have other children are they likely to be similarly afflicted?" and to assure them that the defect under consideration is not hereditary. There are other cases, such as cases of cystic fibrosis of the pancreas, gargoylism, Charcot-Marie-Tooth type of muscular atrophy and many others, in which the physician cannot give a reassuring answer. To complicate the matter still further, there are, of course, certain manifestations which in one patient may be the result of heredity, in another the result of mutation, and, in still another, perhaps the result of non-hereditary injury of the fetus in the early course of development. Unfortunately for the physician who attempts to advise families in matters concerning the inheritance of defects, these are not transmitted in man in such a nicely predictable fashion as they are in inbred strains of laboratory animals.

It appears to be a conservative estimate that 60 percent or more of mentally defective children are so because of heredity. Some investigators have placed this fraction of retarded children as high as 80 percent of the total. It is true that environment is important in the mental growth and development of the child, but it is also true that the best environment can do no more than bring out the child's full potential. Conversely, it is true that the child with normal potential can achieve far less than he is capable of if he is in a highly unfavorable environment. It is also true that a child with normal or superior potential for mental development may have that favorable situation altered by natal or postnatal injury, usually by asphyxia, encephalitis, meningitis, intercranial hemorrhage, and so on. Fortunately, the incidence of severe mental deficiency of the imbecile or idiot range is rare, probably no more than 5 percent of the total.

The most standard and well-known example of mental deficiency is the child who suffers from what is ordinarily designated as mongolism, a term obviously applied because of his superficial resemblance to members of the Mongolian races. There is some evidence that mongolism may be inherited. I have seen several instances of two such children in one family, and there are in medical literature reports of one or more instances of a woman, herself a mongoloid, giving birth to a similarly afflicted child. Sorsby said that the incidence of mongolism among the siblings of affected children is about 1 percent. This seems to be due in part at least to the fact that the incidence of mongolism increases sharply with the age of the mother. Again, Sorsby is the authority for the statement that any woman who becomes pregnant after the age of forty years runs a statistical chance of 1 to 6 percent of having a mongoloid child.

The repeated occurrence of seriously defective children, including monstrosities, is not unusual. Yannet said, "Studies of pregnancies resulting in abnormal children, including the mentally retarded, have shown a significant incidence of such conditions as early maternal bleeding, suggesting imperfect placental attachments; toxemias of pregnancies, including eclampsia; and prematurity." Most physicians have had the experience of observing families in which two or more defective children are born. Murphy said that in families already possessing a malformed child, the birth of a subsequent malformed offspring takes place with a frequency which is in the neighborhood of twenty-five times greater than that of the general population. He was not referring to mongolism specifically, but this same general rule holds. Others have estimated that the woman who has given birth to one mongoloid child runs a risk of as high as 1 to 20 that she may repeat. This is, of course, is very marked contrast to the incidence of mongolism in the population generally, which is approximately 1 per 800 births.

It is seldom safe for the physician to treat the matter of inheritance of defectiveness lightly with some such remark as, "This couldn't happen to you again in a million years," or some other nonspecific statement intended to reassure the parents unless, indeed, such is known to be the case. I think it is necessary to tell any parents of a defective child that the fact that they have produced a defective child, whether it be on the basis of genetics, iso-immunization, unfavorable placental implantation, and so on, has statistically reduced their chances of producing normal children in the future. In some instances, this reduction will not be sufficient to warrant the physician's advising strongly against future pregnancies. With respect to the birth of a mongoloid child, it has been my experience that the chances are better for subsequent children to be normal when the parents are in their twenties than they are when the mother is in her late thirties or early forties.

As mentioned previously, most mental deficiency apparently is the result of heredity. It is well known that when both parents are defective nearly all of the children (95%) will be abnormal. If one parent is mentally defective and the other is normal, the children will be about evenly divided with respect to mental deficiency and normal potential. It is perhaps worth remembering that even when both parents are apparently normal there still exists a 1 to 3 percent chance that deficiency may occur in the children of that couple. This is not meant to deny an equally well-known fact that some of the world's intellectual giants have unexpectedly come from apparently average parents. It seems that there are several "leavening" influences which tend to keep the population from becoming eventually divided into two groups, the one extremely brilliant, the other extremely retarded. It is well that this is so.

QUESTIONS AND ANSWERS

The following are questions commonly asked by parents, and the answers are based on views and opinions developed at various conferences and round-table discussions.

Question: How can the physician best handle the problem presented by the birth of a mongoloid child?

Answer: Needless to say, the diagnosis of mongolism should be established before the parents are advised of this catastrophe. If necessary, consultation should be obtained; in fact, it is usually advisable to have more than one opinion if there is doubt about it. Bakwin has outlined a course of procedure which might well be a guide for physicians. He said that the parents should be told frankly and with as much kindness as possible about the true condition of their child. Certain offensive words like idiot, mongol, monster, and others, should be avoided, since they will aggravate the hurt to the parents, and they do not mean the same thing to the layman that they do to the physician. It may be possible to ease the situation a little by pointing out that the mongoloid child is not deformed in the ordinary sense, nor is he in any sense a monstrosity. He simply has signs and symptoms which inevitably point to a severe limitation of his ability to learn that which he must learn and to become independent and self-sufficient.

It is extremely important that parents be told that the etiology is not established and that there should be no feeling of guilt or the thought that the child's condition resulted from an overt action or thoughts of rejection which the parents might have had. At some time in the discussion, but possibly not at the first session, matters of heredity and the possibility of subsequent children being similarly afflicted must be brought up and discussed fully. Eventually, the subject of institutional care must be introduced, and it may well come up even at the first conference with the parents. As a rule, this subject needs to be approached very carefully with the idea that the family and physician are attempting to make proper provision for a child with mental handicap rather than with the idea that they are trying to get rid of a defective, unwanted child. Above all, the physician should impart to the parents his sympathetic and continued interest in their problem and their child, and the fact that he expects to advise them repeatedly until the problem is satisfactorily solved.

Question: Admitting that eventual institutionalization is the best solution for the severely mentally retarded child as represented by the mongoloid, when should such a child be removed from the family to a custodial institution?

Answer: Not all physicians agree as to how this question should be answered. A generation ago, most pediatricians followed the thinking of Brenneman and many others who felt that such children should be separated from the family at the earliest possible moment, preferably taken from the lying-in hospital to an institution or to a boarding home pending admission to the institution. There has been some change in this view, and many pediatricians, psychiatrists, and others feel that such precipitate action is harder on the mother of such a child than a course which permits the parents to take the child home and to keep him until they are able to understand the problem fully, and to accept by degrees the necessity for placing the child in a protected environment for his own good as well as the good of the other members of the family. This school of thought fears that the abrupt removal of the baby from the maternity hospital leaves the mother with the feeling that she produced something so defective and possibly monstrous that the doctors do not want her to see the child and, indeed, feel that it should be hurriedly removed to some place of relative concealment. Also, she may have some lingering doubt that the diagnosis was correct.

There is nothing repulsive about the ordinary mongoloid child, and, in most instances, the parents can take him home and take care of him until such time as they can fully accept the physician's recommendation that the world will not be receptive of him and is more likely to appear to him to be cold and rejecting, and that he will be better off and happier in the institutionalized environment where he can be with children like himself and where the tempo is suited to his capabilities and he is understood rather than pitied, scorned, and rejected. There is one practical consideration — it is not possible to place all mentally defective children in institutions. There just are not enough beds for them.

Attentions should be paid to the observations set forth by the professorial staff of the state home and training school institutions to the effect that the mongoloid or mentally defective child who can stay with his own family until he is four or five years of age is usually in somewhat better mental and physical condition than the child who comes to the institution in infancy. Florence Stewart, Director of the Lockland School, Geneva, New York, has still another reason why the family may, in the long run, feel better about their child if they have not rushed him out of the home. She said, "My experience has convinced me that parents who keep such a child at home as a loved member of the family until he is three or fours years of age are better able to accept his handicap and relinquish the later care with less pain because they have the satisfaction of having given several years of tender care. . . ."

Question: What about the child with spina bifida and myelomeningocele?

Answer: Many children with this common combination of anomalies are normal mentally and will remain so if they escape complicating hydrocephalus. When the child has a gross anomaly such as to render him shocking and possibly repulsive to his mother, the problem of what to do is further complicated. When the deformity is gross and of such character as to be incompatible with successful surgical or other treatment, the situation calls for removal of such a child from the family, usually without the mother having seen the child. There certainly is no way to obviate severe mental trauma to the parents in such instances, but, with the exception of an unusually mentally stable mother, such infants should not be taken home. Large myelomeningoceles or teratomatous growths must indeed strike horror and terror into a mother's heart. The problem is not so simple when the infant with a myelomeningocele appears to move his lower extremities and hydrocephalus has not developed or may not do so. In this instance, it is desirable to have the mother care for the infant unless the physician believes she is not up to it. A few such children do escape hydrocephalus, and the meningocele sac may be removed at a later date.

REFERENCES

1. Aldrich, A. A.: Preventive medicine and mongolism. *Am J Ment Defic, 52*:127 (October) 1947.
2. Jolly, D. H.: When should the seriously retarded be institutionalized? *Am J Ment Defic, 57*:632 (April) 1953.
3. Editorial: The mentally retarded child. *J Pediat, 42*:521 (April) 1953.
4. Editorial: Early home care or institution for the retarded child. *J Pediat, 42*:396 (March) 1953.
5. Benton, A. L.: Concept of pseudofeeblemindedness. *Arch Neurol Psychiat, 75*:379 (April) 1956.
6. Kirk, S. A., Karnes, M. B. and Kirk, W.: *You and Your Retarded Child; a Manual for Parents of Retarded Children.* New York, The Macmillan Company, 1955.
7. Buck, Pearl: *The Child Who Never Grew.* New York, John Day Company, Inc., 1950.
8. Rogers, D. E.: *Angel Unaware.* Westwood, Fleming H. Revell Company, 1953.
9. Bruckner, L. S.: *The Triumph of Love; an Unforgettable Story of the Power of Goodness.* New York, Simon & Schuster, Inc., 1954.
10. Strauss, A. A. and Kephart, N. C.: *Psychopathology and Education of the Brain-injured Child. Progress in Theory and Clinic.* New York, Grune & Stratton, Inc., 1955, Vol. 2.
11. Levinson, A.: *The Mentally Retarded Child; a Guide for Parents.* New York, John Day Company, Inc., 1952.
12. Reed, S. C.: *Counseling in Medical Genetics.* Philadelphia, W. B. Saunders Company, 1955.
13. Sorsby, A.: *Clinical Genetics.* St. Louis, C. V. Mosby Company, 1953.

Chapter 13

The Physician and Parents
of the Retarded Child

J. WILLIAM OBERMAN

 D URING the last twelve years much progress has been made in assessing the potential ability of the retarded child and applying this toward the development of community programs to help him realize this potential. Sparked by the National Association for Retarded Children and given major impetus by programing and funds from the Children's Bureau, a mushrooming of multidisciplinary clinics devoted to diagnosing and planning for the retarded child has occurred throughout the country. These clinics examine the child from medical, social, psychological, and educational points of view, interpret to parents the nature and magnitude of the condition, and attempt to set up a comprehensive plan for future management of the child.

However, many children are taken long distances to clinics for the mentally retarded by their parents, and after confirmation of the diagnosis, return to their homes where professional persons who have specialized in work with retarded children may not be available. Thus it remains to the family physician or pediatrician to counsel and advise the parents as their mentally retarded child grows older.

What can the family physician or pediatrician do when presented with a child obviously mentally retarded or one suspected of being so, if in his community such specialized services are not available? Does helping the parents and child require a vast

Note: Reprinted by permission of the author and *Children, 10*:109-113, 1963.

Dr. Oberman is Director of the District of Columbia Clinic for Retarded Children, Bureau of Maternal and Child Health, District of Columbia Department of Health.

body of information which he cannot hope to have at his command? Must he take extensive refresher courses in mental retardation to answer the inevitable and seemingly interminable parental questions about the child and his future?

When the retarded child is passing through the first few years of life, it is most difficult for any person to answer the questions of ultimate prognosis uppermost in parents' minds. Nevertheless, these early years are crucial for the child, since during this period of life his basic personality patterns begin to emerge. If in addition to a delay in development, the retarded child must cope with a liberal dose of parental anxiety and feelings of helplessness, his entire adjustment can be channeled into areas of behavioral abnormality which will lead inevitably to early institutionalization.

The pediatrician or family physician who sees retarded children can and must play an important role during these early years. By virtue of his training and experience in normal child development, he can contribute to the normal personality development of the retarded child, especially if he already has an established relationship with the family and has gained their respect and confidence. Through his knowledge of the home atmosphere, he can anticipate problems that may arise and can give the parents many practical suggestions for managing the child. Many parents who, because of their feelings of guilt and anxiety, would not be able to seek help from a child guidance clinic or social agency can lean on the strength of their family physician or pediatrician, and thus accomplish many changes in their behavior toward the child even though they do not gain any real insight into their own feelings. Direct suggestion, even when it conflicts with basic parental feelings, can often be accepted (1).

The birth of a child is a momentous occasion in the life of a family. Long before birth, parents idealize the child and make elaborate and often fanciful plans for his future. Many parents see their child as an extension of themselves and as an opportunity to live out their own fantasies and wishes. While many normal children do not live up to the often unrealistic expectations of their parents, who therefore must gradually relinquish their cherished plans, parents who receive a diagnosis of mongolism at their child's birth or mental retardation early in life have their dreams and fantasies brought to an abrupt end. Thus, when a diagnosis of mental retardation is made, it is the parent who suffers a blow rather than the child (2).

Consequently, parents who seek help for a retarded child are usually in a state of heightened emotions. They frequently expect and fear the worst and are already calling forth the usual feelings of shame or guilt which people suffer if something goes wrong in connection with the birth process. One recent study of the initial subjective reactions of a group of parents whose children had been diagnosed as mentally retarded has shown that about half expressed feelings of rejection toward the child associated with shame or guilt, and a large proportion of the others worried about reactions to the child of their other children, relatives, and friends (3). Some parents are unable to overcome their frustration and disappointment at the child's inability to attain their ambitions for him; he remains a source of irritation to the family and may even precipitate its disruption.

DIAGNOSIS

When the physician first suspects mongolism in a newborn infant, he may want to seek confirmation of his diagnosis by consultation with a colleague. His next step must be to interpret the diagnosis to the parents during the neonatal period or shortly thereafter, preferably to both of them together. After the initial shock has subsided, the parents will inevitably deluge him with questions concerning the "why" and "how" of it, and having to do with the child's chances for health and adjustment in later life. In addition to talking these problems over with them in considerable detail, he may find that providing them with a copy of the booklet *The Mongoloid Baby* (4), which answers the questions most frequently asked by parents on this subject, is a great help to them.

In the case of the nonstigmatized retarded infant, the diagnosis is usually one gradually suspected, frequently not until after the child is a year old. The physician then has the difficult task of deciding whether a developmental aberration is a physiological variant or is, in fact, true mental retardation. Perhaps the most pertinent finding in early diagnosis is the observation, as recently noted by Illingworth (5), that the child who is mentally retarded from birth or shortly after birth *is behind in all fields of development* except occasionally in the gross motor field. On the other hand, the child retarded only in a specific field of development (walking, talking), may represent only a physiological variant and should not be considered mentally retarded unless his further course of development so indicates. When a suspicion of mental retardation arises, the physician should seek the services of a qualified psychologist to confirm his impression or refer the child to a multidisciplinary evaluation clinic if one is available.

Without entering into the controversy of the reliability of infant testing as a predictor of future intellectual potential, this author is in agreement with those who believe that the great majority of infants whose development is found to fall *within the mentally defective range* (developmental quotient less than 70) in the first two years of life are likely to be found to be mentally retarded in later years (6). Certain premature infants of low birth weight, infants with a history of "maternal deprivation," and those with chronic debilitating physical disease may be important exceptions. When there is uncertainty psychological testing repeated six to twelve months after the initial tests may clarify the diagnosis.

However, when a diagnosis of mental retardation has been made and interpreted, the physician's work has just begun. Many physicians do not relish the task of helping parents with retarded children because they feel that there are serious gaps in their knowledge of the growth and development of the retarded child. But they do have considerable knowledge of *normal child development* and can bring this to bear most satisfactorily on the management of the *abnormal child.*

TELLING THE PARENTS

When the physician tells the parents about a diagnosis of mental retardation, he frequently meets with denial and then sometimes becomes the target for parental criticism and hostility. This is particularly true if he presents the diagnosis only, giving no suggestions as to how the child should be handled or what kind of plan should be made for him. In a recent study, Koch and his co-workers (7) have commented on the frequent dissatisfaciton of parents with the way pediatricians and general practitioners deal with the problem of the mentally retarded child and on the parental bitterness toward what they regard as the cursory nature of the examination and presentation of facts. In the case of the nonmongoloid child, who seldom exhibits recognizable physical abnormalities, parents and physicians frequently arrive at a suspicion of mental retardation together. However, the parents often become anxious long before the physician, who sometimes retreats behind the phrase "he'll grow out of it." When the diagnosis is eventually made, the parents often express animosity toward the physician who did not listen to their fears.

Some physicians react to the diagnosis of retardation in a child with an abrupt recommendation for institutionalization. While this may be indicated in some situations, the recommendation is a far-reaching one and should be made only after such factors as attitudes of the parents toward the child, the social background of the family, the welfare of the child's siblings, the economic status of the family, and the availability of satisfactory institutions have been taken into account. Such a recommendation is often made without considering the possibility that the retarded infant may profit considerably from the mother-child relationship in the first years of life and that his presence in the family is not likely to interfere seriously with the normal emotional development of older or younger siblings. Studies such as those of Schipper (8) and Saenger (9) have emphasized the good adjustment of many retarded children and young adults living with their families.

Helping parents face up to the diagnosis cannot be done quickly. For example, at the District of Columbia Clinic for Retarded Children, which provides continuous follow-up services to retarded children and their parents as long as they are requested, the initial interpretation may take as long as an hour to an hour and a half. During this time the parents are encouraged to express their feelings of hurt and disappointment as well as to ask any and all questions concerning the child's future potential. And the clinic's services to parents do not end with the initial interpretation. Many parents receive brief or continuing social casework in order to work out their feelings, the child development specialist sets up home-training regimens (10), parents are seen in groups so that they may explore their mutual feelings toward their children and how to deal with problems of behavior and development (11), brief psychotherapy is made available to selected children, and a variety of other services are given. Parents are encouraged to contact the clinic at any time the child exhibits a developmental crisis or at any time educational or training plans are indicated.

Thus, the actual evaluation is both a learning and a therapeutic experience for parents, since they have a chance to air their views of the child's deficiencies and to compare his development with the development of normal children. Rarely after this is a parent unable to realize, at least intellectually, that his child is retarded.

However, we have found subjective parent reaction at the time of interpretation at the clinic to vary from complete acceptance of the clinic's findings and whole-hearted cooperation in planning for the future life of the child to one of complete rejection and subsequent "shopping" to other agencies. Some parents persist in their fantasies that the child will "grow out of it" and that the retardation is not as severe as the clinic has found. They frequently use the interpretation session to criticize one or more aspects of the evaluation and to ignore many of the findings.

COUNSELING AND TIME

Curiously, during this often very emotional session, parents seem to be directing their comments to the world at large rather than to any specific clinic member — their reason tells them what their feelings will not allow them to believe. Particularly is this true of fathers, who frequently cling to the hope of future normality. It is at this time that counseling, whether given by a trained social worker or by any other professional person with the ability to listen, sympathize, and respond wisely, is most valuable.

It is this author's impression, however, that even following a careful evaluation and continuing follow-up service by skilled personnel, the most important factor in the ability of parents to plan realistically for their child is *time.* Many parents, while initially rejecting the diagnosis, after a period of time in the home, where they can appraise the child and compare him to his normal siblings and playmates, are able to see and to say that their child is abnormal. An important element in the effects of time is the fact that the retarded child of preschool age *passes through the same stages of development as do normal children,* even though at a slower rate. For instance, when a parent has been able to observe his child's attainment of a particular self-help skill such as toileting, he is able to say to himself that the problem is not after all hopeless. Being more hopeful, he is at the same time more able to admit that his child is retarded.

Many parents who have initially rejected the diagnosis of mental retardation return to the clinic a year or so later proudly demonstrating the recently learned skills of their child. Some parents who are unable or unwilling to talk to their disappointment or guilt at having produced a retarded child are able to focus on his accomplishments and plan ahead for his future life. It is most important, therefore, that the "pot be kept boiling" during the early developmental years when the child who ultimately will have great difficulty in school can be compared more favorably with his normal siblings.

ANTICIPATORY GUIDANCE

How different is the retarded child from normal children in the preschool years? In one sense he is no different. For, while his rate of neuromuscular development is delayed, the stages through which he passes are the same. As the normal child does, he will sit before he crawls, crawl before he stands, and stand before he walks. At the time of walking he is most likely to respond to attempts to toilet train him. Thus, the physician with even rudimentary knowledge of child development can give the parents "anticipatory guidance" by applying this knowledge to interpret the next step in the training of the child. He can supplement his interpretation by giving them easily obtainable and readable booklets on normal child development (12, 13) which deal with many of the needs of parents of a retarded child in the preschool years.

The frequent contacts with parents and child provided by ordinary well-child visits provide a natural setting for discussions of developmental problems. In these, the physician need only provide continuing sympathy, support, and encouragement to the family. While advice should be geared to the level of parental anxiety, it should always be presented in terms of normal stages of development. The parent can compare his child's progression in these stages with those of normal children, especially if the child has older, normal siblings, and see that after all this is first and foremost a child — a handicapped child, to be sure, but a child nevertheless.

The services of public health nurses are invaluable in helping parents of retarded children, especially when they visit the home and provide practical advice and demonstrations of how to set up self-help routines — self-feeding, toileting, dressing. This not only helps the mother in managing the child but also indicates that someone is interested in her problem and is willing and able to help her meet it. Information contained in such booklets as *The Mentally Retarded Child at Home* (14) also proves quite useful in this respect.

In talking with the parents, it is not necessary to use scare words such as "brain damage" or higher scientific phrases which the parent may misinterpret or not understand. Parents should be encouraged to watch their retarded child grow and to enjoy him just as they would a normal child, treating him in terms of his mental age and allowing him to progress at his normal rate of speed. "Behavior problems encountered in the preschool period are most often characteristic of the developmental stage for the child's mental age or a reflection of abnormal pressures applied by parents who are treating him as a child of his chronological age. The younger a retarded child when diagnosed and the earlier the physician is able to help the parents set up simple regimens in the home, the greater is the likelihood of a child's developing a healthy personality and being able at school age to adapt to and enjoy the school setting for which he is qualified.

The occasional hyperactive, distractible, retarded child whose retardation has an organic basis presents special problems in management by virtue of his speeded-up pace of living and requires a modified approach involving firmness and limit-setting techniques often alien to many parents. The paradoxical effects of such central nervous system stimulants as dextroamphetamine and methylphenidate are frequently very useful for quieting the hyperactive behavior of such a child.

During his contacts with the family the physician must continue to remember that the parents' acceptance of a child's mental retardation will be gradual. Whether or not it proceeds at the rate he thinks he should, the important thing to watch is whether the parents are following through with plans for training in self-help skills and are treating the child in a way that will foster a healthy personality development. Each parent must find his own way to this acceptance, and there are as many different ways as there are parents.

The physician should be prepared to keep his own plans for the child flexible. For example, he may feel that a young child's place is with his mother in the home all day, failing to realize that the presence of a child who remains an infant for a long period of time may be a chronic source of physical and emotional strain on the mother. A substitute mother in a daytime foster family home or day care center can allow the mother the breathing spell she needs. Should the physician at any time become aware of increasing parental tension or inability to deal with the child in the family, referral of the parents to an appropriate community family service or child welfare agency for counseling or planning for institutional placement is indicated.

As the child grows and approaches the age at which children need group experience, the physician should try to help the parents find a nursery school in the community which will accept retarded children, to help prepare the child for entering a specialized class in the public school. Helping the school-age retarded child more and more becomes the responsibility of the educator and vocational rehabilitation worker as the child grows older, the physician's role becoming one of normal health supervison. With optimal care and training, many retarded children as adults become productive members of society; and when they do, the physician can look back with pride at his role in fostering their normal personality development in the preschool years.

REFERENCES

1. Mead, B. T.: Physicians attitudes decisive in treating children's emotional problems. *Feelings,* June 1962.
2. Werkman, S. L.: Symposium: the physician and mongolism. *Clinical Proceedings of Children's Hospital of the District of Columbia,* February 1961.
3. Graliker, B. V.; Parmelee, A. H., Sr.; Koch, R.: Attitude study of parents of mentally retarded children. II. Initial reactions and concerns of parents to a diagnosis of mental retardation. *Pediatrics,* November 1959.
4. U.S. Department of Health, Education, and Welfare, Social Security Administration, Children's Bureau: The Mongoloid baby. CB Folder No. 50. 1960.
5. Illingworth, R. S.: *An introduction to Developmental Assessment in the First Year.* William Heinemann, Ltd., London, England. 1962.
6. ————— : *The Development of the Infant and Young Child, Normal and Abnormal.* E. S. Livingston, Ltd., Edinburgh, Scotland, 1960.
7. Koch, R.; Graliker, B. V.; Sands, R.; Parmelee, A. H., Sr.: Attitude study of parents with mentally retarded children. I. Evaluation of parental satisfaction with the medical care of a retarded child. *Pediatrics,* March 1959.
8. Schipper, M. T.: The child with mongolism in the home. *Pediatrics,* July 1959.
9. Saenger, G.: *The Adjustment of Severely Retarded Adults in the Community.* Albany, New York State Interdepartmental Health Resources Board, 1957.
10. Dittmann, Laura L.: Home training for retarded children. *Children,* May-June 1957.
11. Anderson, Alice V.: Orientating parents to a clinic for the retarded. *Children,* September-October 1962.
12. Spock, B.: *Baby and Child Care.* (Revised edition, paperback.) New York, Pocketbooks, June 1962.
13. U.S. Department of Health, Education, and Welfare, Social Security Administration, Children's Bureau: Your child from one to six. CB Publication No. 30. 1962.
14. Dittmann, L. L.: The mentally retarded child at home. U.S. Department of Health, Education, and Welfare, Social Security Administration, Children's Bureau. CB Publication No. 374. 1959.

Chapter 14

Observations Concerning Counseling with Parents of Mentally Retarded Children

STANLEY C. MAHONEY

 T HE parents of mentally retarded children are no longer forgotten people. Professional workers concerned with the mentally retarded child have become increasingly aware of the similar feelings and reactions experienced by most parents in our society upon learning they have a retarded child. From a period when little professional attention was given to the anxiety and confusion experienced by the parents of a retarded child, we have come to a time when parental counseling is usually accepted practice. Similar psychodynamic patterns, repeatedly found, have led to a "special psychology" of counseling with parents of retarded children.

In this paper, which is an outgrowth of the author's observations and experiences in counseling with parents of retarded children, an attempt is made to further refine our understanding by pointing out some differences among parents of retarded children. It is felt that a recognition of these differences is of utmost importance if our counseling efforts are to be maximally realistic and beneficial to both parent and child. For the most part, parents of mentally retarded children have been considered a

Note: Reprinted by permission of the author and the *American Journal of Mental Deficiency, 63*:81-86, 1955. Copyright 1955, American Association on Mental Deficiency.

Mr. Mahoney is with the Psychological Service Center, Fort Hays Kansas State College, Hays, Kansas.

rather homogeneous group with similar feelings and reactions to a similar traumatic situation. It is the thesis of this paper, however, that unless we go beyond the similarities involved and relate the parents attempts to cope with their feelings in this traumatic situation to their total psychological functioning as people, and not just as parents, then we will not be as effective as we might be as counselors.

First, let us look more closely at our conception of parents of mentally retarded children. Are they as homogeneous as our categorization and our literature might imply? It would seem that they are as normal, as average, as maladjusted, as neurotic as are all parents — before the birth of a mentally retarded child. With this latter traumatic event, they suddenly become members of a common group — they are now parents of a mentally retarded child. But in so viewing them, are we not perhaps glossing over many real differences which exist beyond a situation they share in common and toward which they might have similar feelings and reactions? There is a danger, it would seem, in relating to these people, in perceiving them, in thinking about them, solely as parents of a retarded child. In our endeavor to help them cope with the anxiety and confusion aroused in response to a retarded child, we are frequently in danger of forgetting that they are not only parents but also individuals uniquely different from each other, despite in many cases, similar reactions to a similar traumatic situation.

Parents of mentally retarded children, like all parents and all people, differ greatly with regard to the adequacy of their own personal adjustment to themselves and to others. Many of these people have been able to effect an adequate adjustment to themselves and to others, and have led relatively productive lives enriched by interpersonal relationships which they have found personally satisfying. They have been able to assume a responsible adult role in our society and have achieved some measure of happiness in their everyday lives. For these parents, the birth of a mentally retarded child is a traumatic and painful incident which may, in some cases, precipitate a temporary situational maladjustment. The parents may temporarily resort to a variety of defensive reactions to alleviate the pain and anxiety they are feeling and may temporarily be incapable of realistic planning for their child. With time, however, and perhaps with the help of a counselor, they are able to become more tolerant of their feelings and are able to do what has to be done in the best interest of all concerned. When the parents have been well-adjusted people who have been able to achieve a happy and satisfying life, the trauma of the birth of a retarded child is relatively clean-cut, so to speak, and counseling can usually proceed to a stage of rational planning. Rheingold (2) and Kelman (1), among others, have clearly presented the general process of such counseling.

Some individuals, however, have been unable to effect a personally satisfying adjustment to themselves and to others previous to the birth of a retarded child. To varying degrees their lives have been devoid of happiness and their behavior has been characterized by a painful, fruitless search for peace and security. Frequently lonely people, who have been unable to establish satisfying interpersonal relationships, they have been unable to assume the responsibility for seeking the psychological help which they need. A very different therapeutic situation presents itself with these parents than with parents who are relatively well-adjusted people. Here, more than ever, we must be sensitive to the various meanings the retarded child may have in the individual's total psychological functioning. We must remain especially aware of the multiple determinants of behavior, and not become lulled into a false sense of security by the perception of a familiar psychodynamic pattern.

Consider, for example, the frequently encountered pattern of overprotective behavior toward the retarded child. Most often this has been found to be reflective of rejecting and hostile feelings toward the child which the parent is unable to accept or tolerate. Consequent guilt feelings are assuaged and forestalled through a leaning over backwards, as it were, to care for and to protect the child. Thus a behavioral pattern of overprotection and over-indulgence frequently serves to thwart and render more difficult the direct expression of contrary underlying feelings of repulsion and rejection. But there are tremendous differences in the degree and intensity with which this behavioral pattern is observed among parents of retarded children. The more well-adjusted parent may be consciously aware of his ambivalent feelings toward his child, and he may struggle painfully to do what has to be done. Other parents may be able to cope with their feelings and control their behavior only after seeking help from a counselor. Still other parents rigidly adhere in a self-righteous manner to unusual degrees of protective and indulgent behavior, remaining totally unaware of the implications of their behavior and becoming highly resistant to any implications that they might find counseling helpful.

As a rule of thumb, and as a working hypothesis in need of more rigorous verification, it can be postulated that the more intense the defensive reaction toward the child and the longer its duration, the more probable it is that the retarded child has become an integral part of the parents total psychological functioning. That is, it is more likely that the dynamic relating to the retarded child have become closely and vitally involved in the parent's total adjustment process as a person. It would seem that the parent who has effected the most satisfying adjustment before the coming of a retarded child will be most capable of experiencing the pain and anxiety aroused without severe personality decompensation and readjustment. The parent who has previously been unable to effect a stable, satisfying adjustment will be most likely to undergo severe personality disturbance and readjustment and will more often tend to involve the retarded child into their total psychological functioning in a more pervasive and persistent manner.

Perhaps first of all, then, we must, if we are to be most effective as counselors, "forget" as much as possible our rational categorization of the individual across from us as "a parent of a mentally retarded child" and respond to him as an individual in his own right. Trite though it may be, we must concern ourselves with the whole person. We hear a great deal about the stereotypes held by the public toward the retarded child and his parents; let us recognize that we also have our stereotypes, our prejudgments as to how these parents are feeling and reacting, our interpretations made upon previous knowledge and experience as to what it means to have a retarded child. Although our stereotypes may be more accurate, they can still become a hindrance in an individual counseling situation if we are not careful; we as counselors are human too and are not immune to misapplying and superimposing preexisting frames of reference. In those cases, which unfortunately are not rare, where the parent has not been able to effect a relatively satisfying adjustment before the birth of the child, we are frequently in danger of supporting a neurotic adjustment pattern and helping neither parent nor child when we focus all our attention upon feelings related to the child. Let us remember that the parent is also a person, and recognize that the birth of a retarded child may have implications to the person far beyond his role as a parent.

The following case illustration will perhaps make some of the foregoing remarks more meaningful, and it will serve as a reference point for further discussion.

Mrs. A., a middle-aged woman of rather plain appearance, came for counseling as to when her 8-year-old daughter would be ready to attend public school. Her child had been seen previously by several physicians and psychologists, and there was a general concensus of opinion that the child was mongoloid and functioning in the low moron range of intelligence. Furthermore, this child appeared to be emotionally disturbed as well as mentally retarded; she clung to her mother continually in a demanding and manipulating manner, refusing to do anything for herself or by herself. Mrs. A. defiantly and defensively stated she overprotects her child, "always have and always will," knows that it is not good for the child, but "she's my only child and I just feel she's too good and too innocent to play with other children." Mrs. A. had flatly refused to consider institutionalization: "If you mention it, I'll leave at once, like I did the others." She expressed her desire to do anything for her daughter's good, emphasizing that she was prepared to sacrifice her own happiness to make life better for her daughter.

Mrs. A. described herself as having been "the ugly duckling" among several sisters. In growing up, she compared herself unfavorably to her sisters, fought openly with them, and blamed them for her difficulties. She did not complete high school, again blaming her "bad looks" and her sisters. She worked as a domestic helper after leaving school, became very shy and withdrawn, brooded about her homeliness and attributed her lack of happiness to her physical appearance. "It would have been different if I wasn't so ugly." When in her mid-thirties she married a man much older than herself, and in his words, continued to question him as to why he married such an ugly person. Following her daughter's birth, and upon learning the child was mentally retarded, she apparently suddenly lost her concern over her physical appearance. According to her husband, "now everything is because of the child. If someone doesn't like her, it's because of the child; if someone looks twice at her, it's because they know about the child. First it was her looks, and now it's the child."

Mrs. A. is obviously a very disturbed woman who has been unable to effect a satisfying adjustment, either to herself or to others. In a rigid, bitterly self-righteous manner, she avoided taking any responsibility for her own happiness, but successively attributed the source of her dissatisfaction to her sisters, her physical appearance, and now to her mentally retarded child. Her intense overprotection of her child, her refusal to consider institutionalization, and her expressed desire "to do anything to make life better for my child" are feelings and reactions which are not uncommon among parents of retarded children. However, in Mrs. A.'s case this is much more than a temporary reaction to a traumatic incident. Mrs. A. has not only been unable to accept her child as a person with limited capacities, she has not only reacted to underlying feelings of hostility and rejection, but she has also made this child a part of her own adjustment pattern. The child has become an integral part of her own defense system and has become vital to her own adjustment. The child has been rejected as a person, but embraced as a psychological crutch.

In dramatic and bold relief, Mrs. A.'s functioning illustrates a phenomenon found in many cases where the parent has been able to achieve only a marginally satisfying life in a rather neurotic manner prior to the coming of a retarded child. Namely, there is a rather sudden shift in the symptomatic behavior of the parent, and the retarded child becomes the external, concrete anchoring point for a multiplicity of difficulties. In Mrs. A.'s case, her physical appearance served as an external referent for all of her difficulties and problems before the birth of her child. Then, after the birth of her child, her physical appearance suddenly became of relatively little importance and her child became the anchoring point for her inability to effect a satisfying life for herself. In a manner characteristic of many emotionally disturbed people, Mrs. A. avoided the more painful task of coming to grips with her own feelings by finding an external referent for her problems. The common dynamic, "It is not me, I'm doing my best, it is this other thing that stands in my way," underlies her use of her sisters, her physical appearance, and her retarded child.

The question can be raised as to why Mrs. A. would not favor institutionalization for her child if she felt her child to be the source of her difficulties. Logically this would seem to make sense, but the determinants of her behavior are psychological and not logical. Mrs. A. is a woman who needs a "cross to bear," so to speak, in order to maintain her neurotic adjustment to herself and others. The suffering involved in "bearing the cross" is more easily tolerated by her than the anxiety which would be aroused in assuming greater responsibility for her own happiness and behavior. She does not perceive the contradictions in her behavior, and she sincerely believes that she is motivated purely "for the child's best interests"; contradictions, distortions, and vicious circles leading nowhere are the price she unknowingly pays for the illusive and precarious security she has achieved.

For most all parents of retarded children, except for those who are outrightly and overtly rejecting of the child, the question of institutionalization is threatening and anxiety-arousing. For the average, relatively well-adjusted parent, it is a painful step. The dynamics in such a situation have been known for some time, especially as they relate to the parents unresolved guilt feelings and to their tendency to project themselves into the place of the child who is going to the institution. The chronically disturbed parent who has taken the child as a crutch, however, has an understandably greater burden at this point, and separation from the child is of truly traumatic proportions. The parent who has found in her retarded child "a new meaning in life," a focal point for activity and endeavor, or a straw to grasp at in her psychological confusion has become more dependent upon her child than the child has upon her. To institutionalize the child is to threaten the parent's psychological existence, to take away her crutch, her "meaning in life." The question here is not how the child will manage without the parent, but how the parent will manage without the child. It is at this point that the chronically maladjusted parent is especially in need of support and help.

More often than not, the psychodynamics are not as sharply etched as in the case of Mrs. A. where only the main theme has been presented. The retarded child usually takes on a variety of meanings in the psychological functioning of the chronically disturbed parent in a much more subtle, complex, and insidious manner. Frequently the retarded child serves simply as a concrete focal point for attention and activity which is socially acceptable, providing a welcome relief from a vaguely dissatisfying and empty life. The retarded child may give the parent "a purpose in life," "a meaning for living," or "a cause to fight for," and thus become a crutch to the psychologically crippled parent. This would seem to occur most often when the marital relationship has become a treadmill of going through the motions and is devoid of any real satisfactions for the parents. Although a consuming interest in mental retardation on the part of the parent may sometimes have beneficial results for the child, too often the child becomes merely a pawn in the parents defensive operations.

Again, as a rule of thumb and a working hypothesis in need of more rigorous verification, it can be postulated that the greater the shift of symptomatic behavior in the parent from previous external referents to the retarded child, the less can counseling be realistically oriented toward the needs of the child and the more the parent will need intensive treatment. That is, the more the child is used as a psychological crutch by the parent, the more the child becomes a part of the parent's total psychological functioning, and the greater will be the difficulties in working with the parent toward the best interests of the child.

To recapitulate, when the parent has previously effected a relatively satisfying adjustment to himself and others, the retarded child may be temporarily experienced as a traumatic threat to one's well-being. Temporarily, and to varying degrees of intensity, a diversity of defensive behavior may be utilized to cope with this perceived threat. However, the parent gradually becomes better able to focus upon the realities of the situation and to tolerate the pain and anxiety frequently entailed in doing what is generally agreed upon as being best for the child. Here counseling of a generally supportive nature, with opportunity for the expression of feeling, will usually be effective and attention can be increasingly focused upon realistic planning for the child.

In cases where the parent has been unable to effect a satisfying adjustment prior to the coming of the retarded child, however, a very different therapeutic situation presents itself. The child, experienced at first as a threat, is later incorporated as a crutch. Here supportive counseling will generally be of little value, since the parent is unable to make effective use of it. In some cases legal action may be necessary for the child's well-being, despite the parent's protests. In all cases, the chronically disturbed parent will be in need of intensive psychotherapeutic help, and the crucial factor will be his or her capacity to make use of it.

REFERENCES

1. Kelman, Howard R.: Some Problems in Casework with Parents of Mentally Retarded Children. *Am J Ment Defic, 61*:595-598, 1956-57.
2. Rheingold, H. L.: Interpreting Mental Retardation to Parents. *J Consult Psychol, 9*:142-148, 1945.

Chapter 15

Continuing Treatment
of Parents with
Congenitally Defective Infants

LAWRENCE GOODMAN

 T HE birth of a congenitally defective infant trans-
forms a joyously awaited experience into one of catastrophe and
profound psychological threat. The apprehension of failure that is
a normal part of the psychic anticipation of parenthood turns into
reality — and the family finds itself in crisis. A demonstration
treatment program sponsored by the New York State Department
of Mental Hygiene provided an opportunity to see clinically 140
families in the process of adjusting to the birth of a mongoloid
infant. All had sought state institutionalization, although about
forty withdrew their applications following casework contact.
Families from the regular clinic case load, who never openly
considered placement, did not appear to differ greatly in the
extent of their disturbance and in their use of counseling. The
study population is, therefore, considered to be reasonably
representative of families confronting the crisis of a congenitally
handicapped child. Selected cases will be presented throughout
this paper to illustrate how the offer of help was responded to in
terms of each family's adaptation to crisis and their patterns of
coping with it.

Note: Reprinted with permission of the author and the National Association of Social
Workers, from *Social Work,* Vol. 9, No. 1 (January 1964), pp. 92-97.

Mr. Goodman is Director of Social Work at the Mental Retardation Center of the New
York Medical College, New York, New York.

INITIAL PARENTAL REACTION

Greta Bibring considers the entire period of gestation as one of strain and enhanced narcissism for the mother. Significant endocrine and general somatic, as well as psychological, changes occur. The pressures continue after delivery and disappear gradually in reciprocity with the child's development (1). Thus, the natural course of discharge of tension, as the mother responds to her normal child and achieves the emotional satisfaction of experiencing expected maturational milestones with him, is denied the parent of a child with severe birth defect. The heightened emotionality of the father — as a result of his own anxiety and in response to his wife's needs — is also denied its normal release.

Grief, mourning, and planning for the future must be lived through simultaneously and can be overwhelming in their impact. Engel describes "uncomplicated grief" as running a consistent course, modified mainly by the abruptness of the loss and the nature of the preparation for the event.

> It generally includes an initial phase of shock and disbelief — followed by a stage of developing awareness of the loss, characterized by feelings of sadness, guilt, helplessness, etc. Finally there is a prolonged phase of recovery during which the work of mourning is carried on and the trauma of the loss is overcome (2).

Grief faced by parents of a defective child is much more complex.

Solnit and Stark define the parents' experience as one of loss of the wished-for, expected baby at the same time as the birth of a feared, threatening, anger-provoking child. There is no time for working through the loss of the desired child before there is the demand to invest the new and handicapped child as a love object — attempts to withdraw libido from the lost normal child are disrupted by the demands of the living blighted child (3).

Parents search within themselves for nonexistent answers to "Why has this happened to me?" "How did it happen?" "What have I done?" Previously worked-out feelings of self-doubt and inadequacy may be reactivated as they view the damaged child as an extension of themselves. It is as though their flawed self-image has taken form and shape and can no longer be concealed. Marital disruption can occur if the child is seen as a symbol of underlying failure in the marriage. Conscious or unconscious death wishes toward the child intensify the anxiety.

This is not to imply that there must inevitably be a pathological reaction. Sorrow and a sense of crisis are natural responses to a trafic experience. During such periods, however, the balance in personality integration usually goes through a phase of disorganization. In helping families at this point of turmoil, the social worker faces both an especially difficult challenge and a unique opportunity. As Gerald Caplan points out, during an important life crisis pathogenic sequences can originate or become aggravated, but there can also be a sudden acceleration of personality maturation (4). The necessity for treatment as soon as possible to help the family move toward healthy solutions becomes crucial.

Much has been written about the importance of the initial informing of parents, usually by the physician (5-7). In retrospect parents are often critical of the doctor's failure to discuss developmental and prognostic implications frankly and realistically. They frequently report a callous, perfunctory attitude that intensifies their disturbed reaction to the diagnosis. In such instances, the physician may feel a sense of having failed the family and may be attempting to deny his own emotional involvement. While the most thoughtful and sensitive early handling can only mitigate the impact of what has occurred, it can help establish a framework for the family to engage the healthier part of their ego in the first vital stages of crisis response.

The role of the physician takes on a more lasting effect if his desire to rid the family and himself of this symbol of failure results in a premature recommendation that the child be institutionalized. At this time of strain and regression the doctor can be viewed as an omnipotent figure. The family may feel compelled to move toward an emotionally self-destructive decision to place the child before they have the opportunity to face the crisis on a reality level. Even when parents appear to have rejected the child completely, their underlying guilt, denial, and struggle make it imperative for them to have appropriate counseling before determining their course.

There have been attempts to systematize patterns of family crisis response and ways of adapting (8-9). Such frames of reference, which can help an understanding of family dynamics immeasurably, are of little immediate use to the physician and social worker who must act at the height of the parents' emotional intensity. Recognizing the existence of a crisis and the normal reactions of grief and sorrow following a calamitous event, the worker must still individualize the family's strengths, weaknesses, and potentials. This includes an assessment of the family's ability to respond to crisis in terms of (1) the damage to the ego caused by having produced a defective child, (2) the almost infinite variations of guilt, (3) facing the prospect of a lifetime of concern for the needs of a handicapped person and continuing emotional reaction to it, (4) capacity to recognize anger, resentment, and intense frustration, and (5) social, economic, ethnic, and possible genetic influences and implications.

CLINIC PROGRAM

The program of the clinic has utilized individual counseling, group counseling and therapy (for couples), and home counseling. Individual treatment has given parents the opportunity to ventilate emotions freely and to be given support in the expression of hostility and bitterness. They have been accepted as parents of a living child, one worthy of love and attention. The workers have attempted to relate them to specific content for an understanding of mongolism and mental retardation and to face the distortions in their conception of the child so that the decision to institutionalize — if it is followed through — will be reality based. If it becomes clear that deeply pathological response is being dealt with, the goal may be to motivate for intensive psychotherapy. However, this is rarely feasible.

Frequently what appears to be a psychotic reaction may be a transitory phase in parents with borderline personalities. Denial, isolation, projection (including ideas of reference) may be used to an extreme degree. Disowning the child totally, claiming that the nurse has "switched babies," or insisting that everyone is conspiring to mislabel an obviously normal child are not completely uncommon. Yet as such parents are held to reality, they can often be helped to reestablish what probably at best have been tenuous controls.

Group counseling has obvious advantages for parents who feel themselves suddenly cut off from the mainstream of the uncomplicated and conventional life around them. They are given the opportunity to meet with other families struggling with the same trauma. In structuring the groups it is, of course, ideal to include one or two couples who are willing, under the direction of the group leader, to help other families incorporate their own healthy solutions. It has also been found of value to set up the groups so that there will be some balance between families who already are moving toward a decision for home care and those who will go ahead with placement. This introduces dynamic conflict, which the leader uses to point out that there is no single solution — that each family must come to terms with its own reality (10).

COUNSELING IN THE HOME

The home counseling activity has been a practical response to the needs of part of the patient group. It has been an attempt to cut through the self-destructive pattern of withdrawal and isolation by reaching out aggressively for the client. The mongoloid child can be viewed as an outcast. Through the parents' association with him, which reactivates early feelings of separateness and not belonging, they too feel shunned and closed off from the rest of society. In addition, the intensity of the emotional reaction may be so immobilizing that it is not possible for the parents to reach out for desperately needed help. The following shows how home counseling was able to help one family feel the necessity for constructive action.

Mrs. E is the 34-year-old mother of a 10-month-old mongoloid child. She is an unsophisticated, dependent, somewhat limited woman who has been depressed and partially immobilized since the birth of her son. She is obese and suffers frequent petit mal seizures. Mr. E is vaguely supportive and passive, one of the few fathers in the project to be involved only minimally. It was with great effort that Mrs. E was able to bring the boy to the clinic for evaluation. She has rarely left the house since his birth and lives a considerable distance from the clinic. The needs of her two normal children were being denied as she became more and more involved with Louis — a low-functioning child with severe somatic involvement, who needed constant supervision. Although placement in this case was clinically indicated, Mrs. E was wavering in her decision.

Weekly interviews in the home were set up with Mrs. E. At home she appeared overburdened and poorly organized, but was warmly affectionate to all the children. With increasing trust in the worker, she was able to discuss her ambivalence around placement, but as the time for separation approached she regressed further. With much support and encouragement she was able to relate her severe separation anxiety to her own feelings of abandonment as a child when she was hospitalized for epileptic attacks. She could also express her fears that her child's defect was related to her own handicap and that she had failed her husband. With continuing intensive support and bolstering, and with much reiteration of the necessity for placement in this case, Mrs. E was able to follow through.

Home visits continued as Mrs. E was helped to handle her fears that the child was being neglected, that he might go into "shock" from loneliness, that he might die soon, alone. Later there was guilt over feeling relieved of the constant burden of his care. The working through of grief continued.

With much nurturing from the caseworker, a functioning level of adjustment and independence was reestablished. Mrs. E was able to use the worker's support to propel herself toward constructive action in all areas of functioning — for ventilation of feelings of guilt, inadequacy, and separation panic, and for the development of sufficient insight to enable her, after a prolonged crisis period, to face her mongoloid child realistically and free of disabling conflict.

REJECTION OF CASEWORK

Contact may be rejected completely by those families responding to the situation by immobilization or avoidance. There is an inability to seek clarifying information about the diagnosis or to strive for understanding the social and psychological implications of the condition. There is little examination of feelings of guilt, anxiety, or shame, in spite of the obvious underlying tension. The following cases illustrate this orientation.

Mr. and Mrs. A are a bright and sophisticated couple who showed frequent hostility and sarcasm during the intake interview. Their 2-month-old child had been in a private infants' home since birth, pending admission to the state school. They made it clear early in the interview that the child will remain there. "We only came to the clinic to hear what you have to say — if you promise us that you can change her physical appearance or raise her intellectual level, we will bring her in for study." Both parents had been informed at birth of the diagnosis and decided immediately, with little awareness about mongolism, not to take the child home.

In this case, the parents were too defensive to permit an expression of feeling other than generalized, displaced hostility to emerge. The future detrimental effect of the unresolved conflict that was being closed out can only be speculated on.

Mr. and Mrs. B placed their child in a private infants' home as soon as they learned the diagnosis. Everyone has been told that the child is dead, and Mr. and Mrs. B obviously are trying to view her this way. In the course of the interview it was clear that they knew nothing about mongolism and did not care to know anything about it. They seem to have built a defensive wall between themselves and their child in an attempt to preserve their vulnerable intactness.

Mr. and Mrs. C presented a similar veneer, but as a result of the worker's persistence (and a breaking into awareness of their conflict) agreed to attend a parents' counseling group after their child was placed in the state school. Mr. C assumed a didactic role in the first meeting. In an emotionally detached way he insisted that placement of his child had been right and that the other parents in the group were being misled into considering alternatives. He insisted that he was attending the session to help others now that his problems were solved.

Mrs. C went along with her husband during the first meeting. In the second session, however, she revealed some of her confusion and despair at having produced a mongoloid infant, which she viewed as a punishment. In the third meeting she broke into anguished weeping, saying, "The way I act is a front. I have tried to keep my feelings on ice because I couldn't bear to look at my suffering, but it's there."

Mr. C could not risk exposure of his own wavering adjustment and withdrew from the group, but was seen in a few individual sessions to help him restructure his defenses. Mrs. C entered one of the other clinic groups for mothers alone, and has been helped to greatly increased self-awareness and understanding of the dynamics of placement.

OPTIMAL ADJUSTMENT

Families at the other extreme, who participate most readily, are those with an awareness of deeply conflicted feeling, a willingness to use their accelerated energy in a search for information and new sources of inner strength, and the ability to focus on the problem.

Mr. and Mrs. D learned immediately after the birth of their child that he was a mongoloid. Following the strong urging of their obstetrician, who insisted that the child would develop better if he were placed immediately, they planned to arrange for placement as soon as possible. It was only after the intervention of the hospital social worker that they decided to disobey the physician's instructions and see the child. They found him not to be a monster at all, and began to experience a strong attachment toward him. He remained in the hospital for three weeks while the D's investigated placement facilities and, as they put it, tried to regain some perspective in their thinking. None of the private nurseries they visited seemed satisfactory, and it was decided to take the boy home while awaiting state school placement.

The D's accepted the clinic's offer of evaluation and services eagerly and asked many questions about mongoloids — what could be anticipated developmentally, what kinds of educational and social programs were available, and so on. They requested pamphlets and asked the clinic to recommend readings. They were affectionate and relaxed with the child, and during their participation in a parents' counseling group withdrew their application with the state Department of Mental Hygiene.

Pride in their son's progress became possible while their expectations remained realistic. As they have learned to feel more at ease with the boy, friends, relatives, and their two older children have also been able to show warmth and acceptance of him. There is no shame or reticence in discussing him with anyone. They admit to discouragement at times when they contemplate his future, but are obviously able to handle their anxiety. They verbalized their appreciation for the clinic's support and for the opportunity of meeting and sharing the experience with other couples faced with the same problem. They suggested that the clinic could be of further help if it set up supplementary parent education groups to discuss specific problems of management.

In this case what is dealt with are intact and resilient parents who are not likely to be encountered in treatment agencies unless they have produced a handicapped child. Yet even they went through a period of impaired judgment and regression. It is impossible for them now to conceptualize their willingness to follow the doctor's suggestion and attempt to dissociate themselves completely from their child. Had they followed through, much guilt and self-recrimination obviously would have resulted later.

SUMMARY

Families of congenitally defective infants have had a tragic occurrence fatefully thrust upon them, and a crisis situation suddenly exists. Even parents with a high level of intactness go through an initial phase of regression and disorganization. It is vital that counseling begin as soon as possible so that the family can be helped to mobilize its strengths for combating threat on many levels. The family's self-concept is shaken, social position and mobility are endangered, individual adjustment patterns may be permanently damaged.

The decision to institutionalize without the opportunity to face anger, guilt, and conflict can be particularly destructive. At this time, the family looks primarily to the physician for guidance and direction. Since he, however, cannot be expected to assume the required carework function, the hospital social worker must intervene. In planning programs of continuing treatment the value of home counseling, in situations characterized by withdrawal and avoidance, should not be overlooked. Group counseling, for those able to participate, has obvious and unique advantages for parents of the handicapped.

REFERENCES

1. Some Considerations of the Psychological Processes in Pregnancy. In *Psychoanalytic Study of the Child.* New York, International Universities Press, 1959, Vol. XIV, pp. 113-121.
2. Engel, G. L.: Is grief a disease? *Psychosom Med, 23(1)*:18-22, January, 1961.
3. Solnit, A. J. and Stark, M. H.: Mourning and the Birth of a Defective Child. In *Psychoanalytic Study of the Child.* New York, International Universities Press, 1961, Vol. XVI, pp. 523-537.
4. Caplan, Gerald: Patterns of the parental response to the crisis of premature birth. *Psychiatry, 23(4)*:365-374, September, 1960.
5. Zwerling, Israel: Initial counseling of parents with mentally retarded children. *J Pediat, 44(4)*:469-479, April, 1954.
6. Giannini, M. J. and Goodman, Lawrence: Counseling families during the crisis reaction to mongolism. *Am J Ment Defic, 67(5)*:740-747, March, 1963.
7. Koch, Richard, *et al.*: Attitude studies of parents with mentally retarded children. *Pediatrics, 23(3)*:582-584, March, 1959.
8. Parad, Howard J. and Caplan, Gerald: A framework for studying families in crisis. *Social Work, 5(3)*:3-15, July, 1960.
9. Caplan, Gerald: Patterns of parental response to the crisis of premature

birth. *Psychiatry, 23(4)*:365-374, September, 1960.
10. Giannini and Goodman, *op. cit.*

Chapter 16

Parent Counseling as a Means of Improving the Performance of a Mentally Retarded Boy
A CASE STUDY PRESENTATION

ANNE C. FRENCH, M. LEVBARG, and H. MICHAL-SMITH

W ITHIN recent years, good custodial care for the handicapped has given way to a new goal which aims first at rehabilitation and social integration and views custodial care as a measure of last necessity. With efforts to implement this new objective, it has become increasingly clear that if programs to promote development and social adjustment of the handicapped child are to succeed, they must include some psychiatrically orientated guidance for the parents. This is true because the parents of the handicapped suffer a unique disability in planning for these children. The parents of average children have the resource of their own life experience as a basis for social, educational, and career planning for their offspring. By contrast, parents of the handicapped must plan for children, who are in some respects so deviant from average, that planning for them cannot follow patterns drawn from parental experience. As a

Note: Reprinted by permission of the authors and the *American Journal of Mental Deficiency, 58*:13-20, 1953. Copyright 1953, American Association of Mental Deficiency.

Drs. French, Levbarg and Michal-Smith are from the New York Medical College, Flower and Fifth Avenue Hospitals, and the Clinic for the Mentally Retarded, New York, New York.

result, parents of the handicapped feel "at a loss" on a very realistic basis, and with this sense of inadequacy come feelings of guilt and anxiety.

A special effort has been made to study and meet the problem of providing support for parents of the children under care at our clinic. The first step in planning was recognition of the practical impossibility of offering full-scale psychiatric help for the parents of all the children in care. The practice established has been to focus help offered by the clinic staff (pediatricians, psychologists and social workers) on giving the parents a realistic insight into the child's assets and disabilities, as these affect his present behavior and future prospects. In cases where the parents have serious emotional problems, in addition to those associated with their concern for the child, they are referred to the psychiatric service for more intensive help.

Our procedure is to use sessions in which we interpret diagnostic evaluations of the child to the parent as occasions for exploring parental attitudes toward the child and his disability. Where attitudes which are unrealistic, overprotective, or rejecting are uncovered, these are noted and shared with other members of the staff team working on the case. It is then decided whether the problem of parental reorientation can be adequately handled in subsequent routine interviews, or whether intensive individual counseling is indicated.

Regardless of whether counseling is carried out in the course of interviews which are part of the regularly scheduled program of the clinic for all parents, or undertaken on a more intensive basis through additional sessions, the focus remains the adjustment of the child. An attempt is made to give the parent some insight into personal emotional problems which may specifically affect acceptance of the child. However, intensive therapy for the parents themselves, when necessary, is handled by the Department of Psychiatry. Direct counseling is also used in suggesting specific measures for effecting improved behavior, greater self-help, or freer self-expression on the part of the child. When a directive approach is used, the measure suggested is always related to the general underlying problem and offered as a sample of management rather than as a formula.

While the scope of our parent therapy is thus deliberately limited, the program has proved of substantial value to a majority of our parents, as judged by observed improvement in the adjustment of the children. The following case is presented as an example of the degree to which practical social functioning can be improved through parent guidance, in a child of conspicuously limited intellectual endowment.

Perry is a well-developed fourteen-year-old white, male, who was first seen at the clinic for the mentally retarded at the age of 12½ years. He was a full term baby, and delivery was normal.

Developmental History:		*Clinic* *(on admission)*	
Lifted head	1 mo	Recognized parent	9 mo
Sat up	8 mo	Recognized noises	3 mo
Turned over	2 mo	Recognized hands	3–6 mo
Crawled	14 mo	Followed objects	6 mo
Stood	19¼ mo	Toilet trained	2½ yr
Walked	19¼ mo	Responded to commands	?
Spoke words	5 yr	Ate alone	3 yr
Spoke sentences	7 yr	First teeth	6–7 mo
Age when started ABC's	11 yr		

History (to present time):
  8 mo—Child started to sit up and rock back and forth. Mother consulted a pediatrician.
  2½—Examined by psychologist and determined that child would be slow. Predicted school placement at 7 years.
  3 —Examined by neurologist and retardation established.
  4½—Placed on medical therapy.
  5 —Hospitalization for diagnosis and cause. Examination negative, retardation established, etiology unknown.
  9 yr—Neurologist substantiated the above findings. Felt child educable and trainable for job placement.
  9 yr—Psychological testing and placed on drug therapy.
  11 yr—Returned to first neurologist who felt that child with training could become self-sufficient.

Unusual Behavior: Temper tantrums if he is frustrated or hurt. He usually has them with the mother. When angry he will bang his head or bite his hand. Occasionally he touches the genitals. He doesn't play with children, and he has a short attention span.

Childhood Contagious Diseases:

Whooping cough	3 yr
Chickenpox	7
Mumps	7½
German Measles	11

Past Illnesses of Note:

Throat infections	6 mo
Pneumonia	9 yr

Operations:

Tonsils and Adenoids	11 mo
Mastoid	2½ yr
Undescended Testicle	6 yr
Hernia	6 yr

Laboratory Findings:

Electroencephalogram	Within normal limits
Roentgen findings Skull	No evidence of intra-cranial calcification observed.
Wrist and Hands	No evidence of osteal or periosteal pathological process observed. Bone age normal with chronological age.

Cholesterol normal
Blood count normal
Urinalysis normal

Medical Findings:
Chest, heart, abdomen, extremeties, neurological — all within normal limits.

Diagnosis: Cerebral Agenesis

Psychological Examination: Intelligence

1. November 1950 Revised Stanford-Binet Intelligence Scale (Form L)

C. A.	12—8	
M. A.	3—7	Basal III—6
IQ	28	Ceiling VII

Perry was extremely distractable, talkative, and it was necessary to call his attention to the test. He showed little inhibition of his own ideas and action. At times he gave several bizarre answers which seemed to stem from the attractiveness of his own distractions. His mental abilities appear to be widely divergent. He can repeat only 2 digits (2½ yr. level) while his apprehension was almost passed at the 7 year level. Score is representative of the level at which he is functioning.

2. October 1951 Revised Stanford-Binet Intelligence Scale (Form L)

C. A.	13—6	Basal IV
M. A.	3—6	Ceiling

Friendly and cooperative, but easily distractable. He approached the testing situation with the play attitude of a much younger child. This spotty performance is a measure of his distractability and lack of effort, as well as of intellectual deficity. His potential seems to be greater than present testing would indicate. He was able to give an intelligible account of radio and television programs; demonstrated some knowledge of sports, and in general, gave the impression of function at about six or seven years old. Impression is that the boy is functioning well below capacity level due to lack of discipline and habit training.

3. January 1952 Revised Stanford-Binet Intelligence Scale (Form M)

C. A.	13–9	Basal III–VI
M. A.	4–9	
IQ	35	Ceiling VII

Cooperative and displaced concern about his failures or success. Continuously speaks about television programs. Distractibility present and his test behavior seems to be an expression of capriciousness, rather than solely due to intellectual disability. He converted the test materials to his own uses, interrupted test instructions to tell jokes, etc.

4. April 1952 Wechsler Intelligence Scale for Children

C. A.	14–0
Verbal IQ	55
Performance IQ	50
Total IQ	48

Approach was much less capricious than it had been in the original session. He still showed an inclination to stray off along lines of his own interest, but returned to the task at hand without protest, when urged to do so. The possibility that this better performance reflects a difference in the tests used on the two occasions is discounted by comparison of the figure drawings at the first and second testing. The drawings at the first session consist of uncontrolled, imcomplete, and box-like figures, all of which are complete as to social features, appendages, and body parts, all of which are executed with good line control. Further, when each of these figures was completed, he recognized the end of the task and turned the page over to the examiner, instead of attempting to embellish the page. The age level reflected in these drawings is between the seventh and eighth year, a performance which falls within the attainment range seen on the intelligence test. The impression of the examiner is that the boy's optimum level of function is probably between 60–65 I.Q., and that continuation of the present training program will raise it to this level.

When originally seen, Perry was so capricious and distractable that Rorschach administration was impossible. However, he did consent to make a figure drawing. His first drawing, identified as "a man" approximates the maturity level of a five-year-old, but lacks the decisiveness which is commonly found at this age. The head and body are joined directly without a neck, arms are lacking, and the trunk is more or less "set upon" feet, one of which does not even make contact with it. Clothing representation is confined to a line marking the waist, and a tall, brimless hat, set askew on the head. When he had completed the figure, Perry seemed to be dissatisfied with it, and added a few random lines in the background. When asked to draw a girl or lady, he responded with a random box like figure. It appeared that this was an evasion of the task rather than a distortion of an intended human figure, as he failed to identify it as a person when questioned.

Six months after the original drawings, Perry was seen for retesting and new drawings were obtained. The intervening period coincided with what his mother described as miraculous improvement in his behavior, with cessation of tantrum behavior and the emergence of a definite sense of responsibility. The change in the figure drawings is as striking as the behavior changes reported. The maturity level has increased approximately two years, the parts of the figure are well integrated, the whole drawing shows a marked increase in decisiveness, and both male and female figures are drawn with an attempt at sex differentiation through clothing. Instead of the shapeless circles which served as feet for the first figure, both feet and legs are shown. Arms are also present, though attached to the head in the manner of a very young child's drawing.

The improvement noted in the second set of drawings is sustained and extended in a set obtained exactly one year after the original testing. In this final set, the figure is for the first time shown as smiling, clothing elaboration has increased, showing growth of social perception, and fingers have been added to the arms, indicating emergence of some feeling of competence in environmental manipulation. Finally, the size of the figure has decreased so that it no longer fills the page, indicating a decrease in the boy's drive to dominate the environment.

On this occasion, Perry was both cooperative and communicative, so the Rorschach was presented. He accepted all of the cards and while his responses were simple and literal in content, they were neither foolish nor bizarre. His first response to all ten cards was "a map," but after giving it he would proceed to give additional responses. This pattern indicates that the perseveration was an expression of defensiveness, and a need to gain reassurance from the tried formula before venturing to something new, rather to a poverty of ideas. This is a device which is also used by children of average ability. Another expression of this timidity appears in the fact that Perry's best form elaboration centers on tiny detail, suggesting that feelings of inadequacy keep him from being able to apply himself to any but the smallest tasks. On the basis of his full performance, it may be said that while the boy is both immature and insecure, he shows enough flexibility to develop assurance through favorable experience. The likelihood of such experience is good, for he shows a capacity for personal relatedness, and good patterns of basic socialization. Finally, his intellectual capacity and associative resource appear to be above the level of his present reality function, so that with continued guidance and encouragement he may be expected to show a substantial growth in self-sufficiency.

Two considerations prompted the decision to work intensively with Perry's mother. The first was a change noted in the mother's attitude toward the boy, in which what had originally appeared as very good general acceptance, was replaced by acute anxiety relating to his temper tantrums and general lack of control. The seond indication for intensive work was the psychologist's impression that Perry's potential was substantially better than the test scores indicated, and that his poor test showing was due to a capriciousness which suggested lack of proper training. It was therefore decided to schedule additional counseling sessions to help the mother develop a management program which would guide Perry toward increased self-control.

When the treatment goal was outlined to Perry's mother, she rejected it as unrealistic and impossible and sought to prove her point by a lengthy description of his tantrums. She revealed that the violent manner in which he tore at his clothing and threw himself about so frightened her that her own self-control would be lost, making Perry the inevitable victor. Since the boy was reported to have shown tantrum behavior throughout his childhood, reasons were sought to explain the mother's sudden anxiety regarding behavior which she had been able to accept formerly. Mrs. S. then disclosed that when marked pubertal changes became apparent in the boy, the tantrums which she had previously disregarded as "childishness" took on a new significance. Her son's uncontrolled behavior now appeared to her as a forecast that he would become an adult maniac, beyond social tolerance and institutionalized under restraint.

The first step in handling these fears was to make the mother understand that the boy had not in fact changed or deteriorated, and that it was her own attitude which had changed. This served to allay her fear that he was becoming worse. The next step was to help her understand the reasons for tantrum behavior in general, and to have her see that tantrums are not characteristic of the retarded, but can occur in all children. When this point had been made, Mrs. S. herself asked what measures could be used to prevent and control tantrums, indicating a shift from her original attitude that the situation was beyond remedy.

Perry's tantrums were then discussed as a device used by the boy to attain his own ends. This was followed by a discussion of the role of firmness and habit training in building the frustration tolerance needed to help Perry attain self-control. It was suggested that the mother and father collaborate on a program in which tantrum threats would be ignored, while demands for cooperation in areas of common family interest, such as choice of television programs, be enforced with a new firmness. It was further suggested that the boy be given specific incentives to demonstrate his capacity to share in the family responsibility and meet his need for successful achievement. Three specific suggestions were made: (1) that Perry be made responsible regularly for making his own bed, a chore which he enjoyed but performed on a sporadic basis; (2) that he be given a regular allowance weekly, instead of ten cents per day; (3) that his father regularly find ways to utilize his services in making stock arrangements in the family's stationery store, a job which Perry enjoyed but was seldom allowed to share because of his inefficiency.

The program as outlined above was instituted and enforced by the family over a three-month period. At the end of this time, Mrs.

S. reported what she characterized as a "miraculous change in the boy's character" with a cessation of tantrums and development of general social cooperativeness. The improvement noted by the mother was confirmed by observation of the boy, who was quieter, more tractable, and had increased in cooperation enough to score thirteen points above his previous high on the intelligence test, due to better concentration and motivation.

At the time of this interview, Mrs. S. appeared calm and self-possessed, in marked contrast to the picture of panic anxiety which she had presented three months earlier. In reviewing with her the improvements which she reported in Perry, care was taken to emphasize the fact that they had resulted from a change in her own attitude and manner of handling, rather than from any magical character transformation. A return was then made to the subject of the mother's original anxiety, namely Perry's future, and the change which he had already shown was used as a demonstration of the role which training and management would play in determining it. A plan was discussed with the mother for extending the areas of the boy's self-sufficiency, by giving him responsibility for covering hair cuts and small personal necessities from an increased allowance, giving him more opportunity to work with his father in the store, and encouraging him to think and act more independently regarding amusements, and so on.

At a conference one month later, the mother reported that Perry's school teacher had sent for her to comment on marked improvement in school attention and achievement. Mrs. S. also reported that Perry was showing a new awareness of his own social role and said that on one occasion, when the family had had company, he came to her after the departure of the guests and said, "See, tonight I didn't babble at all, did I?" This report was made the basis of discussing ways to aid Perry in social integration. It had been noted that his attempts at conversation were never bizarre, but had the empty content which reflects lack of experience. It was suggested that the boy be taken on trips about town and given a better opportunity to enlarge his experiental background, so that he would be able to contribute in some measure to general conversation without feeling that he was "babbling."

At this interview Mrs. S. also reported that she and her husband had been so heartened by the boy's improvement that they had determined to explore possibilities of sending him to a summer camp with a work-training program. While no camp of this character was located which was operated to serve retarded children, one camp had been found which would accept a few retarded children who appeared to be able to profit by the program. Perry had been interviewed by the director of the camp and accepted. The program is one of outdoor activity, centering around forestry and lumbering so that the individual child may work at his own speed and still remain within the framework of the general program. Both Perry's parents and the camp director felt that such a program would have great value for the boy, as a means of showing the practical values of cooperative action in a setting which would also give him an opportunity to enlarge his social experience through associations with boys of his own age.

The fact that Perry's mother had been able to initiate and carry through this camp placement was interpreted as evidence that she had overcome the anxiety crisis which she had shown at the beginning of treatment. Every effort was made to have her understand that Perry's improvement was the fruit of her own effort, and to make her feel that his progress was something which she could view with justifiable pride and a sense of achievement.

SUMMARY

The case described is that of a fourteen-year-old boy who is under care in the Clinic for Mentally Retarded Children at Flower and Fifth Avenue Hospitals, New York. He is presented because of marked improvement in his behavior and adjustment during a one year period, in which his mother received guidance and supportive therapy. This service to the mother was on a counseling basis, directed toward helping her evolve better methods of training and discipline.

The good results obtained in this case are ascribed to our Clinic policy of integrating the findings of pediatricians, psychologists, and other personnel who may deal with the child, and having all of the services involved collaborate in planning for handling the case.

The case is offered as an illustration of the value of parent counseling as a means of securing improved functional efficiency in mentally retarded children.

Chapter 17

Small, Short-term Group Meetings with Parents of Children with Mongolism

MARY L. YATES and RUTH LEDERER

VARIOUS means have been used to help parents cope with the knowledge that they are the mother and father of a retarded child. These may include the group approach or individual counseling, both of which have been successful. An attempt was made to find out whether in a clinic settihg short-term, undirected group meetings would help both parents of retarded children. Since parents of children with mongolism (1) raised similar questions with regard to the developmental prognosis of their child, regardless of their degree of acceptance of the diagnosis, it was decided to include such parents in a first attempt to try out these groups. It was felt that four couples should be the maximum number included in any one group because the emphasis in the meetings was to be on the sharing of experiences, and more than this number would perhaps be a deterrent to this goal.

A series of three evening sessions was planned with each of three groups, meeting at monthly intervals, so that both parents could attend. In the course of a year ten meetings were held. A total of sixteen parents participated, all of whom had had their children evaluated in the clinic and had received interpretation.

Note: Reprinted by permission of the authors and the *American Journal of Mental Deficiency,* 65:467-472, 1961.

Mary Yates and Ruth Lederer are affiliated with the Bureau of Maternal and Child Health, Government of the District of Columbia, Department of Health.

The children represented ranged in age from one year to four years, with the exception of one child who was seven. There were five boys and four girls included.

Services for the Retarded Child is a special program of the Bureau of Maternal and Child Health of the Government of the District of Columbia Department of Public Health.* The clinic offers diagnostic as well as treatment and follow-up services. The diagnostic study is an unhurried process, often involving several contacts with the various staff members, because it is felt that these appointments can be of therapeutic value as a step in preparation for interpretation. Interpretation is given by the pediatrician-director, and efforts are made by the staff members immediately concerned to help parents carry out the recommendations. In many instances parents need help in accepting and understanding the diagnosis and this is offered through continued casework service. Or, if the child is in need of stimulation in developing self-care skills, help in this direction is provided.

Following interpretation, parents' reactions may vary from seeming acceptance to hostile rejection and inability to use help. The question was raised as to whether it is possible, regardless of the degree of acceptance, understanding and awareness of the situation a parent may have, to provide something, in addition, to facilitate their ability to restructure their way of living to include this experience.

Although in the last few years the public has become more enlightened about mental retardation, much misconception still persists. Mongolism, for example, is still even among professionals equated with idiocy. Historically, the term *mongolism* embodies characteristics which have been associated with the concept of the fool or idiot. Because of this, the parents of these children have to cope with their own feelings about their child as well as with the ambivalance shown toward him in their contacts outside of the home.

---

*The staff consists of a pediatrician-director, two social workers, a psychologist, a child development worker, a nursing consultant, and a psychiatric consultant. This clinic also has at its disposal other special services which are available within the Health Department and include speech and hearing, neurology, electro-encephalography, physical and occupational therapy, orthopedics, ophthalmology, and cardiology.

In other situations group meetings have been utilized successfully in helping parents. It was felt that the group process might be of use here to assist parents to find their equilibrium more easily and handle more appropriately their feelings about what has happened to their child.

PURPOSE, GOALS AND FORM OF THE MEETINGS

The purpose of these meetings was to encourage parents to share their experiences and concerns with each other by permitting them to assume responsibility, not only in conducting the meetings, but also in bringing up subject matter for discussion. It was hoped that parents would feel free to bring up common concerns, what they did about them, their feelings about having such a child and that the very sharing with each other would help them make a more satisfying adjustment. All of the families who participated in these meetings were told individually about them and their structure. It was emphasized that these were their meetings, a time during which they could bring up and discuss any concern they might have about their child, and that all parents invited had a child with mongolism. Thus the groups were to be composed of parents who met the following criteria: children with the same diagnosis, both parents able to attend when possible and who were not so severely disturbed about the diagnosis as to need special individual help.

As members of the group, the staff participants did not function in their usual professional roles of psychologist and social worker, but rather as sponsors of the group taking leadership only to get discussion going and to keep it along lines within limited goals. The social worker assumed the responsibility for the meetings, and the psychologist participated as cosponsor. They acted as sympathetic listeners, redirected questions back to the group, took initiative at the beginning of the sessions and at the end, answered questions and gave information only if it was obvious that the group had misinformation or lacked knowledge about the subject.

The meetings were held in the conference room of the clinic, and as the parents arrived they were invited to sit around the conference table. In order to stress the informality of these meetings, light refreshments were available, and informal conversation was encouraged because it was felt best to wait until the majority had gathered so that all parents could have equal benefit of the exchange of ideas. This went on until such time as the sponsors indicated at the meeting would begin. Although the sponsors had in mind some time limit as to when the meetings would draw to a close, they were not rigid about this. Sessions were permitted to go on until they reached a logical and natural termination point, and it usually turned out that they lasted for approximately one hour and one half. At the close of the meetings, there was always a pulling together of what had gone on. This was done either by a parent or the social worker. However, if the social worker took responsibility for doing this, every effort was made to include the parents in the summing up.

PATTERN OF THE INITIAL MEETINGS

The initial meetings of all three groups seemed to follow a similar pattern. The sponsors usually had to take more initiative in the initial session of each group than during the remaining meetings of the series. They opened with a review of the purpose for which the group had been called together and with clarification of the role the sponsors would take. It was then suggested that the parents describe their child in order that he might be identified for the group. This was eagerly responded to by the parents. Some took this quite literally and described him in physical appearance, size and weight, while others immediately brought up problem areas.

One of the concerns presented first in all three groups centered on growth and development. The earlier questions in this area usually involved the onset of the basic achievements in motor development skills, that is, at what age a child sat up, walked, talked and the like. This immediately set up a contact point between the parents. It was more than just an exchange of information, a sort of emotional interchange. Most of them had not known the parents of any other child with mongolism, and this was their first opportunity to really discuss mutual concerns. This led to a very rapid feeling of relatedness among them and enabled them to quickly move into other areas.

Almost immediately following this physical description of the child, the question was raised as to when the others had learned of the diagnosis. Another question that came up early was whether they had told anyone else, and, if so, how they had handled it. These questions were emotionally charged and were brought up by the parents who had experienced difficulty in dealing with them. There was usually a parent in the group who had been able to handle his own anxieties in this area who could help clarify the underlying feelings the parents had about this. Those involved seemed able to listen to what was said.

Having shared this kind of information with each other seemed to release a certain tension that had existed and they began to participate very actively in discussion. In a first meeting, they seemed to cover the whole gamut of concerns: diagnosis and timing of being told the diagnosis, their feelings about having such a child, not only now but at the time they were given the diagnosis, rate of development, resources, and schools. They also raised questions about what can be expected of their child in the near future as well as in terms of long-range plans, reaching into adolescent and adult years. One group broached the possibility of some type of insurance plan.

These subjects were really just skimmed over, and gave the impression that these questions had been on their minds and they had to get them out. It was usually very difficult for the first session to break up because there seemed so much more still to be said.

THE PATTERN DURING A SERIES OF
THREE MEETINGS

In all three groups, the trend seemed to be that most areas that were discussed in later sessions had already been touched upon in the first meeting. The emotional tone of the first meeting was one of a positive feeling for the sponsors and for each other. They seemed glad to have an opportunity to meet with other parents with similar problems. It was more or less a sharing with people who feel very close, but not in an intimate way. The deeper feelings they might have about their particular situation did not usually come up. Although many factors enter into this, one might be that they were grateful for the opportunity to share information with others who can be sympathetic out of experience.

At the second meeting, the same subjects were raised that had been brought up during the first sessions but, in addition, some of the more serious details as well as their more deep concerns came out. They tended to look to the sponsors for answers, and when redirected to the group, they displayed hostile feelings toward them. Since the sponsors did not assume responsibility for answering questions or taking over, usually some member of the group assumed leadership, and they were able to work out some of their feelings and answers to the questions. Those persons who took the role of leader seemed to rise to the position and to gloss over some of their deeper feelings about their own situation in order to help some of the others with theirs. The way they handled this was to display extreme acceptance of having a retarded child, pointing out some of the assets and actually to distort some of the situation.

The subject of whether they had found it necessary to conceal the fact that they had a retarded child came up. How had they handled this and what were their feelings about sharing this information with others? They wanted the details of whether you tell other members of the family and members of the community and, if so, how one goes about it and how much one tells. It was the parent leaders who were able to help the other members of the group look at this more realistically and work out how this could be handled. Although this was not resolved to the point where some of the more reluctant parents would agree that they would tell others, there was a feeling of relief from having expressed their feelings about why they had not told others about the child. This was a rather uneasy session, one during which they had to face up to reality. No matter how they attempted to couch many of their problems and feelings, someone of the group always saw through it. The parents seemed to look forward to the third session. They appeared to need each other, and they even planned what they would cover.

The last meeting of the series was usually a more intellectual type session, during which there was some attempt to solve their problems and an evaluation of what had come out of the meetings. The solutions they offered were usually beyond their immediate problems, reaching into adolescence and adulthood. There was some cirticism of the sessions, what they had expected of them and still needed and, also, some criticism of the role the sponsors took. They seemed to have expected more informative and instructional-type sessions, but they were able to see what the sponsors meant by setting up limited goals within which they themselves would attempt to face their situation. Once having "hashed out" what had gone on in these sessions, they seemed to feel that they had gained some benefit from this type of meeting. Often they felt that some of the needs that had not been met in these brief sessions could be found within existing community resources such as the Association for Retarded Children or could be fostered through such facilities.

EVALUATION

The impressions gained are based upon a limited number of cases and therefore are tentative.

Small, short-term, undirected group sessions, spread over a three-month period, with both parents attending appeared to the sponsors to be quite helpful and useful. This approach would seem to work best with persons who have some ability to put their feelings into words. The number of meetings was limited because goals were limited, and the sponsors wanted to help these parents during their period of adjustment to the diagnosis and its implications. Three meetings seemed to be ideal because the first meeting served to throw open the problems; the second, to delve more deeply into certain aspects of the problem; and the third, to help them pull together and integrate what had been accomplished during the sessions and begin to think more realistically about the future.

With the first group, a fourth meeting was held in compliance with the demands of the parents. During this session the parents planned for expansion of the group. They were interested in increasing the members, bringing in speakers on various topics, and also in changing the role of the sponsors to include discussion of the more emotionally charged issues. As this did not fall within the purpose and goals of this project, the sponsors discussed with the parents the resources in the community where this could be met. It would appear that this type of group might not be able to maintain its nondirective character beyond three sessions, but would tend to become more therapy-oriented or educational-informative in nature.

The focus in these group meetings was to encourage parents to discuss their feelings about thier child and help them come to grips with the situation. The small-group sessions were effective because the size made it a face-to-face relationship, yet, enough different from a one-to-one relationship as to present a nonthreatening situation conducive to sharing and enabling parents to bring up areas of concerns one might anticipate they must have.

The meetings did not change the parents' basic attitude but did enable them to see, for example, that although it was "terrible" to have such a child, it was all right to feel this way and seemed to relieve some of their shame and guilt. Although their problems and feelings were not resolved, in some it had been so bottled up, they had been unable to express any feelings except hostility, withdrawal, and denial. As the meetings progressed, there seemed to be less need for denial toward other people and a more realistic appraisal of their situation and their feelings about it. As a result, the parents seemed better prepared to consider the next steps in planning. For example, they seemed more aware of their own needs in relation to such planning and in a position to recognize the need for direct help whether it be in relation to their feelings about the diagnosis or help in the area of management. They also seemed able to look at the broader implications of mental retardation and to wonder what they could contribute as parents in areas outside their immediate situation.

In the group setting, with both parents present, the sponsors became more aware of how difficult it is for fathers to accept the diagnosis of mental retardation, since they tend to cover up their real feelings. Their early comments were more general, and they had a tendency to intellectualize their problem. Mothers, on the other hand, responded in a more personal way. Their comments were closely related to specific incidents from their experience with their child. Fathers and mothers looked upon the sponsors differently, too. The mothers used the sponsors in their role more appropriately and the fathers tended to place the sponsors on a more social level. One factor of significance which emerged from these meetings is that fathers do want to be included in planning for their children. It was pointed out that fathers were not always able to participate as much as they would like, but they felt strongly that they wanted to be the ones to decide to what extent they could be involved rather than have it assumed that they could not participate.

At a first meeting, either the father or the mother seemed to take over and the couple functioned as "one," with the less verbal parent reinforcing the other. In later meetings, the husband and wife spoke up as individuals, free to express their own ideas regardless of whether their comments were in agreement with the spouse. In once case they even sat on opposite sides of the table. The emphasis was on clarifying their own thoughts. This was made possible because they gained support from the other couples. What occurred was different from, for example, mothers supporting mothers and fathers, fathers. At the end of the sessions, they again seemed to be united, voicing more or less similar feelings.

It is important for parents to be able to attend meetings together. Although the couples seemed to speak to the point of the reality factors in the situation, when only one person of a couple was present, the members of the group seemed to jump to supporting that person more quickly. Also, when there are couples present, the core of the issue is forced because they do not have to accentuate their sex-linked role.

These meetings appeared to help parents in their adjustment during the period following interpretation. The spacing of the meetings at monthly intervals seemed to give them time to absorb some of what they had brought up during the meetings. The role the sponsors took was different from their professional one in the clinic. It took time for the parents to accept this, and occasionally their hostility was aroused. But they went along with this, selecting their own leaders who were able to assume the role they wanted the sponsors to take. Because in the third session they were able to evaluate what had gone on quite objectively, being able to discuss both the negative and positive aspects of the meetings, it was felt that steps toward adjustment had been initiated.

At first the parents felt a very strong link with each other because of the factor of mongolism. Discussion was unproductive when they attempted to analyze and understand the physical attributes of mongolism per se. Only when they realized the futility of this were they able to examine the basic issue of retardation and discuss their children who had varying degrees of retardation rather than "having to deal with a mongolian idiot."

It should be remembered that the children represented by the parents in these groups were still young. The children themselves had not yet had to face the community. The parents will, perhaps, again have to analyze their feelings in terms of mongolism when they meet situations as their children grow older.

This type of group can be effective as a regular part of such a clinic program and is thought of only as an intermediary step in the process of adjustment.

REFERENCE

1. Schipper, M.T.: The child with mongolism in the home, *Ped, 24*:132-144, 1959.

PART III
COUNSELING PARENTS OF CHILDREN WITH EPILEPSY AND CEREBRAL PALSY

Group Sessions for Parents of Children with Epilepsy

GASTON J. BAUS, L. LaVERGNE LETSON, and EDITH RUSSELL

T HE need for a consistent and organized educational program for parents of children with epilepsy has been recognized for some time. The children and parents seen by the psychologist in the Psychiatric Clinic as a part of the integrated service of the Clinic focused attention upon this need. The Jerry Price Seizure Clinic of the Los Angeles Childrens Hospital instituted a program of orientation for parents of children with epilepsy by means of group sessions in March, 1955. This program is believed to be original and the first to be described in this country. Its success and the parent response have been encouraging. We are reporting the outline of the sessions in the hope that such a program, or similar group sessions, might be useful in other clinics.

The primary aim of the group sessions is the correction of prejudice and misunderstanding, and the relief of tension in the parents of children with epilepsy, which is an important part of the overall therapy. Prior to the institution of group sessions, this function was handled by the physician during the clinic visits. Epilepsy and the principles of its treatment were explained.

The social worker worked with some of the parents at the request of the physician and the psychologist. The psychologist's

Note: Reprinted by permission of author and *Journal of Pediatrics, 52:*270-273, 1958. Copyrighted by the C.V. Mosby Co., St. Louis, Mo.

The authors are affiliated with the Jerry Price Seizure Clinic and the Department of Pediatrics, Children Hospital, Los Angeles, and University of Southern California School of Medicine, Los Angeles, California.

role was limited to seeing those parents referred to the Psychiatric Clinic by the physician for emotional or intellectual evaluation. In some instances, this was followed by therapy sessions with the psychologist.

The frequency and consistency of questions and problems presented by the parents relative to the care of such children became apparent to the members of the clinic. The presence or absence of serious emotional or intellectual disturbances in the child did not influence the parent's primary concerns. Parents were noted to have concepts of a child's illness clouded by misunderstanding after as much as two years' attendance in the clinic. It was concluded that this phase of the medical care was obviously weak.

The success of group therapy in other fields encouraged us to feel that the technique might be applied to this problem. The concept of group sessions was suggested by the psychologist who is a regular member of the Seizure Clinic staff.

In order that epilepsy might remain the primary subject, it was elected to exclude those parents whose children had, in addition, cerebral palsy, blindness, severe hearing deficiency, diabetes, marked mental retardation, or other gross disorders. It was felt that the group discussions would become too complex if such additional conditions were brought up by the parents. There is particular reason to avoid the suggested association of mental retardation and epilepsy to the parent of a child with average intelligence.

OUTLINE OF GROUP SESSIONS

After some experimentation, the following procedure was adopted. Excluding the parents of children with the above-mentioned additional problems, the parents of all new patients to the Seizure Clinic are interviewed by the social worker after the first visit with the doctor. At this time the orientation course is outlined and the importance of regular attendance for the sake of continuity is emphasized. Transportation, "sitter," and working-time problems may be involved. If these things can be arranged, an appointment is made for the next available series of sessions.

The course consists of five weekly meetings, lasting from one to one and one-half hours. Registration is limited so that the parents of no more than eight children participate. The atmosphere is that of round-table discussion with questions and interruptions welcomed. At the first two sessions, one of the clinic physicians, a pediatrician as well as an epileptologist, speaks on the medical aspects of epilepsy. At the next two sessions, the psychologist discusses the management of the child, the emphasis being on the child rather than on epilepsy. The focus of the last session is the relationship of the child within the total family group and the community, with the social worker leading the discussion. The psychologist and the social worker are present at all the sessions and have the opportunity to observe those parents who may benefit from additional help on an individual basis.

To encourage the thorough participation of the parents, all distracting factors are eliminated. Observers are excluded, as are the children. It is desirable to keep the situation from reverting to that of the clinic visit or lecture room.

First and Second Sessions

At the first two meetings of the group sessions, conducted by one of the clinic physicians, the primary purpose is to introduce the parent to the clinic and to give him reliable information concerning epilepsy and its treatment. A brief description of epilepsy and its treatment is outlined. The diagnostic devices and techniques used in arriving at this diagnosis are explained to the parents and their questions are answered. The different kinds of seizures, their frequency and duration are described. The principles of medication and treatment are discussed. That these medications are not habit forming is emphasized especially. The parents are instructed in the care of the child during convulsions.

Parents are encouraged to ask questions whenever they desire. Recurring questions relative to specific aspects of epilepsy will indicate the need for further discussion of particular problems. Typical questions which indicate the primary concerns of parents are as follows: To what extent should physical activity of the child be curtailed? Will the child die in a convulsion? Will he recover? Is epilepsy hereditary? Will the convulsions cause heart damage? Will they lead to nervous or mental illness? What adverse effects, if any, may be expected from the medication?

In the informal discussions it is felt the parent obtains a clearer conception of the problem. Through accurate specific knowledge he rids himself, to some extent, of prejudices and misconceptions associated with epilepsy and gets practical help in learning to care for the child. That he is able to share his problems with others in some measure gives the parent support at an important time, that is, when treatment of the child is being instituted and the parent is adjusting to the care of the child with this condition. The group sessions with the physician are essentially factual and informative.

Third and Fourth Sessions

The psychologist introduces a new phase in parent education and therapy in the third and fourth group sessions. Practical and specific advice on management problems are considered. These two sessions also serve as a screening device for disturbed family situations that could be handled more effectively early in the patient contact with the clinic. The parent is given the opportunity to ventilate his feelings in the group sessions, and he is then encouraged to examine them. Criticism or support from other parents has a salutary effect upon the parent. The psychologist structures these sessions according to the needs of the group.

Two major concerns are consistently apparent in the sessions with the psychologist. Discipline is the primary problem of these parents. Parental insecurity and uncertainty are frequently apparent relative to control of the child's behavior, especially when administration of discipline appears to precipitate a seizure. Discipline is discussed in its general aspects. The parent is encouraged to ask questions about his particular situation. He can thus present his feelings and attitudes to the psychologist who, with the aid of the group, works at making him feel more comfortable with the idea of discipline. He is made more aware of feelings he may have which interfere with discipline. Attitudes are subject to critical inspection, and all members of the group are invited to participate in this procedure.

The second most important problem is behavior, normal and abnormal.

Parents of children with epilepsy are sensitive to what they think might be a deviation from the normal. An attempt is made to point out reasons for a child's behavior other than the fact that he has seizures. The object is to allow the parent to accept the idea of individual behavior as a rational part of the growth process in every child, including his own.

Another subject that generally needs discussion is the parent's attitudes and emotional conflicts about epilepsy. The objective atmosphere of discussion and criticism aids the parent in attaining perspective necessary to free himself of unhealthy attitudes. Relieved of these, he will be able to offer the child increased emotional support.

Other topics discussed are the fear of convulsions, over-protectiveness, and relations of the child with other children in the family. The child's emotional development is largely a result of the emotional relationships he has within the family, and this is stressed to the parents. The goal of the group sessions with the psychologist is to help the parent accept the problem of his child's having epilepsy more intelligently and objectively. The parent will then be able to give him the necessary emotional support and special care that this particular problem presents.

Fifth Session

The social worker conducts the fifth and final session of the group sessions, which is concerned with total family life and social adjustments. At this meeting the parents are given suggestions about interpreting the term *epilepsy* to relatives, neighbors, and friends. Information is given about available resources of the community, public school programs, camp facilities, and community groups interested primarily in epilepsy. At the conclusion of this session, parents are given a brochure to take home.

The brochure is written in nontechnical language and is a summary of much of the medical and psychological information covered during the group sessions. It was compiled on the basis of typical parent questions and concerns that had been observed and recorded during the first year of group sessions. The parent is encouraged to read it and to bring back to the clinic further questions he may have. The continuing interest and help of the Social Service Department is emphasized to the parents for any future problems they may have.

SUMMARY

At the Jerry Price Seizure Clinic of the Los Angeles Childrens Hospital, the need for a consistent and organized educational program for parents of children with epilepsy was recognized. Customary clinic visits with the doctor were inadequate for this purpose. Courses of group sessions were initiated. This procedure has been carried out for two years and has been found effective in its original aims.

It is felt that the parents of children with epilepsy are able through the group sessions to correct their misunderstandings and prejudices and relieve their tensions to some extent.

The course is divided into five sessions, and attendance is limited to the parents of eight children. The first two sessions are conducted by a physician who is also an epileptologist. At these sessions the physician deals with essentially factual and informative material. He encourages the parents to ask questions and answers them informally. Group discussions are emphasized.

The next two sessions are conducted by the psychologist. The two most frequently discussed problems are discipline and behavior. Through discussion and ventilation the parents are helped to accept the problem of the child with epilepsy more intelligently and objectively, resulting in increased emotional support for the child.

The final session is conducted by the social worker, who focuses attention upon the child's social relationship and informs the parent of the facilities and services available to them for help with the child. The continuing interest of the Social Service Department in any future problems that may arise is likewise emphasized.

It is believed, after a period of more than two years, that the group sessions for parents of children with epilepsy are of material aid and have fulfilled the objectives for which they were designed.

Chapter 19

A Group Work Experience
for Mothers of
Adolescents with Epilepsy

LYDIA SANTIAGO DE COLON, RICHARD D. TRENT,
and LUIS SANCHEZ LONGO

Numerous recent publications have described
the prejudices, misunderstandings and misconceptions concerning
epilepsy widely held in the United States and elsewhere (1-6).
Epileptics are regarded with suspicion and fear; many people still
believe that the epileptic is insane or cursed by the devil.

Parents of epileptics are not always free of these prejudices and
misconceptions, despite the fact that the epileptic's parents have
had contacts with physicians. Livingston (5) of Johns Hopkins
Hospital has pointed out that the parent's attitude toward the
disease, the work in which the physician can gain cooperation and
confidence of the parents, and the advice the physician can give to
the parents to allow the child to lead as normal a life as possible
are all crucial for the successful social management of epileptic
children.

It has also been recognized that emotional problems act as
precipitants to seizures in some patients. If the psychological
environment of the epileptic's home is one of fear, tension, and
prejudice, the successful management and rehabilitation of the
epileptic become more difficult. As Yahraes (7) pointed out:

Note: Reprinted by permission of the authors and *Boletin de la Asociacion Medica de
Puerto Rico, 56*:51-57, 1964.

The authors are associated with the Section of Neurology, Department of Medicine,
School of Medicine, University of Puerto Rico, Rio Piedras, Puerto Rico.

219

"There are cases in which emotional tension brings on seizures. For these patients the doctor needs to find out not only the medicine which controls the seizures, but also the psychological treatment which will relieve the mind."

There is a need for consistent and organized educational programs for parents of children with epilepsy. The limited information usually given to parents of epileptics during brief office calls is not sufficient.

A pilot investigation which included a multiple therapeutic approach for the treatment of epileptic adolescents was completed recently. The treatment approach consisted of three phases: the utilization of pharmacotherapy, group psychotherapy for adolescent epileptics, and group work with the mothers of the adolescent epileptics. This report, describing for the most part the first dozen sessions of the group, is concerned only with the third phase of the research project, group work with mothers of adolescents with epilepsy. This phase of the treatment program had two major purposes: (1) to correct the prejudices and misunderstandings of group of parents of adolescent epileptics concerning epilepsy, (2) to reduce the anxiety and tension in parents.

METHOD OF STUDY

Two methods were used to study the progress of the program: participant observation and the recording of these observations, and the use of an attitude test. A transcript of the group's major transactions was prepared by the group leader after each meeting.

This transcript included the major concepts discussed, the attitudes and biases expressed by mothers, and their emotional social behavior in the group. During several sessions an observer sat with the group and took extensive notes on the group's transactions.

The parents of ten adolescents girls with epilepsy were invited to participate in this group experience. Concomitantly each of the epileptics was being treated with pharmacotherapy, and some were in psychotherapeutic groups participating in the multiple treatment program. Despite an invitation to both parents, only the mothers attended the meetings. The mothers varied in age from thirty-five to forty-nine years. Their educational backgrounds were diverse: two were college graduates, three had attended high school, one had had no formal education and was illiterate.

Each mother was asked to complete a fifty-item Attitudes Toward Epilepsy Test. This test was developed in order to determine objectively the parents prejudices, misconceptions, and beliefs concerning the disease. The attitude test was based upon actual statements which had been made by the parents of epileptics in the past. The test was pretested in this section before its use. The mothers were asked to read each statement and to indicate whether or not they agreed with the statement. The following are some of the items which appeared on the test: "To have an epileptic child is a disgrace to the family." "Epilepsy is caused by heart trouble". "Epilepsy can be cured easily by spiritualism." "Epileptics are cursed." "Most epileptics are stupid." "Epileptics are queer an strange." "Epilepsy is God's curse on the parents." "Epileptics have special powers." "Epileptics are mysterious persons." "Epileptics are crazy." Table 19-I shows some of the major items of the test with which 50 percent or more of the mothers agreed. It should be noted that each of the respondents is a parent of a diagnosed epileptic and that each mother has had repeated contacts with physicians in the district hospitals of the island. Also it should be indicated again that some of these mothers were fairly well educated. Despite these facts, almost all of the mothers tested agreed with many of the prejudiced, stereotyped misconceptions presented in the attitude test.

THE COUNSELING PROGRAM

The counseling program began formally in February, 1962, and has continued to this date. The mothers meet twice a month for a one-hour informal round-table discussion. The group leader of all sessions has been this section's social worker. Below is a summary of some of the most significant interpersonal transactions which occurred during these group meetings.

The first session was devoted to the formation of the group and to the explanation of the program's purpose. All mothers accepted the idea and promised to participate regularly. At the end of the first meeting, the mothers suggested the following topics be discussed in the forthcoming meetings: Epilepsy versus mental disease, different attitudes of parents toward epilepsy, and epilepsy and marriage.

The second and third meetings were devoted primarily to the above topics. Of great interest was the fact that several mothers considered epilepsy a mental disease and that their own children were mentally insane. One mother suggested the group give itself the name "Mothers of Epileptics Club." This proposal made a greater impact on the group. One mother denied that her daughter was an epileptic; several others objected strenuously and indicated that their daughters would feel very inferior.

The major concerns expressed by these mothers in the first three sessions were their terror and pain when an attack occurred, the inability of public school teachers to handle their daughters when an attack occurred in school, their shame and disgrace that one of their offspring was an epileptics, and their suffering because they were mothers of epileptics. The mothers were particularly fearful of sending their daughters to school. They expressed the worry that their daughter might have attacks on the street or on the road. Some considered their daughters defenseless and hence in need of constant supervision and protection. Three mothers indicated that they were afraid of some man's attacking their daughters after a convulsion.

In these sessions much information was obtained concerning the mothers' method of handling their daughters. Several indicated that they "protected" their daughters by hiding the fact that the daughter was an epileptic from friends, neighbors, and even from relatives. Some commented that one could only give more love, more security, and understanding to the child while others argued that the epileptic can only be managed through the use of consistent and firm discipline.

Four to six group sessions were devoted primarily to giving the mothers objective, factual information concerning the causes of epilepsy and the principles and methods of treatment of the disease. A physician from this section gave an informal lecture to the group on the background of the functioning of the human brain and upon the cause of epilepsy. The mothers asked questions and discussed the concepts presented by the physician's lecture. An educational film on epilepsy was shown which brought out more misconceptions the mothers had about epilepsy. Several mothers indicated that one could get epilepsy through the saliva of an epileptic and that the disease was highly contagious. These discussions taught the mothers that the epileptic "howl" is caused by lack of respiration during the attacks, that the frequency of seizures is related to menstruation and high anxiety, and that drugs can control the attacks. One mother indicated she would now insist that her daughter take her medication regularly and that she, the mother, would no longer go to "spiritualists" and "religious miracle workers" in the hope of obtaining a complete cure for her daughter.

By the end of the sixth session it became clear that several of the mothers developed resistance to the program. This matter was discussed in detail by the group and the following appeared to be the major reasons:

1. Two members were dissatisfied because they were sure that their daughters were not epileptics. Despite the presentation of objective, expert evidence, their denials continued.
2. The illiterate mother felt too timid and embarrassed to participate frequently in the group. She assumed that any question she may have had was silly due to her lack of schooling and would be considered by the other group members as a demonstration of her ignorance.
3. Almost all members of the group admitted that learning about their daughter's disease was a very painful process. Many had hoped simply to avoid the truth. Several cried upon learning that a complete cure in most instances was impossible at present.

Two group sessions were then devoted to improving and handling the mothers' resistances. The project psychologist attended these sessions and afterwards discussed the resistances with the group leader and the psychotherapist of the adolescents' psychotherapeutic group.

The attitude test toward epilepsy was repeated during the ninth group session. The results were compared with those of the first. The results were gratifying. Only two of the mothers indicated that they still adhered to their previous misconceptions. However, it should be recognized that intellectual acceptance is not the same as emotional acceptance. By the ninth session, one mother still insisted that her daughter was not an epileptic. This comment prompted one of the others to declare that "some of us need help more than our daughters."

The tenth and eleventh sessions of the group were devoted to the discussion of their daughters' future plans. Most interesting in this discussion was the fact that every mother expressed the idea of letting her daughter decide what she herself wanted to do. This was a rather startling reversal of opinion, since in the early group sessions each mother had described how the daughters must be protected, even overprotected.

It was also during the tenth and eleventh sessions that mothers mentioned spontaneously how these sessions had made them feel better. One mother put it this way, "It is easier to be the mother of an epileptic when you know there are other mothers who have the same problems you have." The mothers also mentioned that now that they understood their daughters' illness better, it was much easier to handle them. It was apparent that some of these mothers in fact did feel much more at ease in their relations with their daughters.

The twelfth session marked a major turning point in the activities and focusing of the group. The mothers had shown much concern about the lack of knowledge, prejudices and fears about epilepsy held by the general population of Puerto Rico. The mothers had repeated continuously that most Puerto Ricans reject epileptics and felt much fear and hostility toward persons with this disease. The mothers wanted to know if they could do something about this community problem. After much discussion the group decided to work toward the creation of a Puerto Rico Epileptic Parents Club. The proposed aim of the club would be to help educate the Puerto Rican public and to aid doctors, parents, and patients to solve the social and psychological problems of epilepsy. Subsequently the club has been organized and its work has begun.

SUMMARY

The need for enlightment on the subject of epilepsy in Puerto Rico is great. Few health problems are so incrusted with such an accumulated mass of prejudice, ignorance, and misinformation. Even the mothers of epileptics, as the results from this study show, are not free from these prejudices despite the fact that many have had repeated contacts with physicians.

The major purpose of this report was to describe the group process employed in helping the mothers of ten adolescents with epilepsy. This process was part of a three-phase program aimed at treating these patients. The mothers met in an informal group setting with a social worker on a semimonthly basis. The purposes of this program were to overcome the mothers' misinformation concerning the disease and to reduce their fears and anxieties.

Each mother was given an attitudes test on two occasions in order to obtain an objective measure of attitude changes which may have occurred. Each session was recorded by the group leader.

Nine of the ten mothers seemed to have changed greatly in terms of their attitudes and feeling about the disease. One mother, despite the same ten months of participation in the group, still insists that her is not an epileptic.

TABLE 19-I

ITEMS FROM ATTITUDE TEST GIVEN TO MOTHERS OF
EPILEPTIC ADOLESCENTS

	Positive Answer (%)
An epileptic almost always has an epileptic child	80
The cause of epilepsy is unknown	80
Epilepsy is a very mysterious disease	80
All epileptics have convulsions	70
If an epileptic eats very little, he will have fewer convulsions	60
Epileptic children should be protected at all times	50
Epileptics should be placed in a special hospital	60
Epileptics are incapacitated their whole life and cannot be rehabilitated	50
An epileptic is not good for anything	50
Epileptics go crazy if they do not receive treatment	50

The mothers of epileptics were able through the group sessions to overcome many of their misconceptions and fears about epilepsy. We believe, on the basis of testimonials given by these mothers, that the adolescents with epilepsy have benefitted from their mothers reduction of tension and anxiety. In nine to ten cases, it would appear that these group sessions have led to a general reduction of tension within the home. The best medical care is of little avail, in our opinion, if the epileptic is exposed continually to a psychologically detrimental home environment.

REFERENCES

1. Baus, G. J., La Vergne, L. and Russell, E.: Group sessions for parents of children with epilepsy. *J Pediatrics, 52*:270-273, 1958.
2. Cohen, H.: Epilepsy as a social problem. *Brit Med J, 5072*:672-675, 1958.
3. Lampe, J. M.: Education and epilepsy. *J School Health, 29*:220-223, 1959.
4. Lennox, W. G.: Epilepsy and the epileptic. *J Am Med Assoc, 162*:118-119, 1956.
5. Livingston, S.: The social management of the epileptic child and his parents. *J Pediatrics 51*:137-145, 1957.
6. Pond, D. A.: Social problems of the epileptic. *Med World, 83*:221-225, 1955.
7. Yahraes, H.: Epilepsy — *The Ghost Is Out of the Closet.* New York, Public Affairs Pamphlets. Pamphlet 98, 1951.

Chapter 20

Group Therapy with Parents: An Approach to the Rehabilitation of Physically Disabled Children

DORIS H. MILMAN

THIS communication will report an experience with group therapy of parents of physically disabled children in a chronic disease hospital. Slavson's (1) definition of group therapy corresponds most closely to the sense in which it is employed here: "Treatment through interviews in groups where problems are ventilated, inner pressures and anxieties released, and guidance given by therapists as well as by patient participants."

Group therapy is not a new technique, having been used by Schilder (2) and others in the treatment of adult psychoneurotic patients. In the field of child psychiatry Amster (3) in 1944 and others employed the technique of group therapy in the collective or group guidance of parents of children receiving psychotherapy.

In November, 1950, group therapy with parents was undertaken at a chronic disease institution for the twofold purpose of clinical investigation and psychotherapy. The group was composed largely of parents of cerebral palsied children, but children with other conditions were also included, i.e. spina bifida with paraplegia, and poliomyelitis. The common feature in all of these youngsters was a disability in the area of locomotion, but some of them suffered in addition from visual, auditory, and/or speech disorders, and varying degrees of mental retardation.

The parents met in groups of ten to twenty for one and

Note: Reprinted by permission of the author from *Journal of Pediatrics, 41*:113-116, 1952. Copyrighted by the C.V. Mosby Co., St. Louis, Mo.

one-half hours two evenings each month. The group was heterogeneous as to socioeconomic, educational, and intellectual levels,
but nevertheless maintained cohesion because of the common
interest. A pediatric psychiatrist led or moderated the discussion
attempting to keep the tone of the meetings informal yet orderly.
The usual procedure was for the physician to propose a topic or
facet of the problem as a point of departure and then to let the
group itself carry the burden of the discussion. The therapist
participated only to the extent of summarizing or restating the
parents' ideas or raising further points. In general, the approach
was nondirective, and every effort was made to have the parents
formulate their own answers to the questions they raised. Initially,
some parents seemed bewildered by or resentful of the lack of
direction but later came to see its purpose. In the beginning several
parents were quite reserved, but as time went on, they became
more confident and outspoken. Parents often disagreed with one
another, sometimes gently and occasionally quite vigorously. At
no time, however, did the differences of opinion threaten the
cohesiveness of the group. Proof of the appeal and value of this
format is the fact that the parents were invariably reluctant to
terminate the meetings.

EXPLORATION OF PARENTAL ATTITUDES

This communication will attempt to contrast the aims with the
actual accomplishments of the program. In the investigative area
two questions were raised. The first of these was What are the
emotionally significant attitudes of parents of disabled children?
These attitudes were expressed guardedly or not at all in the
beginning, but later came out more freely. The parents expressed
feelings of shame and painful self-consciousness in the presence of
others. They recognized that a physical disability is conspicuous
and often unesthetic. Many parents also said that they dreaded the
inquiring looks of casual passersby in the street. Some parents
admitted that they themselves had a feeling of distaste for their
children's appearance. One mother of a six-year-old spastic
paraplegic expressed this idea as a question: "Isn't it a disgrace,"
she asked, "to see a big girl like Anita playing in the street on her

hands and knees?" This mother was tearful in telling of her shame and embarrassment. Her concern for the opinions of others was expressed also as a dread of being pitied or ridiculed. Many parents were concerned lest the knowledge of this social stigma be communicated to the children themselves and cause them added suffering.

Perhaps the most telling attitude which these discussions revealed was the parents' interpretation that having anomalous children is evidence of their own inadequacy. They regarded their inability to reproduce themselves perfectly as a kind of personal failure. On the occasion when this material was brought out by members of the group and then restated by the therapist, there were tears in every parent's eyes, indicative not only of profound feeling, but also of the emotional release which is one of the therapeutic aims.

Many parents also suffered guilt feelings, and in this connection, the attending obstetrician was most often the target. There was no evidence that this group of parents experienced greater feelings of rejection toward their children than an average group of parents. However, since participation in the group was purely voluntary, it is possible that the consciously rejecting parents failed to attend the group at all. An element of subconscious rejection was inferred in cases where parents anticipated social ostracism of their children. In this connection it was interesting to note the range of attitude toward their plight among the parents: from complete, even smug, acceptance, to abject despair, to bitter resentment, to self-pity, to a "why should this happen to me?" reaction. These varying parental reactions correlated well with the reported degree of social acceptance which each child experienced, where the range again varied from total acceptance to total ostracism without regard to the degree of disability. A good example of this is the case of Joan, our most severely handicapped child, who has no speech and no voluntary motor control. On the ward she has always been well accepted and befriended. Her mother, who is an exceptionally warm, motherly person, reports that her social acceptance at home is completely satisfactory.

The second investigative problem was to discover parental

defense mechanisms, to learn how these parents compensated themselves. Here, too, the reactions were varied. Some parents became overprotective and fostered the child's infantile dependency. It is postulated in this regard that a parent finds the child's helplessness more acceptable and more plausible if he can continue to regard the child as a baby.

Another means of parental compensation was concentration on an exaggeration of the child's intellectual capacities. Parents in this category showed a striking departure from reality, regarding children with IQ's between 40 and 50 as normal.

Most of our parents used as an outlet for their anxiety preoccupation with and sometimes overdependence upon rehabilitation agencies and techniques. One father was constantly requesting "homework" assignments for his child: drills and exercises that he could apply during visiting hours and weekends at home, in the desperate hope of hastening the child's progress. He rejected completely the staff's suggestion that, since the child was already undertaking a full program, his function was to provide recreation, sociability, and other emotional values.

Some parents released their anxiety by devoting a great deal of energy to fostering the program of the Cerebral Palsy Association and to the organizational details of the parents' therapy group.

A form of defense, or more properly escape, which caused the staff a great deal of concern, was the tendency of many parents to resort to prolonged hospitalization for their children. Of course in many instances in-patient care was both necessary and desirable but often the parents used their own anxiety or physical limitations, real or fancied, as the reason for the child's hospitalization.

THERAPEUTIC AIMS

The following were the chief therapeutic aids: First of all, group therapy was undertaken to minimize individual feelings of isolation and difference, the hypothesis being that the parent derives a feeling of strength and solace from discovering that he is not unique in his tragedy. As a corollary to this proposition, it was anticipated that the group experience would demonstrate to each member the universality of his feelings and attitudes and thereby dilute some of their intensity. In support of the validity of this proposition, there is the report of a social worker from another institution concerning one of these parents. This mother, who was our most fearful and tearful, reported that she had benefited a great deal, particularly from the discovery that others experienced the same unhappiness and shame as she. It appears, then, that therapy directed toward the working out of these and other negative attitudes is an important area for future attention.

Steps were taken to channel feelings more constructively by guiding the group into undertaking the following exercises and activities:

1. Analysis of and planning a program for visiting the hospitalized child.
2. Analysis of and program for integrating the child into his ultimate social milieu.
3. Analysis of the child's role in the family.
4. Analysis of the child's emotional needs.
5. Analysis of the child's educational needs.
6. Analysis of the child's social needs.

The practical results of these exercises in terms of release of parental anxiety through constructive activity and in terms of enrichment of the children's lives were significant. In particular, the following achievements can be cited: greater interest in visiting hours, more frequent home visits and outings for hospitalized children, organization of a Boy Scout Troop in the hospital with one of the fathers acting as den leader.

As a further therapeutic step an educational series was undertaken to acquaint the parents with the scope and detail of the rehabilitation program. Physical medicine, pediatrics, physical therapy, occupational therapy, Board of Education, and nursing staffs each sent a representative to one or more meetings.

The final point in the therapeutic program was to help each parent to achieve a realistic and objective understanding of his own child's present status and future expectations. This, too, is an area for further study and work. It is the one objective that may need to be achieved in an individual rather than in a group setting, but the groundwork can be accomplished in the group. A case in point was that of a ten-year-old boy with spastic quadriplegia whose father had always held tenaciously to the idea that the boy was bright and intellectually hopeful. After many group discussions on the expected achievements of these youngsters, this father was able, in private conference, to accept the fact that the boy's IQ was only 50 and to envision realistically his future prospects.

SUMMARY

A pilot program of group therapy and education was undertaken for the purpose of discovering the outstanding parental needs and difficulties and attempting to resolve them. A great deal was learned that was of value and the parents' response, both in enthusiasm and in understanding of themselves and their children, was sufficient to warrant continued attention to this type of treatment.

REFERENCES

1. Slavson, S. R.: *Am J Orthopsychiat, 13*:650, 1943.
2. Schilder, P.: *Am J Psychiat, 93*:601, 1936.
3. Amster, F.: *Am J Orthopsychiat, 14*:44, 1944.

Chapter 21

Emotional Conflicts of Handicapped Young Adults and Their Mothers

MARIAN H. MOWATT

EMOTIONAL problems of children with cerebral palsy and other handicaps have been studied for a number of years, and help has been provided through discussion groups for their parents and occasionally for patients (1-3). But relatively less research has been done concerning emotional conflicts and less help given to these families after the children grow beyond school age.

A series of discussion groups planned by the Mothers' Unit of the Cerebral Palsy Center in Seattle, followed by a similar series for handicapped young adults enrolled at the Center, gave an opportunity to compare the concerns of the mothers with those expressed by the sons and daughters. Both series were sponsored by the Family Life Education Department of the Seattle Public Schools, which provides instructors for community groups interested in working on family problems, and both were led by the author, a clinical psychologist experienced in group psychotherapy.

The discussions revealed, in brief, that both groups have characteristic emotional conflicts, that an uncomfortable dependence upon each other is the most conspicuous common problem, that the mothers' conflicts give the appearance of being more disturbing than the patients', and that group discussion of the problems with a trained leader can help to clarify and relieve

Note: Reprinted by permission of the author and the *Cerebral Palsy Journal, 26*:6-8, 1965.

Dr. Mowatt is associated with the Community Psychiatric Clinic, Seattle, Washington.

some of the discomfort.

The Cerebral Palsy Center, a United Good Neighbor Agency operated by the United Cerebral Palsy Association of King County, provides a five days per week sheltered workshop for people over the age of eighteen, offering paid work through jobs done for local industries, speech therapy, physical therapy, academic classes, arts and crafts and recreation. Cerebral palsy patients too handicapped to hold regular jobs are accepted, no matter how severe the disability. People with a variety of other handicaps may enroll if no other agency is available.

The Mothers' Unit, with about thirty members, helps with fund-raising, publicity, recreation, and transportation. An average of twelve mothers attended each of the eight biweekly discussions. Of the total of 120 enrollees, attendance averaged twelve for their six weekly meetings. Since both groups were voluntary, there was not a one-to-one relationship between mothers and enrollees, but seven families had representatives in both groups. The parents of some of the enrollees were not living. Five commuted daily from a nursing home.

The "young people" ranged in age from nineteen to sixty-two years, with a median age of twenty-seven. The majority had cerebral palsy. Other diagnoses included epilepsy, mental retardation, multiple sclerosis and various kinds of brain damage. Eight were in wheelchairs. More than half had speech impediments, ranging from a halting but clear delivery to almost total unintelligibility. To the latter group, the others listened with utmost patience, until the first person to understand interpreted the message to the leader. One member plainly indicated his reaction through his facial expression and a variety of grunts. Thus absence of speech was no contraindication for group participation.

In both groups some members regularly sat near the leader and were eager to contribute; others characteristically preferred to sit outside the circle or near the door. Some appeared interested by said little or nothing during the entire series. Interesting parallels between mothers and offspring were noticed. One mother and her child sat on the fringes of their respective groups, seemed inattentive, and sometimes left early. The son of a woman who drew out and responded warmly to the other mothers, expressed concern for his colleagues in his own way by fetching ashtrays and making room for wheelchair patients.

The members were free to bring up any topic, and discussions ranged widely in content from the question of how to get the wheelchair people to the coffee breaks to the emotionally "loaded" areas described below. The groups usually began with practical matters, then gradually permitted feelings to be verbalized.

The most serious concerns of both groups were in two areas usually worked through and more or less solved by late adolescence – the achievement of independence from the family and the handling of sexuality. Perhaps because the Center took care of vocational problems for the time being, vocational goals did not figure to any extent in the discussions.

As the mothers described their interactions with their sons and daughters, they revealed their anxiety about separating from them. At the first meeting, a mother described their situation as different from that of all other parents, whose problem children eventually grow up and leave the nest. Gradually the mothers admitted to feeling "stuck" with their children, both for the daily care and for the long haul of the years. They could see no way out of this, yet they realized that parents do not live forever, and that the nest would eventually leave the young. As they discussed this dilemma, it became clear that anxiety rather than realistic considerations made it difficult for them to prepare their offspring for the inevitable separation in the future. When the leader focussed on feelings about small steps toward independence, such as taking a vacation, many of the mothers felt that this was out of the question. Many had had no vacation in years. Leaving the patient with a "sitter," with one another, or in a nursing home was seen as unloving, as providing inadequate care, or as unacceptable to the child. While some of the less severely handicapped were asking for apartments of their own, or a chance to room with another family, even a trial run at such an arrangement was hard for most of the mothers to accept. Feelings of guilt seemed to infuse the mothers' reactions toward giving themselves a "break," apparently because of the partially hidden resentment toward their strenuous care-taking job. The guilt was reflected in one mother's typical exclamation — "But you can't resent a helpless child!"

The same negative feelings were no doubt partially responsible for the tendency of some mothers to give more help than necessary to the young people, and to give in too often when the patients were cranky and demanding. Many mothers realized that they should not stay home in the evening every time their young adults objected and should not give any more than absolutely necessary help with dressing. Giving in usually led to further resentment in the mothers, and more dependency in the offspring, often with angry bickering on both sides. In the group, a beginning was made at viewing these impasses objectively, and untangling some of the motivations which caused them.

Occasionally the mothers were surprised to find that the children could do more than had been suspected. Once when a severely handicapped youth's brace was removed for repairs, he found that he could hold a paintbrush and paint with his toes. Midway in the series of meetings, one of the mothers took her first trip out of town in years. "I said to myself, 'Why can't I?'," she announced to the group on her return. Her family got along remarkably well without her. Incidentally (or perhaps not), her son mellowed from a hostile, withdrawn stance in his group to active, interested participation.

While many mothers accepted the burden of bathing and toileting their young adults rather than installing appliances which might have allowed more independence here, some objected to the job of providing transportation when the sons and daughters asked to go out or to visit friends on weekends. Thus an avenue of growth toward independence was cut off. In this connection the mothers brought out their dislike of exposing the handicapped boy or girl to the curiosity, the patronizing attitude, or the cruelty of the public. Whether or not they were projecting their own feelings on to others, the result was to keep the offspring more closely tied to the mothers.

The mothers' concerns about sexuality first came up in connection with a recent episode — two enrollees had been found embracing on the grounds. Indignation was the first feeling expressed, followed by suggestions of ways to prevent future occurrences. This negative attitude, and the ambivalence revealed by some of the mothers about the eventual marriage of their children, seemed to be another reflection of their guilt-based need to keep their youngsters close. Adult sexuality and marriage would surely separate the children from the home.

As the discussions explored these matters, some of the mothers, in varying degrees, were able to approach a more realistic acceptance of their sons and daughters as adults with needs and lives of their own.

Another source of anxiety for the mothers was their feeling that their husbands did not support them in their difficult dealings with the handicapped offspring. Some of the fathers were seen as antagonistic toward their children when they refused to give in, and resentful toward their wives' continual involvement. No doubt many fathers were coping with uncomfortable mixed feelings about their handicapped children. Several of the mothers suggested a discussion group to include fathers as well mothers.

In many ways the enrollees' discussions revealed the other side of the coin. At every meeting they enthusiastically advocated more independence for themselves. They freely expressed resentment at not being allowed to go places where they felt capable of handling themselves, such as downtown on the bus. Several called their mothers overprotective, and were jealous of the greater freedom given to their unhandicapped siblings. Some mentioned their desires for apartments of their own and for vacation trips. The young people admitted that their lack of experience made them "younger" in some ways than their contemporaries, but strongly disliked being patronized or infantilized. They were particularly annoyed at people who thrust unwanted help upon them. In this connection one enrollee thoughtfully remarked, "It's harder for us to get along by ourselves, so we need more, not fewer chances to learn than normal people do." Their own part in the infantilization — the demanding, overly dependent tactics so irritating to the mothers — was not mentioned by the patients. This suggests that conjoint meetings of parents and offspring together would clarify some of the issues through mutual confrontation.

Sexuality came up early in the enrollees' discussions, with spontaneous jokes about current pairs and triangles at the Center, and reappeared often, as in any normal adolescent group. One patient summarized their feelings — "We may be handicapped physically, but we have normal emotions!" As the group moved toward a consideration of marriage, it appeared that the discussions gave a greatly appreciated chance to express ambivalent feelings about this important matter. Several wondered if it would be fair to ask a partner to give constant physical care. Some of the men brought out their resentment at having to be cared for by a wife rather than playing the culturally accepted masculine role.

While the meetings apparently helped the young people to move ahead in the task of gaining confidence with the opposite sex, there were some complaints about the parents' opposition to their progress in this direction. For example, two pleasant young women, handicapped in speech and motor control by cerebral palsy, had been invited to the movies by young men. In each case the mother, instead of rejoicing, had refused permission, fearing that the man would take advantage of the handicapped girl. The girls bitterly resented missing the rare chance to have the fun of a movie date. Again, an opportunity to practice independent behavior was lost, as well as a chance to learn how to relate to men while mother was still available to give instruction.

An important concern explored more fully by the patients than by the mothers was the need for better communication with people. Many expressed a wish to spend more time with friends, and particularly with nonhandicapped people. They complained of those who walk away instead of listening, and of those who merely pretended to understand. The lively exchanges in the group attested to the strength of the need. The high enthusiasm to share ideas was never dampened by the incredibly prolonged and intense muscular effort on the part of many to bring out each word. Often the leader's job was to regulate traffic when several wanted to talk at once.

While the young people, like their mothers, were concerned about the attitude of the public toward the handicapped, they appeared to be rather more casual. Many felt that recent books and other publicity had made the public more accepting, and they were able to laugh at some of the untoward reactions of normal people toward the handicapped.

COMPARISON OF THE TWO GROUPS

The most noticeable difference between the two groups was in the atmosphere, and this seemed to be not entirely a function of the differences in age and role. The mothers, intelligent, attractive women who had accomplished the very difficult task of raising a physically handicapped child, presented a rather stoical, restrained front. There was less ventilation of anger than among the enrollees, and less mirth. The young people freely expressed anger toward parents, siblings and roommates. One wheelchair patient told of successfully kicking another one across the room in a dispute. Laughter and friendly ribbing prevailed. At the end of the series some of them (but none of the mothers) mentioned that they had come to know and like each other better through the group. No doubt the mothers should receive due credit here. Somehow they had succeeded in giving the offspring more freedom to speak out than they allowed themselves.

Very probably the difference in spontaneity means that the mothers were coping with more serious inner conflicts than the patients. Apparently the typical mother had not completed the work of "mourning" the lost dream of having a normal child. The natural grief, anger, shame, and guilt which inevitably arise with such a disappointment had left a powerful residue. Far from being faced, expressed, and assimilated, the mourning had never been completed, and the feelings had been fought and defended against over the years. Denial of the negative feelings and reaction formation against them were the chief defenses, leading to the inhibition of affect and the unrealistic efforts to help and to keep the children close. Guilt, overprotection, and resentment seemed to feed upon each other in a never-ending, underground cycle. Often the children, like any youngsters, had easily discovered this maternal weakness and had exploited it to control their mothers, giving further impetus to the resentment-guilt phase of the cycle.

The crippled young adult, while unsure of his self-image, frequently thwarted by realities, and often misunderstood by others, nevertheless revealed himself in these brief sessions as less conflicted, less inhibited and with greater zest of life than most of the mothers. Born that way, he had no dream to mourn.

It was the impression of the leader that those from the nursing home, while more severely handicapped, were more interested in and eager to be a part of the world outside themselves than those who lived at home. The latter remained focussed on their conflicts with parents, and had "unfinished business" to do concerning their own part in prolonging the dependency.

Both groups were helped to some extent to accept themselves and their negative feelings and to look for new solutions through the support and mutual acceptance provided by the group and the objectivity offered by the leader. Unfortunately a few people after expressing strong affect, left the groups before they could be helped to deal with these emotions. Both series were too short to do more than begin the process of change.

SUMMARY

Group discussions for mothers of young adults with cerebral palsy and other handicaps, followed by a similar series for the patients, were used to explore problems in the areas of independence from the family, expression of sexual interests, and social communication.

Because the mothers apparently harbored more unresolved, conflicted feelings than their children, they expressed themselves with less spontaneity than the young adults. Their inner conflicts appeared to be more crippling emotionally than the young people's physical handicaps.

Group participation, possibly including parents and young people conjointly rather than separately, offers a unique opportunity to alleviate some uncomfortable feelings, and to promote more independent functioning for both generations.

REFERENCES

1. Bice, Harry V.: Group Counseling with Parents of the Cerebral Palsied. In *Psychological Problems of Cerebral Palsy*. A Symposium, sponsored by the Division of School Psychologists, American Psychological Association and the National Society for Crippled Children and Adults, Inc., Chicago, Easter Seal Society, 1952, pp. 23-44.
2. Wilson, E. L.: Group therapy experience with eight physically disabled

homebound students in a prevocational project. *Exceptional Child,* *29*:164-169, 1962.
3. Zeichner, A. M.: Observations on individual and group counseling of the individual with cerebral palsy. *Exceptional Child, 23*:35-352, 383, 1957.

Chapter 22

A Letter to the Parents of a
Brain-injured Child

MERLIN J. MECHAM

Dear Mr. and Mrs. Smith:

Since your last visit to the Speech and Hearing Clinic, I have received the reports of Mike's psychological and medical examinations which we recommended he should get. They verify our original supposition that Mike's difficulty stems primarily from a brain injury acquired before, during, or shortly after birth.

You asked me to help you in the better understanding of your child's problems. Well, I must reemphasize that I cannot do this adequately alone. You will need not only the help of the speech pathologist, but also that of psychologist, medical doctor, and other sympathetic specialists whom I will mention a little later on.

It must be remembered that no two children are ever exactly alike. Even identical twins are different in many ways — perhaps as different in some things as two children who are completely unrelated. It is difficult in this short time to make many specific suggestions that may be of help to you. However, there are some generalities which might be relevant and which take into account at least some of the difficulties with which you and your child are confronted.

Your physician will tell you that brain damage is a condition resulting from injury to some of the cells and pathways of the brain. This may occur in one or more areas and as a result of one

Note: Reprinted by permission of author and *Cerebral Palsy Journal, 16*:25-26, 1955.

Dr. Mechan is with the Department of Speech, Speech Pathology and Audiology, University of Utah, Salt Lake City, Utah.

or more of numerous causes. A brief mention of some of the causes may be appropriate here. Lack of oxygen is one of the most frequent causes. Brain cells are more vulnerable than any of the other cells in the body. If a newborn child does not breathe within four minutes after birth, some of the brain cells are likely to die. If he does not breathe within eight minutes, severe and extensive brain damage is bound to result. There are many things which may impair or hinder the supply of oxygen to the brain which I will not try to enumerate here. Also, physical injury of the brain cells themselves may result from mechanical trauma such as instrumental or birth canal lacerations obtained during the birth process, or from infectious conditions such as meningitis or encephalitis. German measles, if developed in the mother during the first three months of pregnancy, frequently has a handicapping effect on the fetus and is very likely to cause damage to the nervous structures. Regardless of cause, brain cells, once damaged or killed, can never be restored to their original function. The ultimate performances of these cells are destined to be lost or distorted.

I would like to say in all earnestness, Mr. and Mrs. Smith, that there is always more than one human being affected when injury occurs in a newborn child. It is not only the child, but his parents and perhaps the whole family, including aunts and uncles, who are stunned by the bolt of misfortune which strikes suddenly and without warning. It could as well have been the Browns or the Hannahs down the street, for this misfortune is no respector of persons, creed or financial status. And it seldom strikes twice in the same place.

I was particularly interested in what the author of the book entitled *The Other Child* described as the tragedy felt by the parents. He remarked that as the sins of the fathers pass down to the latest generations, so the behavior disturbances of the child are commonly considered to plague the child's forebears. This is a notion which engenders feelings of guilt and helplessness in the parents. They become paralyzed into accepting as a genetic calamity a physiological fact which is as accidental as the broken leg, and as hereditary as the measles.

Human beings are prone to strive for an optimal adjustment to any situation. In chaotic circumstances this effort for optimal adjustment may be shortsighted and detached from any breadth of ultimate long-term adjustments. It is sometimes tough to face the apparent misunderstandings of "unknowing people." Reactions which arise purely from curiosity on the part of people often emerge in the form of such questions as "Can he walk? Can he talk? Why does he drool?" Then more boldly "What's the matter with him? What made him that way? Is it hereditary?"

It is often said that knowledge breeds sympathy and understanding. I believe that unsatisfied curiosity may breed contempt and rejection. One of the happiest experiences of one parent occurred when a neighbor child was heard to explain to other children who were playing in a group with her child, "Bobby is sick and some of his muscles don't work very good. But if we let him play with us and try to help him, we can make him walk better." This statement, though likely a mere repetition of the answer of the child's own mother to her question about little Bobby, seemed enough to satisfy the curiosity of the other children.

Brain injury affects the child in many ways. There are various centers in the brain, for example, which have a major control over various types of behavior and abilities. One center is mainly responsible for emotions, another — muscle control. Specific centers are responsible for perception and communication or the use of languages. Injury to the brain may alter the function of anyone or many of the various brain centers. It is for this reason that we usually refer to the brain-damaged child as a multiply handicapped child. The brain, of course, is responsible for our intellectual functions. These children most often show a jagged intellectual profile, that is, they may have difficulty performing some obviously easy tasks and at the same time be successful with other more difficult ones. Generalizing and shifting from one concept to another may be very difficult for them.

Language difficulty resulting from brain damage is called *aphasia*. Children who have aphasia are usually deficient in more than one communicative function, for example, reading or writing as well as speech. In speech there are two predominant types of aphasia: (1) the inability to express or expressive aphasia, and (2) the inability to understand heard speech or receptive aphasia.

Expressive aphasia may manifest itself mainly through a lack of speech. There may be crude grunts accompanied by some kind of gestures. A child with this type of aphasia develops a fairly good gesture language. He can understand what he hears and is generally well oriented as to what is going on in the speaking world around him.

Receptive aphasia is manifest by the inability of the child to understand the speech that he hears. The receptive aphasic child is unresponsive and unattentive to the spoken word although he may well hear and recognize sounds and noises in his surroundings. He may know when the telephone rings or when daddy pulls up in the driveway outside. When an airplane flies over, he may go to the door to watch it. The speech of this child is usually characterized by a conglomeration of jabbering and bizarre gesturing. He may be able to mimic speech perfectly well at times in parrot fashion. However, because one must be able to understand heard speech before one can learn to talk, this child does not have any intelligible and meaningful spontaneous speech. He, like the expressive aphasic child, may have a gesture language, usually more crude and less distinguishable than that of the expressive aphasic child. Children with only a partial involvement in the expressive or receptive abilities are referred to as dysphasic rather than as completely aphasic. Although in the above description I have separated expressive and receptive aphasia as distinct entities, very rarely do they occur separately in children. If the motor area of the brain is injured, speech and communication will be further complicated by dysarthria and muscular involvements.

The *treatment program* for the brain-damaged child is important. The program will involve a team of specialists including the psychologist, the pediatrician and other medical specialists, the speech pathologist, occupational therapist, physical therapist, and the special education teacher. A well-rounded program includes (1) a thorough program of medical treatment and training under the guidance of the pediatrician, neurologist and orthopedic surgeon, (2) psycholgical counseling with the parent for the purpose of channeling the child into the avenues of care and training which are best suited for him, (3) training in speech and language communication, (4) special education and/or social development, and (5) prevocational and vocational counseling and training. Our clinic is fortunate in having the services of most of these specialists available to give aid and advice in regard to proper programming for your son Mike.

Of course, Mike's speech and language development are very important aspects to be considered at the present time. He needs to be able to express himself and you will soon be thinking about his possible entrance into school. In addition to the therapeutic help which he gets in speech, he must get rich readiness creating experience at home. He must go through the normal developmental stages of (1) prelanguage exploration and manipulation such as babbling in speech, the drawing of figures and shapes in writing, and picture-word association in reading; (2) isolated language understanding and production, such as individual sound production in speech, printing of letters in writing, and learning of letters and words in reading; and (3) use of proper language structures in meaningful speech, reading and writing communication. Without special and patient help from both the parent and the therapist, these normal developmental patterns are not likely to materialize efficiently. There must be close parent-therapist cooperation in a clinic-home training program.

It has been demonstrated that the brain-damaged child, in spite of his special difficulties, will still respond to established principles of learning. Strong discipline is often not nearly as effective as the mere process of ignoring the child. An unusual amount of attention is nearly always the demand of these children just as you said was the case with Mike. A spanking may be a more satisfactory mode of attention and less effective as a disciplinary measure than nothing at all. Conditioning is an effective avenue of training. Repetition and routine in his daily activities will enable him to remain organized.

It must also be remembered that the shadings of social conformity come from day-by-day buffering experiences which a child encounters in everyday situations. He must learn to make *acceptable* adjustments to the many little social problems which occur, at the time that they occur. Any unusual experiences will make patterns of normal conformity difficult. A child who has abnormal perceptual and emotional faculties must learn to compensate through special channels of experiences just as a child who is blind must learn to see through other senses. For instance, tracing a word with his finger may facilitate the aphasic child's learning to read the word. Inhibitions over impulsiveness and distractibility may be developed by working under specially constructed surroundings at first and then gradually moving into more complex or normal school and social situations. A child who is auditorily handicapped can be given rich intellectual stimulation and exercise through visual, motor-kinisthetic, and other senses. Above all, it is imperative that he have an abundance of carefully guided social experiences.

Finally, an atmosphere of understanding and acceptance of the child for what he is must be forthcoming before any of his problems can be tackled. Goals must be planned realistically according to what the child is physically, emotionally, and mentally able to do. One parent in our clinic has insisted on setting up her child's goals according to aspirations which were developed even before he was born. This is possibly an attempt to satisfy the needs of some one other than the child. In fairness to the child, it is usually good to set up what would be a minimum goal for him. The parent may then help him to do better if he possibly can, but should not require him to do better. After all, our ultimate goal for Mike, as for other brain-damaged children, is that he be written back onto the role of human beings as an individual who needs and receives love, affection, and acceptance just as any one else. Once this goal is reached, he will find his place in society.

Yours sincerely
Merlin J. Mecham, Ph.D.
Speech Pathologist

Chapter 23

Therapeutic Aspects of Parent
Associations for the Handicapped

ALFRED H. KATZ

I N connection with a study of the growth and development of parent groups in fields of physical and mental handicap (1), individual interviews were conducted with fifty parents of handicapped children and with three groups of such parents. These parents were all members, and active to some degree, in associations of parents in the fields of cerebral palsy, muscular dystrophy, mental retardation and severe emotional disturbance (childhood schizophrenia). The primary focus of the interviews, and of the study as a whole, was upon the early history and development of the self-organized groups, their relationship with professional agencies, and professional workers – physicians, teachers, social workers, and so on. Nevertheless, in the course of these interviews – which were exploratory and fact – rather than attitude – centered, it was inevitable that some impressions would be gained regarding the emotional aspects of participation in these groups as experienced by parents.

The presentation that follows discusses some of these aspects and attempts to relate them to an analytic framework.

The most striking and widely recurrent theme in the individual and group interviews with parents was the therapeutic value of the self-organized groups for those who participate in them.

This characterization of the helping aspect of the group's values

Note: Reprinted by permission of the author and the *Cerebral Palsy Journal, 22*:6-7, 13, 1961.

Dr. Katz is Professor, Social Welfare in Medicine, University of California Medical Center, Los Angeles, California.

was expressed repeatedly in the course of the interviews with parents and by professionals, especially those who had had contact with individual parents in the groups and knew of their personal situations. Both group support — the assistance of others — and catharsis — the release of hitherto blocked feelings with consequent relief — seem to occur among the members of all of the groups studied, and to be important concomitants to active membership and participation. These psychological factors seem to be important elements in making possible organizational progress for the groups, through stimulating the readiness of parents to contribute time, effort and finances to them.

PSYCHOLOGICAL FACTORS FOR PARENTS

From the interviews, understanding was gained of the source of these therapeutic values in the common factors in the experience of parents of handicapped children. Even parents who made the impression of being highly intelligent and well-adjusted stated that they had experienced serious traumas when they found that their child was born crippled or suffered a crippling disease. These examples illustrated the point made by Guensberg (2): "It is a known fact that the agonies suffered by mothers in some instances surpass by far the emotional disturbances of the child." From the incidental descriptions of the disruption of family living, commented on by several interviewees, it was indicated that notably parents, but also siblings and other family members, of children born with or acquiring a severe handicap, are subject to such trauma. The resulting anxieties seem to be intensified when the handicap is conspicuous, permanent and socially stigmatized, as in mental retardation, and the more obvious and extreme effects of cerebral palsy. One mother of a cerebral palsied child stated in the interview that she had not taken her child outside the house, except for medical attention, for a period of six years, prior to becoming active in the U.C.P.-N.Y.C. She stated that she "could not stand the pitying glances of people in her apartment building and on the street."

Such hypersensitivity or anxiety was frequently heightened for these parents by the attitudes of other members of their family, relatives, and neighbors or other lay persons in the community. Several parents also commented that they had experienced negative attitudes and what appeared to be callous reactions on the part of professional persons from whom they sought guidance and assistance. The comments of those interviewed in the course of this study are similar in character to many such reports in the literature on subjective perceptions or rebuffs and rejection of such parents in their early contacts with professional workers.

With this combination of hypersensitivity, anxiety, shame, and the sense of rejection, many parents came to the early meetings of the self-organized parent associations and used them, perhaps unwittingly, to achieve emotional catharsis.

Marshall (3) has well expressed these initial therapeutic aspects brought about by group participation:

> Through the group relationship great emotional support is provided. One can express anxiety and pent-up aggression without increasing a sense of guilt because the group is accepting and understanding. From open disucssion one can sometimes reduce emotional conflict by simply listening to experiences of others. The personal and individual aspects of problems lose their force when others share the same difficulties. One can ask freely, "why does my child not walk?" "why does he not hold his toys?," or "why do I have feeding problems?" when one is sure of sympathetic understanding. In such a situation, where so many common experiences exist, there is keen desire to help each other in working out these difficulties.

There is great therapeutic value for parents in the feeling that they belong to a group.

It was noted throughout the worker's interviews that considerable confusion ensured for parents from contradictory or indefinite diagnosis of their children's condition by professionals, or by the immediate advocacy by physicians or nurses of institutionalization for the child. In this respect, the data from these interviews parallels similar findings by professionals regarding the psychological situation of parents of the handicapped, and the therapeutic benefits found in group activity. Samburg, who conducted a casework service for parents of mentally retarded children, believes that "faulty communication of diagnosis (by professionals) contributes more than any other single factor of parents' difficulties in handling the problem of their child's retardation" (4). One of the key factors in the inadequate communication of diagnoses, he finds, is that physicians and other professionals working with mental defectives "are poorly equipped in their training for real comprehension of the prognostic meaning of the various types and degrees of mental defect with which they deal" (5). Samburg adds that the "active participation of these parents in a parent association can do much to help clients in comprehension and diagnosis, aspects of home management that prove the most troublesome, and in developing healthy and constructive activities of a social or group nature" (6).

Hormuth, who worked in a clinic with the parents of mentally handicapped children, found that "these parents of mentally handicapped children had been so frozen by frequent rejection of their problem by professionals and oft-repeated advice to institutionalize the child, that, though through the usual case work approach they gave intellectual recognition of their overprotection, they were unable to move from their accustomed reactions and habit patterns" (7), until they were involved in group activities and in discussing proposed facilities for their children.

Bice (8), among a considerable number of other students, found similar difficulties among mothers of cerebral palsied children, based on a combination of the physical difficulties and psychological stresses associated with the care of their children. A review of the clinical literature dealing with the psychology of the parents of the handicapped makes clear that the difficulties that have been described exist very widely and generally. The few relevant materials dealing with the organization of such parents into groups are also uniformly in agreement, from the writer's observation, on the therapeutic values of group participation.

Peck, a psychiatrist with considerable interest and experience in the use of group-treatment methods, pioneered in the provision of group therapy for the parents of schizophrenic children, a service which later grew into one of the parents associations with which the writer's study was concerned. The functions and results of therapy groups for these parents were evaluated by Peck and his associates (9) as follows:

The method of group therapy has been found particularly effective to deal with common reactions — confusion and intense feelings of guilt, hostility, social isolation and hopelessness. In the groups a positive and realistic attitude towards the child's illness develops. The recognition of the common character of their problem diminishes the sense of uniqueness and builds relationships between the individual members as well as strengthens identification with the group. This process allows for emotional release, the expression of previously suppressed feelings, the attainment of insight. Ability to handle community pressures constructively develops, accompanied by a move toward social action to improve community facilities for the care of schizophrenic children.

As these clinical experiences reveal, the therapeutic effects of group discussion and identification do much to improve the situation of parents of the handicapped, their inner family relationships, and relationships with the outside world. As the material of the writer's interviews demonstrates, the self-organization of the parents makes it possible for them to channel their emotional drives into means of bringing about changes in the social environment. In and of themselves, these changes help to relieve some of the pressures experienced by the family, through the organization of direct services — clinics, recreation groups, schools and so on. The therapeutic accomplishment for the family then becomes a double one — first, through group participation, some of the oppressive feelings of hopelessness, isolation and shame are relieved. And secondly, concrete help in the burdens of daily care of the child is achieved. While a comparatively small number of individuals were seen, generally speaking, it can be stated that the experiences of the groups studied and the interviews with members confirmed this analysis of the therapeutic values for parents of membership in activity and identification with organizations. It is important to note that many professionals interviewed in the course of the study credited the groups with these values. One professional, however, expressed skepticism on this point, believing that identification with a parent group intensifies anxiety and morbid preoccupation for parents.

Because of the small numbers of persons seen, and the fact that exploration of this point was not systematic in the interviews, it cannot be claimed that these incidental findings are more than suggestive confirmation of a widely-held impression regarding an important aspect of the groups' functioning. Subject to the same reservations, these findings tended to confirm one of the sub-assumptions of the working hypothesis that the overall study was concerned to test, namely, "Leadership in these groups may provide an outlet to parents and relatives for feelings of frustration, and of inability as isolated individuals to cope with the adjustment problems of their family members and themselves. As such the groups have a socializing and therapeutic value of an important kind."

The preponderance of attitudes expressed by parents in the course of the interviews indicates that not only did they experience catharsis and relief of anxiety and tensions, most of them also, despite their criticisms or reservations, related to the parent associations in a positive way. This positive feeling has undoubtedly been one of the major factors in the successful growth of the several organizations studies.

GROUP TECHNIQUES IN THE ORGANIZATIONS

It is noteworthy that the leaders of the parent associations studied have been alert to the values of group experience and participation either intuitively, because of their closeness to the problems of parents, or through the guidance of professionals. These groups have set up specific educational projects which accomplish their ends through meeting the needs of the parent participants for both information, and emotional expression, and support. Although there are differences among them as to level and intensity of the "therapeutic aspects," parent education courses, more formal group therapy programs, and group counseling for adult victims of the diseases all are found.

Such classes, discussions, or therapy groups in the parent associations have proven a vital and magnetic part of their programs to parents and adult sufferers; all have waiting lists of potential participants, and the organizations have found that from such groups they have been able to recruit active workers and volunteers.

It is important to note that discussion or therapy groups are not considered by their sponsors to be a substitute for individual counseling or therapy but rather are seen as effective supplements to these. While the group programs reach numbers of parents, individual information and counseling services are offered simultaneously to many parents by the organizations either directly, or through services they support. The value of individual casework services is fully accepted by the parent groups and is attested to in a growing body of professional literature their workers have produced. The self-organized parent associations, in fact, have been laboratories for the study and development of a simultaneous approach to the group and the individual.

REFERENCES

1. "An Investigation of Self-Organized Groups of Parents and Relatives," by Alfred H. Katz, D.S.W. dissertation, N. Y. School of Social Work, Columbia University, 1957. Published by Charles C Thomas, Fall, 1960, as "Parents of the Handicapped."
2. Guensberg, Marcus: Emotional implications of handicaps, *The Crippled Child, XV*(1):20, Feb. 1951.
3. Marshall, Frances: Why is my child different? *Exceptional Child, XIV*:216-24, April, 1952.
4. Charles, Samburg: *An Experiment in Helping Parents of Mentally Defective Children.* New Haven Guidance Center for Retarded Children, 1954.
5. Ibid.
6. Ibid., p. 5.
7. Hormuth, Rudolph P.: Case Work Approaches in a Community Clinic for Mentally Retarded Children," *Am J Ment Defic, 20*(6):254, March 1954.
8. Bice, Harold V.: Groups Counseling with Parents of the Cerebral Palsied. In *Psychological Problems of Cerebral Palsy.* Chicago, Nat'l. Soc. for Crippled Children and Adults, 1952, pp. 27-28.
9. Peck, Harris B., Rabinovitch, Ralph D. and Cramer, Joseph B.: A Treatment Program for Parents of Schizophrenic Children, *Am J Orthopsychiat, XIX*(4): Oct. 1949.

Chapter 24

Understanding Parents
ONE NEED IN CEREBRAL PALSY

ERIC DENHOFF and RAYMOND H. HOLDEN

U NDERSTANDING parents is one need in cerebral palsy. To contribute in any measure to the habilitation program of the child who has cerebral palsy, the professional person must understand the fears, anxiety, and doubts of the parents of these children. On the other hand, parents of children with cerebral palsy must understand that progress for their child can only be made if their child's needs are met in a warm, loving environmental climate, which can only be provided by them.

UNDERSTANDING INFANCY

A child's happiness is predicated by his parents' reactions to his behavior. This philosophy embraces all children, especially the ones handicapped by cerebral palsy. The moment the baby is born, most parents decide that their child will be brought up the "right" way. Such a decision is usually based on their own feelings about children in general or their own childhood in particular rather than a knowledge of the development needs of the newly born baby. Thus, it is not unusual for babies to be exposed to restrictions or excesses during the period of early growth and development.

These parent-imposed regulations often lead to anxiety and insecurity in the growing child. Fortunately, most babies survive the occasional bunglings of parents during the early months. With

Note: Reprinted by permission of the *Cerebral Palsy Journal, 16*:9-11, 25, 1955.

Dr. Denhoff is Medical Director and Mr. Holden is Staff Psychologist at the Meeting Street School for Cerebral Palsy, Providence, Rhode Island.

time, there gradually evolves a happy, relaxed, accepting parent-child relationship. Within this framework of happy family environment, the average healthy child emerges as a secure, vigorous, and fairly well-adjusted adult.

When a child has cerebral palsy, his emotional developmental background may differ from normal children. As might be expected, parent worries are much more intense with these children. Worries first start when the baby does not respond to the normal amount of mothering. Therefore, even before the diagnosis of cerebral palsy is suspected, the mother already has a feeling that her baby is not well. The baby cries excessively, fusses a good deal, and feeds and gains poorly in spite of formula changes, frequent diaper changes, and patient handling. When there is no alleviation of the irritability with maturation, mothers of babies with cerebral palsy become so distraught and overtired that they frequently are now unable to meet even the basic requirements of the infant. Frequently they convince themselves they are poor mothers and give up the struggle to meet the baby's needs as a result of their initial frustrations in bringing up baby. These mothers do not realize that it is because of a damaged brain, and not because of their own inadequacies, that the responses of their infant are atypical.

When the clinical picture of cerebral palsy emerges sufficiently for the doctor to make a diagnosis, some mothers react to the news by becoming extremely upset, while other mothers seem to respond coldly and unemotionally. However, all of these mothers inwardly feel sorry both for their crippled baby and for themselves. Sooner or latter maternal overprotection emerges as a pattern found as a recognized part of the cerebral palsy picture. Excessive overprotection interferes with the future development of the baby and tends to obscure any progress the infant may make in his own right.

The father's role during these early months is also a difficult one. Since nature has designated a passive role for the father with the baby during the early years of development, he usually finds his major contribution to the cerebral palsy problem in his family as one of giving solace to his wife. This job is not an easy one, since the father must constantly reassure and reexplain to his wife the medical connotations of cerebral palsy when he himself is unsure of the fact. His own anxiety about the role he plays may lead to short temper with his wife. As a result, there may be a rift in parent solidarity. Soon one may find the father spending little time at home, utilizing the pressure of business as the excuse to escape from the family turmoil. This is unfortunate because, when the time comes for the father to assume his normal authoritative role in bringing up the child, he finds that he is unable to cope with the problems that have emerged about him. There are some fathers who throw the blame for this tragedy on their wives rather than on themselves. They refuse to recognize their own responsibility. By constant criticism they hardly permit a normal mother-and-child relationship to develop.

PARENT ATTITUDES

Parents' poor attitudes have proved a stumbling block to the successful treatment-training program of youngsters who have cerebral palsy. A number of years have been spent in trying to understand the reasons for them. In essence, the major number of problems with parents stem from the difficulties arising in the newborn and infancy periods as described. There are some parents, however, who were disturbed even before they had a child. Having a handicapped child serves them well, since they can transfer their own problems onto their youngster. In this latter group, treatment is rarely successful, since the parents themselves unconsciously refuse to permit improvement. Fortunately, these parents are not commonly found. However, whenever a therapeutic program that should be going well for a child is failing, this pattern of parent behavior must be looked for.

The conclusions about parent attitudes were made from a study of thirty-five children who were admitted to the first group for treatment and training of cerebral palsy youngsters at the Meeting Street School for Cerebral Palsy (1).

Four to six years later, after the children were no longer in nursery school, it was found that 67 percent of the group were making an adequate adjustment in the public school system. In retrospect, most of the parents of these successful children could be regarded as "good" or "fair" parents when rated on their attitudes during the period the child attended nursery school. Eleven children failed to make a good adjustment. In seven cases, the parents were rated as "poor" while their child attended nursery school. The four other children who failed in school proved mentally too low to adjust to formal schooling, even though they had been able to participate in the nursery school.

Analysis of the complaints of the seven "poor" parents consistently revealed the same dissatisfactions with the nursery school: (1) there was not enough emphasis on physical training and too much emphasis on play, (2) transportation problems were "so insurmountable" for the family that the school should be entirely responsible for it, (3) the fees were excessive ($1.00 per visit), (4) the medical program was not satisfactory, (5) other children in the group were more handicapped than their child, and they did not wish their child to mix with the more handicapped children, and (6) the goals of the school in no way coincided with the goals the parents had set for their child. In addition, the staff noted that: (1) these children were never ready when the bus came for them, (2) their clothes were frequently messy and children were often unkempt, and (3) the mother failed to remain at the school when requested, but disappeared to do shopping at the earliest opportunity.

A rating scale which compared "good" parents with "poor" parents has been utilized to differentiate these parents. It was noted from the ratings that, in the "good" parents group, parents got along well with each other and with their child. There seemed to be unanimity in the family acceptance of the child as he was. There was an obvious effort being made to permit the handicapped child to be part of the family, school and community. The child was permitted to perform as much on his own as possible without the parents pushing to achieve this. The "good" family accepted competent medical advice and followed through with suggestions. They trusted professional personnel and soon became part of the therapeutic team. They had sufficient drive and stamina to originate "helpful aids for their child," without extra professional help, and would make certain that their child received the maximum benefits from the program as it was outlined at the moment.

On the other hand, the "poor" families were outstanding in having a high incidence of husband-wife discord. The responsibility for cerebral palsy care usually fell on the mother. Not infrequently, she would state that the father or paternal grandparents blamed her for the child's plight. Another disturbing item in this group was the limitations of exercises or play activities of the child at home because of the failure of the father to build or obtain the necessary home aids. Frequently this group of parents consulted several doctors or cultists over a period of two or three years. Usually the parents permitted very little medical diagnostic studies for the child, although they constantly complained about the inadequacies of the medical profession. Some parents superficially well-read about cerebral palsy used one doctor's opinion against another's to maintain a program of do-nothing. Table 24-I outlines the characteristics of "good" parents versus "poor" parents.

TABLE 24-I

PARENT ATTITUDES

Good Parents	Parent Attitudes	Poor Parents
Accept child as he is	Acceptance	Refuse to acknowledge degree of child's handicap
Realistically appraise developmental abilities	Developmental Understanding	Unrealistically expect miracles in spite of developmental limitations
Provide warmth and security in interfamily activities	Parent and family relationships	Promote tensions and competition within family circle
Encourage and make opportunities for self-help	Participation	Overprotect and limit self-help activities
Carry through with recommendations in spite of attendant difficulties	Initiative and stamina	Discourage easily when progress not immediately evident
Accept guidance and advice	Professional trust	Are unable to face unpleasant opinions

PARENT PROGRAMMING

Experience with parent attitudes has given us some insight into their many problems. To minimize detrimental parent attitudes, more emphasis is being placed on parent-staff relationships in the early programming for children with cerebral palsy. "Poor" attitudes must be avoided from the very onset. By guiding both the parents and their handicapped child along constructural pathways, perhaps this can be done. As a result, a planned program for all new parents to the school was introduced. This consisted of group sessions under the guidance of trained psychiatric workers (2). Mothers and fathers of the patients were placed in separate groups so that there would be no limitation placed on expression of feeling about family life. The groups usually consisted of about ten fathers and a similar number of mothers who met weekly for sixteen sessions. No attempt was made to give active psychiatric guidance. Rather, the group leader attempted to guide discussion into areas that involved the cerebral palsy problem and methods of handling it in the family.

Several series of group sessions were held over a period of two years. In the group, the therapist could weed out from the start the few parents who were severely disturbed about their problems. For these parents referral for individual psychiatric help was suggested. The majority of average parents, endowed with a normal amount of tension and anxiety about their child with cerebral palsy, appeared to enjoy a few sessions. Once they had clarified in their minds what their cerebral palsy problem was, they appeared to relax and join freely in the disucssion. Generally, most parents soon felt pity for the other parents who had more severely handicapped children. However, before the sixteen sessions were completed, attendance had dropped markedly. The excuse given for absenteeism was that the meetings were inconvenient and wasteful of time, since many of the sessions did not include discussions about their particular child.

It must be emphasized that the sessions were not held primarily for general information about cerebral palsy or about specific children. Rather their purpose was to assess parent attitudes and to introduce an aura of permissiveness about expression of negative as well as positive feelings on the part of the parents.

Recently an attempt is being made to reach new parents through the medium of a handbook. The handbook simply presents to the parents the relationship of the doctor, psychologist, nursery school teacher and the various therapists with their child. It is hoped that the printed page may give more security and guidance to the parents than parent talks alone.

Through the pamphlet, the parents are introduced to the school and its purposes. The first chapter deals with normal and abnormal growth and development. The next chapter, "The Doctor Talks to Parents," defines cerebral palsy and discusses the handicap. The reasons and need for detailed diagnosis as well as a discussion of prognosis and treatment goals is included. Then follows factual discussions of the role that physiotherapy, occupational therapy, speech therapy, nursery school and recreational therapy plays in the school. The particular theme throughout the pamphlet concerns the practical aspects of "cerebral palsied" development. Home exercises are labeled developmental exercises and emphasize play techniques for mother and child rather than accentuating formal "P.T." or "O.T." exercises. Speech development is explained by correlations of the reasons for proper use of sucking, swallowing, mouthing, and other oral attitudes that are used by the baby in growing up. It is pointed out to the parents that the nursery school's function with children with cerebral palsy as with normal children is to help the child find his proper relationship to other children, as well as finding his own place in his own little world.

DISCUSSION

The information gathered on parent attitudes actually evolves into a philosophy of the treatment of children who have cerebral palsy. Experience has taught that there are certain requirements that must be fulfilled first if some measure of success is expected in the habilitation program. It is imperative that first the patient receive a detailed medical survey. The discussion with parents of the results of medical studies should be factual but placed on a "positive" level. In discussing babies and young children particularly, stress should be made on favorable development attitudes rather than unfavorable "mental" criteria. The parents must be left with a feeling that, although medical and psychologic tests may be definitive, nevertheless they are not always the last word. Rather, the attitudes of the family towards the child and the behavior of the child towards the family and society may make the difference between success or failure ultimately.

It is urgent to recognize early the cloud of guilt and guilt-complexes that lie over many parents of handicapped children. Results of evaluations can be utilized to lessen a factor that handicaps many parents. For example, in many instances, uncontrollable causes may be found in a case, rather than neglect or accident. On the other hand, the failure to find a cause may leave more parent guilt than playing up an inconclusive reason for the child's handicap. Parents must not be left with the feeling that cerebral palsy in their child was due to their own or their physicians' negligence.

Treatment should be started as early as possible. Although some physicians feel that a child receives little benefit from any therapy until three or four years of age, our experience differs. These early years can be spent profitably in preparing parents to understand the problems of their child, and in preparing the child to participate with the other children in a group.

The home exercises outlined in the physical and occupational therapy chapters are better called developmental exercises. These are designed to give the parent a positive program to do at home, while nature is helping the child capture the developmental items that belong to him. They are designed to give the parents a tie with the school until the youngster is developmentally ready to belong to a group.

They are given to the parents so that we can eliminate the "do-nothing now" attitude and substitute a "let's get going" atmosphere. The latter attitude gives the parents little time to think of their misfortune. It also helps them to "show off" the progress their child is making under their own hand at home.

Perhaps the most important thing that happens to most infants during the developmental phase of the treatment program is the slow, but gradually improving, reactions to new people. Most youngsters cry when placed in new unfamiliar situations. Soon after three years of age, they emerge from the "hanging-on-to-mama's-strings" stage to wanting to participate in play with other children. Many infants who have cerebral palsy, because of their physical, mental, emotional, and environmental handicaps, have difficulty in climbing this phase of the developmental ladder. The regular visits involved in the developmental sessions, which are designed for preparation for the group, help the patient reach this most important rung in the ladder. Within six to nine months, the therapists no longer find a crying, tense, fearful infant accompanied by an anxious, resistive mother. Rather, this is replaced by a smiling, happy, playful youngster accompanied by a warm, prideful mother. This will be the result when one has succeed in meeting parent needs.

CONCLUSIONS AND SUMMARY

Understanding parents' needs as well as the child's needs is an important part of a successful habilitation program in cerebral palsy. This can be accomplished best through a planned program for parents based on an understanding not only of the developmental needs of their children, but their own need for being "good" parents.

REFERENCES

1. Denhoff, E., and Holden, R.: Factors in Success-Adjustment of Cerebral Palsied Children, *Exceptional Child, XXI*:5-7, 1954.
2. Rubin, E., and Koret, S.: Unpublished data. Meeting Street School Parent Group Studies.

Chapter 25

How Parental Attitudes
Interfere with Counseling

ANDREW FLYNN

IT is important that children with cerebral palsy prepare to do some specific kind of task, if possible the same as nonhandicapped. Some of them go through adolescence without any thought of work or preparation for occupation because of their disability. They do not look into the future and see themselves playing an active, useful role in life. This unfortunate attitude is often fostered by the parents.

It is in this area that counselors run up against their biggest difficulty — parents with problem attitudes. This is a hindrance not only in the initial counseling situation but also in later follow-up after the individual has not been able to keep a position after it has been secured for him. The problem attitudes occur in many forms, some conscious, others, and the majority I like to believe, unconscious. A few of the main problem attitudes and their probable effects on the child and the counseling situation are discussed here in their various forms.

At times the form takes rejection. When parents reject a child, he is likely to be aggressive, annoying to those about him, attention getting, hostile, hyperactive, jealous, or rebellious. It seems that these children are driven abnormally by compensatory behavior to attract attention, gain group acceptance, or to see parents and therapist upset about them. This rejection may take many forms and may be on a conscious or unconscious level. This is in part a matter of degree. It may be physical, involving the

---

Note: Reprinted by permission of the *Cerebral Palsy Review, 17*:130-143, 1956.

child itself, or it may be economic, showing itself in lack of clothing, food, and so on. All this means that the child views the work from a narrow ledge, as it were, and when this narrow ledge is uncertain or unfriendly, the result is poor adjustment to surroundings, especially in a stress situation such as a new position that may have been "begged" by a counselor or social worker.

Another group is in direct contrast to those who reject their children — they magnify their responsibilities. These parents tend to overaccept their children and take themselves too seriously. Maternal overprotection shows in excessive contact, infantilization, and prevention of social maturity. This type of mother frequently overcoaches adolescents, prepares his lesson, interferes with any independence, and is in conflict with the counselor who is going to help her "baby" get away from her. In many families parents of these handicapped children are filled with a sense of hopelessness that finds expression in an emotional pattern based on pity. Often, too, these reactions are complicated by feelings of guilt. From this myriad of circumstances, there result situations which not only impair the possibilities for any constructive program but also create serious difficulties for the counselor.

A third group of parents cannot see their children as separate and distinct personalities but as miniatures of theselves. These parents seek to relive their lives in those of their children. They wanted to be a doctor or a lawyer and never made the grade. Consequently, from the time their child is born, he is pushed in that direction in spite of his physical condition or mental equipment.

Among other types who give a guidance counselor difficulty is the possessive parent, who relates the child to himself, always making the child aware that he "belongs" only to the parent. These people do not like interference from outsiders and unconsciously, and sometimes consciously, undo all the counselor has done.

Overindulgent parents anticipate the offspring's every need and help to keep him dependent and immature. The handicapped child is made to feel that he needs the parent more than he really does. He is never encouraged to attempt tasks for himself, to think for himself, or express any opinions. Some of these children, by the time they reach adolescence, have become dictators within their home as a result of these over indulgent parents. Their wish is every one's command. When it comes time to leave the home, it takes a great deal of counseling and guidance because these adolescents refute authority. They have been used to giving orders without being questioned and now find it difficult to change as is required in a vocational situation for guidance and later in the actual working situation.

Paradoxically, some parents approve of independence as the end result but seem unable to approve of the inevitable in between steps. Ask a mother if she wants her child to be a capable useful happy individual and she will undoubtedly answer Yes. Yet in the next breath, she will forbid the child from doing this, that or the other thing that will be the first step toward the end goal. It would be well for parents to maintain a future perspective and to think of their children in relation to that future; then they would see that a desired end must have intermediate steps. They must be willing to accept the counselors' recommendations and put aside their own unrealistic hopes and thwarted ambitions; they must stop being parents with problem attitudes and become parents with proper attitudes.

PART IV
COUNSELING PARENTS OF CHILDREN WITH SPEECH, HEARING, AND VISUAL HANDICAPS

Language Disorders and Parent-Child Relationships

DOROTHEA McCARTHY

RECENT research and clinical investigations bring out increasingly the fact the language, and particularly its oral form, speech, is an important indicator of the state of an individual's mental health. Clinicians are just beginning to read the linguistic barometer. Goodenough (18), for example, considers that "some form of the free-association method offers one of the most promising approaches yet available for the study of personality differences." She has developed refinements of the familiar word-association tests (17), which show that patterns of associations of words have diagnostic significance with reference to the broad aspects of personality. It is also becoming evident that the emotional climate prevailing in the home provides experiences which have important influences, not only on the child's personality adjustment, but also in his language development.

The cultural milieu in which children are growing up in present-day America places increasing emphasis on the vital importance of all forms of communication: listening, speaking, reading, and writing. Increasingly large numbers of individuals of normal mentality and sensory endowment are experiencing difficulty in acquiring facility in the various essential forms of

Note: Reprinted by permission of the author and the *Journal of Speech and Hearing Disorders, 19*:514-523, 1954.

Dorothea McCarthy is Professor of Psychology, Fordham University Graduate School. This article is adapted from a paper presented at the 1953 Convention of ASHA, New York City.

communication. This phenomenon has in turn given rise to the several professions concerned with remediation, such as speech therapists and remedial reading teachers who, together with clinical psychologists and psychiatrists, are concerned with alleviating the various language disorders. Evidently something is going wrong in one phase or another of the language development of increasingly large numbers of children.

LANGUAGE DISORDER SYNDROMES

When the child whose speech is not developing normally is examined carefully, it is usually found that there have been anomalies of language development present in one form or another throughout his life (3, 9, 27, 43). Whether a child is referred to a speech therapist, to a psychologist, or to a remedial-reading teacher is largely a matter of timing. It is a question of when a particular symptom becomes intolerable to someone in the environment and what facilities are available in the community.

Language disorders rarely appear singly or in isolation. In the clinic at Fordham three fourths of the nonreaders had also shown delayed speech, lisping, stuttering or articulatory defects at one time or another (27), but no one had been sufficiently concerned to seek help for the earlier symptoms. The majority of these children had two or more such oral symptoms in combination with the reading disorder which eventually brought them to the clinic. It was also found that about one fifth of the stutterers had had difficulty in learning to read and two thirds of them had additional speech symptoms. Yedinack (43) found 40 percent of a group of second-grade poor readers also had articulatory defects, and 38 percent of a group of cases identified as having articulatory defects also suffered from reading disabilities. Huyck (21) cites a summary by Rutherford, which states that 25 percent of dysphemia cases have reading and writing defects or other speech defects and 18 percent of dysarthria cases show similar syndromes. The more general term *language disorder* seems preferable therefore, since it helps to focus attention on the entire syndrome and its causation rather than on a single symptom which happens to be predominant at a particular time.

These language disorders tend to appear in children who manifest certain types of personalities. Some present a pattern of shyness, timidity, immaturity and tension, which often conceals pent-up hostility and anxiety. Others present a picture of aggressiveness, bullying and predelinquency, in which their tension and anxiety are shown overtly in antisocial behavior (27).

It appears profitable, then, to study the home backgrounds of these children for clues as to why some develop language disorders and others do not.

INFANT SPEECH

Speech involves probably the most intricate motor coordination of which human beings are capable, and its symbolic nature is the distinctive feature which sets man apart from animals. It is a phenomenon which has its onset in most normal children (that is, among those who are not mentally defective or deaf) some time during the second year of life.

The speech mechanisms are first used in infancy for other biologically important functions, namely breathing and eating (35). Children do not begin to use real language until after several things have occurred in their physical and motor development. Respiration must first become well established and be under satisfactory control. Front teeth must also be acquired and form a front wall of the oral cavity so that dental and post-dental sounds can be uttered (26). Babies do relatively little articulate babbling until after they have had considerable exercise of tongue and jaw muscles in the mastication of solid food. Apparently the use of nasal sounds is associated with the child's assumption of the erect posture in sitting and standing. Speech, then, is the most refined and last acquired use of the complex organs involved, and it occurs in a total developing organism according to regular, but as yet relatively little understood, laws (26). It stands to reason, however, that the kind of nurture the child receives during this important formative period will have much to do with determining the facility with which he acquires speech. Emphasis must be placed not only on the nurture in physical terms, such as the kinds of food offered him and at what ages, and on the amount of time he is propped up in a sitting position, but also on the way in which these things are done. It these ministrations are given by a smiling, affectionate mother, or mother substitute, who has a genuinely good relationship with the child, he develops linguistically more normally than when the same physical care is given impersonally as a duty by a disinterested person.

Aldrich, Norval, Knop and Venegas (1) have shown that the more individualized nursing care babies get in a hospital nursery, the less crying they engage in. Naturally, the less they cry the more waking time there is available for spontaneous babbling. Irwin's amazingly painstaking technqiues (22, 23) have done much to unlock the mysteries of infant speech, and they show that many of the differences in language development which cruder techniques have revealed among older children, especially the differences between upper and lower socioeconomic classes, are present even in the first six months of life.

CHILDREN WITHOUT FAMILIES

Brodbeck and Irwin (6) have shown that babies who have been brought up in normal family environments vocalize more, and in a more advanced manner than babies reared in an institutional setting. Fisichelli (13), who also studied the speech of infants, found her institutionalized babies using fewer phonemes in their babbling and showing lower consonant-vowel ratios than the Brodbeck and Irwin subjects who were living in family situations.

Freud and Burlingham (14) in England, Roudinesco and Appell (32) in France, and Goldfarb (16) in New York have all shown that young children separated from their families and raised in institutions are seriously retarded in all aspects of their development. When they are given an improved regime with more "mothering" care from attendants, they improve in motor development, but their language development shows the least improvement and tends to show more or less permanent impairment. Buxbaum (7) states that "severely neglected children and those whose attachments to adults are interrupted and infrequent . . . are slow in learning to speak and may remain retarded in speech throughout their lives." These children she describes as "anxious, insecure, inhibited children who were punished for self expression or suffered the pangs of hunger, cold and loneliness."

Williams (41) and his associates at Iowa also showed retardation of orphanage children at the preschool level in vocabulary and in other aspects of language development. These institutionalized children may be thought of, then, as those who enjoy a minimum of individualized adult contact in early childhood.

AMOUNT OF CONTACT WITH MOTHER

At the opposite extreme, there are "only" children brought up in their own homes who experience the most intensive contact with the mother and other adults over the longest period of time. Davis' study (8) indicates that only children, particularly only girls, are the most accelerated in language development. Such children are seldom found among the clients of speech and reading clinics. Between these two extremes are single children with siblings who have the concentrated attention of their mothers in infancy, but who must share the mother's attention with brothers and sisters either from birth or from an early age. Such children are in between institutionalized and only children in their language development.

Another interesting group are the "multiple birth children," such as twins, triplets and the famous Dionne quintuplets (5, 8, 28). All of these groups who must always share the mother from earliest infancy show retardation in language development, and the degree of retardation seems to vary directly with the number of same-aged children involved. It would seem, then, that there is something of a gradient related to the intensity and duration of the mother's attention.

QUALITY OF MOTHER-CHILD RELATIONSHIP

The mother is normally the child's first language teacher in our culture, and it is she who furnishes the example for the baby to imitate (39). It is her voice that he echoes back in his babbling, and her smile and fondling which most often elicit his cooing and other prelinguistic utterances. Studies indicate that it is not merely this quantitative aspect of the mother-child relationship which is important, but that the quality of that relationship undoubtedly has a significant influence on the acquisition of language (36). The mother reflects her own personality in the kind of nurture she gives her baby (34). The very way she approaches motherhood, whether she welcomes or dreads the child's arrival, whether she feels adequate to care for him, or whether she is tense, worried and uncertain in everything she does for him, whether she is happy and talks to him as she goes about her tasks or pushes the baby carriage, whether she is silent and preoccupied while giving physical care or is impersonal and merely allows the child to vegetate most of the time are the kinds of things which are important in determining whether his language development will thrive, or be stunted, or distorted in some unfortunate way.

The smothering, overprotective attitude of mothers whose children lisp or cling to other forms of infantile speech is familiar to clinical psychologists and speech therapists. Such children are literally kept babies emotionally, and their speech is merely one reflection of what such overprotective mothers are doing to the developing personalities of their children (42). The dire effects of too-ready anticipation of the child's needs, and the failure to require him to speak and express these needs, as well as the bad effect of repeating the child's baby talk back to him instead of giving him the correct model to imitate are also well known. The emotional immaturity of parents who go in for that sort of child-caring practice is all too evident. Such children are best helped by assisting their parents to release them and to permit them to grow up emotionally, as was so well shown in the excellent study by Wood (42). The roots of such problems are usually found in the childhood experiences and parent-child relations of the previous generation.

It should also be remembered that the mothers of stutterers are usually overprotective, especially in regard to matters of health (10). They are tense, perfectionistic parents, however, whose overprotectiveness is often a disguise for real rejecting attitudes. Many stutterers, in spite of severe hostility toward their parents, are so ambivalent as to be unable to leave home even as adults.

Others who do succeed in breaking home ties, often experience real improvement in their speech problem as they take this step toward emotional maturity.

Another pattern of parent-child relationship, which is perhaps less well understood than that of overprotectiveness, is that of the parent who ignores, neglects, or overtly rejects the child. Some children who find themselves in such a hostile world develop a 'basic anxiety' so well described by Horney (20). These children may withdraw into mutism and perhaps eventually become schizoid personalities as described by Despert (11). Others attempt to retaliate against the hostile environment and become aggressive and hyperactive, indulging in excessive use of gestures and motor behavior with a minimum of language, which they often use only to express hostility and resentment either in content or manner of speech. Deprived of parental affection, these children never develop respect for parental authority, and carry over hostile attitudes towards teachers and other parent surrogates in the community. They do not develop wholesome friendships, and usually drift into patterns of delinquent behavior, as their limited facility in dealing with words and symbols renders them unable to socialize well or to profit by the highly verbal curriculum of the school (27).

It has long been known that homes of low socioeconomic status (25), bilingual homes and homes in rural areas, tend on the average to produce children whose linguistic development is considerably slower than that of children from upper socioeconomic levels, those in urban areas, and those from homes in which only one language is heard. Data are just beginning to emerge, however, as to the dynamics of the cultural patterns present in different kinds of homes which seem to be causally related to the linguistic development of children. For example, children in lower socio-economic levels ask fewer questions than those in upper socio-economic levels (25). Could it be that they receive fewer and less adequate answers?

Milner's interesting study (29) of the home life of children who as first graders were in the lowest third of their classes in language achievement scores, showed that these children did not have breakfast with their parents, and that they did not engage in two-way conversation with significant adults in their homes before or after school. They were likely to hear only a few commands or directives, were exposed to considerable corporal punishment, and had little opportunity to use language themselves. In contrast, the children scoring high in language achievement did engage in two-way conversation with important adults in their homes, they did eat meals with their parents regularly, had much more opportunity to use language meaningfully in the home, and their discipline was on the verbal rather than on the physical level.

Lafore (24), who studied parent-child relationships of preschool children in more favored homes, found that even well-intentioned parents who apparently loved their children very much, were often extremely ignorant and inept in the ways in which they handled their children. Although greatly concerned about their children's intellectual development, they made relatively few attempts to assist them in language growth. Parent-child contacts helpful to language growth were the least frequent of all the types studied.

Apparently, lower socioeconomic status itself is not causally related to poorer speech among children of the lower classes. It is likely that concomitant patterns of family life similar to those experienced by Milner's poor readers and which are more prevalent in lower socioeconomic groups are the more important influences. These kinds of human relations which provide few stimulating situations affording children opportunities for effective speech can and do occur at all socioeconomic levels but are most often found in less favored homes. In order for children to thrive linguistically, the home must foster the desire to acquire language skills, and parents must help children build meaning into words in their everyday life situations.

EXPERIENCES AFFORDED BY THE HOME

The fact that variety of experience is important in enlarging children's vocabularies has long been understood, and schools take many steps to broaden the young child's experience in order to add to his vocabulary. Homes, of course, differ tremendously in the variety of experiences they afford young children. They differ, not only in toys, gadgets and furnishings available, but also in the opportunity to travel, to go on vacations, to camp, to the seashore, and other places, where new things are to be seen, and new activities are engaged in. Such experiences extend the child's knowledge and his store of usable words. With the increasing mobility of the population, babies now live an appreciable percentage of the time in cars. Although they may not put down as deep roots as children of former generations did, they certainly have more varied experiences which are linguistically stimulating.

With the disappearance of domestic help, fewer and fewer babies are being cared for by ignorant and often illiterate nurses whose speech affords a poor model, and they are spending more hours with their parents than was true a generation ago. These factors in the changing social scene probably mean that there are fewer children coming to school with extremely limited experiences. Vacations are enjoyed by increasing numbers of families, and with the five-day week there is more leisure time for parents to spend with their children and to take them to zoos, museums, and other places which extend their experiences. The mere fact of the availability of these leisure hours, however, does not assure the child's optimum language growth. The important thing is how those hours are spent.

The vicarious experiences of television are now beginning to impinge on the present generation of children. It is certain, however, that larger and larger numbers of children are having their ears bombarded with language a larger percentage of the time than formerly, and they are enjoying excellent visual aids to the comprehension of that language, so that seldom nowadays is a child found whose experience is as seriously limited as that of many underprivileged children of a generation ago. The gap is being narrowed between favored and underprivileged homes economically and in many other respects, yet there are still many linguistically and emotionally underprivileged children at all socioeconomic levels. Their deprivations are more subtle and therefore harder to detect and to understand.

The mother who encourages her children's excessive use of television to keep them 'out of her way' is not merely depriving them of opportunities to practice language; she is depriving them of herself and is not giving them the real, vital interpersonal experiences such as story-telling, picnics, tea-parties, and the like, which constitute the very essence of family life. What the benefits and disadvantages of these many changes in our contemporary social scene will be, only time can tell.

NEIGHBORHOOD INFLUENCES

As the child gets older and has additional contacts outside the home, it becomes increasingly important for him to identify with his peers. Now, the neighborhood contacts become definite influences on the child's speech, and the geographical location of the home and its similarity to or difference from those in the environs will have a bearing on the child's speech. An interesting study by Anastasi and D'Angelo (2) on the language development of five-year-old Negro and white children showed that the Negro children were more retarded than the white children when both groups were isolated from each other. Negro children living in housing developments with, and associating in playgroups with white children, however, showed no language retardation. Possible selective factors, such as admission of superior Negro families to mixed housing developments, however, were not controlled.

Studies of the misarticulations of older children usually present a discouraging picture. Sayler (33), for example, found little improvement in the articulation of children from grades seven to twelve, and Spriesterbach and Curtis (38) report that older children are more consistent than younger children in their misarticulations. Perhaps findings of this sort can be accounted for in terms of the waning of home influences in adolescence. Hockett (19) observed the marked flexibility of the young child's phonemic system which he says develops by splits and contrasts until a reasonable facsimile of the adult phonemic system heard in the environment is attained. He found, however, a loss of flexibility by the age of puberty when the sounds of one's own speech sound "right" or "wrong," according to how closely they resemble those used by the peer group. This is the age, then, when parents with high speech standards and teachers experience unbeatable competition from the neighborhood associates. A few hours in the classroom, at home, or with a speech therapist can scarcely counteract the powerful influence of the many more hours spent with the gang as the adolescent strives for independence.

BILINGUALISM

The problems in language development and speech encountered by the child from a bilingual home are also familiar. All studies indicate that children who are exposed to two languages simultaneously in the preschool period show retardation in both languages, and that even the combination of the two vocabularies does not compensate for the lack of terms in a single language. In the past, the emphasis has been on the intellectual confusion of the bilingual child, but more recently his problem has been reconsidered in terms of emotional dynamics. It has already been pointed out that the language heard in infancy has deep emotional roots. These cannot be discarded easily as the child enters an environment in which another tongue is spoken, and deep emotional harm may be done to the bilingual child if he is forced to suppress all verbal expression associated with the parental culture. These early emotional associations by which children identify with their parents and their early environment are the basic reasons why foreign accents are often so difficult to overcome. If children are made to feel that the language of their parents is taboo, they may develop severe feelings of guilt about using the parental tongue, yet unconsciously and emotionally they cannot give it up completely (7).

Spoerl (37) has shown that bilingual college students are much more maladjusted than monolingual students, and the maladjustment was most evident in the area of intrafamily adjustment. Bilingual students showed extreme scores on tests of social values, some having accepted and identified with the parental culture and others having rejected it. Spoerl states that the major conflict for such cases is within the home. Lack of identification with the parent environment is often coupled with a rejection of the cultural backgound of the parents, and the parental speech becomes for the bilingual child a symbol of the parental culture. Most of the maladjustment, Spoerl considers, is environmentally determined and is not the result of mental conflict engendered by the complexities of thinking or speaking in two languages. In association tests she found that bilingual students, significantly more often than monolingual students, respond to the word *language* in terms descriptive of *the act of speech.* This she interprets as indicating that there is in his mental organization a residual effect of the emotional turmoil and mental effort which must have been present in the early days of his school career when English was not for him a facile medium of expression.

It appears then, that speech defectives, when studied carefully for home adjustment, family background, and personality factors, seem to show marked abnormalities in these areas as well (3, 9, 11, 15, 30, 31, 37, 42). Brief examples from several of the major language disorder categories may serve to clarify this point.

Delayed Speech

Beckey (4) compared fifty children with delayed speech with fifty who spoke at the normal age. She found that such children cried easily, tended to play alone, and did not want as much adult attention as the normal speakers. They suffered from many respiratory ailments, had young, nervous mothers, and came from family stock in which there were other speech defectives, left-handed individuals, and mental defectives.

Stutterers

Glasner (15), who studied fifty young stutterers two to five years of age, found that 54 percent had feeding problems, 27 percent were enuretic and 20 percent had exaggerated fears or nightmares. Moncur (31) compared forty-eight stuttering children five to eight years of age with a matched control group. It was found that every stuttering child exhibited several symptoms of maladjustment in addition to his speech problem. Significantly more of the mothers of the stutterers than of the control group employed harsh disciplinary measures, threats, shame, humiliation or corporal punishment. They admitted more inconsistency in discipline and more conflict with the father over discipline. They tended to be more indulgent and pampering, especially in regard to eating habits, and there were more illnesses, accidents, and unfortunate health conditions affecting the households of stutterers. Despert (10), in her study of fifty stuttering children, states "probably the most common finding is anxiety, primary, not secondary to the speech difficulty, which is reported by all investigators." She concludes, "pressure on the part of neurotic, often compulsive, mothers at critical periods of the speech development in somatically sensitized individuals is viewed as a catalyzing agent for speech and associated pathology." In another study Duncan (12), who studied the responses of stutterers to the Bell Adjustment Inventory, found that all the items which successfully differentiated stutterers from nonstutterers had to do with family relationships.

Poor Readers

Among nonreaders, Missildine (30) found that nearly all of his group harbored severe affective disturbances involving some member or members of their families. Twenty out of thirty came from homes where the mothers were overtly hostile or of a coercive, perfectionistic nature. Stewart (40) describes the parents of bright children who are poor readers as "more indulgent, overprotective and capricious than they are rejecting." Beck (3), who studied the nursery school records of fifth-grade poor readers, found that they had presented a variety of symptoms indicative of parent-child conflict even in the preschool period.

SUMMARY

In conclusion, it may be said that (1) language disorders are extremely complex and do not appear in isolation, (2) children presenting nonorganic language disorders often seem to have disturbed family relationships which render them emotionally insecure with various patterns of accompanying symptoms of maladjustment, (3) the home atmosphere as determined by the personalities of the parents seems to be the most important single factor influencing the child's acquisition of language, and (4) therapy directed toward the language symptoms seems to be most effective when it is preceded or accompanied by psychotherapy, either group or individual, for the child and for his parents.

REFERENCES

1. Aldrich, C. A., Norval, M., Knop, C., and Venegas, F.: The crying of newly born babies: IV. Follow-up after additional nursing care had been provided. *J Pediat, 28*:665-670, 1946.
2. Anastasi, A. and D'Angelo, R.: A comparison of Negro and white preschool children in language development and Goodenough Draw-A-Man IQ. *J Genet Psychol, 81*:147-165, 1952.
3. Beck, H. K.: Relationship of emotional factors in early childhood to subsequent growth and to achievement in reading. Ph.D. Dissertation, Univ. of Mich., 1950. (Microfilm)
4. Beckey, R. E.: A study of certain factors related to retardation of speech. *JSD, 7*:223-249, 1942.
5. Blatz, W. E., Fletcher, M. I. and Mason, M.: Early development in spoken language of the Dionne quintuplets. In Blatz, W. E., and others. *Collected Studies on the Dionne Quintuplets.* Toronto, Univ. of Toronto Studies in Child Development, Ser. No. 16, 1937.
6. Brodbeck, A. J. and Irwin, O. C.: The speech behavior of infants without families. *Child Develop, 17*:145-156, 1946.
7. Buxbaum, E.: The role of a second language in the formation of ego and superego. *Psychoanal Quart, 18*:279-289, 1949.
8. Davis, E. A.: *The Development of Linguistic Skill in Twins, Singletons with Siblings, and Only Children from Age Five to Ten Years.* Minneapolis, Univ. of Minn. Press, 1937.
9. De Hirsch, K.: Specific dyslexia or strephosymbolia. *Folia phoniatr, 4*:231-248, 1952.
10. Despert, J. L.: Psychosomatic study of fifty stuttering children. *Am J Orthopsychiat, 16*:100-113, 1946.
11. ———: Schizophrenia in children. *Psychiat Quart, 12*:366-371, 1938.
12. Duncan, M. H.: Home adjustment of stutterers versus non-stutterers. *JSHD, 14*:255-259, 1949.
13. Fisichelli, R. M.: A study of prelinguistic speech development of institutionalized infants. Ph.D. Dissertation, Fordham Univ., 1950.
14. Freud, A. and Burlingham, D. T.: *Infants without Families.* New York, Internat. Univ. Press, 1944.
15. Glasner, P. J.: Personality characteristics and emotional problems in stutterers under the age of five. *JSHD, 14*:135-138, 1949.
16. Goldfarb, W.: Effects of psychological deprivation in infancy and subsequent stimulation. *Am J Psychiat, 102*:18-33, 1945.
17. Goodenough, F. L.: Semantic choice and personality. *Science, 104*:451-456, 1946.

18. _____: The use of free association in the objective measurement of personality. In *Studies in Personality, Contributed in Honor of L. M. Terman.* New York, McGraw-Hill, 1942.

19. Hockett, C. F.: Age grading and linguistic change. *Language, 26*:449-457, 1950.

20. Horney, K.: *Neurosis and Human Growth.* New York, W. W. Norton, 1950.

21. Huyck, E. M.: The hereditary factors in speech. *JSD, 5*:295-304, 1940.

22. Irwin, O. C.: Infant speech. *Sci Am, 18*:22-24, 1949.

23. _____: Speech sound elements during the first years of life; a review of the literature. *JSD, 8*:109-121, 1943.

24. Lafore, G. G.: *Practices of Parents in Dealing with Preschool Children.* New York, Bur. of Publ., Teachers Coll., Columbia Univ., 1945.

25. McCarthy, D.: *The Language Development of the Preschool Child.* Minneapolis: Univ. of Minn. Press, 1930.

26. _____: Organismic interpretations of infant vocalizations. *Child Develop, 23*:273-280, 1952.

27. _____: Personality and learning. In *Amer Counc Educ Stud* (Ser. I), No. *35*:93-96, 1949.

28. _____: Some possible explanations of sex differences in language development and disorders. *J Psychol, 35*:155-160, 1953.

29. Milner, E.: A study of the relationships between reading readiness in grade one school children and patterns of parent-child interaction. *Child Develop, 22*:95-112, 1951.

30. Missildine, W. H.: The emotional background of thirty children with reading disabilities with emphasis on its coercive elements. *Nerv Child, 5*:263-272, 1946.

31. Moncur, J. P.: Environmental factors differentiating stuttering children from non-stuttering children. *Speech Monogr, 18*:312-325, 1951.

32. Roudinesco, J., and Appell, G.: Les repercussions de la stabulation hospitalière sur le développement psychomoteur des jeunes enfants. *Sem Hop Paris, 26*:2271-2273, 1950.

33. Sayler, H. K.: The effect of maturation upon defective articulation in grades seven through twelve. *JSHD, 14*:202-207, 1949.

34. Shirley, M. M.: The impact of the mother's personality of the young child. *Smith Coll Stud Soc Wk, 12*:15-64, 1941.

35. Shohara, H.: A contribution to the genesis of speech movements and the genesis of stuttering. *JSD, 7*:29-32, 1942.

36. Spitz, R. A.: Anaclitic depression: An inquiry into the genesis of psychiatric conditions in early childhood. In Freud, A. and others (Eds.): *The Psychoanalytic Study of the Child.* New York, Internat. Univ. Press, 1946.

37. Spoerl, D. T.: Bilinguality and emotional adjustment. *J Abnorm Soc Psychol, 38*:37-57, 1943.

38. Spriesterbach, D. C. and Curtis, J. F.: Misarticulation and discrimination of speech sounds. *Quart J Speech, 37*:483-491, 1951.

39. Stengel, E. A.: Clinical and psychological study of echo-reactions. *J Ment Sci, 93*:598-612, 1947.
40. Stewart, R. S.: Personality maladjustment and reading achievement. *Am J Orthopsychiat, 20*:410-417, 1950.
41. Williams, H. M.: Development of language and vocabulary in young children. *Univ. Iowa Stud. Child Welfare, 13*(2), 1937.
42. Wood, K. S.: Parental maladjustment and functional articulatory defects in children. *JSD, 11*:255-275, 1946.
43. Yedinack, J. G.: A study of linguistic functioning of children with articulation and reading disabilities. *J Genet Psychol, 74*:23-59, 1949.

Chapter 27

Parent Counseling by Speech Pathologists and Audiologists

ELIZABETH J. WEBSTER

IN the course of their clinical work, speech pathologists and audiologists must have frequent contacts with parents of children with communication disorders. These contacts are a vital part of the clinical role. How clinicians handle them makes a marked difference in the clinical contribution.

Clinicians refer to their work with parents by a variety of terms. For example, Rittenour (17) distinguishes guidance as the information-giving, recommendation-making functions which help parents define and cope with the facts of their children's problems, and counseling as the process of helping parents "explore and alleviate their sense of helplessness, anxiousness, and self-condemnation." Some clinicians (15) subsume the guidance and counseling functions under the term *therapy,* while others (4, 5) use *counseling* to refer to all the clinician's work with parents. In this paper *counseling* will be the general term used. Specific functions included under this heading will be outlined in some detail, since the functions a clinician serves are more basic than the label by which they are designated.

Contacts with parents vary in length. Clinicians may have only brief interviews with parents on a one-time basis, as in most diagnostic interviews. Or they may do long-term counseling; that is, they may have continuing, regularly scheduled meetings with

Note: Reprinted by permission of the author and the *Journal of Speech and Hearing Disorder, 31*:331-340, 1966.

Elizabeth J. Webster, Ph.D., is Associate Professor of Speech, University of Alabama, in the Children's Division of the Speech and Hearing Clinic.

individuals or with groups. Contacts with parents also vary in purpose. Clinicians serve such purposes as giving information, assisting parents in coping with issues which face them in light of this information, and helping them clarify their roles with their children. Because these contacts with parents are a vital part of the clinician's contribution, it is imperative that he be conscious both of the nature of his parent contacts and of his goals for each such contact.

The first purpose of this paper, then, is to outline a point of view regarding counseling with parents of children with communication disorders. Because a point of view emerges from the assumptions upon which it is based, some assumptions will be made explicit regarding (1) parents of children with communication disorders, (2) ways in which counseling can benefit these parents, (3) tools for promoting communication, and (4) the role of the clinician as parent counselor.

The second purpose of this discussion is to suggest ways in which speech pathologists and audiologists can implement this point of view in a continuing series of counseling sessions with groups of parents. A brief assessment will be made of some of the differences between counseling with one person and counseling with persons in a group situation.

PARENTS OF CHILDREN WITH COMMUNICATION DISORDERS

First it is assumed that whatever other problems these parents may have, they are caught in a vicious circle of breakdown in communication with their child. This assumption is based on the following premises: (1) Wherever there is a speech or hearing problem there is some degree of breakdown in communication. (2) This breakdown leads to difficulties in interpersonal relationships. (3) Difficulties in interpersonal relationships lead to further breakdown in communication.

The parent contributes to the child's problems and vice versa. This statement does not imply that parents are the cause of the child's difficulties with communication. There are numerous causative factors. As Wolpe.(21) states, "It is neither the parents nor the child who are responsible for the emergence of a problem . . . It is a two-way channel, and the parent is neither entitled to total credit nor to total blame for his child's behavior." In any case, whatever has caused the child's communication problem, it can be assumed that at the time clinicians see the child, that child and his parents are experiencing some degree of anxiety in their communication and thus in their relationships with each other.

Parents bring these difficulties with their child to visits with clinicians. When parents seek out speech pathologists and audiologists, they are aware that their child needs help. They may not be seeking help for themselves. Wolpe (21) postulates that, ". . . anxiety has been mobilized in the parents to the degree that they seek help with the objective of getting the child's behavior so changed that the parental anxiety can be dissipated." Clinicians must recognize that many parents who contact them do not assume at the outset that they need help for themselves.

Many of these parents experience a great deal of guilt. They wonder what has caused their child's problem, how they have contributed to it, what they have done wrong. For example, one mother said with some bewilderment. "I guess I must be treating her wrong – the doctor says so – so does my mother – but I swear I don't know what I've done differently with her than with the other children." Parents also seem afraid that whatever it is they have done to their child, they cannot keep from doing, and so they will continue to "cause the child's problem."

It seems obvious that if parents are laboring with such feeling as guilt, fear, and bewilderment, they must also have defenses against these feelings. Thus it is assumed that they will confront the clinician with some defensive behavior. They may show hostility rather than reveal their anxiety, or appear overly aggressive when they are almost paralyzed by fear.

These parents are trying to cope with their problems in the best ways that they know. However, they can be helped to deal more creatively and productively with those problems. But it must be remembered that parents, not clinicians, do the rearing of the child. Clinicians can serve a vital role in helping parents to clarify issues in their child rearing; they can work to support parents' efforts to do the best that they can do. But to the extent that clinicians openly or subtly demand to take the lead in directing the child rearing, they do in fact devalue the parents and attempt to usurp parental rights.

Finally, it is assumed that parents have in them a drive toward greater health. It is important to help them to recognize this drive and to permit them to realize their potential for growth. Parents with whom I have worked have had at least four basic motivations which they could be helped to utilize. These are termed basic motivations because they frequently are obscured by such forces as anxiety, guilt, and defensive behavior. The first basic motivation is the desire to do what is right for the child; the second, to understand and accept other human beings, including the child; the third, to communicate more effectively with the child; and the fourth, the desire for fulfillment for themselves as well as for their child.

The first three seem self-explanatory, but perhaps a word of explanation is needed about the last one. Parents often say such things as, "I live only for the children," "If my child gets better, that's all it will take to make me happy," or "My family is all that matters to me." Often mothers seem to lose themselves in their children. However, the writer's experience is that whatever parents may say, they want to be recognized as unique and worthwhile human beings apart from their roles as parent, housekeeper, breadwinner. They have needs for their own self-growth and satisfaction. One mother illustrated this when she said, "I like it in this group that we use first names. Mostly out places I'm only 'Bryan's mother' or 'Mrs. _____', and here I feel like just me." Another mother, who had questioned her rigidity in making her children, aged seven and twelve, take daily naps, revealed some of her unique needs when she said, "I guess I'm so rigid about the . . . naps because you see this is the only time during the day I can be all by myself . . . my husband is gone and it's different to be alone in your own house, and maybe I'm funny, but I like it . . . and it's different than when he's there at night after the children go to bed." When asked what it meant to her to have time alone she said, "I don't know that I can say . . . but like free of any worry . . . or to think your own thoughts . . . not to have to talk or answer questions . . . I don't know, it's just the only real freedom I feel all day." As this mother talked, it seemed apparent that the nap for the children was not as crucial as was the feeling of freedom for her. Parents have needs for themselves, to be themselves. They can be helped to recognize, understand, and utilize these needs to their greater satisfaction.

WAYS IN WHICH COUNSELING CAN BENEFIT PARENTS

Experience has shown that counseling can help parents modify the vicious circle of poor communication with their child and establish, or reestablish, better communication. There are three important ways that participation in counseling can provide assistance.

First, it can help parents to verbalize frankly about issues in their relationships and forces which motivate them, such as their own needs, goals, and fears. Perhaps this is the most important thing that counseling offers parents: it provides them with a situation in which the clinician is willing for them to be themselves, to disclose their own thoughts and feelings, and to speak of their needs, anxieties, fears, joys, and successes. As Beasley (3) stated, "to the extent that parents themselves are granted acceptance and respect they will be more free to give this to their child. . . Since the problems of a child in language and speech originate and exist in an interpersonal setting, modifications of this environment may be highly important if change in speech is to take place . . . the speech therapist's knowledge and understanding of the parents can do much to bring this about." It is only as parents become aware of their own feelings and of issues in their relationships that they can clarify them. Only as they clarify their part in the relationship can they deal more creatively with their child. Their own openness in communication with an understanding clinician can lead them to communicate more openly with their children. Thus they can participate in creating a different interpersonal setting for communication with the child.

Second, counseling can provide parents with important information. They need facts, simply and honestly presented, about their child's specific disorder. They can begin to clarify issues only when they have this knowledge. This information also can alleviate, at least temporarily, their anxiety and guilt. However, just having facts is not enough. Parents also need help in organizing and assessing what the information means to them.

The third way that participation in counseling can help parents is to provide opportunities for them to experiment with tools for promoting better communication. Clinicians can introduce tools in the counseling situation and encourage their use. However, the professional person's role is that of introduction and experimentation with tools; he cannot make others accept his ideas.

TOOLS FOR PROMOTING COMMUNICATION

It is obvious that every aid the child acquires, be it a hearing aid, pharyngeal flap surgery, or more adequate articulation, also assists the parents. There also are some less obvious tools which parents can acquire to assist them in their communication with their children. Much time should be spent with parents on these more subtle aids, among which are (1) attempting to understand the child's feelings and to verbalize this understanding to him, (2) trying to accept the child's feelings even when his behavior is unacceptable, (3) giving the child times with the parents when they can concentrate on communicating with him, (4) giving the child opportunities to communicate at times when he has a chance to feel success and satisfaction, and (5) attempting to communicate with the child on his level. Each of these tools will be discussed briefly here.

Understand What Child Feels and
Verbalize This Understanding

Routinely parents say they accept the idea that the verbalization of emotions is an important part of communication. Many, however, do not encourage the expression of emotions, or understand what they might do when the child expresses them. If parents are to communicate more fully with their child, they must acknowledge his emotional, nonrational side. They also must encourage him to verbalize about this. Further, when the parent attempts to put his understanding of what the child might be feeling into words for the child, he promotes better communication between them. In time this will help the child verbalize his feelings for himself. Parents can be helped to speak of their understanding simply and on the child's level. If the clinician is going to encourage the parent to try to verbalize what the child may be feeling, he must also help the parent to practice doing this in a simple and direct fashion.

Accept the Child's Feelings
Even When His Behavior is Unacceptable

It is difficult to differentiate between behavioral symptoms and the emotions experienced by the child; for example, a child may fight when he feels hurt, isolated, or afraid. Parents need help in understanding the implications of this principle. They need many chances to discuss ways that they can limit behavior while still accepting and feeling compassion for the emotions which lead to the behavior.

Give Child Times With Parents When They Can
Concentrate on Communication With Him

Often mothers think that they must devote every waking moment to their children; they cannot freely do this. Often, although they invest a great quantity of time with their children, they are distressed about the quality of the time. A mother expressed it as, "So much of what I say to him is 'don't', or 'you can't' . . . and I'm really not listening to him . . . and he knows my mind is on something else, he feels it . . . and that's bad for him and me both."

Parents can be encouraged to share with the child short periods of time which are the child's to use as he likes. Short times, freely given, can be more productive than longer times when the parent cannot really participate in the child's world. It is the quality rather than the quantity of time for communication between parent and child which makes a significant difference in the child's growth and development.

Give Child Opportunities to Communicate
When He Has a Chance to Feel Success and Satisfaction

Most parents can be helped quite easily to structure situations which are relatively free from pressure for the child in which he is free to communicate as he can. They can find much for which to give the child genuine praise. Perhaps a mother summed up this point when she reported, "His grandmother came this weekend, and Joe got quiet like always . . . Only this time I didn't nag him to talk to her like I always do . . . and the more I tell him to talk, the less he talks . . . So, while Joe was watching TV, Mama (the grandmother) asked him what was on, and he told her and told her. My, how he talked! When I told him I thought he talked good to grandma . . . and I really meant it . . . he just said, 'Oh, Mama', but he grinned all over like he really liked it." If children learn from the reinforcement of successful experiences, certainly parents can do much by structuring situations in which the child has a chance to feel that he communicated successfully.

Attempt to Communicate With Child on His Level

Wyatt (22) has pointed out that adults help children overcome their communication difficulties by using speech closer to that which the child is using. Often parents seem to think this means they must talk baby talk to their child. It does not. Parents can best understand the principle of corrective feedback by observing the clinician providing such feedback. Parents' observation of a clinician should be coupled with repeated opportunities to practice behaving in this way.

THE ATTITUDES AND ROLE OF THE COUNSELOR

The essential requisite for those who do counseling is positive regard and respect for the persons they counsel. The clinician must attempt to communicate his faith in the parents' ability to manage their lives productively and meaningfully. He must wholeheartedly attempt to provide a situation in which they feel free to recognize and disclose what is meaningful to them. He must permit them to express their feelings as well as their thoughts. Beasley (2) says, "The (clinician) should listen to what people are saying — really listen— and attempt to understand the emotional import of the topics parents choose to raise, the problems they describe, the observations they make about their child, and the relationships among family members on which they comment." The clinician's attitudes and verbalizations should encourage the parents' attempts to discover and clarify their ideas and feelings.

The clinician introduces tools that may be helpful to parents. He also takes the lead in attempting to maintain a laboratory situation in which parents may test the use of such tools. Another requisite for the speech pathologist or audiologist who serves as counselor, then, must be broad knowledge of the content of his field. He must be skilled in his clinical area — able to convey facts and to answer questions completely and accurately.

The clinician will make educated decisions about which of parents' questions to answer directly and which ones to help parents explore for themselves. It is no justice to a parent to let him struggle with a question which the clinician's training equips him to answer. For example, direct questions such as, "Is my child's speech development delayed?" deserve a direct answer. The skilled professional person will willingly share his knowledge. He will also give the parent opportunities to talk about what the information means to him. On the other hand, the clinician should know that there are many questions for which there is no one valid answer because they are largely matters of opinion or preference. These are the questions which parents should discuss in order to find their own solutions. For example, the clinician can ask the parent his ideas on such questions as, "What should I do when my child plays with matches?" or "What should I say to him when I can't understand what he's telling me?" Parents will have to do what they can in these matters anyhow, so it seems illogical for the clinician to impose his solutions on them.

The clinician must realize that changes takes place slowly. It can be neither forced nor hurried. Parents often verbalize insights long before they do anything about changing their behavior. For example, a mother suddenly realized, ". . . they say I should be more permissive, and maybe I should . . . (pause) . . . Y'know, I've just gotten the idea I'm too permissive — Why, I'm letting them walk all over me!" This insight did not lead to an immediate change in attitude or solution to the problem; however, it did seem an idea of potential importance to her. If the clinician's goals include helping parents to clarify issues for themselves, he must be patient with the process.

Finally, a word of caution about the content of counseling sessions seems in order. Because so much of parents' verbalization is problem centered, it is easy to think this is all they want to discuss. Such a problem centered approach overlooks important aspects of parents' worlds. They also have their joys, successes, humorous incidents, and prideful moments to relate. Parents need to be conscious also of the good that is in their lives. They can learn from this, too. If the clinician tries to remain parent centered, he will listen to what parents choose to talk about — the successes as well as the failures, the joys as well as the problems. He will be able to laugh with them even as he is able to view their suffering with compassion.

THE CLINICIAN'S ROLE IN GROUP COUNSELING

The group situation is similar to the two-person exchange in many ways. In both situations the clinician wants to respect individuals; he wants to understand not only what each person says but also what it means to him. In the multiperson situation this task is more complex because the counselor has to respond to more people. In both situations the clinician wants to introduce tools for their potential value to parents. The number of persons may make this more difficult, as some individuals wish to spend time on one fact while others are ready to move on.

An advantage of the group situation is that parents often help each other to clarify issues. They offer support to each other. In short, they can serve to provide more than one counselor.

On the other hand, parents may conflict with each other in the group situation. The clinician must decide how he is going to handle these conflicts. He has at least these options: (1) he can ignore negative feelings between persons and go on as if they were not operative, (2) he can make these feelings the only issues which are explored in the counseling time, or (3) he can recognize and verbalize his understanding of the conflicts, and yet not devote the whole of the counseling time to them. The third option seems most desirable. When there are serious communication problems between parents and children, the majority of the counseling time should be used for raising and clarifying these issues. Thus, the effective clinician must hold the attitudes and respect the tools of psychotherapy, but group parent counseling must provide for discussion of issues other than difficulties between group members. Parents need the psychotherapeutic benefits of group membership. However, they also should learn about their child's specific communication disorder. They need help in assimilating the information the clinician has to offer them. They need chances to discuss what their child's problem means to them. Therefore, the clinician must provide a structure which permits parents to disagree with each other, but he must provide also for discussion of important content which is unique to these people.

If parents are to learn from each other, there must be group interaction. The clinician leads in developing a group climate which fosters both verbal interaction and the trust necessary to disclose thoughts and feelings. The clinician cannot provide for group interaction by lecturing. Neither does he encourage it by remaining the dominant member of the group. He must be willing to relinquish some of his authority. The clinician sets the example for the group by honoring the contributions of each parent. He often returns questions to them for discussion rather than attempting to give all the answers. Skill in handling questions makes a vast difference in how quickly group members talk with each other rather than just with the clinician. The clinician notices and reinforces group members' support to each other and their attempts to understand and clarify the statements of another.

Care must be taken not to overlook parents who find it difficult to talk in a group. The more quiet people must be helped not to feel isolated. The clinician can honor the ways that they do participate; for example, he can note a person nodding in agreement, or frowning as if puzzled about a point, and ask him to verbalize his thoughts. If he wants to help the quiet people talk more, he must let them do it as they feel they can. He must guard against putting them under so much pressure that he further diminishes their ability to verbalize. It may be helpful to the clinician to remember that problem-solving can also begin in silence.

The clinician must remain part of the discussion group. If he refuses to engage in discussion, to share himself, and to give examples, he separates himself from the group and is less useful. In group counseling as in work with individuals, the clinician maintains a position which is not scolding or preaching, neither is it laissez-faire. Rather, he is an open, warm, accepting participant.

CONCLUSION

The question sometimes arises, "Can't the speech pathologist or audiologist do damage to parents by attempting to counsel with them?" The answer depends in part on how one defines counseling. If counseling means the imposition of prescriptions without care for the person for whom they are prescribed, one may indeed do damage. The nonaccepting, noncompassionate clinician runs the risk of hurting parents; so does the one who focuses concern on the child to the exclusion of concern for the parents. The speech pathologist or audiologist who leaves to others the interpretation of the information his field has to offer may do parents great harm. The same can be said for the clinician with limited knowledge who gives faulty information.

On the other hand, it is virtually impossible for one person to damage another by listening to him, by trying to understand what the world looks like to him, by permitting him to express what is in him, and by honestly giving him the information he needs. In this view of counseling, the clinician serves as an accepting listener. He delays his judgment of parents and tries to accept them as they are and as they will become. Further, the clinician uses the tools and knowledge of his profession as well as his clinical concern for parents. Whatever tools the clinician chooses to introduce, his goals should include helping parents increase their consciousness of their own attitudes, feelings, and behavior. As parents become more conscious of these factors, they can clarify issues in their communication with their children. Thus they can create a different interpersonal situation in which their children communicate.

Finally, for some parents clarification of issues leads to marked modifications of behavior; for others it does not. And the clinician cannot know with certainty which of these outcomes will prevail. If he demands sweeping or rapid changes, he will be doomed to frequent disappointment, just as he will be if he sees no improvement. These are sobering and humbling realities. At this stage of knowledge the clinician who counsels parents must have, or acquire, a tolerance for the ambiguous results of his counseling efforts.

Perhaps a prime requisite for the speech pathologist or audiologist counseling parents is respect for himself as a participant in a drama of which the final act has not been written but in which his role may make a vital difference.

SUMMARY

A point of view regarding parent counseling by speech pathologists and audiologists has been presented. Assumptions were made explicit about parents' problems, the benefits of counseling to them, and the role of the clinician who serves as counselor. Several ways to implement this point of view in long-term counseling with parents in groups have been suggested.

REFERENCES

1. Backus, Ollie: Group structure in speech therapy. In L. Travis (Ed.), *Handbook of Speech Pathology.* New York, Appleton, 1025-1063, 1957.
2. Baruch, D. W.: *New Ways in Discipline.* New York, McGraw-Hill, 1949.
3. Beasley, Jane: Relationship of parental attitudes to development of speech problems. *J. Speech Hearing Dis,* 21:317-321, 1956.
4. Bice, H. V.: Group counseling with mothers of the cerebral palsied. Chicago: Nat. Soc. Crippled Children and Adults, 1952.
5. Campanelle, T. C.: *Counseling Parents of Mentally Retarded Children.* Milwaukee, Bruce, 1965.
6. Chess, Stella, Thomas, A., and Birch, H. G.: *Your Child is a Person.* New York, Viking, 1965.
7. Frieden, Betty: *The Feminine Mystique.* New York, Norton, 1963.
8. Fromm, E.: *Man for Himself.* New York, Rinehart, 87-88, 1947.

9. Fromm, E.: *Escape from Freedom.* New York, Rinehart and Co., 1941.
10. Goldman, R., and Shames, G. H.: A study of goal-setting behavior of parents of stutterers and parents of non-stutterers. *J Speech Hearing Dis, 29*:192-194, 1964.
11. Goldman, R., and Shames, G. H.: Comparisons of the goals that parents of stutterers and parents of non-stutterers set for their children. *J Speech Hearing Dis, 29*:381-389, 1964.
12. Jersild, A. T.: *When Teachers Face Themselves.* New York, Teachers College, 1955.
13. Jourard, S.: *The Transparent Self.* Princeton, D. Van Nostrand, 1964.
14. Martin, E., Ward, Louise, and Johnson, T. E.: The self as a central concept in speech therapy. In D. Barbara (Ed.): *New Directions in Stuttering.* Springfield, Charles Thomas Publishers, 126-128, 1965.
15. Matis, E.: Psychotherapeutic tools for parents. *J Speech Hearing Dis, 26*:164-170, 1961.
16. McDonald, E. T.: *Understand Those Feelings.* Pittsburgh, Stanwyx House, 1962.
17. Rittenour, Marjorie: Counseling with parents of children with abnormal speech and language development. *J Med Assoc Ala, 34*:62-65, 1964.
18. Rogers, C. R.: *Client-Centered Therapy.* Boston, Houghton-Mifflin, 1951.
19. Rogers, C. R.: *On Becoming a Person.* Boston, Houghton-Mifflin, 1961.
20. Wicks, Frances G.: *The Inner World of Childhood.* New York, Appleton-Century-Crofts, 1927.
21. Wolpe, Zelda: Play Therapy, psychodrama, and parent counseling. In L. Travis (Ed.), *Handbook of Speech Pathology.* New York, Appleton, 1957, pp. 1015, 1016.
22. Wyatt, Gertrud: The Wellesley research project in the treatment of stuttering children and their parents. Presented at the ASHA Convention, 1962.

Chapter 28

An Open Letter to the Mother of a "Stuttering" Child

WENDELL JOHNSON

Dear Mrs. Smith;

I deeply appreciate your concern about the speech of Fred, your four-year-old boy. You say that he is healthy, alert, and generally normal by any standards you know about. But you feel that, in spite of all this, he stutters.

It will interest you to know that the great majority of four-year-old children regarded as stutterers by their parents fit that general description. I want to say to you what I should say to the mothers of the many thousands of other "Freds."

Toward the end of this letter I am going to make a few suggestions which I believe might prove helpful. If you are like other intelligent and conscientious mothers, however, you would like to understand clearly what is back of these recommendations before you try them out on your own child. For that reason, I shall introduce the suggestions by giving you certain information.

This information has been obtained in the course of several years of research. Certain studies made of very young children regarded by their parents as stutterers have been particularly revealing. In summarizing the main findings of this research, I shall try to emphasize those points which will help you most to understand the problem that you feel you have with Fred's speech.

Note: Reprinted with permission of the author. Copyright 1962.

First of all, I want to try to put you at ease by stressing that our research findings indicate that children and adults who are thought of by themselves and others as stutterers are not generally abnormal or inferior. Concerning this point, I should like to make as clear a statement as possible — and I make it on the basis of several hundred scientific studies, including a series of investigations involving some one thousand mothers and fathers and five hundred of their young children. Half of these children had been classified by their parents as stutterers andhalf as non-stutterers.

The statement I have to make is this. About seven out of every one thousand school children are classified as stutterers. I think any expert can be quite safely challenged to examine one thousand children who have not yet begun to speak and to pick out the seven among them who will be regarded as stutterers five to ten years later. In fact, I should be willing to let the expert examine the children after they had begun to speak but before any of them had come to be labeled as stutterers. I should not want him to talk with the parents, but he could examine the children as much as he liked in search of any physical abnormalities that he might suppose to be causes of stuttering. And if he were asked to pick out those who would later be thought of as stutterers, my best judgment is that he could do little better than make pure guesses.

Indeed, I doubt that any examiner could go into a room in which there are one thousand adult men and women and pick out the seven stutterers whom we shall include in the group. He may use any physical or psychological tests he prefers on each person, except that he may not hear him speak or obtain information about how he speaks or feels about his speech. I should be surprised if the examiner could make clearly better selections with his tests than he could by means of eenie-meenie-minie-moe.

So far as I know persons classified as stutterers are not significantly different as a group from persons regarded as nonstutterers, aside from their speech behavior and the way they feel about their speaking experiences. In fact, even the speech of most young children who are taken by their parents to be stutterers is essentially and for the most part not unusual — but it does become more or less unusual in most cases after their parents begin to think of them as stutterers.

This last point is particularly important. I mentioned above that we have made several studies involving some five hundred young children regarded by their parents either as stutterers or normal speakers. As the first findings came in we were frankly puzzled. We soon discovered that it was difficult in most cases, often impossible, to see any difference between the speech of children *newly classified* as stutterers and the speech of other children.

We decided to make a series of precise studies of the speech fluency of normal youngsters. Since this had never been done, nobody knew just how smoothly young children do talk. We found that two-, three-, and four-year-old children in a large nursery school spoke on the average with about 50 repetitions per 1,000 words. It was taken for granted by everyone that these children were normal speakers. They repeated suh suh sounds like that, or or or words, or two or two or more words. We found no child who never did this sort of thing and those who repeated the most did it more than 100 times per 1,000 words. These are norms — figures for fairly representative normal children.

Now, we were greatly puzzled by the fact that most of the youngsters whose parents believed they had begun to stutter appeared to be speaking as fluently as that — at the particular moment of the particular day *when their parents first thought of them as "stutterers,"* so far as this day or moment could be determined. After a great deal of research, we were forced to conclude that these children were in general like other children — and that even their speech itself was in most cases apparently like that of other children during the general period when they were first regarded as "stutterers."

This is not to say that they were talking perfectly. It is only to say that when we compared them with other youngsters of their age, and when we took account of the circumstances in which they were speaking, their speech behavior seemed "understandable or acceptable for their stage of development and under the circumstances." They were more disfluent — hesitant and repetitious — sometimes than other times, and this is true of children generally. To all appearances, most of the parents had applied the label "stuttering" to essentially the same types of speech behavior that other parents apparently take in stride and do not call "stuttering."

We were faced with the question of whether the name used by a child's parents in referring to him or to his manner of speaking could make any difference. Does not a rose by any other name smell just as sweet?

Our research findings suggested that, Shakespeare notwithstanding, a rose by certain kinds of other names does not smell the same at all. If you regard your child as a "stutterer" you are likely to get one kind of speech development, and if you evaluate him as a "normal" or "good" or "acceptable" speaker you will probably get another kind of speech behavior.

I can illustrate what I mean by telling you briefly about two cases. The first is that of Jimmy, who as a pupil in the grades was regarded as a superior speaker. He won a number of speaking contests and often served as chairman of small groups. Upon entering the ninth grade, he changed to another school. A "speech examiner" saw Jimmy twice during the one year he spent in that school. The first time she made a recording of his speech. The second time she played the record for him, and after listening to it, told him he was a "stutterer."

Now, if you can remember the first time you tried to speak into a speech recording machine you can understand what seems to have happened. In the studies referred to previously, all the children spoke with hesitations, repetitions, "uh-uh-uhs," and so on. It is easy to see how the apparently inexperienced examiner misjudged Jimmy who was, after all, a superior speaker as ninth graders go.

He took the supposedly "expert" judgment to heart, however. The examiner told him to speak slowly, to watch himself, to try to control his speech. Jimmy's parents were quite upset. They looked upon Jimmy's speech as one of his chief talents, and they set about with a will to help him, reminding him of any little slip or hesitation. Jimmy became as self-conscious as the legendary centipede who had been told "how" to walk. He soon developed tense, jerky, hesitant, apprehensive speech – the kind that a speech pathologist would call stuttering in the clinical sense of the word.

The second instance involved Gene, a three-year-old boy. His father became concerned one evening because now and then Gene repeated a sound or a word. (He had been doing this all along, of course, but his father had not noticed it before.) The father reported that Gene did not seem to know he was doing it and was not the least bit tense about. The next day the father remarked to the family doctor that Gene "was beginning to stutter." Taking the father's word for it, and evidently taking for granted that the father meant the same thing he did by the word "stutter," he told the father to have Gene take a deep breath before trying to speak. Within forty-eight hours Gene was practically speechless. The deep breath had become a frantic grasping from which Gene looked out with wide-eyed bewilderment.

These are real cases, and in their essential features — though not, of course, in specific detail — they seem to be representative. We were mystified as our investigations went on and such results as I have sketched kept coming in. Not only were practically all of the so-called stuttering children, at the time when someone first began to think of them as stutterers, speaking like other children who were not thought to be stuttering, but also we could find no evidence that they had suffered more injuries and diseases. Moreover, contrary to the traditional theory that stuttering usually begins as the result of serious illness, severe fright or shock, and the like, we found that just as an amazing proportion of traffic accidents occur on dry, straight highways, in daylight, in the country, in good automobiles, so in most cases *the problem* called "stuttering" develops in ordinary homes, under conditions that are not dramatic, in children who are apparently not unusual and who speak as well as other youngsters of their age.

The so-called stuttering youngsters were so puzzling just because they appeared to be so normal — until we decided to give up the assumption that they should necessarily be abnormal. Then the mystery began to lift. Slowly we saw more and more clearly what was staring us in the face. I suspect that it had been overlooked for so long — for centuries, in fact — just because it is so obvious.

What we had overlooked, and what we now noticed, was simply that in case after case stuttering, as a serious problem, developed *after it had been diagnosed.* The diagnosis of stuttering – that is, the decision made by someone that a child is beginning to stutter – is one of the causes of the stuttering problem and apparently one of the most potent causes.

Having labeled the child's hesitations and repetitions as "stuttering," the listener – somewhat more often the mother than the father – reacts to them as if they were all that the label implies. She seems to do this – to react to *the label* that she herself has decided to use – without realizing that she is doing it at all. By her very facial expression and tone of voice, as well as by what she tells the child, she tends (without meaning to certainly!) to convince him that he is not speaking "well enough" and that she disapproves of the way he speaks. She disapprove of it because she disapproves of the label she herself has given it. In her zeal to "control" what she now calls his "stuttering," she might, with the very best of intentions, even influence her child to feel that she no longer loves him, or at least that she is disappointed in him.

Her label "stuttering," you see, implies to her that her child needs help, and she, of course, is eager to help him because, like you, she loves her child deeply. She may show the child how to inhale and how to exhale, how to speak more slowly, how to breathe "with the abdomen" or "with the chest," how to place the tongue for certain sounds. She may urge him – perhaps with considerable urgency – to "relax" and "take it easy," or to stop and start over, or to "think out" what he intends to say before he tries to say it. Occasionally a parent might, shall we say, scold her child if he does not speak smoothly after all these "helpful" instructions. The major and unfortunate result of all this is that the child "catches" her own attitude of anxiety and disapproval of his speech when he does not speak smoothly.

As soon as he has acquired this attitude, he too begins to have feelings of uneasiness and disapproval. He begins to make ingenious attempts to speak according to the standard of fluency which his mother appears to favor. He tries hard. He does so want to do the thing properly – so his mother will smile again. Naturally, he exerts effort, he strains. Of course, he cannot strain without holding his lips together tightly, or holding the tongue against the roof of the mouth, or constricting the muscles of his throat. He cannot exert effort in certain ways without holding his breath.

By doing these things, he interferes with his speech even more. He feels that he is "stuttering" worse, therefore, and so he makes greater efforts to "keep from stuttering," and these greater efforts, in turn, are felt by him – and are regarded by his mother and father and other listeners – as "more severe stuttering." His mother, understandably, tries harder to "help." She urges her husband to pay more attention to "the stuttering" and "do something about it." Maybe she talks to her close friends about it, and they also try to be "helpful." Any child reacts to all this, if only slightly, and some children become quite tense and unsettled. In some cases the child finally reaches the point where he is straining much of the time and so speaks with what appears to be great difficulty.

This, then, is a general account of how *the problem* called "stuttering" usually begins and develops. I believe this sketch might help you to understand better the problem which *you and Fred* are experiencing. If other factors also are operating in your situation they are to be given due consideration.

In giving you this information, I have by no means intended to say that you have done something for which you are to be criticized. On the contrary, it is to be taken for granted that you have acted from the finest of motives – the love you feel for Fred. Fred knows this and you know it. You have done the best that you have known how to do. My sole purpose in writing as I do is to help you see how best to help Fred, which is what you want so very much to do.

If I have outlined then, in the main essentials at least, the problem with which you have to deal, I believe the following suggestions will prove helpful:

First, it is far from likely that Fred speaks the way he does because of any physical fault. You might, perhaps, have other reasons for taking Fred to see a physician. If he has any need for medical attention, it should be provided for him. Nothing should be done, however, to suggest to him that he is frail if he is not, that he is sick if he is well, or that he should get more rest and sleep than he actually needs.

Second, do nothing at any time, by word or deed or posture or facial expression, that would serve to call Fred's attention to *the interruptions* in his speech. Above all, do nothing that would make him regard them as abnormal or unacceptable. If he has begun to notice his own hesitatings, help him to feel that they are understandable under the circumstances and so, of course, acceptable. In doing this, however, do not make the mistake of "protesting too much." You can make Fred self-conscious about his speech even by praising it — if you praise it to excess. Err, if you must, on the side of approving it a bit more than is justified.

I am not suggesting that you "pay no attention to Fred's stuttering." You may often be given advice in these exact words. The people who give it to you have good intentions. Meanwhile, the wording of the advice is not quite right, in my judgment. Here is what I mean: If Fred repeats and hesitates (speaks disfluently) in the ways that are more or less ordinary for his age and for the sorts of situations in which he is talking, he is simply not doing anything that might usefully be called by such a grave-sounding name as "stuttering" in the first place. He is just speaking normally, and normal speech is more or less disfluent. If he is more hesitant in speech than most children are, and especially if he hesitates with strain or tension, look about him, and at yourself, and try to find out the reasons. Then do what you can to remove them. Do not "pay no attention" to the *unusual* reactions Fred is making to the *unusual* things in his surroundings that need to be changed.

Third, in order to see Fred and his speech in proper relation to the things and persons about him, and to develop a proper perspective in viewing Fred's hesitating and repeating, you should observe carefully the following:

1. The conditions under which he hesitates and repeats.
2. The times when he speaks smoothly and easily.
3. The ways in which he is, generally speaking, a "regular boy."

4. The times when other youngsters of his age also speak hesitantly and repetitiously more or less the way Fred does, especially when they are "excited," or "talking over their heads," or when frustrated and under other such conditions.
5. The times when Fred does not speak fluently but yet does not fail utterly or "go all to pieces" — rather, he repeats sounds or words or says "uh-uh-uh" more or less smoothly (or did before and at the time when you first began to wonder whether he might be a "stutterer").

Fourth, do not label or classify Fred as a "stutterer." If you do, you will have a very powerful tendency to treat him as if he were as abnormal and unfortunate as the label suggests, and this may affect badly the way he feels about himself and weaken his self-confidence. This is a great and needless risk. Instead of saying vaguely and ominously that he "stutters," say more clearly and calmly what you mean, that under certain conditions *(and describe these specific conditions)* he repeats sounds or words, says "uh-uh-uh" — or whatever it is he does *(and describe specifically what he does)*.

You are your own most affected listener, and when you tell yourself that Fred "is a stutterer," you do something to your feelings about him that you do not do when you tell yourself that he repeats words or says "uh-uh" in talking about a new family of squirrels he is excited about and does not know how to describe to you while you're busy trying to fix dinner — or to his father who is watching television or reading the newspaper and not paying much attention to what Fred is saying. It is pretty difficult for you, too, to talk smoothly about something you consider very important to someone who does not pay much attention to what you are saying. It is hard for you to do that without a certain amount of hemming and hawing and backing and filling even when you know very well what you want to say and when you know exactly the words you need to use. Much of the time Fred does not quite know what he is talking about, and he needs words he has never used before.

What you tell yourself about Fred is a matter of such profoundly fundamental importance that I could not possibly emphasize it too much. The way you classify Fred — and the names you give to what he does — will determine very largely the way you feel about him and react to him. This is as true of his speaking as it is of everything else about him. If we label a boy a thief, no good will come of it because it will become harder and harder for him to do anything honest or honorable in our eyes. If we frequently call a youngster "stupid," it will be very unlikely that we will ever see the intelligent ways he behaves. Just so, if we think of a child as a "stutterer," we will worry about him, keep our ears tuned for the bobbles and imperfections in his speech, and literally not hear what he does well when he speaks.

Fifth, you are already "tuned in" to the disfluencies in Fred's speech that you call "stuttering." Take a tip from the noted speech pathologist, Dr. Dean Williams, and "tune yourself in" to the disfluencies in Fred's speech that you would call "normal" or "normal under the circumstances for a child of Fred's age." The chances are that you will notice more and more "normal repetitions and hesitations" and fewer and fewer "stutterings" as time goes on — and Fred will sense the difference this will make in you and your feelings about him, and he will find it easier to talk to you with your new feelings.

Sixth, there are certain conditions under which practically any child tends to speak smoothly and other conditions under which he tends to speak hesitantly. You will find it wise, therefore, to observe the following simple rules:

First of all and above all, try to be the kind of listener your child likes to talk to. You know a great deal about how to be this kind of listener, but it may be that no one has ever helped you realize how tremendously important it is to Fred — and to you, and to the two of you together — that you be such a listener wherever he talks to you.

He should never have reason to doubt that you love him and that you enjoy hearing him talk.

Read to Fred whenever you can. In reading or speaking to him enunciate clearly, be interested in what you are reading, and avoid a tense, impatient, or loud voice. Enjoy this reading and make it fun and companionable. Do some of it every day, preferably just before bedtime, if possible.

Do not say, "No, you can't" or "Don't do that" when it really would not matter if he did go ahead and do what he wanted to. Try to keep "Stop that" and "Don't do that" remarks down to a fourth or less of all the things you say to Fred — and see what you do say to him then, most of the time. You will probably enjoy the time you spend with Fred much more if you do this.

Say, "That's fine!" to Fred much more often than, for example, "Do not be so careless and awkward!" Rewards are far better than punishments.

Avoid asking Fred to "speak pieces" for company or to "show off" in other ways.

Do not keep him in a state of excitement by too much teasing, nagging, bullying, or too much "running and jumping."

See that Fred's brothers and sisters are not always "bossing" him, or not always talking when he wants to talk.

In general, try to avoid situations that are needlessly or unduly frustrating, exciting, bewildering, tiring, humiliating, or frightening to Fred.

When you take Fred to strange places or ask him to do something that is new to him, prepare him for it by explaining ahead of time.

When he is "talking over his head" be patient, and now and then supply him with a new word which he has not yet learned but which he needs at the moment. To a reasonable extent and *in meaningful ways* help him to add to his vocabulary — preferably at those times when he needs words he has not yet learned in order to tell you things he has never tried to say before.

As for "discipline," so far as possible help Fred to discipline himself. Help him to understand how others feel and to be considerate of them. If Fred is to be loved, he must be lovable. Help him learn how to be.

My last suggestion may sound quite drastic, but I believe you might find it worthwhile: Try at all times when it seems practical to be as friendly and considerate toward Fred as you would be toward a house guest.

Unless the speech problem that *you and Fred are in together* is in some way exceptional, or has developed into a truly serious form, these suggestions should prove helpful. You will not, I am sure, expect more from the printed page than would be reasonable — and you will remember that Fred is only human. His speech — or yours or mine — will never be as fluent as a faucet. All children hesitate and repeat and stumble more or less in speaking — and so do all adults. Even the most silver-tongued orator makes an occasional bobble. But if within six months or so you feel, for any reason, that Fred is not talking as smoothly and easily as he should, I hope you will consult a speech clinician — preferably, of course, one who is certified by the American Speech and Hearing Association.*

Yours very sincerely,
WENDELL JOHNSON

*The American Speech and Hearing Association is the recognized professional organization of speech pathologists and audiologists in the United States. The address of the Association is 1001 Connecticut Avenue, N. W., Washington 6, D. C.

Chapter 29

Counseling Parents of Stuttering Children

ERIC K. SANDER

W̲HAT is the clinician's role in the prevention or early treatment of stuttering? He cannot with clear conscience reassure parents that their stuttering child will 'outgrow' the problem.* Or, if in his mind no problem exists (in the child), it will probably not suffice simply to tell parents that they have "nothing to worry about."

The task of counseling parents of children thought to be stutterers needs to be outlined more thoroughly than has been done. Schuell (25), in a short article, formulated a series of three structured interviews which could be used as a basis for working with parents of stuttering children. Additional thoughts are offered in an article by Brown (5) and in the texts of Van Riper (26), Johnson (19), and Berry and Eisenson (2).

When parents cooperate in a counseling program with insight and determination, the outlook for the young stutterer is most favorable. Johnson (15) observed forty-six stuttering children

Note: Reprinted by permission of the author and the *Journal of Speech and Hearing Disorders, 24*:262-271, 1959.

Eric K. Sander (M.A., University of Iowa, 1959) is a graduate clinical assistant, Cleveland Hearing and Speech Center, Western Reserve University. Grateful acknowledgment is made to Professor Wendell Johnson of the University of Iowa for his assistance with the preparation of this article and most particularly for the use of his file of recorded interviews with parents of stuttering children.

*In 1938 Bryngelson (6) hazarded the guess that 40 percent of stuttering children could be expected to overcome their difficulty without the help of a clinician. More recently, Glasner and Rosenthal (11) reported that of a group of 149 first-grade children who at one time were thought by their parents to have "stuttered," 81, or over one-half, had stopped stuttering without the benefit of professional assistance.

shortly after the onset of the difficulty. He reports, "At the close of the study (the median period of observation was two years, four months), speech was judged to have improved in 85 percent of the cases and to be 'normal or nearly normal' in 72 percent." Johnson attributes the improvement to be largely the result of parent counseling. In a study of sixty-nine stuttering children, Jameson (14) reports that "normal or near normal speech" was acquired by twenty of twenty-five children who were referred within one year of the onset of stuttering but by only "44 percent of those who first attended after more than one year had elapsed." Continuing, she states that "normal or near-normal speech was acquired by 82 percent of the children who attended for advice before five years of age and by 37 percent of those who began treatment over five years."

That the adult stutterer faces at best a laborious, imposingly difficult process of recovery emphasizes the necessity for prompt preventive measures. Two distinct reasons for early counseling are stated by Jameson (14):

1. The speech of a young child with a stammer is not fully stabilized. His hesitations are usually repetitive and seldom accompanied by anxiety; consequently, when environmental pressure on his speech is reduced, he is more likely than an older child to regain normal speech.

2. The mother of a younger child is, as a rule, willing to accept advice on his management at home. When, however, an older child who has been stammering for some time attends for treatment, not only is his stammering more firmly established, but if the mother has been in the habit of correcting it, she probably finds it difficult to change her attitude.

EXAMINING THE CHILD

In evaluating the fluency of a child's speech, his age should be considered. Davis's early study (9) established the general trend (with the exception of syllable repetitions alone) of a decrease in nonfluency with age. Observations by Metraux (23) from a study of the language development of 207 preschool children confirm and supplement the findings of Davis. Metraux found a marked decrease in repetitions among children after the age of four. Whereas repetition of words and phrases at twenty-four and thirty months is a compulsive sort of thing (the repetition may often be broken by introducing a new subject or object), at forty-two months repetitions are more likely to be related to other persons and social situations, demands for attention, information or encouragement. After the age of six most children do not differ greatly in fluency from adults.

Johnson (19) reports data on the average number of non-fluencies for forty-two young stutterers ages two to eight, matched with forty-two nonstutterers. The average child in the stuttering group prolonged or repeated parts of words approximately ten times more frequently than the average of the nonstuttering group. On the other hand, no significant differences existed between the two groups in the average amount of revision and interjection. The problem of establishing criteria for "stuttering" versus "normal nonfluency" in a general or basic sense is spelled out in a study by Johnson and his associates (17), in which the data referred to here and similar data from ninety-four additional subjects are reported.

The speech clinician should arrange, if possible, to record the child's speech so that the instances and types of nonfluencies can be closely studied. Careful observation is needed to determine the presence of avoidance reactions distinctly related to the child's speaking efforts: grimaces, hand movements, elbow shrugging, lip compression or preformation, eye blinking, disturbed breathing, and so on. Such observations are in order not so much to decide whether or not the child *is* a stutterer (the question is ill-phrased) but (1) to gain insight into the presence of any circular reactions by the child toward his own speech behavior and (2) to secure a clear perception of what the parents may be reacting to in the child's speech.

Brown (5) believes that the examiner "should be as informal as possible" and careful not to exert "too much pressure" on the child's speech. The beginning clinician is likely to evaluate the child's speech solely by conversing with him in a relaxed atmosphere. A more complete speech examination, however, might take into account the child's reactions to pressure, his performance under stress. By applying the same pressure devices used in desensitization therapy,* it may be possible to reproduce, as Berry and Eisenson (2) put it, "in token if not in complete form, the type of behavior in the child's home or school environment to which he reacts unfavorably."

The child's apprehension or sensitivity to his speech interruptions may determine whether he needs to be included in the therapy program. Much can be learned from the child himself if he is old enough to be interviewed. It might be interesting to ask him, "Why are you here with your mother?" or "Why did you come to see me?" The writer recalls one incident in which the child glibly answered, "Because I stutter. I don't talk right." The mother, who insisted that the child knew nothing of his difficulty, was openly nonplused.

COUNSELING PROCEDURE

As with the physician who is able to cure pneumonia while helpless with the common cold, our direct therapeutic methods have been aimed primarily at the older stutterer. It is easy to become absorbed with the dramatic symptomatology of the adult stutterer and blinded to more profitable avenues of early treatment. Only recently has adequate attention been focused upon problems associated with the onset and early treatment of stuttering.

When confronted with a young stutterer,† usually it will be necessary for the therapist to deal with the attitudes and behavior of the parents. Those aspects of parental behavior which adversely

---

*The method of desensitization therapy, as originally outlined in Van Riper's text, (26) aims to develop in the child a callous resistance to environmental fluency disruptors. The child is subjected to carefully controlled gradations of environmental pressure of the sort that may be precipitating his particular nonfluencies.

†The problem of definition is crucial at this point. According to Johnson (19), a child, before being classified as a stutterer, should show unmistakable anxiety-tension reactions in relation to his speech nonfluencies and be definitely regarded as a stutterer by his parents, teachers, or other responsible persons. It is, of course, obvious that if parents regard the child as a stutterer they have a definite need for counseling regardless of the actualities of the child's speech.

affect the child and influence his speech must be altered if he is to make a satisfactory adjustment. Lack of collaboration with parents of young stutterers is a shortcoming of many speech therapists. In the school situation, the family may not even be consulted. The young stutterer, however, cannot be disattached and adequately treated apart from his essential relationship with the parents.

A few words of general procedure seem in order before entering into a discussion of the counseling process. To begin with, the therapist must always determine whether the child's speech can rightly be considered disturbed. A careful examination of the child should not only precede the interviews but is an absolute necessity if we are to guide the direction of the counseling sessions. It would seem both futile and unrealistic, for example, to attempt to convince a parent that her child's nonfluencies are perfectly natural if he is already reacting to his speech, struggling or displaying a habitually excessive degree of tension. If the child's speech is within normal limits, treatment justifiably concerns itself entirely with the parents, their attitudes and speech evaluations.

Brown (5) recommends that the examination of the child's speech be done in the presence of the parents and then repeated alone. He continues, "The behavior of the parents during the child's nonfluencies should be observed, and the child's reactions to their behavior." The parents may later be asked, "Is this the sort of thing you're concerned about?" or "Does he do more of this at home?" Letting parents listen to a recording of their child's speech and asking them to indicate those moments when he is "stuttering" is often enlightening.

Parents are not likely to come to the speech.pathologist with any degree of insight. The novice or over-anxious therapist must constantly remind himself to "apply the brakes," so to speak, never exceeding the parent's capacity for learning or acceptance. When parents are lacking in insight, seeking help but unprepared to acknowledge their role, it will often be desirable to have the child brought to the clinic initially, regardless of his speech, and somehow occupied. In this way, parents, waking to an unpleasant situation, are less likely to break subsequent appointments.

The counseling relationship should be structured. Schuell (25) suggests a series of at least four interviews with several follow-up conferences at three- to six-month intervals. More conferences may be necessary depending upon the complexity of the problem.

In some cases parent-education groups may be organized, but the limitations of such an approach should be recognized at the outset. Through intimate contact and awareness of the individual problems of parents, more effective counseling is usually accomplished. Clark and Snyder (7) describe the advantages of an informal group therapy program for parents of preadolescent stutterers in which a permissive atmosphere prevails and the therapist does a minimum of interpretation. They report, "Each parent sees faults and shortcomings in the others, he feels less guilty about his own, and is therefore better able to admit them and cope with them."

The need for bringing the father into active participation in the counseling program is emphasized by Clark and Snyder. A similar observation is made by Glauber (12), who reports that "when the father did take a consistent and active interest in the stuttering child, the prognosis was invariably more favorable." Clark and Snyder (7), Glauber (12) and Despert (10) all paint a dominant mother and passive father picture as the typical accompaniment of stuttering. LaFollete (22) in this connection reports that the fathers of older stutterers when compared with a control group on the Allport Ascendance-Submission Test showed greater submissive tendencies. Yet the evidence does not warrant the generalizations of Clark and Snyder to the effect that stutterers lack well-defined masculine identification or that they are somehow the victims of a father-child disturbance.

EVALUATING THE PARENTS

Some speech therapists never get beyond the "don't-label-him-a-stutterer" type of counseling. Often, after a period of calm observation, the nonfluencies subside and are recognized as a passing phase toward maturity. But most frequently the need arises for doing more than imparting *do's* and *don't's* or passing out pamphlets. The case history is an important tool of the counselor for discovering and evaluating the significance of causal and precipitating factors related to the stuttering from which productive insight is gained and beneficial modifications can be made in the home environment.

Parents of stutterers are often critical and almost always overeager about the way their child is speaking. It is difficult to pass off these attitudes as mere products of the end result. Considerable information regarding the parents, the child and the home situation needs to be obtained. It is assumed that the reader enters this discussion with some information on the essentials and techniques of effective interviewing. Johnson, Darley and Spriestersbach (20) offer some particularly valuable suggestions for case history interviewing of parents of stuttering children.

Simply telling the parents early in the counseling program how stuttering often develops is not nearly as effective as having them trace back, if possible, the onset and development of the problem in their own child. They should be given an opportunity to reevaluate their thinking in concrete vivid terms related to the child's own history. When did they first focus attention on the child's speech? Just exactly what happened in the *beginning?* Under what conditions? How did it sound? Can the parents imitate it?

With older children the memories of parents are usually hazy. It may not pay to unearth the beginnings, to stir up unstirred guilt feelings. If the parents have not delayed in coming for advice, however, it is often possible to pinpoint the date of their first concern by associating other events with the onset. What parents observe in the beginning are usually simple, relatively effortless repetitions (8). They may insist that these repetitions are something the child had never done before, yet most probably he did (4). To be correct, then, the initial parental judgment of stuttering is probably coincident with the first attentive observations by the parent of the child's early nonfluencies. We might ask: Why were the parents so attentive? Did they have any reason to be concerned about the child? Was he ill? Did he have an accident? Are the parents inclined to worry generally about their children? Is there stuttering in the family background?

Whatever it was that the child did in the beginning, what did the parents do about it? How did they react to it? Darley (8) found that in forty-eight of fifty families, suggestions calculated to help the child "overcome his stuttering" was made by one parent or both. The accounts of how parents react, their ways of thinking, are often interesting. They may have the vague notion that what they first noticed and called stuttering continued to occur, that the child constantly "stuttered" from that point on.

What do parents believe is causing their child to stutter? In many cases this will not tell us a great deal about the child, but it will help us to evaluate and understand the parents and the way they have approached their child's problem. Parents are likely to externalize their problems, project their own anxieties to the child. Darley (8) reports, "Only 16 of 100 parents attached importance to the parental role (not necessarily their own) in the development of the child's stuttering, and not even all of those 16 parents considered that role to be necessarily the primary causal factor."

So blinded may parents be by a tenacious belief that their child's speech is somehow disordered that they are often unable even to describe what it is he is doing. Their expressed feelings are but verbal blindfolds; they tell us little about the child. "He stutters." "He has difficulty." "He starts with the first word wrong." "He has good days and bad days." It is generally a nondescriptive, evaluative language that parents use. They seem to have a particular need to become conscious of the distinction between "fact" and inference, between description and evaluation.

An understanding of the parents would be incomplete without some idea of their standards of fluency. Bloodstein, Jaeger, and Tureen (3) report that parents of young stutterers are more inclined to react to nonfluencies as stuttering than are parents of nonstutterers. What concepts do the parents have of normal speech? How do they want Johnnie to talk? How would Johnnie have to be talking before the parents could consider his speech as normal? Such information is not for the counselor's benefit alone; the point cannot be overstressed that these parents need to discover themselves, become aware of their excessively high standards of fluency, and revise them accordingly.

COUNSELING PROGRAM

By now we have given up the search for an unidimensional

answer to that all too familiar question, "What causes stuttering?" We need not fret over subtle dilemmas which have little practical consequence. Whether the child is, as Van Riper (26) suggests, being driven to "the acquisition of adult forms of speech at too early an age," or, as Johnson (19) expresses it, influenced by parents who "have persuaded themselves that the child's speech is disordered," is not of life or death importance. In either instance, parents must recognize the essential normality of early nonfluent speech, stop direct attempts at correction, eliminate or reduce apparent fluency disruptors, and give the child a position of love and security in the home. Even the psychoanalysts (12) share some common ground as far as treatment is concerned when they attribute stuttering to the maternal relationship and recognize that parents themselves must undergo treatment.

The general objectives of the counseling program thus seem clear. Following the framework suggested by Johnson (19), we might reduce our purposes to two basic aims:

1. Parents should be supplied with the information they need in order to appreciate the nature of normal childhood speech. They are helped by knowing the essential facts about normal speech development, especially as far as fluency is concerned. They are helped, too, by knowing about the more important conditions under which children — and adults for that matter — are more and less fluent in speech.

2. Parents should be led, so far as possible, to recognize their own insecurities, their excessive psychological need to have their child speak extremely well and perhaps to excel in other ways too, and, in general, their specific discontents and the reasons for them.

The order in which these two goals have been presented is important. An effective approach involves a *positive* stress, a realistic appraisal of the child's assets. Feelings and behavior deeply rooted in past beliefs are not easily modified. An accusing finger should never be pointed at the past mistakes of parents. It is far better to change the attitudes of parents through a consideration of what Johnnie is doing right, not what they have done wrong. "They need to be encouraged to accept their child as he is, and to rejoice in his growth and the possibilities of his future," as

Johnson (16) has put it.

In order to appreciate fully the part they play in the development or prevention of stuttering, parents must first recognize the essential normality of early speech hesitations. A twofold problem exists: (1) What sort of information should parents be given? (2) How should this information be presented? Much information relating to stuttering and nonfluent speech behavior is available in texts and research articles (4, 9, 17, 18, 19, 23). Most parents are in want of such information and can usually benefit from it, provided the therapist is sufficiently sensitive to their needs and feelings and has established a warm and open relationship with them. The ingenious therapist must present the necessary information in such a manner that it will be accepted and acted upon by parents.

Nearly two decades ago Carl Rogers (24) wrote a few wise words on the limitations of a strict educational approach in dealing with the feelings or emotions of parents:

> To the beginner in clinical work, education of the parent would seem the answer to a great many of the problems which children present . . . . There would seem to be only one real risk to be considered in the use of such techniques. If a parent is given information which runs strongly counter to his own emotionally determined attitudes he will not only reject the information but may reject the worker as well. To this extent a direct educational approach may block further therapeutic effort, and this must be borne in mind in deciding upon treatment.

The futility of imparting on an intellectual level advice which the parents are not emotionally prepared to accept must be recognized. At no time should the parents be cornered or made to feel guilty because of something they have done. Unless diplomacy is used, the parent, once put on the defensive, will immediately be alienated. As Kanner (21) says, "a mother may be thrown into a state of guilty anxiety without comprehending the basic origin of her panic. Nothing is gained even if she expresses verbal agreement. True and helpful insight can come only from within." Our task is to get the parents implicated but not deeply disturbed, informed but not guilt ridden.

The interview following the case history is usually devoted to a discussion outlining the development of speech, the normality of repetitions and perhaps a few beginning words concerning our present knowledge of how stuttering develops. Some questions might first be addressed to the parents. "How many times do you think the average child at the age of two or three repeats (every hundred or every thousand words)?" "Do you think normal children repeat at all?" After the therapist has secured an idea of what the parents think, they should be told basic information about early speech development. The following transcript, from an interview by Wendell Johnson, may be suggestive:

> There's been a lot of research done on your children and the way they talk and how speech develops. In children between the ages of two and five years, they *all* repeat. Repetition, in fact, begins with the birth cry. The birth cry is repeated over and over again. It has to be. During the first year, depending upon how you define a repetition and allowing for variations, it's pretty accurate to say that about half of all the infant's vocalizations are repetitions. A child doesn't say 'da.' He says 'da-da-da-da.' This is normal. This is utterly normal. This is essential. Without this you would have abnormality.
>
> Now there is no given Tuesday when the child stops it. He does this all his life. Between the ages of two and five years when children are learning to talk in words and sentences they all repeat – sounds, words, phrases. The average child at that age repeats a *s-s-sound* like that or or words like that *or-two or-two or-two* or more words like that. He does this – up to 100 times per 1000 words is within the norm, a little over 100. They all do it. The mean is from 35 to 50 depending on the type of testing situation. Now that's quite a bit, you see.

Berry and Eisenson (2) use a somewhat different approach:

> We ask parents to think about and tell us in what activities aside from speaking the child is likely to be repetitious. Parents, through such a procedure are likely to become consciously impressed that their child, in common with most normal children, can beat a drum *ad nauseam,* can ride a tricycle *around and around and around,* can listen to the same records *over and over and over* again, and can enjoy listening to the same story told or read to them without alteration of word or syllable, time after time and day after day. Parents must be helped to realize the normality of repetition – that its presence in speech is not in and of itself to be evaluated as an abnormal phenomenon.

Often a mother will be found who hesitates a good deal more while speaking than does her child. In such cases, assuming the mother considers herself a nonstutterer, it may be particularly helpful, as Berry and Eisenson (2) phrase it, 'to have them turn a mirror and reflect on their own speech.'

HOME SITUATION

Too much hurrying, stimulation and excitement is disrupting for the child and should be avoided whenever possible. Parents should eliminate family quarrels and conflicts in the presence of the child which contribute to an emotionally charged home environment; they need not, however, and should not, shelter the child in an overprotective fashion from all "undesirable" influences. Gottlober (13) gives this exposition of how over-protection may follow the diagnosis of stuttering:

> It is quite common to have a parent report that the patient's blocking becomes more frequent when he suffers a disappointment or is punished. When things go smoothly days pass without a sign of hesitancy. The cause and effect become obvious and gradually the entire family is cudgeled into doing the little despot's bidding. No one wants to be responsible for making him 'stutter.'
>
> If an effort is made to understand and treat a child properly from the beginning, this type of behavior need never develop. By bending over backward later and giving him many times the original attention and sympathy he should have got originally, he is only being encouraged in his maladjustment.

Everyone enjoys being listened to. Parents can help a young stutterer by displaying an interest in his message rather than by registering pity for his difficulty. Speech situations will be less frustrating for the child if parents will refrain from interrupting him before he finishes his thoughts. Of course, if the child, lacking words, finds himself groping for a noun, parents may aid him in building a vocabulary.

Counseling implies more than prohibitions. It is necessary to bring about certain positive, constructive changes in the child's environment. Parents should plan to spend more time together with their child. Schuell (25) suggests some activities that might be initiated during the counseling program.

Beasley (1) comments:

> While one or the other parent may be with the children almost

constantly, the time spent together more frequently involves a doing *for* them rather than a doing *with* them . . . Often parents can see their way clear to working with the child on a task a teacher may have suggested, or they may spend long hours transporting the child for weekly lessons to a distant center, but they fail to realize the value of a similar amount of time spent with the child for enjoyment and relaxation.

By attracting the child's interest in some useful activity within his realm of achievement, parents can help him experience emotionally satisfying accomplishments. Success breeds self-confidence. Everything should be done at home to give the child successful speaking experiences. The talking he does should be both enjoyable and rewarding. In those situations when the child speaks with relative ease he should be encouraged to talk; when he appears to be unusually nonfluent, it is best not to stimulate him further, although he should never be discouraged.

The constructive aid of parents should be enlisted to discover conditions which exist in the home. Van Riper (26) has set forth a list of six everyday situations conducive to nonfluency. It might be useful to mimeograph information of this sort to aid parents in carrying out situational analysis assignments. An effective assignment consists of having parents observe for a week the situations in which their child appears overly hestitant; also, those situations in which he speaks quite fluently. These assignments serve a twofold function: (1) Probably most important, they help parents to separate fact from inference through careful observation. Parents, like all human beings, tend to respond to their own anxiety states. In a sense they are too observant; in another sense, not careful enough in their observations. (2) These assignments aid in the elimination of environmental pressures which disrupt the fluency of the child's speech. By recording these circumstances in detail, detrimental influences can be established and eliminated. Parents will do things differently as they come to recognize and correct their past mistakes.

Caution must always be exercised before upsetting the family situation. The fundamental task is to alter the parental conviction that a child is grossly peculiar if he displays some speech hesitations. The therapist cannot hope to eliminate all of the child's nonfluencies. But the parents can learn to reduce their criterion of what is normal.

Brown (5) suggests that parents cultivate an objective attitude by observing the repetitions in the speech of normal children outside the family. It might be wise to have them actually tabulate the number of interruptions in their child's speech and in the speech of other children. Perhaps the therapist might arrange a visit with the parents to a preschool nursery. To have the concerned parents of a hesitant, yet normal-speaking child observe a severe stutterer with pronounced anxiety-tension reactions would further impress upon them how stuttering in the apprehensive adult differs from the simple and relatively unconscious repetitions of all children.

Telling parents to avoid showing concern for the child's speech is not enough. As Johnson (19) says, "They must not be concerned." And this requires a basic reevaluation of their attitudes. Quite often parents will insist that they have done nothing to show their concern for the child. But a beginning swimming student, concerned lest he drown, is not likely to float; so too, an anxious mother, deeply disturbed by her child's speech, will find it difficult, if not impossible, to keep a poker face. It should be explained to parents how their evaluations have a self-reflexive effect both upon themselves and upon the child.

It is a good idea to avail parents of literature on stuttering and general semantics to the extent that they can grasp and comprehend the information. Literature, well chosen, is a great help to the intelligent parent and will make subsequent interviews more meaningful by providing an effective basis for communication. Books and pamphlets should not be given out indiscriminately, however, without a consideration of aims and a prior review of their content with the parents.

SUMMARY

Some suggestions, based in large part upon the research and counseling interviews of Professor Wendell Johnson, were outlined for counseling parents of children thought to be stutterers. Central to this discussion has been the suggestion that parents learn to describe the behavior of their children, particularly with respect to speech, apart from their own evaluative reactions. The speech clinician must impart to parents essential information on stuttering and early speech development. In order to make speech a pleasant and rewarding activity for the child, undesirable influences in the environment must be modified and positive changes introduced.

REFERENCES

1. Beasley, J.: *Slow to Talk.* New York, Teachers College, Columbia Univ., 1956.
2. Berry, M. F., and Eisenson, J.: *Speech Disorders: Principles and Practices of Therapy.* New York, Appleton-Century-Crofts, 1956.
3. Bloodstein, O., Jaeger, W., and Tureen, J.: A study of the diagnosis of stuttering by parents of stutterers and nonstutterers. *J Speech Hearing Dis, 17*:308-315, 1952.
4. Branscom, M., Hughes, J., and Oxtoby, E.: Studies of nonfluency in the speech of preschool children. In W. Johnson (Ed.): *Stuttering in Children and Adults.* Minneapolis, Univ. Minnesota Press, 1955.
5. Brown, S. F.: Advising parents of early stutterers. *Pediatrics,* 170-175, 1949.
6. Bryngelson, B.: Prognosis of stuttering. *J Speech Dis, 3*:121-123, 1938.
7. Clark, R. M., and Snyder, M.: Group therapy for parents of pre-adolescent stutterers. *Group Psychol, 8*:226-232, 1955.
8. Darley, F. L.: The relationship of parental attitudes and adjustments to the development of stuttering. In W. Johnson (Ed.): *Stuttering in Children and Adults.* Minneapolis, Univ. Minnesota press, 1955.
9. Davis, D. M.: The relation of repetitions in the speech of young children to certain measures of language maturity and situational factors. *J Speech Hearing Dis, 4*:303-318, 1939; *5*:235-246, 1940.
10. Despert, J. L.: Psychosomatic study of 50 stuttering children. *Amer J Orthopsychiat, 16*:100-113, 1946.
11. Glasner, P. J., and Rosenthal, D: Parental diagnosis of stuttering in young children. *J Speech Hearing Dis, 22*:288-295, 1957.
12. Glauber, I. P.: Dynamic therapy for the stutterer. In G. Bychowski and J. L. Despert (Eds.): *Specialized Techniques in Psychotherapy.* New York, Basic Books, 1952.
13. Gottlober, A. B.: *Understanding Stuttering.* New York, Grune and Stratton, 1953.
14. Jameson, A. M.: Stammering in children — some factors in the prognosis. *Speech, 19*:60-68, 1955.
15. Johnson, W.: A study of the onset and development of stuttering. In W. Johnson (Ed.): *Stuttering in Children and Adults.* Minneapolis, Univ. Minnesota Press, 1955.

16. Johnson, W. (as told to Jerome Ellison): I was a despairing stutterer. *Sat Eve Post,* January 5:26-27, 72, 74, 1957.
17. Johnson, W., et al.: *The Onset of Stuttering.* Minneapolis, Univ. Minnesota Press, 1959.
18. Johnson, W.: *Toward Understanding Stuttering.* Chicago, National Society for Crippled Children and Adults, 1959.
19. Johnson, W., Brown, S. F., Curtis, J. F., Edney, C. W., and Keaster, J.: *Speech Handicapped School Children* (2nd ed.). New York, Harper and Brothers, 1956.
20. Johnson, W., Darley, F. L., and Spriestersbach, D. C.: *Diagnostic Manual in Speech Correction.* New York, Harper and Brothers, 1952.
21. Kanner, L.: *Child Psychiatry.* Springfield, Charles C Thomas, 1948.
22. LaFollete, A. C.: Parental environment of stuttering children. *J Speech Hearing Dis, 21:*202-207, 1956.
23. Metraux, R. W.: Speech profiles of the preschool child 18 to 54 months, *J Speech Hearing Dis, 15:*37-53, 1950.
24. Rogers, C. R.: *The Clinical Treatment of the Problem Child.* Boston, Houghton-Mifflin Co., 1939.
25. Schuell, H.: Working with parents of stuttering children. *J Speech Hearing Dis, 14:*251-254, 1949.
26. Van Riper, C.: *Speech Correction: Principles and Methods* (3rd ed.). New York, Prentice-Hall, 1954.

Chapter 30

Group Therapy for Parents of Preadolescent Stutterers

RUTH M. CLARK and MURRY SNYDER

F ATHERS are parents too. This, of course, is no revelation. Yet in the past we have tended to overlook the implications of this obvious fact. Since the mother is more closely and frequently in contact with the child, it has been assumed that on her shoulders rests major blame for an adjustment difficulties he may have, and in recent years there has been a plethora of articles, lectures, and books on the evil of that mother-dominated relationship once so aptly termed "momism." In keeping with this trend, parent counseling has often meant mother counseling almost exclusively.

We at the National Hospital for Speech Disorders have been no exception in following this practice. For a number of years, we have had a parent counseling service for mothers of our younger stutterers but have brought fathers into the treatment situation only in individual cases. However, as we have become increasingly impressed with certain clinical observations of stutterers, we have begun to reevaluate the role of the male parent and to bring him more actively into treatment. This we have done primarily through the medium of group-therapy sessions.

The one clinical observation that has particularly impressed us is

Note: Reprinted by permission of the authors and *Group Psychotherapy,* 8:226-231, 1955, J. L. Moreno, M.D., Editor, Beacon House Inc. Publisher.

The authors are associated with the National Hospital for Speech Disorders, New York, New York.

Read at the Annual Meeting of The American Society of Group Psychotherapy and Psychodrama, May 7, 1955.

the fact that a disproportionately large percentage of male stutterers show a lack of well-defined masculine identification and that almost all display inordinate fear of authority figures, pointing to some basic disturbance in the father-child relationship. Too, the adult stutterer, in retrospect, typically expresses more hostility toward the father figure than toward the mother, and as treatment progresses, he often brings to light material which indicates that there has been a realistic basis for this hostility. That there is a basis for it is further suggested by material elicited in our group-therapy sessions for parents.

The sessions — usually confined to ten or twelve parents — are held in the evenings, and parents are urged, but not required, to attend. The absence of dictatorial policy is this respect imposes decisions on the parents which are highly revealing of basic attitudes toward the child. More mothers than fathers attend, often reflecting the father's indifference to the child's problem or his unwillingness to accept responsibility for helping the child to resolve it. The parents, both fathers and mothers, of some children are consistently absent, and these are typically parents who are most rejecting or, in a few instances, who are themselves so seriously disturbed that they dare not face the danger of mutual criticism or run the risk of self-discovery. These parents, of course, are seen individually, to the extent that this is possible, but often the same factors which prevent them from coming to the group sessions militate against the effectiveness of even individual counseling.

The central activity of the group-therapy session is informal discussion. Sometimes a parent brings to the group a problem which has implications for everyone present. Sometimes the therapist propounds a question — for example, "What is there about your child which disturbs you?" Beyond this, the therapist enters very little into the discussion, except to draw into it the more retiring members of the group and prevent others from completely dominating it or using it to air their views and problems exclusively. The therapist does a minimum of inter- pretation, the group itself largely taking over that function. For example, in one session, a father admitted that he was extremely critical of his son, attributing this to the fact that he himself was a perfectionist. His wife and other members of the group pointed out that what he termed perfectionism was in reality intolerance. The therapist did not attempt to suggest directly that the intolerance, in turn, had deeper implications. However, by interposing a question intended to make evident the father's more accepting attitude toward another child in the family, he brought into focus the significance of his intolerance toward the son who stuttered.

The most consistent parental attitudes revealed in these sessions have been rejection and domination, the two often being synonymous. These may be expressed directly, but more often are demonstrated in undue criticism or overprotection of the child, or in setting too high standards for him, imposing the parental will on him, or taking excessive disciplinary action against him. Whatever the form parental rejection or domination takes, there is undue repression of the child's drive for self expression and undue pressure on him to meet the parents' needs or to conform to their conception of what he ought to be. As one parent stated in a group-therapy session: "We have certain set rules. When the child goes against our wishes, we get upset. Many times, even though we know we are wrong, we get so angry that we won't give in, particularly when they don't want to listen to us."

A series of comments made in another therapy group illustrate this basically rejecting or dominating attitude so often noted in the parents of children who stutter. Discussing some of the characteristics of their children which they found disturbing, the parents stated:

Mrs. P.: "My boy is so slow in everything he does that I get impatient. His father can't tolerate anything he does either because he's a fast type of man."

Mr. S.: "The only objection I have to my son is that he isn't a normal speaker."

Mrs. C.: "My daughter is very set-minded; you can't tell her anything."

Mr. M.: "My boy is so childish in his attitudes. I'll give you an example. The other day he accidentally stepped on something that belongs to his little sister. His sister, as a natural reaction, hit him. He didn't actually hit her back, because he is bigger than she is, but the tendency was there. And he wouldn't apologize. If we do make him say he is sorry, he doesn't mean it."

Mrs. S.: "Paul is sloppy. His table manners are terrible. He won't use his fork when he should, and he won't use his knife right."

Mrs. P.: "I guess that we all more or less feel the same way. The children just won't listen to us. They won't see it our way."

As a corollary to the parents' rejecting attitudes, guilt feelings are prevalent. These stem from the parents' vague awareness that something is lacking or is undesirable in their behavior toward the child. Guilt feelings seem to be associated also with the actual fact of having a child who stutters. This attitude is analogous to that of many parents of children who are mentally retarded or have physical defects.

Parents of stutterers very definitely feel "different" about the child with this handicap than about their other children, and they react differently toward him. They reject him *as a stutterer.* In fact, they tend to reject him even before the appearance of the speech disturbance, and this rejection would seem to be one of the principal factors which precipitate it. In this respect, fathers often play a more important role than we have heretofore suspected.

This may be explained, at least in part, by certain characteristics of the child who stutters. Research tends to show, and our clinical observations tend to confirm, that stuttering children as a group have relatively poor motor coordination. Parents frequently conplain that their stuttering child is awkward and ungainly, that he is a poor athlete, and that he is last to be chosen on teams when games calling for athletic prowess are played. The child, sensing a certain lack of adequacy in himself, tends to be fearful of situations calling for motor proficiency; he typically shuns competition in these areas and assumes a generally passive role. To many fathers, this behavior and the lack of motor adequacy underlying it are unmasculine and hence unacceptable.

The father may react by criticism of the child, or by trying to push him or shame him into conforming to the parent's conception of what a "real boy" should be. All too often, the father's rejection takes the form of putting a distance between himself and the child, either by actual absence from the home or by failure otherwise to give him adequate attention. It appears to be true that the fathers of stutterers, as a group, are farther removed from their children than is the average male parent. As a result, the boy who stutters is frequently deprived of a masculine figure with whom to identify. Instead of identifying with the male parent, he may develop a fear of him and, subsequently, of all father surrogates.

The father's attitude almost inevitably forces the mother into an overprotecting role, a role in which she often has to assume sole responsibility for the child and his problems. Thus, while on the one hand she may be overprotecting and solicitous, on the other hand, she is frequently resentful and angry at having to cope with the child's problem without adequate assistance or cooperation from her husband. She may manifest her resentment toward the child in various ways. The result is that the young stutterer often feels basically unaccepted by either parent, but clings to the mother in self-protection.

In this respect, a transcript of a recent group-therapy session for parents is significant. An excerpt from it is particularly revealing of the attitude of one father toward his stuttering son.

> David, the child in question, is 8 years of age and the older of two siblings, both boys. Although of superior intelligence, he has a severe reading disability as well as a stutter. He displays an inordinate need to reveal how much he knows, in an effort to gain approval and acceptance. He has been subjected to excessive parental criticism, especially on the part of the father, and resents it, manifesting his resentment in obstinacy and intolerance for the ideas of others. In the group, he does not play with the other children, but rather leads and drives them, reflecting in this respect the behavior of his father toward him.
>
> The father, a postal clerk, is 44. He rejects David as the boy he is and tries to mold him into a different type of child. The mother, 34 years of age, is more understanding but is confused and overwhelmed by the demands made by a perfectionistic, intolerant husband and by the responsibilities of motherhood, and she frequently reacts to her son's behavior with irritation.

The parents were discussing the matter of how much they should expect from a child:

> *David's Father:* My attitude and my behavior and my handling of David are diametrically opposed to what you have been saying. Many

times I admit I am very harsh with him, so harsh, in fact, that my wife could throw me out the window. Maybe I am a hard taskmaster, as I said before. Being a perfectionist, I know it is my fault. I don't pride myself on it. But I am just innately that way. What upsets me with David is not what he does so much as for not thinking it out in advance.

Now, right back to what's always thrown at the parent: what do you want from an 8-year-old? It may be a selfish viewpoint, it may be a very hard viewpoint, but what Davey may suffer now, I still want to condition his mind to a point where he does not unthinkably do things. He'll stop and think a little while. If it requires punishment many times, I still want to instill one thing in his mind, and it is: Think before you jump.

Again, I say it is not the anger with what he does so much. I expect childish things from an 8-year-old. It is not what he does, but has he thought of anything prior to the action.

A Mother (Interrupting): I believe that this takes many, many years of living, and I don't think you can expect it from a child.

David's Father: I don't disagree with that view at all. Let me put it this way: I intentionally become angry with him. *Intentionally* become angry with him. To point out that if a little thought had gone into what he was doing, it would not have turned out this way . . . And I intentionally do get angry and do bawl him out. As I say, it's a hard row for him to hoe, but . . .

Another Father: I think you are harming the child, and it's upsetting him.

Several Parents: (An excited interchange of comments).

David's Father: I have heard all these arguments. I don't disagree with them, believe me. As my wife will say many times, "With another child you wouldn't do that." And I wouldn't. Now, as to my insistence that he do something at certain times, that he stop and think, that he do things methodically, with aforethought, not impulsively, let me just generalize and throw it back into a larger vista of thinking. Believe me, Davey's stammering has never represented any problem to me because I may foolishly go along thinking he will outgrow it, and I look at it as only another problem for me to handle while I am training my child.

Other Father: You think you are really training that child?

David's Father: Yes, I do.

Other Father: I think you going against the discussion we had in our first meeting. You're really forcing the child to do things your way. You may not like it, but you're forcing him and it's putting him under that nervous strain. I think you're making him all the more nervous.

David's Father: Putting pressure on him? I admit that he strives to attain certain things.

Other Father: You're trying to put him years ahead of himself, and I think that's a mistake.

David's Father: Now, Mr. Snyder says to speak openly and I speak openly when I say that his stammering to me is only one problem in my child's life for me. If I thought that stammering was going to be a very big thing in his life, my attitude would be a little bit different. But, basically, my mind is not concerned with his stammering, believe it or not. He irritates me many times. When I want him to express himself freely and clearly and confidently, sure I could reach down his throat and pull that sentence out . . .

Other Father: But what if, for example, we say that nervousness is the thing that causes stammering and you knew for a fact that it was nervousness that causes stammering, would you let down a bit on your pressure of the child?

David's Father: No; I *know* that nervousness is the background of stammering.

Other Father: You *know* that it is making him nervous? And you think you're helping him?

David's Father: I think that when he gets over a bigger stumbling block, he'll be instilled with a little more confidence than he would ordinarily have.

A Mother: Is your son sensitive? He must be.

David's Father: Sure, he's sensitive. But I can't go along 24 hours a day, shielding my son from harm or hurt, and I expect him to condition himself to the point where he will accept hurt and take it for what it is. You say it is pretty hard for an 8-year-old. I agree. Maybe he's carrying a lot now, and maybe my insistence is a little more of a load to carry, but I feel that if he were to carry just that little bit harder lot, when he does get into his teens he'll have just that much more confidence in himself and that sense of value above children of his age . . .

Therapist: There has been a silent partner in all this, . . . and I wonder if we could get her comments?

David's Mother: I find that my husband keeps saying that he's a perfectionist, and I become very irritated . . . I don't feel he's a perfectionist. I believe he is intolerant. He's expecting too much. I say to my husband, "You're 40 years old and you want to make the child think like a 40-year-old . . ."

This is a very direct expression of one father's rejection of his son and his attempt to dominate him. Many other fathers, while more subtle in being so, are equally rejecting. A parent in point is the father who protested against the treatment David is receiving; he himself meets out essentially the same type of treatment to his own son but in less frank and obvious fashion, a fact which became evident to him as the group-therapy sessions continued.

Herein lies one of the values of the sessions: in discussing the problems of one another, parents gain insight into their own attitudes and behavior toward their children. In this connection, the group has an advantage over individual therapy in that as each parent sees faults and shortcomings in the others, he feels less guilty about his own and is therefore better able to admit them and cope with them. In consequence, this type of therapy, although it is necessarily superficial and not intended to bring about far-reaching personality changes in the parents, in most cases does markedly change their attitudes and behavior toward the child who stutters. By doing so, it appreciably alters the emotional tone of the child's environment and leads to a closer relationship between parent and child. This, in turn, is reflected in lessened anxiety and tension on the child's part and in gradual improvement of his speech.

Chapter 31

Procedures for Group Parent Counseling in Speech Pathology and Audiology

ELIZABETH J. WEBSTER

MUCH of the parent counseling done by speech pathologists and audiologists involves one clinician interacting with one set of parents for one or two conferences. This type of counseling occurs, for example, in diagnostic interviews where the speech pathologist or audiologist and the parents of a child with a communication disorder discuss the child's disorder, the results of speech and/or hearing testing, and the clinician's recommendations.

In addition to such individual contacts, many clinicians also are called upon to counsel groups of parents of children with communication disorders. Often this group work is done on a continuing or long-term basis; that is, a group of parents is seen for a specified number of sessions, perhaps regularly for the length of time that their children are enrolled for speech and/or hearing therapy.

Earlier (5), I discussed assumptions upon which both individual and group parent counseling may be organized and suggested tools which may be introduced to parents. I suggested that the clinician (1) work to implement attitudes of respect and support for

Note: Reprinted by permission of the author and the *Journal of Speech and Hearing Disorders, 33*:127-131, 1968.

Dr. Webster is associated with the University of Alabama, University, Alabama.

Acknowledgment is made to Glenda Waters, Carole Oliver, and Faye McCollister for their help in preparing this manuscript.

parents, (2) encourage and support parents' attempts to verbalize and to clarify issues relating to communication with their children, (3) provide necessary information, and (4) be aware of his limitations in counseling.

My purpose here is to suggest how group discussion and role-playing can be utilized in working with groups of parents in the setting of a speech and hearing program, particularly with groups of parents seen for long-term counseling.

GROUP DISCUSSION

Informal discussion is the chief medium in group parent counseling. Such informal discussion is facilitated by holding parent meetings in a room with comfortable furniture and chairs arranged so that each person can see all other persons in the group.

The clinician implements his belief that the group exists to serve parents by asking them to bring topics for discussion and by encouraging them to verbalize their concerns and questions. The clinician serves as discussion leader who insures that each parent has a chance to speak and who encourages group members to listen and respond to the speaker. The clinician must remember that parents have varying skills in verbalization and must not require all to be equally sophisticated in discussion.

The clincian helps to build a positive group spirit by pointing out similarities in the concerns felt by different parents. Initially parents tend to think of the differences between them; but as McDonald (4) pointed out, when the clinician gives parents the opportunity to discuss that which is important to them, they find much commonality in their concerns, fears, disappointments, and hopes. Further, when parents are encouraged to discuss topics they select, discussions usually move from being almost exclusively child centered to being more parent centered; that is, parents discuss their children less and discuss themselves more.

The clinician's leadership is not just laissez-faire leadership. He shares responsibility for bringing discussion topics to the group and introduces content that he considers important. The clinician is the only group member aware of some information that parents should know, and he should not assume that parents can discover and explore all of this content by themselves. For example, the mother of a child with a repaired cleft palate told a group that her son was to have pharyngeal flap surgery during the next school vacation, and she was worried about "what it is for and what it will do to him." The clinician realized the mother needed information, so he explained the procedure and its potential benefits. When he had finished, the mother said, "Good. I understand the reason for it, and some of the mystery is taken away." The point here is that a speech pathologist or audiologist shares the knowledge which he feels might be helpful to parents, whether or not they suggest such content for discussion.

It is the clinician's responsibility to introduce tools he thinks will help parents. In an earlier article I suggested introducing the following tools for promoting better parent-child communication: (1) listening to try to understand what the child thinks and feels, (2) trying to accept the child's thoughts and feelings while not necessarily accepting his behavior, (3) trying to verbalize understanding of the child's feelings, and (4) trying to verbalize to the child more on his level rather than on an adult level (5).

These tools can be discussed in a variety of ways. For example, in parent groups that I conduct, the tool of listening to try to understand is introduced early. I ask parents to try to understand the meanings of events to their children and to speculate about the feelings their children have in certain situations. Parents are asked to practice this way of listening to each other as they talk in the group and to try to verbalize their understanding of the meanings and feelings conveyed by other parents. Then parents are given the assignment of listening to and trying to understand a person outside of the group and of reporting their experience to the group. This reporting provides another possibility of free group discussion. For example, one mother reported:

> Sunday when people were visiting, Jim walked around saying, "I'm so big, I'm so big," over and over. I was about to holler at him to quit when I thought about how we were supposed to understand what somebody was feeling, so I tried to figure it out. I guess (he felt) good, and big, and maybe real proud to show off.

Another mother told the group,

> I ran into the grocery in a big hurry and ran into a woman I hadn't

seen in months, and she started telling me her troubles with her son, and I got so interested listening to her (she reported some information the woman gave her and commented at length about the compassion she felt for the woman). It got me in trouble, though . . . my husband was so mad when I was late getting home.

Experience indicates that these listening assignments serve to promote discussion about such related topics as times when parents really have listened to others, times they have refused to listen or have been too busy to do so, and about how they feel when people will not listen to them. Such practice exercises can serve the clinician's purposes of helping parents increase their group interaction and discussion, their awareness of the feelings of others, and their ability to verbalize such awareness.

However, it should be noted that the clinician who encourages parents to speculate about their children's emotions must not lead them to assume either (1) that their children experience the same emotions they do, or (2) that they can know positively what their children feel. Rather, the clinician helps parents to speculate about the emotional realms of children. He also supports the recognition by many parents that emotions are acceptable even though some of the resultant behaviors are unacceptable.

ROLE PLAYING

A second procedure for working with parent groups is role playing — that is, the acting out or demonstrating of situations. The clinician should point out to parents that he is asking them to participate in a demonstration process; he probably should not dwell on the label for the process, as it often symbolizes to people that they must be actors. The clinician's goals in role playing are to help parents gain understanding of behavior and to experiment with varied behavioral approaches to situations.

Role playing involves three steps: (1) the warm-up period, in which the leader helps the group delineate the situation to be acted out, assigns roles, and helps each person begin to create his role; (2) the actual acting out of the situation; and (3) discussion of the situation. This often is a circular process, in that new situations to be "role played" may be suggested in the discussion.

Discussion is an integral part of role playing, used both in the initial warmup period and in the final step of the procedure. However, role playing goes further than discussion in that it requires bodily action. One value of role playing is that it provides for participation at the level of demonstration as well as at the level of discussion. As Wolpe (6) states, "Unlike a discussion group, which often remains solely on an intellectual level, role enactment insures emotional participation in the very dramatic management of the scene. . . ." Another value is that role playing "is here and now, natural and spontaneous" (2).

Although role playing has the advantage of encouraging emotional involvement, it also has limitations, and the clinician must use this procedure with caution and sensitivity. Many people are terrified by the thought of being asked to act out a role; this fear will probably prevent them from exploring ideas through the medium of role playing without a great deal of help from the clinician. Again, parents may feel anxious about revealing negative aspects of themselves. Another danger arises from the fact that role playing may reveal differences between people and may induce feelings of separation in parents who disagree with the majority of the group. The clinician must be skillful enough to help parents cope with such feelings. Further, parents often assume that there are right and wrong ways to play roles. If the clinician also holds this assumption and insists that parents play a role in the "right" way, he puts tremendous pressure on them and probably defeats his purpose of helping them clarify their ideas and behaviors.

Perhaps the greatest danger in role playing is the opportunity it affords the clinician to manipulate parents. The clinician who uses this procedure must continue to reexamine his attitudes, for he cannot disguise his negative judgment of certain parents, his hostility toward others, or his demands that parents change. Such attitudes will show in what he asks a parent to do in the way of role playing. For example, if the clinician's bias is that a mother is to blame for her child's communication problem, he can easily manipulate the role played scenes to that the mother shows up poorly.

It is imperative that before the clinician uses role playing, he must have experienced the playing of roles himself, as it is through his own experience that he will understand the nature of role playing and its potential benefits and dangers. However, in professional practice the clinician usually should not participate in the actual playing of roles. Rather, he should serve as director or leader, because when he is involved in the action, he is less able to respond to the whole group and to see many sides of the situation in an unbiased manner.

Situations to be role played often arise from parents' discussion. For example, the father of a deaf boy reported that he thought people often stared at his child and several other parents stated that this was a problem for them, too. The clinician suggested that this father show what his son did, asked another parent to be a person staring at the child, and asked a third person to play the father. The three role played a situation in a grocery store. In the ensuing discussion parents stated what they thought each participant felt in the role played situation, thus giving them an opportunity to clarify their impressions.

In addition to suggesting the role playing of situations which have been discussed, the clinician may suggest that parents role play situations which illustrate specific points. For example, the clinician can ask parents to explore the use of simple language patterns with children through the role playing of situations in which they attempt to speak in a simplified fashion. The tool of listening to understand can be illustrated through role playing a situation in which one person tries to listen to another. Through role playing the clinician can help parents to experiment with such concepts of discipline as that of trying to provide freedom within limits. For example, in groups I conduct, parents are assigned to report on one time that they were able to set and maintain a rational limit, stating why they set the limit, how they explained it, and why they felt good about the incident. Some parents have reported verbally on their experience, while others have shown (i.e. role played) what happened.

Corsini points out that role playing can be used by clinicians of various theoretical orientations (1). He gives suggestions for ways of introducing and conducting role playing (2).

The clinician must remember that all group members need not

role play in order to benefit from the procedure. Often persons who have not participated in the action have contributed quite easily to the discussion, thus participating in a way which is comfortable for them. Further, many parents have reported that, although they were unable to participate either in the action or in the discussion, some of their ideas were clarified from watching others role play. Clinicians should respect and accept a parent's refusal to participate in role playing, and should consider it as reflecting that parent's need.

The judicious use of discussion and role playing, then, provides the speech pathologist or audiologist with procedures for helping parents explore and clarify both their ideas and their behaviors.

REFERENCES

1. Corsini, R. J.: *Role Playing in Psychotherapy.* Chicago, Aldine, 1966.
2. Corsini, R. J., Shaw, M. E., and Blake, R. R.: *Role Playing in Business and Industry.* New York, The Free Press, 1961.
3. Ginott, H. G.: *Between Parent and Child.* New York, MacMillan Co., 1965.
4. McDonald, E. T.: *Understand Those Feelings.* Pittsburgh, Stanwix House, 1962.
5. Webster, Elizabeth J.: Parent counseling by speech pathologists and audiologists. *J Speech Hearing Dis, 31*:331-340, 1966.
6. Wolpe, Zelda: Play Therapy, Psychodrama, and Parent Counseling. In L. Travis (Ed.): *Handbook of Speech Pathology.* New York, Appleton, 1957.

Chapter 32

A Speech Pathologist Talks to
the Parents of a Nonverbal Child

HARRIET W. DUBNER

THE following is a letter I have found useful as an aid for counseling parents of nonverbal children. The underlying condition may be cerebral palsy or another handicap such as deafness, mental retardation, perceptual difficulties, emotional disturbance, or lack of stimulation due to neglect or overprotection. I make no reference to etiology in the letter since all too often it is not known or, if it is, the diagnosis may not be acceptable to the parent.

The purpose of the letter is to help the parent understand the child's difficulty without any threatening labeling. I have also found it helps alleviate, in those cases where it is present, some of the parent's guilt feelings about his child, and an awareness of the techniques enables him to take positive action in helping his child.

Dear Friend:

Your child does not speak and you are concerned and rightfully so. For if he does not speak, how can he grow up to become an independent human being? We all know that communication is one of the first steps on the long, long road to independence.

Note: Reprinted by permission of the author and *Rehabilitation Literature, 30*:360-362, 1969.

Mrs. Dubner is currently engaged in private practice and is consultant speech pathologist at The Forum School, Ridgewood, N.J. She formerly was speech therapist at The Cerebral Palsy Center of Bergen County.

NATURAL DEVELOPMENT OF LANGUAGE

Communication begins when we try to express our needs. When we are very young, we cry, and, lo and behold something happens. We get picked up, cuddled, cleaned, and fed, and, if we're lucky, cooed at. It does not take the average child long to learn that crying is meaningful and useful to him. This noise-making ability we have becomes a tool for satisfying some pretty important needs. Hmmm! Let's try it again. Here comes Momma. Hopefully, while she's satisfying our physical needs, she is cooing at us. This is pleasurable for the young child. He will smile and coo back at her.

Very early in life the child learns he can derive satisfactions from making this other kind of noise. We can communicate our enjoyment of each other, and the means by which we do this, in turn, becomes enjoyable. The human learns to use sounds for communication by such reinforcement. We use them very early in life as tools for getting our physical and social needs satisfied. The more successful we are at it, the more we enjoy using the tools.

As time goes on, we learn that certain sounds we feel and hear ourselves make and certain sounds we hear others make can bring specific satisfactions. When we are about one year old we begin to use these sounds, knowing they will help us get what we want. This is human speech and we are well on the way toward verbal communication.

This is the normal process of language development and it is an extremely complicated process. It assumes normal growth physically, mentally, and emotionally. Any slight deviation in any area may interfere with the natural development of language. Sounds forming the basis of language make many demands on the child before he can successfully transform them into meaningful language.

First of all, the infant needs to be able to do the following:
to Make sounds.
to Feel himself making them.
to Hear himself making them.
to Hear others making them.
to Recognize them.
to Remember them.

to Repeat them.
to Imitate them.
to Enjoy making them.
to Enjoy hearing them.
to Enjoy the satisfactions they bring.
to Associate them with the satisfactions they bring.
He needs to be able to need sounds.

THE ROLE OF THE SPEECH PATHOLOGIST

If the child has trouble meeting any of the above requirements, his language development will be affected and he may require the services of a speech pathologist.

How Do We Help?

We analyze the child's language behavior as we see it, hear it, and test it, as it is described to us by his parents, teachers, and doctors and as it is clarified by his medical history and psychological reports. We do this in an attempt to determine the specific areas of difficulty and then we try to strengthen the weak spots. The procedures vary with the specific needs of each child. But there are universal therapeutic principles of which you, his parents, should be aware.

How Can You Help?

You can help the child with language problems by remembering how children usually learn to speak in their first year of life. At that point repetition of sounds seemed to bring certain satisfactions to them. We must now duplicate this process even though the needs of a growing child are more sophisticated than they were as an infant. His world has expanded, and he needs more than just being cleaned and fed and cooed at. But too often the physically or emotionally handicapped child still makes his demands in the old infantile way. Only too often, he has no need to learn new and better ways, because those around him, in their anxiety to please, have always responded and are still responding to those now inadequate baby sounds and gestures.

Help Him Say "I want"

One of the prime objectives of therapy is to break this pattern of response. We try to show the child he can get his wants satisfied in a superior manner through the use of verbal language. At the beginning it is still necessary to respond to the old ways of communication, but we start the change by delaying the response to the gesture, to the grunt, or to the groan that has been substituting for language. In addition we can tell the child, "You don't have to point or grunt. You can say 'milk.' " Even if the child does not immediately respond to this request for the word, we are giving him the special training he seems to need for verbalizing his needs. When we do respond to his inadequate forms of expression we give him the words he should be using: "Johnny wants milk." "Here is the milk." "Mommy is giving Johnny milk."

In this way we are giving him not only what he wants but the words he needs in order to get what he wants. In time he may learn to associate these words with the satisfactions he gets. When that happens, hopefully, he will make an attempt to make those words himself. Then he should be responded to quickly, so that he is given the opportunity to learn that the use of words can be very satisfying. At this point we are not to be concerned with how he says the words. We are looking for an attempt at imitation. We may have to continue our repetitions over a long period of time to help the child improve his articulation.

This procedure of speaking to your child while giving him what he wants teaches him that the use of language is enjoyable because it enables him to say "I want —" and to have his wants satisfied more efficiently than if he just grunted or pointed.

Help Him Say "Look at me"

We can also show him that using language can be fun because it enables him, in effect, to say, "Look at me!" This is another important need of any child. Of course, first you must really look at him, see what he is doing or trying to do, and then describe it to him. "Johnny is playing in the mud." "Johnny is picking up a spoon." "Johnny is making a pie." "Johnny is making a mud pie." "Johnny is playing in the mud." By repeatedly describing to him that which is important to him you are giving him the words he needs to communicate.

Think of it this way. Suppose making a mud pie is fun. You, an important person in the child's life are repeating words at the same time. The child is getting a lot of attention. That is fun. After many similar experiences, he may connect the three experiences. He may want to repeat the words, too, since everything connected with it was so satisfying. Your pleasurable reaction to his attempt at imitation will help convince him using words can be fun. And so without calling attention to or correcting his speech you can help develop it by describing to your child what he is doing.

A word of caution is necessary. The repeated descriptions should be those acts the child enjoys, not those you would have him do. Telling him "Put your toys away" over and over again is not going to leave him with any sense of language enjoyment.

Help Him Understand "Now" and "Later"

Many of our children have behavior problems because they do not know what to expect. Too often the child who does not speak elicits the response of no speech from those around him. This is a natural response, but, how unfortunate! The child who needs the most language stimulation often gets the least.

This leads to problems other than lack of models for him to imitate. He may have many temper tantrums because he does not know what to expect. For example, he may be entertaining himself and then suddenly be forced to stop because Mother has other plans for him, such as lunch. Or he may be enjoying a ride in the car and become furious when he is made to stop and leave the car. The child with a communication disorder does not know what is about to happen to him.

The use of "now" and "later" is an invaluable aid in preparing the child for coming events. Tell the child, "Now Johnny is playing," "Later you will stop and eat lunch," or "Now you are riding in the car," "Later you will get out and see Grandma."

Give Him the Opportunity to Make Choices

Whenever possible give the child an opportunity to distinguish one object from another. For example, if he's hungry, ask him, "Johnny, which do you want? The cookie or the banana?" Show him what it is you are talking about at the same time you are talking and certainly respond immediately to his efforts at communication. While you accept his efforts at communication, or even if no efforts at communication are made, continue verbalizing for him.

Another note of caution: while verbalizing for your child your own language should be repetitious, brief, and consistent. A cookie should not be a cookie one time and a cracker another time. The sentences you use should be short and clear so that the child does not become overwhelmed by a great many sounds. The language should be repetitious so that the child is repeatedly presented with concise but consistent stimuli.

These procedures are not different from those we use naturally with any young child. The usual child with nothing handicapping him will respond very quickly and usually learn to communicate at an early age. The child with handicaps to overcome, however, needs a greater concentration of this kind of stimulation. He needs to be shown how to say "I want —" and "Look at me" over a longer period of time than other children. He needs more help in understanding what is going on about him. He needs more help to learn that sounds and words can help him control his environment.

These measures provide him with this kind of help. If he is not too greatly handicapped and he catches on, then he really is on his way toward growing up and becoming as independent as is possible for him.

I do hope this letter will prove helpful to you.

My best wishes to you and yours,
Sincerely,

Harriet   W.   Dubner

Chapter 33

Emotional Adjustment of the Mother to the Child with a Cleft Palate

GLADYS C. KINNIS

THAT parents of a child born with a congenital defect face difficulties over and above the rearing of a normal child is obvious. Not only do they frequently have hospital bills and costly appliances to pay for, and years of corrective treatment to deal with, but they are faced with the necessity of imparting courage and self-confidence to their child, who, while born different from many of those around him, must learn to take his place in the world with others.

The child born with a congenital defect needs, like every child, to be given a feeling of belonging as the first requisite for a healthy adjustment to life. We know that infants are highly sensitive to the emotional reactions of those nearest them, and before they have learned to walk or talk, they have begun to sense the security that a warm and loving parent can give. We know, too, that they are sensitive barometers to fears and anxieties in adults, reacting all too quickly to any conflicts parents may have. The child who has a congenital defect will take his cue from the attitude he finds in his own home. If this attitude is cheerful, matter-of-fact, and engendered by loving acceptance of him, he more easily will acquire self-confidence in his relationships with persons outside the home. But many parents, shocked by the sight of a cleft palate

Note: Reprinted by permission of *Medical Social Work, 3*:67-71, 1954.

Mrs. Kinnis is a caseworker of the Social Service Department, Royal Victoria Hospital, Montreal, Canada.

or cleft lip and beginning to realize that this congenital malformation will affect one of the most important aspects of their
child's life — communication through speech — find their minds in
turmoil and their thoughts far from cheerful.

Because we have had more opportunity to get to know the
mother than the father, both while she is in hospital and later
when she brings her child to clinic, we have become particularly
aware of her problem. Our focus, as medical social workers, has
been in terms of helping her to make the emotional adjustment
necessary. We know that in a very deep sense she has had the wish
to bear a child, healthy, normal, and in her own image. A baby
physically less than perfect is at once, so it seems to her, a
reflection on her adequacy as a giving person, and in the long run a
reflection on her adequacy as a woman.

It is possible, then, that her initial reaction to learning that her
child has been born with a cleft lip or palate may be composed of
disappointment, anger, and frustration. She may even feel
antipathy toward her child, followed by a sense of guilt that she
should react thus to her own flesh and blood. She may wonder
how she and her husband will cope with the situation. It is at this
point that she can be actively helped by the hospital team of
physician, nurse, and social worker. She may have turned already
to the physician, asking him why this should have happened to her
child, and since it has, what can be done about it. She will be glad
to know whatever medical fact he can tell her, and her mind will
be eased when he explains what modern plastic surgery and speech
training can do. She may also receive constructive hope from him
through learning of a definite date when the first operation can be
undertaken. The nurse, by her warm acceptance of the baby, can
stand as a positive symbol to the uncertain mother of the reactions
of persons outside the hospital. With the social worker the mother
may share, bit by bit, her own mixed feelings about the baby and
what lies ahead.

With or without help, and depending on her own capacities, the
mother may become more accepting of the situation, taking
delight in her baby as he is. Or she may attempt to deny the
situation by refusing to take the baby home with her until after
the first plastic repair has been done. Whatever her reaction, we

must meet her where she is, helping her to make the best adjustment that she can. In any case, it is doubtful if she can be expected to work through her feelings about her child while she is still in hospital or even in the period immediately following. The follow-up program in the Cleft Palate Clinic, which affords the child a check-up from time to time as regards further plastic surgery, dental care, speech training, and general medical care, also provides the opportunity for discussions between mother and social worker. We believe that our initial point of contact with the mother should be while she is still in hospital. In the past, however, this has not always been possible, and so we find mothers and children coming to the Cleft Palate Clinic, many of them involved in an intricate web of feeling "different."

Perhaps, when a mother first comes to clinic, her problems are not very apparent, and it would be hard to see her as one needing help. She may give her child the best of care and be alert to carrying out the physician's exact orders as regards further clinics and hospitalization. If there are no financial or obvious social problems, she may appear to have no need to talk to a social worker. Indeed, it is not always easy to establish a relationship with her, for in the period of time since the birth of her child, she may have assembled a set of thoughts and feelings which act as defences to what lies deeper. While these defences may operate fairly successfully for her, the hidden feelings have usually gained force, showing themselves in innumerable small ways, but strong enough to communicate themselves to her child. When we see him, some of his mother's fears may already be showing in his behavior and he will have begun a kind of suffering which may last for the rest of his life.

Jimmie is a seven-year old boy who was born with a deep cleft lip and cleft palate. He is awaiting a final plastic surgery operation after which he will begin speech therapy. He is a quiet, nicely-mannered, nice-looking child whose upper lip is mildly scarred and whose speech has the sound characteristic of a cleft palate. His mother says he is very good at school work but does not seem to want to mix with other children. Mrs. D. brings him to clinic regularly and seems anxious to help him in every way. But she tells us that neither she nor Jimmie eat breakfast the morning they come to clinic and she usually has a splitting headache afterwards. However, she is glad that Jimmie is always so good at clinic. She says he has never been any trouble. In the course of our conversations, she confides that one of her greatest fears is that he will some day find the photograph that was taken of him as a baby before his lip was repaired and which she always carries in her handbag.

It usually comes as a revelation to a mother like Mrs. D. to learn that her feelings of fear and disappointment on first seeing her baby were by no means unnatural and are something which she shares in common with many mothers of such children. Mrs. D. may find it hard to admit that she never really got over that first feeling of disappointment. Only hesitatingly will she confide that the clinicing, the hospital bills, the worry each time there is an operation have been a strain on both her and her husband. When she asks "Could the doctor fix the lip so it wouldn't show?" or "Will Jimmie's speech really improve and how long will it take?" she is actually asking us to understand and help her, for she is a fearful and, to the extent that love excludes fear, an unloving parent. It is usually a crucial point in her understanding of her relationship with her child when she can relate, step by step, her feelings on first seeing him. The potency of these feelings can be gauged by the vividness with which, no matter how many years later, the experience is related.

We find another aspect of emotional maladjustment in the mother who refuses to come to clinic or who frequently misses appointments. If she does come she may grudgingly comply with the physician's recommendations or find several reasons for not being able to carry them out. If her child begins speech lessons, he may drop out of the class before the therapist has had time to help him.

Mrs. B., who lives on the outskirts of the city, did seem to have a good reason for finding it hard to come to clinic. When we were able to offer her a taxi, she hesitatingly agreed to keep the appointment. However, she arrived two hours late for clinic, even though she had been given careful instructions as to time and place. As a result she did not see the physicians. Her child needs further operations and speech training, but now Mrs. B. says she has no time to come to clinic. She is not at home when the social worker visits even though an appointment is made ahead of time. Mrs. B. may have very real fears about another operation for her child or she may have financial worries which she does not want to disclose. On the other hand, she may never have been able to accept the fact that her child was born with a congenital deformity, for her own life experiences, when she lacked sympathetic understanding herself, may have ill-prepared her for assuming this additional burden. Whatever the causes of her staying away from clinic, she herself needs the experience of a warm and helping relationship before and at a time she is expected to carry through the various medical recommendations for her child.

A mother, in her attempt to come to grips with what may be for her an almost unbearable situation, may often search around for some reason for her child's defect. Not infrequently she is aided and abetted by friends and relatives who offer some superstitious theory as to why the child was "marked." Very often this may be directed to the behavior of the mother or father before the child was born, often with the unhappy result that both parents and particularly the mother blame themselves unnecessarily. This in itself has ramifications. Each parent may bear an unspoken reproach toward the other, or more likely each has a feeling of guilt that he or she may have been the cause of their child's defect.

> Mrs. Z. was brought up in Poland and has adhered to many of her old-country customs. Eighteen years ago, when her daughter was born with a cleft lip, Mrs. Z. recalled how during her pregnancy she walked in front of her husband while he was cutting wood. To this day, they both reproach themselves for having been so careless for, according to their culture, they ought to have foreseen the consequences of such an act. Now, after this length of time it would hardly help Mrs. Z. to remind her of what she was told when her child was born, that medical knowledge does not put any stock in her theory. Her belief has served for too long to both comfort and punish her. But perhaps its significance has grown less as she has been able to talk about her relationship with her daughter and to see the development of the girl's personality and character.

In our work we have seen that the mother of a child born with a cleft palate can learn to replace negative attitudes with more positive ones by being encouraged to explore her own feelings about her child. In addition, she needs to have held up for her the more objective mirror of how we regard her child, not as "different" or unusual, marked with a special stigma for the rest of his life, but as an individual with many potentialities, not the least being capacity for growth and happiness.

Chapter 34

What Parents Should Be Told About Cleft Palate

NOAH D. FABRICANT

KNOWLEDGE of the existence of cleft palate in a newborn infant often comes as considerable shock to parents. For many people cleft palate brings to mind a squeamish recollection of some person once seen or known who had difficult-to-understand speech, a facial deformity as likely as not accompanied by "hare-lip," and which aroused a mixed emotion of pity and revulsion. Unfortunately, cleft palate has had this implication for many people only because they have not been adequately informed about the vast possibilities the child with a cleft palate actually has today to develop into a normal person. In this connection, physicians can play an important educational role by outlining to parents the modern-day facts about the management of cleft palate infants and children.

To begin with, it is perfectly natural for parents to wish for the birth of a normal baby and to be intensely disappointed with the information that their new offspring has either a cleft palate or cleft lip or both. Certainly, parents should be told that cleft palate is no respecter of social class and occurs at all economic levels in approximately one birth in every ten to twelve hundred newborn infants. While the number of theories have been advanced to explain the failure of tissues to join together, none have been established with finality. Nor should parents assume that cleft palate is causally related to intermarriage of cousins, feeble-

Note: Reprinted by permission of the author and *Eye, Ear, Nose and Throat Monthly,* *32:*526, 534, 1953.

Dr. Fabricant is Associate Editor of *Eye, Ear, Nose and Throat Monthly.*

mindedness, or syphilis. The presence of one condition does not presuppose the presence of another, and an infant with cleft palate is no more likely to be mentally defective than any other newborn infant. In reality, cleft palate does not run in families; about 80 percent of cleft palate babies are born to families without a known history of the defect. As a general rule, the parents of an infant with cleft palate need not fear to have other children on that account, the persons who have a cleft palate usually need not be concerned about having children of their own, particularly if there is no history of the defect in the family of the mate.

According to Backus, one of the best ways parents can achieve an unemotional acceptance of the problem is to start behaving at once in a matter-of-fact way, mentioning casually to other people the presence of a cleft palate or lip in the newborn infant. The news itself should produce less gossip value if it is accepted openly at once. Indeed, parents who become adjusted to the idea of having a child who has a cleft palate will often raise a child who will develop into a well-adjusted person. Like charity, adjustment should begin at home, and for parents adjustment should start from the day of the newborn infant's birth. The infant should be treated as nearly as possible as if he were normal, and the parents should be instructed not to become oversolicitous or over-protective.

In children with cleft palate a number of special problems are likely to develop. For example, such children are prone to infection and especially infections of the middle ear. As much as possible, upper respiratory infections should be treated with a sense of immediacy. This is also true of exposure to contagious childhood diseases. Indications for tonsillectomy and adenoid-ectomy should be established only after sufficient joint consulta-tion between otolaryngologist and oral surgeon.

It is important that parents be made to understand that the best type of cleft palate surgery is performed by a specialist skilled in cleft palate surgery, especially since surgical repair of a cleft palate or lip involves more than "closing a hole." The responsibility in great measure for providing as normal and attractive a facial appearance as is possible to obtain falls, of course, upon the oral surgeon himself. Also upon him rests the responsibility for constructing palatal tissue that is capable of normal function and eventually of normal speech. Parents should be reassured that fatalities from cleft palate surgery are extremely rare.

In addition to the services of the oral surgeon, it is important that the parents obtain the advice and services of a dentist from the time of the eruption of the first tooth at about six or seven months of age until full development of the jaws has occurred. The dentist should be an individual who comprehends the special dental problems associated with the cleft palate condition. From time to time, the dentist in turn finds it necessary to call for the assistance of an orthodontist in the management of special dental problems.

Parents of cleft palate children should consult a speech clinic during the first few months of a child's life and should not wait until defective patterns of speech have developed before seeking help. Backus points out that in relation to cleft palate, the speech clinic can serve most effectively, if its role is both preventive and corrective, with emphasis as much as possible on the preventive aspect. Since speech is a developmental process, and since it is influence by various factors, this relationship between parents, child, and speech clinic will extend over a period of several years.

Today, summer residential clinics are available in many states for cleft palate children. For young adults and adults with cleft palate, a number of college and university clinics offer an intensive type of instruction. These facilities have contributed greatly to the progress made in the field of cleft palate defects.

Chapter 35

The Family and the Deaf Child

ROBERT P. LISENSKY

MOST sociologists have not been particularly interested in action or in the clinician's role. There are a number of reasons one can give for this, but one of the most important may be the scientific stance. The problem of values has always been evaded and especially by the social scientist. The modern scientist claims that values may not be derived by science, and therefore science should have nothing to do with them. Actually, this is without foundation of fact. Values appear in everything the scientist does, from the choice of his problem, to the evaluation of his data, to the treatment of his conclusions. This does not mean that the social scientist is to yield and need not insist that the social scientist be rigorous in method as well as detached in his gathering and appraising of data; but it does mean that the values of the society really give the direction, the scope, and the very significance to scientific analysis.

An excellent illustration of this lack of interest is the dearth of research found concerning the problem of dependency in our society. However, a most recent expression of a new birth of concern in the area of rehabilitation was a conference on "Sociological Theory, Research and Rehabilitation" held in Carmel, California in March, 1965, under the auspices of the Vocational Rehabilitation Administration and the American Sociological Association. The main concern was the potential contribution of sociology to the field of rehabilitation.

Disability is a social ailment. Dr. Sussman, in summarizing the conference, states that "rehabilitation involves the activities of almost every organized major institutional system in the society, and because of this, the sociologist has a rare opportunity to

Note: Reprinted by permission of the author and *Volta Review, 68*:673-678, 1966.

theorize, research, and advise on the meaning of these societal activities for rehabilitation as an institutional system and a process" (1). With the advantages of relating sociological findings to the field of rehabilitation thus held to be an accepted position, I would like to relate these findings and concepts to the problem of deafness. I hope that I might stress the desire for research in this area along with creating an interest in the relevance of sociological theory.

Two years ago, I was introduced to the aspects of deafness when I assumed the role of consultant to a program seeking to develop a social and personal hygiene curriculum for a state residential school for the deaf. The program was established under the auspices of the United States Office of Education as a demonstration project. The major purpose was to develop a set of tools that might be used in classroom procedures and thus deal directly with the sex education of deaf children.

One of the overriding elements in the conversations about the personal adjustment of the deaf was the consensus on the part of the educators of the deaf that it seemed to be the school that played the major role in establishing personal adjustment patterns in deaf students. The responsibility for the socialization of the deaf child shifts, for a number of reasons, from the family to the school. However, it was also suggested that the school should take steps to involve the family in the educational process and to encourage the deaf child to identify strongly with his family group. Although this is the ideal pattern, it is possible that the question could be raised, especially with the residential school type of student, that the American cultural pattern of family life might make this somewhat an unrealistic pattern.

The family is the basic institution of society. It is basic because the family is universal, the smallest in size of all social institutions, has early access to the child during a time in which he is psychologically accessible, and the major source of emotional commitment and social control. Yet, although it is basic, the family has been involved in vast changes in its structure and function. These changes affect the relationship between the family and the deaf child.

The present industrialized urban society has called forth a small immediate family of father, mother, and minor children with great fluidity in adapting to constant changes both in residence and occupational roles. In 1790 the average family had 5.8 members; in 1840, 4.9; in 1950, 3.5; and in 1960, 3.6. This increase in the average family size in the last decade cannot be considered to be a trend, however, for the estimate for 1980 is 3.8 (2). To emphasize the isolation of the American family, along with its limited size, the statistics also demonstrate an increasing tendency for couples to live apart from others even in a time when there has been an increase in teenage marriages and in the size of the population sixty-five years of age and over. The ideal pattern of the single-dwelling place occupied by the family owning it is evidenced in the increase of the proportion of owner-occupied housing units from 44 percent in 1940 to 62 percent in 1960 (3).

With the increase of urbanization and industrialization, the traditional family functions also changed. The shifts in the household as an economic unit are most noteworthy. Not only do we have a change from a family that served primarily as a unit for the production of goods and services for home consumption to a unit for the consumption of goods and services, but there has also been a devaluation of homemaking. This change is seen in the increase of the percentage of married women in the labor force. In 1890, 4.6 percent of all married women were in the labor force; by 1950, this number increased to 24.8 percent. Since World War II, by actual number, married women outnumber single women in the labor force by several million (4). This potential economic emancipation of the woman emphasizes the change not only in the homemaking role but also in the role of mutual affection as based on marital harmony rather than economic security.

The protective function of the family has also changed. Once illness, old age, or financial crisis was the responsibility of the family. Today it has become the task of the federal and state agencies and the private insurance companies. "Total payments for unemployment, old-age assistance, and old-age and survivors' benefits under the Social Security Act and related state laws for the years 1936, 1940, and 1950 were respectively 8.3, 629.0, and 4,382.6 millions of dollars" (5). These same staggering figures are present in the increase of life insurance policyholders and the amount paid to these policyholders. The family does not have the physical facilities or the funds to care for its members.

This trend toward welfare agencies is also reflected in the change of direction in legislation for vocational rehabilitation. The earliest legislation was concerned for the disabled who could become independent. Recent legislation demonstrates the new concern for the impact of disability on the family as well as the individual. Employability as a criterion of eligibility for humanitarian efforts is becoming a thing of the past. These changes "reflect a shift in values from the unqualified idolization of rugged individualism to a growing concern for the welfare of others as part of a societal morality" (6).

This transfer of the protective function from the kinship unit to nonkinship units suggests that the tendency for major responsibility of the care of deaf children shifting from the family to the school will continue. The usual interpretation for this shift has been attributed to the problem of communication. To suggest that the residential school for the deaf take steps to involve the family in the educational process and to encourage the deaf child to identify strongly with his family group faces not only the difficulty of communication but also a change in the interpretation of the protective function. *Our society permits a transferral of responsibility.* Add to this the frustrations of the family with a nonhearing child and his hearing sibling, the sense of guilt about neglecting the hearing child in favor of the deaf child and the problem multiplies. Studies in the area of diabetic children reflect these family difficulties (7). Although the problem will be related to such things as the onset of illness or the degree of deafness, it is apparent in a child-centered society that the possibility of seeking the protective function from other agencies is accepted as a necessity.

There are times when those dealing with the deaf attribute to the disability many problems which merely reflect larger societal problems. Difficulties in relating the family to school programs is almost universal in our culture. This frustration of accepting a diminishing role of the family sometimes prohibits the educator of the deaf from working in areas that he assumes sacred to family life. Sex education outside the family is most often criticized because it is the family's role and should not be infringed upon by outside agencies. That this is not true is reflected by the willingness on the part of the family to transfer this function to a more specialized agency. In our social and personal hygiene programs, we found that of the sixty families asked to give permission for their children to take part, all accepted.

What is the role of the family today? Despite the loss of certain functions, the American family has adapted itself to a new level of operation which is, in many ways, more specialized but in no sense less important. The transfer of a variety of functions from the family to other structures of society need not represent a decline in the family. These changes have created in the family a more specialized agency than before, possibly a new type of family that maintains the important functions or what might well be called the root functions of the family system. Talcott Parsons states that "the basic and irreducible functions of the family are two: first, the primary socialization of children so that they can truly become members of the society into which they have been born; second, the stabilization of the adult personalities of the population of the society" (8).

The functions of the family have moved from those centered on activities on behalf of society to those concerned about activities on behalf of personality. The intimacy that persons need to maintain their stability is found chiefly within the family. We have become a child-centered society and there is little indication that this situation will change. The family is the cradle of personality development. It is the family that must inculcate basic disciplines, instill aspirations, teach skills, and define the social roles. It is the family that has the obligation to provide the continuing intimate interpersonal relationships between persons which are the foundations for personality development.

What is the relationship of the residential school for the deaf to this process of the socialization of the child? Many of the skills of manipulation, of awareness, are taught in the intimate interactions between parent and child. Basic to this skill development is language, for it serves not only as a means of communication but as a container of the cultural heritage of the people. If growth in knowledge is related to break-through in language development, the educator of the deaf is indeed parent and school.

However, there is more to this question of fulfilling the role of the family, on the part of the educators of the deaf, than this issue of knowledge transmission. There is the need to accept greater responsibility for the development of the ingredients of character, responsibility and respect for the feelings of others within the personality of the child. It has been found that there are two basic roles that must be performed in all small task-oriented groups. The one is understood as an expressive role and the other as an instrumental role. The expressive roles are related to emotional components of behavior while the instrumental roles are those related to behavior for achievement of specific tasks. Sussman suggests that "the extended kin family provides the emotional support and care for its members and, therefore, is most likely to carry out expressive roles while reliance is placed largely on other systems such as the hospital, medical, welfare, and the like to meet the instrumental needs involved in long-term illness and disability" (9).

What this suggests, however, is that the educator of the deaf must be aware of this expressive role. He must ask the questions: Who will endow the nonhearing child with achievement motivation? Who supports or who internalizes the norm so that the individual becomes self-operative? There seems to be emphasis on vocational rehabilitation with less regard for social rehabilitation. Successful rehabilitation demands that the individuals be able to operate independently in society at all levels. Louie J. Fant, Jr. expressed this concern in an article entitled, "The Meaning of Responsibility — Can It Be Taught?" He suggested that the educator of the deaf "must create an atmosphere in which identification with adequate models is likely to occur," that the educator of the deaf must "devise and implement love-oriented techniques of discipline for the development of conscience-controlled behavior and abandon wherever possible materialistically oriented techniques of discipline which promote self-directed control of behavior" (10). There is a vital necessity to be aware of the expressive role as over against the instrumental role with its emphasis on the task of earning a living, formal instruction, and discipline. Social behavior is a product not only of environmental and genetic factors but also of norms and values that the individual learns in his society.

A major role for the educator of the deaf is to reinterpret the goals and the rules of society and adapt them to the capacities of the individual and to his special circumstances. This role teeters on the edge between frustrations and satisfaction. One of the phrases most often repeated as I worked with the deaf was: "You do not understand the deaf because you have not worked with them" To those who do work with the deaf, the statement goes like this: "You do not understand the deaf, because you are not deaf." It is possible for the educator of the deaf to crystallize roles for the deaf child which might stigmatize that person. There is no doubt that we have seen some individuals who find the illness role to be advantageous (11). However, the effects of the subculture of the deaf and his social institutions also determine the definition of disability.

Some writings suggest that one might conceive of the deaf person as deviant. Freidson states that "by definition, then a person said to be handicapped is so defined because he deviates from what he himself or others believe to be normal or appropriate. In this sense, the concept of deviance is central to rehabilitation activities" (12). This deviation is accepted by society and no penalties are imposed on the individual because of his behavior, but it does suggest a social marginality.

I would be happier to use Florence Kluckhohn's term "variant" rather than deviant, but the use of the term does pose some questions (13). It is not the physical attributes of disability that are so important as is the definition of the situation. It is possible for the educator of the deaf to provide a role that expresses the traditional stereotype of the deaf. It well might be the hearing world's "way of doing a thing" rather than that of the nonhearing. We must use a frame of reference that fits the nonhearing. We must understand what deaf people want of themselves, their interpretation of the rehabilitation goal that they see appropriate. We must accept the fact that often the deaf child with whom we work has more insight into the actual cultural world which the society permits them to achieve than does the teacher. It is necessary to learn to reward those strivings that are within their range and overcome the possibility of imposing a specific type of deviant role. Scott, in discussing the blind, states, "rehabilitators of the blind who have the same beliefs about blindness that the laymen does are not agents of social change. They are agents of the community who make blind persons out of people who cannot see" (14).

Rubin Hill, in an article entitled "Social Stress on the Family," raised a question of how families react to "crisis-stress" and informed us that no crisis situation is the same for any given family so that the event is not the problem but the family's "definition of the situation." He developed a formula: A (the event) → interacts with B (the family crisis-meeting resources) → interacts with C (the definition the family makes of the event) → produces X (the crisis). The crucial issue is within the family itself, the elements of B and C. If the family defines the event as crisis, it is crisis. He found that the family that was crisis prone did not have a sense of unity and was not capable of shifting its position (15).

We must seek a consensus, a common definition of the role of the deaf child. We must avoid the crystallizing of a deviant pattern for the deaf. We must introduce the widest experiences possible for the deaf child. We must expand, especially in working with the deaf, the horizons of the child, to move him in and out of the variant value orientation to that of the dominant value orientation of the culture. We must develop within the child a responsibility to adult life rather than a hostility. In our process of education, we miss this mode of development in our confusion about readiness. Breener states, "The curriculum revolution has made it plain even after only a decade that the idea of readiness is a mysterious half-truth. It is a half-truth largely because it turns out that one teaches readiness or provides opportunities for its nurture; one does not simply wait for it. Readiness, in these terms, consists of mastery of those simpler skills that permit one to reach higher skills" (16). We must leave the child with as many free choices as possible as he looks at the varieties of ways in which we behave.

It is important that we stir the desire for research and theorizing in the area of rehabilitation. Those who have worked with the deaf have much to offer in the attempt to understand the impact of dependency on the individual, the family and the society.

REFERENCES

1. Sussman, Marvin B.: Outcome and Outlooks, *Sociology and Rehabilitation.* U. S. Department of Health. Education and Welfare, 1966, Grant No. RD 1684-6, pp. 236-237.
2. United States Department of Commerce, Bureau of the Census: *Historical Statistics of the United States. 1789-1945* (1949), Series B 171-181, p. 29, and Bureau of the Census, Series P 20, No. 106 (January 9, 1961). p.2.
3. United States Department of Commerce, Bureau of the Census: *Statistical Abstract of the United States, 1962,* Table 1071, p. 758.
4. Bredemeier, Harry C., and Stephenson, Richard M.: *The Analysis of Social Systems,* New York, Holt, Rinehart and Winston, Inc., 1962, p. 207.
5. Burgess, Ernest W., and Locke, Harvey J.: *The Family,* New York, American Book Company, 1960, p. 466, quoted from U. S. Department of Health, Education, and Welfare, Annual Report. Washington, D. C., 1958, pp. 17-81.
6. Straus, Robert: Social Change and The rehabilitative Concept, *Sociology and Rehabilitation,* U. S. Department of Health, Education and Welfare, 1966. Grant No. RD 1684-6, p. 24.
7. Sussman, Marvin B.: Sociological Theory in Deafness; Problems and Perspectives, *Research on Behavioral Aspects of Deafness.* Proceedings of a National Research Conference on Behavioral Aspects of Deafness, May, 1965, Sponsored by University of Illinois. pp. 67-68.
8. Parsons, Talcott, and Bales, Robert F.: *Family, Socialization and Interaction Process.* Glencoe, The Free Press, 1955, pp. 16-17.
9. Sussman, Marvin B.: *op. cit.,* p. 69.
10. Fant, Louis J., Jr.: The Meaning of Responsibility — Can It Be Taught. *Proceedings of the Forty-Second Meeting of the Convention of American Instructors of the Deaf.* U. S. Government Printing Office, Washington, 1966, pp. 461-462.
11. Parsons, Talcott: *The Social System,* Glencoe, The Free Press, 1951, pp. 428-473.
12. Freidson, Eliot: Disability as Social Deviance. *Sociology and Rehabilitation,* U. S. Department of Health, Education and Welfare, 1966, Grant No. RD 1684-6, p. 72.
13. Kluckhohn, Florence Rockwood: Dominant and Variant Value Orientations. Clyde Kluckhohn and Henry A. Murray: *Personality in Nature, Society and Culture,* New York, Alfred A. Knopf, 1959, pp. 342-357.
14. Scott, Robert A.: *Comments About Interpersonal Processes of Rehabili-*

tation, Sociology and Rehabilitations, op. cit., p. 138.

15. Hill, Rubin: Social Stress on the Family. *Social Casework, 38*:139-150, 1958.

16. Bruner, Jerome S.: Education as Social Invention, *Saturday Review of Literature,* February 19, 1966, p. 72.

Chapter 36

Counseling the Parents
of Acoustically
Handicapped Children

LeROY D. HEDGECOCK

W HILE the subject of this discussion does not allow me to contribute nor even to review a vast body of new knowledge, it does permit a report of significant strides in the application of our knowledge. In recent years there has been a growing interest in the problems of deafness with particular attention to the preventive, corrective, and rehabilitative measures that apply to these problems.

It does not require an exhaustive survey of facilities to reveal that an increasing number of agencies and individuals are providing improved equipment and procedures for dealing with the hearing problems of children. A questionnaire distributed in 1950 to accredited medical schools in the United States and Canada showed that twenty-seven individuals in fifteen institutions were serving in the capacity of nonmedical consultants or teachers in speech and hearing therapy (4). Several medical centers have speech and hearing clinics and some conduct classes for the deaf and hard of hearing. A number of schools questioned offer lectures on speech and hearing problems and provide observation in this field for medical students.

Note: Reprinted by permission of the Editor, *Transactions, American Academy of Opthalmology and Otolaryngology, 56*:66-72, 1952.

From the Section of Otolaryngology and Rhinology, Mayo Clinic.

Presented at the meeting of the Committee on Conservation of Hearing of the American Academy of Ophthalmology and Otolaryngology, Oct. 14, 1951, Chicago, Ill.

Audiologic services under sponsorship of educational institutions and state departments of education as well as public health and private agencies have undergone extensive growth since the end of World War II. Outstanding in this development have been college and university speech and hearing clinics which serve most of the larger communities and many smaller communities throughout the United States. Also of note are the preschool and extracurricular programs in speech and hearing therapy offered by numerous local chapters of the American Hearing Society. During the year 1950-1951 in eighteen states, departments of health were carrying on programs in conservation of hearing (6) and in thirty-one states, departments of education were conducting some type of program in speech and hearing rehabilitation (5). The National Society for Crippled Children and Adults, Inc., had facilities for speech and hearing therapy in eighteen states during 1950-1951 (7). I have no data on the activities in this field of the public, parochial, and private schools, but it is apparent from the demand for teachers trained in speech and hearing therapy that such work is being expanded in the school systems throughout the country.

While it cannot be said that all of these facilities and services are standardized, it is true that reliable information on suitable equipment and procedures is readily available to all. A recent textbook on public school audiometry by Dahl (3) should do much to bring about more uniform and more reliable audiometric procedures. A book by Watson and Tolan (14) on hearing tests and hearing instruments describes in considerable detail most of the equipment and techniques used for clinical evaluation and diagnosis of hearing disorders. A manual for planning a clinic for the rehabilitation of the acoustically handicapped by Bergman (1) deals suitably with the development, the function and the organization of audiology clinics. The combined bibliographies of these books provide a comprehensive listing of the recent research and writing on the subject of hearing tests.

In 1949 Utley (13) prepared a concise review of tests and procedures for determining auditory acuity of young children. The procedures described include the use of percussion toys, squeaking toys, whistles, horns, bells, pitch pipes and meaningful sounds, such as tapping the feeding bottle, clapping the hands, whistling, and vocalizing. A variety of situations are described in which observations of a child's responses may provide reliable clues to the acuity of hearing. "The Peep Show" technique is reviewed. Testing of speech reception is discussed and encouraged whenever the vocabulary and language development of the child permits. Utley also reports on several of the early attempts at objective audiometry by the use of the electroencephalograph and the skin galvanometer. During the last two years the galvanic skin resistance technique in audiometry as described by Bordley and Hardy (2) has undergone considerable trial and validation. The results have proved to be reasonably reliable in determining the functional condition of the auditory mechanism without dependence on intentional response of the individual being tested.

Briefly, this technique utilizes a conditioned response obtained by associating sound stimuli with electric shock. After conditioning is established, the sound alone, if it is heard, will produce a sweat response which is normally elicited by electric shock. This response can be measured precisely by the resistance of the skin to a minute electric current. In this way it is possible to determine the lowest levels at which sounds can be heard and thus to plot an audiogram.

Despite certain limitations and difficulties of administering the above test, I believe it is correct to say that this procedure in the hands of experienced examiners has passed the experimental stage. It is being used clinically now at a number of audiologic centers.

With the information obtained by one or several of the audiometric techniques added to that obtained by a thorough case history and otologic examination, it frequently is possible to answer the question of what caused the loss of hearing. With still greater certainty it becomes possible to determine what can be done in the way of treatment. Finally, a basis is provided for intelligent planning of rehabilitative procedures.

Despite the fact that knowing the cause of a loss of hearing does not insure its amenability to treatment nor necessarily alter the course of training, still it is important to determine the cause if possible. In addition to the doctors', teachers' and parents' interests in the matter, children themselves are likely to inquire about it. Certainly the possibility of hereditary factors is of interest to the entire family and to society in general. It seems a serious injustice to permit a deaf individual to reach adulthood and parenthood with naive or completely erroneous impressions as to the nature of his handicap.

Of greater importance from an educational standpoint than the cause of deafness and frequently imperative in the determination of the cause are the matters of degree and type of loss of hearing and the age of the child at the onset of the impairment. Either in the absence of suitable medical treatment or at the conclusion of treatment which does not produce complete cure, the suitability of a hearing aid and the availability of proper training facilities become matters of prime importance. The evaluation of both of these approaches to the problem depends to a large extent on the degree and type of deafness and on the age at which the child loses his hearing. If a child has enough residual hearing to acquire speech and language through the auditory channel either with or without the use of amplification, the educational problem is vastly simpler than if speech and language must be developed primarily through senses other than hearing. If the loss of hearing occurs after a child has developed a fairly sound basis of oral communication, the handicapping effect is less severe than if it occurs before oral communication is established. On the other hand, it is likely that a child who has never heard or who loses his hearing early in life undergoes decidedly less emotional disturbance than one who has learned the importance of oral communication before his hearing suffers. Of course there are all degrees of the developmental stages here implied, and loss of hearing may occur at any stage of the process. This fact complicates an analysis of the problem, but in no way diminishes the significance of these variable factors in understanding what impairment of hearing means to an individual and to those with whom he associates.

An accurate and authoritative evaluation of the hearing of a child suspected of having hearing disability is an important first step in bringing the parents to grips with the problem. It is the only hope available for ending the frequently futile search for a diagnosis of normalcy and preoccupation with unrealistic hopes for curative treatment.

Contrary to some belief it surely is an ultimate kindness to parents to be told as early and as accurately as possible the condition of their child's hearing. Certainly it is the only approach that does justice to the child. Acceptance of the situation must be followed by understanding of the problem and of the procedures to be employed in alleviating or compensating for the condition. The discovery or the confirmation that their child has a hearing impairment frequently causes an emotional reaction on the part of parents which must be resolved to some extent before intelligent understanding and management is possible.

Serious responsibility falls on the physician in interpreting the problems of deafness realistically and at the same time hopefully. Feelings of bewilderment and despair must be and can be combated by assurance that loss of hearing need not interfere with adequate growth and development of a child nor with happiness and usefulness as an adult. Realization of this fundamental point can be established more effectively if parents either have visited or can arrange to visit homes and schools where children with similar handicaps are living and learning. If the child in question has total or severe loss of hearing, discussion with a teacher or counselor of the deaf or with an adult deaf person may be of great help. It is helpful also for parents of handicapped children to meet with one another. The sharing of a difficult task may not only make it bearable but frequently facilitates its accomplishment.

By whatever means available it is essential that parents of acoustically handicapped children come to face the matter calmly. Only by doing so can they learn to behave in a manner which will provide the security necessary for the wholesome development of every child. If parents show either by attitude or deed that they are not happy with their child, the child inevitably will sense that discontent, and it will instill in him a feeling of inadequacy. On the other hand, if parents wholeheartedly accept the child as he is and look on the handicap as a challenging obstacle, the child will share that attitude and will be ready to help in overcoming the obstacle.

As individuals and as groups, parents must take the responsibility of educating their neighbors and friends in matters that will facilitate communication with their acoustically handicapped children. There is need for intensive effort along this line to help make the hearing world a pleasanter place for those with impaired hearing. A striking example of this need is seen in the lack of effort on the part of most hearing people to communicate orally with a deaf person. A great many individuals become known as "deaf mutes" and behave as if they could not talk while in fact they may have spent many years learning speech and have been considered able to talk satisfactorily by the standards of their teachers. The failure of a hearing person to understand readily a deaf person's speech usually causes both to give up without sincere effort. After a number of such failures, the deaf person is likely to become discouraged and quit trying to talk. In turn, the hearing person is likely to conclude promptly that the speech of all deaf people is unintelligible. This vicious circle of failure needs to be broken. Probably no one can do more in this respect than wise parents who thoroughly understand the problems imposed by loss of hearing on a child and at the same time can recall the indifference of people not closely associated with this handicap. Of course it is equally important that the acoustically handicapped person be taught to accept responsibility for helping the hearing world to understand and adjust to his differences.

I do not mean here to delve into all the intricacies of the emotional life of children, but a brief review may be helpful. It is generally agreed that the basic emotional needs of handicapped children are the same as those of all children. Josselyn (9) has stated those needs briefly as "(1) to be loved and to love in return," and "(2) to strike out against situations which are unpleasant." The most important job for the parents of a deaf child is to recognize these needs and to find ways of meeting them. Parents who can sincerely love and accept their child without reservation are ready and usually able to cope with the handicap itself. Lassman (10) writes: "Studies have revealed that many emotional problems of the deaf adolescent and adult socially, academically and vocationally have their roots in their parents' attitudes toward the handicap."

Many of the methods as well as the principles of handling acoustically handicapped children may be adapted from those applying to children in general. For example, the use of well-established, though flexible, routines in matters of rest, play, eating, dressing, washing and toilet activities is basic in efficient management of all children. Adherence to routine activities is probably even more important to the well-being of children with limited communicative skill than to those who converse normally. In the matter of discipline, too, the same practices apply for the most part regardless of physical differences. The practice of genuine friendliness, patience and tolerance along with fairness, firmness and consistency can generally be expected to result in acceptable behavior from all types of children. The similarity is seen again in the need for activity. All healthy children are especially active before they learn to talk. Since the deaf child is retarded in development of speech, it is to be expected that his period of excessive activity will be prolonged. Thus in the handling of a deaf child, the approach should be in terms of guiding the activity rather than curbing it. Provision of suitable toys and play facilities and direction in games of action are appropriate means of meeting this need.

In addition to the general principles of management, parents of a deaf child want to know what to do to promote development of the speech and language of their child. They should talk to him, sing to him, and play with him even more than they would with a normal child. This talk and play should utilize all of the senses with particular emphasis on vision and touch and any residual hearing he may have. They should interest the child in watching and imitating facial movements and in hearing and feeling the vibration of sound. They should grasp every opportunity to broaden his interests and experiences both with things and with people, particularly with other children. These experiences may be used as stimuli for development of speech and language. The emphasis upon speech, important as it is, should not obscure the fact that there are other forms of expression which play a vital role in early efforts at communication. Abundant use of gestures, pantomime, and facial expression will demonstrate to even a very young child that he can express himself and make many of his wants known in an acceptable manner.

The responsibility of parents to their child is essentially the same whether or not the child attends a nursery school. However, enrollment in a suitable nursery school should be helpful in teaching a deaf child to play and work constructively with other children. If there is no special school available to the young deaf child, it may be wise to enter him in a nursery class along with children who have normal hearing. At the preschool level a handicap in communcation need not entirely prohibit profitable experiences. If the child in question is physically and emotionally mature enough, probably he will adjust adequately by watching and imitating other children in individual and group activities. If he lacks the necessary maturity for satisfactory group activity, it may be necessary for the mother or a special assistant to attend nursery school with him until he is ready to participate on his own. The success of an early venture in school will depend to a large measure, of course, on the attitude and ingenuity of the teacher in charge.

If suitable nursery school facilities are not to be found in the community, it generally is advisable for parents to follow the guidance of a correspondence course providing home-training material for deaf children. The John Tracy Clinic (11) in Los Angeles makes such a course available to anyone who writes for it. It is advisable also for mothers to attend one of the short-term training programs for parents of preschool deaf children which are offered each year by a number of schools for the deaf. In 1950 such courses were offered by twelve public residential schools and by fifteen denominational or private schools. Information regarding these courses may be found in the January issue of the *American Annals of the Deaf* (8) or may be obtained by writing to the editor of that journal.

Sometime before a deaf child is ready for entrance to elementary school, the parents should inform themselves on the types of schools or classes available to him. There are two general types of special schools for deaf children. One is a day school which operates on the same basis as the regular public schools. The other type is a residential school where children both live and attend classes. There are private, denominational, and public schools of each type. Certain obvious differences exist in the educational approach and scope of the different types of schools. The day school concerns itself mainly with so-called academic matters, leaving the more personal and social areas of guidance to the home, while the residential school accepts a greater responsibility for the all-around development of the child. The difference often is largely relative inasmuch as children attending residential schools may go home on weekends, holidays and, of course, during the summer months.

Beyond these organizational distinctions there are differences in philosophies and emphasis of training from school to school. For this reason it is especially desirable for parents to visit the school in which their child is most likely to be enrolled. If circumstances permit a choice of facilities, it probably is wise for parents to investigate each prospective school from the point of view of the particular needs and desires of the individual child and his family.

In making this assessment parents might well be cautioned to keep the welfare of the child in mind more strongly than their own desires. It is perfectly natural and proper for parents to dread the thought of their child being away from home. As a result of this feeling, they are likely to be willing to accept less adequate facilities near home than might be available to them elsewhere. In this connection, too, there is strong appeal and certain logic in the concept that deaf children develop more normally by attending school with children who hear normally than by attending a special school with other deaf children. This reasoning can be supported only if the assumption is made that by attending school with hearing children they also are sharing similar experiences of all kinds. It is important that a child play and work on a relatively equal basis with other children in order to develop and maintain a stable emotional life. Since so much of school life, both academic and social, dependent upon oral communication, it becomes almost impossible for a child with severe hearing loss to compete or even to share experiences comparable with associates who hear normally.

This reasoning is not intended to convey the belief that all deaf children should be educated in schools separate from those for other children, but it suggests that reasons for accepting less than the best facilities available should be examined closely. Generally, the best facilities for educating deaf children are to be found in special schools of sufficient size to permit suitable grouping on the basis of age, achievement and social maturity. Larger schools are likely to offer more diversified programs and better physical equipment and thus be more adaptable to individual needs.

Information regarding all of the special schools, special classes, and educational clinics and camps for acoustically handicapped children in the United States and Canada is conveniently tabulated yearly in the January issue of the *American Annals of the Deaf* (8). This information includes the location, the size and type of school, the number and training of the teachers, the scope and emphasis of the educational program, as well as many other details. A similar directory of schools is given in Myklebust's book, (12) *Your Deaf Child; A Guide for Parents.* This book also contains much other information and excellent advice for parents of deaf children. There are other sources of information on this subject — too many to review here. Either of the publications just mentioned will serve as an index too much of the printed material as well as to individuals and organizations which can be of help to parents and advisers of acoustically handicapped children.

REFERENCES

1. Bergman, Moe: The audiology clinic: a manual for planning a clinic for the rehabilitation of the acoustically handicapped. *Acta oto-laryng. (Suppl.), 89*:7-107, 1950.
2. Bordley, J. E. and Hardy, W. G.: A study in objective audiometry with the use of a psychogalvanometric response. *Ann Otol, Rhin Laryng, 58*:751-760, 1949.
3. Dahl, Loraine A.: *Public School Audiometry: Principles and Methods,* Danville, Interstate Press, 1949, pp. 290.
4. Doctor, P. V.: Medical school personnel in speech and hearing problems. *Am Ann Deaf, 96*:3-4 (Jan.) 1951.
5. ———: State Departments of Education having a speech and hearing program, 1950-1951. *Am Ann Deaf, 96*:33 (Jan.) 1951.
6. ———: State Departments of Health having a conservation of hearing program, 1950-1951. *Am Ann Deaf, 96*:34 (Jan.) 1951.
7. ———: State societies of the National Society for Crippled Children and Adults, Inc., having a speech and hearing program. *Am Ann Deaf, 96*:35 (Jan.) 1951.
8. ———: Tabular Statement of American Schools for the Deaf, Oct. 31, 1940, Miscellaneous Information. *Am Ann Deaf, 96*:262-269 (Jan.) 1951.

 9. Josselyn, Irene M.: The big emotional problems of children. In *If You Have a Deaf Child* (Pamphlet), Urbana, University of Illinois Press, 1949, pp. 47-59.
10. Lassman, Grace H.: *Language for the Preschool Deaf Child,* New York, Grune & Stratton, 1950, p. 4.
11. Montague, H.: Correspondence Course for Parents of Preschool Deaf and Hard of Hearing Children, John Tracy Clinic, 924 W. 37 St., Los Angeles 7, Calif. Revised 1948.
12. Myklebust, H. R.: *Your Deaf Child; A Guide for Parents,* Springfield, Charles C Thomas, 1950, pp. 132.
13. Utley, Jean: Suggestive procedures for determining auditory acuity in very young acoustically handicapped children. *Eye, Ear, Nose & Throat Monthly, 28*:590-595 (Dec.) 1949.
14. Watson, L. A. and Tolan, Thomas: *Hearing Tests and Hearing Instruments.* Baltimore, Williams & Wilkins Co., 1949, pp. 597.

Chapter 37

Psychological Problems of the Parents of a Blind Child

ARTHUR A. EISENSTADT

IN any study of the problems and reactions of a group of people, one must realize that different individuals facing the same pressures may exhibit many different reactions as there are individuals. Kurt Lewin (1) once observed that we do not have a special "group psychology" so much as a psychology of individuals in a group situation, which supports this same viewpoint. However, it is possible to examine which tensions, drives, attitudes, and reactions are strongly present in a given situation, and to point out which of these are most frequently observed in such a setting. It is on such a basis that this paper will report, not only how the parents of blind children react, but also what pressures and forces are most likely to produce certain reactions which shall be here described. To this end, let us briefly examine three areas: the status of blindness, parental reaction to this problem, and the psychoeducational implications which parents and teachers must recognize and manipulate.

The official New Jersey state department definition of a blind person describes him as one who "has 20/200 vision or less in the better eye, with refraction or field limitation induced to 20 degrees" (2). A less technical description, which has been "... continuously used by doctors, teachers and government and

Note: Reprinted by permission of the *International Journal for the Education of the Blind,* 5:20-24, 1955, published by the Association for Education of the Visually Handicapped.

At the time of the first publication of this article, Dr. Eisenstadt was a professor at Rutgers University, New Brunswick, New Jersey.

private workers . . . states that 20/200 means that if a person, even with glasses, can read at a distance of 20 feet only the large type that a person with normal vision can read at 200 feet, he is considered blind" (3). The number of blind persons is a figure which exceeds most lay expectations. In New York State, where the census of the blind is fairly carefully kept, well over eighteen thousand individuals have been counted (4). Also, in terms of the number of parents involved, "blindness is no respecter of age. Although it is not common to childhood, blindness can and does occur at birth and throughout life" (5). Over a three-year period in New York State, 236 blind children under seven years of age were reported, while another 163 were found between seven and seventeen (6). Further, not only is the number of parents of blind children significantly large, but there is indication that the figures will increase. Although some congenital causes such as venereal disease transmitted to the foetus (ophthalmia neonatorium) have been greatly decreased, certain other defects whose cause and prevention are unknown have appeared. Retrolental fibroplasia is the most prominent of these, and each year brings to light an increasing number of these cases (7). Even from so sketchy a review, it is apparent that parents of blind children comprise a substantial group. What about these parents? We know that most handicapped children have emotional and psychological problems, and we are making progress in meeting those problems, but what about the parents? Here is a brief description of what happens to many of them.

> It is natural, in fact almost inevitable, that when parents discover they have a blind baby they are not only sorrowed but shocked. . . . Almost all young parents who find their child is blind are shocked and confused. . . . It is the tendency of most of us faced with misfortune to rebel, and to wonder why it had to happen to us (8).

The reactions just described and their usual sequelae roughly comprise four stages. First, there may be a profound and almost numbing sense of *shock and grief.* The parents may feel an intense sense of loss, of sorrow, and of incredulity. "It isn't so. There must be some mistake. It just couldn't happen to us. This is the end of everything." These are typical remarks made or thought about while the parent is still adjusting to the initial realization of the handicap. In response to the feeling that everyone must be wrong about the child's blindness, the parents very often go from one specialist to another, hoping against hope that someone has a "special" and unique knowledge which will dispel the ugly reality they refuse to accept. The results are harmful both financially and emotionally, and if the child is older, will be psychologically unwholesome for both parent and child.

The second stage is one of *bewilderment and helplessness.* Despondence generally gives way to a kind of acceptance, and the first question is, usually, "What do we do about it?" The answers are often gained with great difficulty. First, the parent must overcome his diffidence and embarrassment enough to go outside himself and ask questions. Also, the doctor may be largely or entirely concerned with the medical picture, and views his role exclusively in terms of medical, surgical, or physiological therapy. It is a rare eye specialist, in the writer's experience, who offers guidance of a social and psychological nature. Fortunately, state departments of education, residential schools for the blind and private agencies such as the Lighthouse and the American Foundation for the Blind in New York City, are superbly ready to counsel the parent. It is well that they do so, for the feeling parents experience at this time has been vividly depicted by the Flaxmans, who wrote about their own problem: "Surely there must be something that can be done. There must be someone who can help us. . . . This aspect of the situation we wish to stress. Time, patience, love, and a solid foundation of a way of life took care of the initial waves of hopelessness" (9). Eventually, depending in degree on the parent's aggressiveness and initiative, a fund of helpful and often conflicting advice and data is amassed. With this new and frequently incomplete knowledge, the parent finds himself beset by new and rather tortuous aspects of his problem.

Phase three of the parent's evolution, now that he has learned something of the social and emotional obstacles to be overcome, is characterized most prominently by the parents' *fears.* Armed at this point only with half-information and vague reassurances that "things will turn out all right," the parents may have visions of an isolated, unhappy child. They may picture the child as a social stigma, forcing them to curtail their own activities, keeping the child discreetly out of sight when company comes, perhaps moving to a new community in order to escape the pity of those who knew them before the catastrophe occurred. They may envision the child as a crushing financial burden, steadily and relentlessly draining away the family income in special books, toys, education, and medical services — and where the community does not help them, this is just what may happen. Then again, they may feel, and this is a corrosive fear indeed, a sense of divine punishment. They may come to believe that because of certain sins or misdeeds of their own, Providence is now visiting a terrible punishment upon them by putting the curse of blindness on their child. With such a feeling, that "the sins of the parents have been visited on the children," it is not hard to visualize a parent who finds it impossible to deny his child anything under the sun. Perhaps the worst fear of all is that which exists when one parent suspects the other of being the one whose guilt brought down this form of divine punishment. Unless psychological perspective is restored, emotional discord and eventual schism may be the unhappy result.

Thus we come to the fourth and final period — the longest and most wearing of all. It is epitomized by the word *tension* in all its manifold aspects. Obviously, the parents have been brought to a state of great anxiety over the child's development. At home, eating, dressing, playing, and talking have presented a bewildering galaxy of minor vexing, frustrating and heartrending problems. To watch a child grope around patiently and endlessly for a toy lying just a few inches away from it, to watch a toddler walk straight into a table, edge, wince, and go about his business taking for granted that all people bump their way painfully through the house, to watch other sighted children play gaily and without fear on the sidewalk and know that your child is forever barred from such carefree play — these are tense, enervating, and joyless moments which parents repeat a thousandfold. Eventually, either in a residential or special public school, the youngster is cared for by others with training and competence such as the parent has probably never seen before. For the first time, the responsibilities he or she has had for years are shifted to other shoulders. The reaction is varied and sometimes startling. A sense of profound relief may be felt, followed by a realization that bone-deep weariness now has a chance to dissipate itself. Then, like the pendulum pushed too far in one direction, comes the reverse swing. Some parents experience a sharp disinterest, an apathy to what is going on. Others develop a fear-filled concern or a hypercritical attitude toward those caring for their child, and may even become quite annoyed with the individual who is now sharing their burden. Whatever the pendulum's position, the parents are in emotional imbalance until they comprehend the three true facets of responsibility: delegated, shared, and personal.

Let us now examine the educational implications which these brief observations suggest. A federal study has found that the training procedure where exceptional children are involved "should be based upon competent psychological, educational, social and medical study" (10). As the writer sees it, the parents of the exceptional child must be given the same kind of analysis in terms of *their* needs, too, for when they are upset, the strongest educational and emotional influence on the young child is rendered ineffective. An indication of how important is their role may be found in the statement by two specialists that "Under adequate *parental* guidance, the normal blind child should be ready to enter school at approximately the same age as a seeing child" (11). (Italics added.) Not only should parents and other close associates understand the child's psychological problems, they must also be aware of his mechanical limitations as well. Testifying to the impact of this area of influence is the preface of a revealing brochure on communications methods which reads, "Prepared for friends and families of the blind" (12), and explains the technical problems of reception, comprehension, and expression of the visually handicapped.

Coupled with this understanding of the child's needs must be an alert awareness on the parents' part of the problems which face them. Easily the most tempting error the parent can make is that of excessive indulgence. In a monograph on the sightless, Totman notes that "one of the biggest pitfalls of the parents of a blind child is the danger of indulgence. Parents . . . permit . . . extra pleasures and favors and excuse him from duties . . . which is poor training and . . . will accentuate his unlikeness to his brothers and sisters" (13). The answer to this situation is found in the perceptive admonition of Speer, who advises "discipline yourself, and then you will be able to discipline your child. It is hard not to pamper and spoil a handicapped child, but life will be more pleasant for the whole family, and the child too, if you can make yourself treat him as a perfectly normal youngster" (14). A succinct recommendation is that offered by Habbe, who tested many handicapped children for psychological deviations: "The best attitude is to avoid the extremes of sentimentalism and neglect" (15). Gertrude Van den Broek, for many years a counselor in the field of the blind, cautions parents to be ready "to build in him the sense of your loyalty and confidence" (16).

Some indication of the psychological needs of the handicapped may be found in the following recommendations:

1. Give the child a positive feeling of security.
2. Make the child feel that he is loved and wanted by the family.
3. Make sure that the child is free of fear and regressiveness regarding his blindness.
4. Give the child ample and varied opportunity to develop his creative and original capacities.
5. Avoid being arbitrary in your attitude and treatment.
6. Build a sense of self-reliance and personal worth.
7. Avoid pushing the child beyond his depth and potential
8. Answer questions frankly — do not give an impression of secrecy or reluctance regarding the handicap.
9. Emphasize improvement, not perfection.
10. Be sure to enrich the child's life with as many experiences as possible.
11. Be prepared for obstacles, setbacks and frictions — accept them as inevitable and devote your energies to solving them.
12. Share your experiences with other parents, and mutual aid will often result.
13. Plan ahead — visualize experiences to come and prepare for them.

14. Weigh many decisions in terms of what the sighted child can be expected to perform.
15. Keep the rounded perspective before you – let social, mental, physical, and emotional competence be your goals.

When all is said and done, no list of rules or tensions can ever be complete or accurate for all children. Like his sighted friends, each blind child is a distinct and different personality, and should be treated as such. For those who are near him – parent, teacher or friend, the opportunity is present to guide and to counsel, to help and to forbear, and in so doing, to grow in stature with him.

REFERENCES

1. Lewin, Kurt: *Social Psychology*, New York.
2. Department of Institutions and Agencies, *A Handbook of Services of the New Jersey State Commission for the Blind,* Pub. No. 52, New Jersey, undated. Unpaged.
3. Yahraes, Herbert: *What Do You Know About Blindness?* New York, Public Affairs Pamphlet No. 124, 1937, p. 3.
4. State Department of Social Welfare: *What About Blindness in Our State?* Commission for the Blind, New York City, undated, 5 pp.
5. *Op. cit.,* p. 2.
6. *Ibid.*
7. Taylor, Josephine L.: Director of Education, New Jersey Commission for the Blind, by interview, April, 1952.
8. Van den Broek, Gertrude: *Guide for Parents of a Preschool Blind Child.* New York State Department of Social Welfare, New York, 1945, p. 13.
9. Flaxmann, E. and G.: *Your Child is Deaf.* Superintendent of Public Instruction, Springfield, Illinois, 1951, unpaged.
10. United States Office of Education, Federal Security Agency, Bulletin, 1940, No. 6, *State Supervisory Programs for the Education of Exceptional Children,* Washington, 1941, p. 53.
11. Lowenfeld, B., and Potts, P. C.: *The Education of the Blind Child.* New York, American Foundation for the Blind, Inc., 1947, p. 5.
12. The Lighthouse of the New York Association for the Blind: *Communication Methods for the Blind.* New York, 1951, 16 pp.
13. Totman, Harriet E.: *What Shall We Do With Our Blind Babies?* New York, American Foundation for the Blind, Inc., 1938, p. 8.
14. Speer, Edith L.: *A Manual for the Parents of Preschool Blind Children.* New York Association for the Blind, New York, 1947, p. 14.
15. Habbe, Stephen: *Personality Adjustment of Adolescent Boys With*

Impaired Hearing. New York, Columbia University Teachers College, 1937, 85 pp.

16. Van den Broek, Gertrude: *op. cit.,* p. 14.
17. Sibilio, J. P.: Mental Hygiene Attitudes Toward the Child with Hearing Difficulties, *Reprint No. 255, Washington,* American Hearing Society, 1952, and Utley, Jean.: Do's and Don'ts for Parents . . .", Illinois, University of Illinois reprint, 1952. Unpaged.

Chapter 38

Infancy: Counseling the Family

FRANK CERULLI and ESTELLE E. SHUGERMAN

IN any discussion of the blind child we rely principally upon our experiences of the last one and a half years. We are indebted to Dr. Philip J. Kahan, Supervising Medical Superintendent, Queens Hospital Center, New York Association for the Blind, and to the board of education of New York City for the opportunity of broadening our own experiences and knowledge.

The education of the blind child, as that of all living creatures, begins at birth. His parents' attitude towards him, their threshhold of acceptance or bitterness about his blindness, will have a profound effect upon his development. It is, therefore, essential that the parents be informed of the child's condition as early as possible, and with complete candor. The earlier this is established, the earlier they can begin to readjust their thinking, to accept their child's disability emotionally. We must be aware that the parents will encounter tremendous difficulties when they discover that the child is blind; they will have feelings of grief, guilt, torment, and hopelessness, and will meet with added frustration and guilt when told by a physician that because the child is blind he should be put away.

In counseling these parents, it is important to help them to realize that the needs of a blind child are primarily the same as those of a sighted child, and that in the first few years of his life he needs, above all, the feeling of security stemming from the affection of his family, and from an environment which has been designed to allow him to develop his potentialities to the full. It may be helpful if, at this early stage, it is pointed out to the parents that the child himself is not conscious of what he is

---

Note: Reprinted by permission of *New Outlook for the Blind,* 55:294-297, 1961.

missing, and that it is they, the parents, who suffer most. Overprotectiveness, overindulgence, pity, and sentiment do untold harm.

In the case of the premature infant, even with respect to those who are not physically handicapped, a definitive diagnosis as to intellectual level, where the question of retardation is raised, is not made until the age of three. We know from other studies that the blind baby develops at a slower pace than the sighted infant. In a situation where there is an added physical handicap, the parents must be encouraged to stimulate the child's development to the utmost. Whatever positive feelings the parents may have had towards the blind infant are distorted to the point where overprotectiveness and overindulgence develops because of the underlying rejection of the child. The resultant effect is that the child's development becomes more stunted and more stultified.

Parents will be more accepting of their handicapped child if the child shows physical and mental development, if he is responsive and learns to do things. In order to accomplish this, the parents need intensive counseling. If this is the firstborn child, the parents would be groping in their handling of the infant even if it were not handicapped; their burden is intensified when the handicap exists. During a sighted child's early years, particularly in the first two years of living, most of his learning occurs without conscious effort and is very largely stimulated by vision. The blind baby is deprived of this stimulation. His interests are confined to listening, feeling, smelling, and tasting. To partially prevent his interests from being turned in upon himself, it is necessary for the parents to stimulate the other senses to a greater degree than with the normal infant. The blindisms develop because the baby is bored; if he has nothing to do, he tends to play with himself and listen to sounds. The blind child has a greater need to be talked to than the sighted infant, he needs to be held more; and since he has no vision, he cannot grab things, so that the mother would have to place things in his hands, all the while talking to the infant. He also needs to be picked up more than the sighted infant because it will give him a feeling of security, of being wanted, and takes his interest outside of himself. This should be started at the age of three months.

We must also consider the fact that the parents may become overzealous and expect the child to accomplish more than he is capable of doing. It is, therefore, our feeling that counseling must be done by someone who is aware of what to expect of the so-called normal infant, and be able to relate it to the handicapped infant, who may or may not have been born prematurely.

The question of psychotherapy with these parents and children, we have found, cannot be approached in an orthodox manner. It is very well to resolve the guilt of the parents for having brought a handicapped child into this world, but this in no way gives them knowledge of how to cope with the child. Concrete suggestions which will make their daily lives more bearable seem to be in order. The parents should be encouraged to give the baby as much physical freedom as possible. He should be encouraged to explore his environment at the earliest possible stage of development. We should consider at this point that the blind child, as others, needs to go through every stage of physical, mental, and emotional development. If this is started at an early enough age, the blind child will learn to navigate in his environment with ease. If he is helped to identify objects tactually and associate these with the proper names, much heartache will be avoided in the future. There is also the possibility that if the child does not learn this at an early stage of development, no amount of teaching, counseling, or therapy will restore the situation to a more normal level. An important aspect of the maturing process is the ability to socialize with one's peers. This seems to be one of the major difficulties encountered by the blind child. It is, therefore, necessary that the parents, through the aid of the counselor, expose the child, from the age of two to three, to other children. This must be done in a continuous fashion.

All aspects of the development should be entered into by the counselors from infancy up. The counselor must have an awareness of the special difficulties involved in helping the blind child to walk, talk, feed himself, and be toilet trained. In all of the developmental phases of the blind baby, the parents must be constantly reminded that the development of the blind child will be slower than that of the sighted child.

We are in a position of treating three children who demonstrate the foregoing points remarkably well. In the case of A, who came to us at the age of seven and a half, we found a very subdued, withdrawn youngster who verbalized a great deal but not in relation to other people; she lived in her own fantasy world. In going over the past history of this child's development, it was ascertained that somewhere between the age of two and three a change in the child's behavior occurred. Until that age, apparently she had made a normal adjustment to living. It is possible that with the birth of a sibling, A felt rejected and left out of the picture and suddenly withdrew into her own little world. She came from the kind of family where intellectual development was stressed over and above all other aspects of living. Our goal, therefore, was to break through her fantasy world and encourage her to live in reality and to relate to others. In discussing this with the mother, we were able to establish to our satisfaction that apparently all the proper things were done for the child to help her development in all areas until the birth of the new sibling. We feel that the trauma of sharing the parents, in addition to possibly further pressure to achieve intellectually, caused the emotional disturbance to develop. It is only after a year and a half of treating both the mother and the child, with outside forces contributing in a positive way to what we were trying to effect, that we were able to break down the resistance of the parents. At the time that A was able to express her hostility towards the mother, immediate improvement in her emotional reactions was noted. She has continued to express her feelings openly. At this time A, although still not able to play constructively with her peers, is a better adjusted child.

In the case of B, this child was subjected to one of the most traumatic experiences that a youngster can have. She was placed in an institution at an early age. The father of this child stated that when his child was born blind, he attended every possible group meeting held for the parents of blind children. He feels that he gained nothing from these experiences other than to have discussions about his feelings of guilt with respect to having fathered a blind child. He stated that if concrete suggestions had been made, the parents could have handled the child more adequately. The parents are vague with respect to the child's emotional disturbance. This is a youngster who has been diagnosed as having a neurological condition, as being mentally defective and/or psychotic. We find that she is none of these, but rather a child with good native endowment who is emotionally disturbed but not mentally ill. During treatment it has become more and more apparent that B has not had sufficient exposure to the common garden variety of objects and experiences in the environment. Her lack of knowledge is not due to retardation but rather to ignorance because she has not been taught. We find it very difficult at this time to overcome this area of neglect. As stated above, if learning of certain things does not occur at the proper age, it is very difficult, almost impossible, to instruct the child when he is older. Much resistance, negativism, and insecurity is reflected in any learning situation. It has been noted, however, that B is not as rigid in her behavior, i.e. she accepts changes in the environment more readily and without panic, she adjusts to new outside situations in a healthier fashion, and recently she has begun to verbalize her feelings with respect to learning, stating: "I can't do it, I don't know how."

In the case of C, the parents were told immediately after birth to place her since the situation was a hopeless one. Aside from their guilt over having borne a handicapped youngster, one can readily imagine what their feelings were when they were given the above suggestion by their pediatrician. They could not place the child, kept her, but were resentful, bitter, and ashamed. In this case we were dealing with rejecting parents and an overprotective grandmother. We can only assume that, although the grand-mother's attitude towards C was not one that we would recommend, she at least was a positive factor in the early years of this child. It was necessary, when we accepted the case, to interview the grandmother as well as the parents and to indicate to her certain things that we wanted accomplished and other things eliminated. This child has been with us for a short time only and we have noticed a change in her, especially in her ability to socialize. It was necessary to be very firm with the parents and the child as well, and to remove certain adverse elements in the environment.

We have given a brief summary of three cases that are being

worked with intensively. One demonstrates acceptance by pressure as far as intellectual achievement is concerned, with no awareness of the social needs of the child. The second case demonstrates the situation of ignorance, guilt, rejection, and ultimate placement. The third case highlights a situation where the parents were told that the situation was hopeless but were unable to give up the child, so that they were in a state of conflict, intensifying their guilt feelings.

In conclusion, we feel that the blind child should be treated as a normal child with the awareness of the handicap, so that special provisions can be made to permit normal maturational development. We feel that no progress can be achieved, either in early infancy or in the age group of our children, unless the parents are given specific, concrete suggestions with respect to helping their children learn about their environment. In the last analysis, it is the parents who have the most influence in the child's life. Without the foregoing, he will vegetate.

Chapter 39

Preadolescence:
The Caseworker and the Family

JOSEPHINE CATENA

OUR concern here is with the group of multiply handicapped blind children who are forming a larger and larger proportion of the caseloads of the social agencies for the blind. In this paper I will discuss essentially the early period of casework contact. While I am dealing primarily with the families of children from seven to twelve years, many of the problems are common to the families of the multiply handicapped blind child of any age.

These parents have suffered the trauma and pain of learning of their child's blindness. Then came the years of watching the child grow, lagging in his development behind sighted children and, in most cases, behind other blind children. As the child becomes older, his problems become more manifest, and by the time he reaches school age, parents are usually aware, on some level, that he has some problem in addition to his blindness. Their awareness now becomes strengthened by various community influences, and the parents are faced with a second trauma, which intensifies their feelings of guilt, inadequacy, anger, and anxiety.

Consider the case of Johnny M., a victim of RLF, now nine years old. Upon learning of his blindness, his parents had suffered shock, some depression, and a break in their marital relationship. They were able to overcome these reactions to some degree but were never able to meet the needs of a child, whose handicap was a severe threat to their already low self-esteem. Thus, around the age of three, Johnny began to show signs of behavior disturbance.

Note: Reprinted by permission of *New Outlook For The Blind, 55*:297-299, 1961.

During his early childhood, Johnny's father was his sole consistent support, as his mother vacillated greatly in her attitude and approach toward him. At the age of seven, Johnny suffered his first convulsive seizure, and was subsequently diagnosed as brain damaged. This, along with Johnny's increasingly difficult behavior and minimal academic success affected his father so strongly that now Mr. M. feels hopeless about Johnny, has very little patience with him, and is almost unable to give the child support in his efforts to cope with his environment.

In this case, as in many others, the caseworker found that she had to deal with the parents' denial of the child's problems. Despite their own problems in handling his tantrums, teasing behavior, and periods of withdrawal, and despite the efforts of social workers and teachers to make them aware of Johnny's disturbance, the M's resisted seeking help for Johnny. It was only after a threatened removal from school, and an actual removal from day camp that the weight of overwhelming evidence made their denial untenable.

The parents of the multiply handicapped child of this age come to the agency with much anxiety and strong negative feeling. They are confused and worried by their child's inability to function adequately. Sometimes they have been through other diagnostic work-ups which have resulted in conflicting diagnoses. They are reluctant to go through another frustrating experience, and yet painfully eager to hear an opinion which will reassure them about the future and offer some solution for the present. At the same time they are fearful of hearing that the prognosis is poor or that there is no help.

These parents, too, have suffered much rejection by the community by the time their child reaches this age range, from relatives, neighbors, and friends as well as from schools and recreation programs. Thus, the parents often come to the agency with lack of trust and with feelings of hopelessness. Their own experiences with their child may only reinforce their defeatism. When they make an effort to reach out to the child, they may experience frustration at the child's lack of response; the parents then react by giving less to the child, which adds to the child's problem, further decreasing his ability to respond.

The picture is sometimes further complicated by the presence of long-standing personality problems in the parents or in marital conflicts.

How can the caseworker help in such a complex situation? In the period of initial contact, the main purpose is to collect relevant data for the diagnostic work-up and to help the parents relate to a source of help. For both these purposes, the establishment of a relationship which gives strength to the parents is crucial. The caseworker must demonstrate an understanding of the parent's needs, fears, and negative feelings, and help the parents express these on whatever level they can. She must also be reassuring and hopeful, wherever this is realistic. At the same time she must not stimulate unrealistic hopes by denying negatives.

CHANNELING EMPATHY

Here the caseworker's job is made more complex by her own reactions. It has been the common experience of caseworkers in our agency to find feelings of depression, frustration, and anxiety aroused in them by the serious nature of the children's handicaps and the damaging effects on the families. We have found that by airing these mutual experiences with each other, we have been able not only to prevent their interference with our work, but to use them to enhance our worker-parent relationships.

The recognition of our own feelings helps us appreciate the parents' need to go slowly in facing all the pain of having a multiply handicapped child. This becomes especially important when the interpretation of diagnosis is made. Most parents cannot integrate this immediately, and may need a number of sessions during which they can ask questions to clarify the meaning of the diagnosis, can disagree, and can experience as much of their feeling reaction as is possible for them. Here again, the social worker's willingness to face the problem with them, honestly, with appropriate attention to both positive and negative aspects, is of great importance. This job is, of course, considerably easier when the possibility exists to offer a concrete program to the parents and to the child. In many cases, parents are unwilling to accept counseling or guidance for themselves unless a program is provided. The parents' ability to accept a special program is directly related to their ability to accept their child's problems.

The final part of the initial phase of casework contact is preparing the parents for participation in the special program. As this may often include continued counseling for the parents, the most effective preparation has been the steady involvement of the parent in the relationship with the caseworker. If this has been possible, the parents understand what is to come because they have already experienced the process. They must also be prepared, in most cases, for a long period of special treatment for themselves and their child, and for the establishment and appreciation of limited goals.

At this time, the problem of the multiply handicapped blind child is one of the most serious we have to face. By turning our attention to this problem, let us hope we can find more ways to offer help to this needy group of parents and children.

Chapter 40

Genetic Counseling with Specific Reference to Visual Problems

ELIZABETH JOLLY

T HE increasing significance being given to genetic counseling by agencies and individuals in the health professions is undoubtedly due not to any upsurge in human concern over problems of heritability but rather to the recent almost revolutionary increase in our understanding of basic and clinical genetics.

The truth of it is that man, for whatever pre-Mendelian myths he may have subscribed to, has never been anything less than actively interested in the makings of his own individuality, including those portions of it, good or bad, that were visited upon his children. Only in the last decade, however, have the diverse branches of biologic research begun to provide him with a healthy measure of meaningful answers and practical help. As a matter of fact, the mounting rate at which new biologic information is now becoming available limelights an inevitable problem: communication between the finders of facts and those from whom the facts are sought.

Because concern over one's heredity is most likely to be verbalized where a disease or defect is involved, it is the physician to whom ·one usually turns for genetic information. Unfortunately, with few exceptions, the physician has had little or no

Note: Reprinted by permission of the author and *Sight-Saving Review,* *36*:150-154, 1966.

Presented at the Annual Conference of the National Society for the Prevention of Blindness, New York, March 31, 1966. Dr. Jolly is chief, Public Health Medical Services, Contra Costa County Health Department, Martinez, California.

training in basic or clinical genetics. Nor will he have until the medical curriculum has been revised to prepare him better for this task. To complicate matters, many of the new findings of clinical genetic significance are not being reported in the journals with which he is familiar but in the literature and the language of the cytogeneticist, the biochemist, and the molecular biologist. And, for the majority of physicians at least, there is not even a handy resource in the community to turn to for consultation on clinical genetic matters.

CONTRA COSTA PROGRAM

It was in the belief that the public health agency has an obligation to aid and support the individual physcian in this area, if it is going to meet its own responsibilities in this rapidly evolving field, that the Contra Costa County Health Department in California initiated its Genetic Consultation and Counseling Service in 1963. The purpose of this program has been simply to help physicians in handling a greater proportion of the genetic problems and questions that confront them by providing them with information having potential use in counseling, in early case-finding, and in prevention.

Because of the various interpretations sometimes given genetic counseling, it may be wise to define the term as it is used in the program. Put simply, it is providing an affected family or individual with any information, limited or extensive, based on the genetic nature of a given desease or predisposition. For example, the physician who tells his patient that the given affection "tends to run in families" is alerting the patient to a possible increased risk to others in the family, and therefore, whether he labels it so or not, he is giving genetic counsel. By the same token, the patient who voluntarily tells his physician that "no one else in my family ever had this problem" is − whether or not he is aware of it − seeking the kind of information which, however simply put, must be considered by our definition to be bona fide genetic counseling. Under this broad definition the indication for it is an everyday occurrence in most physicians' offices. It is important to point out that such counseling should always be done in a way that allows the family or the individual to make his own decisions in personal matters such as procreation and mate selection (1).

REFERRAL PROCEDURE

The services of the Contra Costa program are available to any family in the county on referral of their physician. They are also available on request of the public health nurse to families with chronic or congenital problems who are health department clients.

Once referred, the family is visited by a public health nurse for the purpose of obtaining a family pedigree showing all members through at least three generations as well as the presence not only of the disorder in question but of all other chronic or congenital disorders known to have affected any of them. The pedigree is submitted to the department physician who is responsible for the program to be analyzed in conjunction with any available medical reports and the literature. Final interpretation includes, wherever possible, information on how the disease or its predisposition is inherited, who else in the family is at risk, how much of a risk this appears to be, what methods have been described for detecting normal carriers or potential cases, whether or not there are measures for preventing or postponing symptoms in potential cases so detected, and what local resources exist for each course of action the family may decide to pursue.

A copy of the pedigree and its interpretation are then sent to the referring physician for his use in counseling the family and for whatever medical action he may feel is indicated. In the case of health department clients, the interpretation is sent to the physician whom the family normally consults, whether private or clinic, along with a letter explaining the family's concern. The interpretation is also sent to the nurse obtaining the pedigree, who is available on request to reinforce the physician's counsel.

While direct genetic counseling is not routinely provided, the department physician is available to counsel families where there is no personal physician or where the referring physician requests it.

STUDY OF 337 FAMILIES

Because the program began as a demonstration project to

evaluate the service itself and to acquaint the community's physicians with what it is and offers, health department clients were selected as its first recipients. As a result this group comprises the majority of families studied to date. The majority of private referrals have come from physicians who have received this service in connection with some family in the former group.

To date 337 families have been studied, with index cases representing a wide diversity of chronic and congenital disorders and defects.

While heritable disorders of the eye characterized by visual loss, excluding simple refractive errors, were noted in the index case or members of his immediate family in about one fifth of all pedigrees, the types of disorders seen, particularly among index cases, have undoubtedly been influenced by the kinds of health department services offered (e.g. the Crippled Children Program). Suffice it to say that the conditions seen included a wide range of eye problems, having a distribution not too far different from that expected in the population at large. These included twenty-six families with primary glaucoma, twenty-five with strabismus, five with congenital cataract, four with familial amblyopia, and one to three each with nystagmus, albinism, coloboma, retinitis pigmentosa, galactosemia, ptosis, congenital glaucoma, and congenital optic atrophy. With equal probability this number of families could have included instances of many other heritable disorders of the eye for no less than 246 pathogenic genes are known to express themselves in ocular abnormalities (2).

While the fact of treatability of a condition per se enhances the likelihood that an affected family will come to the attention of the health department and be included in the genetic study, it is still worth noting that the majority of families seen represented conditions which are amenable to therapy and that, for at least a proportion of these conditions, optimal results depend upon promptness of diagnosis and treatment.

In light of the pedigree findings, and a known mode of genetic transmission, it has been possible in most of these families to identify which as yet unaffected relatives are at risk for the same disorder and therefore good candidates for medical surveillance as well as preventive measures or early case treatment if the risk materializes.

An interesting sidelight of the service to date has been the enthusiastic response of families to the process of pedigree study. Many of them were "amazed" to discover that help can often be given families with inherited disorders and predispositions. Even though the inclusion of many of the families who are health department clients was a result of nurse interest rather than an overt expression of family concern, active cooperation has been the rule. Only two or three families have declined to participate, and many have gone to some length beyond their interview with the nurse to get additional information for the sake of pedigree completeness.

The high level of family cooperation seems to be motivated by several factors. Not infrequently, for example, families seem to welcome the process as a means of airing anxieties in a situation which is both sympathetically and constructively oriented. Also, participation in a study with research prospects seems to please them. For the vast majority of families the potential for possible information about themselves which may be helpful either to them or their descendants appears to be particularly significant (3).

The reaction of nurses to the process of pedigree study has been equally encouraging (3). Pedigree taking, for example, has been observed by public health nurses to improve their interviewing skills, to increase their understanding of intrafamily relationships, to create opportunities for health education, and to improve their rapport with the *total* family.

COOPERATION OF PHYSICIANS

About eighty physicians to date have been sent interpreted pedigree material. Precisely how they use this material and with what results has yet to be measured. Such an evaluation will require not only additional financing but a length of time sufficient to reveal actual changes in the pattern of physician use with continued demonstration. The spontaneous expression of satisfaction from many of the physicians in the community, however, has permitted at least an impression of favorable physician response. The greater frequency of private referrals from physicians who have already received the service than from physicians who have not would also seem to be an indication of program effectiveness. So perhaps are the expressions volunteered by families of satisfaction with the information they have subsequently received from their physicians, and, likewise, the spontaneous reports we have received of new cases found as a result of the study.

In Contra Costa County the ophthalmologists have shown a special interest in the genetic approach to eye disorders, particularly glaucoma, and the relatively large number of glaucoma pedigrees seen, representing chiefly private referrals, was the result of a joint project which these ophthalmologists initiated and designed, aimed at prevention of glaucoma in the community.

DIVERSE EYE DISORDERS

In surveying the gamut of conditions represented by all pedigrees studied to date, one cannot escape a final impression not only of the frequency with which disorders affecting vision occur but of the diverse nature of those disorders. One sees, for example, diseases limited to the eye, diseases in which involvement of the eyes is only one of a host of other manifestations, and diseases in which visual loss occurs as a sometimes complication. At one extreme one encounters disorders of vision that are typically congenital; at the other, those that typically affect the end of the life span. One sees disorders demanding immediate diagnosis and treatment as well as those that allow relatively long periods of observation. In short, one sees visual problems, or the potantial of such problems, in many different shapes and sizes and forms.

The job of prevention based on the genetic approach cannot be relegated to any one specialty. The ophthalmologist will probably not be aware of the newborn at high risk for buphthalmos if the obstetrician, or the pediatrician, was not himself aware. The prediabetic state, precursor to active diabetes and therefore to all its ocular and other complications, may not be detected by the internist or the general practitioner if he is unaware that close relatives are diabetic and that the predisposition is indeed inherited. Early peripheral visual loss in glaucoma will often be prevented where the family physician considers a positive family history sufficient grounds for requesting ophthalmologic consultation for the normal-sighted patient.

LOOKING TO THE FUTURE

There is no reason to doubt that new measures of detection and therapy will continue to be developed for an increasing number of genetically determined diseases leading to or associated with loss of vision. There is also little doubt that the physician of the future will ultimately have sufficient training in basic and clinical genetics to allow him to identify on the basis of their genetic probability those individuals most likely to profit from such treatment *before* the fact of disease. If we are going to achieve this latter state at the same pace that biologic research promises to give us the first, however, several things need to be done.

First, we must hasten the integration of clinical genetic teaching into the medical school curriculum; and real integration rather than isolated teaching is needed. There is probably no disease that is not influenced in some way by individual genotype, and the teaching of clinical genetics therefore cannot be limited in its application to selected age groups, disease specialties, or isolated departments within medical schools.

Second, we must promote the concept among students of medicine that prevention is every physician's business, that prevention, over the long haul, may be the only means at his disposal for maintaining high quality care in the face of ever-increasing demands being made on his time.

Third, we must emphasize to the public that helpful information and prevention *are* available for many genetically determined ocular diseases, that recognition of a hereditary influence is often the first prerequisite step in the direction of such help, that the family itself can take an active part in prevention simply by keeping its members informed of any problem which, having affected *one* of them, could affect *others.*

Last, as an interim measure at least, we must make available to physicians everywhere a reliable source of clinical genetic consultation in the form of ready-to-use practical information, utilizing whatever agency, specialist, facility or other resource is best equipped in the given community to do this job.

In short, there is much to be done, there is much to be said for doing it, and there is a part in the doing for almost everyone.

REFERENCES

1. Reed, Sheldon: *Counseling. In Medical Genetics* (2nd ed.), Philadelphia, W. B. Saunders Company, 1963.
2. Francois, Jules: *Heredity. In Ophthalmology* (translated from the French edition *L'Heredite en Ophthalmologie).* St. Louis, C. V. Mosby Company, 1961.
3. Jolly, E., Blum, H. L., Keyes, G., and Smith, G.: Experiences of Public Health Nurses in Obtaining Family Pedigrees. *Public Health Reports, 80* (1):41-44, Jan., 1965.

PART V
COUNSELING PARENTS OF CHILDREN WITH CARDIAC, DIABETIC, HEMOPHILIC, AND ASTHMATIC HANDICAPS

On Borrowed Time:
Observations on Children with
Implanted Cardiac Pacemakers
and Their Families

RICHARD GALDSTON and WALTER J. GAMBLE

THIS study was undertaken with the hypothesis that the threat to life posed by cardiac arrhythmia or arrest in children with complete heart block would be a source of anxiety sufficient to cause a high incidence of the signs and symptoms of dysfunction and regression in the ego.

METHOD OF STUDY

From 1960 to 1967 the sixteen children and two adults who

Note: Reprinted by permission of the authors and the *American Journal of Psychiatry,* *126*:104-108, 1969. Copyright 1969, The American Psychiatric Association.

Read at the 124th annual meeting of the American Psychiatric Association, Boston, Mass., May 13-17, 1968.

The authors are with the Children's Hospital Medical Center, 300 Longwood Ave., Boston, Mass. 02115, where Dr. Galdston is chief, inpatient psychiatric consultation service, and Dr. Gamble is associate in cardiology. Both authors are also with Harvard Medical School, where Dr. Galdston is associate in psychiatry and Dr. Gamble is associate in pediatrics.

This work was supported in part by Public Health Service grant HE-10436 from the National Heart Institute, awarded to Dr. Gamble.

The authors wish to express their appreciation to Dr. Robert E. Gross, surgeon-in-chief in cardiovascular surgery, and Dr. Alexander S. Nadas, cardiologist-in-chief, Children's Hospital Medical Center, for their support of this study.

had internal cardiac pacemakers implanted at the Children's Hospital Medical Center were interviewed on the wards at the hospital and during their visits to the Pacemaker Clinic.* The psychiatrist participated in ward rounds and outpatient clinics as a member of the cardiac team and also conducted individual interviews with patients and their parents. The observations of parents, nurses, ward personnel, and house staff were added to those made directly.

No effort was made to conduct interviews in depth or to search for fantasy material other than that presented in the course of unstructured, sympathetic interviews. The focus of the interviews was on behavior, mood, appetites, interests, and the ways of contending with the stresses posed by the state of exogenous cardiac pacing.

Five of the patients required pacemakers because of congenital atrioventricular block in the absence of other significant heart disease. Thirteen others required them because of complete heart block as a complication of surgery performed for major heart disease.

In the study there were nine males and nine females, ranging in age from two and one-half to forty years at the time of initial implantation of the pacemakers. The pacemakers employed consisted of a generator source, which is a small encapsulated box containing five or six small mercury batteries, and the electronic circuitry. Silastic or teflon-coated wires carry the electrical impulse to the heart where the bared ends of the wires are sewn directly into the myocardium. The generator box is usually implanted subcutaneously in the axilla or abdomen; it is usually palpable and bulges visibly.

Of the eighteen patients, twelve have required revisions, with an average interval of only 5.6 months between surgical procedures. Of the malfunctions, slightly fewer than 70 percent have been due to broken or retracted wires from the batteries to the heart. Thirty percent (30%) have been due to battery exhaustion or component failure. The batteries have had an average longevity of 14.4 months. None of the patients has died because of cardiac arrest or

---

*Besides the authors, Miss Madeline Hyland, M.S.W., Mrs. Dorothy Patton, R.N., Dr. Louis Plyzak, and Dr. Bert Litwin are with the Pacemaker Clinic.

arrhythmia. The cost for an average pacing duration of 30.6 months has been an average of 4.8 operative procedures, including 1.9 thoracotomies per patient.

Despite the acute and chronic stress posed by this condition and its complications, none of these patients developed hyperactivity, tics, enuresis, encopresis, nailbiting, antisocial behavior, conversion symptoms, or lasting disturbances in sleeping or eating. Aside from an unwillingness to care for themselves as much as they might for brief periods following surgery, the children displayed no evidence of sustained regression in any of the readily identifiable ego functions. They went about their business in a remarkably steadfast fashion, seemingly unaffected by an awareness of either their condition or the electrical contrivance it necessitated.

Their parents also accommodated to the situation without significant regression. They mastered the idea of heart block, artificial pacing, and the presence of an internal battery-driven pacemaker without significant evidence of major decompensation in psychic functioning. There were no signs of gross depression, paranoid reaction, destructive acting out, breakdown of family operation, alcoholism, or other evidence of failure in maintenance of ego function.

However, they knew of the constant threat of a lapse in cardiac rhythm and failure of circulation sufficient to maintain consciousness or life itself; these parents and their children existed, aware of this fact, without recognizable sacrifice of ego integrity. Whatever demands their anxieties exacted, these were met without the development of those regression symptoms in the functions of the ego so often encountered in hospital pediatric experience. This report, then, is a testimony to the courage of these children and their parents, with an attempt to describe the manner in which they accomplished this feat and some speculation about the implications concerning anxiety and its management.

The patients and their parents relied upon a triad of psychological processes as their major protection in accommodating to the threat presented: (1) identification with a medical attitude, (2) intellectualization, and (3) denial of affect.

These defenses were employed in concert, and each depended upon the other. They afforded a psychic posture that made for an active response to the requirements of contending with the frequent hospitalizations, surgery, disabilities, restrictions, and the ever-present uncertainty of future life.

IDENTIFICATION WITH A MEDICAL ATTITUDE

The very presence of the technology of cardiac pacemakers signifies the commitment of physicians to the concept of discovery and development. This attitude is conveyed to the patient and his family in many ways throughout the course of hospitalization, surgery, and convalescence. The anticipation of the invention of new ways, equipment, and procedures is both explicit and implicit in every contact between patient and physician. It is conveyed in the very proposition of cardiac surgery, and it taps into a deep-seated fantasy of rebirth, which can be detected in certain parents' expectations that the surgery performed for cardiac defects will also cure other problems — those of an ornery child, an ugly child, or a rebellious adolescent.

This was demonstrated most clearly in the patients with tetralogy of Fallot who had undergone several surgical procedures culminating in an operation referred to as "total repair," which was complicated by heart block necessitating the implantation of a pacemaker. Several of these parents had requested that the total repair be performed, citing reasons far removed from their child's cardiac disability.

This identification with the medical attitude of active, optimistic innovation was manifest in the ingenuity with which the parents managed their lives to match the requests of the doctors. In the two years the clinic has existed, there has not been a single instance of missed appointments.

Often parents displayed great pride in their ability to present the same picture of steadfast attention as their doctor. In word, gesture, attitude, and expectation, these parents have come to match and mimic the medical attitudes of optimistic activity in their approach toward the care of the cardiac pacemaker and its owner.

INTELLECTUALIZATION

Of those features characteristic of the medical attitude, exercise of the intellect was most actively embraced by the parents. Some of these people were not particularly intellectual by inclination or experience, yet they amassed an impressive knowledge of cardiac function and electricity. The image of the heart as a pump is readily grasped and with it an appreciation of many aspects of hemodynamics. Parents became interested in the figures obtained by cardiac catheterization, pulmonary pressures, and so on.

Similarly, the structure, function, and longevity of the batteries driving the pacemaker were topics that most parents mastered. They often posed questions about the autonomy of the apparatus and its liability to interference by radios, transmitters, and other sources of electricity in the environment. Implicit in these questions lay a deep concern about the source of life — what was running whom? Several of the patients showed this in their preoperative questions about the pacemaker, asking if they would run the pacemaker or if it would run them.

Related to this sense of the source of cardiac rhythm was an awareness of time. Rate, rhythm, and time were recurring concerns. One adolescent boy experienced the failure of his pacemaker as a stoppage of his wristwatch, which he checked and wound and rechecked until finally he appreciated the fact that his heart rate had fallen by half.

Another boy, in the hospital for repair of a broken wire, drew a picture of a cat, stating, "This is my cat with a pacemaker which pokes the heart and makes it go. Dogs don't need pacemakers. Cats go slower and need pacemakers." He asked, "Do lions and tigers in the woods need a pacemaker?"

The idea of a limited battery operation time troubled many because of the assumption that there could only be so many heartbeats before the batteries became exhausted and that a slower rate meant greater battery longevity.

DENIAL OF AFFECT

The effective care of these children required their parents' active participation in the supervision of their cardiac status. This made necessary a fairly thorough understanding of the problem, which included the inherent dangers. An appreciation of all these items might well be expected to produce affects of alarm, despair, anger, or dismay to the point of distraction. Such was not the case. Uniformly these people displayed a remarkable ability to register and assimilate pertinent facts without evincing these emotions.

Their recognition of the facts bore eloquent testimony in the care with which they adhered to the doctor's recommendations and the relevance of the questions they asked, Informed and alert in their pursuit of medical advice, they made very few distortions of the explanations and recommendations they received.

What happened to the affects that should have accompanied the facts? None of these people were noticeably cold. They demonstrated ready access to emotion about other issues; isolation of emotion was not a prominent trait in their characters. A certain amount of emotion was displaced. One family displayed considerable turmoil about their daughter's lop ears. They focused chagrin, worry, attempts to conceal, and anxiety about possible corrective surgery for this minor cosmetic defect.

Some emotion was dissipated in the rituals of pulse taking, checking, and recording.

A certain amount of emotion was dealt with through counterphobic maneuvers. One girl and one woman took actions that caused electric burns shortly after pacemaker implantation. The girl crossed the wire from a radio with that of an electric fan, causing a short circuit that burned her fingers while she was convalescing in her hospital bed. The woman received a serious electric shock after plugging in a washing machine to divert hot water into her tub while she was taking a bath. Her doctors had prohibited her from bathing herself during convalescence, but she had always done everything for herself, her husband, and children. Neither of these electric shocks affected the operation of the pacemaker.

Many of the children treated their problems with humor, referring to themselves as "Ever-Ready," "Dynamo," "Dry Cell," and "Hot Shot." One boy signed his valentine card to a girl, who also had a pacemaker, "To my transistor sister."

These attitudes and mental practices allowed for the flurries of feeling that accompanied the daily events described. Over the years it appeared that the relative calm with which these adversities were surmounted was achieved through an intensification of relationship within the family and around an idea. The idea was expressed simply and repeatedly by doctors and nurses in word and practice: "Treat him *as if* there were nothing wrong." "Treat him like *any other* child." This notion, bracketed as it was with specific recommendations for restrictions and cautions, provided a core of belief that presented the challenge: Believe in his future and it shall strengthen you.

This belief, shared by doctors, parents, and child, afforded bonds of fidelity among the members of the family. They showed great pride in their ability to fulfill the prescription of avoiding (within the limits of prudent behavior) the restrictions of fearful inhibition. The signs and symptoms of unaccountable cardiac symptomatology referred to as cardiac neurosis were found in only one patient over the seven years (1, 2).

Somehow these people perceived the laws of electrical conduction and cardiac function as an external danger against which the family drew together to unite their forces in battle. Their response can be likened to that described among civilians during the German occupation in World War II (3).

> During the occupation the Danish population was seized with a feeling of unity, with an interest in political events which in many cases was in contrast to earlier isolation and emptiness, with an increased pride in being a valuable member of a threatened nation and culture. In concordance with the experience of other countries, this reaction is held responsible for the real decrease in psychiatric morbidity and for the increased threshold observed in 1940. . . .
>
> There is no doubt in my mind that this increased feeling of solidarity − in contrast with earlier isolation and disinterest − and the feeling of being a valuable member of a cultural nation in danger were factors causing the decrease in psychiatric morbidity during the first years of the war.

The mothers displayed great acuity in their capacity to monitor their children's heart rates. One detected her daughter's missed heartbeat in a test situation by noting a change in the frequency with which the child blinked her eyes. All the parents maintained continuing and accurate surveillance of the vitality with which their child met daily life. Only in two instances did it appear that this concern was intrusive or excessive. Their ability to maintain an attitude of alert, appropriate clinical concern unaffected by personal parental anxieties was most striking.

This phenomenon of detailed factual knowledge held in a climate of steadfast parental love without regression under anxiety remained an imposing testimony to the human capacity to know, to feel, and to endure. At no time did any of the parents seem to be unfeeling, flat, or isolated. It rather appeared that they held their affects in escrow to allow for the demands of the immediate adversity. The release of emotion was kept in a continuing state of abeyance.

The use of this triad of defenses: identification with the medical attitude, intellectualization, and denial of affect was supported by mutual faith. The child's belief in his parents, the parents' belief in the doctor, and the doctor's belief in the future allow for that comfort of closeness afforded to those who hold to and are held by a common hope.

REFERENCES

1. Bergman, A. B., and Stamm, S. J.: The Morbidity of cardiac nondisease in school-children, *New Eng J Med, 276*:1008-1013, 1967.
2. Cardiac Neurosis in Children, *Lancet, 2*:430, 1966.
3. Svendsen, B. B.: *Psychiatric Morbidity Among Civilians in Wartime.* Denmark, Aarhus University, 1952.

Chapter 42

Psychotherapy of Parents of Allergic Children

HYMAN MILLER and DOROTHY W. BARUCH

THIS paper is based on observations emerging out of fourteen years of integrating psychotherapy into the management of allergic children. The senior author has been in a singularly favorable position to do this, practicing as he does both medical allergy and psychotherapy. Since there are many allergic children in his practice, he has, with the cooperation of the coauthor, had rich opportunity to observe the emotional interrelationships between parents and their allergic children and to explore problems that deal with the psychotherapy of parents along with the child.

During the years, we have seen that when the usual medical treatment for allergy fails, the key to a child's improvement often lies in the field of the emotions. The child's first need in this area is to feel that he as a person is loved as he is: with all his varied feelings, the ones he learns to call "bad," as well as those called "good." He fears that if he shows hostility he will be discarded. Therefore, beside the tender loving care that must come to him, we have found that the most important single emotional factor that precipitates or prolongs physical symptoms is the child's repression of anger at his parents.

This requires a word of explanation. As we brought out in an earlier paper, (1) the allergic child characteristically blocks the normal hostility which all children feel at moments toward their parents. When a parent is the target of angry feelings, the child

Note: Reprinted by permission of the author and *Annals of Allergy, 18*:990-997, 1960.

finds it very threatening to own up to this fact. He feels he will alienate his parents. He tries to hide his anger even from himself. He may divert it onto substitute targets, displacing it for instance onto siblings. He may disguise it through misbehavior which troubles his parents. These efforts, however, prove inadequate to relieve inner tension. He then turns to exacerbations of physical symptoms, using his allergic constitution in an unconscious and unsuccessful attempt to establish emotional homeostasis. He turns his own body into the target of his anger, discharging the hostility against himself, punishing himself for feelings which he is ordinarily too afraid to admit to consciousness. Very rarely can the allergic child say with any discharge of affect, "I'm mad at my mother or my father" or elaborate what in fantasy he would like to do to them in his anger. But when he comes to the point where he feels safe in telling about his feelings, then we have repeatedly seen his symptoms decrease.

To feel safe, the child must sense with certainty that his hostile feelings are accepted by an adult in whom he has confidence. A therapist may serve temporarily, but in the end the child must be convinced that his parents "can take it." For he leans and relies most on them, after all.

For this reason, in the regular routine of allergy practice, when an emotional factor is seen to be present, part of our procedure has been to talk with the parents about the fact that hostility toward parents is felt normally at times by all children in the process of growing up. We have found it helpful, too, to explain that allergic children have unusual difficulty in expressing this without subterfuge or disguise.

We try to be very sensitive in observing the parents' reactions to these ideas. Some parents respond positively and nondefensively. It is relatively easy to help this group of parents get to the point where they are able to state with sincerity to their child that he naturally is sometimes angry at them. They are able to feel within themselves that this really is natural.

They can, in addition, grasp the idea that a firm differentiation must be made between *feelings* and *actions*. All feelings, even the wishes and fantasies about the often primitive and "gorey" things children would like to do in their anger, must be differentiated from what can really be acted out. It is permissible for instance to talk about feelings, to tell stories or to make pictures of what a child would like to do in his angry moments. These are nonharmful modes of discharge. They do not physically touch the parents. But kicking, hitting, destructiveness or any actually harmful or hurtful acts must be barred. They invariably produce additional fear. "You'd like to but you may not really." This statement and holding to the firm limits of action implied in it is essential in order for a child to feel safe in bringing hostile feelings out.

A small episode illustrates the appreciation of such techniques by one mother. She glances at her watch on the way out after her five-year-old boy has had his injection of antigen. She exclaims, "Oh dear, it's too late to go to the toy store." Her child, as if by accident, pushes his smaller brother. "Here, here," says the mother easily, "I know you're mad at me because we can't go to the store. But you mayn't push your brother instead. You can tell me straight out...." The child glares at her. "I don't like you at all." "I know you don't now," the mother nods, with confirming acceptance.

With this type of acceptance of feeling along with the limiting of hurtful acts, as accompaniment to the allergy treatment, this boy had been clear of asthma for the past year. Allergy treatment alone prior to this had failed.

During the interim, his mother, in her office visits with the child, had been exposed to an informal type of psychotherapy. Her confidence in the allergist had permitted her to talk about herself as well as about the child, and to reach feelings within herself which had hitherto been repressed. She had gotten, for instance, at previously hidden hostile feelings she herself had felt as a child to her parents. With this realization she began to sanction with real conviction her child's feeling of hostility to her. Soon then in his turn he had begun to feel safe in bringing his feelings out. He knew with equal conviction that she would understand. Then, in her turn, she noticed that his symptoms diminished and she grew more and more able to accept with equanimity the unmasked verbal expression of her child's anger toward her.

In some cases parents reach out for the principles involved in all of this but cannot so readily accept them with emotional conviction. There is rather, a pseudoacceptance, a matter of technique without inner confirmation of feeling. There is a note of insincerity present which the parent may not even realize but which the child invariably perceives. His symptoms in consequence keep recurring. In still other cases, the mere mention that hostility toward a mother or father is possible, proves too disturbing to a parent. In either instance, we can be quite certain that tender spots within the parents' own emotional reservoir have been touched.

Then deeper and more formal psychotherapy is indicated. In most cases, the mother only has entered treatment; in some recalcitrant cases, both parents. In some cases, the child as well has had psychotherapy on a continuous basis; in other cases, the child has had only occasional psychotherapeutic sessions. In still other cases, after the diagnostic sessions, no psychotherapy has been attempted with the child. Recovery, we considered, lay in the psychological readjustment of the parents.

Obviously it is in the cases where the two parents and the child are all in psychotherapy that the nature of the emotional interplay can be best understood. In our office, one of us has worked with one parent, the other of us with the other parent and the child. Some parents have individual therapy only; some have group therapy; some have a combination of both. Active collaboration between the therapists continues constantly. We confer together daily on the same day as the sessions, before the material grows cold. This often reveals how the pieces of the emotional puzzle fit together. It shows the interrelationships not only of events but of feelings and fantasies, and it often contributes therapeutic leads.

In the past fourteen years we have had many allergic children with one or the other parent in psychotherapy. In ten families, however, we have had both mother and father in intensive treatment. In fifteen additional families where the mother (or in two cases the father) has been in continuous therapy, we have had enough contact on an occasional basis with the other parent to get insight into his psychodynamics. It is from these twenty-five families (involving 29 allergic children), where we have been able to study both parents psychologically in an extended and intensive way, that the following material is drawn.

Among the twenty-nine children involved, there were twenty with asthma as the dominant allergic syndrome. (One of these had equally severe allergic neurodermite.) The remaining nine children had hay fever as the dominant allergic syndrome. It should be pointed out here, however, that even though there is usually the one dominant syndrome, we find periods when the major syndrome is replaced by or complicated by a severe exacerbation of what is usually a minor syndrome. Such shift in symptoms we have found to be connected often with shifts in fantasies that are unconsciously shared by parents and child.

In the tremendous mass of interwoven material involved in these cases, there stands out clearly the fact that the parent unconsciously makes use of the child for his own emotional purposes. He often unconsciously wants to have the child retain his symptoms. The child in turn unconsciously wants to keep them. The illness often becomes the place where the unrealistic purposes of parent and child coincide.

A case report here will serve to illustrate this. In the family of the boy with asthma and neurodermite, the mother as a child had many times heard it said that she'd not been wanted. In her loneliness she turned to her older brother. For one thing, during her childhood, and his adolescence she had extensive sex play with him and would enjoy — as she put it — "getting his mess all over her. It made us more like one person," she said. "Both of us cruddy." "Without my brother I was a nothing," she said, "I thought I'd die if we were ever separated. He was like a part of me or I of him, we were so attached. When he got married and left me I think I wanted to kill him." On a deep level, the attachment to her brother represented a symbiotic relationship which she felt she could not do without.

When she married she strove unconsciously to make her husband into a brother whom she could keep with her always. When her child was born, however, her husband was very preoccupied with business, for unconscious reasons of his own, and once more she felt abandoned. So she turned voraciously to her child and fantasied him almost like a part of herself which she would never have to lose.

When she first brought him into the office at the age of two years and three months, she was strangling him literally, clutching him so tightly to her. On his side, he was clinging, one arm down inside the neckline of her dress, his hand digging into her breast. He was wheezing heavily and was slightly cyanotic. The skin eruption was extremely severe. Both symptoms had started when his mother had needed to wean him at nine months and allergy treatment had then been instituted. As she realized later, at this time she had been very disturbed at the child's growing old enough to necessitate the separation from her breast. Recently, however, the skin eruption and asthma had both become far more severe. This had happened when she recognized that she was again pregnant. She fantasied the new pregnancy as in intrusion — something that threatened to separate her more from her boy.

When the psychotherapist reached for the child to take him into the playroom, she protested the separation, "But *I've* got to carry him," she said. Still later she saw that what she had wanted even more deeply was to be carrying him inside her. She wanted none of him as a growing-up individual who might leave her as her brother had. The eczema helped her identify him as the "messy" brother she had "owned" earlier. The asthma gave her the excuse she needed for holding him to her. "So close," she said, "that I try to breathe for him."

The father encouraged this, for the pattern helped also to satisfy his fantasies. A critical experience in his childhood had been the death of his mother after a prolonged illness, during which she had repeatedly said to him, "I'll never live to see you grow up." Frightened, he wanted, as he put it, "time to stand still" so he could keep his mother. He did not want to grow up.

When he married, he thought of his wife as a girl friend. They were two youngsters having sex play together. Suiting both their fantasies, their sexual pattern concentrated on foreplay, and intercourse, in general, was incomplete. When she unexpectedly became pregnant with the boy and was tired and listless, it reminded him too much of his mother when she had been ailing and sick. It was at this time he ran from his wife into his work.

Then, after his son was born, he fantasied the child as himself and his wife as his young mother before she'd become ill. As long as his son remained a baby, needing to be held, diapered and cleaned up, the father was content. He didn't want the child to mature any further. For if he did, it would prove that time had not stood still. The persistence of the eczema after the child's infancy then served the father's unconscious purpose. By identifying with the eczematous "mess," the father did not grow old either.

Thus the child through his physical symptoms fed the fantasies of both his parents. And yet, even though he wanted the closeness as they did, he felt the smothering quality that came from his mother. It went against his natural striving for independence. And so, it also made him angry. But this he dared not express for fear of the separation and abandonment he felt would come as result. In his play therapy he showed the conflict in his feelings. He would curl up like a baby inside its mother, saying, "This is my goodest way to be." But then he would fantasy being smothered and would start to wheeze. As time went on he would crawl repeatedly into a nest of pillows, his wish to "go in" matching his mother's wish to still have him inside her. Then he would throw aside the pillows and would stamp on them madly, saying, "You, you, you terrible witch, you're not going to capture me and keep me where I can't breathe." Moreover he would act out her wish to have a "messy" relationship. He would get undressed and immerse himself in a tubful of clay, rubbing it over himself, pretending to be a mother rubbing her messy baby.

With longterm psychotherapy, the mother was able to give up her symbiotic fantasies of boy-inside her or part of her. Concomitantly she became able to accept the child as a separate person who was entitled to his own feelings of hostility to her. With this his asthma stopped, recurring only at extremely rare intervals when his mother regressed.

Meanwhile, the fantasies associated in the child's mind with the skin eruption gradually moved from the mother to the father. He imagined playing baseball with his father. In these games he would throw "mud" or "pooch balls" at his father, "messing him all up." Thus, in his mind too, his father and he both became babies and time stood still.

At other moments, he fantasied attacking his father tooth and nail and eating him up to get his "strongness," as he put it. Through messing and clawing at his own skin, he continued to court and fight his father, satisfying the father's still persisting desire to stay young through him, and at one and the same time trying in his own fantasy to "scratch out his father," but then, in typically allergic fashion, turning the hostility onto himself.

Finally, the father who had come into therapy later than his wife, began to let time take its stride. On his part, he became acceptant of his child as a child with feelings that were at times naturally hostile. With this the child's skin eruption markedly improved.

In another case, more briefly, an asthmatic mother wanted her little asthmatic girl of three to act out for her the "little mad demon" she herself had not dared to be. One of her own persistent fantasies reaching up from childhood was of her mother drowning and her father showering her with all the gifts he ordinarily gave to her mother. Then, however, she would grow panicky, would want her mother back but would fear that her mother would be angry at her. At this point in her still recurring fantasies she would shift her daughter into the role of returning mother whose anger she feared. And so, although she would with one side of her stir the child into outbursts of the little mad demon, she would with the other side of herself, back frantically away from any anger which the child-mother-figure openly directed at her. She would find her own way out of her emotional dilemma by retreating into asthma herself.

When her husband would start to show his affection toward her child, she would fiercely snatch her away. She could not stand her fantasied mother being preferred.

On his side her husband did not protest this. For to him his wife represented his mother protecting him from further injuring a younger sibling whom he had actually hurt as a child.

In her turn, the child was angry at her mother for coming between her father and herself. In her sessions she showed that her fantasies coincided with her mother's. She played that she wanted to drown her mother, would grow frightened, then would talk as if she were drowning herself and would develop asthmatic attacks.

These persisted until her mother became more able to receive her hostility without putting the alternating pictures of her own "demon" and her own mother onto her.

Incidentally, in this case, as one would suspect, a major reason for the mother's long concentration on the child was to avoid making a relationship with her husband whom she took as the father she felt guilty about having wanted earlier. This too needed working through in order for the mother to give up her hostile dependent attachment to the child and to become able to accept her child's hostility.

To cite some of the fantasies from just one more family: The mother often took her asthmatic son (almost four when her therapy started) as her younger brother whom she had recurrently dreamt of throwing out of the window. "I see him lying on the ground," she said. At other times she took him as the father whom she had wanted to own.

Her husband on his part had lost his father in infancy and had slept in his mother's bed until his late teens when she had died. When his own son was born, he was disturbed. He unconsciously wanted any other child out of the picture in order to remain the only child himself. He also feared the child's growing older and becoming an adult rival, although he ambivalently wished that the boy might take the role of husband rather than himself. For, he still carried inside him the old fear that a wife must kill a husband as he had fantasied his mother had killed his father in order to take him into her bed.

The boy felt the frightening countercurrents and grew deeply angry. He dreamed of throwing his father out of the window. "I see him lying on the ground," he said, dramatically using the very same words as his mother had used. "No," he said, "That's not the father on the ground, that's the boy lying on the ground." And he would wonder in great bewilderment, "Who throwed him?" And then as if he had actually shared his mother's dream, "Did the mother throw the little boy out?"

He feared this would happen to him should he show his anger. He wanted his mother to throw his father out for him and grew angry at her for not doing so. But instead of expressing his anger directly, he got sick with asthma. Apropos of this, when he was seven, he said, "When I'm sick I'm just a poor little helpless child and nobody'll have the heart to throw me out."

As the mother and father became aware of these and other fantasies, they became able to sanction and accept the child's verbal expressions of hostility, yet at the same time to limit the acting out. And the asthma cleared.

From the mass of data in our cases, we can draw some generalizations concerning psychotherapy with parents of severely ill allergic children. The parents of this group are themselves severely ill emotionally. Psychotherapy with them is long and involved. It is usually important that it go on even after the child is improved. It is usually important that it go on even after the child is improved. Otherwise regressive patterns in the parents continue and create recurrent pressures for the child.

Since their inability to relate well to each other in marriage abets their turning to the child, therapy needs to help them become able to invest a healthy amount of emotional energy in working on the marriage relationship. Often they cannot accept the child's hostility because to them the child represents themselves, and they cannot accept the anger they felt toward their own parents with its concommitant fantasies when they were small. Often their child represents to them a parent to whom they were hostile and yet attached. Then the child's hostility seems to them like rejection from a parent. Often the mixed animosity and clinging wishes they feel toward the child lead them to make a show of loving him, particularly of overprotecting, of giving him whatever he wants. Limitations and forbiddings seem "too cruel," especially because underneath such forbiddings lie their own explosive hostilities.

When a parent can give up the child as part of himself, when a parent can give up the child in the image of his own parent, when the parent has become able to love the child maturely, then he can let the child be himself and grow as himself and speak for himself, as he feels in all honesty, then the allergic symptoms no longer are needed to serve mutual purposes. The child can then make better use of his allergy treatment to get well.

REFERENCE

1. A study of hostility in allergic children. *Am J Orthopsych, 20:*506, 1950.

Chapter 43

An Experiment in
Group Therapy with the
Mothers of Diabetic Children

ANGELA HEFFERMAN

INTRODUCTION

T HIS project came into being in the following way. Among the patients of the Montreal Children's hospital are a considerable number of children suffering from diabetes mellitus. They are under the care of the Department of Metabolism. The usual procedure is to admit them to hospital for an initial period of stabilization, after which they continue to attend the Diabetic Clinic as outpatients. During the child's stay in hospital, the mother receives practical instruction in the technique of insulin injection, urine testing, and dietetics. The nature of the disease is carefully explained to her. This program of education is continued later, when the child has become on outpatient. Yet in spite of all this, the physicians in charge of the Department of Metabolism were not satisfied. They felt that something more was needed to help the mothers of these diabetic children to accept the illness and to manage it more adequately. The Department of Child

Note: Published by permission of the author and *Psychotherapy and Psychosomatics,* 2:155-162, 1959.

Dr. Hefferman is associated with the Department of Child Psychiatry, The Montreal Children's Hospital, and the Department of Psychiatry, McGill University, Montreal, P.Q., Canada.

The author's thanks are due to Dr. Eleanor R. Harpur, Director of the Department of Metabolism, and to the staff of the Department of Metabolism for their cooperation and assistance.

Psychiatry was therefore called into consultation and it was decided to try the experiment of handling these mothers by a group therapy technique.

MATERIAL

The subjects of the group were the mothers of twenty diabetic children. The children comprised eleven males and nine females, ranging in age two years eleven months to fifteen years seven months, with a mean age of nine years five months. The average duration of the illness had been 12.9 months at the time when this project was commenced, but several mothers entered the group within a week or so of the initial diagnosis. The age of onset of the illness varied from eighteen months to twelve years. The mothers came from varied socioeconomic and racial backgrounds, their only common bond being that they each had a diabetic child.

TECHNIQUE AND MANAGEMENT OF THE GROUP

Each mother and child was first assessed by individual psychiatric interviews occupying two to four hours apiece. The children had already received a very comprehensive metabolic investigation and electroencephalograms were available in most cases.

The mothers were formed into a therapy group which met every week for two years, except for the summer holidays. New members periodically entered the group and three of the original members lost contact for various reasons during the second year. A hard core of six of the original members scarcely missed a single meeting throughout the two years.

The psychiatrist who handled this project was chosen because she had had considerable past experience in the medical care of diabetics. The group was run on the "democratic" pattern (as distinct from a didactic or autocratic method). The psychiatrist remained as nondirective as possible, encouraging intragroup discussion from the outset, but answering when directly appealed to. The psychiatrist also manipulated the group to the extent of drawing shy members into the discussion or coming to the rescue of a member who was being too violently attacked by the rest of the group.

AIM

To help improve the parental management of the diabetic child and his illness, and to promote a relaxed, accepting and confident attitude to the situation, by amplifying the mother's "diabetic education" was the aim of the program, to be accomplished through the use of group-therapy techniques and by uncovering and dealing with psychological difficulties associated with the child's illness.

GROUP DYNAMICS

From the very start, discussion was general and animated. After a few meetings, various patterns of reaction to the psychiatrist and of interaction between the mothers themselves became apparent.

One example of this was Mrs. A. She always sat very close to the therapist, almost huddling up to her and glancing sideways as if for permission before speaking. It became apparent as the weeks went by that Mrs. A. was exceedingly dependent upon her pediatrician. She was afraid to alter the insulin dosage by a single unit without telephoning him for permission. Although her child had had diabetes for two and a half years, Mrs. A. had less real grasp of the principles of management than many with half that experience. She said that her pediatrician "did her thinking for her." His attitude towards her, as represented by her statements, was a paternalistic one. Mrs. A's child unconsciously used her illness to keep her mother in constant attendance. She would refuse to eat her meals after her insulin has been given. If the mother attempted to go out, the child would vomit. The least emotional upset at home was followed by glycosuria. Mrs. A. had been brought up by very strict parents; she had been schooled at home because of an orthopedic condition. She described her own mother as an obsessive, very critical person and remarked "that's why I am so afraid of everything, I had so much criticism that it took my confidence away." Another woman in the group, Mrs. C., whose strong masculine identification was consciously based on her relationship to her father, developed a protective attitude towards the timid Mrs. A., defending her when other members of the group criticized her lack of initiative and reassuring her when she expressed her fears.

Another mother, Mrs. B., elected herself a sort of vice-president or aide de camp. She always sat at the opposite end of the table from the psychiatrist and was very ready with offers of assistance. It became evident that the other mothers were ready to accept this, so the therapist decided to give Mrs. B. certain administrative jobs in connection with the group, such as telephoning them all when the time of a meeting had to be changed. This women's relationships with most of the people in her environment, including her diabetic son, were marked by a very strong ambivalence. This was also apparent in her behavior to the therapist and the other members of the group. Although she was friendly and very eager to be helpful, there was a marked underlying hostility and aggressiveness, often expressed in the form of jokes. Mrs. B's father died when she was a small child; she said she was devoted to her mother but described her as extremely strict and rigid. When the mother died, Mrs. B., then aged thirty, suffered a reactive depression.

There was an interesting reaction between the group and another mother, Mrs. D. This woman was extremely antagonistic to her diabetic daughter. She would dominate the group for most of one session with her emphatic denunciations of the child. Then, as her great hostility and restricting overprotectiveness became apparent, the other mothers would become restive and critical, and finally make a concentrated attack upon her. After this experience she would miss a couple of meetings and would then reappear and unburden herself again. When she was not present, the other mothers would discuss and criticize her freely, which led them to explore their attitudes towards their own children. Mrs. D. was the saboteur of the Diabetic Clinic. The other mothers would report indignantly to the group that Mrs. D. had whispered to them to "take no notice of that diet nonsense" and described how she would buy her child a large bag of potato chips and encourage her to sit in the clinic eating them before the eyes of the other diabetic children. Mrs. D. seemed to be in a constant state of rebellion and protest against the world in general, and this was reflected in her attitude towards her daughter's doctors and had a very unfortunate effect on the girl's mental and physical condition.

During the group meetings, the mothers exchanged a great deal of information and experience. Many misapprehensions, some quite bizarre, were cleared up in discussion with the psychiatrist. Those who were new to the problems of handling a diabetic child gained valuable help from other more experienced members. All felt that they had received both support and relief from the discovery that other people had similar problems to their own.

SUBJECTS DISCUSSED BY THE GROUP

It is not possible, in the time available, to give more than a broad summary of the actual subjects taken up by the group. There was, however, a definite sequence to them.

For the first few meetings the emphasis was mainly on technical points in the management of diabetes. Insulin, diets, and comas were all discussed at length. They were all eager to tell their own histories until the noise became deafening. They exchanged cooking recipes and discussed different types of syringe. Some confused ideas were cleared up. For example, one woman thought that the aim of giving insulin was to keep sugar in the urine; this was a misinterpretation of the advice that it is safer to have a trace of sugar in the urine overnight. The financial burdens of having a diabetic child were frankly discussed. Since some of the mothers arrived in their own cars and others walked part of the way to save bus fare, this was an educational experience for all concerned. After the group had passed beyond this stage of preoccupation with the mechanics of the disease, the arrival of a new member would cause a temporary reversion to it, in response to the newcomer's needs.

From discussing diet and injections the group moved on to discussing their own and their children's reactions to these things. It was significant that the mothers were more upset over the need to refuse food to the children than they were over the injections.

This was understandable, since the need for dietetic restriction strikes at the primary relationship of mother and child, that of the feeder and the fed. The mother with a very young diabetic child felt especially frustrated and unhappy as she tried to meet by verbal explanation the primitive rage and tears of a hungry child. They resented being forced to appear as a withholding mother who refused to give food and the affection which it symbolized. One such woman described how, after the nightly battle over the now forbidden bedtime snack, the child lay upstairs crying for the food and the mother sat downstairs "crying and chewing her nails." The effect of the child's disease on the family and on family activities was discussed. It was noticeable all through the group sessions that the fathers were rarely mentioned. Possibly, this was because the care of a sick child is traditionally the task of the mother. However, in the case of an adolescent boy who was afraid to give himself injections and could not be trusted to test his own urine specimens, the genital significance of these procedures led one to question whether they should be carried out by the mother.

One subject which came up quite early was the effect of the illness on sexual life — various questions about sterily, heredity and even hermaphroditism were asked. A girl of only nine had upset her mother by saying that she could never get married because she would be too ashamed for her husband to know about her tests and her needles. Another had been told by a schoolmate that she could never have a baby. The mother's own attitudes to these matters were revealed. When the question of sterility arose, the masculine Mrs. C. muttered "some people would be glad."

When the mothers had gained sufficient confidence in the group and in the therapist they entered upon a stage of comparing and criticizing their various physicians. This was, of course, a difficult stage for the psychiatrist from the ethical point of view and required careful handling. One frequent complaint was that different doctors gave conflicting instructions; but when the different incidents were examined it usually turned out to be a case of incomplete understanding, as in the case of the woman who thought that insulin was meant to keep the sugar in the urine. Another complaint was that some doctors adopted too domineering or lecturing an attitude, which may have been true of some. But since diabetes mellitus is a disease which forces the doctor to adopt a didactic and relatively omnipotent role, it renders him particularly liable to become the object of transference reactions. We have already mentioned some examples. Some of the hospital dieticians came in for similar criticism. There was a general feeling that medical advisers tend to be overrigid and frightening in their initial instructions, in their desire to impress the parents. One mother said "the child would be starving and so upset that she got sugar in her urine, whilst I was afraid to give her anything. Later, when I gave her an apple, feeling very guilty, there wasn't any sugar." The mothers felt that in some cases their practitioners had gone too far in alarming them. They described some pathetic little scenes, when in their anxiety they had punished small and uncomprehending children.

Many sessions were spent on the question of behavior problems. Almost every kind of behavioral difficulty was described. The therapist made a point of asking the group to consider whether any given item of complaint was basically related to the diabetes, whether it was a neurotic symptom caused by other factors, or whether it represented normal childish behavior. Up to this point the function of the group might be described as preventive psychiatry, but in this area of behavior disorder, it moved into the field of therapy proper. In considering the reasons for the childrens' behavioral difficulties, the mothers were led into discussing their own attitudes and feelings towards the children and at this point, for the first time, they found reason to talk about their husbands. Consideration of the mothers' own personalities and their effect on both the children and the disease came into the discussion. Some of the conclusions surprised them. For example, the mother with an obsessive compulsive personality, who is usually praised as a "good diabetic mother" by the doctors because of her rigid adherence to instructions, may in fact have an adverse effect on the disease because of the tension and resentment which her driving manner causes in the child.

Some of the emotional problems discussed appeared to be definitely connected with the disease. There were children who attempted consciously or unconsciously, to control the home by making use of their disease. It was found hard to strike a balance between making the children sufficiently aware of their illness for their own protection on the one hand, and on the other, causing them to adopt the role of an interesting invalid. Some refused to take any responsibility for their own care. They projected their resentment of their illness onto the mother and acted as though the diabetic restrictions and injections were punishments imposed by her. One such mother discovered that her adolescent daughter had been giving her specimens of tap water to test, instead of urine. After discussion with the group this very conscientious lady was persuaded to wash her hands of the matter and place the whole responsibility on the girl, a procedure which proved very successful. Several mothers reported that for the first few months after diagnosis, the children were submissive and conforming; then, when they found that they were still alive and that nothing terrible had happened to them, they became rebellious, refusing to provide specimens, and cheating on their diet. Some mothers claimed that definite personality changes occurred after the onset of the disease. Some found that the child became more mature and adult; others complained that a previously good-tempered child became bad tempered, rude, and disobedient. When neurotic difficulties already existed between mother and child, the disease and its management became an additional weapon on both sides. Sometimes the attitude of siblings produced difficulties. Unhappy scenes arose on such matters as birthday cakes and chocolate Easter eggs, which were forbidden to the diabetic. One mother said "if only the doctor would tell us these little things, as well as all the stuff about injections and urine tests."

The attitude of outsiders had an important influence. Only a few reported ridicule of the diabetic child. But some children refused to attend parties because they were embarrassed by the oversolicitous attitude of their hostess. The teen-age diabetics, especially, felt socially handicapped. One boy could not bear to enter the restaurant where his group of friends met, but left them and walked the streets until they emerged.

OBSERVATIONS AND RESULTS

Even intelligent parents with conscientious pediatricians have many misconceptions about diabetes mellitus, which require a great deal of time for their ventilation and elucidation.

The parents' personalities and attitudes to the child and the illness, and the state of the mother-child relationship can have a marked influence on the physical progress of the disease.

In some cases, the mothers themselves seemed to be acting out, in relation to their pediatricians, various unresolved conflicts from their own childhood and sometimes the pediatrician was unwittingly encouraging this. During the period of group therapy some of this acting out was transferred to the psychiatrist or to the group.

The staff of the Metabolism Department were very satisfied with the results of this experiment, stating that they felt they could now pick out the mothers who had taken part in it from others who had not. The group mothers were more relaxed and confident in their management of the disease. They had a better perspective and were no longer upset by the minor day-to-day crises. They showed a greater insight into their children's behavior and handled them better. It was felt, therefore, that group therapy with parents of chronically ill or handicapped children has a useful place in the management of such cases.

Chapter 44

Social Adaptation in Hemophilia

FLORENCE B. GOLDY and ALFRED H. KATZ

FOR the past two years the Medical Center and the School of Public Health, University of California at Los Angeles, have been studying the social and vocational adaptation of the hemophilic adult, a study which has many implications for the care of hemophilic children. The project, supported by a Federal grant from the Vocational Rehabilitation Administration, has been conducted in two parts. Under the first part a questionnaire survey was carried out on 1,100 hemophiliacs aged sixteen and over. The 100 questions had to do with their vocational, educational, and social experiences.

The second part of the study has involved detailed investigative interviews with forty hemophiliacs who were selected as representing relatively good or poor social adjustments. The focus of this phase, to be reported on here, was to learn more about the relationship between early childhood experiences and broad social adjustments in later life. The authors recognize that such recollections are of limited value, since adults recall their earlier life selectively. Nevertheless, these memories seemed worth exploring as having significance for parents and professional persons concerned with children with chronic illness.

GENETIC AND MEDICAL ASPECTS

Hemophilia is an inherited disorder of the blood in which a vital

Note: Reprinted by permission of the author and *Children,* 1963, 189-193, published by U.S. Department of Health, Education and Welfare.

Dr. Goldy is Research and Clinical Social Worker and Dr. Katz is Associate Professor at the School of Public Health, University of California at Los Angeles.

This investigation was supported, in part, by a research grant (No. 647) from the Vocational Rehabilitation Administration, U.S. Department of Health, Education, and Welfare.

clotting factor is lacking. It is transmitted through the mother to male children and usually makes itself apparent shortly after birth. About 60 percent of the known cases have a family history of "bleeders," but the other 40 percent are "new" cases which have arisen presumably from genetic mutation or perhaps from hidden inheritance through generations of female carriers. At present, there is no way of detecting female carriers by laboratory tests, or of identifying potential mutation subjects (1).

Contrary to our expectations, the family experiences of known hereditary hemophiliacs were not significantly different from the experiences of the "mutants." The mothers in both groups were generally more protective and attentive than the child felt necessary. Mothers who felt guilty because they knew they were carriers showed no significant difference in their mother-child relationships than mothers who had not known they were carriers. Nor were mothers who had known a hemophilic father or uncle significantly different in this respect from mothers who had never known anyone with hemophilia before its diagnosis in their son.

Most of our subjects could vividly recall the change in medical management that occurred with advances in blood-banking techniques. Up to fifteen years ago, hemorrhages resulting in painful swelling, unless extremely severe, were seldom treated by doctors. During bleeding episodes the young hemophiliac usually stayed in bed, with home remedies for pain being administered by parents. If the bleeding was massive and pain became unbearable, the child was hospitalized. The incidence of death from continued bleeding was high. Parents and children lived in constant fear.

Today medical treatment can often shorten bleeding episodes, prevent some residual damage, and lessen the crippling effects of hemorrhages. While the possibility of death from bleeding has not been altogether eliminated for hemophiliacs, the new treatments have greatly increased their life expectancy and chances for productive living. Nevertheless, the hemophilic child typically has recurrent and unpredictable episodes of bleeding that halt the usual routine of life. He is constantly exposed to doctors, clinics, and hospitals. To date, there is neither cure nor the possibility of prevention.

THE STUDY'S SUBJECTS

Hemophilia was diagnosed at birth (or within the early months of life) in about three quarters of the study's subjects. Early symptoms of external bleeding had usually been noted at circumcision, but as the child developed, internal rather than external bleeding was usually his major problem. While just sitting up could cause tender hematomas, spontaneous bleeding beneath the skin or from internal organs was the most disruptive problem in early childhood. Internal bleeding was experienced as more limiting, painful, and disabling than bleeding from external wounds. If, in the recollection of our subjects, the bleeding involved a knee or ankle joint, countless periods of extended bed rest, transfusions, and other medical treatments were required. Bleeding which affected joints in the upper extremities, such as elbow, shoulder, or wrist, were easier to live with in childhood, they reported, since this did not require them to stay in bed and so be separated from the family and its routine.

Because hemophilia is little understood by the general public, it is often feared that hemophiliacs will bleed to death if externally injured. Hemophiliacs themselves, however, are more concerned about the "spontaneous" internal hemorrhages of unknown origin. Sustained problems from internal bleeding such as permanent loss of sight from a hemorrhage into the eye, or permanent kidney damage, were found in members of our study group, but most common were orthopedic disabilities, such as a rigid ankle or knee joint resulting from recurrent internal bleeding.

Despite these problems, many hemophiliacs learned early in life to conceal the fact of their illness as they became aware of people's fears about how gingerly they would have to be handled. Concealment was practiced in childhood to gain acceptance from peers; in adulthood, to avoid rejection from potential employers and social acquaintances. Our subjects drew parallels between the consequences of their misunderstood and limiting physical disorder and of such disorders as epilepsy, deafness, or cardiac disease. Thus, the problems of the hemophilic child do not seem to differ greatly from the problems faced by others who are chronically ill but normal in appearance.

PARENTAL SUPERVISION

The patterns of parental attitude reported by our subjects could be placed in three broad categories: (1) overprotective, (2) realistic or permissive, and (3) indifferent. They saw the roles of mothers and fathers very differently. Mothers were usually expected to be overprotective and to set limits on their young sons' activities because of their fear of physical danger. The fact that mothers had caused them psychological trauma by saying "no" was more easily accepted — "she wasn't a boy ever and couldn't be expected to know how important this game was to me"; but fathers who repeatedly denied physical activity was described with great resentment. They were regarded as traitors to their sex and as having denied the masculinity of their young sons.

When parents had differed, mother saying "no" and father "yes," the boy had felt he was masculine like his dad: but when both parents were overprotective, the boy's urge to maleness or independence had been throttled. The fact of parental disagreement seems to have been less important to the child than the emotional support he felt when his father risked the unknown and recognized his developmental needs.

One of the most important findings of this study was that the key to achieving social competence and independence for the hemophilic boy is a father (or father figure) who recognizes his maleness or who does not show concern about his activities. Among our "good adjustment" group, fathers were remembered as either permissive or indifferent, but among the "poor adjusters" (classed as dependent-unemployed, and usually living in the parents' home), overprotection from both parents was commonly described.

CHILDHOOD EXPERIENCE

"Can my son have a normal personality development in spite of his hemophilia?"

This is one of the first questions asked by parents of a hemophilic child. Recent research and theory in behavioral science would indicate that the answer to this question is influenced by many factors.

In our own research, the elements regarded by hemophiliacs as most strongly influencing their personality development when young was the parents' attitude about permitting normal childhood play. Whether special provisions made within the family for the sick child encouraged or played down a sense of difference was also highly important. While these factors were not the sole contributors to adult adjustment, they were the chief factors stressed by our subjects.

Most of our subjects had been diagnosed as hemophiliacs very early in life and reported they had "always" known they were "different" from other children. The degree to which they felt different did not correlate with the number or severity of illness episodes they had experienced, but was associated with the degree of isolation they had experienced or of restriction from kinds of activities boys usually enjoy. Most of our subjects reported they had been capable of setting their own limits of activity "by the age of six or seven" because the consequences of injury were so painful. They could not protect themselves against spontaneous bleeding, but could and did avoid body contact injuries. In remembering injuries which occurred when they "broke a parent's rule," they said that often it was not the prohibited activity per se that brought about painful consequences, but the tension caused from disobedience. They also reported that as adults they were similarly accident prone when under tension, but competent in self-protection at other times.

Another key to feeling "male" lies in sharing experiences with other boys from preschool age until adulthood. A large number of our sample of "good adjusters" felt that their parents encouraged them to join with other children, while most of the "poor adjusters" recalled parental opposition. If not permitted to join other children because parents consider the risk too great, the hemophiliac, who like any child wants to be with other children, internalizes the concept of being "totally different" instead of a child who has a difference but also has many likenesses to his peers.

Even when very young, the child with a *visible* handicap can be accepted by other children without being expected to join in all their activities; but the "normal appearing" child has no visible excuses. Since most young boys' play is gross motor activity, the issue of how far the hemophilic child can go is posed early and decisively.

The key problem for parents of hemophiliacs is in drawing a fine line between necessary caution and harmful overprotection. When our subjects were asked what advice they would give to parents of hemophiliacs, many stressed the importance of developing independence by allowing the child to learn himself what his limits are. One subject advised, "Try to teach him self-discipline and give him lots of love." Another commented, "I knew what I could and couldn't do, but my parents felt my body should be wrapped in cotton-wool, even if it meant missing all the good times kids need."

SCHOOL EXPERIENCE

The years from age six until the teens were recalled as their hardest by our subjects. In this period they derived little gratification from being good students, since their peers placed a much higher value on other accomplishments, especially in athletics. Most of our subjects considered themselves scholastically advanced as children because they read a lot when they could not play. On the other hand, they had attended school only irregularly, and had obtained little satisfaction from their school-work. Those who had gone to schools with large structured classes had had more difficulty in school adjustment than those who had attended one-room schools. The latter, being in classes with children of various ages and grades where students were expected to learn different things, did not feel conspicuously different when the teachers individualized their work for them.

The grade school years were usually evaluated by our subjects according to how much activity they missed and how excluded they had felt. If the parents restricted or forbade after-school play, the youngster felt alienated from his peers. But the child who because of his parents' intention or indifference was allowed to join other children had a chance to identify with other boys.

Three men in the sample who had not attended school beyond the third grade are employed and finding satisfaction in adult roles, and so are classed with the "good adjusters." All three reported that when they were children, their parents had expected them to act like boys even though they were too ill to go to school.

The following case stories illustrate contrasting parental approaches and their effects.

Mr. P is a pale, thin, attractive man with no apparent physical deformities. He lives with his widowed mother and his married sister and her family. He spends his day viewing TV, reading, or "just doing nothing but watching people pass by on the sidewalk in front of the house."

When he was a child, Mr. P was never expected by his parents to do anything except watch. He was not allowed to play with other children for fear he would get hurt. By the time he was 6 or 7, he was afraid to join the neighborhood boys because he did not know how to play their games with them. Gradually he withdrew to watching through the window.

At age 10, Mr. P was enrolled in school for the first time at the recommendation of the local school authorities, but was so frightened by the "big kids" that he never returned to class. His parents made no effort to send him back. He received what education he got from a home teacher and from correspondence courses in accounting and bookkeeping. When he was 24, he tried to work for three days but quit because the office crew were not especially cordial and because his parents felt he should not "push" to get to the office by 9 a.m.

Now at 32, Mr. P feels that life is passing him by. He has nothing to do and no interests. His family still tends to watch him if he tries to sweep the porch or carry out the garbage because they fear he will hurt himself. He wishes he had been expected to play outside, to assume household chores, to attend public school, to develop active hobbies, instead of being encouraged only to protect himself physically.

Mr. A, age 35, walks with a pronounced limp and carefully lowers himself into a chair. He came to the interviewer's office after working hours. He is a tool dyer and has been employed in the same firm for the past nine years.

Mr. A described his childhood as "never having a parent at home." His father seldom "bothered to come around" and his mother "was always working or out." He had many episodes of bleeding into weight bearing joints as a result of which he often used crutches. He did not attend school because no "truant officer bothered us after the years I had been in the hospital" and my parents "weren't around to make me go."

Mr. A remembers waiting each day for 3 o'clock to come around, for then the neighborhood boys would be home and he could play with them. He liked fishing and sliding down sand hills on boxes, but best of all he liked just being with his "buddies."

Before he reached his teens, Mr. A. was "hanging around a garage" with older boys and developing a skill in fixing cars. Once in a while he helped his father, who was a mechanic. Since crawling under cars was too difficult for him, he gradually converted his interests to tools. Though he had no formal training as a tool dyer, he made himself into a tool expert, and is now proud of his earning capacity and his productivity.

Even though Mr. A's "indifferent" parents did not provide him with much love and security, he became an apparently competent person because they did not smother him or isolate him from social contacts.

TEEN-AGE EXPERIENCES

Among physically normal children, adolescence is frequently an emotionally painful and difficult period, but, as Beatrice Wright (2) has shown, this is not always true of the handicapped child.

Our subjects generally found the teen years easier than their earlier years. Many of them made their first fully reciprocal and satisfying friendships then. Formerly, play activities were chiefly physical, but in their teens many of their peers had hobbies and interests which they could share – stamp collecting or motor cars, for example. Scholastic accomplishment now had rewards, since in some high schools the "bright" student with a broad range of knowledge may attain status.

The feelings about being "different" did not disappear but did diminish as the hemophiliacs grew older and found more bases for social relationships. Gradually they became aware that other boys were also feuding with their parents over limits on independence – hours, use of the car, family participation – and this was reassuring because it helped them experience a bond with their contemporaries.

In the course of adolescence, peer group approval became as important as paternal approval had been earlier. If allowed to mix with other teen-agers, the hemophiliacs tended to adopt the peer group outlook on employment, schooling, and other topics.

Cars had an even greater meaning to the hemophilic teen-ager than to his unhandicapped compeer. The democracy of wheels served both as a leveler and as an opportunity for increasing social status. There were many more drivers among those of our subjects classified as "good adjusters" than among the "poor adjusters." In addition to its practical value, driving seemed to help the handicapped teen-ager to express his desire to be like and to spend time with his peers.

VOCATIONAL COUNSELING

Gains from having had professional vocational counseling was noted by some of our subjects, but the timing of counseling interventions was often regarded as inappropriate. Many of our subjects had not received help in vocational planning until they were in dire need of employment and were seriously disadvantaged by their lack of skills or education. Vocational counseling had been beneficially used by eight of the forty hemophiliacs interviewed, but the most helpful counseling was reported as having been started during the junior high school years (ages 12-15). During this age period, the youngster could accept a trainee or student status because he was at an age when young people are expected to be financially dependent and when school attendance is the usual routine of his age contemporaries regardless of their financial status. The hemophiliac who did not have vocational discussions until he was in his late teens often felt then that he was too old to start a long educational program and went into unskilled work. Many of our subjects commented that "they (the counselors) waited until it was too late for me to change."

Help in early vocational training and planning was regarded by our subjects as necessary in a total treatment program for persons with a chronically limiting disorder. They described the ideal vocational counselor as one appropriately informed both about job prerequisites and potentials and about the limits imposed by specific diseases. However, they stressed the fact that *the self-image of the patient has to include being potentially employable before he can respond to vocational guidance and training in a realistic way.* Again, we were made aware of the family's great influence on individual potential for independence and competence.

Our subjects included many young adults who had found work on their own, some of whom recognized they had made poor job choices because of lack of guidance. Also included were hemophiliacs who had received vocational guidance and training, but who had not sought employment because they felt unable to work in the field of their training. Isolating occupations, such as watch repairing, were reported to be bad choices because the handicapped person needs to make social contacts through his work experience; moreover, for hemophiliacs constant sitting, in a confined area, may be physically damaging. Self-employment, after enough training to permit work at a livable level in occupations in which frequent absences would not matter, was often cited as ideal for the hemophiliac. Twenty percent (20%) of our subjects had attained this goal.

Here is one success story:

> Doctor Z is a research chemist with a commercial drug firm. As a young child he used crutches occasionally and was confined to bed frequently, but he "made it through high school." His family expected him to help on the farm, and he managed both chores and schoolwork. During high school he showed interest and ability in the physical sciences, and the school guidance officer encouraged him to compete for a scholarship to college. The undergraduate course took him eight years due to dropouts from illness, and the graduate work even longer, but he is now well established.
>
> Doctor Z supervises a research laboratory and explains that he can "supervise by telephone for a few days when necessary." Married, with young children, he assumes a responsible position in the home, in the community, and on the job.
>
> Doctor Z advises young people with chronic handicaps to expect to reach educational goals more slowly than others, rather than to take on the unrealistic burden of trying to keep up with other students.

REHABILITATION AND COUNSELING

Most state departments of vocational rehabilitation extend services to handicapped persons who have reached the age of sixteen; but many persons who have had lifelong handicaps do not make application for services until much later in life. We saw hemophiliacs who were unaware of this source of help, who felt too defeated to try to qualify for training, or who were likely to continue to be dependent the rest of their lives because they were unable to visualize a different role for themselves. With some intensive help, these men might be rehabilitated to gainful employment, but at their age changing a dependent to an independent self-image through counseling is a long and difficult process.

Complex life adjustment problems obviously confront every hemophiliac as well as other chronically ill persons. If a professional counseling service were readily available at the time of diagnosis and thereafter, parents would have the opportunity to explore their reactions to the handicapped child, to gain emotional support during crises, and to learn to plan and provide a home climate that fosters independence and growth. This preventive approach would reduce the necessity for rebuilding a damaged self-image in adulthood. Somewhere within our public and voluntary efforts for handicapped children, we should be able to find the wisdom and resources to implement it.

REFERENCES

1. Canadian Hemophilia Society: *Hemophilia Today*. Montreal, Canada, Mar. 1, 1962.
2. Wright, Beatrice A.: *Physical Disability: A Psychological Approach.* Harper & Bros., New York, 1960.

PART VI
COUNSELING PARENTS OF CHILDREN WITH SEVERE AND TERMINAL ILLNESSES

Helping a Mother Face Medical Crisis in a Child

BETSY SAFRAN and FRANCES SPIEGEL

IN casework practice, our focus is essentially twofold — the individual's inner personality equipment and the environmental factors inherent in his situation. The problem in treatment is to assess the reality of each and to attempt to help bring about as harmonious and life-giving an interplay as possible. In this discussion we are concerned with the helping process in a situation in which there exists an acute, realistic environmental crisis, in this instance that of the effect upon a parent of the sudden, incapacitating, and fatal illness of a young and previously healthy child. Several aspects of this situation characterize its particular treatment problems. One such factor is the time element. The crisis is sudden, affording an acute change in the situation of the patient and those concerned. The need for help is imminent and pressing, limiting the therapist's flexibility in terms of time. Despite the pressure for prompt relief, however, there are barriers to the patient's amenability to treatment.

In the setting here concerned, that of a hospital* medical ward, the family member enters treatment motivated solely for alleviation of the medical trauma, rather than out of direct interest in his own emotional adjustment. In addition, his readiness for

Note: Reprinted by permission of the *Journal of Jewish Communal Services, 33*:180-184, 1956.

The authors are associated with the Mount Sinai Hospital, New York, New York.

Presented at the National Conference of Jewish Communal Service, Atlantic City, N. J., May 25, 1955.

*Case material from the Social Service, Psychiatric and Pediatric Departments of Mount Sinai Hospital, N. Y.

help is limited by the strong need for defense in the face of tragedy. The individual's entire interest is in a catastrophic event which would be taxing even to the most resilient of personality structures. It remains the case worker's problem in such cases to guard against being likewise overwhelmed by the outer trauma and to retain a focus to the total individual and total situation. Though our direct treatment goal, in a medical social work wetting, may be of help with an immediate situation, this cannot be achieved except through a focus to the whole.

It is in the life crisis that the emotional resources are most acutely taxed. Our awareness of the psychic interplay is critically essential and at the same time critically challenged in these cases. Regardless of the particular make-up of the individual, a situation of acute trauma inevitably calls for the erection of defense. The individual strives in his moment of crisis to preserve his identity. Defense in the threat of danger and loss is natural and helpful. It is in the quality of the defense that we receive our clues into the psychic structure of the individual and our guides into the treatment process. It is the degree to which the defense appears appropriately related to the outer problem and the degree to which it promotes or hinders healing which help us determine the need for help. Regardless of its effectiveness, however, the defense in itself is a protective device and cannot be relinquished unless a more effective support is substituted. This support can best be provided through the treatment relationship.

We shall attempt to illustrate such a treatment situation with a case illustration: We shall call the child Diane — an 11-year-old girl who entered our hospital with post-measles ascending myelitis. On admission she was completely paralyzed from the neck down, and was placed in an artificial respirator. Her paralysis followed a case of the measles, prior to which she had been in excellent health. The diagnosis was established quickly and prognosis was felt to be poor. No hope was held for improvement and ultimate fatality was considered inevitable.

It was noted that the mother, Mrs. Mason, was a high-strung woman with personality difficulties of her own which were complicating her adjustment to an innately traumatic situation. Referral for casework was initiated by the disturbing nature of her response and was for the purpose of helping her adjust to the limits of Diane's situation. It is at this initial point that we first glimpse Mrs. Mason's responses and receive clues as to the nature of her inner equipment for meeting the problem. Mrs. Mason's outstanding reaction was one of an attempt to control the entire situation from diagnosis on through ward routine and treatment of the child. She refused to accept the medical diagnosis and prognosis when this was realistically presented to her. She insisted that Diane would get well, and exerted pressure on the child and the staff to take measures which would hasten recovery. She herself made unrealistic living plans regarding Diane's rehabilitation and pressed the child to strive for improvement. This pressure increased tension in the child and aggravated her problem in adjustment to the trauma. She became increasingly anxious, irritable, and resistant. The liaison psychiatrist attached to the ward observed the interrelation between the child's behavior and the mother's influence. Mrs. Mason was referred for casework treatment and was seen two times weekly for ten weeks. The social worker had no direct treatment function with the child, who was seen regularly by the liaison psychiatrist.

Before discussing treatment, a brief summary of the family background: Mrs. Mason, a 39-year-old woman, had been divorced from her husband for five years. Mr. Mason was a business man, who lived alone and supported her with alimony. There was one other child, a girl, aged 10. Mrs. Mason lived with the two children in a six-room private home owned by Mr. Mason. She lived on a high economic scale in an upper-middle class suburban neighborhood. She supplemented her income through private sale of antiques. There was little contact between Mrs. Mason and her former husband except in business matters. Mrs. Mason herself describes an emotionally deprived background. She was the youngest of eight children, isolated from her siblings because of age difference. The emotional milieu was cold. Her mother was a self-sufficient woman who devoted little time or feeling to Mrs. Mason. Her father was described as a weak, dependent man whose role in the family was subdued by his wife. Mrs. Mason's attitude toward him was one of contempt. She stated that she never felt loved, always felt the need to be self-reliant, for there was no one to whom she could turn for help. Mrs. Mason carried into her adult life her need to conceive of herself as self-sufficient; a "doer rather than a leaner," in her words. She married, at a young age, a man whom she described with contempt as a weakling. She spoke of having married for position rather than love. She prided herself on the degree of emotional control she could exert upon herself; expressed no regret at her broken marriage, in which she initiated the request for severance, after fourteen years of marriage. Though she maintained relationships with other men, she admitted to no interest in remarriage, described a coldness and emotional sterility in most of her relationships.

Mrs. Mason was an attractive, youthful looking woman. She was meticulously groomed; dressed fashionably. Her manner was self-contained, aloof, and somewhat dramatic. She was intelligent and tended to intellectualize. People responded to her with an awesome deference. The significant point in diagnosis is that her outer facade was well controlled and retained throughout the crisis she passed through. Her attention to her wardrobe, for example, was something she clung to tenaciously and appeared to increase when anxiety mounted.

The degree of this superficially effective control gave us initial insight into the general nature of her defense mechanism. It is the extent to which this defense interfered with optimum adjustment that it became a destructive element which necessitated treatment. It was on the basis of this destructiveness that Mrs. Mason was originally referred for casework help. Her awe-inspiring personality had succeeded in virtually dominating ward routine and was interfering with treatment of the child. Mrs. Mason closely supervised Diane's care, spending most of her waking hours on the ward and allowing little help from her husband or other family members. She literally took over nursing duties, causing near-rebellion on part of nursing staff. Her anxious pressure for improvement was causing mounting tension in the child, herself and all others concerned. Any suggestion for change met with hostile resistance.

Upon her referral to the caseworker, Mrs. Mason could in no way openly accept this situation as one for help with her own adjustment, but rather conceived of it as an additional instrument through which she could exert pressure for improved care of Diane. At onset of treatment, Mrs. Mason's need for control was strongly evidenced in her resistance to the interview situation per se. She attempted, at first, to control time, setting, subject matter. She tried to evolve the relationship into a friendly, social one, and attempted to induce worker to conduct interviews informally over lunch. Throughout, we were uncritical but firm in setting certain limits with which we were consistent. We feel that this uncritical but firm consistency was crucial in treatment of Mrs. Mason. It is at this initial point that the milieu of treatment is established. If we had been moved by the pressure of her tragedy and the rigidity of her defenses to yield to her seeming need for a more relaxed, social milieu, we would have automatically blocked the establishment of the kind of rapport which would be most therapeutic to Mrs. Mason. If Mrs. Mason had been allowed to control this situation as she had all previous ones, this would have confirmed her conviction that there is no helping agent strong enough to cope with her problem; her insecurity and need for rigid defensive controls would have been perpetuated.

After much initial testing, Mrs. Mason began to yield to the limits for the treatment relationship. When she met with acceptance within these limits, she allowed herself freer expression of feeling and exposure of problems.

Mrs. Mason's progress in her adaptation to Diane's illness was gradual. At first she was openly fearful that we would pressure her into giving up hope for improvement. In her first interview she warned us that if this was our purpose in seeing her, she wished no further contact. She expressed resentment of the medical staff, who she felt were trying to impose upon her acceptance of their hopeless attitude. We did not directly challenge her defensive resistance to the prognosis; instead, we geared discussion to the present rather than the future and encouraged her to include, in her concept of the present, her life as a whole. There was discussion of her own practical needs, of her relationship with her husband, and, in particular, of her relationship with her younger daughter. Mrs. Mason revealed a negating attitude toward this younger child, whom she had always identified with her guilt-ridden self, as opposed to Diane, whom she had idealized as representing her own frustrated strivings for perfection. When Diane was stricken, Mrs. Mason rejected her own welfare and that of the other child as being unworthy.

In discussion of this guilt and self-rejection, Mrs. Mason was able, with increasing freedom, to examine herself more objectively in terms of her past background and current functioning. She began to use interviews frankly for treatment and to give open expression to personality problems which had existed prior to the present crisis and which were continuing to impede her adjustment. The chief theme of these discussions was the unrealistic pressure she had always, in all areas, exerted upon herself for superlative and all-controlling performance, her inability to accept herself for herself, and her lack of belief that others could be strong enough to help her. Mrs. Mason was able to make connections with her familial background, i.e. her development in an emotionally starved milieu, in which she was thrust upon her own resources for survival and had contempt for her father and resentment of a rejecting mother. Mrs. Mason exposed more completely the degree to which she had guarded against deep attachment in her adult relationships. She admitted that though she had attracted attention and admiration from both men and women, she had never been able to respond with deep love feeling. She was able to express guilt over the degree of her emotional detachment in all her close relationships. Of prime significance here is the extent of her self-recrimination over her prior handling of the sick child. Though she had idealized Diane's potentialities and fostered their fulfillment, Mrs. Mason condemned herself for some inner awareness of inadequacy as a mother and a woman. The interview situation offered Mrs. Mason an opportunity to expose these feelings and to view her behavior in the framework of her total life perspective. This somewhat relieved her self-blame. She began to identify with the worker's accepting attitude and to modify her own self-rejection. She was able to increasingly include concern over her own total welfare and that of her younger child. There gradually evolved a marked change in her daily adjustment to Diane's ward routine. She became less anxious, released some control over Diane's care, spent less time on the ward, and allowed more help from her husband and family members. There was improvement in her relationship with the nursing staff and lessened tension in Diane herself. In general, Mrs. Mason became more realistic in her attitude toward Diane's illness. She expressed realization that she had needed to deny the prognosis in order to save herself from breakdown. With time, she was able to state that despite Diane's minimal signs of improvement, she recognized the possibility of limited recovery, if any.

After ten weeks of treatment, Diane died without immediate forewarning. Mrs. Mason's response was controlled but not rigidly so. We feel that Mrs. Mason's response to Diane's death was cushioned by the preparation she had received in the previous weeks of treatment. Of chief significance was the relief of guilt and her resultant ability to value life apart from, or in addition to, Diane. In the moment of Diane's death, her energy thus remained more attached to existing life than it would have without preparation.

Following the child's death, there was a pause in treatment of about four weeks during which Mrs. Mason did not visit the hospital. The worker suggested that Mrs. Mason contact us should she wish an interview. She did so, and we had two interviews with her, both initiated at her request. In these interviews she was able to express grief and emotion. She was profoundly depressed but able to reach out for help. She expressed awareness that she had emotional problems which had always hindered her adjustment and were continuing to do so. Her expression of this awareness led to discussion of referral for psychiatric treatment. She had at various times considered this, but had never been able to follow through. Mrs. Mason continued to express some resistance to yielding to treatment for herself, chiefly in her feeling of guilt about focusing to her own need now that Diane was gone. With the worker, she was able to work this through to the extent of seeking private psychiatric help. Our treatment function was necessarily terminated at this point. Despite the fact that Mrs. Mason's total needs were considered in treatment, our focus remained throughout, somewhat tied to the crisis which had initiated contact. With the passing of the crisis, it was important for Mrs. Mason to relinquish her ties connected with it and to move on to further help. This could best be provided by a therapist in a new setting whose function would be directly related to her personal adjustment. The referral to a psychiatrist rather than another casework agency was determined by the purely intrapsychic nature of her problem at this point. Mrs. Mason's ability to seek such help reflects some carry-over of the treatment experience per se into her total life functioning.

The differentiating factor in the treatment problem illustrated is the advent of a crisis which, in itself, is highly traumatic. The ability to adjust to such a trauma is largely determined by the individual psychic makeup. Regardless of individual differences, however, several significant elements emerge for discussion. One such element is the natural need for defense in the face of threat. This defensiveness may be immobilizing and destructive, but it is necessary for self-preservation. The defense cannot be relinquished unless substitute support is offered. Such support can be provided through a treatment relationship which is sensitively adapted to the needs of the individual. Through this relationship per se, a modification of defenses can be worked through, resulting in improved adaptation to the problem at hand. In the case illustrated, Mrs. Mason's denial of the reality situation was a strengthening of her usual defense patterns in an attempt to control the tragedy with which she was faced. Her defensive reaction added to the strain of the situation, but temporarily protected her from collapse. Any attempt to immediately deprive her of her defenses directly related to the child would have met with failure. However, this rigid need for defense was indirectly handled through the treatment relationship per se. As Mrs. Mason allowed herself to loosen controls within this relationship, and found herself supported and accepted, she was able to modify her reactions to the traumatic event. Ultimately, her lessened need for self-defense enabled her to seek further personal help.

In addition to a rigid strengthening of defenses, there are several factors in this situation which limit accessibility. The individual's focus at the point of contact is to an outer event affecting another individual rather than to his own need. The ability to focus to his own adaptation to the problem is hindered by the overwhelming nature of the crisis and by the tendency toward self-denial when a family member is stricken. This tendency varies with the individual and depends largely on the extent of his guilt-feeling. It is only through relief of such self-condemnation that the person can be helped to view life as a whole rather than binding himself completely to the stricken one. Mrs. Mason, for example, could allow her self interest in her own life only after expressing her self-blame and realizing that she could not rightfully hold herself fully responsible for all that had happened in her own life. The roots of such guilt as she suffered stem from deeper origin than the immediate trauma and can be approached only superficially in brief contact. However, even limited handling can result in relief and improved adaptation. In particular, the ability to face fatality is aided to the extent to which remaining life has retained its meaning. This meaning can be retained only if the individual allows himself to leave the departed one and focus to other life needs.

The experience of crisis inevitably causes some stirring up of psychic patterns. This emotional stirring can, if sensitively handled, often result in growth and movement which otherwise would not have been stimulated. Though our direct treatment goal may be limited to help with the presenting crisis such help can be provided only through a focus to the whole. A hoped-for result of effective treatment is a carry-over into the strengthening of the total personality.

Chapter 46

Behavioral Observations on Parents Anticipating the Death of a Child

STANFORD B. FRIEDMAN, PAUL CHODOFF, JOHN W. MASON,
and DAVID A. HAMBURG

THERE are few tasks in the practice of medicine as difficult as trying to help the parents of a child afflicted with a disease which is invariably fatal. Since the physician cannot change the reality of the tragic situation, he frequently feels totally unable to lessen the parental suffering. However, understanding the nature of the stress as experienced by the parents, and appreciating that there are characteristic ways in which they cope with the situation, should enable the physician to offer helpful support in a majority of cases.

Forty-six parents of children with neoplastic disease were involved at the National Institutes of Health (NIH) in a study of the adrenal cortical response under conditions of chronic stress, and this work has been reported elsewhere (1). The present paper is concerned with the clinical impressions gained over a two-year period while this study was in progress and the implication of these findings to physicians caring for children with similar diseases, adding to what is presently in the literature (2-8).

Note: Reprinted by permission of the authors and *Pediatrics, 32*:610-625, 1963.

The authors are associated with the Adult Psychiatry Branch, Clinical Investigations, National Institute of Mental Health, United States Public Health Service, Department of Health, Education and Welfare, Bethesda, Maryland, and Department of Neuroendocrinology, Division of Neuropsychiatry, Walter Reed Army Institute of Research, Walter Reed Army Medical Center, Washington, D.C.

SUBJECTS AND GENERAL METHOD OF STUDY

The forty-six subjects represented one or both parents of twenty-seven children, all of whom had been referred for treatment with chemotherapeutic agents to the Medicine Branch of the National Cancer Institute. In all cases, the child had previously been hospitalized elsewhere for clinical evaluation, and the suggestion for referral was most frequently made by a physician at the time he communicated the diagnosis to the parents. In a minority of cases, the matter of referral was initiated at a time later in the child's clinical course. Within twenty-four hours of each child's admission to NIH, the parents were informed of this study by the principal investigator and invited to participate. During a ten-month period in 1960-1961, a total of thirty-six children (including 2 siblings) were admitted for the first time to the pediatric ward of the National Cancer Institute. Of these, the parents of one child did not wish to participate in the study, while the parents of seven other children were unavailable for formal inclusion, though most could be interviewed occasionally.

The median age of the twenty-six mothers was thirty-three years, and that of the twenty fathers, thirty-five years. As seen in Table 46-I, there was broad representation of socioeconomic level, though the majority of parents were high school graduates and from families where the estimated annual income was forty-five hundred dollars or more. Approximately two thirds of the parents lived in an urban or suburban environment, and a majority professed the Protestant faith. One mother and three fathers were married for the second time.

Nineteen of the twenty-seven children, including the two who were siblings, had acute lymphocytic leukemia, one had acute myelogenous leukemia, six had metastatic "solid" tumors, and one child was found to have a benign lesion following an erroneous referral diagnosis of leukemia. The median time from when the parents learned the child's diagnosis from the referring physician and admission to the National Cancer Institute was two and five weeks for the children with leukemia and "solid" tumors, respectively. The group of children with leukemia appeared to

TABLE 46-I

DESCRIPTIVE DATA ON THE TWENTY-SIX
MOTHERS AND FATHERS

Data	Mothers		Fathers	
	No.	*%*	*No.*	*%*
Age				
Range	23–49	–	25–49	–
Mean	33.4	–	36.0	–
Median	33.0	–	35.3	–
Education				
<High school	8	31	7	35
High school	12	46	7	35
>High school	6	23	6	30
Income (Est.)				
<$4,500	6	23	5	25
$4,500–$7,500	16	62	12	60
>$7,500	4	15	3	15
Environment				
Urban	15	58	13	65
Suburban	3	12	1	5
Rural	8	31	6	30
Religion				
Protestant	23	88	17	85
Catholic	3	12	3	15

experience a clinical course consistent with a recent review of this disease by Freireich *et al.,* (9) though somewhat modified by the constant development of new therapeutic techniques. All the children with "solid" tumors had widely metastatic lesions and were referred for systemic chemotherapy. The sex distribution, age at the time admitted, and the average number of siblings for this group of children is shown in Table 46-II.

Thirty-five parents, twenty mothers and fifteen fathers, lived some distance from NIH and were admitted to a ward of the National Institute of Mental Health, where they resided during all or a portion of the time their children were hospitalized. Eleven parents, six mothers and five fathers, who lived in the immediate vicinity of NIH were available for study to a lesser extent and were

TABLE 46-II

DESCRIPTIVE DATA ON THE TWENTY-SEVEN CHILDREN

Data	Diagnostic Group			
	Leukemia *(N=20)*	*"Solid" Tumor* *(N=6)*	*Benign Lesion* *N=1)*	*All Groups* *(N=27)*
Sex				
Male	12	2	. .	14
Female	8	4	1	13
Age (in years)				
Range	1.5–16.0	2.0–7.5	. .	1.5–16.0
Mean	7.0	5.0	. .	6.5
Median	5.3	4.5	4.0	5.0
Siblings				
Average number	2.4*	1.7†	. .	2.2
Patient only child	1	. .	. .	1
Patient oldest child	4	2	. .	6
Patient youngest child	9	3	1	13

*Includes three stepchildren in one family; two in a second family.
†Patient and sibling adopted in one family.

seen on what we have considered an "outpatient" basis.

The period of observation for the parents living on the ward ranged from approximately one week to eight months; two months was the median time for the mothers and one month for the fathers. The parents spending a total of four to eight months on this ward had their stay interspersed with periods at home when their children were ambulatory.

The ward for the parents was two stories above the children's ward and was designated as a "normal volunteer" floor. There were generally six to eight parents staying on this ward at any given time, and the floor was arranged so that each couple, or two mothers, could have a single room with an adjoining bathroom. The parents were usually on the pediatric floor with their children during visiting hours (11 a.m. to 1 p.m., and 3 p.m. to 8 p.m.), but spent most of the remaining hours on their own "normal volunteer" ward, though they were entirely free to leave the Clinical Center at any time.

The parents studied in the ward setting were interviewed by one of the investigators (S.B.F.) in his office at least once a week and were seen on the ward almost daily. In addition to these interviews and observational notes, the nurses on the "normal volunteer" ward made and recorded observations, and each morning the parents filled out a brief questionnaire regarding their activities during the previous twenty-four hours. The parents seen on an "outpatient" basis were interviewed approximately once every two weeks when their children were hospitalized, and there was the additional opportunity to see these parents during periods when their children were in remission and living at home. All parents were also observed interacting with their children on the pediatric ward, though no systematic attempt was made to study the children.

The interviews were primarily concerned with each parent's perception of his child's illness and clinical course, the defenses utilized by the parent to protect him from the impact of the stressful situation and the threatened loss, and the individual's ways of dealing with the many problems that arise when caring for a seriously ill child. Further information was obtained at weekly group sessions open to all the parents and led by one of the investigators (S.B.F.); this investigator was also in frequent contact with the ward physicians,* the nurses caring for the children, and with the social worker assigned to the pediatric ward.

Although the parents of the children with leukemia and metastatic tumors faced many of the same problems shared similar experiences, this paper will primarily discuss the parents of the children with leukemia. An attempt will be made to generalize from our observations, with an emphasis on the findings that are most relevant to the problems of clinical management. No claim is made that the psychodynamics underlying the observed behavior have been fully described; data regarding the specific symbolic

---

*The ward physicians at the National Cancer Institute have the title of Clinical Associate, having completed internship and at least one year of residency prior to their NIH experience. During each year of this study, there were three ward physicians assigned to the children's floor, each spending nine months on this and an adult service.

meaning of the threatened and actual loss for each of the parents were generally not available.

In cases where we contrast our findings with those of others, we would like to emphasize that differences probably existed in the populations under study and the unique setting in which our study was conducted. However, though the parents living on the "normal volunteer" ward were in a somewhat artificial setting, the general applicability of our findings is supported by the similarity of behavior observed both in the parents studied on the ward and in those studied while they continued to live at home.

EARLY REACTIONS OF PARENTS

Learning the Diagnosis

In general, the parents stated that they had some prior knowledge about leukemia and therefore suspected their child might have this disease before actually hearing it from a doctor, and, in this sense, they somewhat anticipated the news. However, without exception, the parents recalled a feeling of "shock" or of being "stunned" when hearing the definitive diagnosis. Only an occasional parent reported a concomitant feeling of disbelief, though in retrospect most parents feel that it took some days before the meaning of the diagnosis "sank in." Thus, in this study, the majority of parents appeared to intellectually accept the diagnosis and its implication, rather than to manifest the degree of disbelief (5,6) and marked denial (2) described by others. Only later did they consciously begin to hope that the diagnosis might be in error.

In cases where the referring doctor discussed leukemia and its clinical course in detail, the parents later realized that little of this general information was comprehended at the time. Certain immediate decisions had to be made, particularly whether the child was to be referred to NIH, and only that information which aided the parents in handling this immediate situation appeared meaningful. The fathers generally took the major responsibility for such decisions at this time, and also tended to offer emotional support to their wives.

Upon arrival at NIH, there was a tendency to be overwhelmingly impressed, and this was associated with revived hope, expressed by statements such as, "If any place can save my child, it will be here." During the period of this study, this reaction was anticipated by the ward physicians who pointed out shortly after the child's admission the realistic aspects of the situation and the present limitations of the chemotherapy.

These statements by the ward physician that NIH was not omnipotent often invoked an immediate reaction of hostility, sometimes expressed by saying that *"only* God could decide" their child's future. However, after a period of a few days to a few weeks, all but a minority of the parents then praised the ward physician for having taken this approach. They felt that they had "now heard the worst," and no longer had to contend with the dread that there was some unknown, even more devastating news, yet to come. Our impression was that this direct approach gave the parents confidence in their ability to master subsequent developments and tended to discourage unrealistic and maladaptive behavior patterns.

Three fathers, two of whom were not formally included in this study, reported a marked hostile component during their early reaction to learning the diagnosis. One confessed to an immediate urge to "blow up the world," another overtly threatened to attack his child's physicians, and a third partially succumbed to the impulse to injure others by deliberate recklessness while driving. All three of these fathers had a history of significant psychiatric problems, two in the form of overt paranoid behavior. Though it was not unusual for a parent to show evidence of hostility directed towards others, the open frank expression of such thoughts and impulses always reflected psychopathology in our experience.

Guilt

Once the diagnosis of leukemia was made, the parents would, almost without exception, initially blame themselves for not having paid more attention to the early nonspecific manifestations of the disease. They wondered whether the child would not have had a better chance of responding to therapy if the diagnosis had been made sooner. Although such reactions of guilt were extremely common, and the deep emotional basis of such feelings has been emphasized by others (4), most parents in this study readily accepted assurance from the physician that they had not neglected their child. Particularly reassuring to the parents was the information that the long-term prognosis in most cases of childhood leukemia is essentially the same no matter when the diagnosis is made.

Thus, in the majority of parents, guilt was not manifested by prolonged and exaggerated feelings of wrong-doing but was more characteristically a transient phenomenon. The various etiologic possibilities which were considered included genetic and controllable environmental factors, but most parents did not dwell on their own possible contribution to the development of the disease and were able to minimize their feelings of guilt. However, we are aware that the degree of guilt reported in a study such as this is dependent upon the intensity with which each subject is studied, the depth of interpretation by the investigator, and the definition of the term itself.

Notwithstanding the above qualifications, a minority of parents did display obvious indications of guilt that were more than transient, and which appeared as persistent self-blame for the child's illness. As one mother said, "It is God's way of punishing me for my sins." More often, a parent would blame himself for not having been more appreciative of the child before his illness. Things had not been done together, the buying of toys had been postponed, or perhaps the child had been disciplined too severely. This attitude frequently led to overindulging and overprotecting the now ill child, with no limits put on his behavior. The ward physician would sometimes comment on such extreme practices, but this parental pattern, to the extent that it was generated by underlying guilt, was exceedingly resistant to change.

Seeking Information

The ward physician had at least one lengthy interview with the parents shortly after each child was admitted and, later, periodically discussed the child's condition with the parents and was readily available to answer any further questions. The parents were generally aware of and appreciative of these efforts, but their remained what appeared to be an insatiable need to know *everything* about the disease. For many weeks, there was, characteristically, an extensive search for additional information, especially about therapeutic developments.

This search took many forms, but most noticeable, at least to the medical and nursing staffs, was the exchange of information among parents on the floor solarium which served as a waiting room for the parents between the morning and afternoon visiting hours. Here the "new" parents would glean information from the group, not only about leukemia and its therapy, but also regarding hospital policies and organization. Information from the three ward physicians and the nurses would be pooled and minutely evaluated for consistency. However, it was inevitable that a parent would not be completely objective in relaying information, and an individual's fears, defenses, neurotic tendencies, and lack of a general medical background would not infrequently lead to misinterpretations and overgeneralizations, limitations that most parents recognized in this mutual sharing of information.

Friends and relatives served as an abundant source of "information" about leukemia, often given with the intent of cheering up the parents. For instance, a parent might be told of a patient who lived for years with leukemia, the informant failing to say that the patient had been an elderly man with a chronic type of the disease. This kind of "information" was of little practical use to the parents and contributed to their tendency to deny the disease, a point which will be discussed later.

Newspaper and magazine articles were read many times if they were even remotely related to leukemia or childhood cancer, and relatives, friends, and acquaintances from all parts of the country would send such clippings. Furthermore, particular attention was paid to *where* the reported work had been done, with parents openly inquiring whether the doctors at NIH were aware of a "latest development." There were repeated requests for written authoritative information about leukemia, as it was recognized by the parents, particularly the mothers who usually had the responsibility of keeping their husbands informed, that there was a limitation on how much could be accurately retained after talking with a doctor.

It was noted that parents would become confused and anxious whenever they perceived divergent "facts" or opinions regarding their child's condition, even if the differences were negligible or imaginary. For instance, one couple became quite agitated when a doctor said their child had a bacteremia and then a second physician referred to the same process as septicemia. Similarly, the parents would perceive minor or major variations in degrees of pessimism or optimism at any given time among the doctors.

The seeking of information can be understood partly as a realistic attempt to learn as much as possible about leukemia in order to better master the situation and care for the ill child. However, the process of learning about leukemia appeared constructive only up to a point, and a sudden upsurge of parental questions often reflected increased anxiety or conflict, which could not be resolved by the aquisition of more detailed information about the disease.

PSYCHOLOGICAL MANAGEMENT OF THE ILL CHILD

The Hospitalized Child

An almost universal concern of the parents was the question of how much the children knew, or should know, regarding their diagnosis. Anxiety about this problem was considerable, although obviously influenced by the particular parents involved, the age of the child, and the help received in this area from the physician. The majority of parents, even those who realistically accepted the nature of the tragedy, shielded their children from ever hearing the word "leukemia," though in the hospital setting this was at times all but impossible. Our impression is that *some* acknowledgment of the illness is often helpful, especially in the older child, in preventing the child from feeling isolated, believing that others are not aware of what he is experiencing, or feeling that his disease is "too awful" to talk about. Unfortunately we have no data which clearly help answer the question of how best to inform children of their illness, but others (10-12) have suggested approaches, though primarily applicable to the adult with a fatal disease, and Marmor (13) further comments on the difficulty of the physician's task in deciding what to tell the cancer patient and his family.

Another common problem was that the younger children with leukemia frequently openly rejected their parents, making such statements as, "I hate you and I don't ever want to see you again," with the result that the parents would feel that they had, in some way, failed their child. This pattern of behavior appeared most commonly after the children had been ill for some time, and seemed in part related to the parents' inability to prevent painful procedures and prolonged hospitalization with consequent damage to the usual childhood faith in parental omnipotence. Furthermore, we have speculated that the children sensed their dependence on the medical and nursing staff and were therefore fearful of expressing hostility directly toward these individuals.

This ability of even young children to perceive the transfer of authority from their parents to the professional staff manifested itself in many ways. Within a remarkably short time, the children would, for instance, directly ask the nurses and doctors for permission to deviate from their diet or to partake in various recreational activities. The parents were accordingly bypassed and would often feel that they were no longer important to their children. Even when the children developed symptoms at home, they might ask the parents to call "my doctor," again reflecting their awareness that the parents' ability to help them was limited.

Diagnostic and therapeutic procedures were painful to the parents as well as to the children. Parents differed on whether or not they desired to be with their children during such procedures, although they usually would not express their wishes unless explicitly asked. Some parents were markedly relieved when they were not expected to be present at such times; others became less anxious if they were allowed to stay with their children and comfort them.

Parents of the younger children often mentioned the difficulty they experienced each evening when they had to leave a child crying in protest or despair. The parents would generally make an effort to continue the usual routine of putting their child to bed, usually with the help of a favorite toy or doll, and within a week or two most children accepted the fact that the parents had to leave each evening. However, a minority of children and parents never appeared to tolerate this daily separation.

The Child in Remission

Parents would eagerly look forward to the time that their child would go into remission and be discharged from the hospital, but their pleasurable anticipation of this event was frequently tempered by considerable concern regarding the necessity of again assuming the major responsibility for the child's care. They feared that without warning some acute medical problem would arise, and any past feelings of inadequacy associated with failure to recognize the original symptoms were reawakened.

Discipline was a common problem when the child returned home, especially if the parents hesitated to set reasonable limits on the child's behavior. The overindulged child would increase his demands on the family until rather belated disciplinary measures had to be instituted, sometimes only after the other children in the family had grown openly resentful of the special favors received by their apparently well sibling.

Overprotection usually accompanied the overindulgence, with activities such as swimming and bicycle riding being prohibited as they might "tire" the child. Ecchymoses resulting from normal activites created anxiety in the parents who associated the bruises with leukemia, and in many cases, this anxiety may have unconsciously led to unnecessary curtailment of the child's physical activity. Furthermore, the fear that the child might overhear his diagnosis sometimes led to discouraging attendance at school and other activities. Thus, returning home for some children meant living a rather isolated and restricted life, and the added strain for the parents led a few of them to be aware of longing for the relative security of the hospital.

DEFENSE PATTERNS AND COPING MECHANISMS

Coping Behavior

Coping behavior is a term that has been used (14-15) to denote all of the mechanisms utilized by an individual to meet a significant threat to his psychological stability and to enable him to function effectively. Such behavior would consist of the responses to environmental factors that help the individual master the situation, as well as the intrapsychic processes which contribute to the successful adaptation to a psychologic stress. The stressful episode in this study, evoking such adaptive and defensive reactions, has been defined as the totality of events associated with being the parent of a child with a fatal disease, and includes both the external events and the associated inner conflicts, impulses, and guilt.

The success or failure of this coping behavior may be evaluated in at least two ways. The observer may judge whether the behavior allows the individual to carry out certain personal and socially defined goals. In the setting of this study, one frame of reference was the relative ability of the parent to participate in the care of the ill child and fulfill other family responsibilities. Though value judgments on the part of the observer are constantly invoked when using such criteria, this area is certainly of major concern to the physician caring for the child with leukemia.

The effectiveness of coping behavior may also be evaluated in terms of the individual parent's ability to tolerate the stressful situation without disruptive anxiety or depression, regardless of whether the behavior is socially desirable. Such judgments were made in studying the parents' hormonal response (1,16), where it was found that pathological as well as socially desirable coping patterns were associated with stable 17-hydroxycorticosteroid excretion rates, *if* such behavior was effective in protecting the individual from anxiety and depression. Optimally then, coping behavior not only enables the parent to deal effectively with the reality situation, but also serves the protective function of keeping anxiety and other emotional distress within tolerable limits.

The "shock" of learning the diagnosis and the associated lack of emotional experience has already been mentioned, and this may conveniently be classified as an extreme degree of isolation of affect, a mechanism by which the apparent intellectual recognition of a painful event is not associated with a concomitant intolerable emotional response. Only after a few hours or days was there profound emotional feeling and expression associated with the intellectual awareness of what had happened, this usually occurring only after the necessary arrangements had been made for the child's immediate treatment. This lack of affective experience continued to be a conspicuous defense, and enabled parents to talk realistically about their children's condition and prognosis with relatively little evidence of emotional involvement. Thus, the parents were frequently described by the medical and nursing staffs as being "strong," though occasionally this behavior was interpreted as reflecting a "coldness" or lack of sincere concern. The parents were also often aware of this paucity of emotional feeling, frequently explaining it on the grounds that they "could not break down" in the presence of the children or their physicians. However, that there was some uneasiness about their apparent lack of emotional expression was suggested by the fact that parents would occasionally verbalize their confusion and even guilt over not feeling worse.

In an occasional parent, the process of intellectualization was extreme, as if the parent was trying to master the situation through complete understanding. Here, there was not only the usual desire for medical knowledge, but a persistent tendency to discuss leukemia in a detached and highly intellectualized manner, at times clearly identifying with the physicians. For instance, the parent might wish to examine a peripheral blood smear, since he "always wondered how our body works."

Over a period of time the parents became increasingly knowledgeable about leukemia, and would often request rather detailed information regarding their child's condition, especially about laboratory results. Inquiries about a hemoglobin level or leukocyte count were common, and in addition, occasionally such data would spontaneously be given by a doctor in order to help explain the more general situation. This led to attempts, generally unsuccessful, on the part of some parents to predict what therapy their child should receive next, with confusion and suspicion when their "medical judgement" disagreed with that of the physician. Having once received such detailed information, the parents tended to expect a daily briefing, and would exhibit at first disappointment, then anger, when this routine was interrupted. Such concern over details did serve a defense function by allowing the parents, as well as the doctors, to avoid the more general, but also the more tragic and threatening aspects of the case. However, our impression was that, overall, more anxiety was generated than dissipated by this practice.

Another defense, less ubiquitous than isolation of affect, but also generally present in greater or lesser degree, was the mechanism of denial, by which is meant the intellectual disclaiming of a painful event or feeling. A few parents openly denied the seriousness of the illness and prognosis; in these individuals there was always a history of a similar defense pattern during past episodes of stress. Such parents did not seem to "understand" the importance of various procedures and thera- peutic plans, and were therefore prone to direct hostility towards the physicians.

Motor activity also appeared to often serve a coping function, the parent usually being partially aware of the motivation behind such activity. Thus, one mother realized that when her child was acutely ill, she would markedly increase the amount of time she spent sewing and knitting. This intermittent activity served to physically remove this mother from the threatening situation and to give her "something else to do and think about."

The mothers readily participated in the overall care of their children and the importance of such activity to the parents, such as allaying existing guilt, has been emphasized by others (3-5,7). This type of activity appeared most supportive to the mothers who, in contrast to their spouses, found the nursing role consistent with their past experiences and self-image.

It should be emphasized that defensive activity does not always, by any means, interfere with adequate and effective behavior. Rather, there appears to be an optimal range of defending or "buffering" one-self from the impact of having a child with a fatal disease. Deviation from this range in one direction, by denying reality, interferes with optimal participation in the care of the child by not allowing the parent to fully meet the responsibilities and demands associated with the situation. On the other hand, when a parent lacks adequate defense patterns applicable to these circumstances, his ability to care effectively for his child is also significantly hampered. This latter situation was vividly illustrated by one father who wanted to stay by his boy's bedside, but found it intolerable to do so because he would be preoccupied with thoughts of the boy ultimately dying. The only way this father could decrease his own anxiety was to stay away from the Children's Ward, leaving his boy alone for relatively long periods of time.

Social Influences

As has been discussed, the adjustment seen in most of the parents characteristically included a relatively high degree of intellectual acceptance of the diagnosis and prognosis. Realistic arrangements, including those directly related to the care of the ill child, were therefore facilitated. However, this acceptance was not easy to achieve and came about only after a good deal of emotional struggle, expressed as "We had to convince ourselves of the diagnosis." It is therefore pertinent that relatives and friends did not usually help in this process, but rather, were more likely to hinder the realization of the child's condition.

Typically, the children's grandparents tended to be less accepting of the diagnosis than the parents, with more distant relatives and friends challenging reality even more frequently. The tendency for the degree of reality distortion to increase with the remoteness of its source from the immediate family almost made it appear that some of the parents were surrounded by "concentric circles of disbelief." Friends and relatives would question the parents as to whether the doctors were *sure* of the diagnosis and prognosis and might suggest that the parents seek additional medical opinion. Comments would be made that the ill child, especially if he was in remission, could not possibly have leukemia as he looked too well or did not have the "right symptoms." Individuals cured of "leukemia" would be cited, and in a few cases, faith healers and pseudomedical practitioners were recommended.

Although parents generally perceived most of these statements and suggestions as attempts to "cheer us up and give us hope," they found themselves in the uncomfortable position of having to "defend" their child's diagnosis and prognosis, sometimes experiencing the feeling that others thought they were therefore "condemning" their own child. Thus, the parents were not allowed to express any feelings of hopelessness, yet, as will be discussed later, they were paradoxically expected to appear grief-stricken.

Grandparents not only displayed more denial than the parents, but often appeared more vulnerable to the threatened loss of the loved child. Therefore, many of the parents felt that they had to give emotional support to the grandparents at a time when it was most difficult for them to assume this supportive role. Our impression is that this marked degree of emotional involvement on the part of the grandparents helps explain the observations of Bozeman *et al.* (2), who noted that the mothers in their study did not often turn to their own mothers for support or guidance. In spite of this, grandparents generally were informed of the diagnosis almost immediately, though parents would occasionally first tell "people we hardly knew . . . just to make sure that we could get through it."

Though society did not allow the parents to give up the hope that their children might survive, it also assumed that they would be grief stricken. Therefore, the parents were not expected to take part in normal social activities or be interested in any form of entertainment. The relatively long course of leukemia made this expectation not only unrealistic, but also undesirable in that some diversion appears necessary in allowing the parents to function effectively in the care of the ill child. Illustrative of this area of conflict was the experience of one mother, whose child had had leukemia for one year. She gave a birthday party for one of her other children and was immediately challenged by relatives who "could not understand how my family could have a party *at a time like this.*" Such remarks often produced anxiety, guilt, or confusion in a parent, leading this same mother to remark "that being a parent of a leukemic child is hard, but not as hard as other people make it."

An additional problem was that friends and relatives often beseiged the parents with requests for information about their child. Parents would have to repeatedly describe each new development, listening by the hour to repetitive expressions of encouragement and sympathy, and occasionally having to reassure others that the disease was not contagious. This arduous task was ameliorated in the cases where a semiformal system evolved where some one individual, often a close friend or a minister, would be kept up to date so that he in turn could answer the multitude of questions.

Although it was clear that friends and relatives sometimes aggravated the parents' distress, they also provided significant emotional support in the form of tactful and sympathetic listening and by offering to be of service, as has been described in detail by Bozeman *et al* (2). The major source of emotional support for most parents during the period of hospitalization appeared to be the other parents of similarly afflicted children, with the feeling that "we are all in it together" and with concern for the distress experienced by the other parents, a mode of adjustment discussed in detail by Greene (17). The parents learned from each other, and could profit by observing the coping behavior manifested by others in the group. Thus, the common fear of "going to pieces" when their child would become terminally ill was greatly alleviated by watching others successfully, albeit painfully, go through the experience.

Search For Meaning

The parents generally found it intolerable to think of their child's leukemia as a "chance" or meaningless event. Therefore, they tried to construct an explanation for it, displaying a certain amount of urgency until one appropriate to their particular frame of reference could be accepted.

A few parents were content with what might be termed a "deferred explanation"; that is, they accepted and appeared satisfied with the knowledge that it would be some years before a scientifically accurate answer was available to tell them why *their* child had acquired leukemia. Parents in this category were all relatively well-educated and were able to evaluate the current thoughts regarding the etiology of leukemia, coming to the *conclusion* that definitive proof of causation was still lacking. However, this did not constitute an acceptance of leukemia as a "chance" phenomenon, but rather implied an ability to wait for the accumulation of more knowledge regarding the etiology of the disease.

A greater number of parents appeared to need a more immediate and definite answer. They would eagerly and unconditionally accept one of the more recent theories concerning the etiology of leukemia, such as "viral theory," with some additional explanation as to why it was *this* particular child, rather than some other child, who developed the disease. Most parents constructed an explanation which was a composite of scientific facts, elements from the parent's past experiences, and fantasies. Though in the majority of cases their concept of etiology served to partially resolve any feelings of being responsible for the child's illness, the synthesis sometimes appeared to reflect parental self-blame. In these instances the guilt appeared to be less anxiety provoking than the total lack of a suitable cause for the leukemia, and therefore guilt may at times be thought of as serving a defense function for the individual (18).

Religion

The attempt of parents to attribute meaning to the fact that their child developed leukemia was inseparable from their religious beliefs and orientation. Most parents expressed the sentiment that religion was of comfort to them, occasionally making such statements as, "It helps us be more accepting" and "At least we know he will be in Heaven and not suffering." These statements seemed to be sincere reflections of the help that the parents received from their religious beliefs, though these same parents did not characteristically discuss the child's prognosis in religious terms, nor were topics of religion often brought up spontaneously in the interview situation. In contrast, a few individuals primarily thought about their child's illness in a religious context, with statements made that "This is the Lord's way of protecting him from an even worse fate." In these parents, there was a tendency to accept the illness as God's will, with the acknowledgment that one could not expect to fully understand His ways.

Although a strong religious orientation made the illness more understandable for some parents, having a child with leukemia caused other parents to doubt their previously unquestioned religious faith and these doubts sometimes led to transcient expressions of guilt. However, to our knowledge no parent actually renounced his religion as a result of this experience. In fact, it was common for a parent to report an eventual "return to religion," and express sympathy for any of the other parents who did not have sufficient religious faith to help them in this time of need.

Hope and Anticipatory Grief

The element of hope as it refers to a favorable alteration of the expected sequence of events, though hard to evaluate, is of general clinical importance (13,19) and was universally emphasized by the parents. Comments would be made such as "Without hope I could never keep going . . . though I know deep down nothing really can be done." Unlike massive denial, hope did not appear to interfere with effective behavior and was entirely compatible with an intellectual acceptance of reality. That the persistence of hope for a more favorable outcome does not require the need to intellectually deny the child's prognosis is of clinical significance, as it differentiates hope from defense patterns that potentially may greatly distort reality. Hope actually helped the parents accept "bad news" in that the ward physician would often couple discouraging news with some hopeful comment.

As the disease progressed in the children, there was usually a corresponding curtailment of hope in the parents. Whereas at first they might hope for the development of a curative drug, as the child became increasingly ill, the hope might be only for one further remission. Parents would note that they no longer were making any long-range plans and that they were living on a day-to-day basis. The hopes regarding their children would tend to be so short-term and limited that parents would find themselves preoccupied with a question such as whether their child would be well enough that evening to attend a movie, rather than think about his ultimate fate. This gradual dissipation and narrowing of hope appeared inversely related to the increasing presence of what has been called anticipatory grief (20).

The amount of grieving in anticipation of the forthcoming loss varied greatly in the individual parents, and in a few, never was obvious at any time during the child's clinical course. However, in most, as noted by others (6), the grief process was usually quite apparent by the fourth month of the child's illness, frequently being precipitated by the first acute critical episode in the child's disease. Grieving then gradually evolved as the disease progressed and any death on the ward often had a potentiating effect.

The signs and symptoms of this anticipatory mourning process were not as well defined as in an acute grief reaction. However, it was common for parents to complain of somatic symptoms, apathy, weakness, and preoccupation with thoughts of the ill child. Sighing was frequently observed, and many parents would occasionally cry at night and appear depressed. At other times there seemed to be an increase in motor activity and a tendency to talk for hours about the ill child, an observation consistent with the findings of Lindemann (20).

The process of resigning oneself to the inevitable outcome was frequently accompanied by statements of wishing "it was all over with." The narrowing of hope and the completion of much of the grief work was described by one mother who stated: "I still love my boy, want to take care of him and be with him as much as possible . . . but still feel sort of detached from him." In spite of feeling "detached" from her child, this mother continued to be most effective in caring for and comforting her child, with no evidence of physical abandonment. Richmond and Waisman (4) have commented on the usefulness of this anticipatory mourning in stepwise preparing the parent for the eventual loss, and the few parents in our study who did not display such behavior experienced a more prolonged and distressing reaction after the child actually died.

TERMINAL PHASE

Terminal Episode and Death

The parents realized that the clinical condition was much more serious when all of the established chemotherapeutic agents had been exhausted, this event marking what might be considered the beginning of the terminal phase of the illness. Characteristically at this time, there was an acceleration of the grief-work or the actual precipitation of mourning in those few individuals who previously had denied the prognosis, and to the staff, the parents often appeared resigned to the fact that their child would die. Often, as previously described (4), parents would become increasingly involved in the care of other children on the ward, and occasionally a parent would openly express the desire to resume a more normal life and return to the other children at home. Though these feelings prevailed, there still were residuals of hope, if only that the child might "just smile once more" or "have one more good day." During this terminal period, the knowledge that the doctor "who knows the case best" would be in daily seemed of particular importance. However, in spite of this appreciative attitude, the parents were also less understanding and easily became annoyed when even minor things did not go exactly according to plan. There were apt to be frequent, though brief, expressions of irritation or anger, often followed by spontaneous denial of such feelings. These transient manifestations of hostility might have been related to the direct challenging of an underlying unrecognized belief in the omnipotent nature of the doctors and the hospital, or in some cases, a displacement of unconscious resentment and ambivalence from the ill child to the medical staff.

In this setting, the child's death was generally taken calmly, but with the appropriate expression of affect. Outbursts of uncontrollable grief or open expressions of self-blame were the exception, and usually there was some indication of relief that the child was no longer suffering. There were arrangements, telephone calls, and decisions to be made, and characteristically the father again assumed the more dominant and supporative role, just as he had shortly after the diagnosis had first been made.

The death of the child therefore did not appear to be a severe superimposed stressful situation, but rather an anticipated loss at the end of a long sequence of events. This was also reflected in the 17-hydroxycorticosteroid excretion rates (1), in that there was not one parent who showed a marked rise during the last day of urine collection, which frequently included the time the child had actually died, nor were plasma corticosteroid elevations observed several hours after the child's death (21). These findings might in part be due to the parents not yet experiencing the emotion, as many of them remarked that they "just cannot believe that it's all over . . . it just hasn't hit yet."

Follow-up Observations

The parents of the children who died relatively early in our study were invited to return to NIH for a three-day period. Twenty-three parents were thus approached; eighteen, including eight couples, accepted and were seen three to eight months after the end of their children's illness. In addition, three parents who lived in the immediate vicinity of NIH were also available for study during a comparable period.

The grief reactions following the actual loss of the children, as related by these parents, were very similar to, though in some cases not as intense, as those following a sudden loss (20), and the mourning usually became much less pronounced after three to six weeks. There was a tendency for feelings of guilt and self-blame to be verbalized, often for the first time, and as other (22) have noted, repeated reassurance from the doctor was frequently quite comforting during this period. One might speculate that in some cases an unconscious or barely conscious wish for relief of tension through the child's death during the terminal phase provided the motivation for such expressions of guilt during the mourning period.

Of the eighteen parents who return to NIH after their child's death, sixteen felt that the return had been a helpful experience. Some of these parents believed that they "would have been drawn back," even if they had not been invited to again participate in the study. This feeling existed in the face of a "dread about returning," sometimes accompanied by a tendency to think of their child as still a patient at the hospital. In these parents, there was a feeling of relief soon after arrival at NIH, expressed as "It wasn't anywhere near as hard as I thought it would be," followed by statements to the effect that returning to NIH "has put a period on the whole affair . . . it now seems more real that Jimmy is not with us." In our opinion, this suggests that an unconscious remnant of denial persisted in many parents, reflecting a previous denial process that was not always readily apparent when the child was still alive. This apparent acceleration in the termination of the grief process was not reported by two parents who did not appear to have accepted their loss to any significant degree, though approximately six months had elapsed since the death of their children.

Though our follow-up observations are still limited and confined to twenty-four couples, it is known that five mothers became pregnant either during or immediately following their child's illness. There is not sufficient data in three cases to judge whether the pregnancy was planned, but in the other two there was a deliberate effort to conceive. One additional couple attempted to adopt a child approximately four months after their own child had died, and in one other family, the mother is attempting to become pregnant some six months after their youngest child died.

None of the parents who have thus far participated in our follow-up study have reported an increased incidence of somatic complaints or minor illnesses, nor have any of the parents developed any acute medical problems requiring hospitalization subsequent to the actual loss of their child. However, it is recognized that the follow-up period has been of inadequate length to make any statements regarding the possible relationship of unresolvable object loss and the grief reaction to the development of disease, as has been suggested by Schmale (23) and Engel (24).

IMPLICATION FOR PHYSICIANS AND CONCLUSIONS

Each parent of a child with a fatal disease reacts to the tragedy in a unique manner, consistent with his particular personality structure, past experiences, and the individualized meaning and specific circumstances associated with the threatened loss. In general, optimal medical management depends on the physician's awareness and evaluation of certain aspects of this specific background information. However, the parents of children with leukemia do share many similar problems that are inherent in the situation, and certain modes of adjustment commonly occur in a characteristic sequence. The parental behavior, though not stereotyped, is therefore predictable to some degree.

Characteristically, most parents are unable to incorporate detailed information regarding the disease and its clinical course during the first days after learning the diagnosis. The physician should therefore concentrate on explaining the child's acute condition and keep his guidance relevant to the immediate problem, helping the parents with whatever decisions must be made. Sufficient time and privacy should be available to allow the parents to ask their questions, repititiously at times, since this is one of the processes by which they come to accept the tragic diagnosis. If referral to a larger medical center is contemplated, the parents should be led to have realistic expectations, neither anticipating a "cure" nor frightened by statements that "nothing can be done."

After the child's medical management has been decided and the immediate problems subside, the parents should be furnished with sufficient information about leukemia* to allow them to realistically help in the care and handling of their child. Such information also aids them in resolving any feelings of guilt or sense of responsibility for their child's illness. However, requests for detailed medical information, such as the daily laboratory findings, should be discouraged and evaluated in terms of what underlying needs the parents are attempting to fulfill. The physician should appreciate the frequent attempts of parents to find some "meaning" or "cause" for their child's illness, and unrealistic etiologic explanations should only gradually be questioned. In order to avoid unnecessary confusion and anxiety, all medical information should, whenever possible, be communicated to the parents by the same physician.

The physician should be alert to the problems of the hospitalized child, and parents should be informed, when

*A publication entitled *Childhood Leukemia: A Pamphlet for Parents* is available to physicians for distribution to parents from the Information and Publications Office, National Cancer Institute, Bethesda, Maryland.

indicated, that overt manifestations of apathy, depression and hostility are often the natural consequence of prolonged illness and hospitalization in children. Apparent bypassing of parental authority, or even open rejection of the parents by the child, may precipitate episodes of anxiety and guilt in the parents, and every attempt should be made not to further undermine the parental role. During the child's hospitalization, nurses can be particularly helpful in guiding parents, especially fathers, in effective participation in their child's care. At the time of discharge, parents should be instructed about the physical and emotional care of their child, reassured regarding their adequacy to meet the demands of the situation, and advised of the availability of prompt medical help during this period. Special emphasis should be paid to discussing what activities are reasonable for the child, with the aim of preventing undue restrictions and overprotection.

Coping mechanisms observed in parents should be viewed in terms of how such behavior contributes, or interferes, with meeting the needs of the ill child and other family members, yet not neglecting to appreciate the protective function such behavior has in keeping anxiety and depression within tolerable limits for the individual parent. There are many appropriate ways for parents to master the situation, and advice should be consistent with the individual's particular coping pattern, with attention paid to the expectations and demands that may be made by friends and relatives. An acceptance and understanding of anticipatory grief can further enable the physician to help parents adjust to their inevitable and painful loss, though the child's physician should not modify his course of treatment because of this anticipatory mourning experienced by the parents. Expressions of guilt or hostility should not be considered abnormal unless they are extreme and persistent; in these cases further evaluation, and perhaps psychiatric consultation, is indicated.

The physician should not underestimate the importance of his mere presence, to both the child and the parents. Parents particularly need his support when their child first becomes seriously ill, even though in reality a remission is likely to follow. Though the physician must keep somewhat "emotionally distant" from the family he is treating in order to maintain his own effectiveness and objectivity, his empathy and understanding are vitally important in caring for the child with a fatal disease and the child's family.

REFERENCES

1. Friedman, S. B., Mason, J. W., and Hamburg, D. A.: Urinary 17-hydroxycorticosteroid levels in parents of children with neoplastic disease: a study of chronic psychological stress. *Psychosom Med, 25*:364, 1963.
2. Bozeman, M. F., Orbach, C. E., and Sutherland, A. M.: Psychological impact of cancer and its treatment, III. The adaptation of mothers to the threatened loss of their children through leukemia: Part I. *Cancer, 8*:1, 1955.
3. Orbach, C. E., Sutherland, A. M., and Bozeman, M. F.: Psychological impact of cancer and its treatment, III. The adaptation of mothers to the threatened loss of their children through leukemia: Part II. *Cancer, 8*:20, 1955.
4. Richmond, J. B., and Waisman, H. A.: Psychological aspects of management of children with malignant diseases. *Am J Dis Child, 89*:42, 1955.
5. Knudson, A. G., Jr., and Natterson, J. M.: Participation of parents in the hospital care of fatally ill children. *Pediatrics, 26*:482, 1960.
6. Natterson, J. M., and Knudson, A. G.: Observations concerning fear of death in fatally ill children and their mothers. *Psychosom Med, 22*:456, 1960.
7. Bierman, H. R.: Parent participation program in pediatric oncology: A preliminary report. *J Chron Dis, 3*:632, 1956.
8. Greene, W. A., Jr., and Miller, G.: Psychological factors and reticuloendothelial disease: IV. Observations on a group of children and adolescents with leukemia: An interpretation of disease development in terms of the mother-child unit. *Psychosom Med, 20*:124, 1958.
9. Freireich, E. J., *et al.*: The effect of chemotherapy on acute leukemia in the human. *J Chron Dis, 14*:593, 1961.
10. Rosenberg, A.: Psychological problems in terminal cancer management. *Cancer, 14*:1063, 1961.
11. Dameshek, W., and Gunz, F.: *Leukemia,* New York, Grune & Stratton, 1958, p. 311-313.
12. Hoerr, S. O.: Thoughts on what to tell the patient with cancer. *Cleveland Clin Quart, 30*:11, 1963.
13. Marmor, J.: The Cancer Patient and His Family. In *The Psychological Basis of Medical Practice.* Edited by H. I. Lief *et al.* New York, Harper & Row, 1963.
14. Visotsky, H. M., *et al.*: Coping behavior under extreme stress:

Observations of patients with severe poliomyelitis. *Arch Gen Psychiat,* 5:423, 1961.

15. Hamburg, D. A., Hamburg, B., and deGoza, S.: Adaptive problems and mechanisms in severely burned patients. *Psychiatry, 16*:1, 1953.

16. Wolff, C. T., *et al.*: The relationship between ego defenses and the adrenal response to the prolonged threat of loss: A predictive study. Presented at the Annual Meeting of the American Psychosomatic Society, Atlantic City, 1963.

17. Greene, W. A., Jr.: Role of a vicarious object in the adaptation to object loss: I. Use of a vicarious object as a means of adjustment to separation from a significant person. *Psychosom Med, 20*:344, 1958.

18. Chodoff, P.: Adjustment to disability: Some observations on patients with multiple sclerosis. *J Chron Dis, 9*:653, 1959.

19. Menninger, K.: Hope. *Am J Psychiat, 116*:481, 1959.

20. Lindemann, E.: Symptomatology and management of acute grief. *Am J Psychiat, 101*:141, 1944.

21. Friedman, S. B., Mason, J. W., and Hamburg, D. A.: Unpublished data.

22. Solnit, A. J., and Green, M.: Psychologic considerations in the management of deaths on pediatric hospital services: I. The doctor and the child's family. *Pediatrics, 24*:106, 1959.

23. Schmale, A. H., Jr.: Relationship of separation and depression to disease: I. A Report on a hospitalized medical population. *Psychosom Med, 20*:259, 1958.

24. Engel, G. L.: Is grief a disease?: A challenge for medical research. *Psychosom Med, 23*:18, 1961.

Acknowledgment

The authors are deeply indebted to the parents who participated in this project, and to the clinical associates who cared for their children on Ward 2-East. Dr. Myron Karon of the Medicine Branch of the National Cancer Institute offered his continuous support and facilitated many aspects of this study. We also gratefully acknowledge the encouragement and support given by Drs. C. Gordon Zubrod, Emil Frei, III, and Emil J. Freireich of the National Cancer Institute. Mr. Paul C. Hartsough tabulated much of the data, and Mrs. Joanna Kieffer, Miss Susan Rusinow, and Mrs. Martha Mantel were responsible for the office and secretarial work. The authors are also indebted to Mrs. Mary Miller and her nursing staff on the "normal volunteer" ward and to Mr. Lawrence Burke of the Social Service Department. Drs. George Engel, Arthur Schmale, and Gilbert Forbes were kind enough to critically review the manuscript.

Chapter 47

Psychologic Aspects of
Management of Children with
Malignant Diseases

JULIUS B. RICHMOND and HARRY A. WAISMAN

T HE management of patients at any age with malignant disease is a trying experience for the physician as well as for the patient and his family. When such disorders arise in childhood special problems are presented. Therefore, it occurred to us that observations made during our management of forty-eight children with leukemia (1) and many children with other malignant lesions would be of value to others faced with similar clinical problems. Although many patients in this study were hospitalized for metabolic observations of the effect of folic acid antagonists administered experimentally, we do not imply that prolonged hospitalization is necessary or desirable. Because of the tragic nature of this group of diseases, it is not a simple matter to undertake a carefully controlled study of emotional reactions of either patient or family; it is hoped that some relatively innocuous methods of measurement may be developed and applied in the future. This report, however, is based solely upon our clinical impressions.

As death from infectious, nutritional, and metabolic disturbances decreases in incidence, malignant disorders assume

Note: Reprinted by permission of the author and the *American Journal of Diseases of Children, 89*:42-47, 1955.

From the Department of Pediatrics, College of Medicine, State University of New York at Syracuse (Dr. Richmond) and the Department of Pediatrics, School of Medicine, University of Wisconsin (Dr. Waisman).

relatively greater significance in the practice of the pediatrician. One author has indicated that 3 percent of surgical patients admitted to a children's hospital had malignant disease and stated that "it is probable that cancer in childhood will become an even more frequent cause of hospital admissions" (2). If leukemia, lymphoblastomas, and other nonsurgical malignant disorders are added, hospital practice is increasingly concerned with the management of children with potentially fatal diseases and their families. In this light it is striking to note that so little has been written concerning this aspect of pediatric practice, although Alvarez has recently presented an interesting discussion of this and similar problems in adults (3).

At the outset it must be stated that these comments will necessarily be general. In dealing with matters as complex as the human personality, the spectrum of reactions is so broad as to minimize the significance of generalizations. Our observations are not intended as a substitute for study and evaluation of each patient and family. Intelligent management is dependent upon some understanding of the background of each individual, as it is in every situation involving the study of human behavior. Indeed, with a knowledge of parental personalities, the experienced observer can make reasonably accurate predictions of what may be expected under emotional stress.

The diagnosis of malignancy necessarily brings with it one of the most deep-seated of all anxieties, that of separation from a loved one. This has deeper meaning than most separation anxieties which parents and children face because of the finality of separation which comes with death. The psychological depth of this reaction indicates the importance of the physician's precision in diagnosis; without an accurate diagnosis it is cruel to arouse anxieties unnecessarily, although publicity and cancer education have made people increasingly aware of and sometimes needlessly anxious concerning the possibility of this diagnosis. This emphasizes the importance of ready availability of diagnostic consultation services in which there is specific competence in neoplasms of children by physicians, since it is impossible for individual physicians to encompass personally all the subleties of malignant diseases of childhood.* The relative significance of these diseases renders it imperative that complete frankness — again, without arousing undue anxieties — obtain in the relationship between physician and parents. Procrastination in diagnosis or imparting inaccurate knowledge concerning the diagnosis often renders future relationships — and indeed the relationship with all physicians — more difficult. Thus, promptness and skill in diagnosis of the physical disorder may have far-reaching effects psychologically in management.

For purposes of presentation, the observations relevant to the patient, parents, physicians, and other personnel will be discussed separately. Obviously this division is arbitrary, since interaction among these persons is continuous. This interaction will be brought into the discussion as is feasible.

THE CHILD

The reaction of the child to malignant disease is dependent to a considerable extent upon the age at which the disease develops, since there are different levels of understanding at different ages. The type of lesion probably is also a significant factor in how the child views the disease. Changes in energy for physical activity (as in leukemia) or obvious physical abnormality (as in sarcoma about the neck or face) must influence how the child views himself and his relationship to others.

Prior to the establishment of the diagnosis in leukemia, it is not uncommon for a child to be lacking in energy sufficient to carry on his usual daily activity. Since the cause for this change in behavior is not recognized, he may be subjected to criticism and to punitive action by siblings or parents (with later feelings of guilt on their part) because he does not respond in his usual manner and assume his usual responsibilities. Or he may be subjected to the comments of other children concerning obvious bodily deformity. Or, if surgery is being considered, the realistic loss of a part of the

---

*If facilities are not available locally for physicians, the Tumor Registry of the American Academy of Pediatrics, Dr. Harold Dargeon, Chairman, 112 E. 74th St., New York 21, provides an excellent consultation service.

body and its symbolic meaning may be productive of great anxiety. Psychiatric consultation may be very helpful in identifying the nature of the child's problem.

In spite of the above factors, children observed by us rarely manifested an overt concern about death. Even among adolescents, who intellectually may know much about cancer, the question concerning diagnosis and possibility of death usually was not raised as it often is by the adult patient. Our suspicion is that this does not reflect an awareness but rather represents an attempt at repression psychologically of the anxiety concerning death. For the occasional child who asked about his diagnosis, a simple descriptive statement was given without provision of a diagnostic label.

In general, children seem to have reacted with an air of passive acceptance and resignation. Associated with this there often seemed to be an atmosphere of melancholia. Some of this may, of course, be the projection of the staff and parents rather than the child's feelings. Since the child's physical energy diminishes so significantly, it may be that much of the child's lack of emotional as well as physical response is due more to this factor than to psychological awareness of the diagnosis.

During diagnostic and therapeutic procedures, we have noted a tendency to greater passivity to the procedures than is present in normal children. Whether this is due in part to resignation or to the lack of physical energy is not known at present. With the progress of the disease, the passivity tends to become marked; it is not uncommon to observe children with extensive lesions and hemorrhage maintained entirely by parenteral fluid therapy, without any significant protestations concerning its discomfort.

PARENTS

One of the physician's most important roles in the management of the child with a malignant disease is the help which he may provide to the parents in their integration of a tragic event into their life experiences. Perhaps at no other time does the previous integration of the personality and of the family unit reflect itself so clearly as it does during the severe emotional stress associated with mourning. The physician should realize that the withdrawal, feelings of unworthiness, and preoccupation with thoughts of earlier experiences with the loved one for a period of time (usually several weeks) is part of the mourning process in the normal person. When these manifestations are extreme, it may be suspected that parental psychopathology is present and that psychiatric help may be necessary. Ordinarily, this period serves as one in which a reintegration of feelings takes place and a gradual redirection of energies externally occurs. It should not be the physician's goal to minimize or to abort what is a physiologic emotional experience. There is perhaps too great a tendency to attempt to spare people from this experience in our culture, which probably is not desirable. Many cultural practices concerning paying respects to the bereaved, centering around the provision of help in ways unique to each cultural group, have respected the emotional implications of mourning.

The physician can help in relieving the suffering of parents who are mourning if he has insight into the feelings which they are experiencing. These feelings initially center about the anxieties concerning parental responsibilities for the development of the illness. These are usually manifested as feelings of guilt. When given an adequate opportunity to express their anxieties, almost all parents will ask questions ranging from "whether it would have been different if we had called the doctor earlier" to "do you think my spanking him may have brought this on?" The deep emotional basis of these questions is revealed by the fact that they arise in spite of the fact that intellectually most of these parents know better. The ventilation of these anxieties has therapeutic value; reassurance within the limitations of our knowledge of etiology is helpful. We refer to this as the physician's "sharing" of anxiety, which has the effect of reducing its intensity. It is important, however, to permit the parents to verbalize sufficiently to determine the specific anxieties. A case in point was the futile attempt of a house staff member to reduce the anxiety of a father whose son was admitted with a prior diagnosis of acute leukemia. The young physician's own anxiety led him to extended explanations of the disease, the lack of a known etiology, and so on, with no results. A senior staff member observing the situation casually engaged the father in conversation and within a few minutes learned that his anxiety centered about whether he was going to be a recipient of "charity" against his will. When assured there was no rule against his paying the hospital bill, he was considerably more comfortable. He had already made a reasonably good adaptation to the child's illness.

A second major concern of parents, as previously indicated, centers about separation and its irreversibility. The rearing of children represents a series of steps in separation from the birth process to the grave. When death comes prematurely, the blow is considerably more potent. Aspirations and plans which have developed over the years are shattered, for what parent has not dreamed of what a child will grow up to be? The physician is therefore called upon to help parents deal with the feeling of emptiness which characterizes the separation from a loved one during mourning.

Malignant disease is not usually associated with sudden death. The physician, therefore, has time in his favor in helping parents through the severity of this separating experience. Although depression or marked anxiety may accompany the initial impact of the diagnosis, the period of illness prior to death may be one of reintegration of parental feelings in which the mourning process takes place substantially prior to the death of the child. This may occur with any prolonged fatal illness and is observed with adult patients and their families too. The fact that the separation itself occurs over a period of time tends to facilitate this. Our experience indicates that parents are often enabled to traverse this difficult emotional experience with much less difficulty in this way. This is in contrast to the feelings on the part of friends or some physicians who, reflecting their own anxieties, feel that it is "better to get it over quickly."

We have found that the involvement of parents in the physical care of the child is extremely important in facilitating parental adaptation. First, this permits the parents to have a feeling that they personally have done everything possible for the child; second, feelings of guilt are somewhat relieved by the expenditure of personal effort in the care of the child; third, in retrospect parents are very grateful for having had the opportunity to spend as much time with the child as was possible; and fourth, an opportunity to observe and to participate in measures directed to relieve pain and discomfort as much as possible is comforting to parents. Except for the unusual instance of very disturbed parents, in whom there were preexisting problems in the parent-child relationships, there was a real feeling of involvement in hospital care of the child. The parents were given an opportunity to participate realistically in the physical care of the child; they were gainfully occupied in routines of bed making, feeding, play activities, story reading, and so on. Thus, parents became integrated into the ward program and communication with ward personnel was enhanced thereby. This tended to effect some interidentification with parents sharing to some extent the problems of nurses, doctors, and other staff, while the staff in turn shared parental problems.

An observation which seemed interesting to us and which further illustrates the advantage of parental participation in physical care relates to the development of parental capacities to care for and to give of themselves to other children. Usually the initial period on the ward was one of involvement solely with their child. After a variable period a desire to help as effectively as they could with the care of other children developed. In many instances it was our feeling that the manifestation of this capacity to give to other children marked a turning point in parental adjustment which reflected acceptance of the child's illness and ultimate death, with the conversion of energy which had previously gone into a form of mourning to more constructive endeavors. This observation is in accord with that noted by Freud (4) many years ago as marking the end of mourning.

Many of these parents ultimately continued their contact with ward personnel and desired to be of service; others found emotional outlets in the provision of gifts to the ward or to children on the ward. In a more organized way a sizable group of these parents have become active in the promotion of research in hematologic and malignant disorders. These activities were never encouraged by the staff in any formal way, but it was interesting that the contacts of parents with others sharing the same problem permitted the development of what seemed to be an organized yet socially and emotionally desirable form of activity.

Because of the considerable anxiety which parents of a child with a malignant disorder faced, we believed it undesirable to add to this anxiety by leaving decisions concerning treatment to them. We are aware of the fact that it is not uncommon for physicians to leave a decision to parents as to whether an attempt at treatment is to be instituted, with potential prolongation of life. We believe that the feelings of guilt which every parent has to some extent are too great to permit the intensification which may occur when the parent is placed in a position of making a decision which may or may not alter the course of the disease. We therefore have assumed the responsibility generally of offering an opinion to parents concerning what we believe to be desirable in management. It has been only in the rare instance when the parent has in a very positive way indicated "If he has to go, we want him to go as fast as possible" that we have not assumed complete responsibility for medical management.

Although parental participation in the care of the sick child is desirable, this should not be at the expense of the emotional and physical well-being of the remainder of the family. Siblings may be particularly disturbed during this period and may require considerable parental support. It is helpful therefore if the physician encourages parents to divide their time among the various members of the family as the situation warrants. This provides a greater sense of sharing of the problem by all members of the family; greater integration of the family unit usually develops as a consequence.

PHYSICIANS

The physician's relationship to the patient and family is considerably influenced by his developmental background. As the family experiences the emotional problems of separation, the physician, by understanding and empathy, also experiences significant reactions. These are especially difficult for the young physician in many instances.

When the disease process is chronic, an opportunity for identification rather than empathy with the patient and family may develop. This may consume a considerable portion of the physician's energy — either by driving him to extreme (and often absurd) lengths to "do something" or by influencing him to "do nothing so that the end will come soon." The response of each person varies in relation to many factors in the patient's and the physician's backgrounds. As an example, overinvolvement with one patient was observed in an otherwise fairly objective physician; it was noted that this physician unconsciously identified the patient with his son, who happened to have the same given name and was of the same age. As a consequence, he went to extremes to "leave no stone unturned" and in the process tended to subject the child to many more therapeutic procedures than were indicated. It probably need not be emphasized that such emotional relationships, aside from being difficult for the physicians, interfere significantly with objectivity in providing medical care.

Senior staff members should also be aware of the dissipation of emotional energy which may occur when a relatively youthful house staff has several children with malignant disease under constant care. Without their conscious awareness, we found that house staff members tended to find many reasons (beyond the reality of physical work involved) for not admitting additional patients with leukemia if they had as many as three such patients under their care. In effect, they were indicating to the senior staff their limits of tolerance for such emotional stress. It was also not uncommon for house staff members to experience a considerable feeling of relief on leaving the services which was disproportionate to its physical and intellectual demands and which seemed greater than that observed prior to our study, when patients with malignant disorders were not so numerous on the ward.

It has been striking to observe the respect and gratitude which parents have for the physician in the face of his inability to provide specific therapy. The opportunity which the physician has to share parental anxieties, his permitting some dependency in a situation which makes real demands for maturity, and his provision of realistic help and interest make for a relationship which is appreciated deeply. This is not unique to the management of children with neoplastic disease; we have also observed it in parents of children with muscular dystrophy, when the physician is often embarrassed by the gratitude of parents in the face of his helplessness in combating the progress of the disease.

OTHER STAFF

Much of the previous discussion applies to other hospital personnel. Nurses play a particularly important role, since they provide much of the physical, as well as psychologic, care of patients. That they should be selected on the basis of their real interest in and love for work with children is an obvious statement, which is not always respected. Patients and parents readily detect feeling tones even if these are not verbalized, and serious doubts concerning adequacy of care may enter the parents' minds when members of the nursing staff are not deeply interested in children.

The acceptance by the nursing staff of the continuous presence of parents was not as difficult as we believed it might be initially. Ordinarily many nurses believe it more efficient to perform all the work involved in patient care without "interference" from outsiders. The severe illness and many needs of the patients, however, convinced them that the children usually received better care when parents were present. Genuine acceptance of parents and considerable sensitivity to and understanding of their problems were observed in the nursing staff after the program was in progress for several months. Hospital administrators were also won over to this policy, even though no adequate facilities were available for parents. Improvisation by the nursing staff to care for parental needs developed spontaneously. The effectiveness of this program with nurses, dietitians, occupational therapists, teachers, aides, and others, we believe, is attributable largely to the example set by the more senior members of the pediatric staff and the identification which the remainder of the staff achieved with them.

SUMMARY

Observations, experiences, and suggestions for management of children with malignant diseases and their families based on a study of forty-eight children with leukemia and children with other neoplastic diseases are presented. Suggestions by which the physician may help such children and families through the trying emotional experiences associated with these diseases and their fatal outcome are discussed.

REFERENCES

1. Poncher, H. G., Waisman, H. A., Richmond, J. B., Horak, O. A., and Limarzi, L. R.: Treatment of acute leukemia with and without folic acid antagonists. *J Pediat, 41*:377, Oct. 1952.
2. Farber, S.: Malignant Tumors in Early Life. In Nelson, W. E., (Ed.): *Mitchell-Nelson Textbook of Pediatrics,* (ed. 5.) Philadelphia, W. B. Saunders Company, 1950.
3. Alvarez, W. C.: Care of the dying. *JAMA 150*:86, Sept. 13, 1952.
4. Freud, S.: Mourning and Melancholia. In *Collected Papers.* London, Hogarth Press, 1948.

Chapter 48

The Psychologic Management
of Leukemic Children and
Their Families

GODFREY P. OAKLEY and RICHARD B. PATTERSON

A FAMILY crisis ensues when it is learned that one of its children has leukemia. The desire to ameliorate the shock has motivated many physicians to study both the children with this disease and their families. Since there are currently no methods of cure or prevention, efforts have recently been made to define the role of the physician and his associates in helping the family accept this tragedy with minimal trauma (1-9).

To evaluate the management of leukemic patients and their families at North Carolina Baptist Hospital, fifteen interviews were held with parents of children who had died of leukemia. The interviews also provided an opportunity to look for regional peculiarities that might require a different approach from that used in other localities. The interval between the child's death and the interview was greater in our cases than in other studies based on follow-up interviews (6,7), and in all but two cases the child's home was visited personally, another departure from the usual method.

MATERIAL AND METHODS

The North Carolina Baptist Hospital, a five-hundred-bed private

Note: Reprinted by permission of the author and the *North Carolina Medical Journal,* 27:186-93, 1968.

From the Department of Pediatrics, Bowman Gray School of Medicine and North Carolina Baptist Hospital, Winston-Salem.

hospital, is the major teaching facility for the Bowman Gray School of Medicine. There is a School of Nursing and a School of Pastoral Care. In the absence of a social service staff, the students and faculty of the School of Pastoral Care perform some of the functions of social workers.

Selection of Subjects

From a group of patients whom one of us (R.B.T.) had come to know during a three-year period as a fellow in hematology or as chief of pediatric hematology, there were twenty-two who met the following criteria: (1) had been diagnosed as having leukemia (or in one case, lymphosarcoma), (2) would have been dead at least eleven months at the time of interview, and (3) had lived within a one-hundred-mile radius of Winson-Salem.

Letters were written to the parents of these twenty-two children briefly outlining the project and requesting their participation. A self-addressed postal card was enclosed. Parents were asked to respond by marking one of three choices: (1) grant an interview in the home, (2) complete a questionnaire if the interview was objectionable, and (3) decline to participate.

Seventeen families agreed to an interview, two letters were returned because of inadequate addresses, and no reply was received in three instances. One parent requested that he and his wife come to the medical school for the interview; another family volunteered to come. These offers were accepted; the other parents were seen in their homes. Two cooperating families were not visited because the pressures of the academic year did not allow enough time.

Characteristics of Children and Families

The patients included ten boys and five girls whose ages ranged from ten months to eleven years three months at the onset of illness. All had received chemotherapy. The length of survival from diagnosis ranged from three to twenty-five months. In all but two cases the diagnosis was acute lymphocytic leukemia. One child had lymphosarcoma; the other, Down's syndrome and acute myelogenous leukemia.

There were three families with four children, two with three children, seven with two children, and three with only one child. Both children of one family were adopted.

The mothers' ages ranged from nineteen to twenty-seven years and the fathers' from twenty-five to forty-six years. One father had committed suicide a year prior to diagnosis. One father had been married prior to his present marriage. All other parents were living together and had been married only once.

One family was Roman Catholic, the others Protestant. All lived in Southwestern Virginia or Western North Carolina. All but one lived in rural areas or towns of less than 10,000 population. The other family lived in a city over a population of between 10,000 and 50,000.

None of the families were wealthy. Some of the parents had college degrees, but the majority were semiskilled or unskilled workers. Commonly both parents worked.

Method of Questioning

A questionnaire was prepared that included biographical data, recollections about the diagnosis, the course of the disease, and the death of the child. Parents were questioned about their activities since the child's death.

The authors visited thirteen homes. We went together and conducted the interviews jointly. After introductions and greetings, the interview followed an outline covering points in the questionnaire. The visit lasted about forty-five minutes.

RESULTS

At this point it should be noted that many of the impressions and observations presented here were not recorded at the time of the events to which they relate. They depend upon what the parents were able to recall. Hamovitch (7) noted in his study, however, that "selective recall" agreed well with observations recorded during the illness.

Feigel (19) has discussed death as a taboo topic. The authors are aware that their own taboos and inhibitions were in operation during both the planning stages of the project and the actual interviews with the parents. In spite of these limitations, the data gathered seem worthy of presentation.

Initial Reactions to Diagnosis

The majority of the patients were referred to NCBH without a diagnosis, but the possibility of leukemia had been suggested to some families. A feeling of shock on learning the truth was universal. They could not believe the diagnosis; they hoped it was not true.

Although parents thought that there was no "good" way to reveal the diagnosis, only one parent was unhappy about the particular method used in her case. The family physician had told the father and paternal grandfather that he suspected leukemia, but told the mother that the child had infectious mononucleosis. That night, after the child had been placed in the local hospital, this mother confronted the doctor and asked bluntly, "Does my child have leukemia?" Honesty on the part of the referring physician and the hematologist was generally considered to be of the utmost importance.

One family did not want to know the diagnosis. "Just tell us what to do; we'll do it." At the time of the interview they still remained reluctant to discuss the diagnosis.

One father, a justice of the peace, noted that he was not "normal" at the time of his son's illness. He resented authority if he thought it to be contrary to the best interest of his son. This man stated that he nearly assaulted a house officer because he, the father, disliked the other man's approach to his son.

Hospitalization

One of the parents, more often the mother, wanted to stay with the child at all times. Suggestions that parents could not remain with their children aroused violent reactions. Many parents were disturbed because the physical plant at NCBH was much older than that of their local hospital: mothers were accustomed to having a bed in the child's room. Not only were no beds available for mothers at NCBH, but the only accommodation for the parent was a straight-backed chair. Private rooms were not desired — "It helped to see other people."

A mother stated that at the time when her shock was greatest, she was a stranger in the medical center. She remembered being tired and hungry after the long ride from home and the hospital admission procedures. Yet directions to the cafeteria were so poorly given that it took her thirty minutes to find it.

One parent complained that rigid enforcement of visitor regulations caused important visitors such as pastors to be "run out" rudely in the midst of significant conversations.

The medical school teaching environment itself was a source of difficulty. At the time of the interview one family was still concerned about the "doctors in white." They could not understand why any physicians other than their private doctor had anything to do with their child. Other parents were aware of the medical school and its teaching methods but still had complaints. Several parents thought that two or three separate, complete physical examinations on return visits were unnecessary, particularly when the child was acutely ill. Mothers objected to giving the complete history to a third-year medical student or house officer on each return admission, especially if the admission was only for a transfusion.

The inconsiderate attitudes of one particular house officer and one nurse were mentioned by several families. In contrast, the interest of the student nurses was appreciated and praised.

The business officer of the hospital drew criticisms from several parents. They complained that the bills were never correct. One parent remembered being called from the room of her dying child to discuss her account.

Clinic Visits

The recollections of clinic visits were essentially positive. One family looked forward to the visit because it was hoped that the child would be helped. One technician who "did the sticking" was held in affectionate regard: "She had a way with children." The visits provided the parents with an opportunity to talk together. On the other hand, the trips were long and tiresome to a few. Others feared rehospitalization. The children dreaded the days when bone-marrow aspirations were done.

Home Life

The home lives of these families were generally centered on the sick child. Both parents and siblings sacrificed time and money for the patient. Parents admitted that the other children were neglected during the illness.

One family reported that their children often came home from school with distressing questions prompted by their classmates (no doubt the result of conversations overheard at home). Frequent telephone calls from friends and relatives necessitated an unlisted phone number in at least one family. Others recalled that the many inquiries were tiresome.

Social events were not enjoyed. Parents "felt guilty" about being happy. One nineteen-year-old mother was disturbed at parties when someone would ask, "Aren't you the one whose child has leukemia?"

Problems and Help

In addition to the emotional strain imposed by illness, these families were faced with such practical problems as finances, transportation, and the matter of running a household, often in the mother's absence. Every family but one had relatives nearby on whom they called for help with transportation and household tasks. Churches, civic funds, fellow employees, often helped financially. The one family with no near relatives happened to live the greatest distance from the medical center. For clinic visits a mother and a daughter rode the bus to Winston-Salem the day before and returned the day of the visit, leaving the other children in the home of a neighbor. Employers were felt to have been generous and considerate about working arrangements for both mothers and fathers.

Emotional help was sought and received from ministers;

however, some parents emphatically pointed out that their minister was unable to function in this role. Some "talked it out" with friends. No one mentioned other members of the family as a source of emotional help. One mother received help from reading her Bible. Another family stated that daily devotions, begun early in marriage, were a source of strength. One father joined a church for the first time in his life during his child's illness; the degree of help received was questionable.

Death and Mourning

Whether death occurred at home, in the local hospital, or at the medical center, the parents often recalled a sense of relief. One father remembered a chaplain's comment that God had given the family "a dirty deal" by letting their son die from leukemia. This was not the father's view, and it angered him.

Details of the mourning process were difficult to evaluate. All families reported a time of activity for several days after the death. Visitors and food were plentiful. This was followed by a variable period of loneliness and isolation as friends stopped coming. In one exceptional case, members of the parents' bridge club visited at three- to four-day intervals after the first few days; the parents recalled the visits as helpful. It was universally agreed that staying busy was very important. Two families had moved from houses that they found unbearable without their deceased children. Another family took a two-weeks' trip after the death occurred.

At the time of the interview all parents were outwardly functioning satisfactorily. There had been no divorces or separations. Two mothers had required hospitalization because of "nerves." One family was so disturbed by the interview that it had to be ended prematurely. Their son had had lymphosarcoma and had been acutely ill during the four months that he lived after the diagnosis. Although it was not uncommon for mothers to weep, none of the other interviews had to be stopped before completion.

Unhealthy psychological situations were found to involve siblings of the deceased children. Two children had nightmares and difficulties with school work. One child kept all her older sister's old toys aligned in a certain order and became furious when neighborhood children disturbed them. Because of the mother's fear of losing a second child from leukemia, she had monthly blood counts made on this little girl.

More than half the families had pictures of the child in view and stated that they were able to talk about the child with friends. In other homes no pictures were seen. Many parents admitted that they rarely discussed their child with others. They had difficulty in talking during the interview.

Family Additions

Among the fifteen families, two mothers were pregnant at the time of diagnosis. One was delivered three weeks before the death of the leukemic child, and the other eight months before death occurred. The parents whose two children were adopted, adopted another child two years after the death. Two other families had babies from eighteen to twenty months after the death of their sick child.

A mother who had one child living stated that she knew she should have another, but her first pregnancies had been difficult. Her history included one spontaneous abortion. She also feared that another child would be abnormal. In another family in which there were no living siblings, the mother wanted other children but the father did not. There had been an earlier spontaneous abortion in this family, too. This father had remained with the child in the hospital a major part of the time — a role the mother usually played. Another mother stated that she had stood all the pain she could and did not want to chance being hurt again. Still another said that her deceased daughter had been "everthing I could want in a girl." No other children could take her place.

Miscellaneous

All but one of the families stated that they had tried to learn everything they could about the disease, consulting medical texts, home medical books, and newspaper and magazine articles. When shown a recent pamphlet on the subject, they thought it would have been useful.

Eleven families wanted to return to the medical center to see their child's physician. Four actually did return. The mother whose husband had committed suicide thought that a return visit would not have been worthwhile. No answer to this question was recorded in two cases. Other parents did not return because they thought the doctor would be too busy to see them.

Many parents asked about new developments in the understanding and treatment of leukemia. Others wanted to know about the risks their other children faced.

Many families who became acquainted while their children were ill kept in touch after they died.

Although not queried specifically, none of the families regretted that their child had received chemotherapy. One grandmother had advised against any therapy, but the parents were glad they had not followed her advice. The parents wanted everything possible in the way of therapy — in one case, to the extent of making a trip to Florida to see a faith healer.

As indicated before, all the children in this study died from a disease their physician could not cure. Nevertheless, there was not one indication at any interview of hostility toward the physician. In fact, there seemed to be a feeling of appreciation for what he had done.

DISCUSSION

The information gleaned from this study will now be integrated with the findings of others into suggestions for the psychologic care of a child with leukemia and his family.

An accurate diagnosis is the foremost factor in dealing with the family. When the clinical picture and laboratory data suggested leukemia, it is necessary to make a definitive diagnosis by bone-marrow examination as soon as possible. This may mean immediate referral to a medical center, or the attending physician may do the study himself. The urgency of a diagnosis in either case is important for two reasons: (1) the family will probably suspect the diagnosis and feel great anxiety, and (2) an early diagnosis and immediate institution of therapy will enable the family to feel later that "everything was done soon enough" (2).

Green and Solnit (11) have recently discussed some of the consequences of a mistaken diagnosis.

With the diagnosis in hand, the physician must inform the family. As Farber (12) states, "The truth should be told . . . kindly, and preferably in a room removed from the hurly-burly of the clinic." He continues that the term "acute leukemia" should not be used until "a relationship based on confidence in the physician has been established."

Orbach and others (2) emphasize that the parents have a "deep need to preserve some hope in the child's eventual recovery." They believe that parents want to keep their children alive as long as possible. That no cure is presently known must be made clear; however, these authors believe that research or experimental therapy should be offered to preserve some hope and let the parents feel that they have done everything possible.

Time should be available to reply to however many questions the parents may ask. Farber (12) says it so well: "Parents must be prepared for the eventual loss of the child — or even the termination of the illness in a very short while — without depriving them of the hope that prolongation of life may in itself preserve the child for benefits of research yet to come."

Orbach and others (2) state that the "period immediately following the diagnosis is a time of intense parental anxiety manifested by hostility toward doctors, failure to comprehend the information given, acute feeling of personal responsibility for the illness, disruption of functioning, or separation fears." One can understand why Davis (13) says these people need "mothering."

The physician must expect hostile attitudes in parents as a normal reaction. He should not become angry. When consultations are requested, he should get them. It is his responsibility to assure the parents that they could not have prevented the illness nor its outcome. His responsibility extends to seeing that the family obtains food, lodging, and sedation if necessary. One mother in this study remembered being lost and lonely after her arrival at the medical center. She was not "mothered" enough. A social service worker is invaluable in such cases. A social worker may also help the mother organize the household chores that need to be done in her absence. Suggestions as to what to tell neighbors, family, and siblings are useful.

After the initial period of protest, most parents accept the diagnosis. It is now that they are eager for information about the disease. The pamphlet prepared by the National Cancer Institute (10) can be of help. As the parents remember little of what has been told them at the time of diagnosis, the physician must be prepared to answer any questions that the parents have, even though they have been answered before.

The importance of parents' being able to identify a single doctor as their child's physician is emphasized in two reports (9,2). He should be the one on whom they can rely both during hospitalization and during stays at home. Many treatment centers have residency programs with a relatively high turnover. Here parents receive less than the best psychologic support in that there is no single physician whom they can identify as their child's.

While there are no easy solutions to the psychological problems attending leukemia, Williams (14) offers some suggestions:

> Desirable plans for medical service at the university hospital include the following: physical segregation of the majority of patients according to the main type of disability, but a pooling of others in general medical units; uniformly excellent care for all patients, with no segregation according to financial status; and major responsibility for the activities of these units under the respective specialty chiefs and general internist."

The emotional need of the hospitalized child has recently been reviewed by Mason (15). He and Richman and Waisman (3) imply that the liberalization of visiting hours has a positive effect on both child and family. The families in this study were universally appreciative of extended visiting privileges and were extremely bitter when, owing to a misunderstanding, they were asked to leave the child's room. Richman and Waisman suggest and Hamovitch (20) shows that the parental participation in the routine care of their child can be helpful to both parent and child. A necessary corollary is an understanding, mature nursing staff who give verbal and silent approval of the parent's help and can assume full care when this best meets the needs of the family. To expect such maturity from all nurses working on a general pediatric ward is no small order.

Another liability of liberalized visiting hours and parental participation in the care of their children is that the other members of the family will be completely neglected. It is also necessary that the mother get adequate rest and nutrition. Parental participation in the care of their children is nevertheless a worthy goal.

Many children experience a remission and subsequent relapse requiring hospitalization. On readmission the fears of separation are revived (2). Several mothers in the present study were distressed by having to repeat the complete history of the case to a stranger, usually a medical student, and again when the house officer and medical student performed separate examinations on these acutely ill patients. Such evidence causes us both to agree and disagree with Feinstein (16). Because the history and physical examination of these patients require the fullest employment of both the art and the science of medicine, one examination would seem to serve the best interests of patient, parents, and student, the latter observing while the physician makes the examination, as suggested by Feinstein. That the history must be repeated in its entirety to the admitting house officer on each readmission, is, however, in our opinion, unnecessary and perhaps unwise.

As death approaches, the family needs the physician. Friedman and others (6) remind us that even though the physician feels that he can be of no more help to his patient, his mere presence in the room every day comforts the family.

Following the advice of Solnit and Green (9), the physician should be sure that the parents are aware of an imminent fatal event. Should they be out of the hospital, he should telephone them to come, having prepared them in advance for such a message. When the parents are in the hospital they will undoubtedly know of the death as soon as, if not before, the physician does. He should come to discuss the circumstances with the family as soon as possible. Solnit and Green advise the physician to be prepared to answer questions and, more important, to listen as the parents initiate their immediate grief reactions. Although these authors recommend that the physician offer to see the parents later, the American literature dealing with the psychologic care of leukemic families has not, in our opinion, given a return visit the emphasis it deserves.

In the present series eleven parents stated that they would have liked to return to talk with their child's physician, and four actually did. Other studies (6,7) report favorable impressions of the follow-up interviews, but fail to include the recommendation that it be a necessary part of the care of these families.

Williams, an Australian pediatrician from the Royal Children's Hospital of Melbourne, appreciates the importance of a follow-up interview. He says:

> I have found that a single interview at the time of death has been incomplete and unsatisfactory from several points of view. There are often a number of questions that can be discussed only at a time when parents have had the opportunity to adjust to the loss of their child, and when the results of the postmortem examination are known. After an initial interview at the time of death, parents have been given the opportunity to talk with me one to three months after the child's death. The majority of them have welcomed such an opportunity, and considerable experience leaves me in no doubt of the value and importance of this second interview.

The interviews reported here were characterized by the parents' having unanswered questions. There were unhealthy attitudes and perhaps pathologic grief reactions among these families.

Robbins (18) says:

> We can no longer divide life into segments such as fetal, neonatal, childhood, adolescence, adulthood, and senescence. Rather, it is a dynamic continuum with the status at any one point in time being influenced by all that went before and in turn, having an effect upon all that follows.

If he speaks the truth, then the follow-up interview would certainly be of value from the standpoint of helping families with psychologic problems needing therapy. Just as important is the role that these interviews can play in preventing unnecessary psychologic trauma to the parents and the siblings of the dead child. The follow-up interview should not be underestimated, and should become a part of the care of these families.

It is well to recall that all patients and their families must be treated individually. One must be able to recognize the exceptions to the rule.

SUMMARY

A series of fifteen interviews was conducted with parents of children who died from leukemia eleven months or longer prior to the interview. The purpose was to evaluate the psychologic care given these patients and to look for regional pecularities.

Mistakes had been made in the care of these patients and especially of their parents. No outstanding regional peculiarities were noted.

Several suggestions for improving the cares of these people were made. The importance of an interview with the parents some months after the death of the child is stressed.

REFERENCES

1. Boseman, M. F., Orbach, C. E., and Sutherland, A. M.: Psychological impact of cancer and its treatment, III. The adaptation of mothers to the threatened loss of their children through leukemia, Part I, *Cancer 8*:1-19, Jan-Feb, 1955.
2. Orbach, C. E., Sutherland, A. M., and Boseman, M. F.: Psychological impact of cancer and its treatment, III. The adaptation of mothers to the threatened loss of their children through leukemia: Part II, *Cancer 8*:20-33, Jan-Feb, 1955.
3. Richmond, J. B., and Waisman, H. A.: Psychological aspects of management of children with malignant diseases. *Am J Dis Child, 89*:42-47, Jan, 1955.
4. Knudsen, A. G., Jr., and Natterson, J. M.: Participation of parents in hospital care of fatally ill children. *Pediatrics 26*:482-490, Sept, 1960.
5. Natterson, J. M., and Knudsen, A. G.: Observations concerning fear of death in fatally ill children and their mothers. *Psychosom Med, 22*:456-465, Nov-Dec, 1960.
6. Friedman, S. B., and others: Behavioral observations on parents anticipating the death of a child. *Pediatrics 32*:610-625, Oct, 1963.
7. Hamovitch, M. B.: *The Parent and the fatally ill child.* Durante, Delmar Publishing Company. Inc., 1964, pp. 77-82.
8. Lourie, R. S.: The pediatrician and the handling of terminal illness. *Pediatrics, 32*:477-479, Oct, 1963.
9. Solnit, A. J., and Green, M.: Psychological considerations in the management of deaths on pediatric hospital services: I. The doctor and the child's family. *Pediatrics, 24*:106-112, July, 1959.
10. Friedman, S., Karon, M., and Goldsmith, G.: *Childhood Leukemia: A*

Pamphlet for Parents, U. S. Department of Health, Education and Welfare, Public Health Service, 1964.

11. Green, M., and Solnit, A. J.: Reactions to the threatened loss of a child: a vulnerable child syndrome: Part III. Pediatric management of the dying child. *Pediatrics, 34*:58-66, July, 1964.

12. Farber, S.: Management of the acute leukemia patient and family. *CA, 15*:14-17, Jan-Feb, 1965.

13. Davis, J. A.: The attitude of parents to the approaching death of their child. *Develop Med Child Neurol, 6*:286-288, June, 1964.

14. Williams, R. H.: The training of the physician: medical education and patient care. *New Eng J Med, 271*:602-605, Sept, 1964.

15. Mason, E. A.: The hospitalized child — his emotional needs. *New Eng J Med, 272*:406-414, Feb, 1965.

16. Feinstein, A. R.: Scientific methodology in clinical medicine IV. acquisition of clinical data. *Ann Intern Med, 61*:1162-1193, Dec, 1964.

17. Williams, H.: On a teaching hospital's responsibility to counsel parents concerning their child's death. *Med J Aus, 2*:643-645, Oct, 1963.

18. Robbins, F. C.: The long view. *Am J Dis Child. 104*:499-503, Nov, 1962.

19. Feifel, H.: "Death." In Farerow, N. L.: *Taboo Topics,* New York, The Atherton Press, 1963, pp. 69-74.

20. Hamovitch: *op cit,* pp. 69-74.

Chapter 49

Psychologic Considerations in the Management of Deaths on Pediatric Hospital Services

ALBERT J. SOLNIT and MORRIS GREEN

ALTHOUGH papers that deal with the dying child and his family have begun to appear in the literature (1-3), the psychologic help given to the family of the dying child is often overlooked or left to "common sense" and improvisation in most hospitals. In the present paper the authors propose to discuss certain practical guides which in their experience have been valuable in aiding the family of the fatally-stricken child.

BEFORE THE DEATH OF THE CHILD

The aid given by the physician to the family of a child who dies in the hospital begins before that event and continues after it. The competence, sincerity, and consideration shown by the medical staff during the period of fatal illness establish the atmosphere in

Note: Reprinted by permission of the authors and *Pediatrics, 24*:106-112, 1959.

The authors are affiliated with the Child Study Center and Department of Pediatrics, Yale University School of Medicine (A.J.S.), and Indiana University Medical Center (M.G.).

The authors wish to acknowledge gratefully the contributions of Evelyn Sturmer, R.N., and Samuel Ritvo, M.D., to this paper.

which this crucial human experience occurs. The most important aspect of this atmosphere is the relationship between the physician and the patient, including his family. This relationship has the potential of helping the family to cope with their grief when the child dies. This is optimally achieved when there is one doctor whom the parents can identify as the child's physician. It is necessary to emphasize the importance of the one doctor when the most efficient hospital service is continuously faced with the weakening of this relationship, because of the many professional personnel actively involved in hospital care of patients. The child's physician provides the medical continuity in the management of the patient in his fatal illness.

Although there is the tendency and opportunity to withdraw one's interest from the fatally ill child in the hospital, the physician's persistent attention and efforts are of real value to the dying child and his family. This is not to say that unrealistic, last-minute procedures are necessary or can make up for a lack of attention earlier in the course of the dying patient. By making the child and parents as comfortable as possible, the physician establishes himself as one who will help them endure the crisis for which they are preparing. Through his skill in communicating with child and parents in this situation, the physician helps the child and family to feel appropriately dependent on the doctor and his staff.

Unless a parent is severely disturbed emotionally, the best preparation he can have for the painful and tragic experience of losing his child is to know what is going to happen next, insofar as it is possible to know. The parents may need to have the diagnosis, as well as the nature of the treatment, explained many times before they will be able to understand and accept the painful reality of the situation. When reality threatens to dissolve permanently the ties to loved persons, a denial of the reality is evoked. The repeated explanation of the diagnosis and treatment help the family to prepare for the death of the child by offering repeated opportunities to experience the painfulness of the loss in a gradual manner. With this preparation the final loss of the child is less apt to be overwhelming.

At the same time that the doctor conveys the thought that the child can be given symptomatic relief, he can tactfully imply the ultimate fatal outcome of the illness. Although truthfulness with the family is an important principle, the doctor tempers it in order to express it to the family at a time and in a manner that is helpful and understandable to them rather than overwhelming. Some tolerate it better if they are given the information all at one time, while others benefit more from a gradual presentation. Certain parents will strongly demonstrate that they do not wish to have the fatal prognosis made explicit until the last days or hours of the illness. If the parents say, in many ways, "Don't tell me, Doctor," they will have to be helped gradually to realize the facts of the situation.

In those instances in which the diagnosis is not apparent, after an initial investigative effort, the doctor can tell the parents that a diagnosis has not been reached, without burdening them with his own diagnostic or therapeutic anxieties. An impression of incompetence may easily be given by the manner in which the competent doctor points out the limitations of knowledge.

One avoids stating a definite prediction as to the length of the illness, as it is never possible to do this with certainty. One also guards against the tendency to give unwarranted reassurance and to promise too much. Where it is practical, the use of a consultant to confirm the diagnosis, treatment and prognosis can be a significant aid to the family in accepting the reality of their child's illness.

At the time of death, it is very important that the physician avoid censoring or criticizing the parents for their behavior; it is determined by deep currents of feeling about death which emerge from their past experiences and cultural heritage. For example, some parents can stay in the room with their child in the final moments, and some cannot. It may be individually and culturally appropriate to wail and dramatize the catastrophe of losing a child for certain families, and for others a tight-lipped silence indicates that it is not considered acceptable to express strong feelings in the presence of other people. It is wisest to let the parents do what they feel like doing rather than attempt to impose one's own wishes upon them.

If possible, the parents should be offered the opportunity to be nearby when a patient is close to death. Sometimes parents are not alerted because of a mistaken belief that their absence will save them unnecessary anguish.

> A 3-year-old girl, who had amyotonia congenita, was hospitalized because of an overwhelming pneumonia. The mother wished to remain with the child in case death occurred. However, she was advised that she could go home and that she would be called if there was a change for the worse. Unfortunately, the child expired shortly thereafter. In talking about this later, the mother expressed her conviction that had she been present, she could have saved her child. She had a difficult time in overcoming her grief, which was aggravated by the guilt she felt in being absent when her child "needed me the most."

INFORMING THE PARENTS OF THE FATAL EVENT

It is imperative that parents be informed *promptly* that their child has died, regardless of what time of day or night this occurs. This should be done by the doctor responsible for the child's hospital care. If he is not immediately available, this responsibility should be that of the physician present at the time of death. To minimize the possibility of parental misinterpretation, it is preferable for the parents to learn the circumstances of the death from one rather than two or more physicians. Although in certain circumstances the nurse will be the one who first tells the parents, the doctor should follow through as soon as he is available. Obviously it is poor practice to delegate this important medical responsibility to ward secretaries or to hospital telephone operators. Where a language barrier exists, efforts should be made to have an interpreter available.

When death has occurred in the newborn nursery, the pediatrician and obstetrician may decide with the father how and by whom the mother should be told. At times the father will want to do this, but in other instances he will request that this be done by the physician or by a clergyman. The parents may or may not ask to see the baby. There is no need to impose the sight of the baby upon them when they indicate that they do not want to see him.

If parents are not present in the hospital at the time of death, usually they should not be told of the death by telephone unless they raise this specific question themselves or unless they live a long distance from the hospital. Rather, the doctor may ask them to come to the hospital. The parents should be prepared for such a telephone call by being told at the time of admission that the doctor will call them whenever he feels they are needed. Therefore, the parents are called as soon as possible and asked to come to the hospital. If they ask, "Has the child died?" their question can be answered directly and sympathetically. Then the opportunity to discuss the illness and death with the doctor can be arranged.

The above factors are often neglected because the task of telling the parents that their child is dead is a grim and difficult one. In telling the parents this grievous fact, the doctor may note a tendency in himself to feel personally responsible for their unhappiness, reacting as though he were the one who brought it about. If the physician is aware of this inclination, he will not have the need to apologize and will tell the parents of their child's death in a simple direct manner that facilitates their understanding of what has happened.

HELPING THE FAMILY AFTER THE DEATH OF THE CHILD

Listening is often more important than talking once the facts have been presented and the physician has expressed his sympathy. Attentive listening then offers the parents substantial support, because it provides the mother and father with an opportunity to grasp what has happened and to express the concerns, questions, and feelings that threaten to overwhelm them. Questions may range from how to make arrangements for the funeral and burial to reflections about why such a tragedy has occurred. The physician will answer questions as he is able, but the attentive quietness of the authoritative physician also demonstrates that the parents can talk or listen to the doctor when they feel ready. This atmosphere will enable the parents to review gradually their feelings and thoughts about themselves and their child. The doctor's readiness to listen promotes this review, which is an effort by the parents to overcome the helpless feeling they have experienced with the dying of their child. When the physician notes that his eagerness to talk to the parents interferes with their ability to express themselves, he should wonder if he isn't dealing primarily with his own feeling of helplessness. If this is true it is appropriate for him to discuss his observations and questions about the child's death with an accepting and respected colleague.

Because the child is frequently experienced as a partial extension of the parent's self, a part of the self that has died, remarks such as "Well, he is better off this way," are usually inappropriate when spoken by the physician. When faced by the death of a child, there are no words that will make the situation all right. The parents have suffered a painful loss as well as a disappointment of their hopes for self-realization through their child. An attempt should be made to sense whether the parents wish the physician to stay for a time, or whether they prefer to be alone.

Although it is not the purpose of this paper to discuss the psychiatric aspects of grief, the pediatrician should be aware of the range and duration of these reactions (4, 5). The reactions of parents to the death of a child will vary considerably according to the particular parents involved, the age of the child and the nature of the illness.

Much more preparation is possible with a lengthy than with an acute illness. By anticipating that the parents may have many questions and feelings of guilt, the doctor will be prepared to help parents express their feelings of loss. In this way the physician can help the family to feel that they are not alone in coping with this tragic event.

When parents ask questions, they are frequently able to verbalize their fears and other feelings, such as sadness, loneliness and self-blame, which characterize this experience. They may ask whether death would have occurred if the child had been fed differently or brought to the doctor sooner, whether siblings might be expected to develop the same illness, and other similar questions. These should be answered patiently, kindly, and realistically. The repetition of questions usually indicates that the parent is attempting to deny the death of his child in order to ward off the painful and frightening feelings of loss. It is as if he asked the question enough times or in the right way the loss of the child could be undone. It is important that, as warranted, the parents receive the doctor's assurance that what they did or failed to do had no bearing on the illness or its outcome. Honest reassurance can be very comforting.

The doctor may suggest that the parents return at another time to raise questions that will come to mind later. These further discussions with the physician are helpful and represent an important part of the grieving that the parents need to accomplish. Grieving refers to the process by which the person copes with the feelings of loss, sadness and helplessness that occur when an important human love object dies. The physician can expect that initially the feelings, thoughts, and memories of the dead person will be heightened, as though in this way the parent will not lose the child. Then there may be a gradual dulling of the sharp edges of these mental images as the memories and phantasies about the child are repeatedly experienced.

The pace of grieving varies enormously. If the child has been ill since birth and has been the cause of much deprivation in the family, one is not surprised to see the grieving condensed into a few days. The relief to the family made possible by the death of a long-suffering child overshadows the grief in many such instances. If the death has been the outcome of an acute, overwhelming illness, it is more likely that the grieving will be more prolonged and more devastating.

Evidence of grief is usually an encouraging sign that the parents are trying to master this extremely traumatic experience by going over and over again in their minds the questions about the illness and memories of the child. This valuable mechanism of working through something that is overwhelmingly painful should not be discouraged. Where difficulty in the grieving process is evident, either as an over- or an under-reaction, the physician should attempt to help the parent obtain further appropriate assistance from psychiatric, social service, or religious resources in the community.

While parents feel grateful to the doctor for his help and support, it is not a contradiction that they may also have feelings of anger and resentment that the doctor is not omnipotent and that he did not save their child. This may be expressed indirectly in their questions and comments. In the diagnosis and treatment of an acute illness, the doctor is commonly envisaged as having magical powers. When the child dies after an acute illness, the parents may experience this as a withholding of the doctor's magic, and they may be initially disappointed and angry at him. In a chronic illness the doctor is experienced as a friend or ally who tries to overcome the illness of the child. Here the child's death is interpreted as a failure of a reliable and powerful friend. Occasionally, the disappointment and resentment a parent feels toward a burdensome defective or ill child will also come to the surface in the mourning period. This is usually only one aspect of the parents' reaction to the loss of their child in whom so much of themselves had been invested.

INFORMING THE SIBLINGS

Although he may not be asked to do so, the pediatrician should be available to help parents inform siblings about the patient's death (6, 7). If they feel unable to do this themselves, the doctor may help the parents decide who could do it best. This should be someone who already has a meaningful relationship with the children.

The principles used in informing the siblings and in helping them to cope healthfully with the loss are similar to those used with the adult. Preparation for the death of the patient is also a crucial aid to the siblings. The age of the sibling, the age of the deceased child, and the type of illness and death will indicate the appropriate way to do this. In the younger child the language of play may be most effective in helping the child to understand his sibling's death. The use of dolls, pictures, and stories can be very helpful in playing out the child's reaction to the sibling's death. In this way he can express his feelings and questions more effectively. Repetition is characteristic of such play or story-telling.

The birth of a stillborn infant to a mother who has other living children frequently leads to the question of how to help the siblings understand the death of the baby. Generally it is an error not to tell the siblings what has happened in terms that are understandable and useful to them. Many instances could be cited in which the withholding of such information has contributed to psychologic difficulties for the surviving child. For example, such children frequently experience the lack of information from the adults as evidence that the mother is hiding something dreadful, such as the murder or rejection of the baby, and in consequence they are markedly concerned about their own future.

Because each child has his own fearful concepts about the nature of death, an attempt should be made to individualize the approach to informing him of his sibling's death. From time to time his anxious concerns will be revealed in questions and in play. The exact words used in the explanation are less important than the relationship to the informant and the informant's capacity to help the child recognize and cope with the death of the sibling. When the adult is overwhelmed by the death of the child or is unable to come to grips with his own feelings about death, he will likely convey his anxiety about death no matter how carefully he chooses his words. The child may not readily understand or accept the fact that his sibling will not return.

Although painful to the parents, the child should be told at an appropriate time that death is final. The parents may also present to the child their personal beliefs with regard to death. When such beliefs represent a painful conflict for the adult, and he finds it difficult to talk about death, professional help may be required in order to help the child understand what has happened to his sibling.

Parents should be prepared for the fact that children react to the impact of the loss of a sibling in different ways, many of which would be inappropriate for an adult. The child may continue to play as before, read comic books, and show no strong evidence of sadness. They may even ask whether the parents are going to get another child to take the dead sibling's place. This behavior represents the need of the child to deflect the impact of the death-loss in the various ways available to him, in order to avoid being emotionally overwhelmed by feelings of depression and anxiety.

The question of whether or not a child should attend his

sibling's funeral may occasionally arise. If the child is old enough to understand how his sibling died, he is usually old enough to attend the funeral if he desires. When a child is afraid, reluctant, or revolted by the idea, he should not be forced to be present. Most children under six years of age are too young; children over nine are often able to benefit from the funeral experience, especially if the services are conducted with the child's needs in mind. In the event that the child wishes to go to the funeral, there can be an advantage to his experiencing the loss of his sibling in a concrete way by attending the funeral services or by viewing the body.

REQUEST FOR A NECROPSY

Request for a necropsy is best made by the physician responsible for the child's care in the hospital. The timing of the request will vary, but it is important that it not seem abrupt. The parents should be given time to recover somewhat from their initial shock. They may then be asked whether they will permit a necropsy. Questions raised about this procedure should be answered patiently and honestly.

In the presence of a proper physician-patient relationship, permission is frequently obtained. However, where a patient has been ill for months or years, the parents may feel that their child has suffered a great deal and that they want nothing more to be done to his body. Permission for a necropsy is less likely to be obtained if the physician with whom the parents have been most familiar is not present at the time of death. As one parent said later, "I would have given permission for the necropsy, but I just didn't know any of those doctors." It may be expected that necropsies will be less readily obtained when death occurs shortly after admission. Under these circumstances the doctors have little opportunity to become acquainted with the parents.

Where the parents are uncertain about granting permission, the physician may indicate that it is a difficult decision to make. He can suggest that they think about it for a while and perhaps talk to their family physician. This evidence that the doctor appreciates the difficulty of such decisions often helps parents to make a judgment which which they are comfortable.

While necropsy findings often contribute to medical knowledge and permit an evaluation of current medical practice, these gains do not offset the effects of the feelings of guilt or helplessness that follow when permission for a necropsy has been obtained through intimidation. When parents have refused permission, the doctor should accept their decision. Although the physician may feel irritated and disappointed that the parents have refused permission for a necropsy, he should guard against indicating this as such criticism may heighten the parents' guilt. This will tend to reduce the physician's effectiveness in aiding the family to cope with their loss.

THE DOCTOR'S REACTION TO THE DEATH

The doctor's reaction to the death of a child in the hospital is determined by many factors, among which are his past professional and family experiences with death. As the motivations for entering medical training usually include the wish to oppose destructive forces in oneself as well as in others, and because one of the doctor's gratifications comes from helping patients get well, the death of a patient may be expected to evoke feelings of defeat and discomfort in the physician. In work with children, the physician's maternal or paternal feelings toward the patient may result in a keener sense of loss. The capacity to emphathize with the parents without loss of perspective is an important attribute of the physician. However, if he becomes involved to the extent of grieving with the parents, his helpfulness will be much reduced.

The doctor's reaction may be expected to differ depending upon whether the death occurred after an acute or after a chronic illness and whether the prognosis had been hopeless or not. When death occurs after an acute illness, especially one not uniformly fatal or one not yet diagnosed, the doctor usually reviews critically the diagnostic and therapeutic work in order to reassure himself and to learn as much as possible from the experience. In doing this he may detect in himself feelings of guilt or disappointment. When guilt and self-criticism are undetected, they may interfere with his work.

Where the doctor feels responsible in some way for the death of a child, it is much more difficult for him to handle the situation with the parents. He may feel, unrealistically, as though the child's death in the hospital could have been avoided. Although a certain amount of self-questioning on the part of the physician may be useful to him, guilt feelings can impair the physician's self-esteem and confidence to the degree that his diagnostic and therapeutic effectiveness with patients is reduced.

While the doctor is more apt to feel responsible when a child dies after an acute illness, his reaction to the death of a child with a chronic fatal illness is more likely to include the feeling of personal loss. In the instance of a chronic illness, the doctor is often puzzled by the parents' reaction when the child dies. They may react initially as though the death were a surprise or shock for which they had not been prepared. The physician's work in preparing the family for the child's death emerges as a bolstering force only after the initial painful reaction. Death is always a shock no matter what the preparation. The capacity to master and integrate the experience of losing a child may, however, be increased by preparation and by a supportive relationship with the doctor. Through his understanding of these factors the doctor is prepared to accept the initial reaction of surprise, bitterness, anger, and resentment on the part of the parents as the beginning of the grieving process, and not primarily as a personal reaction to him.

To be present as the parents experience deep sorrow and to feel helpless in the face of the parents' grieving for their child can be most uncomfortable for any physician. Many doctors deal with their discomforts by being very active. Unless they are *doing* something or *saying* something, they feel uncomfortable and negligent. It would be well for the doctor to recognize that, at times, some of his overactivity represents a means of dealing with his personal discomfort more than an activity designed to help the parents in their grief. The doctor's anxiety about death has many antecedents, one of which is universal: the profound fear and anxiety that we all have for our lives and the intactness of our body. The threats of permanent separation from a loved one, or of dying, are often evoked by the death of a patient.

The reaction of the doctor will be magnified if he has made an error in diagnosis or treatment. Perhaps nothing can be more distressing or cause such self-searching and marked feelings of guilt. He may gain some solace in the fact that even the most sincere and careful physician is fallible. It is of crucial support for younger physicians to have all critically ill children examined by a senior staff member. This permits this great responsibility to be shared and provides the security of knowing that everything possible is being done. For the established practitioner, the use of consultation in the case of critically or fatally ill children may serve the same purpose.

REFERENCES

1. Bozeman, M. F., Orbach, C. E., and Sutherland, A. M.: Psychological impact of cancer and its treatment. III. The adaptation of mothers to the threatened loss of their children through leukemia. Part I. *Cancer, 8*:1, 1955.
2. *Idem*: Part II. *Cancer, 8*:20, 1955.
3. Richmond, J. B., and Waisman, H. A.: Psychologic aspects of management of children with malignant disease. *Am J Dis Child, 89*:42, 1955.
4. Lindemann, E.: Symptomatology and management of acute grief. *Am J Psychiat, 101*:141, 1944-45.
5. Freud, S.: Mourning and Melancholia. In *Collected Papers, Vol. 4.* London, Hogarth Press, 1934, p. 152.
6. Mahler, M. S.: *Helping Children to Accept Death.* New York, Child Study Association of America, 1950.
7. Wolf, A. W. M.: *Helping Your Child to Understand Death.* New York, Child Study Association of America, 1958.

PART VII
GENETIC COUNSELING AND
PARENTS OF CHILDREN
WITH HANDICAPS

Chapter 50

The Impact of Genetic
Counseling upon the Family Milieu

ROBERT L. TIPS and HENRY T. LYNCH

MODERN genetic counseling comprises clinical appraisal of problems of affected individuals on nonaffected relatives within the family milieu. The implications of genetics produce multifaceted emotional stresses permeating the families and fostering interpersonal and intrafamily hostilities to the extent that reproduction of offspring essentially ceases after the birth of the affected member. Through empathetic communication with the family, genetic counseling promotes reasonable acceptance and realistic adjustment, plus a measurable effect on reproductive performances of female kindred.

The major purpose of this study is to present a philosophy of genetic counseling developed during the course of current research in pediatrics and internal medicine. The genesis of this philosophy stems from our experience in the management of family units within a broad framework encompassing the crosscurrents of both the clinical disciplines and modern genetic principles.

The impact of this approach upon the family milieu has been a sufficient magnitude to warrant objective appraisal (1, 2). The

Note: Reprinted by permission of the author and *Journal of the American Medical Association, 184*:117-120, 1963.

A portion of this paper was read before the American Society of Human Genetics, Corvallis, Ore., Aug 30, 1962.

From the Department of Pediatrics of the University of Oregon Medical School and the Department of Genetics of the Oregon Regional Primate Research Center, Beaverton (Dr. Tips), and the Department of Internal Medicine of the University of Nebraska Medical School and the Eppley Institute for Study of Cancer and Allied Disease, Omaha (Dr. Lynch).

search for parameters which lend themselves to quantitation has led to the comparison of reproductive performances in terms of pregnancy rates among adult kindred members of families into which children with genetic or suspected genetic disorders have been born, prior to and after counseling.

MATERIALS AND METHODS

During the period from July, 1959, through June, 1962, approximately two hundred patients and their families were referred for genetic studies (Table 50-I). For descriptive convenience, these families are categorized by the patient's disease as follows:

1. Genetically dominant disorders were observed in twenty-six patients, all of whom had at least one mildly affected parent and one additional case in the family. Sporadic cases were not referred for consultation during the study period.
2. The recessive disease group included thirty-four patients, the majority of whom had no similarly affected family members.
3. Sex-linked abnormalities were diagnosed in six patients. Affected males on the maternal side were observed in each family.
4. Cytogenetic abnormalities appeared as sporadic cases in twenty-eight families.
5. Multiple congenital anomalies were found as isolated cases in fifteen families studied.
6. Diseases of unknown etiology, but with suspected genetic components, were noted in one hundred four families.

Since the disease prognoses and genetic mechanisms are approximately similar in each category, the counseling study procedure was adapted to the disease category, but guidelines were similar in all cases.

Referral by the family physician was supplemented by a direct application for consultation by the family. All charges and fees were eliminated. Applications were accepted only after receipt of pertinent medical records and laboratory data.

The initial consultation visit began with a brief conference

TABLE 50-I

DISTRIBUTION OF COUNSELING CASES
ACCORDING TO PATIENT DIAGNOSIS

A. Dominant Disorders

    1. Friedreich's ataxia 14
    2. Charcot-Marie-Tooth syndrome 3
    3. Retinoblastoma 2
    4. Osteogenesis imperfecta 2
    5. Marfan's syndrome 2
    6. Congenital porphyria 3

    Total 26

B. Recessive Diseases

    1. Cystic fibrosis (mucoviscidosis) 8
    2. Phenylketonuria 3
    3. Galactosemia 2
    4. Glycogen storage disease 2
    5. Adrenogenital syndrome 3
    6. Wilson's disease 1
    7. Rh blood group incompatibility 15

    Total 34

C. Sex-Linked Diseases

    1. Antihemophilic Globulin deficiency 3
    2. Agammaglobulinemia 2
    3. Diabetes insipidus 1

    Total 6

D. Cytogenetic Abnormalities

    1. Mongolism (trisomy 21) 24
    2. Turner's syndrome (XO) 3
    3. Autosomal trisomies 1

    Total 28

E. Multiple Congenital Anomalies

    1. Cleft lip and palate syndromes 4
    2. Congenital heart diseases 5
    3. Multiple anomalies of unknown etiology 6

    Total 15

F. Diseases of Unknown Etiology

    1. Idiopathic developmental retardation 34
    2. Congenital spastic paraplegia 52
    3. Congenital athetosis 18

    Total 104

which included the patient, his parents, and his siblings for the purpose of outlining the method of procedure. It was at that time that very close observation of the psychodynamics of the family group was begun, with particular attention to interpersonal relationships and the character of individual identifications within the group. It is only through continuous observation of manifold emotional factors that the genetic counselor is able to gain sufficient insight into the needs of the family that he, in turn, can effectively reflect these needs into more organized channels of communication.

As the next step, the mother was interviewed privately to review the complete clinical history of the patient, after which the patient was thoroughly examined in her presence and dismissed. The mother's medical history was discussed and directed into a pattern of inquiry relative to the major manifestations of the genetic disease. The pattern was further emphasized by an appropriate physical examination. Finally, the mother's pregnancy history was sensitively explored in chronological order of occurrence with guarded reference to paternity and marriage dates. The inquiry pattern for medical history was meticulously repeated for each infant born. The mother's interview was interrupted at this point.

After all of the siblings had been examined for pertinent physical details, the father's interview was begun. When the patterned inquiry of his medical history was completed, he, too, was examined. During the interview, he was confidentially interrogated concerning previous marriages and extramarital children, after which a family pedigree was constructed utilizing information asked of him with respect to surnames and maiden names, marriages and paternities, birthdates and places, and health histories and deaths of kindred members.

The details of the family history were reviewed personally with the mother with specific emphasis placed on pregnancy histories of kindred members. As members were reviewed, additional cases and formes fruste in the family were detected through suggestions established by the patterned clinical inquiries of the earlier interview. Other genetic conditions were also noted. The first visit was terminated after a brief discussion on methods by which the medical management of the patient could be more effectively implemented in the existing family situations. Attempts at presenting risk figures or referring to genetic data were deferred until later visits.

During the follow-up conferences, usually limited to the mother and the patient, the clinical management was evaluated first, then the discussion was reoriented in order to reconsider the details in reproductive records of the mother and other members of the family. Careful stress on menstrual histories and sexual relations sometimes uncovered additional pregnancies, extramarital paternities, and marital problems. Such discussion focuses attention on reproduction and promotes further inquiry into the genetic problem.

To explain mechanisms of inheritance (4), the mother was taught to diagram gene combination in fertilization simply by displaying the sorts of genes from the ova along one axis and the spermatozoal gene types on the other. Arithmetical probabilities of zygotic genotypes became obvious in the completed diagram. The proficiently instructed mother, recognizing her own genetic potentialities, responded by acting as a teacher to other family members.

In cytogenetic diseases and other abnormalities in which empiric risk figures (5) must be used, explanations were usually given utilizing photographs, karyograms, and descriptions. They required more time and effort, but simplicity and repetition remain essential.

To determine the impact of genetic counseling on the families, the reproductive rate was estimated with respect to first, the prebirth period, which extends from the date of marriage of the parents to the date of birth of the propositus; second, the precounseling period, which extends from the date of birth of the propositus to the date of the initial counseling visit; and third, the postcounseling period, which extends to the date of final follow-up contact. The length of each period was measured as the mean in number of months of marriage per female kindred member for each disease category. The total number of months accumulated in each period represents the sum of months of marriage for the mother and the actual married months for aunts within the time limits. Only the marriage records of the mother and the maternal and paternal aunts were considered.

To determine the reproductive rate for each kindred female (mothers and aunts), the actual number of pregnancies was divided by the number of months during which fertilization was presumed possible by virtue of the nonpregnant state. The number of nonpregnant months was estimated by subtracting the number of gravid months from the total number of married months during the particular period in question. Twelve months were deducted for full-term pregnancies and gestation plus two months for nonterm pregnancies.

The mean and standard deviation of the reproductive rate of kindred females in each disease category were calculated for the prebirth, precounseling and postcounseling periods. Such rates clearly reflect pattern changes in reproduction which occur after the birth of the abnormal offspring and after counseling of the families.

TABLE 50-II

BASIC DATA ON 213 FAMILIES COMPLETING
HEREDITY COUNSELING PROCEDURES

Disease Category of Propositi	Families No.	Mean Age, Propos- itus	Mean Age, Parents	Average Time Consul- tation*	Counsel Period††
Hereditary diseases					
1. Dominant	26	8.2±3.8	33±8	5.0	30
2. Recessive..................	34	4.5±2.6	28±9	6.5	60
3. Sex-linked	6	4.8±1.0	29±4	5.0	45
Cytogenetic abnor- malities	28	5.6±4.2	36±15	6.0†	90
Multiple congenital anomalies	15	4.8±2.6	31±9	5.5†	60
Diseases of unknown etiology	104	5.2±3.1	30±9	5.5	60

*Estimated total time of consultation per family in hours.
†Exclusive of laboratory studies.
††Estimated average period in days to complete consultation.

RESULTS

The distribution of counseling cases according to the disease of the propositus, presented in Table 50-I, reflects family selection based on research interests, diagnostic problems, and parental motivation. Eighty percent (80%) of the total families completed the counseling study after initial referral, wheras 20 percent required two or more referrals.

The logistics of the 213 families completing the counseling procedure (Table 50-II) involved personal contact in a clinic setting for an average of 3.5 hours initially and 1.5 hours per follow-up conference with completion of study in a period of approximately sixty days. The mean age of patients was 5.6 years and of parents, 31.6 years, with minor deviations for separate disease categories.

To complete the assessment for the status of the reproductive rates in all three periods, 96 percent, or 204 of the 213 families, were recontacted in a time interval ranging from fifteen to thirty-six months after completion of the study (Table 50-III). The mean in length of the first or prebirth period varied from twenty-nine to sixty-one months per kindred female in the various disease categories. It is noted that an interval of approximately five years preceded the birth of the propositus in families with dominant disease and with multiple congenital abnormalities, whereas a two and one-half to four years interval characterized the remainder.

The means in reproductive rates during the prebirth period varied from 89 to 115 pregnancies per 1,000 potentially fertile months per kindred female among the various disease categories. These rates serve as control estimations of reproduction during a time prior to the abnormal family status, so that pattern changes which occur in the later two periods may be compared and evaluated.

The means in length of the second, or precounseling, period varied from fifty-three to ninety-eight months per kindred female among separate disease categories. Thus the four and one-half to eight years length of the second period was considerably greater than the prebirth period in each category. However, the method of estimating the reproductive rate precludes a direct relationship of reproductive patterns to the length of the period. The reproductive rate varied from 6 to 25 pregnancies per 1,000 potentially fertile months per kindred female among the categories during the

TABLE 50-III

REPRODUCTIVE PERFORMANCES OF MOTHERS AND
AUNTS IN 204 FAMILIES

Disease Category	Mo o	Months Marriage M	Fertile Months* M	No Preg- nancies M	Repro- ductive Rate† M
Prebirth Period (Parents' Marriage to Patients Birth)					
Dominant 151		56.0±9.6	26.5±5.0	2.53±0.73	0.115±0.035
Recessive 129		29.2±6.3	15.6±4.8	1.54±0.76	0.099±0.023
Sex-linked 18		35.8±5.1	18.2±4.9	1.67±0.62	0.098±0.013
Cytogenetic 139		61.3±8.1	30.9±5.2	3.03±0.71	0.098±0.011
Multiple congenital anomalies 68		48.0±7.6	25.7±5.6	2.28±0.77	0.089±0.009
Unknown etiology 392		38.2±9.7	19.3±8.9	1.83±0.69	0.097±0.017
Precounseling Period (Patients' Birth to Counseling)					
Dominant 154		98.3±9.8	88.3±8.9	0.53±0.48	0.006±0.005
Recessive 136		53.9±6.3	42.1±7.3	0.97±0.46	0.025±0.009
Sex-linked 19		57.2±5.0	51.9±7.9	0.52±0.28	0.010±0.008
Cytogenetic 149		65.8±6.8	56.9±6.3	0.69±0.29	0.012±0.004
Multiple congenital anomalies 74		56.9±7.2	49.5±8.1	0.75±0.31	0.015±0.004
Unknown etiology 409		62.1±5.3	46.8±7.5	0.99±0.40	0.022±0.005
Postcounseling Period (After Counseling Procedure)					
Dominant 156		30.4±1.7	18.1±2.1	1.19±0.11	0.062±0.015
Recessive 139		31.2±1.6	20.3±3.1	1.11±0.17	0.057±0.011
Sex-linked 19		30.8±1.8	19.9±3.0	1.12±0.20	0.053±0.007
Cytogenetic 151		28.9±1.8	21.8±2.3	0.69±0.12	0.029±0.009
Multiple congenital anomalies 74		29.6±1.4	21.6±2.7	0.82±0.15	0.036±0.009
Unknown etiology 411		29.5±1.6	19.7±2.7	1.01±0.19	0.050±0.013

*Potentially fertile months as determined by the non-pregnant months during marriage.
†Ratio of number of pregnancies to the number of potentially fertile months.

precounseling period when the affected offspring was present in the family. Each rate represents a severe and significant decrease in reproduction after the birth of the propositus.

The means in length of the third or postcounseling period varied from 28.9 to 31.2 months, during which the mean in reproductive rate was 29 to 62 pregnancies per 1,000 potentially fertile months per kindred female, as noted for the separate categories. The rates during this period, after families were counseled, all showed a marked and statistically significant rise for each category.

Thus, the data indicate a marked depression of reproductive rate among kindred females after the birth of an abnormal child. The rates rise significantly in association with genetic counseling of parents. There were no marriage disruptions, divorces, or legal separations among the 204 families during the three periods to account for the marked differences in reproduction.

COMMENT

Genetic counseling provides a means of evaluating patients with genetic disease within the framework of the family unit (6, 7). Appraisal of the history of kindred members coupled with critical investigation of the unit assists the family in developing a realistic approach to the problem (1, 2). The referral procedure aims at case selections based on deep parental motivation. The clinical evaluation of the patient and the pertinent kindred members of his family promotes an empathetic means of communication with the family unit. The patterned medical inquiry focuses attention upon the pathogenetic processes without repetitive detail during the interviews. The recall of simple pedigree data by the father, in a structured counseling atmosphere, promotes a catharsis of such a nature that the veneer of defense mechanisms, such as projection, rationalization, repression, and feelings of misdirected guilt and hostility, is circumvented. The review of family data, with stress on reproductive performances, during the mother's interviews provides supplementation and verification, and promotes a similar catharsis and affective experience (3).

Education of the parents relative to the mode of inheritance and causes of cytogenetic anomalies is tempered by their spheres of comprehension and inquiry. This is in keeping with the present counseling philosophy in that it meets the realistic needs of the family unit as opposed to the traditional, cold sterotyped, didactic, mathematical-probability approach (8-10). But even further, the underlying dynamics of the counseling program fosters a psychotherapeutic relationship which lends itself to the amelioration of psychosexual conflicts which often have their origin in the inappropriate assessment of factual genetic knowledge (3).

Selection of intact family units restricts the influence of the intervening variable of disruption of marriage as an obvious factor of reproduction among the 204 parents of patients. The similar absence of divorces and legal separations among their siblings probably reflects the influence of parental counseling.

The methods of ascertainment of families and of reproductive rate calculations limit the comparison of these data with population controls and published results. However, the rates within the active reproductive pools prior to the birth of the affected child serve as control data for subsequent periods.

The second, or precounseling, period which follows the birth of the propositus is conditioned by morbid psychological processes, such as impotency, pregnaphobia, interpersonal hostility, and rejection, based on feelings of guilt and overt accusation. The marked decrease in reproduction during this time reflects the permeating effects of such processes throughout the entire kindred, not only as detected through the failure of the parents to produce subsequent pregnancies, but also as shown by the pregnancy records of their sisters.

The third, or postcounseling, period is characterized by a significantly increased reproductive rate within the kindred. Parents first become aware during counseling that many of their manifold emotional conflicts stem not only from the burden of management of the chronically ill child and the stigmata of mental and physical abnormality but also from the realization of hereditary influence in the pathogenetic processes involved in the illness. They recognize and begin to accept the fact that many of the subtle, subsurface tensions and conflicts within the milieu of their immediate family unit result from distorted concepts of genetic potentialities and from problems in reproductive and sexual adjustment. This awareness fosters a release from apprehension so that constructive adjustments are readily resumed. Although morbid pregnancy risks remain an actuality, these concepts become realistically comprehensible to the parents as they assume a more normal reproductive pattern during the postcounseling period.

Furthermore, as parents become cognizant of solutions regarding adjustments within the family unit, their conprehension extends to include the discordances which developed among other kindred members due to misunderstanding of the genetic dilemma within the family. The properly counseled parents, especially the mother, seek to amend the family discordances through exploration of the subtle nature of apprehensions underlying such conflicts. Reception of these efforts promotes a clarity of understanding whereby the benefits and education of genetic counseling to the parents are fully realized throughout the kindred, and their reproductive patterns thus resume a more enlightened course.

The impact of genetic counseling procedures which are directed to delineate and explore the underlying subtle psychopathologic mechanisms of fear and misunderstanding that permeate the family milieu of patients with genetic or suspected genetic disease can be measurably estimated in terms of reproductive performances of kindred members.

REFERENCES

1. Tips, R. L., *et al.*: Heredity Counseling in Pediatrics: A Review of 300 Families. Read before the American Society of Human Genetics, Corvallis, Ore., Aug. 30, 1962.
2. Tips, R. L., Meyer, D. L., and Perkins, A. L.: Clinical Counseling in Human Genetics. Read before the Oregon State Medical Association, Portland, Sept. 26, 1962.
3. Tips, R. L., Meyer, D. L., and Perkins, A. L.: Dynamics of Genetic Counseling, unpublished data.
4. Herndon, C. N.: Heredity counseling. *Eugen Quart, 2*:83-89, 1955.
5. Fraser, F. C., *et al.*: Congenital cleft lip and palate, *Am J Dis Child, 102*:853-857, Dec. 1961.
6. Kallman, F. J.: Psychiatric aspects of genetic counseling. *Am J Hum Genet, 8*:97-101, June, 1956.
7. Kallman, F. J.: Human genetics as a science, as a profession, and as a social-minded trend of orientation. *Am J Hum Genet, 4*:237-245, 1952.
8. Hammons, H. G. (Ed): *Heredity Counseling.* New York, Paul B. Hoebner, Inc., 1959.
9. Reed, S. C.: *Counseling in Medical Genetics.* Philadelphia, W. B. Saunders Company, 1955.
10. Reed, S. C.: Counseling in Medical Genetics. *Acta Genet, 7*:473-480, 1957.

Chapter 51

Genetic Counseling

R. G. B. CAMERON

THE basis of genetic counseling is the expression of the estimated risk of recurrence in a family of any abnormality suspected to be influenced by inherited factors; in practice it must be elaborated to include any advice likely to assist those faced with the suspicion of such an abnormality in themselves, their progenitors or their children. This is family medicine, in every sense of the word, and sooner or later it will fall within the province of every family doctor to share the responsibility for it.

The birth of an abnormal child is the most obvious reason for seeking genetic counsel, but other apposite circumstances will come readily to mind. Advice may be asked prior to marriage, before starting a family or before seeking a child for adoption; not infrequently individuals are simply concerned with the possible risk of some inherited disorder in themselves, and it is scarcely possible to practice in any field without giving some thought to inherited disease. Many of the questions asked will be found to refer to maladies in which heredity plays a negligible part, but from time to time situations arise which demand as full and accurate an interpretation as the sum of knowledge will permit; any practitioner called upon must bear in mind the gravity of the decisions which may be taken on the counsel he gives, and will do well to remember the criteria for sound genetic prognosis enunciated by Fraser Roberts — namely, exact diagnosis, a full family history and a complete survey of the literature.

Note: Reprinted by permission of the author and the *Medical Journal of Australia,* *1*:697-699, 1963.

Read at the Third Plenary Session, First Australian Medical Congress, May 21 to 25, 1962.

ASSESSING THE RISK

It is mandatory that a full and accurate diagnosis be made of any index case available for study; this will not always be easy. Many of the diseases in question are likely to be outside the experience of many practitioners, and of course it may happen that the question of recurrence is first raised when there is no longer access to any clinical material. The diagnosis, once made, will often go far towards determining the pattern of inheritance, particularly if transmission is known to be along simple mendelian lines; but there are many pitfalls for the unwary or the incompletely informed. Some diseases well known to be often inherited have phenocopies which are not significantly influenced by genetic factors — for example, congenital deafness or congenital mental defect; there are some entities indistinguishable on clinical grounds which have alternate modes of inheritance, and it may be difficult to decide at times whether one is dealing with a fresh mutation. Retinitis pigmentosa and gargoylism are examples of conditions which may be either sex-linked or recessive, and in the latter instance there would be virtually a normal prognosis for all the children born to the sisters of an affected male; however, if the disease was sex-linked, each sister would have one chance in two of being a carrier, as would the female offspring of such as were carriers. Male offspring of carriers would have one chance in two of being affected by the disease.

The apparent absence of a family history of an abnormality which is usually dominant or sex-linked may suggest a fresh mutation and a good prognosis for subsequent siblings, but it may be due to a generation's having been skipped owing to irregular dominance, or perhaps to the fact that one is on this occasion dealing with an individual homozygous for a recessive gene which was previously concealed in a long line of heterozygotes. The risk to subsequent sibs may be one in two in the first instance, and perhaps one in four in the second. When the family history throws no real light on an individual problem, it may be necessary to give an average numerical expression of the risks. Finally, one may be forgiven for suggesting that the putative father may indeed have made no genetic contribution to the child under discussion.

Late or incomplete expression of an abnormality can mean that an individual so affected may become a parent before the abnormality is clinically apparent, and so present the counselor with a *fait accompli*. Huntington's chorea is the classical example of an abiotrophy in which late expression may perhaps lead to a course of action which may not have been undertaken had the facts been fully known, and in my experience there have been cases of polycystic disease of the kidney and hereditary hemorrhagic telangiectasia which were not recognized in a parent before the birth of several children. The implications of this sort of situation are not necessarily serious, but there will usually be need for explanation of the genetic phenomena involved.

More often than not the clear pattern of mendelian inheritance is obscured by the existence of modifying genes and multifactorial inheritance, and the mere diagnosis of an abnormality will not in these circumstances allow a precise definition of dominant or recessive behavior. Again, heredity plus environment is a rather unpredictable combination, and so on many occasions the counselor will be forced to rely on empirical figures calculated from population studies or analysis of individual pedigrees. It will readily be realized that access to the literature is quite essential to sound prognosis. Fortunately, one can take comfort from the fact that obscure inheritance is usually accompanied by risks of recurrence sufficiently small to be of little practical significance.

GENETIC COUNSELING AND THE FAMILY DOCTOR

No special knowledge is required to put genetic problems in their proper perspective, although the initial definition of the situation may need all the resources of the geneticist and the specialized clinician. The family doctor has a most important role, in that he is the one best fitted to interpret the cold facts of a genetic prognosis, which includes an explanation of the clinical abnormality and its prognosis in terms which seem appropriate in the light of his special knowledge of the family; he must discuss the prospect of treatment, the chances of recurrence in other members, and the probable financial and social obligations. He will also have to help the family live with the consequenses of their decision, and this alone may tax his resources to the utmost.

Persons faced with the knowledge of abnormal inheritance often feel very much alone; folklore still contributes heavily to such opinions as they may have, and they are frequently torn by emotions of guilt, fear, reproach, and shame, all of which flourish in ignorance. It is therefore of the greatest importance to stress the accidental nature of any unexpected abnormality. Moreover, it is easy to explain how inheritance derives from one or other parent, or from both, and it is often comforting to be told that everyone is capable of passing on at least several harmful recessive genes; only those unlucky enough to have married another heterozygote ever become aware of their harmful potential. Bad luck carries no stigma, at least in comparison with that imagined in fearful contemplation of the possible sins of the fathers.

It is usual to define the chances of recurrence of any abnormality as a percentage, or in terms of odds, but this may mean little without some yardstick of reference. For instance, a risk of one in twenty becomes comprehensible only when it is compared with an estimated one chance in forty that some serious abnormality will derive from any pregnancy, or with the estimated incidence of the abnormality in the general population. It must be remembered, too, that an optimistically expressed estimation of a 75 percent chance of normality may be at times more appropriate than a gloomy prognostication of one chance in four of abnormality. Sometimes one can present a clearer concept of the significance of these figures by checking them against the values they would represent in the vernacular of the "two-up" ring or the racecourse. The most unfavourable prognosis can sometimes be made tolerable by the prospect of treatment or cure; conversely, a risk may be more acceptable if the abnormality in question is likely to result in early death than it would be if there was a prospect of long years of financial burden and special care.

Many common diseases have a tendency to "run in the family." Among these are essential hypertension, coronary atherosclerosis, diabetes mellitus, peptic ulcer, epilepsy, allergy, gout, cancer, rheumatism, leukemia, pernicious anemia, tuberculosis, nontoxic goitre and primary thyrotoxicosis. This does not purport to be a complete list, but it may serve to illustrate the main argument, which is that the issues raised by most such diseases are not really of critical importance in genetic counseling. Some do, perhaps, cause more alarm than they need do, and in any case all are likely to give rise to queries which must be answered. The risk that children or siblings of epileptics may develop the disease is certainly greater than the random incidence, but nevertheless the chances are not more than one in forty, and on this basis few indeed would wish to add to the troubles of the average epileptic patient by throwing doubt on his right to have children; the average risks do not justify such a course, unless the affected parent is thought to belong to that rare group of epileptic persons who develop their illness late in life and tend to transmit their disorder as a simple dominant.

Cancer is often mentioned as a familial disease and naturally gives rise to a good deal of anxiety on this score; again, one's duty is to be reassuring, except with regard to those few forms of malignancy which are strongly genetically determined, such as retinoblastoma, and the cancer which develops in persons with polyposis of the colon. Hypertension, atherosclerosis and ischemic heart disease can be kept fairly well in perspective, provided that one remembers the link with familial hypercholesterolemia, which may be transmitted as a dominant.

It must be remembered that even a "low-risk" abnormality, like diabetes mellitus or epilepsy, carries a much greater risk of recurrence if there is a family history on both sides; prognosis would need to be guarded, and there may be scope here for the application of some test which may detect the heterozygote.

CONSANGUINITY

Consanguinity is not a very common issue in these days of less rigid geographical boundaries; union of individuals less closely related than first cousins is of no practical significance, for their offspring are subject to risks not significantly greater than those of random matings. However, consanguinity at the first-cousin level does raise some problems, and it is difficult to give appropriate advice; obviously the clinical expression of disease will be increased by the greater likelihood of a double dose of a recessive gene.

The risk to the children of first cousins relative to that to be expected in the general population has been worked out for a number of diseases; when the disease is rare the absolute risk will still be quite small, and of the order of 2 percent or less (2). There is a risk that offspring of cousins may become homozygous for a number of genes that may be subtly undesirable, resulting in increased morbidity and mortality for all sorts of reasons; this is of course apart from the effects of specific abnormalities arising from a double dose of single genes. The problem may be put another way: the overall risk of all abnormalities has been estimated at about twice the random risk; it is rather more for nonspecific mental defect — perhaps three times that present in the general population. The risks are not really very great, but it is nevertheless fortunate that the marriage of first cousins is becoming less common.

ADOPTION

Couples considering adoption should be told, if they are worried, that there is no more risk of abnormality in an adopted child than there would be in one of their own blood; moreover, racial traits, including skin color, behave as multifactorial characteristics, in that children tend to fall between the statuses of their parents, and "throw backs" do not occur unless there is a fresh introduction of the character concerned. Delinquency and criminal tendencies and all other such attributes known or suspected in the actual parents are the products of environment, and need not be expected in the child. If a parent of a child for adoption is known to be of low intelligence, it is quite reasonable to say that mental defectives do not necessarily produce children of as low intelligence as themselves; nevertheless, the presence of mental deficiency in a parent will discourage most prospective adopters, if they are aware of it. It would scarcely be wise to attempt to influence their decision.

EXPERIENCES IN GENERAL PRACTICE

There are a number of diseases, all more or less genetically determined, which are on the records of the practitioners serving a population of some 30,000 in central western New South Wales. These practitioners are resident in a provincial city and its environs. The family names of some of the early settlers are of common occurrence, and there has probably been intermarriage in some of the more remote and inaccesible areas, but there is no real evidence that this is in any way reflected in the incidence of the abnormalities that will be discussed. The list is not complete, the items having been selected and classified so as to illustrate some of the applications of genetic counseling:

Dominant inheritance
  Achondroplasia
  Anonychia
  Capillary telangiectasia
  Polycystic kidney (adult type)
  Acute porphyria
Recessive inheritance
  Mucoviscoidosis
  Adrenocortical hyperplasia
  Spinocerebellar ataxia
  Retinitis pigmentosa
Chromosome mutation
  Down's syndrome
Mental diseases
  Manic-depressive psychosis
  Schizophrenia
  Oligophrenia

Abnormalities due to genetic and
  environmental factors
  Pyloric stenosis
  Harelip
  Harelip and cleft palate
  Cleft palate
  Congenital dislocation
    of hip
  Intussusception
Major nervous system
  abnormalities
  Anencephaly
  Myelocele
  Meningo-myelocele
  Hydrocephalus

The several cases of achondroplasia arose from fresh mutations with no risk of recurrences in siblings or the children of siblings; capillary telangiectasia and polycystic kidney are included as examples of conditions which may not be recognized before children are born to affected individuals. The family with anonychia demonstrated very uniform expression of the disorder, and the pedigree is quite consistent with that to be expected. One isolated case of acute porphyria has been recorded, and may be a useful pointer to diagnosis should suspicious symptoms ever occur in other members of the family.

The parents of one child with mucoviscidosis were told of the "one-in-four" risk applicable to all their children. In fact, they have two others, both clinically normal, although one was found to have a sweat content of sodium and chloride suggestive of the heterozygous state. The parents are only too aware that this is a prolonged, expensive and ultimately lethal disease, and have been told that the frequency of the gene in the general population is high. Unfortunately it is not yet possible to distinguish the heterozygote with certainty, but they would be prepared to advise their children to investigate the presence of the gene in themselves and their potential partners, if it became possible to do so.

One unfortunate couple had two successive daughters suffering from the adrenogenital syndrome, and have, at least for the present, decided against having any more children. They have been told that their chances of having a normal child are still at least 75 percent, and may yet change their minds, as one child has died. Another couple embarked on a second pregnancy fortified by the knowledge that their first daughter was in good electrolyte control and had a good cosmetic result from surgery. They were told that boys might be affected, though not so obviously as girls, and so must be subjected to biochemical check for signs of glucocorticoid deficiency. Their second child was a girl, and is perfectly normal. It is necessary to distinguish the occasional sporadic case of virilism due to maternal overdose of androgens.

Spinocerebellar ataxia and retinitis pigmentosa are both subject to alternate modes of inheritance. The examples encountered seem to be due to a recessive gene. The sex-linked variety of retinitis pigmentosa can be detected in the female carrier by the tapetal reflex.

There have been a number of cases of Down's syndrome. All the parents were given the usual good prognosis for subsequent children with so far happy results. One case was investigated by chromosome studies. At least two mothers, including the one investigated, were quite young, and under these circumstances it may perhaps be well to exclude the rare possibility of translocation of genetic material in both parents, as this would raise the possibility of recurrence, perhaps to 50 percent. This may explain some of the cases of more than one mongoloid defective in a family, and should certainly be investigated when this occurs. It may be apposite at this point to mention a suggestion that the apparent correlation of maternal age and nondysjunction in the gonad may perhaps be in fact due to the total dose of ionizing radiation. This is conjectural, but may be yet another reason for guarding the gonads of potential parents from unnecessary exposure to irradiation; it is reasonable to include advice along these lines under the heading of genetic counseling.

A question was asked about risks to the children of a man with established manic-depressive psychosis. The family was complete, and one felt justified in playing down the risk, which in fact seems quite considerable. Mental deficiency always presents difficulties, both of diagnosis and prognosis. It is essential to distinguish the severe forms due to purely genetic causes, such as phenyl-ketonuria, and those due to purely environmental causes, such as fetal anoxia. The risks of recurrence of nonspecific types of feeble-mindedness are perhaps somewhat greater than the random, and certainly are if the parents are closely related. There is no sound genetic reason for parents of less than normal intelligence to limit their families, or indeed for the sterilization of the mentally unfit, if one thinks that by so doing the racial incidence of feeble-mindedness will be materially diminished. However, there is some justification for advising such parents to limit their families for purely personal reasons, as they may have difficulty in supporting their children.

Pyloric stenosis may be selected as a typical example of the conditions toward which genes and environment both contribute. It is comparatively common, and of course curable. The risks have been assessed from family and population studies, and, after the birth of an affected child to unaffected parents, are about one in twelve for boys and one in fifty for girls. If one parent, especially the mother, has been affected, the risk is increased. The random incidence is between one and four per thousand; all the other conditions listed under the same heading have a similar risk index. The effect of environment is noticeable in such phenomena as the effect of birth order and birth season on some of these disorders; sex predominance is also evident — for example, in pyloric stenosis intussuception and congenital dislocation of the hip (1).

The risk of recurrence of the major nervous system abnormalities is perhaps not great, unless more than one child has been affected. However, parents should be apprised of the chances, with proper emphasis on the significance of the odds given.

GENETICS AND PREVENTIVE MEDICINE

Clinical genetics can be applied to preventive medicine, but our efforts so far have not made much impression on the incidence of death and morbidity from genetic causes, which remains much the same as it was fifty years ago. There are several ways in which the rapidly increasing knowledge of genetics can influence the incidence of disease, one being the application of the results of investigations into the mechanism and biochemistry of the behavior of genes, and another being genetic counseling in the light of such knowledge as we do possess. The effective agent in prevention is, of course, the potential parent. The doctor can give advice based on genetic prognosis, and can do all he can to recognize and control contributory environmental factors; the decision to marry or to have children must remain the prerogative of those directly concerned. The primary aim of genetic counseling must be to help every individual achieve a happy family life, and it is the particular task of the family doctor to maintain the morale of those faced with the need to make decisions which may run contrary to their strongest instincts. Every problem affects individuals, and it is difficult to think of any circumstance in which one has the right to press an opinion as to who should or should not marry or have children. If the sum total of advice is sound, it will benefit the family and the race. Certainly, when the risks of recurrence are small — say, better than one in twenty — there can be a more positive approach, and people should be encouraged to accept reasonable risks. Occasionally one may feel tempted to keep silent, or to play down risks, but this can seldom be wise; not only is one taking a chance with another person's future, but there is a risk that properly given genetic advice may become discredited. Even if the problem is one to which there is no known answer, it is better to say just that than to attempt to conceal the fact that the problem exists. Any advice from an authoritative source is better than silence, or the blind taking of a chance that "lightning never strikes twice." There will be no lack of advice from other sources, whether or not the doctor faces his responsibility.

SUMMARY

The interpretation of genetic prognosis is initially the responsibility of the practitioner first called upon for advice, whether he be specialist or general practitioner. It will almost always devolve upon the family doctor to help the individuals concerned to apply the information given. It may require the expert advice of the geneticist and the specialist to define the problem; some of the difficulties have received brief mention, followed by a discussion of the information likely to be required by those who find themselves in urgent need of genetic counsel.

Some mention is made of the inheritance of common diseases, and the value of the routine taking of family histories, together with the advice which may be appropriate to those concerned with consanguinity, or who are fearful of the risks of abnormal heredity in adopted children.

Examples are given of maladies influenced by genetic factors culled from the records of practitioners in one area, and of the reactions of some of those directly involved, together with those of the practitioner who had to advise them. Finally, genetic counseling is suggested as an incompletely exploited branch of preventive medicine.

REFERENCES

1. Carter, C. O.: Heredity and congenital malformations. *Practitioner, 183*:144, 1959.
2. Motulsky, A. G., and Gartler, S.: Consanguinity and marriage. *Practitioner, 183*:170, 1959.
3. Roberts, J. A. F.: *An Introduction to Clinical Genetics,* (2nd ed.), London, Oxford University Press, 1959, p. 228.
4. Roberts, J. A. F.: Genetic prognosis, *Brit Med J, 1*:587, 1962.

Chapter 52

Genetics and Genetic Counseling

THE concept that all disease has a genetic or hereditary element will come as no surprise to workers in the public health field who are constantly attuned to the multicausal nature of disease and disability. For the majority of conditions the genetic element is usually ill defined, perhaps amounting to no more than an increased predisposition or tendency on the part of certain individuals to succumb to particular conditions, these conditions having a far more obvious exogenous or environmental cause. For instance, while rapid advances in bacteriology during the nineteenth century led to a vast increase in understanding of the transmission and spread of infectious disease, it soon became apparent that while the seed was most important, the role of the soil in the development of disease could certainly not be ignored. One example of this was the early recognition of racial differences in susceptibility to infectious diseases, the Western Highland Scot and the Negro, for instance, being notoriously prone to tuberculosis; and the ravages of the smallpox virus among the indigenous population of this continent provided a setback from which that population has, perhaps, not even yet recovered.

Infectious diseases do not supply the only example of conditions where the genetic element, while undoubtedly present, is still poorly understood. As is well known in Western countries today, the most numerically important cause of death and disability is vascular disease of heart and brain. Here too the

---

Note: Reprinted by permission of the author and the *Canadian Journal of Public Health,* 57:513-518, 1966.

Presented at the annual meeting of the Saskatchewan Branch of the Canadian Public Health Association held in Regina, April 5-6, 1966.

Dr. Ives is Assistant Professor of Pediatrics, University of Saskatchewan, Saskatoon, Sask.

relative advantages of the female sex, as well as the differences in incidence between families and between racial groups, all indicate that the genetic constitution is of considerable importance.

In addition to this large mass of disease where the contribution of genetic factors is not always clearly defined, there are diseases which can be relegated to one or other of two extremes. On the one hand, thanks to concepts put forward by Gregor Mendel just one hundred years ago and to the biochemical advances of recent decades, it is now possible to detect conditions where genetic factors are of prime importance and where, in certain combinations, these factors will cause disease despite any environmental manipulation currently known. Well known examples of this are, muscular dystrophy, Huntington's chorea, and cystic fibrosis.

At the other extreme are conditions where exogenous elements are so much in the ascendancy that it is almost impossible to detect any role for genetic factors. What is the relationship of the genes to the injury sustained by a man, out for an innocuous afternoon walk who, while passing by a building site, is hit on the head by a falling brick? Perhaps his genetically determined thick skull may prove to be his saving grace. This is a facetious example, but accidents, as a group, are not uncommonly regarded as due mainly to exogenous factors. The very resistance which accident figures have shown to many and various environmental adjustments immediately contradicts this assumption and, as experts in this field very well realize, the solution, or at least amelioration of the problem, will probably rest in the better understanding of the genetic factors underlying human behaviour, motivation, educability, and adaptability.

It is not necessary to labour any longer the point that "genes are important." Medawar (1) has summed it up in referring to the common belief that there is a hereditary or genetic element in all human ills and disabilities, this being known as true of some disease and not being known as false of any. Since this concept is certainly not new, why then are we suddenly emphasizing afresh the genetic elements in disease? The reasons underlying our concern at present follow two main channels, though, like any two streams following a closely similar course, these will in time and at high water tend to overflow, merge and become one. Firstly, we must attempt the difficult task of contemplating some of the possible implications of the accelerating and ever increasing acquisition of knowledge about human biology. Secondly, we are already faced with the need to plan our approach to the increasing importance of genetic factors in disease.

THE ADVANCE IN KNOWLEDGE OF HUMAN BIOLOGY

This century has seen the rediscovery of Mendel's evidence for laws governing the transmission of particulate information from one generation to the next and the natural extension and application of this work to man. Following rapidly on this, the molecular mechanisms which cause these laws to operate have become largely understood and the genetic code has been cracked, indicating the way to a complete translation of the information handed on by one generation to the next. Most recently of all, a Nobel Prize has gone to workers who have put forward evidence for a regulatory system which brings the environment back into the picture. These developments, while vast compared with advances in knowledge over previous centuries, are negligible when compared with our still gross ignorance of human biology. Nonetheless, the pace of increase in knowledge is quite un-precedented and, to cite just one example, a directed change in the genetic content of cells is already well within the bounds of possibility. This has been achieved with bacteria and similar attempts with human cells grown outside the body are experimentally feasible. Such an approach could lead to treatment for disease at a far more fundamental level than has ever been possible before.

Unfortunately, as always with beneficial advance, there is another side to the coin, in that by the same means, it may also become possible to modify deliberately the genetic component of human nature, considering it in the widest sense. Most of us here are no better equipped than any man in the street to deal with the philosophy or ethics of such possible interference with human biology as we know it today, or, to forecast what adjustments to human beings may be desirable in the unknown environmental conditions of the future. It is often, and perhaps justifiably, suggested that there is a potential analogy between the present position in biology and the position in physics some years ago when nuclear energy was released in the world as a result of momentous decisions made by a very few, albeit highly informed, men. When it eventually becomes necessary to make even more momentous decisions regarding the kinds of attributes which may be desirable in human beings, let us hope that these decisions will be made in the light of a democratically obtained ethical, philosophical and social preparedness.

At present it can only be hoped that this will be achieved by perpetually demanding clarification of the biological and technical possibilities from the specialists, by disseminating this information as widely as possible and by following it up with rational discussion. Pontecorvo (2) has pointed out that practices such as prenatal care, organ transplantation, and dietary supplementation, are all examples of human engineering on a very minor scale which we have taken in our stride. In the future, the problem is likely to be one of applying such minor changes on a scale greatley accelerated as to time and quantity.

THE INCREASING IMPORTANCE OF GENETIC
FACTORS IN DISEASE

Despite appreciation of the contributions of genetic endowment and environmental hazard to the causation of disease, there would be no dispute that the greatest triumphs of medicine and public health have resulted, almost exclusively, from control of the environment. This control has taken the form of both primary and secondary prevention. Either an external threat has been completely removed, witness the absence of cholera and typhoid organisms from our drinking water, or, should this approach fail, attempts are made to detect the earliest possible signs of disease and to institute appropriate specific therapy.

An immediate effect of the success of this approach has been a significant relative increase in importance of genetic causes of mortality and morbidity. An analysis by Carter (3) of the causes of death in Great Ormond Street Children's Hospital in 1914 and again forty years later in 1954 has been frequently quoted but illustrates this shift in relative importance so well that the findings bear repeating again. In 1914, 68 percent of deaths were attributed to environmental factors, most notably infections, whereas in 1954, following immunization programs and the introduction of antibiotics, this proportion had fallen to 14 percent. On the other hand, the proportion of deaths regarded as wholly genetic had undergone a sixfold increase from 2 percent in 1914 to 12 percent in 1954. Again, the relative nature of this change must be stressed. Similar findings are reflected in the figures for specific disabilities. For instance, in 1922 (4), a survey of causes of blindness in British school children attributed 37 percent of such blindness to congenital and genetic abnormalities. In 1950, thirty-eight years later, a similar survey of the same age group put 68 percent of all cases in this category, but the total amount of blindness had been halved.

Recent estimates (5) have indicated that at present about half of all profound childhood deafness is genetic in origin. While personally unaware of any comparable estimates made thirty to forty years ago, the introduction of such measures as antibiotic therapy for otitis media and good management of hemolytic disease in the newborn make it reasonable to suspect that there has been a similar trend toward a relative increase in genetic causes of deafness. Orthopedic conditions provide yet another illustration for, with the control of inflammatory bone disease and latterly of poliomyelitis, congenital and genetic skeletal defects must inevitably now be more important. It is noteworthy that major philanthropic societies, in both Britain and the U.S.A. have recently extended their support from poliomyelitis and cerebral palsy to include the whole field of development and birth defects.

This relative increase in importance of conditions with a strong genetic element in causation does not indicate an absolute increase in the number of such diseases; however, this possibility must also now cause concern. Although much less dramatic, since each individual condition tends to be rare, genetic diseases are beginning to benefit from advances in therapy. The phenylketonuria story is familiar, and everyone must welcome the avoidance of severe mental retardation. Cystic fibrosis, similarly, provides an even more common example where, in spite of the high mortality, an increasing number of affected individuals are reaching the reproductive years. The possible long-term effects of circumventing natural selection in this manner cannot be ignored.

A particularly interesting group of conditions are those singled out in Carter's analysis (3) of causes of death as being "partly genetic" in nature. This group includes most of the common malformations such as harelip and cleft palate, spina bifida, some congenital heart disease and congenital pyloric stenosis. During the forty-year interval between the two years analyzed in the study, this group had also become relatively more important as a cause of death, contributing 14 percent of deaths in 1914 and 52 percent in 1954. However, this change is less marked than in the other categories described, probably because of a significant reduction in mortality among these common malformations. A recent study in U.S.A. (6) showed a 28 percent reduction in mortality from spina bifida in the first year of life between the first and second halves of the decade 1950-1959. There has, almost certainly, been a further reduction since then. Plastic surgery has so advanced that a child afflicted with a harelip and cleft palate has now almost the same probability of marrying and reproducing as any other member of the population. Similarly, cardiac surgery has made advances so that many victims of congenital heart disease are living to reproduce. In all these conditions, as well as many unknown environmental factors, it is probable that several genes are involved. Transmission of these genes to subsequent generations will surely, in time, cause an increase in the frequency of these malformations. Instructive evidence that this does occur has been published by Carter (7) who has studied the children of the first survivors of pyloric stenosis, following the introduction of the Rammstedt operation in 1912. As might be expected a significant proportion of these children were similarly affected.

We can anticipate both a relative and an absolute increase in the contribution to total morbidity and mortality made by diseases which are either wholly or partly genetic in nature. Before considering whether or how public health workers should concern themselves with this problem, it is necessary to sketch present ideas concerning the origin and value of the inborn differences between human beings.

Genes are the determiners of inherited characteristics and are located, physically, on the chromosomes, within the nucleus of all nucleated cells. Genes occur in pairs, as do chromosomes, one member of each pair being derived from each parent. In human beings there are perhaps 50,000 such pairs of genes, arranged in 23 pairs of chromosomes, but, with the exception of identical twins, no two individuals are ever likely to possess exactly the same complement of individual gene types because constant mixing takes place through the process of reduction division and chromosomal crossing over in the gonads. If individuals are so different, how has it come about that certain populations have particular characteristics? From time to time, new genes are created by the process of change, or mutation, of the old genes. This change affects the characteristics controlled by that gene, and, depending on the environment in which the organism finds itself at that moment, this may prove either harmful or beneficial. If the former, the gene will tend to be eliminated, if the latter it will tend to be retained.

This is an oversimplification of the role of natural selection in evaluation, but does suggest why populations living in different environments have different gene frequencies, even though the environmental force that favored the retention of a particular gene may no longer be apparent. In some instances, the anomalous situation arises where a gene, which in double dose is lethal, is retained in the population at a much higher frequency than can be accounted for by the occurrence of new mutations. Under such circumstances, it appears that the single dose carrier of this harmful gene may actually have some advantage over the completely normal individual. Unfortunately, one rarely knows, or can even guess, what this advantage could be with the one exception, the classic example, the increased resistance to falciparum malaria exhibited by carriers of a single gene for sickle cell hemoglobin. Probably as a consequence, this gene has a high frequency in parts of Africa and other malarious areas of the world, but it appears to be diminishing in frequency among the North American Negro in a nonmalarious environment. In the North American Caucasion population, it is suggested that the gene for cystic fibrosis may act in some similar manner, for it has a higher frequency despite the severe effects seen when it occurs in double dose. Possibly some advantage is similarly conferred by single doses of the genes involved in diabetes or schizophrenia.

This indicates the uncertain ground one would be on if it were advocated that there be wholesale restriction of reproduction by such individuals as the treated phenylketonuric or cases of cystic fibrosis. It is necessary to learn a great deal more about the gene frequencies in various population groups and attempt to relate these to the environmental forces which may have operated in their creation. For example, it has been shown (8) that the majority of grandparents of cases of phenylketonuria treated in London, England, originated from Ireland. This suggests that Ireland may have a higher than usual frequency of the gene for phenylketonuria. If so, why? Is there an increased mutation rate in that part of the world? Is the high frequency (if it exists) due to the effects of so-called genetic drift, or was there at one time or still, an advantage in the possession of this gene in the single dose? By asking and trying to answer questions such as these, a picture of the factors which have contributed to the adaptation of populations under different environmental conditions may be slowly built up. Progress can then be made toward studies of factors likely to contribute to adaptability in man. The populations which provide the most information are those which, for cultural or geographic reasons, have retained a greater degree of genetic isolation. The historical origins, social and cultural changes, with their important moulding effects, may often be better defined in such groups than in large mixed populations. For these reasons and because such groups are rapidly becoming assimilated into larger mixed and mobile populations, the study of the remaining primitive populations has urgent priority.

GENETIC COUNSELING

All public health workers are concerned with the origins of any disease or disability. This is especially so when a group of such conditions forms a significant portion of the total ill health of a given population. Only by considering the causes will approaches to prevention become apparent and here the genetic factors in disease offer new challenges. It is not, at present, possible to prevent any genetic disease by the application of devices outside the control of the individual as is the case with many infections and industrial hazards. As Roberts (9) has remarked, the sole effective agents in the prevention of genetic diseases are potential parents. These agents will only be aware of their role if full use is made of the most important means presently at our disposal for the control or prevention of genetic disease, namely, genetic counseling. Many people have regarded this as merely counseling for birth control, with the implication that at such an interview family limitation is always strongly advocated. This falls far short of the truth. Genetic counseling is primarily a service to individuals in which information is provided concerning the risk of the birth of a child affected with a certain condition, or the odds on a particular individual developing and hence transmitting a particular condition. While counselors can make such odds or risk figures more meaningful by relating them to the risks run by any random individual, the final decision as to whether such odds as can be given are worth taking must, in nearly every situation, be left to the individuals immediately concerned.

The tools of genetic counseling are correct diagnosis and, wherever possible, elimination of conditions with a similar end result caused by other than genetic means, the so-called phenocopy as, for instance, the cataracts caused by prenatal rubella, versus the cataracts caused by recessive genes. An adequate family pedigree is required, and since many conditions are rare, the counselor must have access to the experience of others through the world medical literature.

The conditions in which counseling may be appropriate fall into three main groups. The first comprises conditions caused by single deleterious genes which are transmitted in a regular fashion following the pattern of autosomal dominant or recessive, or sex-linked inheritance. The risks of recurrence may be high but are usually very specific, and it is also frequently possible to provide much positive and optimistic reassurance to unaffected family members. Further refinements in such counseling are being provided by advances in biochemical and other means of detecting externally normal carriers of potentially harmful genes and by the increasing number of situations where parents can be alerted to the possibility of treatment, usually early, if an affected child is born.

The second group of conditions where advice may be requested are those situations where a gross chromosome anomaly has occurred, as, for example, in Down's syndrome. Fortunately, though many of these anomalies are severe, the majority of such conditions are sporadic in occurrence. Appropriate investigation will help to separate out the very small proportion with a high risk for recurrence as, for example, the translocation mongol.

The third, and numerically largest group of conditions about which advice may be sought are those which seem to result from a mixture of environmental and genetic factors. This includes many of the common congenital malformations and also, very probably, many of the commoner diseases of adult life, such as diabetes, schizophrenia and atherosclerosis, where the situation is, also, still far from clear. Because of the complex etiology only average, or empiric risks for recurrence can be given here, but even these tend to be welcomed as an advance on the casual, complete reassurance often offered by the doctor or the equally pessimistic outlook commonly found in parents who have had one malformed child, and in malformed but otherwise normal individuals themselves. Indeed, there is a big field for the positive approach to genetic counseling for, even where marriage and reproduction are not immediate issues, much needless concern may be felt by affected individuals and their families about the cause of their condition and the risks they may run.

In the past most genetic counseling has been confined to a highly selected, university hospital orientated and socially motivated group of patients. Counseling a much wider range of people will provide problems, for there has been only a slight increase in the availability of genetic counsellors. Fortunately, health departments are adept at making useful measures available to large numbers of people, often with a skeleton staff. Despite the establishment of a number of health department programs (9), the premise that genetic counseling is a useful and effective measure has yet to be adequately proved; but, if for the moment this is accepted, how big an time would it be in Saskatchewan and how best could it be provided?

There is no comprehensive register of disease or disability in this province and this would be the first defect to remedy. If only newborns are considered it has been estimated that 1 percent have disease or defects caused by single genes, another 1 percent have chromosomal anomalies and about 2½ percent have one of the partly genetic common malformations. Applying these figures to the yearly births in Saskatchewan it can be seen that at least 600 to 800 sets of parents are potential candidates for counseling. Who is going to do this counseling? There are two lines of approach. Firstly, better training of the medical profession in the basic concepts of human genetics will equip many more physicians to recognize and deal with the conditions caused by single genes which follow Mendelian patterns of inheritance. Many physicians with access to a service chromosome laboratory are also well equipped to recognize and manage the majority of chromosomal anomalies, and it is hoped that many more will learn to do so. Secondly, however, there are many physicians who do not feel adequate to undertake this work and still others who do not have the inclination. For the patients of these doctors, their parents and, if indicated, their relatives, facilities should be available, on a regional basis, where appropriate information and advice could be obtained. Just as public health nurses and others endeavor to ensure that patients are aware of services for diagnosis and treatment, so should it be their responsibility to make people aware of what can be offered by genetic counseling services.

CONCLUSION

The advance in knowledge of human biology is constantly accelerating and there is an obligation on health workers to keep informed, to transmit information, and when the opportunity arises to enter into rational discussion of the possibilities and problems.

Attention must be drawn to the obvious change in importance of genetic factors in disease. To gauge the degree of concern that should be felt over this change, much more must be learned about human adaptability and the respective roles of genes and the environment. To this end a constant surveillance should be kept of the amount of genetic disease in the local provincial population. There is much evidence from present knowledge of evolution that many apparently harmful genes should be tolerated for it is probable that it is only from this gene pool and from the resultant human diversity that men may come who are more appropriate to the unknown future.

REFERENCES

1. Medawar, P. B.: In *The Future of Man,* B.B.C. Reith Lecture, Mentor Books, 1959, p. 30.
2. Pontecorvo, G.: In *The Control of Human Heredity,* New York, Macmillan, p. 81.
3. Carter, C. O.: Quoted by J. A. Roberts: *Brit Med J, 1*:5278, 1962.
4. Sorsby, A.: *ibid.*
5. Fraser, G. R.: *J Med Genet, 1*:118, 1964.
6. Hewitt, D.: *Brit J Prev Soc Med, 17*:13, 1963.
7. Carter, C. O.: *Brit Med Bull, 17*:251, 1961.
8. Carter, C. O.: *Ann Hum Genet, 25*:57, 1961.
9. Roberts, J. A.: *ibid.* 3 and 4 above.
10. Currents in Public Health, Ross Laboratories, 1965, *5*: No. 10.

Chapter 53

Genetic Counseling in Clinical Pediatrics
WHAT TO DO WITH INQUIRIES ABOUT HERITABLE DISORDERS

MARGARET W. THOMPSON

IT is no coincidence that Garrod, who is commonly regarded as the father of medical genetics, was a pediatrician. When at the beginning of this century he noted the peculiar familial distribution of the disorders that he called "inborn errors of metabolism" (6), he was making the kind of observation that can be made much more readily by pediatricians than by other clinicians. Most of the severe genetic diseases are evident at birth or begin in childhood. In practice the pediatrician regularly sees mother and child at once, and without special effort may encounter complete sibships or even larger family groups. And, whether he wishes it or not, the pediatrician is frequently forced to provide genetic counseling when the parents of a child with a genetic defect seeks his advice about the chance of subsequent children being affected, and even on the advisability of having more children.

Genetic counseling has been defined as "the total process of exchange of information relative to the genetic prognosis and its attendant problems" (14). The relevant information upon which

Note: Reprinted by permission of the author and *Clinical Pediatrics, 6*:199-209, 1967.

Dr. Thompson is Associate Professor of Paediatrics and Zoology, University of Toronto; Acting Director, Department of Genetics, Hospital for Sick Children, Toronto, Ontario, Canada.

to base a genetic prognosis is not always at hand, nor is a pediatrician always as well qualified in genetics as in other basic and clinical sciences. Nevertheless, he is usually the best person to give genetic counseling. The physician who knows something of a family's economic, psychologic, and sociologic situation is often able to help the family fit the genetic aspect into the whole medical problem, whereas the genetic counselor who is a non-medical consultant must restrict his contribution to the genetic prognosis alone.

Most parents of genetically defective children have little comprehension of the underlying pattern of inheritance. Genetics is usually not taught in high school or college in a way which is meaningful to young parents a few years later. As the level of education and sophistication in the population rises, we can expect that parents will become more knowledgable about genetics as about many other medical matters. At present, however, in most counseling situations the geneticist must be prepared to teach the parents the basic genetics needed for them to understand their problem.

THE FAMILY HISTORY

Most hospital admission forms and other medical records have spaces where details of the family history may be recorded, but often the kinds of queries on these forms are not pertinent in a given instance — questions about allergies, for instance, in the relatives of a diabetic child. Here are the major components of a meaningful family history, in the light of present day insights:

What are the parents' ages? Late parental age (especially late maternal age) may hint at a chromosomal abnormality produced by nondisjunction.

Are the parents consanguineous? If so, this fact can be a valuable clue to a rare autosomal recessive gene or, less frequently, to polygenic inheritance.

What is the geographic origin of the forebears? Rare genes are more frequent in the near relatives of carriers, or in members of the same geographic isolate, than in the general population.

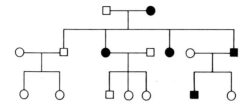

Figure 53-1. A pedigree of hereditary spherocytosis illustrating autosomal dominant inheritance. The trait appears in each generation and is transmitted only by affected members, to half their progeny (on the average). Male-to-male transmission can occur.

All potentially relevant details concerning the patient's sibs, the patient's aunts and uncles and their children, and both sets of grandparents should be recorded. Beyond this the family history may lose in accuracy as it gains in size, but in special circumstances (e.g. a clear-cut autosomal dominant pedigree) it is helpful to extend the pedigree as much as feasible. Relationships should always be stated precisely; e.g. "father's brother" rather than "uncle."

The mother's previous stillbirths and miscarriages should be noted. Any information concerning possible teratogenic insults in early pregnancy should be recorded, though with caution, since this kind of information is notoriously inaccurate.

If the child is a twin, as one child in fifty is, the zygosity of the twin pair should be ascertained. This may require determination of genetic markers in red cells and serum. If a transfusion is indicated medically, the blood samples for analysis must be taken beforehand – an especially important matter when a transplant from one twin to the other is being considered. At the very minimum, the sex of the co-twin should be recorded.

For future reference, a family record is most conveniently summarized in standard pedigree form, as in Figures 53-1 through 53-4.

Usually a clinician is better qualified than a nonmedical geneticist to know just what kind of inquiry to make in a given instance. For example, with a child with cystic fibrosis he can ask more explicit questions about earlier siblings who may have died of respiratory or digestive ailments. When his background knowledge includes some training in genetics as applied to medicine, he will know better just where in the family tree to look for significant observations.

PATTERNS OF INHERITANCE

Genetic diseases fall into three main categories: (1) those dependent upon single genes or gene pairs, (2) those caused by many genes with small effects, and (3) those associated with chromosomal aberrations. Each of these groups has its own special problems of genetic analysis and prognosis.

Single-Gene Inheritance

The typical patterns of single-gene inheritance and the criteria for recognizing the different patterns depend upon (1) whether the gene in question is autosomal or X-linked, and (2) whether it is clinically significant in heterozygotes (dominant) or only in homozygotes (recessive). Since these are independent variables, four main patterns result: autosomal dominant, autosomal recessive, X-linked dominant, and X-linked recessive. (See also Table 53-I)

Autosomal Dominant Inheritance

Autosomal dominant traits are transmitted directly from an affected parent to half his children, regardless of sex. Since human families are so small, an affected person may have no affected child, even though each child has a 50 percent risk of receiving the gene and the trait. Unaffected members of a kindred never transmit the trait. Hereditary spherocytosis is one such disorder (Fig. 53-1).

The typical pattern of autosomal dominant inheritance is not seen often. This is because deleterious dominants, such as achondroplasia or Marfan's syndrome, may impair the affected person's fitness so severely that he does not marry or, if he marries, does not reproduce, either for biologic reasons or by deliberate intent.

TABLE 53-I

PEDIATRIC DISORDERS WITH SINGLE-GENE INHERITANCE*

Autosomal Dominants	X-linked Disorders (mainly recessive)
Achondroplasia	Agammaglobulinemia
Aniridia	Anhidrotic ectodermal dysplasia
Brachydactyly	Color vision anomalies
Epiloia	Duchenne muscular dystrophy
Facioscapulohumeral muscular dystrophy	Glucose-6-phosphate dehydrogenase deficiency
Hereditary juvenile glaucoma	Hemophilia A (AHF deficiency)
Hereditary spherocytosis	Hemophilia B (Christmas disease)
Marfan's syndrome	Hypoparathyroidism
Myotonic dystrophy	Hypophosphatemia
Porphyria (acute intermittent type)	Lowe's oculo-cerebro-renal syndrome
	Nephrogenic diabetes insipidus
Autosomal Recessives	Ocular albinism
Adrenogenital syndrome	**Common Pediatric Syndromes Associated**
Albinism	**with Chromosomal Anomalies**
Cystic fibrosis	
Galactosemia	Autosomal Aberrations
Gaucher's disease	Mongolism (Down's syndrome)
Glycogen storage diseases	E trisomy
Homocystinuria	D trisomy
Maple syrup urine disease	*Cri du chat* syndrome
Metachromatic leukodystrophy	
Phenylketonuria	Sex Chromosomal Aberrations
Pseudocholinesterase deficiency	Klinefelter's syndrome (usually 47/XXY)
Sickle cell anemia	Turner's syndrome (usually 45/XO)
Tay-Sachs disease	
Tyrosinemia	
Wilson's disease	

*For a complete list, see McKusick, V. A., Mendelian Inheritance in Man: Catalogs of Autosomal Dominant, Autosomal Recessive, and X-linked Phenotypes. Baltimore, Johns Hopkins Press, 1966.

Clinically important dominant traits that affect children are likely to be highly variable in age of recognition and in severity of expression. For example, in myotonic dystrophy the onset age in parents and child may differ by more than twenty years. In epiloia (tuberous sclerosis) the spectrum of expression is so wide that a child with tumors in brain, kidney, heart, and skin and severely retarded and epileptic may be born to a parent whose only clinical signs are minor sebaceous adenomata.

Many disorders of vision are autosomal dominants. In one form of hereditary juvenile glaucoma, abnormal development of the mesoderm of the anterior chamber leads to both closed-angle glaucoma variable in onset age and severity, and an unusual characteristic dark blue eye color present from birth (9). Congenital aniridia which usually does not produce severely defective vision until adult life has been traced through at least seven successive generations (19). Hereditary vitelline macular degeneration can be detected in early life by the presence of macular cysts, but visual acuity may be satisfactory until middle life (1). In these conditions genetic counseling can be reliable if the natural history of the disease is understood.

In a pedigree of macular dystrophy currently under investigation here, the gene has been traced through six generations. The family contains eighteen young adults, still with normal vision but each having a 50 percent risk of the double burden of defective vision developing in middle life and of transmitting the disease to half his offspring. It should be possible to reassure half these young people and forewarn the other half, but a physician unaware of the family history of blindness occurring in middle life would not seek to identify those members who are "at risk."

It is not always clear to the members of a family with an autosomal dominant defect that unaffected members who do not have the gene cannot transmit it. For example, a young man of normal stature whose father was one of three achondroplastic sibs, and whose paternal grandfather was also achondroplastic was referred for genetic counseling. Aware of the hereditary nature of achondroplasia, he and his wife were concerned that they themselves might have an achondroplastic child. The achondroplastic father had had only normal children. Might this son, who was normal, have an affected child? Misinterpretations of this nature, when the diagnosis and pattern of inheritance are firmly established, can usually be allayed by explaining autosomal dominant inheritance to the couple concerned.

Autosomal Recessive Inheritance

Autosomal recessive traits typically affect one out of four children of heterozygous parents, and usually do not arise elsewhere in the family tree. These are probably the most common genetic disorders seen in pediatrics. Examples include most inborn errors of metabolism, many neurologic diseases, cystic fibrosis, thalassemia major and sickle cell anemia, the limb girdle type of muscular dystrophy, and many other traits, some of which are rare indeed (Fig. 53-2).

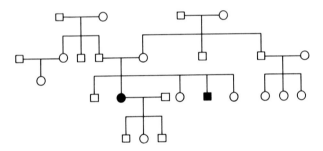

Figure 53-2. A pedigree of limb-girdle muscular dystrophy illustrating autosomal recessive inheritance. The trait appears only in a single sibship, affecting a quarter (on the average) of the sibs of the propositus. It does not appear in earlier or later generations.

Cousin Marriages

Any rare disease-related gene is more frequent among relatives of carriers than in the general population. This is why autosomal recessives, and especially the rare ones, are more likely to affect the children of cousin parents. Cousin marriages produce an undue share of genetically determined diseases. The parents of children in institutions for the deaf or blind are perhaps one hundred times as likely to be consanguineous as parents in the general population.

Cousin matings are encouraged in the Moslem faith: "The marriage of cousins is sealed in the heavens." Hence a wide array of autosomal recessives tend to be encountered in such communities.

Coincidence of two rare recessives sometimes occurs in the children of cousin parents. Since a pair of first cousins have one-eighth of their genes in common, and their children are homozygous at one-sixteenth of all their gene loci, it is not particularly surprising to see more than one rare recessive mutant expressing itself in the children of a consanguineous marriage.

The total additional risk of genetic disease to which the children of first cousins are exposed may be about half the general population risk. It is only fair to add that this risk is regarded as negligible by hardheaded life insurance actuaries, who do not penalize clients because their parents were cousins.

Incest

An important though infrequent aspect of genetic counseling is advising about the adoption placement of children born of incestuous unions. Though firm data are not available to asses the risk of genetic disease in such children, they may well be homozygous for one or more deleterious recessives. The more closely related the parents, the greater the risk of a genetic disease in the child.

X-linked Inheritance

Genes on the X chromosome are distributed, with the X itself, unequally to males and females, and never from father to son. Different frequencies of the trait in males and females and the absence of father-to-son transmission make X linkage easy to recognize. Sixty or more X-linked traits have already been described. In fact the X chromosome is the first — and so far the only — human chromosome to have a book written about it (11).

Females have a pair of X chromosomes just as they have twenty-two pairs of autosomes; males have only one X, and are said to be *hemizygous* for X-linked genes.

The male who has an X-linked mutant gene is affected. When he reproduces, he will transmit the mutant to all his daughters but none of his sons. (The sons receive his Y instead.) With a dominant mutant all his daughters will be affected (Fig. 53-3). With a recessive mutant no daughter will be affected clinically, yet half will be carriers who in turn will transmit it to half their sons (Fig. 53-4). In other words, if the mutant is recessive the daughter of an affected male will be clinically normal; if it is dominant she will be affected. But in either case half her sons will be affected, and half her daughters will be heterozygotes like herself. Sons of affected males will be normal and will not transmit the gene to later generations. Thus whether a trait is X linked or not can usually be determined easily by looking at the offspring of affected males.

There are some diseases for which accurate genetic assessment

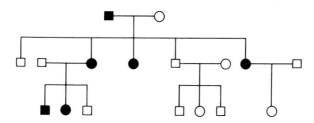

Figure 53-3. A pedigree of hypophosphatemia illustrating X-linked dominant inheritance. An affected male transmits the trait to all his daughters but to none of his sons. Affected females transmit the trait to half their offspring, regardless of sex. This is the least common pattern of single-gene inheritance.

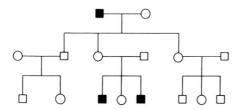

Figure 53-4. A pedigree of the deutan type of red-green blindness to illustrate X-linked recessive inheritance. An affected male transmits the trait through all his daughters to half their sons (on the average). Male-to-male transmission does not occur.

and counseling is of major importance. Duchenne muscular dystrophy, an X-linked recessive in which affected males are usually unable to reproduce, is one such disease. It is typically transmitted through unaffected carrier females to half their sons and, through half their daughters, to half the daughters' sons; but many cases are caused by new mutations in genetically normal noncarrier mothers. This severe and protracted disorder, with its hopeless prognosis, can at present be reduced in frequency only if carrier women can be recognized and advised about the genetic risk. Tests are being developed which will permit identification of these carriers with a relatively high degree of certainty (23).

Mutation

Many severe traits may arise as fresh mutations. The proportion of cases of a specific disease produced by new mutations may be high if the trait severely affects survival and reproductive ability. In achondroplasia, four fifths of all cases, and in Duchenne muscular dystrophy, one third of all cases are sporadic, i.e. caused by a new mutation in a genetically normal parent.

It is not always possible to distinguish between a severe sporadic dominant mutation and a malformation due to some other cause, such as a teratogenic drug, virus infection, or homozygosity for a recessive gene. For genetic counseling, the distinction is important. For example, a condition caused by a new dominant mutation has a negligible recurrence risk with a sibship, but a 50 percent risk in the offspring of an affected person; whereas a recessive trait has a 25 percent recurrence risk in the sibs and a little risk of appearing in the next generation.

Polygenic Inheritance

Many common diseases (and countless normal traits such as stature, intelligence and other continuously variable characteristics) seem to be determined not by genes at a single locus but by many genes with small additive effects. In expression, these traits can often be modified to a greater or lesser extent by environment. There may be a "threshold" beyond which the expression is clinically abnormal (e.g. serum cholesterol level or blood pressure) (4). Many congenital malformations have polygenic inheritance (2).

Genetic counseling with congenital malformations is replete with difficulties. Patterns of transmission often seem irregular. Many clinical categories seem heterogeneous, made up of a mixture of single-gene traits, multifactorial traits, and perhaps a few chromosomal abnormalities. Some cases seem to have a strictly environmental origin. Fortunately, the recurrence risk with polygenic inheritance is usually low (though well above the population risk). Fortunately, also, many polygenic traits can be ameliorated surgically or medically.

It is convenient to discuss the recurrence risk of congenital malformations in terms of multiples of the general population risk (see Table 53-II). Whereas for single-gene dominant traits the risk falls by half for each step of relationship (50% for sibs, 25% for uncles and aunts, 12.5% for first cousins, etc.), in polygenic inheritance the risk falls much more sharply with more remote relationships.

CHROMOSOMAL DISORDERS

Almost as soon as abnormalities of chromosome number and structure could be correlated with certain clinical abnormalities, it became apparent that the various chromosomal disorders are not randomly distributed, but that autosomal aberrations, sex chromosome abnormalities, and leukemia occur more often in the same kindred — and even in the same individual — than pure chance would explain. Thus genetic counseling has a place in the management of patients and families with cytogenetic problems; but chromosomal defects do not show typical mendelian inheritance, and usually have low recurrence risks.

Mongolism (Down's Syndrome)

In mongolism, which is caused by trisomy for chromosome 21 (a small acrocentric chromosome in the G group), the chief epidemiologic observation is late maternal age. Application of

TABLE 53-II

RECURRENCE RISKS FOR POLYGENIC TRAITS IN SIBS

Trait	Approximate Population Incidence per Thousand	Approximate Relative Recurrence Risks in Sibs	Reference
Anencephaly and spina bifida	5	×8	Carter [2]
Cleft lip (+ cleft palate)	1	×30	Carter [2]
Club foot (talipes equinovarus)	1	×20	Carter [2]
Congenital dislocation of the hip	1	×40	Carter [2]
Congenital heart defects	3–8	×5*	Nora and Meyer [16]
Diabetes mellitus			
All diabetes	—	×3	Simpson [20]
Juvenile diabetes	—	×17	
Pyloric stenosis	3	×20	Carter [2]

*Not suggested as empiric risk because several different congenital heart diseases are combined.

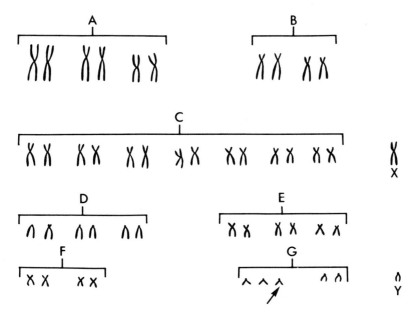

Figure 53-5. Karyotype to illustrate mongolism of the standard 47 chromosome: trisomy 21 type. The extra 21st chromosome is indicated by an arrow. This pattern is found in about 99 percent of all mongols.

computer methods to large population samples should eventually provide precise empiric risks for the birth of a mongol child at different maternal ages. The studies so far reported are based upon rather small series, considering the low recurrence risk involved; and they may also be subject to criticism on the basis of ascertainment, since families with only a single mongol are less likely to be described than those containing several.

The empiric risk of recurrence of mongolism within a sibship seems to be of the order of 1 to 2 percent, regardless of age. As compared with the general population, Carter and Evans (3) have estimated that for mothers under 25 the risk is about fiftyfold, for mothers aged 25 to 34 about fivefold, and for mothers 35 and over only 1.1 to 1.2 times the general population risk for that age bracket. These figures include both standard trisomy 21 and translocation mongolism, in which the additional chromosome 21 is translocated to some other chromosome (see below).

Some instances of familial mongolism are caused by trans-mission of a translocation from a clinically normal parent who is a translocation carrier or translocation heterozygote, carrying the translocation as part of a balanced karyotype. In a series of recent papers (7, 8, 18), the relevant literature has been surveyed in an attempt to evaluate the proportion of cases of mongolism produced by the transmission of translocations. Here are some pertinent generalizations: Some 28 percent of the mongols investigated were born to mothers under thirty years of age, and 72 percent to mothers past that age. Among those with younger mothers, 8.7 percent were translocation mongols, and of these one-third had inherited the translocation chromosome; the remainder had chromosomally normal parents. In other words, about 3 percent of the mongols born to *young* mothers (less than 1% of the whole group) carried a familial translocation, which was

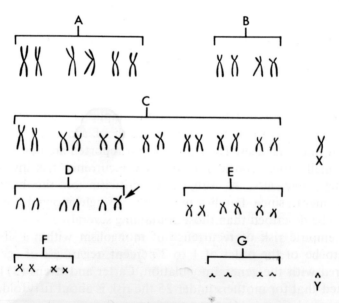

Figure 53-6. Karyotype to illustrate translocation mongolism of the 46 chromosome: D/G translocation type. The abnormal chromosome, represent-ing an extra 21st chromosome translocated to a D chromosome, is indicated by an arrow.

either a D/G translocation (i.e., a translocation of material of a chromosome 21 to a large acrocentric chromosome in the D group, or a G/G translocation involving some other G group chromosome). The three karyotypes seen in mongolism are illustrated in Figures 53-5 to 53-7. Karyotyping of the patient and the parents can show whether a translocation is familial. In the experience of our group, the proportion of all translocations that are hereditary is much less than one-third, closer to one-sixth. If either parent is found to be a translocation carrier, the risk of a mongol child in a later pregnancy ranges from about one in three to one in ten. Translocations appear to be transmitted to an affected child more frequently by the mother than by the father. There is also the risk, theoretically as high as one-half, that a clinically normal child of a translocation carrier will also be a carrier.

The dramatic nature of translocation heterozygosity has overshadowed some important observations which indicate that translocations are by no means always involved in familial mongolism. Soltan *et al.* (21) found *no* translocation in 21 families with multiple cases of mongolism, and in four additional families found *both* a translocation mongol and a standard trisomic. Clearly much has still to be learned about the mechanisms and predisposing factors which lead to mongolism.

With one rare chromosomal abnormality, a 21/21 translocation (or isochromosome), the carrier of the abnormal chromosome can have *only* mongol children. This type of translocation cannot be distinguished microscopically from an ordinary G/G (21/22) translocation. When a parent with a G/G translocation has more than one mongol child, the translocation should be suspected of being the 21/21 type; but if even one child in the family is normal, the translocation cannot be a 21/21 and the prospect that the next child will be phenotypically normal is at least two-thirds.

When should chromosome studies be undertaken to aid in genetic counseling in mongolism? Every mongol child of a young mother and every mongol child in a family with mongolism or other chromosomal abnormality should probably be karyotyped, and if a translocation is found, the parents should also be karyotyped; but for every familial translocation identified by this means, thirty or more negative cases will have to be analyzed, and little information will be gained concerning the recurrence risk of mongolism associated with a standard trisomy 21 karyotype.

A few mothers of mongols have been shown to be mosaics, i.e., to have tissues composed of a mixture of 46-chromosome and 47-chromosome cells. If the mother of a mongol is a mosaic, and the mosaicism involves the gonads, the risk of a second mongol child is above average. Mosaic mongolism can never be ruled out with certainty. Skin cultures are more likely than leukocyte cultures to reveal mosaicism. On the basis of dermal pattern data, Penrose (17) has estimated that about one-tenth of the mothers of mongols may be mosaics.

More rewarding ways of identifying high risk mothers may be developed when factors predisposing to nondisjunction are

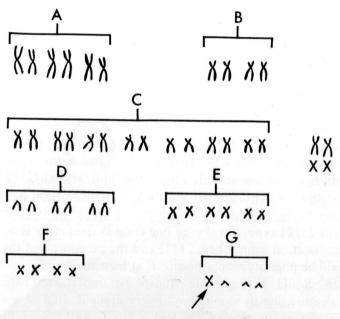

Figure 53-7. Karyotype to illustrate translocation mongolism of the 46 chromosome: G/G translocation type. The abnormal chromosome, indicated by an arrow, may represent either a 21/22 or, less frequently, a 21/21 translocation.

understood more thoroughly. The possible role of viruses in producing chromosomal aberrations has been suggested. Recently Stoller and Collmann (22) offered evidence for an association of hepatitis epidemics in Australia with clustering of births of mongol children nine months later, though this does not seem to be generally substantiated. Fialkow *et al.* (5) have recently drawn attention to the association between thyroid autoimmunity and chromosomal abnormalities, reporting clinical thyroid disease in twenty-one of forty-four mongolism families but in only nine of forty-four control families; and in about 29 percent of women of childbearing age who had had mongol children but only 9 percent of controls.

Other Chromosomal Abnormalities

So far there is little information to permit accurate genetic counseling for chromosome abnormalities other than mongolism. The tendency to nonrandom distribution of chromosomal abnormalities in individuals and kindreds has already been mentioned. In general the recurrence risk is low; about 3 percent is a conservative estimate.

COMPLICATIONS IN PEDIGREE ANALYSIS

Although the rules of mendelian inheritance are simple and clear-cut, it is not always possible to apply them directly in medical genetics. Many complications may obscure straightforward genetic patterns. Some of these are described below.

Genetic Heterogeneity

A single clinical category may include a number of conditions produced by different mutations and thus differing in the basic molecular defect. Careful clinical examination may allow discrimination between closely similar disease entities. For example, Hurler's syndrome (gargoylism) may be inherited as an autosomal recessive or as an X-linked recessive, but corneal opacities appear only in the autosomal recessive type. It is important to distinguish between the two patterns of inheritance, because if the disease is autosomal it will probably not recur in later generations, whereas if it is X-linked, half the sisters of affected boys will be carriers.

Variations in Expression of Genes

The same genetic defect may be expressed differently in different family members. The wide variation in severity of epiloia has already been described. With many clinical syndromes the expression is variable in different members of a family and even more variable in different families. In osteogenesis imperfecta (usually an autosomal dominant) there are abnormalities of the sclera, bones, and skin which must have a common origin in the abnormal product of the mutant gene.

Manifold expressions of a single gene are called *pleiotropic effects.* Within an osteogenesis imperfecta family, members may have no sign of the disease except blue sclerae, whereas others may have numerous congenital fractures and not survive for long. With the latter cases, careful clinical examination of the parents and grandparents may reveal minor stigmata of the disease. When the presence of the gene in an antecedent can be recognized the parents can be told that there is a 50 percent risk that any future child will have the gene; but what cannot be foretold is the severity of its expression.

Attention has already been drawn to the wide variation in age of onset in some genetic diseases. With diabetes mellitus, the variability of onset age has confused the genetic picture so severely that even though diabetes is one of the most common hereditary diseases, its pattern of inheritance has yet to be completely worked out.

Phenocopies

A phenocopy is a trait which mimics a known genetic trait but is not caused by an abnormal gene. The common example is retinoblastoma. Bilateral retinoblastoma is usually inherited as an autosomal dominant, and unilateral retinoblastoma is a phenocopy. When there is a single case of retinoblastoma in a family it is often not possible to decide whether this is of genetic origin or a phenocopy.

Small Family Size

If every human family had a dozen children, carriers of deleterious genes would be much easier to identify. Family histories are often negative only because family size is small. In a family with Duchenne muscular dystrophy, affected boys related through females may indicate which females are carriers; but when there are only a few sons, all by chance may be normal and the typical pattern of X-linked inheritance may not appear.

TREATMENT IN GENETIC DISEASES

Many genetic diseases can be treated with some degree of success. There is a special diet for phenylketonuria, control of serious secondary problems such as respiratory infections in cystic fibrosis, surgery for club feet, plasma for hemophilic bleeding, splenectomy for hereditary spherocytosis, transfusions for thalassemia major, and so on.

Both the medical prognosis in a given disease and the efficacy of treatment have significance for genetic counseling. A trait may be incompatible with life, be fatal in months (Tay-Sachs disease), run a relentlessly progressive course for twenty years or more (Duchenne muscular dystrophy), be relatively mild and non-progressive (mongolism), or even may be fully amenable to treatment. The concern of parents about further pregnancies will obviously be quite different in these different situations.

DETECTION OF CARRIERS

Carrier detection with its important and obvious applications to genetic counseling is an actively continuing area of research in medical genetics.

With an autosomal recessive trait the heterozygote will have the risk of affected children only if he marries a person heterozygous for the same gene. As already brought out, two out of every three normal sibs of children with autosomal recessive disease are heterozygous.

It is now possible to detect heterozygotes for perhaps twenty diseases, and the number is growing year by year. For example, an individual who has a brother or sister with phenylketonuria can be tested to learn whether he is a carrier; if so, his prospective spouse can also be tested to learn whether she is a carrier. Accurate detection of carriers could remove much of the uncertainty from genetic counseling.

PARENTS' ATTITUDES TO GENETIC COUNSELING

The question which arises most frequently in pediatric genetic counseling is that of parents who have produced a defective child and who want to know the risk that the same might happen again. Very often the precipitating incident has made the parents realize for the first time that a defective child can happen in their family as in any other. If the timing is very recent the parents may not be ready to accept — or even to hear — the information they have asked for. Here is one reason why the family physician is in a better position to answer genetic questions than a consultant who is a stranger.

In genetic counseling it is almost a truism that the risk is usually not as high as the parents fear. Indeed, except in a few rare situations such as mongolism in the children of a 21/21 translocation carrier or an autosomal recessive trait in the children of two affected persons, the risk is rarely more than 50 percent, and usually much less. With autosomal recessives, if each parent is heterozygous the risk is 25 percent. With most polygenic traits and chromosomal disorders the risk is of the order of 5 percent. Any pregnancy has about a 3 percent risk of producing a defective child. Data such as these help parents to see their problem in perspective.

Parents are individuals, and their responses to genetic counseling are not always predictable. Some take the attitude, "Why should I stop having children? It isn't my fault that I'm a carrier of hemophilia." Others are pessimists who regard a 3 percent risk as too much of a chance to take ("With my luck, I'd have another child with the same defect"). Many parents refuse carrier detection tests because, "I'd just as soon not know." One mother of our acquaintance does not want her daughter tested to learn whether she is a carrier of Duchenne muscular dystrophy because "if the news got around, it could blight her chances of marriage."

NONPHYSICIAN GENETICISTS

Many attempts to improve physicians' familiarity with genetics are currently under way. For example, genetics has been added to the curriculum of most medical schools, and short postgraduate courses in medical genetics have become common. A growing number of physicians have achieved competence and even distinction in genetics (10). Nevertheless, there are also non-physician geneticists who can provide the busy practitioner with much of the information necessary for genetic prognosis.

A balanced view of the relative contributions of medical and nonmedical geneticists has been provided by Neel (15). "No matter what his starting point, an individual interested in a problem in human heredity is apt to find that he has been led through an intricate nexus into an area where his competence is dangerously low. This is particularly true in the field of medicine. Human geneticists, except perhaps those interested exclusively in the mathematical formal genetics of man, will therefore more and more function as members of a team investigating a complex problem." Such a team approach, with good will on both sides, can function as well in genetic research and counseling as in other medical and paramedical fields.

REFERENCES

1. Braley, A. E. and Spivey, B. E.: Hereditary vitelline macular degeneration. *Arch Ophthal. (Chicago), 72*:743, 1964.
2. Carter, C. O.: The genetics of common malformations. In: Congenital Malformations: Papers and Discussions Presented at the Second International Conference on Congenital Malformations. New York, International Medical Congress, 1964, p. 306.
3. Carter, C. O. and Evans, K. A.: Risk of parents who have had one child

with Down's syndrome (mongolism) having another child similarly affected. *Lancet, 2*:785, 1961.

4. Edwards, J. H.: The simulation of Mendelism. *Acta Genet. (Basel), 10*:63, 1960.

5. Fialkow, P. J., Uchida, I., Hecht, F. and Motulsky, A. G.: Increased frequency of thyroid autoantibodies in mothers of patients with Down's syndrome. *Lancet, 2*:868, 1965.

6. Garrod, A. E.: *Inborn Errors of Metabolism.* London, Oxford, 1909.

7. Giannelli, F., Hamerton, J. L. and Carter, C. O.: Cytogenetics of Down's syndrome (mongolism) II. The frequency of interchange trisomy in patients born at a maternal age of less than 30 years. *Cytogenetics, 4*:186, 1965.

8. Hamerton, J. I., Giannelli, F. and Polani, P. E.: Cytogenetics of Down's syndrome (mongolism) I. Data on a consecutive series of patients referred for genetic counseling and diagnosis. *Cytogenetics, 4*:171, 1965.

9. McCulloch, C. and MacRae, D.: Hereditary juvenile glaucoma. *Trans Canad Ophthal Soc* (unnumbered):79-91, 1950.

10. McKusick, V. A.: Genetics in medicine and medicine in genetics. *Am J Med, 34*:594, 1963.

11. McKusick, V. A.: *On the X Chromosome of Man.* Washington, American Institute of Biological Sciences, 1964.

12. Mørch, E. T.: Chondrodystrophic dwarfs in Denmark. *Opera ex Domo Biol Hered Hum, 3,* 1941.

13. Morton, N. E. and Chung, C. S.: Formal genetics of muscular dystrophy. *Am J Hum Genet, 11*:360, 1959.

14. Motulsky, A. G.: Genetic prognosis and counseling. *Am J Obstet Gynec, 90*:1227, 1964.

15. Neel, J. V.: The detection of the genetic carriers of hereditary disease. *Am J Hum Genet, 1*:19-36.

16. Nora, J. J. and Meyer, T. C.: Familial nature of congenital heart diseases. *Pediatrics, 37*:329, 1966.

17. Penrose, L. S.: *Dermatoglyphics in mosaic mongolism and allied conditions. Genetics Today, Proceedings of the XI International Congress of Genetics.* Oxford, Pergamon, 1965, p. 973.

18. Polani, P. E., Hamerton, J. L., Giannelli, F. and Carter, C. O.: Cytogenetics of Down's syndrome (mongolism) III. Frequency of interchange trisomies and mutation rate of chromosome interchanges. *Cytogenetics, 4*:193, 1965.

19. Shaw, M. W., Grove, J. H. and Borne, G.: A family study of anirida. *Arch Ophth, 65*:81, 1961.

20. Simpson, N. E.: Multifactorial inheritance: a possible hypothesis for diabetes. *Diabetes, 13*:462, 1964.

21. Soltan, H., Wiens, R. G. and Sergovich, F. R.: Genetic studies and chromosomal analysis in families with mongolism (Down's syndrome) in more than one member. *Acta Genet. (Basel), 14*:251, 1964.

22. Stoller, A. and Collmann, R. D.: Virus actiology for Down's syndrome (mongolism). *Nature, 208*:903.
23. Walton, J. N.: Diseases of muscle. *Abst Wld Med, 40*:1-3, 81.

Chapter 54

Genetic Counseling in
Obstetrics and Gynecology

JAMES G. SITES and CECIL B. JACOBSON

INTRODUCTION

G ENETIC counseling is an increasing and expected portion of the practice of obstetrics and gynecology. It has become necessary because the communication of progress in the field is increasing and knowledge in depth is being obtained. The need is also reinforced by the widespread information that four of the last eight recipients of the Nobel Prize in science have been involved in the overall specialty of genetics. The specialist in obstetrics and gynecology is uniquely qualified to better prepare himself for the counselor's role, since he is concerned with the process of life from creation to death. He will be expected to do so as the publicity of abnormalities following the use of drugs, x-ray, and genetic mismatings increases.

Since the practice of obstetrics and gynecology is somewhat divided as to certain phases of reproduction, the aspects of counseling and diagnosis will be considered in relationship to each phase.

PRENATAL CARE

Prenatal care is considered as an integral part of medicine in an

Note: Annals of the New York Academy of Sciences, Volume 142, Article 3, 768-772, copyrighted by The New York Academy of Sciences: 1967; Reprinted by permission.

The authors are associated with the Department of Obstetrics and Gynecology, The George Washington University School of Medicine, Washington, D. C.

effort to produce a healthy offspring which can assume its place in the world as well as to maintain the well being of the mother. In the past, most of the attention has been directed to the lowering of maternal and perinatal mortality rates. As this has been accomplished (and one cannot find fault with the basic premise of this aim), it has become necessary to accept the fact that prenatal care also affords the earliest opportunity for proper counseling and enlightenment on many problems and abnormalities that may occur during or after pregnancy.

The initial history and physical examination still remain an essential part of prenatal care. Too often the history is taken by a nurse who may not know the significance of precise and accurate answers to such questions as the age and health of parents and grandparents, number of siblings and their health, past obstetrical history or abnormalities, abortions and stillbirths, and ethnic and possible consanguinous backgrounds (1). If this information is not taken by the physician, it becomes his responsibility to check it with the patient to determine significant aspects in conjunction with the complete physical examination and laboratory studies that are performed.

A most illustrative example of early genetic counseling that has developed from such observations, resulting in recognition and development of treatment, is in erythroblastosis on an Rh basis. For years, repeated pregnancy losses were noted in certain matings. With an appreciation of the Rh factor and its genetic origin, prognosis by the use of antibody titers and treatment by control of delivery date and exchange transfusions resulted in the saving of many babies who would previously have been lost. This has been climaxed by continued study and development of amniocentesis, intrauterine transfusions, and desensitization at the time of delivery, all of which have further reduced the perinatal mortality. Thus, by study and observation, a problem of genetic origin may be overcome and will not require the forehead tattoo on the homozygous or heterozygous carriers of some of the hereditary diseases, as has been suggested by Pauling (2).

The physician is continually bombarded with questions on the effect of drugs, irradiation, and infections during pregnancy on the developing embryo and fetus. These may arise from casual interest or may lead to the extreme attitude of demanding interruption of pregnancy.

The effects of drugs would appear to be more teratogenic or somatotoxic rather than genetic, mutogenic, or immunogenic. The evidence is not available, however, to prove that in time drugs will not be implicated on an inherited genetic basis, such as in the perpetuation of diabetics by the use of the present antidiabetic drugs. Even though certain undesirable results may be obtained from drugs, as evidenced by Thalidomide (3), progestogens (4), propylthiouracil (5), dicumarol (6) and others, advantages may be obtained by the use of antibiotics, sedatives, hematemics, thyroid preparations, and anticoagulant therapy. As the advantages are weighed against the disadvantages, and a general appreciation of what one is using is obtained, the growing attitude of therapeutic nihilism may be controlled.

Since Stewart suggested the possible relationship between diagnostic pelvimetry and some cases of childhood leukemia (7), there has been increasing interest and concern over the effect of irradiation. Many other investigations have been made, and others will be needed to categorize and confirm the specific effects, whether the exposure by prezygotic or postzygotic.

Brill and Forgotson, reviewing the subject, have reached as a partial conclusion that "induced chromosome aberrations are suggested as one of the primary mechanisms by which radiation action is mediated" (8). As we learn more about cytogenetics and molecular biology, we may hope to understand the manner in which observable cellular damage, such as chromosomal aberrations, expresses itself phenotypically. Until more specific information is obtained, the doctor is obligated to weigh the need and value of x-ray procedures (many of which will still be necessary), at the same time providing the latest in properly calibrated equipment, high-speed films, protection from errant irradiation, and ascertaining the time that they may be done in relationship to menses or conception. The ideal time for the necessary exposure would be in the first ten days of the menstrual cycle or after the first eight weeks of pregnancy, unless the nature of the need requires that they be performed at other times.

Intercurrent infections of many types have been increasingly implicated with congenital anomalies (9). Whereas they may be more teratogenic than genetic, the physician must accept this as a part of prenatal counseling. The attitude will be individualized according to his response to the presented data, but advice will be expected. Particularly in the discussion of rubella during pregnancy, he should formulate definite ideas so that the patient will not detect too much indecision on his part. This is perhaps best explained to the patient by giving her the risk involved in relation to when the disease occurs in pregnancy and what may be expected. If further advice is requested by the patient, then one must decide within the realms of his conscience and the legal aspects under which he practices the indications for continuation or interruption of the pregnancy.

DELIVERY

Early examination of the newborn by the pediatrician has been discussed previously in this Annal by Dr. Doris Howell. This however, does not excuse the obstetrician, who not only has the earliest opportunity but also the obligation to examine the baby he delivers (10). Gellis (11) has pointed out the lack of communication between the pediatrician and the obstetrician in an effort to promote early diagnosis and treatment of many anomalies and illnesses. Immediate examination should alert the obstetrician to early diagnosis of intersex anomalies and true sex chromosome, and autosomal abnormalities. When abnormal genitalia are noted, immediate screening of buccal smears for Barr Bodies may be started. These may be confirmatory or indicate the need for further studies, including chromosome analysis and repeated sex chromatin studies. Where the problem indicates further study, cord blood can be drawn for indicated karyotype analysis, and the placenta and umbilical cords saved for pathologic review. Other studies may be indicated for viruses, enzymes, and other anomalies.

Most of the emphasis in this section of the Annal has been placed on intersexuality, but it is also necessary to emphasize the autosomal abnormalities, particularly one of the more frequent, Down's Syndrome or mongolism. This condition results from chromosomal abnormalities other than those in the sex chromosome and will occur as frequently or even more often than many of the sex anomalies.

For years it has been recognized that mongolism occurs more frequently in the offspring of older patients with an incidence as high as one in forty estimated in mothers of forty-five to forty-nine years of age, whereas the overall incidence is one in six hundred sixty-five, approximately one in three thousand in mothers under the age of twenty-nine (12). Thus on a statistical basis, mongolism can be predicted as to frequency before it has occurred.

Chromosomal analysis should be performed on all babies suggested or affected with mongolism as diagnosed at birth. Most of these will prove to have forty-seven chromosomes with trisomy 21. The risk of recurrence after the birth of one child with trisomy 21 mongolism appears to be about 1 percent regardless of maternal age. However, a certain percentage of these will have translocation-type mongolism and these in turn will require karyotyping of both parents. If a man carrying a translocation gene is found, only occasionally will he have a mongoloid offspring, whereas a woman carrying the same translocation has a 30 percent chance of having an affected child (13).

There are many infants which may be born with evidence of mongolism, but this may not be confirmed by the usual leukocyte karyotypic analysis. In these instances mosaicism must be suspected where certain organs of the individual will have chromosomes of mongolism, whereas the others will not. Thus in counseling the mother of a mosaic, much difficulty is encountered. It is usually accepted that the recurrence risk must be offered as higher than usual until more specific information is obtained.

An attempt will not be made to review other trisomies as they are not seen as frequently as mongolism and reliance must be placed upon the more specialized knowledge of the genetist.

ABORTIONS

Since not all pregnancies will go to term, and since it is estimated that 20 to 30 percent will end in abortion, many women may have questions concerning the genetic aspects of these abortions. To date, evidence from a review of abortions that have been studied in our service has indicated that approximately 25 percent of these abortions are associated with genetic abnormalities (14). In those patients with repeated abortions, it is not only necessary to check the fetus for abnormalities but to take a specific and careful family pedigreed history along with karyotypic analyses as indicated, in order to arrive at a more specific genetic prognosis.

An interesting genetic observation is that spontaneous abortions are more frequent in the offspring of couples in the ABO system where the father is A and the mother is O. Conversely, the likelihood of deimmunization of the fetus of the same couple is decreased, most likely due to the fact that fetal A Rh positive erythrocytes are eliminated from the maternal circulation by anti-A antibodies before sensitization can occur. A plea is made for study of aborted material whenever possible so that more realistic genetic counseling may be provided. A mother who has repeated pregnancy losses in the form of abortions on a genetic basis is just as eligible for counseling as the mother who has the occasional loss at term.

GYNECOLOGIC COUNSELING

With today's emphasis on increased sex education with the associated importance of premarital examination, the physician is encountering opportunities in which he may be of service before marriage occurs. The most frequent age for marriage for the female partner today is eighteen. While it is true that many of these marriages may be taking place where pregnancy has already occurred, it is at the premarital examination that advice can be given and questions answered. Certainly those patients with obvious defects will require study. A careful history, taken in the same manner as during the prenatal examination, will reveal many other problems. An increasing interest is placed on consanguinity, but there is little reason to suspect that marriage beyond first cousins offers an appreciable increase in genetic defects, unless recessive genes are present in both partners. These factors must be explained to those patients who are questioning them, and whereas one seldom will influence the selection of a mate, a better understanding might be obtained.

The gynecologist often encounters the patient who is returning for future advice following a previous pregnancy mishap. Of course, the physician is obligated to make available to the patient knowledge based on his own experiences as well as that obtained from other sources. It is usually considered best to discuss the problem with both husband and wife; when the problem becomes involved beyond the more simple genetic systems; then the aid of a highly specialized, genetically trained physician or nonphysician genetist will be needed. To date, the amount of information for some of the more unusual anomalies is nil, and thus the amount of additional information that the specialist can add may be negligible. However, the satisfaction gained merely from talking with a specialist will often give much relief to the couple seeking information.

In addition to the physical defects one may encounter, the importance of biochemical defects is increasing. Screening for phenylketonuria is already routine in many hospitals, and laws are being passed to make it mandatory in many areas. Not only will more laws be passed to make it mandatory, but public demand and legal action where it is not done will reinforce the increasing emphasis of genetic application in the practice of obstetrics and gynecology.

The direction of early diagnosis and treatment and correction of a genetic mishap is no better illustrated than in phenylketonuria. Once an early and proper diagnosis is made, phenylketonuria can be corrected by diet, resulting in a decrease in mental retardation that would otherwise ensue. This condition is only one of several genetically biochemical defects that can be recognized at present, but it is certainly one of the more important in today's medicine.

Increasing emphasis is being placed on population control, and it behooves the obstetrician and gynecologist today to form ideas and thoughts as to his reaction to this subject. For the first time since 1958, the birth rate in 1965 was below four million. Thus it is evident that interest in birth control is increasing and that many have been using birth control measures. It will be necessary for the physician to face the problem squarely when he is confronted with the indications for contraception, sterilization, and occasionally therapeutic abortion in the presence of genetic defects. As knowledge in the field increases, it is hoped that the accuracy of intrauterine diagnosis of abnormalities and problems may be reached early. It is hoped that instead of eliminating the possibility of pregnancy for some of the diseases that have resulted in malformations in the past, methods may be devised whereby genetic defects may be corrected before conception takes place.

SUMMARY

It is the increasing responsibility of the obstetrician and gynecologist to assume a role in genetic counseling. He is ideally suited for this by the very nature of his specialty, since his contact with patients covers the entire life span of womanhood. It is hoped that he will make an effort to supplement his treatment with counseling, early recognition and diagnosis of abnormal conditions, and treatment of these deformities. It is suggested that by obtaining an adequate history and performing a thorough physical examination of mothers during prenatal care, and of the babies at the time of delivery, a great step may be taken in this direction.

REFERENCES

1. Motulsky, A. G., and Gartler, S. M.: *General Principles of Medical Genetics.* Chicago, Year Book Medical Publishers, Inc, 1962.
2. Pauling, L.: *Medical World News,* p. 55, June 11, 1965.
3. Lenz, W.: Thalomide embryopathy. *Deut Med Wochschr,* 87:1232, 1962.
4. Wilkins, L., Jones, H. W., Holman, G. H., and Stempfel, R. F.: Masculinization of the female fetus associated with administration of oral and intramuscular progestins during gestation: Non-adrenal female pseudohermaphrodism. *J Clin Endo Metab,* 18:559, 1958.
5. Aaron, H. H., Schneierson, S. J., and Siegel, E.: Goiter in newborn infant due to mother's ingestion of propylthiouracil. *J Am Med Assoc,* 159:808, 1955.
6. Mahairas, G. H., and Weingold, A. B.: Fetal hazard with anticoagulant therapy. *Am J Obst Gynec,* 85:234, 1963.
7. Stewart, A., Webb, J., and Hewitt, D.: A survey of childhood malignancies. *Brit Med J,* 1:1495, 1958.
8. Brill, A. B., and Forgotson, E. H.: Radiation and congenital malformations. *Am J Obst Gynec,* 90:1149, 1964.
9. Masland, R. L.: First Asian and Oceanic Congress of Neurology. Japan, 1962.

10. Parks, J., and Sites, J. G.: Genetics and gynecologic practice. *Am J Obst Gynec, 83*:436, 1962.
11. Gellis, S.: Guest Address – Section of Pediatrics – Obstetrics. South Med Assoc, Houston, Texas. Nov. To be published in J Am Med Assoc, 1965.
12. Carter, C. O., and McCarthy, D.: Genetics and preventive medicine. *Brit J Prev Social Med, 5*:83, 1951.
13. Motulsky, A., Hecht, G. F.: Genetic prognosis and counseling. *Am J Obst Gynec, 90*:1227, 1964.
14. Jacobson, C. B., and Barter, R.: Some cytogenetic aspects of habitual abortion. *Am J Obst Gynec*. (In press.), 1967.

Chapter 55

Translocation Mongolism

KENNETH L. BECKER

THE majority of mongolism is due to trisomy "21," which is usually caused by a sporadic meiotic disequilibration. A significant percentage of mongoloids born to young women are familial and are caused by a translocation of the mongolism chromosome. The various forms of translocation mongolism for which pedigree data are available are listed, and cytogenetic mechanisms for their occurrence are discussed. Indications for chromosomal analysis of mongoloids and their parents are suggested, and genetic information is provided which will aid the physician in counseling the parents.

In 1959 Lejeune, Gauthier and Turpin (1) discovered the presence of an additional small acrocentric chromosome in the karyotype of three mongoloid boys. Thus these children had forty-seven somatic chromosomes instead of the normal forty-six, and the additional autosome was later interpreted as being an extra No. 21 of the Denver Standard System of Nomenclature of Human Chromosomes. Enough doubt remains as to the relative size and morphology of the additional chromosome that it is not certain whether mongolism is caused by trisomy 21 or trisomy 22. For this reason the term "mongolism chromosome" seems preferable to the more dogmatic "chromosome No. 21" (2). However, for simplicity of discussion, in this paper chromosome No. 21 will be used with quotation marks.

Note: Reprinted by permission of the author and *Postgraduate Medicine, 40:*459-464, 1966; copyrighted by McGraw-Hill, Inc.

Dr. Becker is Chief, Metabolic Section, Veterans Administration Hospital; Assistant Professor of Medicine, George Washington University School of Medicine, Washington, D. C.

TRISOMY "21" MONGOLISM

It has been demonstrated that the majority of mongolism (perhaps more than 95 percent [3]) is due to trisomy "21," that is, the presence in triplicate of the mongolism chromosome. This chromosomal anomaly is caused by meiotic nondisjunction. Meiotic nondisjunction or, more correctly, meiotic disequilibration (4) is a process by which, during oogenesis or spermatogenesis, the chromatids fail to be distributed equally in order to form two balanced gametes containing an equal haploid complement of chromosomes. In normal gametogenesis the "21" chromosomes would distribute equally among the gametes. However, if during reduction division both chromosomes "21" migrate to one pole and none to the other, the result will be a gamete containing 24 chromosomes, including two "21" chromosomes, or a gamete containing 22 chromosomes without any chromosome "21." (The latter gamete will probably be lethal.) If a normal gamete containing 23 chromosomes and a single "21" chromosome fertilizes the 24 chromosome gamete containing two "21" chromosomes, they will produce a zygote containing 47 chromosomes, including three "21" chromosomes. Such a zygote will become the classic mongoloid.

Trisomy "21" mongolism occurs sporadically, and this form is not likely to occur again in the same sibship, except for the possible occasional family with a hereditary predisposition to nondisjunction. The only known predisposing factor to most cases of "21" disequilibration is advanced maternal age. This is of eugenic value to the practicing physician, who can reassure a woman more than thirty-five years old who had already given birth to a mongoloid child that the risk of her having another mongoloid usually is no greater than the random risk for her age (5). The risk is considerably greater for women less than age thirty-five, partly because of the occurrence of translocation mongolism in this younger age group.

TRANSLOCATION MONGOLISM

Recent studies have demonstrated the existence and genetic

behavior of the more insidious type of mongolism, translocation mongolism, in which the cause is strongly familial (in the sense of frequently being passed from generation to generation). The internist, general practitioner or pediatrician often may provide specific eugenic information on this form of mongolism to a distraught couple with a mongoloid child or a family history of mongolism. The purpose of this paper is to list and elucidate the genetic mechanisms responsible for the genesis and perpetuation of translocation mongolism.

Translocation refers to a structural change in chromosomal morphology resulting from a union of broken chromosomes or fragments of chromosomes. Thus, translocation requires chromo-

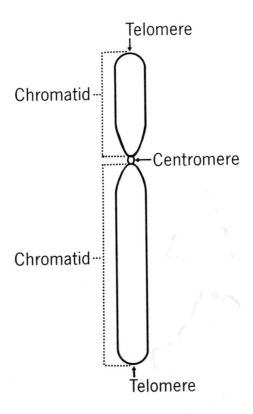

Figure 55-1. Diagram of chromosome (prior to DNA replication).

somal breakage. The distal portion of a chromosome is called a telomere (Fig. 55-1). It is stable and probably cannot unite with a broken chromosomal fragment. A single chromosomal breakage produces a proximal portion of a chromatid containing a centromere and a distal acentric fragment. The acentric fragment consists of a telomere distally and a "sticky" portion proximally. The sticky fragment is not stable and attempts to unite with other chromatin material. The stable telomeres of other chromosomes resist the attempted terminal addition of a fragment to themselves. The sticky chromatid requires union with its own broken-off fragment or with the fragment of another chromosome in order to perpetuate itself as an intact structural entity. Therefore, a single chromatin break usually reunites with its own fragment and is only a transient and apparently harmless phenomenon (Fig. 55-2). This reuniting is called restitution. However, if a portion of two chromosomes should break off simultaneously, each "sticky" end may heal by union with the nonhomologous fragment of the other chromosome. Such a mutual exchange of broken portions of nonhomologous chromosomes is called reciprocal translocation,

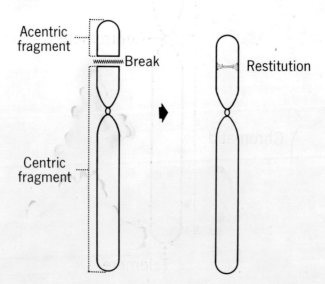

Figure 55-2. Diagram of chromosome illustrating breakage and restitution.

the form of translocation most apt to perpetuate itself. Thus at least two simultaneous breakages are required for reciprocal translocation (Fig. 55-3).

During the late stage of meiotic pachytene, a normal interchange of corresponding segments of *homologous* chromatids takes place which is largely responsible for genetic reassortment; this is called crossing over. Since reciprocal translocation in meiosis involves *heterologous* chromosomes, and since normal crossing over does not occur in mitosis, the meiotic or mitotic reciprocal translocation process has been called a form of illegitimate crossing over.

A reciprocal translocation may result in either two stable monocentric chromosomes (Fig. 55-3) or an unstable acentric fragment and a dicentric chromosome (Fig. 55-4). Chromosomal movement in anaphase requires the presence of a centromere. The acentric chromosome has no power of movement, since it does not become attached to the spindle and will be lost in subsequent mitoses. The dicentric chromosome behaves aberrantly at anaphase because each centromere attaches to the spindle. If one

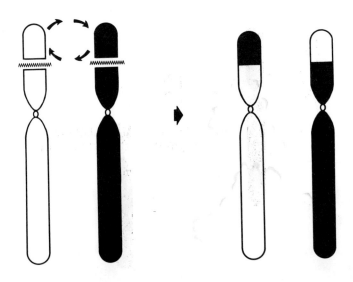

Figure 55-3. Diagram illustration reciprocal translocation.

of each of the two centromeres of a daughter chromosome should pass to opposite poles during anaphase, the chromatin material will form a "bridge" and result in further alteration when telophase occurs. Therefore, the result of a reciprocal translocation which yields one acentric and one dicentric chromatid is eventual elimination of the initial specific chromosomal anomaly either by lethality or by variegation due to endless bridge-breakage fusions. Thus the stable and self-perpetuating reciprocal translocation is the one which results in two monocentric chromosomes.

The breakage which induces such a translocation may occur close to or far from the centromere. If it occurs close to the centromere of two chromosomes, the arms of each translocated chromatid will be nearly complete. Such a translocation process is called a whole-arm rearrangement and is the form most commonly encountered in translocation mongolism. When a whole-arm rearrangement occurs between two acrocentric chromosomes, a

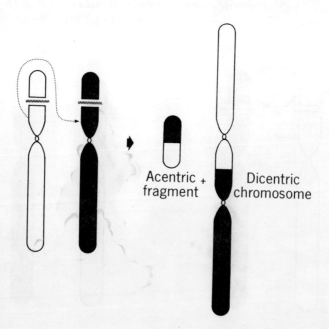

Figure 55-4. Unstable reciprocal translocation.

large metacentric chromosome and a small chromosomal fragment containing a centromere are produced. This latter translocation process is known as centric fusion (Fig. 55-5).

D/"21" Mongolism

In 1960 Polani and associates (6) first demonstrated that chromosomal translocation can result in mongolism. They studied a mongoloid born of a young mother and found the child had forty-six chromosomes, including a normal number of small acrocentric chromosomes, and no apparent trisomy "21."

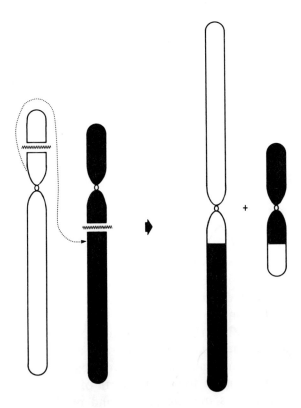

Figure 55-5. Reciprocal translocation between two acrocentric chromosomes with resultant centric fusion. If the smaller chromosome is sufficiently minute it may be lost to future mitotic divisions.

However, a chromosome of the D group (interpreted as being No. 15) possessed two chromatid arms attached to its centromere which resembled in size a small acrocentric chromosome. It was suggested that the etiologic mechanism was a meiotic reciprocal translocation (centric fusion) between an additional chromosome "21" and a D chromosome. In the proband the "21" was present in triplicate, but its addition to the D chromosome superficially camouflaged its existence. The basic genotype for mongolism remained the same — the existence in triplicate of the genetic material carried by chromosome "21."

Carter and associates (7) then elucidated the mechanism of transmission of this forty-six chromosome D/"21" mongolism by demonstrating that the otherwise normal mother and maternal grandmother of a D/"21" mongoloid had only forty-five chromosomes; they were carriers of the anomaly and possessed the D/"21" translocation plus only one discrete "21" chromosome. Apparently, during gametogenesis of an individual several generations back, a simultaneous break in a D chromosome and a "21" chromosome occurred. A reciprocal union took place by which the greater portion of the D chromosome (containing the long arm) united with the greater portion of the "21" chromosome (containing the the long arm). Presumably the smaller fragment of the D chromosome then united with the smaller fragment of the "21" chromosome. Such a union of small fragments, which contain very little genetic material, tends to be lost in meiosis or in future mitotic cell divisions once fertilization occurs.

Although the carrier of a 45 chromosome D/"21" translocation is chromosomally abnormal and contains the karyotype propitious for the appearance of mongolism in the offspring, the carrier is phenotypically normal because very little chromatin material has been lost since the large translocation chromosome contains nearly all of the genetic material of both a D and a "21" chromosome. This forty-five chromosome carrier differs greatly from the normal woman in her propensity toward the birth of mongoloid children. Translocation disturbs meiotic pairing and produces unbalanced gametes. The mongoloid inherits the translocation chromosome D/"21" plus one normal "21" from the mother and one normal "21" from the father.

Translocation mongolism apparently does not depend on advanced maternal age. Indeed, the majority of such carriers give birth to mongoloid children at an early age. Frequently the young mother is the translocation carrier, and it has been estimated that the risk of another mongoloid birth occurring among mothers less than twenty-five years of age who have had a mongoloid child is fiftyfold the random risk (5). Of every three viable offspring produced by a D/"21" carrier, one will be normal, one will be a carrier, and one will be a mongoloid. In addition, the incidence of spontaneous abortion will be greatly increased. The inheritance of D/"21" translocation has usually been through the mother, although the carrier genotype may be present in both sexes. Perhaps the spermatozoa of the male carrier are less viable if they bear both a D/"21" and an extra "21" chromosome. In any case, the male carrier can be told that the risk of his having a mongoloid child is considerably less than that of a female carrier.

"21"/22 Translocation Mongolism

The second form of translocation mongolism, first described by Penrose and Delhanty (8), was an apparent "21"/22 translocation. Again, the mongoloid had forty-six chromosomes. The carrier karyotype for such an anomaly manifests a centric fusion type of reciprocal translocation of "21" and 22. Consequently, the carrier has forty-five chromosomes consisting of the "21"/22 trans-location plus a single chromosome "21" and a single chromosome "22." The risk of a "21"/22 carrier giving birth to a mongoloid infant should be analogous to that of the D/"21" carrier. Transmission appears to occur through both mother and father.

Although it is impossible to prove microscopically, it seems likely that "21"/"21" translocation also may occur. All viable offspring born of a carrier of such a translocation will be mongoloid.

Hamerton, Giannelli and Carter (9) have recently demonstrated that a chromosomal translocation not involving the "21" chromosome may increase the risk of a mongoloid child being born to a person carrying the translocation. They described a mother with a familial D/D reciprocal translocation who gave birth to a trisomy

"21" child who did not carry the translocation. Thus it seems that the presence of translocation in the parent may predispose to nondisjunction.

All of these translocations may involve a common denominator which may implicate the nucleolus. Most of the chromosomes involved in human translocations of all types include acrocentric chromosomes. The acrocentric chromosomes frequently lie in close association with the nucleolus or nucleoli. These are the chromosomes which possess satellites and which primarily contribute to the formation of the nucleolus (10). As White (11) has noted, the interphase nucleolus is in reality merely specialized parts of certain chromosomes and is formed by specific nucleolar organizers in the chromosomes. The nucleolar-organizing zones are believed to be located at the sites of certain secondary constrictions and from regions about the satellites. Are these regions conceivably more active mechanically and metabolically than other chromosomal regions and hence more liable to breakage? The close spatial propinquity of the acrocentric chromosomes (satellite association [12]) further enhances the possibility of a mutual interchange between the fragments produced by such a breakage. A delay in the prophase dissolution of the nucleolus conceivably could be the precipitating cause for such a fragmentation and reciprocal translocation (13).

GENETIC CLUES FOR THE PHYSICIAN

What are the helpful clues concerning mongolism which are available to a physician interested in genetics? A translocation abnormality is most likely to be present when the parents of a mongoloid are relatively young. However, in spite of the fact that most translocation mongoloids are born to young mothers, the great majority of young mothers with a mongoloid child are chromosomally normal and their children have regular trisomy "21" (14). Also, although translocation mongolism is usually familial and is associated with a chromosomal abnormality in a parent, it may occur as a *de novo* phenomenon with parents who are karyotypically normal (15). Nevertheless, chromosomal analysis is strongly indicated in (1) all young parents with a mongoloid child, (2) any parents with more than one mongoloid child, and (3) parents of any age whose family pedigree contains more than one relative with mongolism.

REFERENCES

1. Lejeune, J., Gauthier, M. and Turpin, R.: Les chromosomes humains en culture de tissues. *C R Acad Sci 248*:602, January, 1959.
2. Nichols, W. W., Fabrizio, D. P. A., Coriell, L. L., Bishop, H. C. and Boggs, T. R., Jr.: Discussion: Mongolism with mosaic chromosome pattern. *Am J Dis Child, 102*:452, October, 1961.
3. Hayashi, T.: Karyotypic analysis of 83 cases of Down's syndrome in Harris County, Texas. *Texas Rep Biol Med, 21*:28, 1963.
4. Becker, K. L., Sprague, R. G. and Albert, A.: The chromosomal spectrum of gonadal dysgenesis. *Mayo Clin Proc, 38*:490, October 23, 1963.
5. Carter, C. O. and Evans, K. A.: Risk of parents who have had one child with Down's syndrome (mongolism) having another child similarly affected. *Lancet, 2*:785, October 7, 1961.
6. Polani, P. E., Briggs, J. H., Ford, C. E., Clarke, C. M. and Berg, J. M.: A mongol girl with 46 chromosomes. *Lancet, 1*:721, April 2, 1960.
7. Carter, C. O., Hamerton, J. L., Polani, P. E., Gunalp, A. and Weller, S. D. V.: Chromosome translocation as a cause of familial mongolism. *Lancet, 2*:678, September 24, 1960.
8. Penrose, L. S. and Delhanty, J. D. A.: Familial Langdon Down anomaly with chromosomal fusion. *Ann Hum Genet, 25*:243, 1961.
9. Hamerton, J. L., Giannelli, F. and Carter, C. O.: A family showing transmission of a D/D reciprocal translocation and a case of regular 21-trisomic Down's syndrome. *Cytogenetics, 2*:194, 1963.
10. Ohno, S., Trujillo, J. M., Kaplan, W. D. and Kinosita, R.: Nucleolus-organizers in the causation of chromosomal anomalies in man. *Lancet, 2*:123, 1961.
11. White, M. J. D.: *The Chromosomes.* London, Methuen & Co., Ltd., 1961.
12. Ferguson-Smith, M. A. and Handmaker, S. D.: Observations on the satellited human chromosomes. *Lancet, 1*:638, March 25, 1961.
13. Lehmann, O. and Forssman, H. A.: Familial mongolism and chromosomal translocation also observed in normal boy member. *Acta Paediat, 51*:6, January, 1962.
14. Lehmann, O., Forssman, H. A. and Hallstrom, T.: Chromosome studies of persons with mongolism (Down's syndrome) born to young mothers. *Acta Soc Med Upsal, 67*:285, 1962.
15. Priest, J. H., Bryant, J. and Motulsky, A. G.: Down's syndrome: Trisomy and a de-novo translocation in a family. *Lancet, 2*:411, August 24, 1963.

Index

A

Abortions, 584
Achondroplasia, 560
Accustically handicapped, 366-75
  see also Deaf child, Hearing disorders of
Adoption, and genetic counseling, 539
Albinism, 398
Allergy, 413-22, 537
Anemia, 537
Aphasia, 244-5
  see also Language, disorders
Articulatory defects, *see* Language, disorders
Ascending myelitis, case of, 446-51
Associations for handicapped
  American Association for Mental Deficiency, 101
  American Foundation for the Blind, 379
  American Hearing Society, 367
  American Speech and Hearing Society, 310
  National Association for Retarded Children, 152
  National Society for Crippled Children and Adults, 367
Asthma, 417-22
Atherosclerosis, coronary, 537-8
Attitudes
  parents of,
    asthmatic child, 413-22
    cerebral palsied, 233-40, 257-63
    coronary cases, 408-9
    deaf, 371, 385
    epileptic, 217, 219-26, 228-9
    hemophiliac, 435
    leukemic, 458-78, 485-88, 495-7, 501-4
    mentally retarded, 87-100, 101, 104, 155-59, 171-3, 195-99

speech-handicapped, 274-6, 314-5, 329
  parents, and interference with counseling, 264-66
  toward epilepsy test, 221
Auditory acuity tests, 367-8

B

Blindness, 377-8, 385-90, 391-4
  cases, 388-9, 391-2
  counseling parents, *see* Counseling
  infancy, in, 385-90
  pre-adolescence, in, 391-4
  problems of parents, 377-84, 385-90, 391-3
Brain-damaged child, treatment, 245-7
  see also Cerebral palsy, Epilepsy
Bupthalmus, 400

C

Cancer, 537-8
Cardiac, 550
  arrhythmia, 405
  coronary atherosclerosis, 537
  pacemakers, 405-12
  see also Heart disease, ischemic
Case studies, 95-9, 107-8, 138-40, 174-6, 183-6, 189-99, 348-52, 388-9, 391-2, 439-40, 446-51
Case work
  and family, 391-4
  and mother, 445-53
  rejection of, 184-5
Cerebral palsy, 11-24, 53, 227-41, 248, 255-63, 342, 549
  attitudes of children vs. parents, 233-40
  counseling parents, 227-41, 251, 255-63
  see also Counseling

sexuality in, 235-38
Cleft palate, 348-52, 353-5, 550
  see also Language disorders
Coloboma, 398
Colon polyposis of, 538
Congenital
  cataract, 398
  glaucoma, 398, 400
  optic atrophy, 398
Coping behavior, parental, 465-75
  see also Parent
Counseling
  genetic, 395-402, 523-33, 534-44,
      545-56, 557-79, 580-88, 589-99
    assessing the risk, 535-6
    congenital disorder, 535
    consanguity, 538-9
    and family physician, 536-8
    gynecologic, 585-88
    Huntington's chorea, 536
    impact on family, 523
    in obstetrics and gynecology, 580-88
    and translocation mongolism,
      589-99
    visual problems, 395-402
  misdirective, 78-83
  parent counseling
    problems in, 101-8, 110-16
      see also Parent
    value of 289-90
      see also Parent
  parents of
    acoustically handicapped, 365-75
      see also Deaf child, hearing dis-
        orders of
    allergic and asthmatic, 413, 22
    blind, 378-84, 385-90, 391-4,
      395-402
    cerebral palsied, 227-41, 251,
      255-63
    cleft palate, 348-52, 353-5
    deaf, 356-65, 366-76
    diabetic, 423-31
    epilepsy, 213-8, 219-26
    heart block, 405-12
    hemophiliac, 432-42
    leukemia, 483, 84, 89, 492, 506
    mentally retarded, 110-43, 183-4,
      189-99, 200-9

speech handicapped, 269-84,
    285-98, 299-310, 311-26,
    327-334, 335-67, 348-52
  spina bifida, 227
  see also Parent, counseling
Cystic fibrosis, 549-51
Cytogenetic diseases, 527

D

Deaf child
  education of, 372, 75
  and family, 356-65, 366-75
Death of child
  doctor's reaction, 516
  informing the parents, 510-11
  parent reactions, 446-51, 453-80,
      481-91, 492-506, 507-19
  psychologic considerations in, 507-19
Diabetes, 400, 537
Diabetic child, 423-31
  genetic basis, 537, 552
Diagnostic process
  communication to parents, 127-133,
      163-65, 251, 256, 370, 483,
      501-2
  genetic counseling, 558-9
  hearing disorders, 367-70
  hemophilia, 434
  leukemia, 483, 495, 500
  mental deficiency, 65-77, 118-121,
      162-3
Disorders, genetic, list of, 537, 540
Distrophy
  macular, 562
  myotonic, 562
Down's syndrome, *see* Mongolism
Dysarthria, *see* Language, disorder

E

Epilepsy
  attitudes toward epilepsy test, 221
  genetic basis, 537-8
  group sessions,
    mother of, 219-226, 234
    parents, 213-19
Erythroblastosis, 581
Essential hypertension, 537-8

G

Galactosemia, 398

Gargoylism, 535

Genetics, 395-402, 523-33, 534-44, 545-56, 557-79, 580-88, 589-99
autosomal recessive inheritance, 563
chromosomal disorders, 567
counseling, genetic, 395-402, 523-33, 534-44, 545-56, 557-79, 580-88, 589-99
assessing the risk, 535-6
congenital disorder, 535
consanguity, 538-9
and family physician, 536-8
gynecologic, 585-88
Huntington's chorea, 536
impact on family, 523
in obstetrics and gynecology, 580-88
and translocation mongolism, 589-99
visual problems, 395-402
cousin marriages, 563-4
disorders, list of, 538, 540, 550, 561
hereditary spherocytosis, 560
incest, 564
and mental deficiency, 153-56
mutation, 566
in obstetrics and gynecology, 580-8
polygenic inheritance, 566
visual problems, 395-402

Glucocorticoid deficiency, 541

Goitre montoxic, 537

Grief, parental, 512-4

Guilt, in parents, 27-43, 47, 60, 130, 135, 229, 235, 239, 287, 330, 349, 388, 467, 469, 478, 483

Group therapy with parents
cerebral palsied child, 227-41, 260-3
clinician's role in, 294-7, 336-41, 424-5
diabetic, 423-31
of epileptic adolescent, 219-26
of epileptic child, 213-18
speech handicapped, 294-6, 327-34, 335-41
therapeutic value of, 242-54, 334, 425

Gynecologic counseling, 585-7

H

Handicapped, needs of the, 382-3

Hearing, disorders of, 356-65, 366-76
see also Acoustically handicapped, Deaf child

Heart block, in children, 405-12
see also Cardiac

Heart disease, ischemic, 538

Hemophilia, 432-42
in adolescence, 439-40
case of, 438-9
diagnosis, 434
rehabilitation, 437-8
and school, 437-8

Heredity, *see* Genetics

Huntington's chorea, 536

Hypertension, essential, 537-8

Hypercholesterolemia, familial, 538

I

Institutional placement of child, 124-7, 131

L

Language
bilingualism, 279-80
development, 343-4
disorders, 269-84, 285-98, 299-310, 311-26, 327-34, 335-41, 342-47, 348-52, 353-55
aphasia, 244-45
attitudes, parent, 274-6
bilingualism, and 279-80
cleft palate, 348-52, 353-55
delayed speech, 280
lisping, 270
neighborhood influences in, 278-9
and only child, 272-3
and orphaned child, 272-3
and parent-child relations, 269-82
poor readers, 281
stutterers, 280-3
syndromes, 270-1
infant speech, 271-2
Letter to parents

of brain-injured child, 242-7
of non-verbal child, 242-47
of stuttering child, 299-310
Leukemia, 483, 489, 492-506
acute lymphocytic, 454
acute myelogenous, 454
see also Malignant diseases, in children

M

Malignant diseases, in children, 446-51,
452-80, 481-91, 492-506,
507-19
Manic-depressive psychosis, 540, 542
Marfan's syndrome, 560
Meningitis, 243
Mental retardation (mental deficiency)
cases, 95-99, 107-8, 138-40, 174-6,
183-5, 189-99
causes, classification of, 149
counseling in home, 183-4
counseling parents, 110-43, 189-99
group, 110-16, 200-09, 248
family physician and, 144-59, 160-69
genetics of, 153-56
initial parental reaction, 180-1
mongoloid child, 130, 200-09
genetic origin of, 541, 554, 567-73,
583-4
placement, institutional, 124-7, 131,
157, 174-76
symptoms, 145
translocation mongolism, 589-99
neurotic maternal attitudes, 87-100
pseudomental deficiency, classes of,
149-50
Multiple sclerosis, 234
Myelitis, ascending, case of, 446-51
Myelomeningocele, 158-9

N

National Association for Retarded Chil-
dren, 152
Necropsy, request for, 516
Neoplastic disease, 453
Nystagmus, 398

O

Opthalmologist, 400-1

P

Parent
associations
therapeutic aspects of, 248-54
see Associations for handicapped
attitudes and,
asthmatic child, 413-22
cerebral palsied, 233-40, 257-63
cerebral palsied vs. their children,
233-40
coronary cases, 408-9
deaf, 371, 385
epileptic, 217, 219-26, 228-9
hemophiliac, 435
leukemic, 458-78, 485-88, 495-7,
501-4
mentally retarded, 87-100, 101,
104, 155-59, 171-3, 195-9
speech-handicapped, 274-6, 314-5,
329
attitudes and interference with counseling, 264-66
attitudes toward epilepsy test, 221
children with disabilities, of
allergic and asthmatic, 413-22
blindness, 377-84, 385-90, 390-94,
395-402
cerebral palsy, 227-41, 251, 255-63
cleft palate, 348, 352, 353-55
deafness, 356-65, 366-76
diabetes, 423-31
epilepsy, 213-8, 219-26
heart block, 405-12
hemophilia, 432-42
leukemia, 483, 489, 492-506
mental retardation, 87-100, 110-43,
144-59, 180-1, 183-4, 200-9,
248
poliomyelitis, 227
schizophrenia, 251-2
spina bifida, 227
speech-handicapped, 264-84,
285-98, 299-310, 311-26,
327-34, 335-41, 342-7, 348-52
coping behavior, 464-75
counseling
acoustically handicapped, 365-75
(see also deaf, hearing)
allergic and asthmatic, 413, 22

blind, 378-84, 385-90, 391-4, 395-402
cerebral palsied, 227-41, 251, 255-63
cleft palate, 348-52, 353-5
deaf, 356-65, 366-76
diabetic, 423-31
epilepsy, 213-8, 219-26
heart block, 405-12
hemophiliac, 432-42
leukemia, 483, 489, 492, 501
mentally retarded, 110-43, 183-4, 189-99, 200-9
misdirective, 78-83
problems in, 101-8, 110-16
speech handicapped, 269-84, 285-98, 299-310, 311-26, 327-334, 335-47, 348-52
spina bifida, 227
value of, 289-90
denial, 57-8, 239, 264, 456-62, 467
feelings, 44-51, 228, 233-41, 249, 264-6, 348-52, 388-99, 407-8, 485
grief, 472-3, 475
group therapy, 110-16, 200-9, 210-16, 219-26, 227-41, 294-6
guilt, 27-43, 47, 60, 120, 135, 229, 235, 239, 287, 330, 349, 388, 459-60, 428
hostility, 459
intellectualization, 466
see also Attitudes
letter to parents of,
brain-injured, 242-7
non-verbal, 342-7
stuttering child, 299-310
overprotection, 172, 236, 265, 274-5, 331-2, 386, 389, 464
physician, role of, 117-40, 144-59, 160-9
projection, 59, 484
see also Attitudes
reactions, to death of child, 446-51, 452-80, 481-91
rejection, 275-6, 331-3, 386
see also Attitudes
unconscious conflicts, 136-7
withdrawal, 59, 135
Palsy, *see* Cerebral palsy

Pediatrics
disorders, genetic, list of, 561
genetic counseling, 557-79
Peptic ulcer, 537
Pernicious anemia, 537
Phenylketonuria, 552
Physical handicap, psychology of, 5-9
Placement, institutional, 124-7, 131, 157, 174-6
see also Mental retardation
Poliomyelitis, 227
Polyposis, of colon, 538
Primary glaucoma, 398
Primary thyrotoxicosis, 537
Pseudoretardation, 122-3
Ptosis, 398
Pyloric stenosis, 550

R

Referral, 121
Remission stage, leukemia, 464
Retinitis pigmentora, 398, 535, 541
Retinoblastoma, 538
Rheumatism, 537
Role playing, 338-41

S

Schizophrenia, 123, 552
Sclerosis, tuberous, 562
Slow learners, 115-6
Sociologist and deaf child, 356-65
Speech-handicapped, *see* Language, disorders
Speech therapist
counseling by, 285-97, 311-26, 327-34, 335-41, 342-7, 348-52
letter from, 200-310, 342-7
role of, 344
Spina bifida, 158, 227
Strabismus, 398
Stuttering 280-1, 313-4
case, 331-33
and home situation, 322-4
counseling parents of, 311-26, 327-34, 335-41
see also Language, disorders

T

Thyrotoxicosis, primary, 537
Tuberculosis, 537, 545

U

Understanding   parents   of   cerebral

palsied, 255-63

V

Visual defect, *see* Blindness